Peter O. Müller, Susan Olsen and Franz Rainer (eds.)
Word-Formation – Special Patterns and Restrictions

T0406275

This volume is part of a larger set of handbooks to Word-Formation

Word-Formation
Special Patterns
and Restrictions

Edited by
Peter O. Müller, Susan Olsen and Franz Rainer

DE GRUYTER
MOUTON

ISBN 978-3-11-141370-9
e-ISBN (PDF) 978-3-11-142055-4
e-ISBN (EPUB) 978-3-11-142059-2

Library of Congress Control Number: 2025934168

Bibliographic information published by the Deutsche Nationalbibliothek
The Deutsche Nationalbibliothek lists this publication in the Deutsche Nationalbibliografie;
detailed bibliographic data are available on the Internet at http://dnb.dnb.de.

© 2025 Walter de Gruyter GmbH, Berlin/Boston, Genthiner Straße 13, 10785 Berlin
Cover image: Jasmina007 / iStock / Getty Images Plus
Typesetting: Meta Systems Publishing & Printservices GmbH, Wustermark

www.degruyterbrill.com
Questions about General Product Safety Regulation:
productsafety@degruyterbrill.com

Contents

David Serrano-Dolader

1 Parasynthesis in Romance

Abstract: Parasynthesis is a word-formation process that Romance languages have inherited from Latin. It is characterised by the simultaneous and joint attachment of two affixes (a prefix and a suffix) to a lexical base. In order to define the concept of parasynthesis, several theoretical tenets (e.g., the transcategorisation power of prefixes, the binary branching hypothesis, etc.) must be taken into account. In Romance languages, verbs are the most representative cases of this morphological process; there are, however, other non-verbal formations that have been included in this category.

1 Introduction

Parasynthesis is a linguistic term which goes back to the Greek grammarians, who called παρασύνθεσις the process of forming derivatives, occasionally also compounds, on the basis of compounds (cf. Lindner 2011: 17–19). The result of the process was called a παρασύνθετον. In Latin grammar, this latter term was rendered as *decompositum*. While this terminology continues to be used – parsimoniously – in the same way in most philologies (cf., for example, Henzen 1957: 222 on German "Dekomposita oder Parasyntheta"), in Romance philology it has undergone a semantic change, denoting nowadays a word-formation process whereby a prefix and a suffix are simultaneously attached to a lexical base (cf. Darmesteter 1875; Elliot 1884; Malkiel 1941; Allen 1981; Crocco Galèas and Iacobini 1993; Brachet 1999; Iacobini 2010). The standard example is constituted by Fr. *embarquer* 'to load, board', a verb consisting of a base *barque* 'ship', a prefix *em-* and a suffix *-er*, which is the infinitive ending. Neither **embarqu-*, nor **barquer* are actual, or even possible French words.

David Serrano-Dolader, Zaragoza, Spain

https://doi.org/10.1515/9783111420554-001

This terminological tradition in Romance philology goes back to Darmesteter (1875: 79–80):

> Cette sorte de composition est très-riche: les mots qu'elle forme, et que l'on désigne du nom de *parasynthétiques*, offrent ce remarquable caractère d'être le résultat d'une composition et d'une dérivation agissant ensemble sur un même radical, de telle sorte que l'une ou l'autre ne peut être supprimée sans amener la perte du mot. C'est ainsi que de *barque* l'on fait *em-barqu-er*, *dé-barqu-er*, deux composés absolument uns et dans lesquels on ne retrouve ni les composés *débarque*, *embarque*, ni le dérivé *barquer*, mais le radical *barque*. La langue tire les deux composés immédiatement du radical, sans l'aide d'aucun intermédiaire. [This type of compounding is very rich: the words that it forms, which are called *parasynthetic*, show the special characteristics of being the result of compounding and derivation on the basis of the same root, in a way that neither of them could be eliminated without the word disappearing as such. In this way, from *barque* one creates *em-barqu-er*, *dé-barqu-er*, two compounds completely indivisible, and in which it is not possible to find either the compounds *débarque*, *embarque*, or the derived word *barquer*, only the root *barque*. The language forms those two compounds directly from the root, without the help of any go-between.]

As one can see, Darmesteter's use of *parasynthesis* still follows the Classical tradition, since he considered the *em-* of *embarquer* and the *dé-* of *débarquer* to be prepositions (i.e. Fr. *en* 'in' and *de* 'from') and not prefixes, and hence the combination of *em-* and *dé-* plus *barque* as cases of compounding. However, when during the 20th century elements such as *em-* and *dé-* came to be viewed as prefixes, the term *parasynthesis* was retained and reinterpreted as the simultaneous use of prefixation and suffixation, instead of compounding and suffixation.

This terminological tradition has been consolidated among early 20th-century Romance linguists from different origins, among them Menéndez Pidal (1904: 130), Nyrop (1908: 206) and Thorn (1909: 8). Most Romance linguists have agreed on the need to treat simultaneous double affixation as a necessary condition for parasynthesis, and tried to differentiate these formations from others where the presence of prefixes and suffixes is the result of consecutive processes (cf. Alemany Bolufer 1920: 152; Brøndal 1943: 125; Badía Margarit 1962: 394–395; Lloyd 1964: 736; Malkiel 1966: 314; Tekavčić 1968: 145; Reinheimer-Rîpeanu 1973: 487; Brea 1977: 127–128, etc.).

There were few exceptions to this restrictive view of parasynthesis. Tollemache (1945: 110) starts from a wider perspective, but eventually keeps the name *parasynthetic* for those cases where the affixing processes take place at the same time ("parasinteti simultanei", simultaneous parasynthetics, in his terminology). A real exception is Asan's (1965) proposal who defends a wide definition of parasynthesis that comprises not only formations resulting from attaching a prefix and a suffix simultaneously, but also those where prefixation and suffixation are consecutive processes. Still other scholars, as we will see, have been led to call into question the very concept of parasynthesis (cf. Serrano-Dolader 1995) due to the numerous problems of delimitation that it gives rise to.

Outside Romance linguistics, this special use of *parasynthesis/parasynthetic* is rare, which does not mean that the phenomena referred to do not exist. They are simply treated under different headings such as "prefixal-suffixal formations", etc.

2 Problems concerning the delimitation of parasynthesis

2.1 Meaning

A proper description of the concept of *parasynthesis* requires the formal analysis to be complemented with semantic considerations. The fact that one of the intermediate stages ([p + X] or [X + s]) is attested is not enough to justify the rejection of the parasynthetic character of a formation. It is necessary to verify that such a formation shows the proper meaning that allows one to compositionally derive the meaning of the whole word. Thus, for example, the non-parasynthetic analysis of Sp. *embaldosar* 'to tile' would be shaky if it were only based on the existence of *baldosar* 'to tile', which formally corresponds to the stage [X + s]. It is the semantic analysis of all the members of the word family *embaldosar/baldosar/baldosa* 'to tile/to tile/tile' that allows us to state that the form *baldosar* 'to tile' cannot be considered as the base for the creation of *embaldosar* 'to tile', but that both forms are derived from the noun *baldosa* 'tile', at least from a synchronic perspective. It is irrelevant that etymologists might establish a different derivation process from a diachronic point of view.

On the other hand, the semantic peculiarities of a given formation can allow it to be analysed in different ways. For instance, *desnivelar* 'to unbalance' has two semantic interpretations that correspond to two different morphological analyses: *desnivelar*$_1$ 'to cause to lose balance' (derived from *nivel* 'level' by parasynthesis) vs. *desnivelar*$_2$ 'to reverse the action of levelling' (derived from *nivelar* 'to balance, to level' by prefixation).

2.2 Actual and possible words

Aronoff's (1976: 21) word based hypothesis holds that "[a]ll regular word-formation processes are word-based. A new word is formed by applying a regular rule to a single already existing word". According to this view, it would be sufficient for a complex word to contain an intermediate stage which is not attested to qualify as a case of parasynthesis. Corbin (1980) takes issue with this requirement for intermediate stages to be attested. Her basic starting point is that notions such as "existence" and "non-existence" are ambiguous, and therefore unreliable. For Corbin, attested words and possible, but non-attested words should have the same status in grammar. The fact that an intermediate stage is not attested, therefore, is not considered to be a sound argument in favour of a parasynthetic analysis (cf. Corbin 1980: 191).

The idea of possible intermediate stages is exploited by several authors. In Scalise (1984: 204), for example, parasynthetic forms are formations in two stages: at the first stage (suffixation), a possible, but not necessarily actual word is generated, while at the second stage (prefixation), the whole word is actually generated. According to this account, the derivation of a Spanish word like *engordar* 'to fatten' (from *gordo* 'fat') would go through a non-existent intermediate stage **gordar*.

2.3 Binarism

The binary branching hypothesis, which goes back to the structuralist principle of binarism, states that the branching properties for word-formations are exclusively binary: only one affix may be attached to a word at each step of the derivation. Consequently, it follows that it is impossible to accept ternary structures for parasynthetic formations, since they would show a prefix, a base, and a suffix on the same level. This would imply that two affixes (prefix and suffix) were attached to the base by means of just one word-formation rule.

In his analysis of parasynthetic verbs, Scalise (1984: 202–208 and 1986: 146–150) preserves their binary structure by admitting a non-existent intermediate stage, as we have seen above. The same is true for Alcoba (1987), who, however, considers the non-existing intermediate stage to be formed by the prefix and the base: $[[[Pref] [X]]_X [Suf]]_V$. This analysis rests on the following two premises: 1) The thematic vowel in parasynthetic forms is always verbalizing; 2) The prefix does not take part in the assignment of the grammatical category to the base.

A fundamentally different strategy for preserving binarism is adopted by Corbin (1980, 1987). Her analysis is based on the following two premises, which are the exact opposite of Alcoba's: 1) The prefix can change the category of the base to which it is attached; 2) The infinitive ending is not a derivational but an inflectional suffix. In other words, Corbin proposes to analyse verbs with the form [prefix + base + infinitive ending] as the result of simple prefixation: [prefix + (X)$_{N/Adj}$]$_V$. She denies the existence of verbal parasynthesis altogether.

As has become apparent, Corbin, Scalise and Alcoba agree as far as the binary analysis for supposedly parasynthetic formations is concerned; however, they differ in the structure assigned to the lexical entities that take part in their formation as well as in the categories involved.

3 Parasynthetic verbs in Romance languages

Most discussions on parasynthetic forms in Romance languages focus on verbs, since they are the most representative examples of this process. Three main issues have been discussed in this context: the status of the infinitive ending, the semantic and categorial role of the prefix, and the relationship between parasynthesis and circumfixation.

3.1 The infinitive ending: derivational or inflectional?

Traditional grammar generally assumes that the infinitive ending is derivational. All scholars that define parasynthesis as a simultaneous application of compounding (or prefixation) and derivation (i.e. infinitive suffixation) share this view.

Although this traditional perspective has been kept in some recent work, it is now being increasingly rejected. Corbin, as we have already mentioned, suggests that the infinitive affix should not be identified as a derivational suffix. Therefore, for her, so-called parasynthetic verbs are in reality cases of prefixation: Fr. *embarquer* is assigned the structure [(*en*)$_{af}$ [*barque*]$_N$]$_V$, and *allonger* 'to lengthen' (from *long* 'long') the structure [(*a*)$_{af}$ [*long*]$_A$]$_V$ (cf. Corbin 1987: 129).

For another group of scholars, the verbal suffix aims at signaling the verbal character of the formation: the verb, in order to be one, needs a specific configuration (cf. Pottier 1962: 258 ff.; Reinheimer-Rîpeanu 1974: 18; Thiele 1984: 19; Mascaró 1985).

Another possible interpretation is to argue for the inflectional as well as derivational character of the infinitive ending. If the infinitive is considered to be part of the verbal paradigm, its ending should be classified as inflectional. If, on the contrary, the infinitive is considered to be part of a derivational paradigm, then its ending is derivational (cf. Dubois 1962: 19).

Other proposals postulate the existence of a zero morpheme and examine the role of the thematic vowel.

Hockett (1947), for instance, proposes that Sp. *cantar* 'to sing' has two morphemes, *cant-* and *-r*, whereas the *-a-* ("conjugation vowel") can be interpreted as an "empty morph" (a morph with no specific meaning and without any corresponding morpheme). Hockett (1950) rejects the concept of "empty morph" and includes thematic vowels in a special category called "structural signals": a given thematic vowel informs us that the verbal stem belongs to a specific morphematic class in its inflection.

Reinheimer-Rîpeanu (1972 and 1974) suggests that zero-derivation is involved in parasynthesis just like in the derivation of non-prefixed denominal and deadjectival verbs. Thus, from Fr. *rouge* 'red', we can obtain a verb by means of a verbal derivational zero: *rougir* [*rouge* + Ø + *ir*] 'to redden', just like by means of a verbal ending different from zero: *rougeoyer* [*rouge* + *oy* + *er*] 'to glow red'.

The concept of zero morpheme has also been exploited for the analysis of English formations such as *father* (noun) → *to father* Ø (verb) in Marchand (1955: 7). The problem would directly affect the question of parasynthesis in examples such as *slave* (noun) → *enslave* (verb), because its analysis could be: [*en* + *slave* + Ø], which corresponds to the parasynthetic structure of Romance verbs. For those scholars that support the view that verbalisation is carried out by means of a zero suffix, parasynthesis would no longer be a process restricted to Romance languages: in Romance formations such as *amor* 'love' → *enamorar* 'to cause to fall in love', as well as in English formations such as *noble* → *ennoble*, it could be argued that verbalisation takes place thanks to the action of the same zero suffix (*enamorØar*, *ennobleØ*; cf. Padrosa Trias 2007, for both Catalan and English *en-* prefixed verbs).

The discussion of the inflectional or derivational character of the infinitive ending has led to differentiate between parasynthesis involving a derivational suffix (Port. *en* + *surd(o)* + *ec* + *er* 'to deafen', from *surdo* 'deaf', with derivational *-ec-*) and parasynthesis involving an inflectional suffix (Port. *a* + *baix(o)* + *ar* 'to lower', from *baixo* 'low', with inflectional *-ar*; cf. Valente et al. 2009).

Some of the proposals reviewed above can be included under a wider view of parasynthesis (cf. Serrano-Dolader 1995). The derivational character of the infinitive ending (or part of it, i.e. the thematic vowel) seems plausible. If inflection cannot change the category of the base, it is obvious that in Sp. *líder* (noun) 'leader' → *liderar* 'to lead', *atrás* (adv.) 'back' → *atrasar* 'to put back', *curioso* (adj.) 'curious, nosy' → *curiosear* 'to pry', the category change leads us to think that the element added to the stem should be considered as a derivational transcategorisation device. It seems illogical to accept the derivational character of this ending in these verbs while assigning to it a different character in parasynthetic forms such as *bribón* (noun) 'rascal' → *abribonar* 'to become a rascal', *prisión* (noun) 'prison' → *aprisionar* 'to put into prison, to trap'. A possible interpretation for guaranteeing the parasynthetic character of the whole verbal paradigm – and not just that of the infinitive, which is a simple conventionalised citation form of the paradigm – is to assign the derivational value just to the thematic vowel (cf. Scalise 1984: 205).

As argued in Serrano-Dolader (1995), such a proposal can also be applied to the analysis of parasynthetic forms with an explicit suffix. Thus, in examples such as Sp. *entristecer* 'to sadden' (← *triste* 'sad'), *anochecer* 'to get dark' (← *noche* 'night'), *encanecer* 'to go grey' (← *cana* 'grey hair') or Port. *enrouquecer* 'to become hoarse' (← *rouco* 'hoarse'), *esbravejar* 'to bellow' (← *bravo* 'rude'), the corresponding thematic vowel would be still considered a verbalising element, and consequently, it would not be necessary to assign a transcategorial or verbalising character to the affixes *-ec-* and *-ej-*.

On the other hand, there are conjugated forms where it is difficult to find the thematic vowel. In fact, the verbal derivational form can be instantiated by a thematic vowel (as in the infinitive) or by a zero morpheme, which precedes certain verbal inflectional forms: Sp. *engordAr* 'to fatten', *engordAmos* 'we fatten' vs. *engordØo* 'I fatten'.

In sum, the thematic vowel and the alternating zero morpheme show a double nature: that of a derivational morpheme, if the verb is considered as derived from the previous base; that of a morpheme inherent to the verbal category, if the verb – whether derived or not – is considered as part of its corresponding inflectional paradigm. This solution safeguards the derivational value of the thematic vowel in parasynthetic verbs and protects their status (cf. Serrano-Dolader 1995).

3.2 The role of the prefix

Several linguists have claimed that parasynthesis is a counterexample to the principle that states that prefixation does not allow a transcategorisation of the base. For instance, Hall (1948: 136–165) already considered cases that had been traditionally characterised as parasynthetic as examples of *exocentric prefixation* (cf. also Wagner 1952: 54 and Tekavčić 1972: 146). Corbin, as we have already seen in section 2.3, considers the prefix itself to be responsible for the change in category involved in what are traditionally considered to be parasynthetic verbs.

The opposite view, as we have also seen, is held by Scalise (1984) and Alcoba (1987). Both authors reject the view that the prefix is a transcategorisation device in parasynthetic verbs, but their proposals differ in the structure they proposed for these formations: for Scalise it is [pref. [[X]$_{N/A}$ suf.]$_V$]$_V$, for Alcoba [[pref. [X]$_{N/A}$]$_{N/A}$ suf.]$_V$. There are two similarities: the verbal suffix is the only morpheme that determines the transcategorisation of the base, and the prefix does not modify the category of the base. The difference lies in how the prefix is, in each case, grouped together with the rest of the parasynthetic constituents.

Serrano-Dolader (1995) agrees with these authors in considering the prefix as a non-transcategorising element, but disagrees on their proposed explanations for the structure of parasynthetic formations. For this author, Scalise's proposal does not explain the relationship between prefixed verbs and non-prefixed verbs with the same stem that are not attested, and neglects the widely heterogeneous character of such relations (cf. also Iacobini 2010). On the other hand, Alcoba's proposal does not show any correspondence with examples directly observable in language, because the supposed intermediate stage does not seem to be either attested or possible.

Some linguists (cf. Lüdtke 2005, 2011) have proposed a totally different proposal for the explanation of the prefix in parasynthetic formations. They suggest that these verbs are the result of an agglutination of a preposition with the noun in the base: Fr. *mettre en Bastille* 'to put in the Bastille' → *embastiller* 'to jail', Sp. *meter en barco* 'to put in a ship' → *embarcar* 'to embark', etc. Certainly, this type of process could have played a role in the formation of parasynthetic processes in Latin (*in sinum* 'in the interior of, at the core of' → *insinuare* 'to go deep into, to make advances on somebody', *e limine* 'from the door/entrance' → *eliminare* 'to make go out, place outside', *in gurgitem* 'in the throat/abyss' → *ingurgitare* 'to swallow, dive in'), but it does not seem to be coherent to maintain this line of thought nowadays in the synchronic interpretation of the Romance languages. Many denominal verbs would be left out of this interpretation since the two sets of prefixes and prepositions do not coincide. Furthermore, this type of analysis does not account for deadjectival derivations: Fr. *alourdir* 'to weigh down' (← *lourd* 'heavy'), It. *appesantire* 'to weigh down' (← *pesante* 'heavy'), Port. *encurtar* 'to shorten' (← *curto* 'short'), etc.

As Iacobini (2010) points out, in order to characterise Romance parasynthetic verbs, it is necessary to bear in mind that Latin *ad-* and *in-*, as well as *ex-* with the meaning 'change of state', are different from the rest of the prefixes on the basis of three characteristics: the prefix cannot occur before the verb in a productive manner; the prefix does not express a specific or delimited semantic value; parasynthesis could give rise to verbs that belong to inflectional classes such as verbs in *-ire/-ir* that are not productive except in this parasynthetic construction: It. *appiattire* 'to flatten' (← *piatto* 'flat'), *appuntire* 'to sharpen' (← *punta* 'point'), Fr. *aplatir* 'to flatten' (← *plat* 'flat'), *appointir* 'to sharpen' (← *pointe* 'point'), *alunir* 'to land on the moon' (← *lune* 'moon'), etc.

3.3 Parasynthesis and circumfixation

Besides granting a transcategorial role to the prefix or to the suffix, there is a third possible analysis: the identification of a discontinuous affix that groups together the prefix and the suffix (cf. Bosque 1983: 131–140). Parasynthetic formations would come close to cases of *circumfixation* that exist in languages such as German: *trennen* 'to separate' > *ge-trenn-t* 'separated'. Parasynthesis would not arise because of the simultaneous attachment of two affixes (prefix and suffix), but as a result of only one circumfix that would be the sole responsible for the meaning of the resulting verb.

This proposal has several drawbacks, however. First, a definition of the notion *discontinuous morpheme* such as that suggested by Harris (1945: section 4.1) does not seem to be suitable for parasynthetic formations: "Given some particular environment, if two morphemes X and Y depend on each other so that neither occurs without the other (in that environment), we say that X and Y constitute together one new morpheme Z which simply occurs in the environment." In a series such as Sp. *embalsamar* 'to embalm' (← *bálsamo* 'balm'), *enmascarar* 'to hide, disguise' (← *máscara* 'mask'), *enturbiar* 'to cloud' (← *turbio* 'cloudy'), it is difficult to argue that there is a discontinuous morpheme [*en-...-ar*] based on a supposedly obligatory co-presence of the suffix and the prefix. We have to bear in mind that there are corresponding synonymous verbs without the prefix: *balsamar, mascarar, turbiar*. Second, it is not justified to talk about a discontinuous morpheme when one part has a particular function (transcategorisation) and the other one lacks it. There is nothing that would impede the proposal that these are two independent morphemes that are jointly attached to a base. Both have semantic implications, and only the suffix takes part in the transcategorisation process (Serrano-Dolader 1995). The fact that, in some parasynthetic forms, the content of the prefix cannot be separated from the content of the suffix does not mean that both of them should be taken as only one morpheme. The prefix and the suffix of parasynthetic formations seem to be morphologically independent and fulfill different functions. This implies that their combined occurrence as only one circumfix contradicts the real functioning of both affixes.

On the other hand, it is true that the distinction between parasynthetic and non-parasynthetic verbs rests on a criterion – that of *simultaneity* or *solidarity* of the application of prefix and suffix – that is not always easy to apply. In this sense, Iacobini (2010: 6) proposes to differentiate between true parasynthetic verbs and "verbes à double stade dérivationnel", i.e. verbs with a double derivational stage. The former are those verbs where the prefix and the suffixation process (or conversion) act simultaneously as only one affix. The prefix is an explicit marker of the transformation of a noun or an adjective into a verb. The latter are those verbs such as Fr. *décaféiner* 'to decaffeinate' (← *café* 'coffee'), *désosser* 'to bone' (← *os* 'bone') which result from the previous verbalisation of the noun base, yielding the semantically plausible hypothetical verbs **caféiner* and **osser*, followed by prefixation. Both types of lexical creation processes were already productive in Latin: *decortico* 'to take off the bark' (← *cortex*, stem form: *cortic-* 'bark') is a verb created according to a double derivative stage, while *accommodo* 'to adapt, adjust' (← *commodus* 'convenient, appropriate') is a true parasynthetic.

4 Are there any other types of parasynthetic formations?

4.1 Parasynthetic adjectives

The study of parasynthesis has traditionally focused on verbal derivation, since this is the area where this process is most productive. However, there also seem to be various subtypes of parasynthetic adjectives in Romance languages.

As in verbal derivation, Darmesteter (1877) was the first one to draw attention to the possible existence of parasynthetic formations in the category of adjectives. He mentions formations such as Fr. *sousmarin* 'submarine, underwater', whose meaning cannot be construed as the sum of *sous* 'under' and *marin* 'marine' (as a formal analysis would suggest), but only as "relatif à ce qui est sous la mer", i.e. 'relative to what is under the sea' (Darmesteter 1877: 129, 1891–97: 24–25).

Studies on the lexical morphology of different Romance languages have pointed out several groups of adjectival formations that could be considered parasynthetic (cf. Serrano-Dolader 1995: 155–184, 1999: 4730–4744, 2012a; all the examples are from Spanish):

a) Participial adjectives: *anaranjado* 'orangey' (← *naranja* 'orange'), *achinado* 'slanting, oriental-looking' (← *chino* 'Chinese'), *aniñado* 'childlike' (← *niño* 'child'); *desvergonzado* 'shameless, impertinent' (← *vergüenza* 'shame'), *desalmado* 'heartless' (← *alma* 'soul'), *despiadado* 'merciless' (← *piedad* 'mercy'), etc.

b) Adjectives expressing opposition (*anti-*) and support (*pro-*), where, as also in c. and d., the combination of noun + suffix corresponds to the relational adjective associated with the noun: *antialcohólico* 'anti-alcoholic' (← *alcohol* 'alcohol'), *antifebril* 'antifeverish' (← *fiebre* 'fever'), *antigripal* 'flu remedy' (← *gripe* 'flu'); *progubernamental* 'pro-governmental' (← *gobierno* 'government'), *proclerical* 'pro-clerical' (← *clero* 'clergy'), *propolicial* 'pro-police' (← *policía* 'police'), etc.

c) Adjectives with privative-negative meaning and adjectives with numerical meaning elements: *apétalo* 'with no petals' (← *pétalo* 'petal'), *acéfalo* 'headless' (← *cabeza* 'head'), *imberbe* 'beardless' (← *barba* 'beard'), *informe* 'shapeless' (← *forma* 'shape'); *bimensual* 'fortnightly' (← *mes* 'month'), *trilingüe* 'trilingual' (← *lengua* 'language'), *tetrasílabo* 'tetrasyllabic' (← *sílaba* 'syllable'), etc.

d) Adjectives that include locative-temporal relations: *submarino* 'submarine' (← *mar* 'sea'), *intramuscular* 'intramuscular' (← *músculo* 'muscle'), *interdigital* 'interdigital' (← *dedo* 'finger'), *extrauterino* 'extrauterine' (← *útero* 'uterus'), *precolombino* 'pre-Columbian' (← *Colón* 'Columbus'), *postcolonial* 'post-colonial' (← *colonia* 'colony'), etc.

Each of these groups poses thorny problems in relation to their characterisation as parasynthetic or not, which have given rise to opposite views between those that accept the parasynthetic characterisation of all or some of these groups and those that reject the existence of adjectival parasynthesis in Romance languages. Due to the complexity of the issues involved and the limited space allotted to this article, it is impossible to go into this question any further here.

4.2 Parasynthesis in compounding

All parasynthetic verbs and adjectives discussed above are characterised by the joint attachment of prefixes and suffixes to a lexical base ("parasynthesis by affixation"). The treatment of so-called "parasynthetic compounds" has been more restricted, but equally controversial, in the Romance tradition. *Parasynthetic compounding* can be broadly defined as a lexical process that consists in the blend of two lexical bases – that form a compound that does not exist independently – with a derivational suffix: Sp. [*[[macho] [hembra]] -ar*] 'a male + a female + verbal suffix' → *machihembrar* 'to dovetail' (-*i*- being a linking vowel typical of compounds), [*[[corcho] [tapón]] -ero*] 'cork + plug + suffix' → *corchotaponero* 'relative to the industry of cork plugs'.

This word-formation process seems to be marginal and not very productive in Romance languages, with only a few examples that are difficult to systematise. On the other hand, the underlying structure in formations created by compounding and suffixation does not always correspond to the parasynthetic compounding model, since it is possible for suffixation to precede compounding ([[*casco*] [[*mul(a)*] [-*eño*]]] 'hoof + mule + suffix' → *casquimuleño* 'with small hoofs like

those of mules') or vice versa ([[[*sal*] [*pimienta*]] -*ar*] 'salt + pepper + suffix' →
salpimentar 'to season, spice'); in these cases, suffixation and compounding do
not act jointly and therefore, they do not give rise to parasynthetic structures.

Parasynthetic compounds in Romance languages have been scarcely studied
due to the heterogeneity of the formations that seem to correspond to the double
process of compounding and suffixation. Although the concept of "parasynthesis
in compounding" is not new in Romance linguistic studies (cf. Serrano-Dolader
1995: 199–262), this term – as well as the corresponding concept – has only recently reappeared in studies on Romance, Germanic, and Slavic languages (cf. Bisetto
and Melloni 2008; Melloni and Bisetto 2010).

These formations are closely related to synthetic compounds ("Zusammenbildungen", in German), such as possessive adjectives of the type E. *blue-eyed* and
G. *rothaarig* 'red-haired' or nouns of the type E. *truck driver* and G. *Lastwagenfah-
rer* (on synthetic compounds in German see article 5). Synthetic compounds, however, are not discussed under the heading of parasynthesis, neither in Germanic
nor in Romance linguistics (cf. Gaeta 2010: 219).

Apart from the lack of an accepted terminology, there is also a deep disagreement among scholars when they try to delimit the different subtypes of formations that are likely to be classified as parasynthetic compounds in Romance
languages (cf. Bisetto and Melloni 2008; Melloni and Bisetto 2010; Serrano-Dolader
2012b).

5 References

Alcoba Rueda, Santiago (1987): Los parasintéticos: Constituyentes y estructura léxica. *Revista Española de Lingüística* 17(2): 245–267.

Alemany Bolufer, José (1920): *Tratado de la formación de palabras en la lengua castellana*. Madrid: Librería General de Victoriano Suárez.

Allen, Andrew S. (1981): The development of prefixal and parasynthetic verbs in Latin and Romance. *Romance Philology* 35: 79–87.

Aronoff, Mark (1976): *Word Formation in Generative Grammar*. Cambridge, MA/London: MIT Press.

Asan, Finuţa (1965): Formaţii parasintetice în limba română. *Limba Română* 14: 87–95.

Badía Margarit, Antoni M. (1962): *Gramática catalana*. Vol. 2. Madrid: Gredos.

Batiukova, Olga (2021): Derivation and category change (III): Verbalization. In: Antonio Fábregas, Víctor Acedo-Matellán, Grant Armstrong, María Cristina Cuervo and Isabel Pujol Payet (eds.), *The Routledge Handbook of Spanish Morphology*, 209–221. London/New York: Routledge.

Bisetto, Antonietta and Chiara Melloni (2008): Parasynthetic Compounding. *Lingue & Linguaggio* 2: 233–259.

Bosque, Ignacio (1983): La Morfología. In: Francisco Abad and Antonio García Berrio (eds.), *Introducción a la lingüística*, 115–153. Madrid: Alhambra.

Brachet, Jean-Paul (1999): *Les préverbes ab-, de-, ex- du latin. Étude linguistique*. Villeneuve d'Ascq: Presses du Septentrion.

Brea, Mercedes (1977): La parasíntesis en las *Cantigas d'escarnho e de mal dizer. Verba* 4: 127–136.

Brøndal, Viggo (1943): *Essais de linguistique générale*. Copenhague: Munksgaard.

Corbin, Danielle (1980): Contradictions et inadéquations de l'analyse parasynthétique en morphologie dérivationnelle. In: Anne-Marie Dessaux-Berthouneau (ed.), *Théories linguistiques et traditions gramaticales*, 181–224. Lille: Presses Universitaires de Lille.

Corbin, Danielle (1987): *Morphologie dérivationnelle et structuration du lexique*. Tübingen: Niemeyer.

Crocco Galeas, Grazia and Claudio Iacobini (1993): Parasintesi e doppio stadio derivativo nella formazione verbale del latino. *Archivio Glottologico Italiano* 78: 167–199.

Darmesteter, Arsène (1875): *Traité de la formation des mots composés dans la langue française comparée aux autres langues romanes et au latin*. Paris: Franck.

Darmesteter, Arsène (1877): *De la création actuelle de mots nouveaux dans la langue française et des lois qui la régissent*. Paris: Vieweg.

Darmesteter, Arsène (1891–1897): *Formation des mots et vie des mots. Cours de grammaire historique de la langue française* (troisième partie). Paris: Delagrave.

Dubois, Jean (1962): *Étude sur la dérivation suffixale en français moderne et contemporain*. Paris: Larousse.

Elliott, A. Marshall (1884): Verbal parasynthetics in *a-* in the Romance languages. *American Journal of Philology* 5: 186–199.

Fábregas, Antonio (2023): *Spanish Verbalisations and the Internal Structure of Lexical Predicates*. London/New York: Routledge.

Fruyt, Michèle (2017a): Les verbes parasynthétiques en latin: les interprétations et le 1er type. *De Lingua Latina, Revue de linguistique latine du Centre Alfred Ernout* 13: 1–29 [Online available at: https://hal.sorbonne-universite.fr/hal-03382752].

Fruyt, Michèle (2017b): *Les verbes parasynthétiques en latin: les 2e et 3e types. De Lingua Latina, Revue de linguistique latine du Centre Alfred Ernout* 13: 1–32 [Online available at: https://hal.sorbonne-universite.fr/hal-03382757]

Gaeta, Livio (2010): Synthetic compounds: With special reference to German. In: Sergio Scalise and Irene Vogel (eds.), *Cross-Disciplinary Issues in Compounding*, 219–235. Amsterdam/Philadelphia: Benjamins.

Gibert-Sotelo, Elisabet and Isabel Pujol Payet (2015): Semantic Approaches to the Study of Denominal Parasynthetic Verbs in Spanish. *Morphology* 25(4): 439–472.

Hall, Robert A. Jr. (1948): *Descriptive Italian Grammar*. Ithaca, NY: Cornell University Press and Linguistic Society of America.

Harris, Zellig S. (1945): Discontinuous morphemes. *Language* 21: 121–127.

Henzen, Walter (1957): *Deutsche Wortbildung*. 2nd ed. Tübingen: Niemeyer.

Hockett, Charles F. (1947): Problems of morphemic analysis. *Language* 23: 321–343.

Hockett, Charles F. (1950): Peiping morphophonemics. *Language* 26: 63–85.

Iacobini, Claudio (2010): Les verbes parasynthétiques: de l'expression de l'espace à l'expression de l'action. *De lingua Latina* 3, <http://www.paris-sorbonne.fr/IMG/pdf/Iacobini_parasynthetiques.pdf> [last access 9 Sept 2014].

Lindner, Thomas (2011): *Indogermanische Grammatik*. Vol. 4/1: *Komposition*. Heidelberg: Winter.

Lloyd, Paul M. (1964): An analytical survey of studies in Romance word formation. *Romance Philology* 17: 736–770.

Lüdtke, Jens (2005): Probleme einer funktionellen romanischen Wortbildungslehre: Gibt es *Parasynthese*? In: Carmen Kelling, Judith Meinschaefer and Katrin Mutz (eds.), *Morphologie und romanische Sprachwissenschaft. Akten der gleichnamigen Sektion beim XXIX. Deutschen Romanistentag, Saarbrücken 2005. Arbeitspapier Nr. 120*, 125–139. Konstanz: Fachbereich Sprachwissenschaft der Universität Konstanz. <http://kops.ub.uni-konstanz.de/bitstream/handle/urn:nbn:de:bsz:352-opus-18122/AP_120.pdf?sequence=1> [last access 9 Sept 2014].

Lüdtke, Jens (2011): La "parasynthèse": Une fausse piste? *Romanische Forschungen* 123(3): 312–330.

Malkiel, Yakov (1941): *Atristar – entristecer*: Adjectival verbs in Spanish, Portuguese and Catalan. *Studies in Philology* 38: 429–461.

Malkiel, Yakov (1966): Genetic analysis of word formation. In: Thomas A. Sebeok (ed.), *Current Trends in Linguistics*. Vol. 3, 305–365. The Hague/Paris: Mouton.

Marchand, Hans (1955): Synchronic analysis and word-formation. *Cahiers Ferdinand de Saussure* 13: 7–18.

Mascaró, Joan (1985): *Morfologia*. Barcelona: Enciclopedia Catalana.

Mateu, Jaume (2021): Main morphological formal means (II): Approaches to parasynthesis. In: Antonio Fábregas, Víctor Acedo-Matellán, Grant Armstrong, María Cristina Cuervo and Isabel Pujol Payet (eds.), *The Routledge Handbook of Spanish Morphology*, 28–39. London/New York: Routledge.

Melloni, Chiara and Antonietta Bisetto (2010): Parasynthetic compounds: Data and theory. In: Sergio Scalise and Irene Vogel (eds.), *Cross-Disciplinary Issues in Compounding*, 199–217. Amsterdam/Philadelphia: Benjamins.

Menéndez Pidal, Ramón (1904): *Manual elemental de gramática histórica española*. Madrid: Librería general de Victoriano Suárez.

Nyrop, Kristoffer (1908): *Grammaire historique de la langue française*. Vol. 3. Copenhague: Gyldendalske Boghandel Nordisk.

Padrosa Trias, Susanna (2007): Argument structure and morphology: The case of *en-* prefixation revisited. *Anuario del Seminario de Filología Vasca Julio de Urquijo. International Journal of Basque Linguistics and Philology* 41(2): 225–266.

Pottier, Bernard (1962): *Systématique des éléments de relation*. Paris: Klincksieck.

Reinheimer-Rîpeanu, Sanda (1972): Suffixe zéro? *Revue Roumaine de Linguistique* 17: 261–269.

Reinheimer-Rîpeanu, Sanda (1973): Différents types de parasynthétiques. *Revue Roumaine de Linguistique* 18: 487–491.

Reinheimer-Rîpeanu, Sanda (1974): *Les dérivés parasynthétiques dans les langues romanes*. The Hague/Paris: Mouton.

Scalise, Sergio (1984): *Morfologia Lessicale*. Padua: CLESP.

Scalise, Sergio (1986): *Generative Morphology*. Dordrecht: Foris.

Serrano-Dolader, David (1995): *Las formaciones parasintéticas en español*. Madrid: Arco/Libros.

Serrano-Dolader, David (1999): La derivación verbal y la parasíntesis. In: Ignacio Bosque and Violeta Demonte (eds.), *Gramática Descriptiva de la Lengua Española*. Vol. 3, 4683–4755. Madrid: Espasa Calpe/Real Academia Española.

Serrano-Dolader, David (2012a): Sobre los adjetivos ¿parasintéticos? locativos (*submarino, intramuscular, interdigital*). In: Elisenda Bernal, Carsten Sinner and Martina Emsel (eds.), *Tiempo y espacio en la formación de palabras del español*, 65–78. München: Peniope.

Serrano-Dolader, David (2012b): Sobre los compuestos (para)sintéticos ¿en español? In: Antonio Fábregas, Elena Felíu, Josefa Martín and José Pazó (eds.), *Los límites de la morfología. Estudios ofrecidos a Soledad Varela Ortega*, 427–442. Madrid: Servicio de Publicaciones de la Universidad Autónoma de Madrid.

Serrano-Dolader, David (2016): Viejas y nuevas aproximaciones al concepto de *parasíntesis*. In: Cristina Buenafuentes, Gloria Clavería and Isabel Pujol (eds.), *Cuestiones de morfología léxica*, 9–34. Madrid/Frankfurt am Main: Iberoamericana-Vervuert.

Serrano-Dolader, David (2017): La parasíntesis como proceso lexicogenético (no tan) peculiar. In: Jesús Pena (ed.), *Procesos morfológicos. Zonas de interferencia*, 49–76. Santiago de Compostela: Universidade de Santiago de Compostela.

Šinková, Monika (2017): *Las formaciones parasintéticas en el español moderno (1726–1904)*. Brno: Muni Press (Filozofická Fakulta, Masarykova Univerzita).

Suárez, Janaína (2024): Estructura semántica de los verbos parasintéticos deadjetivales. *Estudios Interlingüísticos* 12: 197–212.

Tekavčić, Pavao (1968): Formazione delle parole nell'istroromanzo dignanese. *Lingua e Stile* 3: 125–180.

Tekavčić, Pavao (1972): *Grammatica storica dell'italiano*. Vol. 3: *Lessico*. Bologna: Il Mulino.

Thiele, Johannes (1984): Reflexiones comparativas sobre verbalizaciones con bases adjetivas en español y alemán. *Linguistische Arbeitsberichte* 45: 19–24.

Thorn, Anders Christopher (1909): *Les verbes parasynthétiques en français*. Lund: Lunds Universitets Arsskrift.

Tollemache, Federico (1945): *Le parole composte nella lingua italiana*. Roma: Edizioni Rores di Nicola Ruffolo.

Valente, Ana Carolina Mrad de Moura, Caio Cesar Castro da Silva, Carlos Alexandre Gonçalves and Maria Lúcia Leitão Almeida (2009): Enfoques sobre parassíntese em português: Da tradição gramatical à lingüística cognitiva. *Revista Virtual de Estudos da Linguagem (ReVEL)* 7: 75–89.

Wagner, Robert-Léon (1952): Remarques sur la valeur des préverbes *a-* et *en-* (<*IN*) en ancien français. In: *Festgabe Ernst Gamillscheg. Zu seinem fünfundsechzigsten Geburtstag am 28. Oktober 1952*, 51–65. Tübingen: Niemeyer.

Francesco Gardani
2 Affix pleonasm

Abstract: Affix pleonasm is a cross-linguistically widespread phenomenon both in inflection and derivation. This article reviews the terminological confusion that has arisen around this term, surveys pleonasm in language in general and, narrowing down the scope, focuses on occurrences of pleonastic affixation in derivation in the languages of Europe. Additionally, theoretical approaches to the motivations of pleonasm are critically discussed.

1 Introduction

While the concept of pleonasm in grammar has not escaped the interest of scholars of language, the terminological landscape surrounding it has been all but homogeneous. As a result, Malkiel's (1957: 84) complaint about the harmful absence of any terminological agreement on the phenomenon still applies to the current state of linguistic research.

The terminological proliferation seems to begin with the introduction of the German term *Übertreibung der Kongruenz* by Franz Nikolaus Finck (quoted in Glässer 1954: 429), followed by *Überkennzeichnung* (Horn 1939: 3–4), and the more widespread term *hypercharacterization*, which translates the German original *Hypercharakterisierung* coined by Eduard Schwyzer (1941) and has also been relabeled *overcharacterization*. More recent coinages encompass *double marking, exuberant marking, multiple exponence, affix repetition*, and sometimes *blending*. Focusing on affixation, Meyer-Lübke (1921, § 34) coined the label *Einreihung*, which Migliorini (1943: 451) rendered in Italian as *inquadramento suffissale*. The term *affix pleonasm*, which is adopted in this article, goes back to the German

Francesco Gardani, Zurich, Switzerland

https://doi.org/10.1515/9783111420554-002

Pleonasmus, originally used in rhetorics and stilistics and later introduced into linguistics, most prominently, by Paul in 1880 (*Pleonasmus von Bildungselementen*; see also the use of *Pleonasmus* with respect to the form *Prinzessin* in Oertel 1830 (s. v. *Prinzessinn*), *dérivation pléonastique* in Nyrop 1908: 36, and *pléonasme morphologique* in Niedermann 1953: 108).

As a matter of fact, these terms are not all strictly co-extensive and scholars of language have both used different labels to cover the same issue and covered only partly overlapping phenomena by recourse to the same terms (see a critique in Tovar 1942: 188). In order to make way through this confusion, the next section reviews which phenomena can be classified under the heading of affix pleonasm or similar labels, and which cannot.

2 The definitional scope of pleonasm

The ultimate etymon of pleonasm is the Ancient Greek πλεονασμός meaning 'superabundance, excess'. Thus, the etymology of pleonasm does not reveal in which ways the excess that it describes occurs.

The most systematic treatment of the topic has been provided by Lehmann (2005), who studies pleonasm at different levels of linguistic analysis and identifies hypercharacterization as "pleonasm at the level of grammar" (2005: 119). Prior to this, by reference to Paul (1920: 162), Haspelmath (1993: 297) defines affix pleonasm as "the semantically vacuous addition of a transparent affix to a word that is already characterized for the morphosyntactic property expressed by this affix". Focusing on cases such as *children*, evolved in Middle English as a compromise between the forms *child(e)r* and *childen*, Hock (1986: 189–190) treats affix pleonasm as a non-systematic process under the heading of blending – a position that Haspelmath (1993: 300) rejects by arguing that pleonasm does not necessarily result from a morphological compromise of two existing occurring forms: for example, Vulgar Latin *esse-re* 'to be' cannot be seen as the result of blending, because Latin does not attest any form **es-re* to combine with the infinitive *esse*. Admittedly, there are cases of affix pleonasm which match true affix blending, for example, in some varieties of German, *rundlicht* 'roundish' (synonymous to standard *rundlich*) shows the suffix -*licht*, which is a blend of the suffixes -*lich* and -*icht* (see Paul 1920: 162; Plank 1981: 77–79; Haspelmath 1993: 307 n. 12). Therefore, affix blending can be considered a hyponym of pleonasm.

Malkiel (1957: 79) provides the following both descriptive and explanatory definition of the phenomenon (that he terms *hypercharacterization*), in which the diachronic dimension is explicitly highlighted:

If a given linguistic formation develops in such a way as to allow, at a certain point, one of its distinctive features to stand out more sharply than at the immediately preceding stage, one may speak of hypercharacterization (or hyperdetermination) of that feature, in the diachronic perspective.

Another term which recurs in the literature is *overcharacterization*, described as "adding a suffix that is strictly speaking superfluous, and hence a pleonastic addition" (Booij 2007: 273).

All these definitions have in common that they do not reveal anything about how to constrain the conceptual scope, that is, the intension of the definition of pleonasm. In fact, phenomena running under the heading of pleonasm can be motivated pragmatically or phonologically: for example, the Spanish plural forms *pie-s-es* 'feet', *cafe-s-es* 'coffee-s', and Old Latin 3PL.PRS *da-n-unt* 'they give' (besides Classical *da-nt*) are prosodically motivated (Dressler, Dziubalska-Kołaczyk and Spina 2001: 123). But, then, is this not motivation enough to discard the characterization of these forms as pleonastic? A way to solve this doubt would be to exclude pragmatic and prosodic motivation from the definitional scope of pleonasm and to only account for both semantic and functional (i.e. morphosyntactic) motivation, but this would not do justice to the synchronic variation appearing in language.

A further aspect relating to the definitional intension of pleonasm concerns the way in which pleonasm is realized. In general terms, the realization of semantic and functional properties can be explicit (or overt) and implicit (i.e. lexical). Based on the distinction between explicit vs. implicit characterization, the following types of pleonastic, that is, over-characterized, marking, can be derived:

1. *Implicit pleonastic marking* is the combination of a lexeme implicitly carrying a semantic or functional value with one element which explicitly (morphologically or syntactically or both) codes the same value. For example, an explicit marker having a value V is combined with a lexeme which inherently contains V: a case in point is the historical addition of the overt feminine marker *-aa* to inherently feminine nouns in Hausa (Newman 1979).

2. *Explicit pleonastic marking* is the addition of double or multiple explicit (morphological or syntactic or both) marking of a value V to a lexeme which does not code V inherently, for example, the Italian NP *tre cani* 'three dogs' with realization of the plural via both the numeral and the suffix *-i*, as well as the Spanish example *cafe-s-es* mentioned above. A further subtype of explicit pleonastic marking would be the realization of V via double or multiple explicit (morphological or syntactic or both) marking on an item which implicitly holds this value. While this option is virtually possible, no case of this type is known to me.

For the sake of completeness, the remaining part of this section briefly discusses what kinds of phenomena can be confused with, but do not count as pleonasm. Crucially, pleonasm must be kept apart from both affix replacement and general loanword integration devices. To the first type belong, e.g., Old Aragonese *alfayante* 'tailor', which resulted from the renewal of *alfayate* through suffixation with *-ante* (Malkiel 1957: 108). To the second type belong, for example, "loanverb markers", such as the suffix *-oa* in Yaqui (Uto-Aztecan) which is added to verbs borrowed from Nahuatl and Spanish in order to facilitate accommodation, e.g., *mediar-oa* [mediate-LVM] 'to mediate' from Spanish *mediar* (Wohlgemuth 2009: 226).

Sometimes scholars apply the label "interference suffix" (see Kolb 1980: 283; Müller 2005: 38) to cases of integration of borrowed lexemes into inflectional classes of the recipient language, e.g., Latin *operāri* > Old High German *opferōn* 'to sacrifice'. This, too, must be seen as a separate procedure, as it is just the result of the application of productive inflectional rules (the infinitive marker *-ōn*) to the base of borrowed items in order to make them fit for syntax (cf. Gardani 2013).

3 Pleonasm in language

In this section, I detail at which levels of language analysis and processing pleonasm can occur, before deepening the phenomenon of affix pleonasm in derivational morphology in section 4.

At the level of discourse, some languages have pleonastic forms acting as discourse markers, for example, in Yiddish, the expletive *es* instructs the hearer that the subject does not represent an entity already evoked in the discourse: *es geyt epes in vald a yid* 'Some Jew seems to be walking in the woods; lit. it goes something in wood a Jew' (Prince 1993: 176); also Dominican Spanish *ello*, European Portuguese *ele*, and Balearic Catalan *ell* all function as markers that encode sentence pragmatics, e.g., Balearic Catalan *Ell no n'hi ha!* 'It does not exist; lit. It not (not) there exists!' (Hinzelin 2009: 17).

In the lexicon, pleonasm often occurs in the form of pure addition of modifiers to lexemes which inherently encode the meaning expressed by the modifier, e.g., *dead corpse, briefly sketch*; Spanish *aniversario anual* 'annual anniversary'; French *conversation orale*; German *mündliches Gespräch* 'oral conversation'; or the additive use of a synonymous grammeme, e.g., Italian *ma però* lit. 'but but'.

An originally lexical item can also be the source of syntactic pleonasm due to grammaticalization. This is famously the case of the French sentential negation *ne … pas* (Rowlett 1998): initially, the noun *pas* 'step', from Latin *pass(um)*, served as a reinforcement in the clause *je ne vais* 'I do not go' → *je ne vais pas* 'I do not go any step'; later, *pas* was desemanticized and acquired the grammatical function of negation; from this time, the negation *pas* is a pleonastic addition to the negative adverb *ne*. Moreover, in the syntax, there is pleonasm in expletives such as the non-standard English 'excrescent *'s*', for example in *Does anyone see what's the tactic is?* This element reinforces or emphasizes the *WH* interrogative word, just as in (non-standard) *how's about, how's come, what's about* (Zwicky 2012).

As has been observed (Lehmann 2005: 137–138), pleonasm is very frequent in the expression of spatial relations. For example, in German, particle verbs license (pleonastic) "directional PPs" (Olsen 1996; Okamoto 2002; Rehbein and Genabith 2006), such as in *Peter lief* [PP *durch den Wald*] *durch* 'Peter ran through the forest'. Similarly, Latin attests the pleonastic realization of spatial relations via the combined use of a preposition and a preverb, e.g., *ex urbe ef-fugere* 'to flee out of town' (Lehmann 2005: 138). Moreover, Latin has what has been called "pleonastic reflexive", e.g., *suo sibi lautum sanguine tepido* [his:ABL.SG RFL bath:PTCP.PST.ACC.SG blood:ABL.SG warm:ABL.SG] 'bathed in his own warm blood': here, the reflexive *sibi* is a fossilized omissible expression of possession (Cennamo 1999: 117).

Frequently, pleonasm occurs in the realization of the values of comparative and superlative, producing syntactic (i.e. analytic) constructions which combine an adverb and an inflected form to express a single predicate, e.g., Middle English *more strenger* (Włodarczyk 2007: 196), substandard French *le plus meilleur*, Spanish *el más mejor* (Lehmann 2005: 139). In other languages, implicit pleonastic marking of the superlative value may occur by adding dedicated inflectional formatives to inherently marked lexemes, e.g., German *(das) bestmöglich-ste* (Lehmann 2005: 140), Late Latin *minimissimus* for *minimus* (Malkiel 1957: 86). Instead, in Modern Greek, we have explicit pleonastic realization of the superlative via double comparative suffixation, e.g., *o kali-ter-o-ter(os)* [good-COMP-COMP] 'bestest' (Petros Karatsareas, p.c.). In south-eastern dialects of Lithuanian, the superlative may be realized, at once, by the simultaneous application of the inherited superlative suffix and a superlative prefix *nai-* borrowed from Slavic, e.g., *nai-gardz-iaus-i obuoliai* 'the most delicious apples' (Grinaveckienė 1969: 222; Wiemer 2009: 353).

Possessive constructions are not immune to pleonasm either, as shown by the syntactic augment in Spanish *su casa + de él* [POSS house + of him] 'his house' (Malkiel 1957: 100), as well as the non-standard southern German 'dative + possessive adjective construction' of the type *dem Peter sein Buch* 'Peter's book'.

In syntax-dependent (i.e. contextual) inflection, we find the perhaps most common manifestation of pleonasm in grammar – viz. agreement. Agreement is the redundant realization of feature values by means of discontinuous affixes in order to facilitate understanding for the hearer (Corbett 2006: 274–275). Nowadays, the most common terms used to describe this phenomenon of morphological asymmetry are "extended exponence" (Matthews 1972), "multiple exponence" (Halle and Marantz 1993), and "exuberant exponence" (Harris 2008). For example, in Batsbi (Northern Caucasian), class marking (contextually: gender-number agreement) can occur in numerous positions within a single verb form, such as in *tišⁿ c'a dah d-ex-d-o-d-anö* [old house(d/d).ABS PV CM-destroy-CM-PRS-CM-EVIDI] 'they are evidently tearing down the old house', via triple affixation with *-d-* (Harris 2009: 267–268).

A particular type of pleonasm is word-internal agreement (Stolz 2007), which has been claimed to result from a process of externalization of inflection (Haspelmath 1993). A well-described case is the realization of definiteness in Lithuanian adjectives. Here, the adjective stem is inflected for case, number, and gender, and this is followed by a suffixal definiteness formative which is again marked for the same features (Stolz 2010: 236), e.g., *bált-os-i-os* [white-NOM.PL.F-DEF-NOM.PL.F] 'white'.

Apart from agreement, the following morphosyntactic features (Corbett 2012) may be realized pleonastically, in the sense of reinforcement of single formatives:

1. case, as exemplified by the genitive (singular) of the Latin pronouns *eius* (< **e(syo)(-s)*), *cuius*, *huius* (Malkiel 1957: 98), or, in German, of both common nouns, e.g., *Hasens* 'of the rabbit', and proper names, e.g., *Mariens* 'Mary's' (Paul 1920: 162);

2. number, in particular the value of plural, as frequently attested in European languages, e.g., Portuguese *alvará-z-es* 'charters', *filhó-s-es* 'fried doughs' (Malkiel 1957: 98); Dutch *kind-er-en* 'children'; northern German *Junge-n-s* 'boys'; moreover, it is particularly recurrent in loanwords, e.g., English *spaghett-i-s*; Dutch *lied-er-en* 'songs'; Afrikaans *vrou-en-s* 'women' (Thomason 1988: 304). In Maltese, there are cases in which templatic morphology is combined with concatenative morphology, e.g., *truf-ijiet* [ends-PL] 'ends', where *truf* is the broken plural of *tarf* and the formative *-ijiet* realizes plural, too (Maris Camilleri, p.c.). In southwestern dialects of Hungarian, we find cases in which the plural is doubly realized via the regular plural formative, *-Ek*, and the plural possessive prefix, *i-*, e.g., in *tehen-i-m-ek* 'my cows' (Imre 1972: 320);

3. gender: some varieties of Italian spoken in Garfagnana give examples of Gilléron's "linguistic therapeutics" (Gilliéron 1921: 11), that is, inflectional class shift of lexemes from a gender-opaque class to a class that marks a certain gender value more neatly, e.g., *fiumo* 'river' for standard Italian *fiume* (masculine): this is an instance of implicit pleonasm, because the inflectional class *libro libri* realizes the gender value masculine on a noun which is inherently masculine (Malkiel 1957: 81).

On the side of verbs, pleonastic realization of person is found, for example, in the Greek dialect spoken in the village of Ochthonia in Euboea, in forms such as *erx-és' tane-s* 'you were coming', which reshape the opaque 2SG medio-passive imperfect form **erxés'tane* by adding the 2SG (final) *-s* formative, yielding more paradigmatic transparency (Pantelidis 2010: 323).

A quite common case of pleonasm concerns the realization of the morpho-semantic feature of tense. MacKay (1979: 487) refers to pleonastic past tense suffixation in child language: for example, *smashted* is due to reanalysis of *smasht* as a present tense form and addition of the past tense formative *-ed* (further examples in Bowerman 1982: 327).

As concerns word-formation, pleonasm is attested in compounding, abbreviation, and derivation. Pleonastic compounds are not uncommon in the languages of Europe: Frisian has appositive compounds of the type *widdofrou* 'widow; lit. widow woman', *einfûgel* 'duck; lit. duck bird'; the Indo-Iranian language Tat forms phytonyms by combining the inherited *dor* 'tree' with specifying lexemes borrowed from Azeri (Turkic), e.g., *qovoq-dor* 'poplar', *balud-dor* 'oak tree'. While these instances clearly count as implicit pleonasm due to the hyperonymic status of the head, synonym compounds, such as the German adverb *schlussendlich* 'end-finally', and the Mandarin Chinese adjective *duo-yu* 'excessive, extra; lit. extra-remaining' (Lehmann 2005: 146–148) are examples of explicit pleonasm.

Cases of pleonasm in abbreviation elaborations are quite frequent, too, e.g., English *PIN number* (*Private Identification Number*) and Austrian German *SPL Leiter* (*Studienprogrammleiter* 'director of the study program'), to mention just a few.

4 Types of affix pleonasm

In line with the scope of the present handbook, this section covers the specific type of affix pleonasm, that is, pleonastic derivational affixation, in the languages of Europe.

Affix pleonasm occurs either when "an affix that normally serves to add a particular unit of meaning gets attached to a root whose meaning already includes that unit" (Covington 1981: 33), e.g., *un-decipher* 'to decipher', Spanish *des-escombrar* 'to dig out' (Rainer 1993: 323), or when multiple derivational markers apply, e.g., German *Prinz-ess-in* 'princess'.

To my knowledge, at least the following parts of speech are attested as displaying affix pleonasm in derivation:

1. nouns, e.g., dialectal English *musician-er* for *musician* (Covington 1981: 35);
2. adjectives, e.g., dialectal English *ungodless* 'godless' (Covington 1981: 35), Latin *aetern-alis* 'eternal' instead of *aeternus*, in which the suffix *-al* explicitly realizes the feature [adjective] (Stotz 2000: 336), or Middle High German *tugenthaft-ic* 'virtuous', in which the suffix *-ic* marks the adjectival status of *tugenthaft* more clearly (Plank 1981: 77);
3. verbs: in Yucatec Maya, the transitivizing suffix *-t* applies to loanverbs which, in the source language, are already transitive, e.g., *alcanzar-t-ik* [achieve-TRR-INCMPL] from Spanish *alcanzar* 'to reach' (Lehmann 2005: 141–146);
4. adverbs, e.g., (colloquial) Spanish *sinduda-mente* 'doubtlessly' (Rainer 1993: 607), English *thusly* besides *thus* (Covington 1981: 35).

As concerns the position of pleonastic affixes, they are mostly suffixes, but we find also interfixes, e.g., Italian *libr-ic(c)-ino* 'small book', prefixes, e.g., *re-continuation*, and, more rarely, infixes, e.g., *fan-bloody-tastic*, where the adjective *bloody* does not change the meaning of *fantastic*, but serves the pragmatic function of intensifying the speaker's feeling of anger or irritation, etc.

In the following, instances of pleonasm are presented according to the semantic/functional values that they realize. Following the line of presentation adopted so far in a coherent way, I start with pleonasm in the realm of valence, which is commonly considered as being located between inflection and derivation. Starting with passive, which is primarily inflectional, we find that in some registers of Turkish, the passive formative *-il/-in* can apply twice in the presence of the abilitive suffix *-(y)Abil*, e.g., *gid-il-ebil-(in)-ir* [go-PASS-ABIL-PASS-AOR] 'it is possible to go' (Aslı Göksel, p.c.). Moving our way down from primarily inflectional towards primarily derivational categories, we find instances of affix pleonasm in the realization of causative. An intriguing case is found in the Romani variety of Selice (Slovakia), where in the perfective forms, two causative allomorphs can be used pleonastically, that is, without yielding a double-causative interpretation: for example, the aorist form *an-av-a-ď-a* [do-CAUS-CAUS-PFV-3SG.PFV] regularly means 's/he had (sth) ordered; lit. s/he makes (so) make (so) bring (sth)' but can also mean 's/he ordered (sth)' (Viktor Elšík, p.c.).

In polysynthetic Adyghe (Northwest Caucasian), pleonasm can affect the expression of participant-internal possibility: for example, in *se maẑᵂe-r qə-s-fe-ʔetə-ŝᵂə-ʁ-ep* [1SG stone-ABS DIR-1SG.IO-BEN-raise-ABIL-PST-NEG] 'I could not raise the stone', possibility is realized by means both of the abilitive suffix *-ŝᵂə* and (a modal use of) the benefactive applicative prefix *fe-* (Yury Lander, field notes).

A clearly derivational operation which is often accompanied by affix pleonasm is derivational gender marking, e.g., German *Hindin* 'female deer' for *Hinde* (Covington 1981: 35), *Diakonissin* 'deaconess' for *Diakonisse* (Malkiel 1957: 86).

Some few languages display pleonastic formation of agent nouns, especially when they denote the agent's profession or rank. Pleonastic agentive suffixation occurs in German, e.g., *Vorfahr-er* 'ancestor' (Paul 1920: 62); Old French *laman-eur* 'pilot' (Malkiel 1957: 107); Spanish VN compounds, by means of the agentive suffix *-ero*, e.g., *picapedr-ero* 'stonemason' for *picapiedras* (Rainer 1993: 268, 487). In Dutch, pleonastic affixation is also found in acronyms which are enriched with the suffix *-er*, resulting in denominal names, such as *UD-er* 'university teacher' (*Universitair Docent*) (Booij 2007: 273).

Processes of intensification such as diminution, augmentation, and iteration are particularly prone to affix pleonasm (Lehmann 2005: 145). Just as, in inflection, pleonastic marking of the plural seems to be the most frequent case of affix pleonasm, in derivation, the champion role is played by diminutive marking. This is richly attested in the languages of Europe: see in Polish child-directed speech *Monisieńko* [*Monika*:DIM:DIM.VOC] 'little Monika!' (Wierzbicka 2003: 53); eastern Yiddish *majlxl* 'little mouth', from Standard Yiddish *moil* 'mouth' + *xǝ* + *l̦* (Jacobs 2005: 69; Herzog and Baviskar 2000: 120); in Lithuanian, *puod-as* 'pot' may be diminuted as *puod-uk-as* 'small pot, cup', but also as *puod-uk-ėl-is* 'small nice pot', via the diminutive suffixes *-uk* and *-ėl* (Gāters 1977: 60–61); in German, forms such as *See-lein-chen* 'small lake', Austrian German *Schatz-i-lein* 'darling; lit. little treasure' are not uncommon; in Icelandic, there are combinations of prefixoids (*pínu-, smá-*) and suffixes (e.g., *-lingur*), e.g., *pínu-disk-lingur* or *smá-disk-lingur* 'tiny diskette', though these cases are far from common there (Þorsteinn Indriðason, p.c.); in Greek, *manulitsa* 'mommy' is formed via *-ul(a)* + *-its(a)* suffixation of the base *man(a)* 'mother' (Petros Karatsareas, p.c.); in Turkish, a sequence of the two diminutive suffixes, *-Acık/-İcik* and *-Cik*, is ungrammatical and would produce an ill-formed form such as **küçücükcük* (from {*küçük+icik+cik*}), but it works when a possessive suffix is added, e.g., *küçücükcüğüm* 'my little tiny one' (Aslı Göksel, p.c.). Interestingly, in Italian, while double diminutive suffixes can effect further denotative diminution, diminutivizing interfixes are denotationally meaningless, e.g., *libr-ino/-etto* (smaller than *libro* 'book') → *libre-ett-ino* (still smaller), but *libr-ic(c)-ino* (not smaller than *librino*) (Dressler and Merlini Barbaresi 1994: 540). Still, they seem to have connotative meaning, e.g., *topo* 'mouse' has two diminutives: *top-ino* and more attractive *top-ol-ino* (Dressler and Merlini Barbaresi 1994: 542).

Pleonastic derivational realization of augmentation can be exemplified with Italian *ultra-bell-issimo* 'most hyperbeautiful' (Lehmann 2005: 137–148). Spanish provides also instances of implicit pleonasm in the realization of iterative via *-ear*, e.g., *interroguear* 'to interrogate', *tergiversear* 'to twist', because *interrogar* and *tergiversar* already have an iterative meaning (Rainer 1993: 459).

A smaller chapter in the present survey of affix pleonasm is the derivation of abstract nouns: examples include Old French *tenebr-our* 'darkness' and *hontage* 'blemish', in which suffixation via *-our* and *-age*, respectively, aims to reinforce the membership of the nouns *ténèbre* and *honte* in the semantically determined group of abstract nouns (Nyrop 1908: 36; Malkiel 1957: 107; Meyer-Lübke 1966, 2: 25–26). In Ossetic, many adjectives can function both as adjectives and abstract nouns, e.g., *fəd* 'evil'. Here, the application of the abstract suffix *-ad* produces disambiguation of the abstract meaning, thus *fədd-ad* means 'evil' only in the sense of 'evilness' (Oleg Belyaev, p.c.).

In the domain of adjectives, we often find what Migliorini (1943: 451) called "cumulo dei suffissi nella formazione degli aggettivi" [suffix cumulation in the formation of adjectives], for example, Middle High German *narrehtic* 'foolish' and *tôrehtic* 'fatuous', with extension of the suffix *-eht* through the suffix *-ig* (originally used to form exocentric adjectives).

A recurrent area of incidence of pleonastic affixes is the integration of loanwords. Quite frequently, affixation exerts an adaptive role in loanword integration, and the trend towards indigenization can give rise to pleonasm. In Ossetic, for example, the adjective *nacionalon* is a synonym of *nacion* 'national', which is regularly formed from the noun *naci* 'nation', via suffixation with *-on*, an Ossetic adjectivizing suffix. Instead, the form *nacional-on* is clearly pleonastic, since there is not a root *nacional in Ossetic; it is probably calqued on Russian *nacional'-nyj*, which is itself an example of pleonastic suffixation in Russian (Oleg Belyaev, p.c.); see also Polish *globalny*, etc. In Maltese, suffixless loanwords from English can be integrated via suffix addition, for example the ethnic adjective *Ġerman-iż* from *German*, in analogy with *Franċiż* and *Ingliż*, borrowed from Italian *francese* and *inglese*. In German, several adjectives borrowed from Latin or French are suffixed with *-isch*, without any semantic modification: e.g., *bestialisch* 'bestial', *musikalisch* 'musical'. Often, adjectives pertaining to the learnèd layer of vocabulary, mostly to technical terminology, display pleonasm, for example German *sphär-oid-isch* 'spherical', instead of *sphär-oid* (Hyrtl 1880: 262), and English *lactiferous* 'conveying milk', *nubiferous* 'bringing clouds', which show, in diachronic terms, an agglomeration of the Latin suffix *-ifer* and the English suffix *-ous*, which was probably fostered by the existence in Latin of an allomorph *-ferus* (although not attested for the two examples mentioned).

Apart from adjectives, affix pleonasm is not absent from the integration of borrowed nouns and verbs either: for example, Turkish speakers can add the agentive suffix *-cI* to borrowed nouns which already denote agents, e.g., *kasap* 'butcher' (from Albanian) → *kasap-çı* (Lewis 1967: 60); in Gagauz, the same suffix *-cI* can attach to loanwords that already denote an occupation, such as *başçıvan-cı* 'gardener': here, the indigenous *-cI* applies to the Persian loan *başçıvan*, consisting of the base *başçe* 'garden' and the Persian suffix *-van*; in Old French, *bolengier* 'baker' results from Old Picardic *boulenc*, on the model of *fournier* (Malkiel 1957: 107). Pleonastically used deverbal derivational affixes can be themselves borrowed items, as is the case of the suffix *-avy*, borrowed from Slavic languages in the Lithuanian dialect of Zietela, e.g., *dėn-avy-ti* 'to lay down' (vs. standard *dėti(s)*) or *griž-avy-ti-s* 'to return' (vs. standard *grižti*) (Wiemer 2009: 360).

5 Why affix pleonasm?

After having provided, without any claim to completeness, a survey of the types of derivational affix pleonasm occurring in the languages of Europe, this final section tries to overview how linguists have approached pleonasm and, in particular, its motivations from a theoretical viewpoint.

For this purpose, I turn to Haspelmath's definition of affix pleonasm, as reproduced in section 2. In fact, this definition suggests that the morphosyntactic features of those word forms that we define as pleonastic, are already realized by primary affixes, to which the secondary (i.e. pleonastic) affixes are claimed to be a "semantically vacuous addition". While the existence of primary affixes is the theoretical foundation for acknowledging the secondary affixes as being *de facto* pleonastic, the status of both primary and secondary affixes needs to be discussed in more detail.

The issue at hand here is whether pleonasm qualifies as a complete or rather a transitory phenomenon in terms both of diachronic evolution and language acquisition. Clearly, in a diachronic perspective, pleonasm can refer to a transitory stage, as can be exemplified with the evolution of sentential negation in French from stage (1), Old French *jo(u) ne vais*, via stage (2), *je n(e) vais pas*, to stage (3), contemporary colloquial *j'vais pas* 'I don't go' (see Malkiel 1957: 90). However, in synchronic terms, one form can be definitive or more variants can be in competition with each other: for example, in contemporary French, both (2) and (3) are possible variants, though they reflect a difference in register.

In scenarios of early phases of language acquisition (Dressler 1997), Turkish children produce forms such as *manav-cı* 'greengrocer-*cı*' (Aslı Göksel, p.c.), English children have plurals such as *feets* or past-tense forms such as *camed* (Covington 1981: 35). These cases, in fact, represent an intermediary stage. Also in language contact, as we have seen in some of the cases reported, pleonasm can be considered, at least partly, the reflex of an intermediary stage: for example, German *verbal*, *nominal* have not been extended via *-isch* (**verbalisch*, **nominalisch*).

These facts lead us to raise the question of whether affix pleonasm exists at all. In other words, do pleonastic affixes have any psycholinguistic salience in the grammars of the speakers or do they only exist in the heads of linguists? Dressler, Dziubalska-Kołaczyk and Spina (2001: 124) argue that "hypercharacterization" (i.e. pleonasm) "is an imprecise concept that is only justified in a very superficial morphotactic or panchronic perspective", because synchronically, the secondary affixes are, in fact, the only markers which are relevant in terms both of productivity and generality.

Thus, if secondary (pleonastic) markers alone realize meanings and values, what are the conditions that make speakers use these markers? What are the conditions under which their occurrence is necessary? While Dressler, Dziubalska-Kołaczyk and Spina (2001: 124) claim that pleonasm is only an apparent phenomenon, thus does not represent a violation of biuniqueness, other linguists consider it to be the source of allomorphy, of uneconomical and non-uniform coding and, thus, a violation of the elsewhere condition (Stump 1989; Haspelmath 1993: 299, 305, 306). In spite of this discord, all authors agree that pleonasm enhances transparency and increases neatness (e.g., Malkiel 1957: 81; Plank 1981: 79). Accordingly, apart from restoring prosodic normalcy, motivations for pleonasm include the replacement of affixes which are either unproductive or exceptional or difficult to parse, as well as their reinforcement (Plank 1985: 69; Thomason 1988: 300; Haspelmath 1993: 298; Dressler, Dziubalska-Kołaczyk and Spina 2001; Dressler 2004). Moreover, affix pleonasm serves systematization in language, as has been observed by Booij (2007: 273) with respect to loanword integration (see also Lehmann 2005: 130 on "safety pleonasm").

In light of the evidence provided in this discussion, neither the pure diachronic nor the pure synchronic perspective helps us to properly understand the very dimension of pleonasm. Instead, it is reasonable to assume an approach in terms of gradual motivation, in order to be able to account for both idiolectal and sociolectal variation (see Fleischer and Barz 2012: 45). In this vein, Haspelmath (1993: 301) proposes a principle of conservatism, according to which innovative forms that are closer to the earlier, more familiar forms are generally preferable than forms that are totally innovative: thus, in Haspelmath's terms, *feets* is better than *foots* for it is more similar to the older form *feet*.

Looking forward to wider cross-linguistic studies providing novel evidence and possibly modifying current claims on the theoretical foundation of affix pleonasm (see Stolz 2007: 249 *contra* Ortmann 1999: 118), it is still certain that pleonasm concerns an "impressive gamut of categories [which is] matched by the variety of languages participating in [it] and, within the lifetime of each, by the number of evolutionary stages testifying to this peculiar encroachment on the norm" (Malkiel 1957: 82).

Acknowledgments

Thanks are due to Peter Arkadiev, Oleg Belyaev, Maris Camilleri, Viktor Elšík, Aslı Göksel, þorsteinn Indriðason, Petros Karatsareas, Ferenc Kiefer, Yury Lander, Paweł Miedziński, Markus Pöchtrager, and Franz Rainer, for their language expertise and for providing examples.

Abbreviations

1	first person	F	feminine
2	second person	INCMPL	imcompletive
3	third person	IO	indirect object
ABIL	abilitive	LVM	loanverb marker
ABL	ablative	NEG	negative
ABS	absolutive	NOM	nominative
ACC	accusative	PASS	passive
APPL	applicative	PL	plural
AOR	aorist	PFV	perfective
BEN	benefactive	PRS	present
CAUS	causative	PST	past
CM	class marker	PTCT	participle
COMP	comparative	PV	preverb
DEF	definite	RFL	reflexive
DIM	diminutive	SG	singular
DIR	directional	TRR	transitivizer
EVID	evidential		

6 References

Booij, Geert (2007): *The Grammar of Words*. Oxford: Oxford University Press.

Bowerman, Melissa (1982): Reorganizational processes in lexical and syntactic development. In: Eric Wanner and Lila R. Gleitman (eds.), *Language Acquisition. The State of the Art*, 319–346. Cambridge: Cambridge University Press.

Cennamo, Michela (1999): Late Latin pleonastic reflexives and the Unaccusative Hypothesis. *Transactions of the Philological Society* 97(1): 103–150.

Corbett, Greville G. (2006): *Agreement*. Cambridge: Cambridge University Press.

Corbett, Greville G. (2012): *Features*. Cambridge: Cambridge University Press.

Covington, Michael A. (1981): *Evidence for lexicalism. A critical review*. Bloomington, IN: University Linguistics Club.

Dressler, Wolfgang U. (1997): "Scenario" as a concept for the functional explanation of language change. In: Jadranka Gvozdanović (ed.), *Language Change and Functional Explanations*, 109–142. Berlin: Mouton de Gruyter.

Dressler, Wolfgang U. (2004): Hypercharacterisation and productivity in inflectional morphology. In: Thomas Krisch, Thomas Lindner and Ulrich Müller (eds.), *Analecta homini universali dicata. Arbeiten zur Indogermanistik, Linguistik, Philologie, Politik, Musik und Dichtung. Festschrift für Oswald Panagl zum 65. Geburtstag*, 515–524. Stuttgart: Heinz.

Dressler, Wolfgang U., Katarzyna Dziubalska-Kołaczyk and Rossella Spina (2001): Sources of markedness in language structures. *Folia Linguistica Historica* 22(1–2): 103–136.

Dressler, Wolfgang U. and Lavinia Merlini Barbaresi (1994): *Morphopragmatics. Diminutives and Intensifiers in Italian, German, and Other Languages*. Berlin/New York: Mouton de Gruyter.

Enger, Hans-Olav (2014): Reinforcement in inflection classes: Two cues may be better than one. *Word Structure* 7(2): 153–181.

Fleischer, Wolfgang and Irmhild Barz (2012): *Wortbildung der deutschen Gegenwartssprache*. 4th ed. Berlin/Boston: de Gruyter.

Gardani, Francesco (2013): *Dynamics of Morphological Productivity. The Evolution of Noun Classes from Latin to Italian*. Leiden/Boston: Brill.

Gāters, Alfrēds (1977): *Die lettische Sprache und ihre Dialekte*. The Hague: Mouton.

Gilliéron, Jules (1921): *Pathologie et thérapeutique verbales*. Paris: Champion.

Glässer, Eduard (1954): Review of Moritz Regula (1951) *Grundlegung und Grundprobleme der Syntax*. Heidelberg: Winter. *Romanische Forschungen* 65: 424–429.

Grinaveckienė, Elena (1969): Lietuvių ir slavų kalbų gramatinio kontaktavimo reiškiniai pietryčių Lietuvoje. In: Vytautas Ambrazas (ed.), *Lietuvių kalbos gramatikos tyrinėjimai*, 219–229. Vilnius: Lietuvos TSR Mokslų Akademija.

Halle, Morris and Alec Marantz (1993): Distributed morphology and the pieces of inflection. In: Kenneth L. Hale and Samuel J. Keyser (eds.), *The View from Building 20. Essays in Linguistics in Honor of Sylvain Bromberger*, 111–176. Cambridge, MA: MIT Press.

Harris, Alice C. (2008): Explaining exuberant agreement. In: Thórhallur Eythórsson (ed.), *Grammatical Change and Linguistic Theory. The Rosendal Papers*, 265–283. Amsterdam/Philadelphia: Benjamins.

Harris, Alice C. (2009): Exuberant exponence in Batsbi. *Natural Language and Linguistic Theory* 27(2): 267–303.

Haspelmath, Martin (1993): The diachronic externalization of inflection. *Linguistics* 31(2): 279–309.

Herzog, Marvin and Vera Baviskar (eds.) (2000): *The Eastern Yiddish – Western Yiddish Continuum*. Tübingen: Niemeyer.

Hinzelin, Marc-Olivier (2009): Neuter pronouns in Ibero-Romance: Discourse reference, expletives and beyond. In: Georg A. Kaiser and Eva-Maria Remberger (eds.), *Proceedings of the Workshop "Null-subjects, expletives, and locatives in Romance"*, 1–25. Konstanz: Fachbereich Sprachwissenschaft Universität Konstanz.

Hock, Hans Henrich (1986): *Principles of Historical Linguistics*. Berlin/New York: Mouton de Gruyter.

Horn, Wilhelm (1939): *Neue Wege der Sprachforschung*. Marburg: Elwert.

Hyrtl, Joseph (1880): *Onomatologia anatomica. Geschichte und Kritik der anatomischen Sprache der Gegenwart, mit besonderer Berücksichtigung ihrer Barbarismen, Widersinnigkeiten, Tropen, und grammatikalischen Fehler*. Wien: Braumüller.

Imre, Samu (1972): Hungarian dialects. In: Benko Loránd and Samu Imre (eds.), *The Hungarian Language*, 299–326. The Hague: Mouton.

Jacobs, Neil G. (2005): *Yiddish. A Linguistic Introduction*. Cambridge: Cambridge University Press.

Kantor, Benjamin (2019): Where does *'Ayyē* come from? Proclisis and affix pleonasm in the Biblical Hebrew interrogatives *'Ē* and *'Ayyē*. *Journal of Semitic Studies* 64(2): 377–399.

Karatsareas, Petros (2019): The morphology of Silliot: Paradigmatic defectiveness, paradigmatic levelling and affix pleonasm. In: Angela Ralli (ed.), *The morphology of Asia Minor Greek*, 148–180. Leiden: Brill.

Kolb, Herbert (1980): Über verbale Interferenzsuffixe. In: Hans D. Bork, Artur Greive and Dieter Woll (eds.), *Romanica europea et americana. Festschrift für Harri Meier. 8. Januar 1980*, 282–292. Bonn: Bouvier.

Koutsoukos, Nikos and Eleni Karantzola (2022): Double marking of the past in Early Modern Greek. *Journal of Greek Linguistics* 22(1): 7–35.

Lehmann, Christian (2005): Pleonasm and hypercharacterisation. In: Geert E. Booij and Jaap v. Marle (eds.), *Yearbook of morphology 2005*, 119–154. Dordrecht: Springer.

Lewis, Geoffrey (1967): *Turkish Grammar.* Oxford: Clarendon Press.

MacKay, Donald G. (1979): Lexical insertion, inflection, and derivation: Creative processes in word production. *Journal of Psycholinguistic Research* 8(5): 477–498.

Malkiel, Yakov (1957): Diachronic hypercharacterization in Romance. *Archivum Linguisticum* 9(1): 79–113.

Matthews, Peter H. (1972): *Inflectional Morphology. A theoretical study based on aspects of Latin verb conjugation.* Cambridge: Cambridge University Press.

Matushansky, Ora (2024): Thematic non-uniformity of Russian vocalic verbal suffixes. *Glossa: A Journal of General Linguistics* 9(1): 1–50.

Meyer-Lübke, Wilhelm (1921): *Historische Grammatik der französischen Sprache.* Vol. 2. Heidelberg: Winter.

Meyer-Lübke, Wilhelm (1966): *Historische Grammatik der französischen Sprache.* Vol. 2. 2nd ed. Heidelberg: Winter.

Migliorini, Bruno (1943): Sulla tendenza a evitare il cumulo dei suffissi nella formazione degli aggettivi. In: Arnold Steiger (ed.), *Sache, Ort und Wort. Jakob Jud zum 60. Geburtstag, 12. Januar 1942*, 442–452. Genève: Droz.

Müller, Peter O. (2005): Einführung. In: Peter O. Müller (ed.), *Fremdwortbildung. Theorie und Praxis in Geschichte und Gegenwart*, 11–45. Frankfurt/M.: Lang.

Naghzguy-Kohan, Mehrdad and Tania Kuteva (2016): On competition and blocking in inflectional morphology: Evidence from the domain of number in New Persian. *Folia Linguistica* 50(1): 65–96.

Newman, Paul (1979): Explaining Hausa feminines. *Studies in African Linguistics* 10(2): 197–226.

Niedermann, Max (1953): Review of Jules Marouzeau (1951) *Lexique de la terminologie linguistique français, allemand, anglais, italien.* 3rd ed. Paris: Geuthner. *Vox Romanica* 13: 103–113.

Nyrop, Kristoffer (1908): *Grammaire historique de la langue française.* Vol. 3: *Formation des mots.* Copenhague: Gyldendal.

Okamoto, Junji (2002): Particle-bound directions in German particle verb constructions. In: Hidekazu Suzuki (ed.), *Report of the Special Research-Project for the Typological Investigation of Languages and Cultures of the East and West. Part II*, 415–431. Ibaraki: University of Tsukuba.

Olsen, Susan (1996): Pleonastische Direktionale. In: Gisela Harras and Manfred Bierwisch (eds.), *Wenn die Semantik arbeitet. Klaus Baumgärtner zum 65. Geburtstag*, 303–329. Tübingen: Niemeyer.

Ortmann, Albert (1999): Affix repetition and non-redundancy in inflectional morphology. *Zeitschrift für Sprachwissenschaft* 18(1): 76–120.

Pantelidis, Nikolaos (2010): The reshaping of the mediopassive endings: Evidence from Modern Greek varieties. In: Angela Ralli, Brian D. Joseph, Mark Janse and Athanasios Karasimos (eds.), *On-line Proceedings of the Forth International Conference of Modern Greek Dialects and Linguistic Theory (MGDLT4), Chios, 11–14 June 2009*, 315–328. Patras: University of Patras.

Paul, Hermann (1880): *Prinzipien der Sprachgeschichte.* Halle/S.: Niemeyer.

Paul, Hermann (1920): *Prinzipien der Sprachgeschichte.* 5th ed. Halle/S.: Niemeyer.

Plank, Frans (1981): *Morphologische (Ir-)Regularitäten. Aspekte der Wortstrukturtheorie.* Tübingen: Narr.

Plank, Frans (1985): On the reapplication of morphological rules after phonological rules and other resolutions of functional conflicts between morphology and phonology. *Linguistics* 23: 45–82.

Prince, Ellen F. (1993): On the discourse functions of syntactic form in Yiddish: Expletive *es* and subject-postposing. In: David Goldberg, Marvin I. Herzog, Barbara Kirshenblatt-Gimblett and Dan Miron (eds.), *The Field of Yiddish. Studies in Yiddish language, folklore, and literature,* 59–86. Evanston, IL: Northwestern University Press.

Rainer, Franz (1993): *Spanische Wortbildungslehre.* Tübingen: Niemeyer.

Rehbein, Ines and Josef Genabith (2006): German particle verbs and pleonastic prepositions. In: Boban Arsenijevic, Timothy Baldwin and Beata Trawiński (eds.), *Proceedings of the Third ACL-SIGSEM Workshop on Prepositions,* 57–64. Trento: Association for Computational Linguistics.

Rowlett, Paul (1998): *Sentential Negation in French.* Oxford/New York: Oxford University Press.

Schwyzer, Eduard (1941): *Sprachliche Hypercharakterisierung.* Berlin: Verlag der Akademie der Wissenschaften.

Stolz, Thomas (2007): Word-internal agreement. *Language Typology and Universals* 60(3): 219–251.

Stolz, Thomas (2010): Pleonastic morphology dies hard: Change and variation of definiteness inflection in Lithuanian. In: Franz Rainer, Wolfgang U. Dressler, Dieter Kastovsky and Hans Christian Luschützky (eds.), *Variation and Change in Morphology. Selected Papers from the 13th International Morphology Meeting, Vienna, February 2008,* 217–244. Amsterdam/Philadelphia: Benjamins.

Stotz, Peter (2000): *Handbuch zur Lateinischen Sprache des Mittelalters.* Vol. 2: *Bedeutungswandel und Wortbildung.* München: Beck.

Stump, Gregory T. (1989): A note on Breton pluralization and the Elsewhere Condition. *Natural Language and Linguistic Theory* 7(2): 261–273.

Szymanek, Bogdan (2015): Remarks on tautology in word-formation. In: Laurie Bauer, Lívia Körtvélyessy and Pavol Štekauer (eds.), *Semantics of complex words,* 143–161. Cham: Springer.

Thomason, Sarah (1988): Double marking in morphological change. In: Ann Miller and Joyce Powers (eds.), *ESCOL 87. Proceedings of the Fourth Eastern States Conference on Linguistics,* 296–305. Columbus, Ohio: Ohio State University.

Tovar, Antonio (1942): Review of Eduard Schwyzer (1939) *Die Parenthese im engern und im weitern Sinne*; (1940) *Syntaktische Archaismen des Attischen*; (1941) *Sprachliche Hypercharakterisierung.* Berlin: de Gruyter. *Emerita* 10: 185–188.

Wiemer, Björn (2009): Zu entlehnten Verbpräfixen und anderen morphosyntaktischen Slavismen in litauischen Insel- und Grenzmundarten. In: Lenka Scholze and Björn Wiemer (eds.), *Von Zuständen, Dynamik und Veränderung bei Pygmäen und Giganten. Festschrift für Walter Breu zu seinem 60. Geburtstag,* 347–390. Bochum: Brockmeyer.

Wierzbicka, Anna (2003): *Cross-Cultural Pragmatics. The Semantics of Human Interaction.* 2nd ed. Berlin: Mouton de Gruyter.

Włodarczyk, Matylda (2007): "More strenger and mightier": Some remarks on double comparison in Middle English. *Studia Anglica Posnaniensia* 43: 195–216.

Wohlgemuth, Jan (2009): *A Typology of Verbal Borrowings.* Berlin/New York: Mouton de Gruyter.

Zwicky, Arnold (2012): Excrescent 's. http://arnoldzwicky.wordpress.com/2012/06/08/excrescent-s/ [last access 30 Sept 2012].

Michel Roché

3 Interfixes in Romance

Abstract: Present in all Romance languages, presuffixal interfixes are meaning-less suffix-like elements which are inserted before the suffix of some derivatives. Their presence is connected to lexical and phonological – prosodic and segmental – parameters. They are a means to offer a more suitable stem to the suffix and to ensure a better integration of the derivative in its derivational series and derivational family.

1 Introduction

One of the most controversial topics of Spanish morphology, the question of inter-fixes has been paid little, if any, attention in other Romance languages. The problems they raise, however, are not specific to Spanish and challenge linguistic description and linguistic theory. For greater accuracy, we shall restrict the scope of this article to presuffixal interfixes as defined in Malkiel's (1958) seminal paper and, first, distinguish the constructions including such interfixes from outwardly similar ones for which they could be mistaken. We shall see, then, how the debate has been renewed by recent developments in morphology, especially morphophonological and paradigmatic approaches, and by the use of extensive data. Most of the examples will be taken from Spanish, Occitan and French, for which literature or personal studies are available, but the linguistic observations would be the same for Catalan, Portuguese or Italian (and probably for Romanian).

2 To be or not to be an interfix

"El español no posee interfijos" [Spanish has no interfixes]: this claim of Martín Camacho's extensive study *El problema lingüístico de los interfijos españoles* [The

Michel Roché, Toulouse, France

https://doi.org/10.1515/9783111420554-003

linguistic problem of Spanish interfixes] (Martín Camacho 2002: 16) seems to invalidate Portolés' thirty-three-page chapter about "La interfijación" [Interfixation] in the authoritative *Gramática Descriptiva de la Lengua Española* (Bosque and Demonte 1999). Before discussing such duelling positions, our first task will be to define exactly the object which is in question.

2.1 The presuffixal interfix

The starting point is Malkiel's definition of the *interfijo*:

> [...] el segmento, siempre átono y falto de significado propio, entre el radical y el sufijo de ciertos derivados, p. ej. el elemento *-ar-* en *hum-ar-eda, polv-ar-eda*, palabras que no es lícito descomponer en *humar-* y *polvar-eda*, por no existir ni haber existido nunca, que sepamos, las fases intermedias **humar, *polvar* come formaciones independientes. [[...] the element, always unstressed and devoid of proper meaning, between the radical and the suffix of some derivatives, e.g., the string *-ar-* in *hum-ar-eda, polv-ar-eda*, words that cannot be broken down into *humar-* y *polvar-eda* since the intermediate stages **humar, *polvar* do not exist and have never existed as independent formations, as far as we know.] (Malkiel 1958: 107)

Before Malkiel, other words had named the interfix itself or the combination of interfix plus suffix (and some are still preferred by linguists who do not acknowledge the notion of interfix). Darmesteter (1890), for instance, used "suffixes intercalaires" [interposed suffixes] for such examples as Fr. *gant-el-et* 'gauntlet' ← *gant* 'glove'; Prati (1942), "antisuffissi" [presuffixes] (e.g., It. *acqu-er-ello* 'watercolour' ← *acqua* 'water'); Pottier (1953) and Badia Margarit (1962), "infixes" (e.g., Pg. *sant-arr-ão* 'zealot' ← *santo* 'saint', Cat. *branqu-ill-ó* 'twig' ← *branca* 'branch'); Adams (1913), "compound suffixes" (e.g., Oc. *pan-at-ièr* 'baker' ← *pan* 'bread'); Graur (1969), "suffixes élargis" [enlarged suffixes] (e.g., Rom. *lung-ăr-et* 'long-DIM' ← *lung* 'long'); etc.

Most of these denominations are ambiguous and confusing. Adams distinguishes "compound suffixes", which are the combination of an interfix and a suffix, from "real double suffixes" (which are the result of two consecutive derivations), but he has no specific term for the interfix itself. Pottier calls "infixes modificateurs" the evaluative suffixes themselves as well as the interfixes which precede some of them. In the French tradition, "formes élargies" can designate variants of a suffix as well as the combination of a suffix and an interfix. The first interest of Malkiel's founding paper was to identify a specific morphological object and name it.

Unfortunately, the word *interfix* has thereafter been used for other inserted elements: the non-etymological velar segment in Spanish verbs such as *tengo*

(Dworkin 1995), for instance, or the marker *-i-/-esc-* in the so-called inchoative conjugation (Allen 1977). It is widely spread, inside and outside Romance, for the linking element of compounds. In the meantime, for the interfix as defined by Malkiel, the word did spread in studies on Ibero-Romance, but the notion itself was bitterly discussed. As regards Italian, the term and its content were adopted by the followers of natural morphology (Dressler and Merlini Barbaresi 1989; Crocco Galèas 1991; Merlini Barbaresi 2004), and rejected or ignored by most other morphologists. In Gallo-Romance, constructions featuring the equivalent of a Spanish *interfijo* had not really been examined until our recent studies. The etymologies of the *Trésor de la langue française* (TLF) exhibit this deficiency. For instance, Fr. *briquetier* 'brickmaker', *pelletier* 'furrier', *malletier* 'trunk-maker', which are obviously constructed after the same pattern (the bases are the simplices *brique* 'brick', *peau* 'pelt', *malle* 'trunk') receive different analyses: *briquetier* as derived from *brique* with the suffix *-ier* and the intercalation of the consonant *-t-*; *pelletier* from OFr. *pel* with the extended suffix *-(et)ier*; *malletier* from *mallette* 'briefcase'.

The result is a great sense of confusion. The use of the same word for different things which have little in common has vitiated the debate on the facts themselves. Leaving aside all that falls within inflectional morphology, and adopting Dressler's distinction between "presuffixal" and "interradical" interfixes, we shall stick to Malkiel's definition and focus only on the former.

2.2 The presuffixal interfix is not a (real) suffix

Most presuffixal interfixes have a suffix-like form. So the result of a construction including an interfix (1a) is superficially similar to the result of two consecutive derivations (1b).

(1)	a. *coque* 'eggshell' → *coquetier* 'eggcup'			French
	libro 'book' → *libriccino* 'booklet'			Italian
	b. *noix* 'walnut' → *noisette* 'hazelnut' → *noisetier* 'hazel (tree)'			French
	libro 'book' → *libretto* 'libretto' → *librettino* 'libretto-DIM'			Italian

The difference, however, is obvious. In (1b), the meaning of the final derivative is calculated from the intermediate form, which is a lexeme. A *noisetier* produces *noisettes*, not *noix*. In (1a), the meaning of the only derivative is calculated from the initial form. The difference does not lie in the fact that an intermediate form is not attested. It would be pointless to introduce a virtual step °*coquet(te)* between *coque* and *coquetier*: the result of the derivation would be the same. *Co-quetier* is to *coque* exactly what *beurrier* 'butter dish' is to *beurre* 'butter'.

Some of the morphologists who do not admit the notion of interfix (e.g., Mascaró 1986) argue that so-called interfixes are, plainly, suffixes. Where others see an interfix, they systematically postulate a virtual intermediate step. This view relies on a conception which takes into account the sole formal dimension of derivation, totally disconnected from its semantic counterpart. But a suffix is not only a phonological string: it is the instrument of a semantic or categorial construction. To be plausible, a virtual intermediate derivative must be plausible both in itself and as the base of the second derivation. In (2), the first derivation would not be possible for semantic or categorial reasons.

(2) ??*testa*   'head'   → **testar* → *testarudo*   'stubborn' Spanish
     ??*poète*   'poet'   → **poétier* → *poètereau*   'poor poet' French
     ??*mangiare* 'to eat' → **mangero* → *mangereccio* 'edible'   Italian

The well-attested derivatives in (3a) cannot be the bases of the derivatives in (3b).

(3) a. *calle*   'street'   → *calleja*   'back street'   Spanish
     b.   → *callejero* 'street directory'
     a. *lop*   'wolf'   → *lobat*   'wolf cub'   Occitan
     b.   → *lobatàs*   'wolf-AUG'
     a. *brique* 'brick'   → *briquette* 'small brick'   French
     b.   → *briquetier* 'brickmaker'
     a. *porta*   'door, gate' → *portina*   'small door'   Italian
     b.   → *portinaio* 'doorman, gatekeeper'

Brickmakers do not make only (or especially) small bricks and the name of the Big Bad Wolf cannot be constructed on that of the cubs. (3a) and (3b) are parallel derivations from the same base.

In (4a), °*gouttelle* and °*gouttette* would separately be plausible (cf. *coupelle* 'small cup' ← *coupe* 'cup'; *chaînette* 'small chain' ← *chaîne* 'chain'), but a two-step derivation *goutte* → °*gouttelle* → *gouttelette* is highly improbable since the meaning of the actual derivative *gouttelette* is the same as that of °*gouttelle* and °*gouttette*.

(4) a. *goutte* 'drop' → °*gouttelle*   'droplet'   French
                        → °*gouttette*   'droplet'
                        → °*gouttelette*   'droplet'

     b. *gos* 'dog' → *gosset* 'puppy' → *gosseton* 'puppy-DIM'   Occitan

The consecution of two evaluative derivations, which is frequent in meridional Romance (4b), is unusual in French and *gouttelette* does not correspond to this pattern.

The crucial point in Malkiel's definition is not "por no existir" – a form could exist without being presently attested – but "falto de significado propio". In spite of its form, the interfix is not a suffix which could act as such in a derivational chain. It is an empty morph.

2.3 The presuffixal interfix is not an infix

It is generally assumed that an infix is an affix which is inserted into a lexeme. Regarding only the derivative, presuffixal interfixes could be viewed, superficially, as infixes. In fact, they differ from infixes in several ways. They are not inserted inside the root, but between the root and a suffix. While infixes, like prefixes and suffixes, have a form of their own and a derivational or inflectional value, interfixes do not: they are always neutral elements and, in most cases, have the form of a suffix.

The word *infix* is no longer used systematically for *interfix*, but both terms can still be found in the analysis of various constructions for which neither is really appropriate. In our view, there are some cases of infixed elements in Romance, such as the often scrutinized Spanish "infixed diminutives" (e.g., *Victítor* ← *Víctor*), but no infixes properly speaking. French *trompinette* 'small trumpet' ← *trompette* 'trumpet' and *poissillon* 'small fish' ← *poisson* 'fish', for instance, exhibit another kind of anomalous infixation, due to the frequency of the endings *-inette* and *-illon* in the lexicon, but the string *-in-* in *trompinette* is the same affix as the suffix *-ine* in *trompettine*, which is also attested, and the string *-ill-* in *poissillon* is the same affix as the suffix *-ille* in *faucille* 'sickle' ← *faux* 'scythe'. They cannot be analysed as interfixes, in spite of their position before a suffix-like ending, since they retain their full evaluative value. In Spanish, Fábregas (2006: 17) calls "infix" the string *-et-* in *corretear* 'to scamper' ← *correr* 'to run' while Portolés (1999: 5066) lists it among interfixes and Lázaro Mora (1999: 4649) among suffixes. The question of verbal suffixation is too intricate to be discussed here, let us just say that we prefer to view the full string *-etea(r)* as a suffix, since it bears the evaluative value of the derivation. But in *despernancarse* 'to spread one's legs' ← *pierna* 'leg', for instance, *-anc-* has no proper meaning and can be considered as an interfix.

2.4 Interfix plus suffix vs. suffix variants

Since the base of Fr. *briquetier*, for instance, is not *briquette* but *brique* (cf. examples (3)), an easy solution would be to consider -*etier* as a variant of the suffix -*ier*. The principal argument against this analysis, since Malkiel, has been descriptive economy: each suffix would have too many variants. Owing to the multiplicity of combinations between interfixes and suffixes, it is simpler to list them separately.

An inventory of interfixes in the different Romance languages would exceed the length of this article, *a fortiori* an inventory of the combinations between interfixes and suffixes (for a partial one, Roché 2005). Their numbers are indeed considerable. In Spanish, a conjunction of Portolés' (1988, 1999) and Rainer's (1993) lists – which do not coincide – comes to 473 combinations. The sole -*ar*- can precede 28 different suffixes (Malkiel 1958: 178–184) and -*ón* be preceded by 41 different interfixes (Portolés 1999: 5044). In French, where interfixation is far less frequent, a dozen different interfixes can be found before the suffix -*on* (Roché 2003a), a dozen before -*ette* in contemporary attestations (Plénat 2005), a score before -*ier*/-*ière* (Plénat and Roché 2004). All of them also appear before other suffixes. Nevertheless, as pointed out by Rainer (1993: 154), the argument of economy is not decisive. If there were good reasons to regard each combination of interfix plus suffix as a variant of a suffix, morphology ought to do so, whatever their numbers. But more important than the numbers themselves is the versatility of interfixes. They have a broad independence from suffixes within the apparatus of word construction, whereas variants are specific to each suffix and closely associated to its history.

Most variants originate in a reanalysis – a coalescence of two suffixes or a miscut between radical and suffix. Fr. -*erie* and -*eraie* typically exemplify two stages in the development of variants: the former superseded -*ie* long ago, the latter is rivaling -*aie* in a growing proportion. Originally, the ending -*eraie*, like -*erie*, was used in derivatives constructed on bases ending in -*ier* (5b), the string -*er*- being a part of the radical. A miscut leads to adding it to the suffix, as in (5c) (Roché 2011).

(5) a. *chêne* 'oak tree' → *chênaie* 'oak grove'   French
     b. [*rose* 'rose' →] *rosier* 'rosebush' → *roseraie* 'rose garden'   French
     c. *bambou* 'bamboo' → *bambouseraie* 'bamboo grove'   French

The string -*er*- is used as an interfix in other derivatives (e.g., *puceron* 'aphid' ← *puce* 'flea', *pâquerette* 'daisy' ← *Pâques* 'Easter', *hachereau* 'hatchet' ← *hache* 'axe', *sècheresse* 'drought' ← *sec* 'dry', etc.) but there are two important differences: (i) before -*on*, for example, -*er*- is one interfix among others (e.g., *bottillon* '(short) boot' ← *botte* 'boot', *pâlichon* 'peaky' ← *pâle* 'pale', *gueuleton* 'feast' ← *gueule* 'mouth', etc.), whereas *-eraie* is the only variant of *-aie* (as *-erie* is the only variant of *-ie*); (ii) interfixes appear after monosyllabic bases only (cf. section 3.2), whereas *-eraie* (as other suffixal variants) may follow any radical (for other examples, Roché 2003b, 2009).

The process which leads to the diffusion of interfixes (cf. section 3.4) is similar to the one which generates suffix variants. It is natural that the distinction between the two kinds of items is not clear-cut. The recurrence of the same interfix before the same suffix leads to the formation of a variant. The Romanian evaluative *-eț*, for instance, is preceded by *-ul-* in an overwhelming majority of derivatives (Graur 1969: 330), so that *-uleț* seems to have become not only a variant of *-eț* but the standard form of the suffix. But we shall see that there are also good reasons to regard the interfix as an extension of the stem. Even though many cases are subject to discussion, the combinations of interfix plus suffix cannot be analysed merely as suffix variants.

2.5 Base + interfix vs. base allomorphy and epenthesis

Symmetrically, the combination of base plus interfix could be assimilated to base allomorphy. At first sight, the morphophonological accidents in Fr. *bombinette* 'bomb-DIM' ← *bombe* 'bomb' and Fr. *criminel* 'criminal' ← *crime* 'crime' are similar: the string *-in-* which appears in the derivative is not present in the free form of the base. Historically, the difference is obvious: the allomorph *crimin-* is inherited from Latin and is the only one for this lexeme, whereas a diminutive of *bombe* can be coined with another interfix (*bombelette* and *bombounette* are also attested). Synchronically, we shall see that both *crimin-* and *bombin-* can be regarded as the stems on which *criminel* and *bombinette* are constructed. So the boundary between interfixation and stem allomorphy is not always clear-cut. But an important difference remains: inherited allomorphy can add a syllable to the stem regardless of its length (cf. Fr. *longitudinal* ← *longitude*, for instance), whereas an interfix is added to monosyllables (and a few disyllables) only (cf. section 3.2).

Epenthesis is another means of modifying a stem, and epenthetic consonants are listed by Malkiel and his followers among interfixes. They have in common with (other) interfixes that they are semantically devoid of meaning. But they differ from them in an important point: they do not add a syllable to the stem. In most cases, their raison d'être is the same as that of latent consonants: to provide an onset to the suffix, in order to satisfy the antihiatic constraint. The only differences between the three examples in (6) lie in the fact that the final consonant of the stem is graphical and etymological in (6a), graphical and non-etymological in (6b), neither graphical nor etymological in (6c).

(6) a. *pot*   /po/ ~ /pɔt/   'pot'   → *potier*   'potter'   French
     b. *canot* /kano/ ~ /kanɔt/ 'canoe'   → *canotier*   'boater'   French
     c. *écho* /eko/ ~ /ekɔt/   'gossip' → *échotier*   'gossip columnist'   French

This is the reason why epenthetic consonants, unlike presuffixal interfixes, are inserted irrespective of the length of the base (e.g., *numéroter* 'to number' ← *numéro* 'number').

However, in spite of the differences between the two phenomena, a continuity between epenthesis and interfixation can be observed in some of the objects in which they are embodied. The choice of /θ/ as an antihiatic consonant in (7a) and its insertion after a sonorant in (7b) are closely akin to the choice of *-ec-* as syllabic interfix in (7c).

(7) a. *café*   'coffee' → *cafecito*   'coffee-DIM'   Spanish
     b. *ratón* 'mouse' → *ratoncito* 'mouse-DIM'   Spanish
     c. *tren*   'train' → *trenecito* 'train-DIM'   Spanish

Being nothing else than phonological material, epenthetic consonants need no other label than epenthetic consonants. To call them interfixes is a matter of metalinguistic conventions, but they must be distinguished from syllabic interfixes.

This survey of different constructions leads to the conclusion that to be or not to be an interfix is neither a matter of presence (or absence) in a list of morphological objects nor a matter of position in the derivative: it depends on the role of the item in a given construction.

3 Interfixes: What? Why? Where?

Having distinguished the presuffixal interfix from other morphological objects, we shall now try to clarify what it is in itself and what role it plays in the economy of word construction.

3.1 The morphemic approach

The Spanish controversy (Lázaro Carreter 1980 [1972]; Martínez Celdrán 1978; Montes 1985; Dressler 1986; Portolés 1988, 1999; Martín Camacho 2002, etc.) has focused for a great part on the morphemic quality of the interfix. To be recognized as an entity of its own, the interfix was supposed to be a morpheme. And consequently, to have the counterpart of its *signifiant*, in an orthodox Saussurean view: a *signifié*. Or, at least, another function which could legitimate its morphemic status.

Portolés (1999) devotes a section to the meaning of Spanish interfixes ("El significado de los interfijos"), but acknowledges that this meaning can be discerned in some of the interfixes only and is due to "un impreciso sema que se cunfunde con el que aporta el sufijo" [a vague seme which merges with that of the suffix] (p. 5058). For Dressler and Merlini Barbaresi (1989: 246), Spanish interfixes have no meaning, but Italian ones may have connotative undertones ("sfumature connotative"). Actually, it is somewhat contradictory to admit Malkiel's definition of the interfix as devoid of meaning – all authors start from these premises – and intend to ascribe a meaning to it. The strings which look like interfixes and have a semantic value of their own occur in other kinds of constructions. For instance, Oc. *femnassièr* 'womanizer' (← *femna* 'woman') is both agentive and pejorative, the agentive value being borne by *-ièr*, the pejorative one by *-ass-*. A two-step derivation (*femna* → *femnassa* 'fat and unattractive woman' → *femnassièr*) would not correspond to the denotatum: the pejoration does not regard the chased woman but her chaser. Thus both suffixes, *-às* and *-ièr*, are full suffixes but act simultaneously, as a suffix cluster. Fr. *noblaillon* (← *noble* 'noble'), *cheffaillon* (← *chef* 'superior, manager'), *poétaillon* (← *poète* 'poet'), etc., which are all three pejorative (through *-aill-*) and diminutive (through *-on*), could receive the same analysis (Roché 2009: 165–167). These are indeed marginal, anomalous formations, but it would not be coherent to see interfixes in them.

Among the other functions attributed to interfixes is the distinction of possible homonyms, if both derivatives were constructed without an interfix: Sp. *llamada* 'call' ← *llamar* 'to call' / *llamarada* 'blaze' ← *llama* 'flame'; Oc. *porquièr* 'pig-keeper' / *porcatièr* 'pig-merchant' ← *pòrc* 'pig'; It. *volpino* 'spitz' / *volpicino* 'fox cub' ← *volpe* 'fox'. But the contrast in meaning is not connected to the choice of a particular interfix, and much more numerous are the examples of synonyms constructed with and without interfix (e.g., Oc. *gatièra* / *gatonièra* 'cat flap' ← *gat* 'cat') or with different interfixes (e.g., Oc. *vimenièr* / *vimotièr* 'osier grove' ← *vim* 'osier'). The distinction of homonyms is a side effect of the presence of an interfix, not the reason of its insertion.

More convincing is the idea that an interfix could adapt a base for a derivation in which the base normally does not enter. Portolés (1999: 5056) gives the example of the Spanish suffixation with *-ón*, which usually selects feminine nominal bases: interfixation enables it to select masculine or adjectival ones (e.g., Sp. *grande* 'tall' → *grandullón, -ona* 'tall person'). In several Romance languages, the interfix *-and-/-end-* helps a verbal base to receive a suffix which is usually dedicated to nominal bases: Sp. *curandero* 'witch doctor' ← *curar* 'to cure'; Oc. *teissendièr* 'weaver' ← *téisser* 'to weave'; Fr. *lavandière* 'washerwoman' ← *laver* 'to wash'; It. *filandaia* 'spinster' ← *filare* 'to spin'. However, the same suffixes can be added to verbal bases with other interfixes, or with no interfix at all, and the same interfix *-and-/-end-* be used in quite different contexts.

These "functions" would concern, furthermore, a minority of the interfixes. As a whole, the dispute about the morphemic status of the interfix leads to a stalemate. The linguists who stick to a strict definition of the morpheme (e.g., Tekavčić 1968: 77: "Un segmento *o è* morfema *o non lo è*" [either a segment *is* a morpheme, or *it is not*]) reject the notion of interfix, but they can hardly account for the constructions where others see an interfix. And the defenders of the interfix have to place it in a particular subcategory – "morfema marginal" [marginal morpheme], "morfema residual" [residual morpheme] (Malkiel 1958: 185, between double quotes); "morfemas vacíos" [empty morphemes] (Dressler 1986: 384) – which makes the notion inconsistent. It is better to recognize interfixes plainly as empty morphs. As pointed out by Maiden (1999), autonomous morphology has cast a new light on such morphological objects and is more apt to acknowledge their role, if they are put back in the phonological and lexical dimensions of word-formation.

3.2 The phonological approach

In its very definition, Malkiel (1958: 107) notes that the Spanish interfix is always unstressed ("siempre átono"), adding a few years later (1970: 75): "As interfixes are, by definition, pretonic [...] they offer a strong [...] appeal to the speakers' sense of rhythm (syllabic count) [...]". In an interfixed derivative, a secondary accent is kept on the syllable which was stressed in the base, and would otherwise be totally unstressed (e.g., Sp. *tos* 'cough' → *tosegoso* /ˌtoseˈgoso/ 'having a chronic cough' vs. °*tososo* /toˈsoso/). In some particular cases, the interfixation blocks an alteration of the base and facilitates its recognition (e.g., Sp. *tierno* 'tender' → *tiernecillo* 'tender-DIM' vs. °*ternillo*, cf. *ternura* 'tenderness'). As pointed out by Allen (1976) in the title of his article, "[i]nterfixes preserve syllables and word roots". However, this "function" of the interfix (Dressler 1986; Portolés 1999) must not be overestimated. The gain in "naturalness" is paid with a loss of faithfulness due to the introduction of a meaningless element.

More important are the observations that Spanish interfixes "sirven para agrandar la pieza radical de una palabra antes del sufijo" [are used to lengthen the radical part of a word before the suffix] (Dressler 1986: 388) or that in Italian "parole trisillabiche evitano l'inserzione di interfissi" [trisyllabic words preclude the insertion of an interfix] (Dressler and Merlini Barbaresi 1989: 245). The examples which follow these assertions show that thanks to the interfix, derivations based on disyllables in (8a) can match the prosodic pattern of derivations on trisyllables in (8b).

(8) a. *padre*   'father' → *padrecito*   'father-DIM'   Spanish
      b. *compadre* 'friend' → *compadrito* 'friend-DIM'   Spanish
      a. *serpe*   'snake' → *serpicella*   'small snake'   Italian
      b. *serpente* 'snake' → *serpentello*   'small snake'   Italian

Detailed investigations of extensive lexical databases have led to more systematic conclusions for Occitan and French. In a corpus of 1503 derivatives with Oc. *-ièr/ -ièra*, 207 are constructed with an interfix, among which 199 have a monosyllabic base (or a disyllable whose unstressed final vowel has been regularly deleted), 8 a disyllabic one, and none a longer one (Plénat and Roché 2004). Among the 8 disyllabic bases, 7 have a vocalic initial. This particularity confirms that interfixation is closely related to the prosodic constitution of the base: the only disyllables which receive an interfix are not, in fact, full disyllables by virtue of being deprived of their first onset (Plénat 1997).

Tab. 3.1: Prosodic conditioning of interfixation in Occitan and French.

suffixation with	base = 1 syllable			base = 2 syllables			base ≥ 3 syllables		
...	total	interfixes		total	interfixes		total	interfixes	
Oc. *-ièr/-ièra*	695	199	29 %	673	8	1 %	135	0	0 %
Fr. *-on*	393	133	34 %	188	4	2 %	14	0	0 %
Fr. *-ette*	1382	434	31 %	984	26	3 %	247	4	2 %

The results are similar in a corpus of 595 derivatives with Fr. *-on* from dictionaries (Roché 2003a) and in a corpus of 2613 derivatives with Fr. *-ette* collected on the Web, most of them neologisms (Plénat 2005) (Table 3.1). The only interfixed derivations with bases longer than one syllable are particular cases: hypocoristic person names, bases with a vocalic initial, or stems with a final /t/ before *-ette*.

It is difficult to determine whether the prosodic template concerns the stem (two syllables) or the derivative (three syllables in French), since the result would be the same. According to Lázaro Mora (1999: 4665), the presence of the interfix *-ec-* (vs. *-c-* or no interfix) in Spanish derivatives with *-ito* (cf. examples (7)) is due to "el control de las dimensiones silábicas de los derivados diminutivos" [the control of the syllabic dimensions of the diminutive derivatives]. In French, observations of several processes of word-formation have led to the conclusion that, in suffixation, a prosodic constraint applies to the base (Plénat and Roché 2003). More properly speaking: to the stem, which is optimally disyllabic. For this reason, we have proposed an interpretation of interfixed suffixation as "suffixation décalée" [shifted suffixation] (Roché 2002; Plénat and Roché 2004): when the base is monosyllabic, the addition of a syllabic interfix results in a disyllabic stem to which the suffix is attached.

This does not mean that *all* monosyllables are lengthened in this manner, but that interfixation tends to satisfy a well-formedness constraint. A constraint which, of course, is counteracted by the faithfulness constraint (nothing ought to be added to the regular form of the constituents). This is probably the reason why the proportion of interfixes varies radically from one sector of the lexicon to another. In the Occitan derivation with *-ièr/-ièra*, when the derivative is a qualifying human noun or adjective (e.g., *lengatièr* 'talkative' ← *lenga* 'tongue'), 63 % of monosyllabic bases are lengthened by an interfix; when it is a classifying human noun (e.g., *vinotièr* 'wine merchant' ← *vin* 'wine'), the rate falls to 43 %; and to 3 % when the derivative names a tree (or another plant). It has been observed as well, among French derivatives with *-ier/-ière*, that the proportion of interfixes has declined regularly from Old French to the present day. And that in Italian (Dressler and Merlini Barbaresi 1989), evaluatives seem to be the only sector in which interfixation is still at work. Hinging upon constraints, not rules, interfixation is subject to their hierarchy, and this hierarchy is highly variable.

We do not have enough information on prosodic constraints in the different Romance languages to generalize these hypotheses, but they would fit all the examples we have found in the literature on interfixes (as far as full syllabic interfixes are concerned, not mere epenthetic consonants). If in the derivative the interfix is considered as part of the stem, a generalization – with very few exceptions – is possible: whatever the prosodic structure of the base and the prosodic structure of the suffix, interfixed derivatives are constructed on a disyllabic stem.

On the segmental side, Malkiel (1958: 176) had noted that in Sp. *goterón* 'drop-AUG' ← *gota* 'drop' (vs. °*gotón*) the interfix separates two identical vowels. A similar dissimilative effect can be observed in French derivatives with *-on* (Roché 2003a), but it is more striking when consonants are involved. In French derivatives with *-ette* (Plénat 2005), when the last consonant (articulated or latent) of a monosyllabic base is /t/, an interfix is added in 89 % of the derivatives (9a). The rate of interfixation is still important (56 %) after /d/ – the other dental stop – but falls drastically after a sonorant. Besides, it is noticeable that the most frequent interfixes before *-ette* are *-el-*, *-in-* and *-oun-*, all ending in a sonorant. The role of the interfix emerges clearly: it prevents the repetition of the same sound, or an almost identical sound, at too short a distance from one another, and affords a more euphonic onset to the suffix.

(9) a. *tarte*   'tart'   → *tartelette*   'tartlet'   French
     b. *tomate*   'tomato'   → *tomatinette* 'small tomato'   French
     c. *croissant*   'croissant' → *croissette*   'small croissant'   French
     d. *cosmonaute* 'cosmonaut' → *cosmonette* 'female cosmonaut'   French

On a disyllabic base, if the final /t/ is articulated in the free form, the dissimilative constraint can counterbalance the prosodic one and an interfix can be added to a disyllable (9b). If the final /t/ is only latent, its repetition is prevented by a truncation (9c), as on longer bases (9d). Interfixation (9a, b) and truncation (9c, d) are complementary means of modifying the stem.

Other observations on the choice of the interfix (Roché 2003a; Plénat and Roché 2004) confirm that it is closely related to the phonological constitution of the suffix. For instance, the most frequent interfix before Oc. *-ut/-uda* is *-ar-* (e.g., *pançarut* 'pot-bellied' ← *pança* 'belly'), which never appears before *-ièr/-ièra*, while the most frequent one before *-ièr/-ièra* is *-at-* (e.g., *boscatièr* 'woodcutter' ← *bòsc* 'wood'), which never appears before *-ut/-uda*. Both vowel and consonant of the interfix must be in harmony with those of the suffix. On the whole, the effect of interfixation is to provide a more suitable stem to the suffix, both prosodically and segmentally.

3.3 The morphophonological approach

To account for Malkiel's canonical example, Sp. *humareda* 'cloud of smoke' ← *humo* 'smoke', three analyses are possible, schematically represented in (10).

(9) a. [[*hum(o)*][*-ar*][*-eda*]]
     b. [[[*hum(o)*]*-ar*][*-eda*]]
     c. [[*hum(o)*][*-ar* [*-eda*]]]

The first one has been eliminated (cf. section 3.1), since the interfix is not a full morpheme. The third one was favoured by Rainer (1993: 156) who, cautiously, tended to see the combination of interfix plus suffix as an allomorph of the suffix. Our last section, which is based on studies posterior to Rainer's book, favours the second one, since the interfix seems to be part of the stem. But the notion of stem is ambiguous and needs to be clarified. As defined by Aronoff (1994), for instance, the stem is both one of the lexical representations of a lexeme and a "sound form to which a given affix is attached" (p. 39). In most cases, these two approaches lead to the same realizations. For the French lexeme GRAND 'tall', the stem /grɑ̃d/ is recorded in the lexicon alongside with /grɑ̃/ and selected to form the derivative *grandeur* (and for the feminine free form *grande*). But this is not always true. Lexically speaking, the French lexeme VALISE 'suitcase' has only one stem – /valiz/ – which regularly appears in the diminutive *valisette*. However, in the colloquial *valoche*, the "sound form to which [the] affix is attached" is a truncated stem /val/. Stem allomorphy is on the one hand intrinsic to the lexeme, inherited from its history (/grɑ̃d/ vs. /grɑ̃/), and on the other, specific to a particular derivation (/val/ vs. /valiz/). The stem as one of the lexical representations of the lexeme, the "lexical stem", may be modified to become an "adapted stem", the radical of a derivative (cf. Roché 2010 for more details and examples). In Spanish, Faitelson-Weiser (1993) establishes a roughly similar distinction between "derivante" and "tema derivativo".

The addition of an interfix is a means – among others – of modifying a lexical stem and adapting it to a given suffixation, providing it with an extra syllable (an "incremento" [increment], in Faitelson-Weiser's words). And the above distinction accounts for the difference between Fr. *bombinette* 'bomb-DIM' ← *bombe* 'bomb' and *criminel* 'criminal' ← *crime* 'crime' (cf. section 2.5) or between It. *agoraio* 'needle case' ← *ago* 'needle' and *corporale* 'bodily' ← *corpo* 'body'. These last two derivatives are put forward by Tekavčić (1968: 78–80) to demonstrate the non-existence of the "cosiddetti interfissi" [so-called interfixes]: "il lessema il cui contenuto semantico è 'ago' viene realizzato *ag-/agor-*" [the lexeme whose semantic content is 'needle' is realized as *ag-/agor-*]. But the stem *corpor-* of It. *corpo* is a "lexical" stem, hereditarily associated to the lexeme, like the stem *crimin-* of Fr. *crime*, whereas *agor-* (for It. *ago*) and *bombin-* (for Fr. *bombe*) are "adapted" stems, particular to one derivation.

3.4 The lexical approach

The keyword for Spanish morphologists who do not accept the notion of interfix, since Lázaro Carreter (1980 [1972]), is "estereotipia", defined by Martín Camacho (2002: 88) as "una forma peculiar de analogía" [a particular kind of analogy]. The first aim of Lázaro Carreter was to deny the existence of antihiatic consonants in Spanish. In *rousseauniano* 'relative to Rousseau', for instance, the *-n-* which precedes the suffix would not be an epenthetic – antihiatic – consonant but the result of an analogy with such derivatives as *calderoniano* (← *Calderón*). The dispute is groundless. The insertion of a consonant between *rousseau-* and *-iano* provides the penultimate syllable of the derivative with an onset, and thus satisfies a universal constraint. And at the same time, the choice of consonant is triggered by the membership of the derivative in the same lexical series as *calderoniano* (and others). The two explanations are not contradictory but complementary.

The same remark can be made for syllabic interfixes. Analogy is not an alternative to interfixation but the way – one of the ways – in which interfixes are selected. Moreover, to say "analogy" (or "estereotipia") is not really explicative without specifying how and why it works. In the case of the Italian examples mentioned above, Tekavčić (1968: 78) invokes analogy for the lexemes in which the string *-or-* is not etymological. But the derivations It. *ago* + *-aio* and *corpo* + *-ale* have nothing in common which could trigger an analogical transfer of the allomorphy *corpo ~ corpor-* to *ago ~ agor-*. Most of Martín Camacho's (2002: 92–118) examples of "estereotipia" are ad hoc linkages in the same manner. Analogy plays a part in interfixation, but it must be situated in the framework of the lexical paradigms along which it displays its effects.

The most important of these paradigms are the derivational series, like that of the Spanish adjectives with *-iano* in the above example. In another already mentioned series, the French diminutives with *-ette*, the choice of *-in-* for an interfix (e.g., *putinette* ← *pute* 'whore') as well as that of /n/ as epenthetic consonant (e.g., *chipinette* ← *chipie* 'brat') or that of infixation when the base already ends in *-ette* (e.g., *starlinette* ← *starlette* 'starlet') are favoured by the presence of several derivatives like *cousinette* ← *cousine* 'cousin' in the same series (Plénat 2005). The ending *-inette* snowballed into an attractive sub-series in which it is fulfilled through several devices. One of Malkiel's (1958: 127–128, fn. 37) examples, Fr. *fermeture* 'closing' (← *fermer* 'to close'), instead of °*fermure*, is due not only to a one-to-one analogy with its antonym *ouverture* 'opening' but to the fact that /t/ is by far the most frequent consonant before *-ure*. It is the same lexical process, a similar reanalysis of recurrent endings, which leads on the one hand to the formation of irregular stems (in addition to *fermeture*, cf. MFr. *fourneture*, Fr. *fourniture* ← *fournir* 'to supply'; OFr. *garneture*, Fr. *garniture* ← *garnir* 'to fill'; etc.), and on the other to the formation of the suffix variant *-ature* (in Fr. *musculature* ← *muscle* 'muscle', for instance).

Let us add that, more generally, the derivational series play a part in the above mentioned prosodic constraint. The disyllabic optimum of the stem is probably a consequence of the predominant structure of derivatives in the lexicon, which tends to be generalized. Horcajada (1987–88) argues that the form of Sp. *panecito* 'bread-DIM' ← *pan* 'bread', for instance, is due to historical accidents, not to a prosodic pattern. But this does not rule out Lázaro Mora's generalization about the interfix *-ec-* (cf. section 3.2): *panecito* (after the more ancient *panecillo*) may have been one of the leader words to have started a sub-series. The majority of derivatives ending in *-ec-ito* do not have a Latin origin. To say that an interfix is added to fit a prosodic pattern is not a teleologic explanation – an approach opportunely put into question by Rainer (1993: 156) – but an observation about the lexical dynamics of derivation.

The other lexical paradigms which play a part in interfixation are the derivational families. Frequently, the interfix is selected among the suffixes which have already been used after the same base (cf. examples (3)). We said that Oc. *lobat* 'wolf cub' cannot be the base of *lobatàs* 'wolf-AUG'. But the choice of *-at-* as an interfix in *lobatàs*, as well as in *lobatièra* 'wolf den', is most probably related to the presence of *lobat* in the derivational family of *lop* 'wolf'. In the family of Sp. *casa* 'house', the augmentative *caserón* owes its interfix to the adjective *casero*, which normally plays no part in its formation, while symmetrically, in the family of *calle* 'street', the adjective *callejero* owes its interfix to the diminutive *calleja*, with no more semantic reason. The process is less visible when the first derivative has disappeared. According to Malkiel (1949), the origin of the rare interfix *-eg-* in Sp. *pedregoso* 'stony', *pedregal* 'stony area' (← *piedra* 'stone') is to be found in the remote Latin derivative °*petricare* 'to pave'.

When the meaning of a previous derivative is close to that of the primitive, both can be (11a), or possibly could be (11b), accepted as the base.

(11) a. *brèç* / *breçòl* 'craddle' → *breçolièra* 'nanny'　　　　Occitan
　　 b. *mule* 'she-mule' / *mulet* 'he-mule' → *(chemin) muletier* 'mule　　French
　　　　track'
　　　　mare 'sea' / *marina* 'sea coast', 'navy' → *marinaio* 'seaman'　　Italian

Received etymologies give *muletier* as derived from *mulet* and *marinaio* from *marina*. But the lexical base of the former is more logically the generic term *mule*, and the meaning of the latter more logically constructed on the basis of *mare* than on any of the acceptions of *marina*. In all cases, the important point is that the choice of the stem is triggered by the prosodic constraint, as confirmed by the examples in (12): the adjective is constructed on a previous derivative when the primitive is monosyllabic (12a), on the primitive itself when it is polysyllabic (12b).

(12) a. *jorn* / *jornada*　　　'day'　→ *jornadièr*　'daily'　　Occitan
　　　　 mes / *mesada*　　　'month' → *mesadièr*　'monthly'
　　　　 an / *annada*　　　'year'　→ *annadièr*　'annual'
　　 b. *setmana* / *setmanada*　'week'　→ *setmanièr*　'weekly'

Slightly different is the case of Sp. *condesil* 'relating to a count'. The base cannot be *condesa* 'countess', since the adjective is semantically connected to *conde* 'count', but one can say that the stem *condes-* is borrowed from *condesa* as well as obtained by the addition of the rare interfix *-es-*. Different again, in another way, is Fr. *angelot* 'angel-DIM' (← *ange* 'angel'), where the interfix *-el-* echoes the Latin stem of *angélique*. In some cases, the Latin stem itself is used as an equivalent of an interfixed stem. To form Fr. *fablier* (13a), the "popular" stem *fabl-* is selected regularly before the "popular" suffix *-ier*. To form *fabuliste* (13b), the "learned" stem *fabul-* is selected regularly before the "learned" suffix *-iste*. With the "popular" suffix *-ette*, the regular derivative *fablette* is attested but *fabul-* is preferred so as to afford a disyllabic stem to the suffix. *Fabulette* (13c) has the same prosodic pattern as the interfixed *fablinette* (13d), which is also attested (notice that in *fablier* the pronunciation of *-ier* as two syllables after a branching onset makes the derivative trisyllabic: /fabli'je/).

(13) a. *fable* 'fable' → *fablier*   'fable collection', *fablette* 'fable-DIM'   French
    b.   → *fabuliste*   'fabulist'
    c.   → *fabulette*   'fable-DIM'
    d.   → *fablinette*   'fable-DIM'

The diversity of processes in these examples confirms that interfixation is one among several possibilities of stem substitution, and that extending the regular stem with an interfix is often an equivalent of borrowing another stem from the same lexeme, or from another lexeme of the same family. When a given interfix is used repeatedly after the same base, the extended stem thus obtained tends to become a "lexical stem", ready for new derivatives. For the above mentioned Spanish lexeme *piedra*, the stem *pedreg-* which is present in *pedregoso* 'stony' and *pedregal* 'stony area' may be considered as an alternate popular presuffixal stem (which surfaces in the Americanism *pedregón* 'boulder', for instance) alongside with *pedr-* (e.g., *pedrera* 'quarry') and the learned stem *petr-* (e.g., *petrificar* 'to petrify').

Interfixation is related, on the right end of the constructed lexeme, to the derivational series (and through them to the suffixes), and on the left end to the derivational families (and through them to stem allomorphy). Fr. *snobinette* 'female snob' has been formed with the interfix *-in-* to join other human nouns in the already mentioned *-inette* series, but from that moment on the stem *snobin-* was ready to be reused in other derivatives of *snob*: *snobinard* 'snob-PEJ', *snobinat* 'snobdom'. This double framed diffusion of interfixes can be compared to that of the Latin type *manualis* in Italian (Rainer 1998), via analogy in the derivational series, via "irradiation from co-derivatives" (p. 82) in the derivational families. Does it mean that "[a]n alternative analysis which is always available is to see the presumed interfix as belonging to the morph on one or the other side, and creating a new allomorph for the relevant morpheme" (Bauer 2004: 57)? Not completely. While the non-etymological -*u*- of Italian adjectives in -*uale* cannot be anything other than a part of an allomorph, the syllabic interfixes have a relative autonomy. But their existence is closely dependent on this double paradigmatic frame.

4 Conclusions

As a result of this survey, some conclusions can be asserted with reasonable confidence, while other questions still await an answer:

- Presuffixal interfixes do not form a class of derivational affixes. They are empty morphs which recycle the form of a suffix (or a former suffix) deprived of its semantic or categorial instruction.
- Interfixation is not a derivational process which could be placed on a par with suffixation or prefixation. It is a means – among others – of modifying the stem presented by the base lexeme. The interfix adds a syllable to the stem and offers a more suitable onset to the suffix (while epenthetic consonants fulfill the second requirement only).
- In such an approach, the notion of interfix is rid of the outdated debate on its morphemic status and can take its place in a lexeme-based morphology.
- The addition of an interfix to the stem and the choice of the interfix depend upon phonological and lexical parameters. The former are both prosodic and segmental, the latter are associated with both paradigmatic dimensions of derivation – derivational series and derivational families.
- Interfixation has no teleologic "functions" and cannot be accounted for by word formation rules. It is the consequence of two kinds of forces which come into play in word-formation: phonological well-formedness constraints (presumably universal) and the influence of the inherited lexicon (proper to each language).
- Interfixes are present in all Romance languages and are not only a collection of historical oddities, the flotsam and jetsam of morphological accidents. They take their place among other stem adjustments, alongside consonantal epenthesis, truncation, substitutions, etc., in contemporary formations as in past ones. But their presence differs remarkably from one language to another, from one period to another, from one sector of the lexicon to another. Additional studies based on extensive data are necessary in order to determine which interfixes are still productive and to what kinds of suffixation they are associated.

5 References

Adams, Edward L. (1913): *Word Formation in Provençal*. New York: MacMillan.

Allen, Andrew (1976): Interfixes preserve syllables and word roots. In: Henry Thompson, Kenneth Whistler, Vicki Edge, Jeri J. Jaeger, Ronya Javkin, Miriam Petruck, Christopher Smeall and Robert D. Van Valin Jr. (eds.), *Proceedings of the Second Annual Meeting of the Berkeley Linguistics Society*, 31–35. Berkeley: Berkeley Linguistics Society.

Allen, Andrew (1977): The interfix *i/esc* in Catalan and Rumanian. *Romance Philology* 31: 203–211.

Aronoff, Mark (1994): *Morphology by Itself. Stems and Inflectional Classes*. Cambridge, MA: MIT Press.

Badia Margarit, Antoni M. (1962): *Gramática catalana*. Madrid: Gredos.

Bauer, Laurie (2004): *A Glossary of Morphology*. Edinburgh: Edinburgh University Press.

Bosque, Ignacio and Violeta Demonte (eds.) (1999): *Gramática descriptiva de la lengua española*. Madrid: Espasa Calpe.

Crocco Galèas, Grazia (1991): *Gli etnici italiani. Studio di morfologia naturale*. Padova: Unipress.

Darmesteter, Arsène (1890): Traité de la formation de la langue française. In: Adolphe Hatzfeld, Arsène Darmesteter and Antoine Thomas (eds.), *Dictionnaire général de la langue française du commencement du XVIIe siècle à nos jours*. Vol. 1, 1–300. Paris: Delagrave.

Dressler, Wolfgang U. (1986): Forma y función de los interfijos. *Revista Española de Lingüística* 16: 381–395.

Dressler, Wolfgang U. and Lavinia Merlini Barbaresi (1989): Interfissi e non-interfissi antesuffissali nell'italiano, spagnolo e inglese. In: Società di Linguistica Italiana (ed.), *L'italiano tra le lingue romanze*, 243–252. Roma: Bulzoni.

Dworkin, Steven N. (1995): Two studies in Old Spanish homonymics. *Hispanic Review* 63: 527–542.

Fábregas, Antonio (2006): Infixes: Right in the middle. *SKASE Journal of Theoretical Linguistics* 3(3): 12–29.

Faitelson-Weiser, Silvia (1993): Sufijación y derivación sufijal: Sentido y forma. In: Soledad Varela (ed.), *La formación de palabras*, 119–161. Madrid: Taurus Universitaria.

Graur, Alexandru (1969): Suffixes roumains élargis. *Revue Roumaine de Linguistique* 14: 327–332.

Horcajada, Bautista (1987–1988): Morfonología de los diminutivos formados sobre bases consonánticas monosílabas. *Revista de filología románica* 5: 55–72.

Lázaro Carreter, Fernando (1980 [1972]): Sobre el problema de los interfijos: ¿Consonantes antihiáticas en español? In: Fernando Lázaro Carreter, *Estudios de Lingüística*, 11–26. Barcelona: Crítica.

Lázaro Mora, Fernando A. (1999): La derivación apreciativa. In: Ignacio Bosque and Violeta Demonte (eds.), *Gramática Descriptiva de la Lengua Española*. Vol. 3, 4645–4682. Madrid: Real Academia Española, Espasa.

Maiden, Martin (1999): Romance historical morphology and empty affixes. In: Sheila Embleton, John E. Joseph and Hans-Josef Niederehe (eds.), *The Emergence of Modern Language Sciences. Studies on the transition from historical-comparative to structural linguistics in honor of E. F. Konrad Koerner*. Vol. 2, 189–202. Amsterdam/Philadelphia: Benjamins.

Malkiel, Yakov (1949): Studies in the Hispanic infix *-eg-*. *Language* 25: 139–181.

Malkiel, Yakov (1958): Los interfijos hispánicos: Problema de la lingüística histórica y estructural. In: Diego Catalán (ed.), *Miscelánea homenaje a André Martinet*. Vol. 2: *Estructuralismo e historia*, 107–199. La Laguna: Universidad de La Laguna.

Malkiel, Yakov (1970): *Patterns of Derivational Affixation in the Cabraniego Dialect of East-Central Asturian*. Berkeley: University of California Press.

Martín Camacho, José Carlos (2002): *El problema lingüístico de los interfijos españoles*. Cáceres: Universidad de Extremadura, Servicio des Publicaciones.

Martínez Celdrán, Eugenio (1978): En torno a los conceptos de interfijo e infijo en español. *Revista Española de Lingüística* 8: 447–460.

Mascaró, Joan (1986): *Morfologia*. Barcelona: Enciclopèdia Catalana.

Merlini Barbaresi, Lavinia (2004): Alterazione. In: Maria Grossmann and Franz Rainer (eds.), *La formazione delle parole in italiano*, 264–292. Tübingen: Niemeyer.

Montes, José Joaquín (1985): Los interfijos hispánicos: Reexamen con base en datos del *ALEC*. *Anuario de Lingüística Hispánica* [Valladolid] 1: 181–188.

Plénat, Marc (1997): L'"extramétricité" des voyelles initiales. In: Chantal Lyche (ed.), *French Phonology. Retrospective and Perspectives*, 239–257. Salford: AFLS and ESRI.

Plénat, Marc (2005): *Rosinette, cousinette, putinette, starlinette, chipinette*: Décalage, infixation et épenthèse devant *-ette*. In: Injoo Choi-Jonin, Myriam Bras, Anne Dagnac and Magali Rouquier (eds.), *Questions de classification en linguistique. Méthodes et descriptions. Mélanges offerts au Professeur Christian Molinier*, 275–298. Berne: Lang.

Plénat, Marc and Michel Roché (2003): Prosodic constraints on suffixation in French. In: Geert Booij, Janet DeCesaris, Angela Ralli and Sergio Scalise (eds.), *Topics in Morphology. Selected Papers from the Third Mediterranean Morphology Meeting (Barcelona, Sept. 20–22, 2001)*, 285–299. Barcelona: IULA-Universitat Pompeu Fabra.

Plénat, Marc and Michel Roché (2004): Entre morphologie et phonologie: La suffixation décalée. *Lexique* 16: 159–198.

Portolés Lázaro, José (1988): Sobre los interfijos en español. *Lingüística Española Actual* 10: 153–169.

Portolés, José (1999): La interfijación. In: Ignacio Bosque and Violeta Demonte (eds.), *Gramática Descriptiva de la Lengua Española*. Vol. 3, 5041–5073. Madrid: Real Academia Española, Espasa.

Pottier, Bernard (1953): Les infixes modificateurs en portugais: Note de morphologie générale. *Boletim de Filologia* 14: 233–256.

Prati, Angelico (1942): Antisuffissi. *L'Italia Dialettale* 19: 75–166.

Rainer, Franz (1993): *Spanische Wortbildungslehre*. Tübingen: Niemeyer.

Rainer, Franz (1998): Paradigmatic factors in the irradiation of allomorphy: The reanalysis of the Latin type *manualis* in Italian. In: Geert Booij, Angela Ralli and Sergio Scalise (eds.), *Proceedings of the First Mediterranean Conference of Morphology (Sept. 19–21, 1997)*, 77–85. Patras: University of Patras.

Rainer, Franz (2021): I suffissi *-arolo* e *-arello* e il problema dell'interfisso *-ar-* nelle lingue romanze. *Revue de Linguistique Romane* 85: 447–506.

Roché, Michel (2002): La suffixation décalée avec oc. *-ièr(a)*. In: Lídia Rabassa (ed.), *Mélanges offerts à Jean-Louis Fossat*, 319–334. Toulouse: Cahiers d'Études Romanes.

Roché, Michel (2003a): De la "bonne formation" des dérivés en *-on*. *Cahiers de Grammaire* 28: 91–112.

Roché, Michel (2003b): L'interfixe est-il une unité morphologique? In: Bernard Fradin, Georgette Dal, Nabil Hathout, Françoise Kerleroux, Marc Plénat and Michel Roché (eds.), *Les unités morphologiques. Actes du 3ᵉ Forum International de Morphologie. Silexicales* 3: 169–178. Villeneuve d'Ascq: Université de Lille III.

Roché, Michel (2005): Interfixe et suffixation décalée dans les langues romanes. In: Teddy Arnavielle (ed.), *Langues. Histoires et usages dans l'aire méditerranéenne. Actes du Colloque La Méditerranée et ses langues, Montpellier, 20–22 mars 2002*, 71–87. Paris: L'Harmattan.

Roché, Michel (2009): Un ou deux suffixes? Une ou deux suffixations? In: Bernard Fradin, Françoise Kerleroux and Marc Plénat (eds.), *Aperçus de morphologie du français*, 143–173. Saint-Denis: Presses Universitaires de Vincennes.

Roché, Michel (2010): Base, thème, radical. *Recherches Linguistiques de Vincennes* 39: 95–133.

Roché, Michel (2011): Pression lexicale et contraintes phonologiques dans la dérivation en *-aie* du français. *Linguistica* [Ljubljana] 51: 5–22.

Tekavčić, Pavao (1968): Sull'analisi morfematica di un tipo di derivati italiani: Il problema dei cosiddetti interfissi. *Studia Romanica et Anglica Zagrabiensia* 25–26: 69–85.

TLF (1971–1994): *Trésor de la langue française.* Ed. by Paul Imbs and Bernard Quemada. Paris: Editions du CNRS (Vol. 1–10) / Gallimard (Vol. 11–16).

Nanna Fuhrhop and Sebastian Kürschner

4 Linking elements in Germanic

Abstract: Linking elements such as *-s* in German *Versicherung-s-vertreter* are found in between the parts of word-formation products in several Germanic languages. Systematic and functional aspects of linking elements are first introduced with respect to German. After that, a survey of other Germanic languages is provided. In parallel across the Germanic languages, the distribution of linking elements is different from that of the inflectional markers they stem from. Linking-*s* is distributed based on morphological (and, in German, prosodic) complexity, suggesting a function as morphological boundary marker across languages. The distribution of syllabic elements is more language-specific and based on semantic, rhythmic, and inflectional characteristics, respectively.

1 Introduction

Linking elements are sound material or graphemes appearing at the boundary between two parts of a word-formation product, cf. *-s* in German *Versicherung-s-vertreter* 'insurance agent'. They are usually considered to be meaningless items, but hypotheses about possible functions exist. Linking elements are frequently found in various Germanic languages, especially in nominal compounds. We provide a detailed sketch of the linking system in German in section 2. Section 3 contains a comparative survey of other Germanic languages.

2 Linking elements in German

German *Versicherung-s-vertreter* is a compound that is made up of two stems, just as its English translation *insurance agent* is. It is worthwhile to note that the

Nanna Fuhrhop, Potsdam, Germany
Sebastian Kürschner, Eichstätt-Ingolstadt, Germany

https://doi.org/10.1515/9783111420554-004

first stem does not surface as *Versicherung*, but as *Versicherungs*. Fuhrhop (1998) introduces the term "compositional stem form" for this form. In this sense, all words that form compounds have compositional stem forms – in most cases these are equivalent to the base form, i.e. they exhibit a "zero link" as in *Schrank-tür* 'cabinet door'. According to miscellaneous counts, 70 % of all German compounds do not employ any kind of linking element (Ortner et al. 1991; Baayen et al. 2007; Kürschner 2003), hence about 30 % of compounds do so. It is quite possible that the same stem may exhibit different compositional stem forms as in *Mann-es-kraft, Mann-s-bild, Mann-deckung, Männ-er-verein*, the last one including umlaut. However, although variation between -*s* and zero link is quite common (cf. *Haupt-seminar-(s)-arbeit*), the number of stems forming compositional stem forms with different linking elements is rather small.

Recent research has shown an interest in functional questions, i.e. questions of which individual or consistent functions linking elements fulfill. There is general agreement on three assumptions: First, linking elements are not merely extant inflectional elements; second, some linking elements are productive; and third, they fulfill one or more functions which are to be investigated.

In the following, we will first introduce the inventory of linking elements in German, establishing a classification (section 2.1). Afterwards, we will address functional questions (section 2.2).

2.1 A classification of linking elements in German

2.1.1 Form and inventory of linking elements in German

Hereafter, only linking elements of nominal first parts are considered. We find the following linking elements: -*s*, -*es*, -*n*, -*en*, -*ens*, -*er*, and -*e* (Augst 1975). These elements differ in frequency of occurrence. As far as the origin of linking elements is concerned, even in today's system, it is evident that linking elements are formally identical to inflectional suffixes in German. It therefore seems plausible to trace the phenomenon of linking elements as such back to inflectional endings, perhaps genitive attributes in the singular or plural. For example, former noun phrases with a preceding genitive may have developed into "genitive compounds" (cf. (1)). After a reanalysis as a complex word, the genitive case markers most likely lost their original function and eventually took on a new distribution. The result of this development is that in current German linking elements are no longer directly related to the inflectional system.

(1) a. des [Teufels] Sohn   > der [Teufelssohn]
       [the devil]$_{\text{GENSG}}$ son]$_{\text{NP}}$ > the-NOMSG [devil-GENSG son]$_{\text{COMP}}$
                                    > 'son of the devil'

or

      b. [der Sonnen] Schein   > der Sonnenschein
       [the sun]$_{\text{GENSG}}$ shine]$_{\text{NP}}$ > the-NOMSG [sun-GENSG shine]$_{\text{COMP}}$
                                    > 'sunshine'

Apart from inflectional suffixes, stem forming suffixes were a source of linking elements. The linking element *-er*, e.g., is reanalyzed from the stem forming suffix *-ir* that preceded case suffixes, e.g., Old High German *lamb-ir-as*, genitive singular form of *lamb*, current German *Lamm* 'lamb' (Wegener 2003), cf. also *-i* in *Bräut-i-gam* 'bride-groom' or *Nacht-i-gall* 'night-in-gale'.

2.1.2 Status of linking elements: (un-)productive and (non-)paradigmatic

In German, there are productive and unproductive linking elements as well as paradigmatic and non-paradigmatic linking elements. At first we will turn to productivity.

Many compounds are lexicalized – some of them with linking elements and others without. Since compounds containing unproductive linking elements are perceived as whole words, these linking elements are of no general interest for morphological research. Hence, it has been an important methodological move to separate productive linking elements from unproductive ones (Fuhrhop 1998).

The linking elements *-n/-en* and *-s* are considered productive. Signs of productivity are:

(i)   A linking element is attached to new words. Neologisms (including suffixes that typically trigger linking elements, see below) are an obvious clue, cf. *Coolheit-s-test* 'test of coolness'.

(ii) In cases of varying compositional stem forms, the form with linking element occurs more often over time than the form without one. E.g., between 1900–1949, *-s* in *Schaden-s-ersatz* 'compensation; lit. damage compensation' occurs in about 15 % of all instances, between 1950–1990 in about 70 % (Nübling and Szczepaniak 2011: 52).

(iii) A linking element can also be found in loan words that enter the German language. In these words, Nübling and Szczepaniak (2009) detect a considerable amount of variation as stated above (cf. *Abitur(-s?-)feier* 'graduation ball').

Paradigmatic and non-paradigmatic linking elements are discriminated from each other based on the inflectional system. A linking element is paradigmatic if it is formally identical with an inflectional ending occurring in the stem's inflectional paradigm. A linking element is non-paradigmatic if it does not constitute an inflectional ending of the word involved (cf. *Versicherung-s-vertreter*, but *Versicherungs). There is only one linking element that is both non-paradigmatic and productive, namely -*s*; in addition, it is the only linking element that is not syllabic.

2.2 Function of linking elements in German

2.2.1 Linking element -*s* in German

a) *König-s-mord, Teufel-s-küche – Liebling-s-getränk*
b) *Freundschaft-s-dienst, Versicherung-s-vertreter, Schönheit-s-wettbewerb, Prüfling-s-nummer*
c) *Religion-s-unterricht, Identität-s-bescheinigung*
d) *??Auto-s-verkäufer – Plastikauto-s-verkäufer, Kuckuck-s-uhr*
e) *??Seminar-s-arbeit – Hauptseminar-s-arbeit*
f) *Fahrt-zeit – Abfahrt-s-zeit, Suchanfrage – Versuch-s-aufbau, Triebwagen – Betrieb-s-wirtschaft*

Using the examples listed in a)–f) above, we would like to demonstrate the various functions under discussion.

a) lists cases that might account for genitive constructions like *König-s-mord – des Königs Mord* ([King-LE]-homicide 'regicide'). However, this cannot apply to *Liebling-s-getränk* because it does not mean 'darling's drink' but 'favorite drink'. Hence, genitive marking cannot be a general function of the *s*-link: first, not all *s*-links can be taken as such (e.g., *Liebling-s-getränk*), second, -*s* is not always employed even if there is a genitive relation involved, cf. *Apfel-kern* (not *Apfel-s-kern) 'apple core', see also section 3.2.2.

b) lists words with suffixes that commonly take linking elements. Aronoff and Fuhrhop (2002) identify these as "closing suffixes" (-*heit*, -*ung*, -*ling*, etc.) – suffixes that are not open for further word-formation suffixes, e.g.,

(2) beobachten   > beobacht-   > Beobacht-ung   > *beobacht-ung-lich
     observe-INF   > observe-STEM   > observe-NOUN   > observe-NOUN-ADJ
     to observe   > observation

In these cases, the linking element reopens closed stems for further word-formation processes, i.e., further compounding, and to some extent also derivation, cf. *frühling-s-haft* 'springlike'.

A different account of these suffixes comes from Eisenberg and Sayatz (2004) who outline a continuum of suffixes and demonstrate that *-ling, -schaft, -tum*, etc. are adjacent to each other if projected on a scale of animacy. This semantic scale coincides with prosodic properties: Midway between the poles (where the collective suffixes in question are positioned), suffixes are stressable and phonologically heavy. Close to the poles, by contrast, suffixes contain unstressable schwa (the agent noun suffix *-er* and the plural suffixes). Following Eisenberg and Sayatz (2004), the form of the suffixes is not accidental. This observation can be connected to the findings of Nübling and Szczepaniak (2009), who demonstrate that linking elements are conditioned by prosodic features (see below). Given that closing suffixes generate precisely those prosodic structures which Nübling and Szczepaniak describe, it seems that the condition described by Aronoff and Fuhrhop (2002) is only indirectly relevant, i.e. the meaning conditions the (non-)derivability as well as the prosodic weight of closing suffixes and thus the specific behavior with respect to linking elements.

c) lists suffixes in loan words that share the characteristics of the linking elements found in b), cf. Nübling and Szczepaniak (2009).

d) lists cases that were highly debatable for a long time with respect to their grammaticality. While it was often argued that linking-*s* is impossible if the compositional stem form is homonymous with a plural form (**Auto-s-bahn*, cf., e.g., Wiese 2000), Wegener (2003) demonstrates empirically that the *s*-link is not primarily conditioned by inflectional, but by phonological factors: It is prohibited if the first part of the compound ends in a full vowel (*Auto* 'car', *Kino* 'cinema', *Uhu* 'owl'). This is exactly the condition in which *s*-plural most often applies (cf. Eisenberg 2006: 164). Conversely, if the stem ends in a consonant, the *s*-link is generally more acceptable (*Kuckucksnest, -ruf, -schrei* 'cuckoo's nest/cry/scream' vs. **Uhusnest, -ruf, -schrei* 'owl nest/cry/scream', cf. Wegener 2003: 434). The acceptability of the *-s*-link is increased additionally when the first part of the compound is complex (cf. Wegener 2003: 445):

(3)   ?Auto-s-verkäufer   [Plastik-auto-s]-verkäufer
      ?[car-LE]-salesman   [plastic car-LE] salesman

e) lists doubtful cases that are covered by Nübling and Szczepaniak (2011). The first parts bear final stress, cf. above.

f) lists cases showing that the probability of linking elements increases if the first element is prosodically and/or morphologically complex.

Based on compounds with varying linking elements, Nübling and Szczepaniak (2008) have demonstrated that linking elements are primarily phonologically and only secondarily morphologically conditioned. According to Nübling and Szczepaniak (2008), the "worse" the phonological word is, the more often -s is selected. In German, good phonological words conform to the ideal foot which is formed by a trochee. In addition to this criterion, monosyllabics also constitute good phonological words. Nevertheless, there are words which deviate from the ideal prosodic structure, namely words in which stress is not found on the first syllable, and words that show secondary stress in addition to primary stress. The above-named suffixes in b) (-*schaft*, -*heit*, etc.) can carry secondary stress, and a few "loan" suffixes such as -*ität* '-ity' attract stress (cf. c) above). Thus, the *s*-link is found regularly in these cases for prosodic reasons. With respect to the cases in d), simple vowels in bisyllabic words (*Auto, Kino, Uhu*) typically do not attract stress, hence they constitute a trochee, and no *s*-link is usually found. If the first part of a compound has more than two syllables and thereby deviates from the ideal phonological word, however, the *s*-links becomes acceptable. Typically, "bad" phonological words are found in morphologically complex words (*Plastik-autosverkäufer*).

In contrast to syllabic linking elements (cf. section 2.2.2), linking-*s* does not improve the word prosodically. Its function is rather that of a boundary marker because it clearly marks the end of the phonological word. The less sonorous the preceding offset, the more prominent the end becomes through -*s*.

2.2.2 Syllabic linking elements in German

The syllabic linking elements in Modern High German are -*es*, -*e*, -*er*, -*en*/-*n*, (-*ens*); -*n* constitutes an allophone of -*en* (cf. (4)), which is why it is included. Out of these linking elements, -*en*/-*n* is considered productive.

(4) a. Doktorand   Doktorand-en
         doctorand-SG, NOM   doctorand-OBL
     b. Biologe   Biologe-n
         biologist-SG, NOM   biologist-OBL

Typically after attaching a syllabic linking element, the first part of a compound ends in a trochaic foot, cf. *Gott-es-dienst, Kind-er-wagen, Schmerz-ens-schrei,* with -*n*/-*en* being the only element which can be productively attached to polysyllabic stems (*Doktorand-en-stipendium* = scholarship for a doctoral student, *Biologe-n-test* = test for/from a biologist). The linking element -*en* is typical for weak masculine nouns that are usually formed with a stressed "loan suffix" (-*and*, -*ist*, -*ent*, Köpcke 1995). The linking element -*n* is employed if the stem ends in schwa, which applies to weak masculine nouns (*Bote-n-gang* 'errand') as well as feminine nouns (*Blume-n-stiel* 'flower stalk'). Feminine nouns ending in schwa occur without linking elements if the schwa represents a suffix like in *Frische-behälter* (5) and *Schwäche-anfall*. Obviously, suffixation "protects" the schwa from further changes. The distribution of the linking element thus occurs complementarily with -*s*, i.e., it is <u>not</u> placed if the first element of the compound is complex. As a consequence the linking element -*n* marks morphological simplicity. According to Fuhrhop (2000), schwa occurring at a link has to be analyzed (besides its interpretation as derivational suffix), as a verbal link, cf. *Bad-e-hose* 'bathing trunks', or rarely as plural, cf. *Städt-e-tag* 'association of cities').

(5) frisch   Frisch-e   [Frisch-e]-behälter
     fresh-ADJ   fresh-SUFFIX   [fresh-NOUN]-container
                 fresh-NOUN   food container

2.2.3 "Common" functions of linking elements in German

Linking elements modify the phonological structure of the first part of the compound: Non-trochaic structures become trochaic if the first part allows for paradigmatic linking elements. In "bad" phonological words, the boundary of the phonological word can be marked more prominently by means of the *s*-link. Frequently, a bad prosodic word structure is associated with morphological complexity. Especially in word languages (as opposed to syllable languages) such as German, morphological complexity correlates with prosodical complexity. Linking elements thus help to recognize morphological boundaries (cf. also Eisenberg 2006: 241) by supporting the phonological boundary (Nübling and Szczepaniak 2008). As such, linking elements have to be analyzed morphologically. In sum, phonologically, the boundary is being supported; morphologically, the linking element is the cement that holds the compound together.

3 Linking elements in other Germanic languages

Linking elements occur in all Germanic languages, but the languages differ with respect to the number of linking elements used and their productivity. As discussed in the previous section, inflectional suffixes are a common historical source of linking elements. And, as also shown for German above, these suffixes develop a distribution which is partly independent of the inflectional system in many languages. Since linking elements are most often found in compounds of the type N+N, we will continue to focus on these constructions while considering other Germanic languages in the following.

3.1 Systematic aspects

The systems of linking elements in the other Germanic languages differ according to the number of elements found, their productivity and the degree to which linking elements are dependent on the inflectional system. As in German, most of the languages employ the unsyllabic s-link as well as syllabic linking elements (e.g., Danish -e [ə] in *fisk-e-suppe* 'fish soup', Dutch -en [ə] in *pann-en-koek* 'pancake'). In West Frisian, diminutive suffixes are used as linking elements as well (Hoekstra 1998: 40–41, cf. also Hoekstra 2001), cf. *bus-ke-griente* 'canned vegetables', *rol-tsje-redens* 'roller skates'. In addition to productive linking elements, lexicalized compounds contain some linking elements which can be considered archaic. In Swedish, for example, old genitive markers or stem suffixes are preserved in *veck-o-slut* 'weekend' (based on *vecka*), *gat-u-barn* 'street child' (based on *gata*).

In most Germanic languages, some of the linking elements are still at least somehow related to the inflectional system. In German and Dutch, for example, -(e)n and -e are restricted to nouns which form their plurals using the same marker. Nevertheless, in languages like Swedish, the connection between productive linking elements and the inflectional system has been lost almost completely: Swedish linking-s is almost never paradigmatic, since case-marking was lost (and -s turned into a phrasal marker) and the plural marker -s is only marginally used. By contrast, there are also languages in which a strong connection to the inflectional system is still observable. A look at Icelandic and Faroese might serve as an example.

A close connection to the inflectional system can be assumed when compounds resemble nominal phrases with a genitival attribute. Icelandic and Faroese retain a rather complex inflectional system including a large number of declension classes. Compounds can be formed with the first part ending in a marker of genitive singular or genitive plural, in conformity with the genitive forms of the respective declension class, cf. Faroese *fjall-a-lamb* 'mountain lamb' (gen. pl. *fjalla*), Icelandic *tölv-u-útskrift* 'computer print' (gen. sg. *tölvu*). While at first sight, these languages seem to preserve nominal phrases at a very early stage of lexicalization, there are also signs that inflectional endings in nominal compounds are reanalyzed as linking elements, cf. Thráinsson et al. (2004: 204–208):

(i) In spoken Faroese, the genitive case is only infrequently used and thus has only a weak status, i.e. genitive markers can be regarded as archaic.

(ii) A genitive marker can appear in singular or plural form. Often, the number semantics are not logically related to the semantic relation between first and second part of a compound, cf. Icelandic *plöt-u-búð* (gen. sg. *plötu*), Faroese *plát-u-handil* (gen. sg. *plátu*) 'record store', where the plural form would be expected.

(iii) Especially *-s* is found with nouns which do not take *-s* as an inflectional marker. For example, *-s* does not occur in any feminine declension class, but is found in compounds with feminine first parts such as Icelandic *keppni-s-höll* 'contest hall', Faroese *gularót-s-pakki* 'carrot pack'.

(iv) Nouns usually appear in the genitive form when the first part of a compound is a compound itself in Faroese, such that the distribution of genitive forms is not (only) morphosyntactically conditioned as with case marking, but governed by conditions of word-formation.

In West Frisian (and in other Frisian as well as some Dutch and Low German dialects), a class of constructions called genitive compounds exists. These constructions are characterized by features which suggest that they are still close to their origin in a word group. For example, stress is not on the first part, as is usually the case in compounds, but on the final part of the construction. The first part additionally always appears in the genitive form, cf. *keamer-s-'doar* 'door of the living room'. Hoekstra (2002) does not analyze these constructions as word-formation units, but as lexical phrases, which are stored in the lexicon as phrasal patterns, i.e. items in between phrasal and lexical units. The genitive markers retain a strong relation to the old case system in these units, but are functionally limited.

3.2 Distributional and functional aspects

Generally, analogy plays an important role in the distribution of linking elements. Especially with respect to the first parts, new word-formation units are often formed in analogy to existing ones (cf. Plank 1976: 217–218; Becker 1992: 10–16), i.e. using the same linking element, including the zero link. Based on the notion of compositional (or derivational) stem forms in the sense of Fuhrhop (1998) (see section 2), new units emerge in analogy to existing stem forms rather than according to more general principles. Nevertheless, it is possible to formulate some tendencies (rather than rules) which show that, in addition to linking in analogy with existing stems, there are certain independent trends specific to the linking elements. This is especially clear with regard to linking-*s* (cf. section 3.2.1), but there are also principles for other elements (cf. section 3.2.2).

3.2.1 Linking-*s*

Those Germanic languages which display a productive system of linking elements show strong parallels in the development of linking-*s*. This linking element is distributed independently of the declension system, i.e. apart from paradigmatic cases it also appears non-paradigmatically. This is especially clear in languages which have lost case marking, such as Danish and Swedish. The following charac-teristics are found in parallel in West Germanic Afrikaans (Botha 1968: 154–183), Dutch (Krott 2001), Frisian (Hoekstra 1998: 39–40), German (cf. section 2), and Luxembourgish (Humbert 2006), and in North Germanic Danish (Kürschner 2003), Swedish (Josefsson 1998) and Norwegian (Faarlund, Lie and Vannebo 2006: 70–73):

1. Linking-*s* is bound to a number of derivational suffixes which are common to many Germanic languages, cf. -*ung*/-*ing*, -*heit*/-*heid*/-*hed*/etc., -*schaft*/-*schap*/ -*skab*/etc., -*tum*/-*dom*, etc.
2. When the first part of a compound is itself a compound, linking-*s* is more frequently found than when it is not a compound.
3. When the first part of a compound is prefixed, linking-*s* is more frequently found than when it is not prefixed.

These three characteristics permit the assumption that linking-*s* has developed into a marker of morphological boundaries in complex words (as described for German above; a conditioning on prosodic structures as has been observed in German has to our knowledge not been subject to systematic studies in the other Germanic languages). As such, linking-*s* can be used to mark a difference in meaning between compounds composed of the same words, but interpreted as [N+[N+N]] (cf. 6a) or [[N+N]+N], respectively (cf. 6b).

(6)   a. *barn+bok+klubb*   'book club for children'
      b. *barn+bok-s+klubb*   'club for children's books'
      (Josefsson 1998)

Although the languages differ with regard to the degree to which linking-*s* consist-ently appears with complex first parts of compounds, it is striking that the development is generally parallel. Note that in Faroese, it is not specifically the *s*-link which appears after complex first parts of compounds, but any (paradigmatic) genitive marker, cf. *ís+fisk-a+last* 'cargo of frozen fish' (Thráinsson et al. 2004: 207).

Apart from complex first parts, linking-*s* is also found with some simplexes serving as first parts of word-formation units, but in this case the distribution is mostly described as more or less arbitrary across languages. It is nevertheless observable, as was the case for German, that the distribution of linking-*s* is often diametrically opposed to the distribution of the inflectional marker -*s*. Since with few exceptions, there have been no feminine declensions with an *s*-genitive in Germanic, the *s*-marker was only found with masculine and neuter nouns. In Modern German, linking-*s* is still almost never found with feminine simplexes (Fuhrhop 1998). Delsing (2002) comes to the same conclusion in a historical study of Swedish. In a comparative study, however, Kürschner (2007) finds that in Danish linking-*s* is less seldom found with formerly feminine simplexes than in Swedish.

3.2.2 Other linking elements

The most frequent linking element -*s* is unsyllabic. By contrast, most other linking elements are syllabic, cf. Danish -*e* [ə], Swedish -*o*, Dutch -*en* [ə], German -*en*, etc. Just as described for German above, they are often still identical with inflectional suffixes. If this inflectional suffix is actually part of the declensional paradigm of a noun, it is interesting to ask whether the linking element is also identical to the inflectional suffix with regard to its function, i.e. whether it also carries inflectional meaning inside the compound. It is often assumed that plural meaning is carried by linking elements which are identical with a plural marker. Experimental studies on Dutch and Afrikaans have shown that linking elements are associated with plural meaning in the first part of a compound. Schreuder et al. (1998) conducted a number of experiments using written compounds. The first part of the compounds could be pluralized with -*en*. In the written form, the linking element varied between <e> and <en>. The results showed that plural semantics were activated when the link was written as <en>, i.e. in the form which is homographic with the plural marker. Jansen, Schreuder and Neijt (2007) conducted an experiment with test subjects who were native speakers of Afrikaans. In Afrikaans, the orthographic form of the corresponding plural marker is <e>. The experiment showed that when confronted with written Dutch compounds containing either the linking element <e> or <en>, a plural interpretation was activated when the linking element was homographic with the Afrikaans plural suffix

<e>, and linking-<en> was associated with singular meaning. These results suggest that paradigmatic syllabic linking elements are associated with plural semantics both in Dutch and Afrikaans. Nevertheless, in contrast with inflection, plural marking is not obligatory in the link, cf. Dutch *spier+groep* 'muscle group' and *mens-en-ziel* 'soul of a human being'.

While plural semantics are associated with linking-*e(n)* in Dutch and Afrikaans, this is less clear in German (cf. Krott 2001: 224). Dressler et al. (2001) conducted a constituent naming task with German compounds showing that plural semantics play no role in compound analysis. For German compounds in which associating linking-*(e)n* with plural semantics makes sense (cf. *Frau-en-heim* 'home for women'), the same response latencies were found as for opposite (*Schlange-n-biss* 'snake bite') and unclear cases (*Vill-en-bau* 'villa building'). Additional support is provided by Banga et al. (2013) who presented novel Dutch compounds to native speakers of Dutch, Dutch-Frisian bilinguals, and German-speaking learners. The subjects were asked to express their preference for a form with or without linking-*en*. A context was provided by which either singular or plural semantics should be evoked. The results showed that plurality played a role in all groups of subjects, but that the effects were considerably smaller within the German group.

While the expression of number by linking elements generally seems possible, there are strong theoretical claims against case marking inside compounds (cf. section 2.2.1 for a discussion of German examples). While number is inherently assigned to a noun, case is a contextually licensed category, i.e. the purpose of case is to determine the relation between a given noun and other entities in the syntactic context. Gallmann (1998) argues that it is impossible to assign a contextually licensed category to a non-head of a compound, and since linking elements are part of the non-heads (i.e. first parts) of compounds, in this view no case marking is possible. Still, so-called genitive compounds in West Frisian might serve as a counter-example (see discussion above and in Hoekstra 2002), and the status of compounds in Icelandic deserves further discussion with respect to case marking in compounds (cf. Indriðason 1999).

In addition to inflectional functions, specifically syllabic linking elements have been claimed to have prosodic functions (cf. section 2.2.2 on German). As such, syllabic linking elements can create trochaic feet from monosyllabic stems, cf. Danish *mælk-e-karton* 'milk package'. Usage of linking elements in this manner is far from consistent, but many syllabic linking elements are almost totally constrained to monosyllabic (or finally stressed) stems, e.g., -*e* in Danish, -*en* in Dutch, and -*e*, -*en*, -*er*, and -*es* in German. Neijt and Schreuder (2007) examine the rhythmic function of Dutch -*en* more specifically, considering an influence from the prosodic structure not only of the first part, but also of the second part of the compound. They find out that linking-*en* is found more often between the parts of compounds in which two stressed syllables clash (cf. *boom* 'tree' + *rij* 'row' → *bom-en-rij* 'tree row') than in contexts in which this is not the case.

Since Dutch -*en* is thus both semantically (plural) and prosodically (rhythm) relevant, Hanssen et al. (2013) conducted a study into the relation between both functions in Dutch. For spoken pseudo-compounds and existing pairs of compounds which are variably realized with or without linking-*en* (cf. *bloem-bak* and *bloem-en-bak* 'flower box'), they tested experimentally whether the perceived plurality is affected by -*en* preventing a stress clash or not. In fact, the results show that when a stress clash is prevented, the perceived plurality is lower than when no stress clash is prevented.

For Danish linking-*e* (realized as [ə]), a semantic distribution based on animacy has been claimed (cf. Kürschner 2005). Native monosyllabic nouns and derivates suffixed by -*ing* tend to appear with a linking-*e* in compounds, cf. *dreng-e-streg* 'boyish prank', *fisk-e-suppe* 'fish soup', *svamp-e-skade* 'damage on mushrooms', *udlænding-e-lov* 'law on foreigners'. The same tendency is also found for the formally identical plural marker -*e* (cf. Hansen 1967: 112), but the use of the linking element is even more consistent compared to the inflectional marker, cf., e.g., *ven* 'friend', pluralized as *venner*, in *venn-e-tjeneste* 'friendly turn'. For Dutch, the results of studies on the effects of countability, animacy, and concreteness have shown that the semantic features of the first part of a compound are relevant to the choice of linking element. Van den Toorn (1982b, cf. also 1982a) suggests that the probability of the appearance of linking-*en* is higher with first parts denoting countable and in particular animate entities, especially when the first part is related to the second part as owner or initiator, cf. *mugg-en-been* 'mosquito leg' or *spinn-en-web* 'spider's web'. Corpus analyses and experimental studies by Krott (2001: 103–120) reveal that the semantics of the right part of compounds has no effect, but that the semantics of the first part is influential: -*s* is more likely to appear with abstract nouns, while -*en* is more often found with concrete nouns. With respect to concrete nouns, -*en* appears with highest probability when the semantics of the left part is characterized by an animate feature. Hoekstra (1998: 39) discusses how the distribution of linking-*s* vs. no linking element in subgroups of West Frisian derived nouns varies with the semantics of the first part of the compound.

4 Conclusions

Various linking elements occur in the Germanic languages, and they are distributed and functionalized in various manners. The distribution and functionalization has been studied in corpora, both with regard to the distribution in the current lexicon and in the historical development of the lexicon. Additionally, experimental studies provide evidence for factors relevant in the production of linking elements, and for morphological, prosodic, and semantic functions associated with linking elements both in production and perception. The link between the corpus-based and the experimentally based lines of research will need to be tightened in future research. In addition, especially the historical development of linking elements is still far from well-studied in most of the Germanic languages. What is more, we can expect new perspectives on linking elements from studies concerning items which appear in the link but do not stem from inflectional suffixes, cf. Renner's (2013) study on -*cum* in English coordinate compounds such as *poet-cum-philosopher*.

5 References

Aronoff, Mark and Nanna Fuhrhop (2002): Restricting suffix combinations in German and English: Closing suffixes and the monosuffix constraint. *Natural Language and Linguistic Theory* 20(3): 451–490.

Augst, Gerhard (1975): Über das Fugenmorphem bei Zusammensetzungen. In: Gerhard Augst (ed.), *Untersuchungen zum Morpheminventar der deutschen Gegenwartssprache*, 71–155. Tübingen: Narr.

Baayen, Harald, Wolfgang Ulrich Dressler, Andrea Krott and Robert Schreuder (2007): Analogical effects on linking elements in German. *Language and Cognitive Processes* 22: 25–57.

Banga, Arina, Esther Hanssen, Anneke Neijt and Robert Schreuder (2013): Preference for linking element *en* in Dutch noun-noun compounds: Native speakers and second language learners of Dutch. In: *Morphology* 23(1): 33–56.

Becker, Thomas (1992): Compounding in German. *Rivista di Linguistica* 4(1): 5–36.

Botha, Rudolf P. (1968): *The Function of the Lexicon in Transformational Generative Grammar.* The Hague: Mouton.

De Belder, Marijke (2023): Linking Elements. In: Peter Ackema, Sabrina Bendjaballah, Eulàlia Bonet and Antonio Fábregas (eds.), *The Wiley Blackwell Companion to Morphology.* [Online available at: https://doi.org/10.1002/9781119693604.morphcom040]

Delsing, Lars-Olof (2002): Svenskt foge-*s*. *Folkmålsstudier* 41: 67–78.

Dressler, Wolfgang Ulrich, Gary Libben, Jacqueline Stark, Christiane Pons and Gonia Jarema (2001): The processing of interfixed German compounds. In: Geert Booij and Jap van Marle (eds.), *Yearbook of Morphology 1999*, 185–220. Dordrecht: Kluwer.

Eisenberg, Peter (2006): *Grundriss der deutschen Grammatik. Das Wort.* 3rd ed. Stuttgart/Weimar: Metzler.

Eisenberg, Peter and Ulrike Sayatz (2004): Left of number: Animacy and plurality in German nouns. In: Gereon Müller, Lutz Gunkel and Gisela Zifonun (eds.), *Explorations in Nominal Inflections*, 97–120. Berlin/New York: Mouton de Gruyter.

Faarlund, Jan Terje, Svein Lie and Kjell Ivar Vannebo (2006): *Norsk referansegrammatikk.* Oslo: Universitetsforlaget.

Fuhrhop, Nanna (1998): *Grenzfälle morphologischer Einheiten.* Tübingen: Stauffenburg.

Fuhrhop, Nanna (2000): Zeigen Fugenelemente die Morphologisierung von Komposita? In: Rolf Thieroff, Matthias Tamrat and Nanna Fuhrhop (eds.), *Deutsche Grammatik in Theorie und Praxis*, 201–213. Tübingen: Niemeyer.

Gallmann, Peter (1998): Fugenmorpheme als Nicht-Kasus-Suffixe. In: Matthias Butt and Nanna Fuhrhop (eds.), *Variation und Stabilität in der Wortstruktur. Untersuchungen zu Entwicklung, Erwerb und Varietäten des Deutschen und anderer Sprachen*, 177–190. Hildesheim: Olms.

Hansen, Aage (1967): *Moderne dansk II: Sprogbeskrivelse*. København: Grafisk forlag.

Hanssen, Esther, Arina Banga, Robert Schreuder and Anneke Neijt (2013): Semantic and prosodic effects of Dutch linking elements. *Morphology* 23(1): 7–32.

Hoekstra, Jarich F. (1998): *Fryske Wurdfoarming*. Ljouwert: Fryske Akademy.

Hoekstra, Jarich F. (2001): Comparative aspects of Frisian morphology and syntax. In: Horst Haider Munske (ed.), *Handbuch des Friesischen. Handbook of Frisian Studies*, 775–786. Tübingen: Niemeyer.

Hoekstra, Jarich F. (2002): Genitive compounds in Frisian as lexical phrases. *Journal of Comparative Germanic Linguistics* 6: 227–259.

Humbert, Adrienne (2006): Die Fugenelemente in den Substantivkomposita des Luxemburgischen. Unpublished MA thesis, University of Trier.

Indriðason, Thorsteinn G. (1999): Um eignarfallssamsetningar og adrar samsetningar í íslensku. *Íslenskt mál* 21: 107–150.

Jansen, Carel, Robert Schreuder and Anneke Neijt (2007): The influence of spelling conventions on perceived plurality in compounds. *Written Language and Literacy* 10(2): 105–114.

Josefsson, Gunlög (1998): *Minimal Words in a Minimal Syntax. Word formation in Swedish*. Amsterdam/Philadelphia: Benjamins.

Köpcke, Klaus-Michael (1995): Die Klassifikation der schwachen Maskulina in der deutschen Gegenwartssprache. *Zeitschrift für Sprachwissenschaft* 14(2): 159–180.

Kopf, Kristin (2018): *Fugenelemente diachron. Eine Korpusuntersuchung zu Entstehung und Ausbreitung der verfugenden N+N-Komposita*. Berlin/Boston: De Gruyter Mouton.

Krott, Andrea (2001): *Analogy in Morphology. The selection of linking elements in Dutch compounds*. Wageningen: Ponsen and Looijen.

Kürschner, Sebastian (2003): *Von Volk-s-musik und Sport-Ø-geist im Lemming-Ø-land – af folk-e-musik og sport-s-ånd i lemming-e-landet: Fugenelemente im Deutschen und Dänischen – eine kontrastive Studie zu einem Grenzfall der Morphologie*. Freiburg: FreiDok. http://www.freidok.uni-freiburg.de/volltexte/1256/

Kürschner, Sebastian (2005): Verfugung-*s*-nutzung kontrastiv: Zur Funktion der Fugenelemente im Deutschen und Dänischen. *Tijdschrift voor Scandinavistiek* 26(2): 101–125.

Kürschner, Sebastian (2007): Grenzgänger zwischen Flexion und Wortbildung: Zur Geschichte des dänischen Fugen-*s*. In: Wolfgang Behschnitt and Elisabeth Herrmann (eds.), *Über Grenzen. Grenzgänge der Skandinavistik*, 349–367. Würzburg: Ergon.

Kürschner, Sebastian (2010): *Fuge-n-kitt, voeg-en-mes, fuge-masse* und *fog-e-ord*. Fugenelemente im Deutschen, Niederländischen, Schwedischen und Dänischen: Ein Grenzfall der Morphologie im Sprachkontrast. In: Antje Dammel, Sebastian Kürschner and Damaris Nübling (eds.), *Kontrastive Germanistische Linguistik*. Vol. 2, 827–862. Hildesheim: Olms.

Neef, Martin (2015): The status of so-called linking elements in German: Arguments in favor of a non-functional analysis. *Word Structure* 8(1): 29–52.

Neijt, Anneke and Robert Schreuder (2007): Rhythm versus analogy – prosodic form variation in Dutch compounds. *Language and Speech* 50(4): 533–566.

Nübling, Damaris and Renata Szczepaniak (2008): On the way from morphology to phonology: German linking elements and the role of the phonological word. *Morphology* 18(1): 1–25.

Nübling, Damaris and Renata Szczepaniak (2009): *Religion+s+freiheit, Stabilität+s+pakt* und *Subjekt+s+pronomen*: Fugenelemente als Marker phonologischer Wortgrenzen. In: Peter O. Müller (ed.), *Studien zur Fremdwortbildung*, 195–222. Hildesheim: Olms.

Nübling, Damaris and Renata Szczepaniak (2011): *Merkmal(s?)analyse, Seminar(s?)arbeit* und *Essen(s?)ausgabe*: Zweifelsfälle der Verfugung als Indikatoren für Sprachwandel. *Zeitschrift für Sprachwissenschaft* 30(1): 45–73.

Ortner, Lorelies, Elgin Müller-Bollhagen, Hanspeter Ortner, Hans Wellmann, Maria Pümpel-Mader and Hildegard Gärtner (1991): *Deutsche Wortbildung. Typen und Tendenzen in der Gegenwartssprache. Vierter Hauptteil: Substantivkomposita (Komposita und kompositionsähnliche Strukturen)*. Berlin/New York: Mouton de Gruyter.

Petersen, Hjalmar P. and Renata Szczepaniak (2018): The development of non-paradigmatic linking elements in Faroese and the decline of the genitive case. In: Tanja Ackermann, Horst J. Simon and Christian Zimmer (eds.), *Germanic genitives*, 115–145. Amsterdam/Philadelphia: Benjamins.

Plank, Frans (1976): Morphological aspects of nominal compounding in German and certain other languages: What to acquire in language acquisition in case the rules fail? In: Gaberell Drachmann (ed.), *Akten des 1. Salzburger Kolloquiums über Kindersprache*, 201–219. Tübingen: Narr.

Renner, Vincent (2013): English *cum*, a borrowed coordinator turned complex-compound marker. *Morphology* 23(1): 57–66.

Schäfer, Roland and Elizabeth Pankratz (2018): The plural interpretability of German linking elements. *Morphology* 28(4): 325–358. [Online available at: https://doi.org/10.1007/s11525-018-9331-5]

Schlücker, Barbara (2023): Compounding and Linking Elements in Germanic. In: Sebastian Kürschner and Antje Dammel (eds.), *The Oxford Encyclopedia of Germanic Linguistics*. [Online available at: https://oxfordre.com/linguistics/view/10.1093/acrefore/9780199384655.001.0001/acrefore-9780199384655-e-954]

Schreuder, Robert, Anneke Neijt, Femke van der Weide and Harald R. Baayen (1998): Regular plurals in Dutch compounds: Linking graphemes or morphemes? *Language and Cognitive Processes* 13: 551–573.

Szczepaniak, Renata (2016): Is the development of linking elements in German a case of exaptation? In: Muriel Norde and Freek Van de Velde (eds.), *Exaptation and language change*, 317–340. Amsterdam/Philadelphia: Benjamins.

Szczepaniak, Renata (2020): Linking Elements in Morphology. In: *Oxford Research Encyclopedia of Linguistics*. [Online available at: https://oxfordre.com/linguistics/view/10.1093/acrefore/9780199384655.001.0001/acrefore-9780199384655-e-571]

Thráinsson, Höskuldur, Hjalmar P. Petersen, Jógvan í Lon Jacobsen and Zakaris Svabo Hansen (2004): *Faroese. An overview and reference grammar*. Tórshavn: Føroya Fróðskaparfelag.

van den Toorn, Maarten Cornelis (1982a): Tendenzen bij de beregeling van de verbindingsklank in nominale samenstellingen I. *De Niewe Taalgids* 75(1): 24–33.

van den Toorn, Maarten Cornelis (1982b): Tendenzen bij de beregeling van de verbindingsklank in nominale samenstellingen II. *De Niewe Taalgids* 75(2): 153–160.

Wegener, Heide (2003): Entstehung und Funktion der Fugenelemente im Deutschen, oder: warum wir keine **Autosbahn* haben. *Linguistische Berichte* 196: 425–457.

Wegener, Heide (2005): Das Hühnerei vor der Hundehütte. Von der Notwendigkeit historischen Wissens in der Grammatikographie des Deutschen. In: Elisabeth Berner, Manuela Böhm and Anja Voeste (eds.). *Ein gross vnnd narrhafft haffen*, 175–187. Potsdam: Universitätsverlag Potsdam.

Wiese, Richard (2000): *The Phonology of German*. Oxford: Oxford University Press.

Martin Neef

5 Synthetic compounds in German

Abstract: The term "synthetic compound" is used for different concepts in the pertinent linguistic literature. This article regards as synthetic compounds complex words of at least three morphemes, where neither the combination of the first two nor of the last two forms an existing free word. Synthetic compounds are typical for West Germanic languages. Different kinds of analyses in different theoretical frameworks have been proposed, some of which are to be discussed in the following. In general, synthetic compounds do not form a genuine morphological category, but can be attributed to other well-established categories.

1 Introduction

In the history of the science of word-formation, many different constructions have been attributed to the concept of synthetic compound. I will give an overview of these constructions as well as a definition of the term "synthetic compound" that covers what I see as the core of this concept. The focus of study will be German, not least because with respect to this language the discussion of this type of word-formation is especially relevant (which, by the way, also holds with respect to Dutch; cf. Booij 2002: 158), but homologous examples from other languages will also be given.

German has a quite rich and productive inventory of means of word-formation (or, more appropriately, lexeme-formation). This holds for compounding (cf., e.g., Becker 1992; Neef 2009) as well as for derivation, but also for a number of other types of lexeme-formation that are more or less productive, especially conversion (cf., e.g., Neef 1999, 2005). There is no monograph on German word-

Martin Neef, Braunschweig, Germany

https://doi.org/10.1515/9783111420554-005

formation written in English to refer to, but many overview works exist in German, among them Fleischer and Barz (2012) and Eisenberg (2013), to mention two prominent standard books. The problem of synthetic compounds is discussed in many textbooks on morphology as well as in a few articles and one monograph (Leser 1990) that are especially devoted to this subject. In this literature on German, synthetic compounds are treated as compounds by some researchers and as derivatives by others, but again by others as a construction type of its own.

For introductory purposes, I give a tentative definition and a prototypical example first. Synthetic compounds are complex words that contain at least three morphemes, with neither the combination of the first two nor of the last two existing as free words. An example is *blauäugig* 'blue-eyed', where the English translation of the German word is a synthetic compound itself, faithfully mirroring the morpheme structure of the German example. In qualification, it should be stated that the possible second member of *blauäugig*, namely *äugig*, actually occurs as a free word, but with a restricted meaning only in specific technical terminologies. The pioneering 18th-century linguist Johann Christoph Adelung (1732–1806) already discusses this in his dictionary (without making recourse to the concept of synthetic compound):

> **Äugig**, *adj. et adv.* Augen habend, ein Wort, welches nur in den Zusammensetzungen einäugig, zweyäugig, hundertäugig, großäugig, triefäugig u.s.f. üblich ist, in den Bergwerken aber auch für sich allein, in der figürlichen Bedeutung für löcherig, bläsig, gebraucht wird. (Adelung 1793: 567)

> [**eyed**, *adj. and adv.* having eyes, a word that is common only in compounds like one-eyed, two-eyed, hundred-eyed, big-eyed, bleary-eyed, etc., but that is used on its own in mines with the metaphoric meaning of holey, blistered.]

Obviously, the meaning of the synthetic compound *blauäugig* does not rest on this meaning of the word *äugig*. Therefore, the free word can not readily be regarded as the base of the complex word. This is the typical situation for synthetic compounds.

2 The term "synthetic compound" and its German equivalent "Zusammenbildung"

The term "synthetic compound" was coined by Leopold von Schroeder (1851–1920). With respect to words like *Machthaber* 'powerholder' and *Besenbinder* 'broom maker', he states:

Da nun hier eine *doppelte Synthese* sprachlicher Elemente vorliegt, indem nicht nur das 1. und 2. Glied der Composition zusammenzusetzen sind, sondern dies 2. Glied erst noch aus Verbalstamm + Suffix geschaffen wird, so schlagen wir für diese Composita die pleonastische Bezeichnung *synthetische Composita* vor. (Schroeder 1874: 206) [Since we find a *double synthesis* of linguistic elements, in that not only the first and the second element of the compound are to be composed but at the same time this second element is formed from a verbal stem + suffix, we suggest for such compounds the pleonastic designation *synthetic compounds.*]

The term "synthetic compound" is nowadays widespread in English linguistics. Bloomfield (1933: 231) may have been the first to use this term in English (cf. ten Hacken 2010: 233). In German, however, it is rarely used in present work. Instead, the term "Zusammenbildung" (lit. 'together-formation') is prevalent, a term that can be traced back to Wilmanns (1896: 2–3; cf. Leser 1990: 19). However, both the English term "synthetic compound" and the German term "Zusammenbildung" are used in the literature for quite diverse concepts. This article is about what I regard as the core concept of "Zusammenbildungen" in German, using the term "synthetic compound" to refer to it (cf. also Marchand 1969: 15; Botha 1984: 146). Occasionally, I will also give examples of constructions that some researchers regard as "Zusammenbildungen" but that do not fall under the concept promoted here. The term "synthetic compound", incidentally, has one disadvantage compared to the term "Zusammenbildung": It implies that the respective words have to be classified as compounds in the first place and not as, e.g., derivatives, a conclusion that is not fixed in advance. The German term is neutral in this respect.

3 Classification

The following list shows different types of synthetic compounds in German. In the data, plus signs indicate morpheme boundaries. Suffixes are translated into English as their semantically nearest equivalents. More structural types are presented in Leser (1990: 5):

(1)   <u>Nouns</u>
       a. N+V+Sx   *Appetit+hemm+er*
                   appetite+block+er
                   'anorectic'
       b. A+N+Sx   *Dick+häut+er*
                   thick+skin+er
                   'pachyderm'

      c. N+V+Sx   *Grab+leg+ung*
                          grave+lay+ing
                          'entombment'

      d. A+N+N   *Alt+weiber+sommer*
                          old+shrew+summer
                          'Indian summer'

      e. Q+N+N   *Fünf+jahres+plan*
                          five+year+plan
                          'five-year plan'

(2)   Adjectives
      a. N+V+Sx   *hand+greif+lich*
                          hand+grab+ing
                          'palpable'

      b. Q+N+Sx   *fünf+jähr+ig*
                          five+year+ed
                          'quinquennial'

      c. N+N+Sx   *asch+farbe+n*
                          ash+colour+ed
                          'ashy'

      d. Q+N+A   *neun+rösser+stark*
                          nine+steed+strong
                          'strong as nine steeds'

(3)   Adverbs
      N+N+Sx   *zeit+leben+s*
                          time+life+ly
                          'lifelong'

The data illustrate the formal diversity of lexemes that are frequently classified as synthetic compounds. At the same time, it shows one of the major problems with this concept: If synthetic compounds are regarded as complex words of at least three morphemes, where neither the combination of the first two nor of the last two forms an existing free word, it has to be made sure that said combinations of two morphemes actually do not exist in the language. Such determinations obviously hinge on the extension of the vocabulary taken into consideration as well as on the specific time of observation. For example, the lexeme *Jahresplan* is not included in the major dictionaries of German, supporting the classification of *Fünfjahresplan* (1e) as a synthetic compound. An internet survey, however, gives a number of relevant uses, thereby questioning this classification. Moreover, if not actually existing words, some of the relevant bimorphemic combinations may be at least possible words, a concept that has to be considered in this context.

In the German examples above, some non-final nominal constituents have a form that differs from the regular stem form, which is the form used for the nominative singular when functioning as the head of a word, thus the rightmost element of a (simple or complex) lexeme. For example, the form *weiber* in (1d) looks like the nominative, accusative, or genitive plural form of the lexeme WEIB, and the form *jahres* in (1e) looks like the genitive singular of JAHR. Traditionally, such additional segments are regarded as discrete units called linking elements or linking morphemes (German "Fugenelement" and "Fugenmorphem", respectively, cf. also article 4 on linking elements in Germanic), frequently analyzed as carrying the said inflectional meaning. This meaning-argument, however, though being convenient for the former case, does not work for the latter, which would call for a plural form. In other examples, nominal stems appear in a form that is not present in the inflectional paradigms as is the case for *jähr* (2b) to the lexeme JAHR or *asch* (2c) to the lexeme ASCHE. Following Becker (1992), among others (cf. Neef 2009: 393), I regard linking elements as a morphological phenomenon on the level of stem forms. Some lexemes like APPETIT have only one stem form for all morphological contexts, others have a specific one for the context "left-hand member of a compound" (like the form *weiber* of the lexeme WEIB) or even a specific one for the context "base of a suffixation" (like the form *jähr* of the lexeme JAHR). Especially with regard to the established vocabulary, a considerable amount of irregularity has to be conceded besides the regular core, under the given analysis as under any other.

4 Analysis

Synthetic compounds contain at least three morphemes. This property gives way to a number of competing analyses. With respect to the data presented in section 3, an analysis with ternary branching is immediately ruled out. In the following, I outline three different types of analyses that more or less explicitly assume a binary structure of synthetic compounds. All these analyses cover a subgroup of relevant data only.

4.1 Synthetic compounds as phrase-based

In the history of Germanic linguistics, the most prominent approach to synthetic compounding regards the relevant words as derivations based on word groups or phrases (cf. Botha 1981: 3; Leser 1990: 25). This view is still present in some more recent work on German (e.g., Römer 2006: 134, 148; Elsen 2011: 29) as well as on English (e.g., Plag 2003: 153). The basic assumption of this approach is that the structure of a synthetic compound is $[[M_1 \; M_2] \; M_3]$, with the first immediate constituent being a syntactic phrase instead of a morphological construction. Thus, the synthetic compound *blauäugig* is said to have the structure $[[blau_{Adj} \; äug_N]_{NP} \; ig]_{Adj}$. An advantage of this analysis is that it seems to be compatible with the semantic interpretation of the word, which can be paraphrased as 'having blue eyes'.

In fact, words with phrasal elements exist in German, namely phrasal compounds (which Römer 2006: 134 consequently subsumes under the category of synthetic compounds, in conflict with my definition above). An overview of the relevant literature on phrasal compounds in German is given in Meibauer (2003), cf. also Wiese (1996), as well as ample illustrative data. Meibauer (2003: 156–158) explicitly distinguishes phrasal compounds like *Rote-Augen-Reduktion* 'red-eyes-reduction' from synthetic compounds like *Dreipunktgurt* 'three-point-belt' (referring to Leser 1990). In the former, the sequence *Rote-Augen* forms a well-formed phrase; adjective and noun are inflected congruously. The sequence *Dreipunkt*, in contrast, is not grammatical as a phrase because *Punkt* is a singular form while *drei* obviously demands a plural form, which would be *Punkte* (the English equivalents show the same behavior in both these cases).

Studies that treat synthetic compounds as phrasal derivations usually focus on words with a suffix as head instead of a stem as in the examples given, but the argumentation would be parallel for such constructions: In the synthetic compound *blauäugig*, the assumed constituent *blauäug* does not behave like a syntactic phrase. Depending on the feature of definitiveness of a preceding determiner, the correct form of this phrase is (*ein*) *blaues Auge* or (*das*) *blaue Auge* '(a/the) blue eye' in the singular and (*die*) *blauen Augen* or *blaue Augen* '(the) blue eyes' in the plural. Obviously, there are clear formal differences between the phrase and the form appearing in the synthetic compound (cf. Booij 2002: 158 for a similar argumentation for Dutch data). In order to maintain an analysis with a syntactic phrase as basis, the transformation of the phrase into a form suitable for a synthetic compound has to be modeled, something that has not yet been attempted in a sufficiently formalized way. Presumably, this formalization is confronted with insurmountable difficulties, indicating that the phrasal account is untenable for formal reasons.

In general, phrasal compounds should be distinguished from synthetic compounds proper; both kinds of construction exist in German morphology but have quite different properties. In particular, whereas phrasal compounds contain syntactic phrases as left-hand constituents, synthetic compounds are not based on such phrases.

4.2 Synthetic compounds as verbal (nexus) compounds

A majority of linguists analyze synthetic compounds as consisting of a simple first constituent and a complex second one. Under this perspective, synthetic compounds fall into two distinct subsets, depending on whether the first element of the second constituent is a verb or not. I continue with a discussion of the type containing a verb in the relevant position.

Lieber (2009: 358) notices that "synthetic compounds in English have traditionally been defined as compounds in which the second constituent is a deverbal element" (see also Gaeta 2010 with respect to German). This definition is quite different from the one I take as basis for this article, though the different concepts have an intersecting set. Frequently, the class of complex words Lieber denotes as synthetic compounds is referred to with a different term. Marchand (1969: 18) equates "synthetic compound" with "verbal nexus compound". Selkirk (1982: 28) uses the term "verbal compound" for a class of compounds "where the non-head constituent may be interpreted as an argument of the deverbal head noun". Olsen (1986: 67) chooses the German term "Rektionskomposita" (lit. 'government compounds') to refer to this concept. The following data illustrate the relation of synthetic compounds and verbal compounds with examples from German (based on Olsen 1986: 66–88):

(4)   a. *Appetit+hemm+er*
         appetite+block+er
         'anorectic'
      b. *Auto+fahr+er*
         car+drive+er
         'car driver'
      c. *Unfall+fahr+er*
         accident+drive+er
         'crash driver'
      d. *Alkohol+fahr+er*
         alcohol+drive+er
         'drunken driver' or 'trucker for alcohol'

All these examples have a deverbal second element. In (4a and b), the non-head constituent is interpreted as the object of the embedded verb. Such an interpretation is ruled out in (4c), while in (4d), both types of interpretation are available. Since the word *Fahrer* 'driver' is a free word in German, only example (4a) is a synthetic compound in a strict sense. This distinction between the different examples in (4) is already given in Bloomfield (1933: 232) who would analyze the words in (4a–d) as "semi-synthetic compounds".

Both *hemmen* and *fahren* are transitive verbs, selecting an accusative object. In syntactic structures, this object has to be realized obligatorily. In morphological structures, sometimes realizing the object is required while sometimes it is not. Such data have been analyzed by means of the concept of "argument inheritance" (Toman 1983: 55; cf. also Hoekstra 1986; Bierwisch 1989). Under such a conception, suffixes may inherit the argument structure of the verb they attach to and pass it on to the dominating node, possibly in a modified way. The German suffix *-er*, for example, attaches to verbs that at least have a subject (external) argument; this argument is not inherited by the suffix. If the verb has an internal argument with structural case (an accusative object), this argument may be inherited by the suffix. Internal arguments of this type with the semantic role "goal", however, are restricted from inheritance (Maling 2001: 455). Other possible arguments of basic verbs (oblique case objects, prepositional objects, a second accusative object) are not also inherited (Leser 1990: 77).

With the transitive verb *hemmen* as the base, the suffix *-er* forms nouns with an obligatory argument that is to be realized in its first order projection (Selkirk 1982: 37). If the deverbal noun *Hemmer* is head of a compound, the first order projection pertains to the non-head position. Therefore, the element *Appetit* in the compound *Appetithemmer* is interpreted as the internal argument of the embedded verb. If *Hemmer* is a "free" noun, the argument has to be realized as an adjacent genitive phrase as *Hemmer des Appetits*. Whether or not this specific phrase is grammatical in German is disputed among linguists working on German (cf. Leser 1990: 64–65). This may be due to the fact that it is uncommon for a noun to be transitive, but this feature is what is predicted from the analysis sketched.

In some cases, lexicalization leads to the inherent saturation of an argument role. This holds, e.g., for the noun *Fahrer* which – although being derived from a transitive verb – can be used as a fully free noun, leading to a variety of interpretations of compounds with this word as head, as indicated in (4b–d), i.e. either as a verbal compound (in the sense of Selkirk 1982) or as a root compound. Olsen (1986: 87) argues that in morphology, the open argument position can also be filled by information that is given only in the previous linguistic context. Such contextual saturation of arguments seems to be less problematic in morphology than in syntax.

Overall, synthetic compounds of the type *Appetithemmer* – a particularly productive case in German – turn out as regular verbal compounds. In effect, the category "synthetic compound" can be dispensed with for this type of data (Leser 1990: 103; Donalies 2001: 134). A similar conclusion may be adequate for Dutch and English.

4.3 Noun-based synthetic compounds

Next I turn to the analysis of synthetic compounds as words with a complex right-hand member in which the first element of this part is non-verbal, confining the discussion to words where the respective element is a noun. The prototypical example for this type of synthetic compounds is *blauäugig*, as introduced in the first section of this article. In German, the suffix *-ig* is particularly productive in synthetic compounds of this type. The transparent core of this derivational pattern can be characterized in the following way: The suffix takes nouns as bases and forms adjectives that denote a possessive relation. For example, the adjectives *bärtig* 'beardy' is based on the noun *Bart* 'beard', and it can be paraphrased as 'having a beard'. The following list shows some relevant data, only some of which will be classified as synthetic compounds in the following discussion:

(5) a. *kurz+bein+ig*
        short+leg+ed
        'short-legged'
     b. *rot+bärt+ig*
        red+beard+ed
        'red-bearded'
     c. *bös+will+ig*
        bad+will+ed
        'malicious'
     d. *rad+förm+ig*
        wheel+shape+ed
        'wheel-shaped'
     e. *fremd+art+ig*
        foreign+kind+ed
        'foreign'

While the adjective *bärtig* is an existing word in German, the similarly structured word *äugig* only exists in technical terminology (cf. section 1) and *beinig* probably does not exist as a free word at all, but only as part of a synthetic compound like in (5a). Leser (1990: 86–93) attempts to explain this peculiar behavior with reference to the concept of inalienable possession as discussed in Ljung (1976) in regard to English adjectives like *blue-eyed* and *bearded*. A possessive relation holds between the basic noun of the adjective and a noun that the adjective modifies in phrasal constructions, for example in the phrase *a bearded man*. Ljung (1976: 162–163) distinguishes two degrees of inalienable possession: The first degree holds when all referents of a noun have as an inherent part or property the referent of the other noun (as is the case for objects and surfaces) or when all referents of a noun are at least expected to have as an inherent part or property the referent of the other noun (like in the relation between human beings and body parts). The second degree holds when a subset of referents of a noun has as an inherent part or property the referent of the other noun, as is the case for males and beards. Besides inalienable possession, there is alienable possession. Adjectives in *-ed* (as well as German adjectives in *-ig*) are impossible for first degree of inalienable possession. Ljung (1976: 162) relates this property to a pragmatic conversation principle that bans tautological expressions. Since all objects that can have legs regularly do have legs, it is tautological to modify a noun with the adjective *legged*.

According to this analysis, synthetic compounds like *kurzbeinig* (5a) do not differ structurally from root compounds like *rotbärtig* (5b), only that *bärtig* is a possible free word while *beinig* is not. The word *böswillig* in (5c) is a synthetic compound although the word *willig* exists as a free word, because the meaning of this word is 'willing' and not simply 'having a will', as would be necessary as the base of *böswillig*. The examples in (5d and e) are usually not regarded as synthetic compounds although their structure fully resembles the other examples in (5) (with *förmig* being impossible as a free word and *artig* only existing with the non-transparent meaning 'dutiful'). Instead, the elements *-förmig* and *-artig* are usually regarded as "semi-suffixes" (e.g., Eisenberg 2013) due to their very high productivity. Apparently, an analysis similar to synthetic compounds like *kurzbeinig* would be preferable since it would render the morphological category "semi-affix" dispensable.

An analysis of the present type of synthetic compounds as morphological compounds with the structure [[*kurz*] [*beinig*]] is not unanimously accepted. Donalies (2001: 135), e.g., rejects this analysis because it does not straightforwardly account for the relevant semantic interpretation. In fact, a short-legged person is not a legged person that is short, but a person that has short legs. This problem of semantic interpretation holds for all the data in (5), not only for synthetic compounds, and is already addressed at length in Botha (1984: 110–135) who reviews the relevant lexicalist approaches of the time that have major problems with the data. More recent theoretical approaches, however, promise a solution.

For example, Giegerich (2009: 191–192) claims that semantic interpretation may generally be independent of morphological structure, invoking the concept of "subsective attribution" for the cases in question. With explicit reference to synthetic compounds, suitable semantic analyses are given by Booij (2002: 158–160, 2009: 213–214) in terms of construction morphology and by Jackendoff (2009: 122) and ten Hacken (2010: 246–249) in terms of the parallel-architecture model. Thus, the persuasiveness of the morphological analysis given for synthetic compounds of the type *blauäugig* depends on further theoretical assumptions concerning the general architecture of grammar. In any case, synthetic compounds turn out as belonging to well-established major morphological categories instead of constituting a genuine concept of their own.

5 Synthetic compounds in other languages

According to the discussion up until now, the two prototypical types of synthetic compounds can be illustrated with the examples *Appetithemmer* and *blauäugig*. These words are compounds of the structure [M$_1$ [M$_2$ M$_3$]], with the exceptional property that the second immediate constituent does not exist as a free word. This feature, which defines the category of synthetic compounds, can be explained with syntactic and pragmatic concepts. Based on this characterization, examples for synthetic compounds from a number of languages other than German can be found in the literature. Synthetic compounds are especially well-established in West Germanic languages. The following table gives relevant examples from some of these languages including a corresponding source for the data.

Tab. 5.1: Synthetic compounds in West Germanic languages.

German	*Appetit+hemm+er*	*blau+äug+ig*	
English	*tree+devour+er*	*blue+eye+d*	Selkirk (1982: 30)/ Bloomfield (1933: 231)
Dutch	*beeld+houw+er* picture+cut+er 'sculptor'	*blauw+og+ig* blue+eye+ed 'blue-eyed'	Booij (2002: 163/ 158)
Afrikaans	*leeu+byt+er* lion+bite+er 'one who bites lions'	*dik+lip+ig* thick+lip+ed 'having thick lips'	Botha (1981: 1)

The fact that the discussion of synthetic compounds focuses mainly on the West Germanic languages may derive from the circumstance that the morphology of these languages is exceptionally well investigated in general. Some sources indicate that synthetic compounds exist in other languages as well. Schroeder (1874: 206–208, etc.) gives examples for synthetic compounds in ancient languages (Greek and Latin), which form the focus of his study. Moreover, there are hints that synthetic compounds exist in some Slavic languages (cf. Leser 1990: 13). In general, the question of whether synthetic compounds exist in other languages as well is not readily answered due to the ambiguous use of the term "synthetic compound". Ralli (2009: 460–461), e.g., has a paragraph on synthetic compounds in Modern Greek, but the data she presents should more aptly be regarded as verbal compounds rather than synthetic compounds. The same holds for Scalise and Bisetto (2009: 36) who claim that synthetic compounds do not exist in Romance languages but restrict their investigation to verbal compounds (cf. also Bzdęga 1999 for Polish). In contrast, Schultink (1986: 482) gives examples for synthetic compounds of type "prefix + stem + suffix" in French that are classified as "parasynthetics" in French linguistics (cf. also article 1 on parasynthesis in Romance). Thus, it is very likely that synthetic compounds as conceived of in this article can be discovered in many other languages as well.

6 References

Adelung, Johann Christoph (1793): *Grammatisch-kritisches Wörterbuch der Hochdeutschen Mundart mit beständiger Vergleichung der übrigen Mundarten, besonders aber der Oberdeutschen.* Vol. 1., 2nd ed. Leipzig: Breitkopf und Sohn.

Becker, Thomas (1992): Compounding in German. *Rivista di Linguistica* 4: 5–36.

Bierwisch, Manfred (1989): Event nominalizations: Proposals and problems. In: Wolfgang Motsch (ed.), *Wortstruktur und Satzstruktur*, 1–73. Berlin: Akademie Verlag.

Bloomfield, Leonard (1933): *Language.* New York: Allen & Unwin.

Booij, Geert (2002): *The Morphology of Dutch.* Oxford: Oxford University Press.

Booij, Geert (2009): Compounding and construction morphology. In: Rochelle Lieber and Pavol Štekauer (eds.), *The Oxford Handbook of Compounding*, 201–216. Oxford: Oxford University Press.

Botha, Rudolf P. (1981): A base rule theory of Afrikaans synthetic compounding. In: Michael Moortgat, Harry van der Hulst and Teun Hoekstra (eds.), *The Scope of Lexical Rules*, 1–77. Dordrecht: Foris.

Botha, Rudolf P. (1984): *Morphological Mechanisms. Lexicalist Analyses of Synthetic Compounding.* Oxford: Pergamon Press.

Bzdęga, Andrzej Z. (1999): Zusammenrückung, -setzung, -bildung. In: Andrzej Kątny and Christoph Schatte (eds.), *Das Deutsche von innen und von außen. Ulrich Engel zum 70. Geburtstag*, 9–23. Poznań: Wydawnictwo Naukowe UAM.

Donalies, Elke (2001): Zur Entrümpelung vorgeschlagen die Wortbildungsarten: Rückbildung, Zusammenbildung, Zusammenrückung, Klammerform und Pseudomotivierung. *Studia Germanica Universitatis Vesprimiensis* 5(2): 129–145.

Eisenberg, Peter (2013): *Grundriss der deutschen Grammatik*. Vol. 1: *Das Wort*. 4th ed. Stuttgart/ Weimar: Metzler.

Elsen, Hilke (2011): *Grundzüge der Morphologie des Deutschen*. Berlin/Boston: de Gruyter.

Fernández-Domínguez, Jesus (2024): A syntactic and morphological account of English nonaffixal deverbal compounds. *Italian Journal of Linguistics* 36: 103–128.

Fleischer, Wolfgang and Irmhild Barz (2012): *Wortbildung der deutschen Gegenwartssprache*. 4th ed. Berlin/Boston: de Gruyter.

Gaeta, Livio (2010): Synthetic compounds: With special reference to German. In: Sergio Scalise and Irene Vogel (eds.), *Cross-Disciplinary Issues in Compounding*, 219–235. Amsterdam/Philadelphia: Benjamins.

Gaeta, Livio and Amir Zeldes (2017): Between VP and NN. On the constructional types of German -er compounds. *Constructions and Frames* 9(1): 1–40.

Giegerich, Heinz (2009): Compounding and lexicalism. In: Rochelle Lieber and Pavol Štekauer (eds.), *The Oxford Handbook of Compounding*, 178–200. Oxford: Oxford University Press.

Hoekstra, Teun (1986): Deverbalization and inheritance. *Linguistics* 24: 549–584.

Iordăchioaia, Gianina, Artemis Alexiadou and Andreas Pairamidis (2017): Morphosyntactic sources for nominal synthetic compounds in English and Greek. *Zeitschrift für Wortbildung / Journal of Word Formation* 1(1): 41–71.

Jackendoff, Ray (2009): Compounding in the parallel architecture and conceptual semantics. In: Rochelle Lieber and Pavol Štekauer (eds.), *The Oxford Handbook of Compounding*, 105–128. Oxford: Oxford University Press.

Leser, Martin (1990): *Das Problem der ‚Zusammenbildungen'. Eine lexikalistische Studie*. Trier: Wissenschaftlicher Verlag Trier.

Lieber, Rochelle (2009): IE, Germanic: English. In: Rochelle Lieber and Pavol Štekauer (eds.), *The Oxford Handbook of Compounding*, 357–369. Oxford: Oxford University Press.

Lieber, Rochelle (2016): On the interplay of facts and theory: Revisiting synthetic compounds in English. In: Daniel Siddiqi and Heidi Harley (eds.), *Morphological Metatheory*, 513–536. Amsterdam/Philadelphia: Benjamins.

Ljung, Magnus (1976): -ed-adjectives revisited. *Journal of Linguistics* 12: 159–168.

Maling, Joan (2001): Dative: The heterogeneity of the mapping among morphological case, grammatical functions, and thematic roles. *Lingua* 111: 419–464.

Marchand, Hans (1969): *The Categories and Types of Present-Day English Word-Formation. A Synchronic-Diachronic Approach*. 2nd ed. München: Beck.

Mattiello, Elisa and Wolfgang U. Dressler (2022): Dualism and superposition in the analysis of English synthetic compounds ending in -er. *Linguistics* 60(2): 395–461.

Mattiello, Elisa and Wolfgang U. Dressler (2025): English synthetic compounds in -er and their German and Italian correspondences. In: Sara Matrisciano-Mayerhofer, Johannes Schnitzer and Elisabeth Peters (eds.), *Patterns, variants and change: Through the prism of morphology. Studies in honor of Franz Rainer*, 295–307. Strasbourg: ELiPHi.

Meibauer, Jörg (2003): Phrasenkomposita zwischen Wortsyntax und Lexikon. *Zeitschrift für Sprachwissenschaft* 22: 153–188.

Meibauer, Jörg and Petra M. Vogel (eds.) (2017): Zusammenbildungen / Synthetic Compounds. *Zeitschrift für Wortbildung / Journal of Word Formation* 1(1): 11–92.

Melloni, Chiara (2020): Subordinate and Synthetic Compounds in Morphology. In: *Oxford Research Encyclopedia of Linguistics*. Oxford: Oxford University Press. [Online available at: https:// doi.org/10.1093/acrefore/9780199384655.013.562]

Neef, Martin (1999): A declarative approach to conversion into verbs in German. In: Geert Booij and Jaap van Marle (eds.), *Yearbook of Morphology 1998*, 199–224. Boston/Dordrecht: Kluwer.

Neef, Martin (2005): On some alleged constraints on conversion. In: Laurie Bauer and Salvador Valera (eds.), *Approaches to Conversion/Zero-Derivation*, 103–130. Münster: Waxmann.

Neef, Martin (2009): IE, Germanic: German. In: Rochelle Lieber and Pavol Štekauer (eds.), *The Oxford Handbook of Compounding*, 386–399. Oxford: Oxford University Press.

Olsen, Susan (1986): *Wortbildung im Deutschen*. Stuttgart: Kröner.

Olsen, Susan (2017): Synthetic Compounds from a Lexicalist Perspective. *Zeitschrift für Wortbildung / Journal of Word Formation* 1(1): 15–43.

Olsen, Susan (2025): Parasynthetic, synthetic and exocentric compounds: diachronic-synchronic considerations. In: Sara Matrisciano-Mayerhofer, Johannes Schnitzer and Elisabeth Peters (eds.), *Patterns, variants and change: Through the prism of morphology. Studies in honor of Franz Rainer*, 55–72. Strasbourg: ELiPHi.

Pafel, Jürgen (2015): Phrasal compounds are compatible with Lexical Integrity. *Language Typology and Universals* 68(3): 263–280.

Plag, Ingo (2003): *Word-Formation in English*. Cambridge: Cambridge University Press.

Ralli, Angela (2009): IE, Hellenic: Greek. In: Rochelle Lieber and Pavol Štekauer (eds.), *The Oxford Handbook of Compounding*, 453–463. Oxford: Oxford University Press.

Römer, Christine (2006): *Morphologie der deutschen Sprache*. Tübingen: Francke.

Scalise, Sergio and Antonietta Bisetto (2009): The classification of compounds. In: Rochelle Lieber and Pavol Štekauer (eds.), *The Oxford Handbook of Compounding*, 34–53. Oxford: Oxford University Press.

Schroeder, Leopold (1874): *Über die formelle Unterscheidung der Redetheile im Griechischen und Lateinischen mit besonderer Berücksichtigung der Nominalcomposita*. Leipzig: Köhler.

Schultink, Henk (1987): Discontinuity and multiple branching in morphology. In: Roberto Crespo, Bill Dotson Smith and Henk Schultink (eds.), *Aspects of Language. Studies in Honour of Mario Alinei*. Vol. 2: *Theoretical and Applied Semantics*, 481–492. Amsterdam: Rodopi.

Selkirk, Elisabeth (1982): *The Syntax of Words*. Cambridge, MA: MIT Press.

ten Hacken, Pius (2010): Synthetic and exocentric compounds in a parallel architecture. In: Susan Olsen (ed.), *New Impulses in Word-Formation*, 233–251. Hamburg: Buske.

Toman, Jindrich (1983): *Wortsyntax. Eine Diskussion ausgewählter Probleme deutscher Wortbildung*. Tübingen: Niemeyer.

Werner, Martina (2017): Zur Entwicklung der synthetischen Komposition in der Geschichte des Deutschen. *Zeitschrift für Wortbildung / Journal of Word Formation* 1(1): 73–92.

Werner, Martina (2020): Three diachronic sources for the development of *-erei*-based synthetic compounds in German. *Word Structure* 13: 347–370.

Wiese, Richard (1996): Phrasal compounds and the theory of word syntax. *Linguistic Inquiry* 27: 183–193.

Wilmanns, Wilhelm (1896): *Deutsche Grammatik. Zweite Abteilung: Wortbildung*. Strassburg: Trübner.

Nicole Dehé

6 Particle verbs in Germanic

Abstract: This article provides an overview and comparison of particle verbs in the Germanic languages, giving examples of the construction in German, Dutch, Afrikaans, Yiddish, English, Icelandic, Norwegian, Faroese, Swedish and Danish. In particular, we will survey some of the basic morpho-syntactic properties of particle verbs, which have given rise to varying syntactic approaches to the phenomenon.

1 Introduction

The aim of this article is to give an overview of the phenomenon of particle verbs (PVs) in present-day Germanic including English. Particle verbs (also: *phrasal verbs, separable (complex) verbs, verb-particle combinations*) are combinations of verbs and preposition-like elements. Together, verb and particle form a close semantic unit. In some languages, notably languages in which the particle precedes the verb in the infinitive, such as German, Dutch, Yiddish and Afrikaans, this is reflected in the orthography. Examples of particle verbs are *send OFF* (German *ABschicken*, Dutch *OPsturen*, Yiddish *AVEKšikn*; particles in small capitals throughout), *look UP* (German *NACHschlagen*, Dutch *OPzoeken*, Icelandic *fletta UPP*, Norwegian *slå OPP*, Faroese *sláa UPP*), *ring UP* (German *ANrufen*, Dutch *OPbellen*, Swedish *ringa UPP*), *drink UP* (German *AUStrinken*, Dutch *OPdrinken*, Yiddish *oJstrinkən*, Faroese *drekka UPP*) and *stand/get UP* (German *AUFstehen*, Dutch *OPstaan*, Afrikaans *OPstaan*, Icelandic *standa UPP*). Particle verbs are a characteristic feature of the Germanic languages (e.g., Harbert 2007: 366; Holmberg and Rijkhoff 1998: 85), but they are also known in other languages or language families, for example Romance and Hungarian. Semantically, a verb-particle combination may be anywhere on a scale from transparent to opaque. Particles may contribute direction-

Nicole Dehé, Konstanz, Germany

https://doi.org/10.1515/9783111420554-006

al, locative, resultative, temporal or aspectual meaning to the complex verb meaning, or the verb-particle combination may have an idiomatic meaning. Accordingly, a threefold distinction between compositional, idiomatic, and completive (or aspectual) verb-particle combinations has been suggested (e.g., Emonds 1985; Jackendoff 2002). As a unit, particle verbs may be intransitive (see (1)), take a nominal object (see (2)) or appear in syntactically more complex variants such as secondary predication constructions or double object constructions (see (3)). (See McIntyre 2007 and 2015 on particle-verb formation, section 2, on semantic and argument-structural properties of particle verbs, and references given there.)

(1) Intransitive PVs
  a. Another opportunity turned UP.
  b. *Der Film fängt   AN.* German
     The film catches Part
     'The film is (just) starting.'
  c. *Ek staan nou OP.* Afrikaans
     I   stand now Part
     'I'm getting up now.'
     (Donaldson 1993: 263)

(2) PVs with a nominal object
  a. *John sparka UT   hunden* Norwegian
     John kicked Part the.dog
     'John kicked out the dog.'
     (Åfarli 1985: 75)
  b. *Hann gjørdi UPP snørið.* Faroese
     He   made   Part fishing-line.the
     'He wound up the fishing line.'
     (Thráinsson 2007: 142)

(3) More complex variants
  a. They made John OUT a liar.
     (den Dikken 1995: 45)
  b. *Þeir hafa sent strákunum peningana UPP.* Icelandic
     they have sent the boys   the money Part
     'They have sent the money up to the boys.'
     (Collins and Thráinsson 1996: 435)

Unlike prefixes and prepositions, particles are prosodically strong, i.e. in a verb-particle combination, main stress falls on the particle and stress in this context may be contrastive. For illustration, consider the minimal pairs in (4) (underlining indicates main stress):

(4) a. German
      umfahren (prefix verb; 'to drive around')
      UMfahren (particle verb; 'to knock down')
    b. Dutch
      omblazen (prefix verb; 'to blow around')
      OMblazen (particle verb; 'to blow down')
      (Booij 2002: 23)

Particle verbs have been dealt with continually in the linguistic literature from various perspectives, such as their morpho-syntactic behaviour and representation, their semantics, but also their behaviour in language processing and acquisition (see, for example, Svenonius 1996b; Dehé et al. 2002; Haiden 2006 for overviews).

One major theoretical challenge arises from the fact that verb and particle are separable and have phrasal properties in the syntax but have characteristics of morphological units at the same time. Questions arise with regard to morphosyntactic constituency ("Does the particle form an initial constituent with the verb or with a VP-internal DP/PP?"; Haiden 2006: 345) and, for transitive particle verbs in particular, with regard to how syntax can account for the surface order.

2 Morpho-syntactic properties of particle verbs in the Germanic languages

All Germanic languages, except Present-day English, have in common that they are verb-second (V2); i.e. in declarative main clauses, the finite verb is preceded by exactly one constituent. English and the Scandinavian languages (Norwegian, Swedish, Danish, Icelandic, Faroese) are SVO throughout, while Dutch, German and Afrikaans are OV in subordinate clauses. Yiddish, along with English and the Scandinavian languages, is generally taken to be SVO, but traces of OV order can be observed in Modern Yiddish, among them the syntax of the passive, periphrastic verbs, clitic floating/climbing, and properties of particle verbs (Besten and Moed-van Walraven 1986; Jacobs, Prince and van der Auwera 1994; Santorini 1992; Jacobs 2005; Diesing 1997).

While particle verbs in general form a characteristic property of the Germanic languages, there is also much syntactic variation in this respect. This variation is partly determined by more general syntactic differences, such as the VO/OV parameter. More specifically, the particle is preverbal in OV languages in non-V2 contexts, but postverbal in VO languages. In all V2 languages, verb and particle are separated in V2 contexts. For transitive PVs in English and some of the Scandinavian languages, there is variation regarding the order of object and particle.

In the following sections, which outline some of the basic morpho-syntactic properties of particle verbs, the languages are grouped according to the VO/OV-parameter setting, except that Swedish and Danish are introduced in a separate section. Based on particle-verb behaviour, Yiddish is grouped with the OV-languages. (Note incidentally that Vikner 2001, against Diesing 1997 and others, takes the syntactic behaviour of particle verbs as one piece of evidence in favour of present-day Yiddish as an OV language.)

2.1 German, Yiddish, Dutch, Afrikaans

In German, Yiddish, Dutch and Afrikaans, particles precede the verbal stem in the infinitive. The particle is postverbal in V2 contexts (see (5)–(8)) and in imperatives. Note that the languages differ with respect to the position of the nominal object in relation to the particle: the object precedes the particle in German, Dutch and Afrikaans but follows it in Yiddish.

(5)   a. infinitive: *ABschicken* 'to send off; lit. off-send'   German
      b. V2:   *Er schickt den Brief AB.*   /
                    He sends   the letter Part
                    *Er ABschickt den Brief.
                    *Er schickt AB den Brief.
                    'He sends off the letter.'

(6)   a. infinitive: *AVEKšikn* 'to send off; lit. away-send'   Yiddish
      b. V2:   *Er šikt   AVEK dem briv.*
                    He sends Part the letter
                    'He sends off the letter.'
                    (Besten and Moed-van Walraven 1986: 119)

(7)   a. infinitive: *opbellen* 'to call/phone up; lit. up-call'   Dutch
      b. V2:   *Hij belt zijn moeder op.* | **Hij opbelt zijn moeder.*
                    He calls his mother Part
                    'He calls up his mother.'
                    (van Marle 2002: 211)

(8) a. infinitive: *AFskakel* 'to switch off'   Afrikaans
     b. V2:   *Ek skakel die lig   nou AF.*
                 I   turn   the light now Part
                 'I'm turning the light off now.'
                 (Donaldson 1993: 374)

The particle is preverbal (non-separable) in contexts where its verb is not in second position, for example, because this position is filled by an auxiliary or another finite verb; see (9).

(9) a. *Er wird den Brief ABschicken.*   German
        He will the letter Part.send
        'He will send off the letter.'
     b. *Er vet AVEKšikn dem briv.*   Yiddish
        He will Part.send the letter
        'He will send off the letter.'
        (Besten and Moed-van Walraven 1986: 119)
     c. *Ik zal   het licht UITdoen.*   Dutch
        I   shall the light Part.do
        'I'll turn off the light.'
     d. *Ek sal   die lig   AFskakel.*   Afrikaans
        I   shall the light Part.turn
        'I'll turn off the light.'
        (Donaldson 1993: 374)

Inflectional affixes such as participle *ge-*, and infinitive markers *zu* (German), *tsu* (Yiddish) and *te* (Dutch, Afrikaans) are inserted between particle and verb; see (10) and (11).

(10) Participles
     a. *ABschicken* 'to send off': *ABgeschickt*   German
        (any other forms ungrammatical)
        e.g.: *Er hat den Brief ABgeschickt.*
              he has the letter Part.sent (participle)
              'He (has) sent off the letter.'
     b. *AVEKšikn* 'to send off': *AVEKgešikt*   Yiddish
     c. *OPbellen* 'to call up': *OBgebeld*   Dutch

  d. *AFskakel* 'to switch off': *AFgeskakel*   Afrikaans
     e.g.: *Het   jy   die   lig   AFgeskakel?*
           Have   you   the   light Part.turned
           'Did you turn off the light?'
           (Donaldson 1993: 374)

(11) Infinitives
  a. *ABschicken* 'to send off': *ABzuschicken*   German
     (any other forms ungrammatical)
     e.g.: *Ich bat   sie, den Brief für mich ABzuschicken.*
           I   asked her the letter for me   Part.inf.send
           'I asked her to send off the letter for me.'
  b. *AVEKšikn* 'to send off': *AVEKtsušikn*   Yiddish
  c. *OPbellen* 'to call up': *OP te bellen*   Dutch
     e.g.: *Zij probeerde haar moeder OP   te   bellen*
           She tried   her mother Part inf call
           'She tried to call her mother.'
           (van Marle 2002: 211)
  d. *AFskakel* 'to switch off': *AF te skakel*   Afrikaans
     e.g.: *Ek heet vergeet   om die lig   AF   te skakel*
           I   have forgotten the light Part inf turn
           'I forgot to turn off the light.'
           (Donaldson 1993: 374)

In OV subordinate clauses, particle and verb are adjacent, with the particle preceding the verb in German, Dutch and Afrikaans (see (12)).

(12) OV subordinate clause
  a. *dass er den Brief ABschickte.*   German
     that he the letter Part.sent
     'that he sent off the letter'
  b. *dat Jan het meisje OPbelt.*   Dutch
     that Jan the girl   Part.phones
     'that Jan rings up the girl'
     (Neeleman and Weerman 1993: 434)
  c. *Ek weet dat hy die lig   nooit AFskakel nie.*   Afrikaans
     I   know that he the light not   Part.turn NEG
     'I know he never turns the light off.'
     (Donaldson 1993: 374)

According to Besten and Moed-van Walraven (1986: 119), Yiddish is different from German, Dutch and Afrikaans in that the particle-verb order is impossible in subordinate clauses; see (13):

(13) a. *az   er šikt   AVEK dem briv*
          that he sends Part the letter
          'that he sends off the letter'
      b. **az er AVEKšikt dem briv*

Moreover, Dutch is different in that it allows an auxiliary between the particle and the verb in subordinate clauses; see the comparison between German and Dutch in (14) and (15).

(14) Subordinate clause
      a. *dat Jan het meisje wil   OPbellen*   Dutch
          that Jan the girl   wants Part.phone
          'that Jan wants to call the girl'
          (Neeleman and Weerman 1993: 435)
      b. dat Jan het meisje OP wil bellen

(15) Subordinate clause
      a. *dass Jan das Mädchen ANrufen will/wird*   German
          that Jan the girl   Part.call wants/will
          'that Jan wants to/will call the girl'
      b. **dass Jan das Mädchen AN will rufen*

In more complex constructions, such as double object particle constructions (here illustrated for two nominal objects in Dutch and German subordinate clauses), the particle is placed next to the verb (see (16)).

(16) a. *dat Jan Marie het zout DOOR gaf*   Dutch
          that Jan Mary the salt   Part gave
          'that John passed Mary the salt'
          (Neeleman 2002: 142); all other orders are ungrammatical
      b. *dass Jan Marie den Tausch ANbot.*   German
          that Jan Mary the trade.off Part-offered
          'that John offered Mary the swap'

Authors disagree as to whether or not particles may be fronted (see, for example, the discussion in Müller 2002: 263–292, Zeller 2001: 88–99, and references given there). A common assumption is that fronting is possible only if the combination of particle and verb is semantically transparent, and if the particle has a contrastive interpretation and receives contrastive stress. See the examples in (17) through (19), where semantically transparent examples are given in a), semantically opaque ones in b). Similar to fronting, speaker judgments vary as to whether or not particles may be modified, but modification is possible only for certain particles and in certain environments, for example when particles are fronted (for details, see Stiebels and Wunderlich 1994, Wurmbrand 1998 for German; Diesing 1997 for Yiddish, among others).

(17) Fronting
    a. *AUF*   *hat Peter die Tür gemacht.*   German
       Part/open has Peter the door made
       'Peter opened the door.'
    b. **AUF haben sie das Stück geführt.* / *Sie haben das Stück AUFgeführt.*
       Part have they the piece lead
       'They performed the piece.'
       (Wurmbrand 1998)

(18) Fronting
    a. *ARAYN iz er gekumen.*   Yiddish
       Part/in is he come
       'In, he came (not out).'
    b. **OP iz dos ayz nit gegangen.*
       Part is the ice not gone
       'The ice hasn't thawed.'
       (Diesing 1997: 384)

(19) Fronting
    a. *AF maak ik mijn huiswerk niet.*   Dutch
       Part make I my homework not
       'I will not finish my homework.'
    b. **OP bel ik mijn moeder niet.*
       Part call I my mother not
       'I will not call my mother.'
       (Booij 2002: 24)

2.2 English, Norwegian, Icelandic, Faroese

In Present-day English, Norwegian, Icelandic and Faroese, particles follow the verbal stem in the infinitive (e.g., English *look UP*, Norwegian *slå OPP*, Icelandic *fletta* UPP, Faroese *sláa* UPP). Due to this order, these languages display contrasts between prepositional verbs and homophonous particle verbs (e.g., English *look UP a word* (*in a dictionary*) vs. *look up the road* (*to see if someone's coming*)). Their syntactic behaviour helps to tell particle and prepositional verbs apart. For example, a preposition always precedes its object, while a particle may either precede or follow a full NP object and must follow an unstressed pronominal object. Moreover, a preposition but not a particle can be fronted together with its object. This is illustrated using an Icelandic example from Thráinsson (2007: 139); see (20)–(21).

(20) Prepositional verb *halda við* 'to support; lit. hold with'
   a. *Tveir menn héldu við   stigann/hann.*
      two   men   held   with stairs.the/it
      'Two men supported the stairs/it.'
   b. **Tveir menn héldu hann við.*
   c. *Við stigann héldu tveir menn.*

(21) Particle verb *halda við* 'to keep up, keep in shape'
   a. *Tveir menn héldu* VIÐ   *húsinu/því.*
      two   men   held   with house.the/it
      'Two men kept the house in shape.'
   b. *Tveir menn héldu því við.*
   c. **Við húsinu héldu tveir menn.*

In all four languages, transitive particle verbs show a surface alternation such that the nominal (full phrase) object may either precede or follow the particle. Pronominal objects are ungrammatical in the position following the particle unless focused and stressed accordingly. See (22)–(25).

(22) a. *Sue looked* UP *the word/*it.*
   b. *Sue looked the word/it* UP.
   c. *I knew that the school board contemplated throwing* OUT *Spanish in order to throw* OUT me.
      (Bolinger 1971: 39; underlined pronoun focused)

(23) a. *John sparka* UT   *hunden /*den.*   Norwegian
      John kicked Part the.dog /it
      'John kicked out the dog.'
   b. *John sparka hunden/den* UT.
      (Åfarli 1985: 75)

(24) a. *Þeir hafa sent UPP peningana/*þá.*   Icelandic
     They have sent Part the money/them
     'They have sent the money/them up.'
   b. *Þeir hafa sent peningana/þá UPP.*
     (Collins and Thráinsson 1996: 430)

(25) a. *Hann gjørdi UPP snørið/*það.*   Faroese
     He   made Part fishing.line.the/it
     'He wound up the fishing line.'
   b. *Hann gjørdi snørið/það UPP.*
     (Thráinsson et al. 2004: 247)

As illustrated for Icelandic prepositional complements in (26) and clausal complements in (27), non-nominal constituents are not allowed between verb and particle:

(26) Prepositional complement
   a. *Jón hélt TIL hjá systrunum.*   Icelandic
     John held Part with the sisters
     'John stayed with the sisters.' (e.g., had room and board there)
   b. **Jón hélt hjá systrunum TIL.*
     (Thráinsson 2007: 97)

(27) Clausal complement
   a. *Jón tók FRAM [að María héfði farið].*   Icelandic
     John took Part that Mary had left.
     'John explicitly mentioned that Mary had left.'
   b. **Jón tók [að María héfði farið] FRAM.*
     (Thráinsson 2007: 97)

Several factors have been suggested in the literature as contributing to the choice
of one word order over the other (for overviews focusing mostly on English, see
Dehé 2002: 76–80 and Gries 2003: chapter 2). Among these factors are phonological factors such as word and sentence stress; morpho-syntactic factors such as
pronominal vs. full-phrase status of the object (see (22)–(25) above), (in)definite-
ness, the heaviness, length or syntactic complexity of the nominal object (illustrated for Icelandic and English in (28) and (29), respectively), the presence of a
directional adverbial, and modification of the particle (see (35) below); semantic
and discourse factors such as the idiomaticity of the particle-verb unit or the
entire verb phrase, and focus or given vs. new information (see (22c) above and
(30) below); and other factors such as dialectal variation (e.g., some Norwegian

dialects prefer the particle-object order, see Svenonius 1996a, 1996b). Based on a large set of English corpus data, Gries (2003) develops a multifactorial statistical approach in order to account for the interaction of some of these factors. He finds that in the multifactorial analysis, morpho-syntactic variables outrank semantic and discourse-functional factors.

(28) NP-Heaviness
    a. ?*Stelpan bar [allar stóru töskurnar*   Icelandic
       girl.the carried all big bags.the
       sem við komum með úr fríinu] INN.
       that we brought from vacation-the PART
       'The girl carried all the big bags that we brought from the vacation in.'
    b. *Stelpan bar INN [allar stóru töskurnar sem við komum með úr fríinu].*
       (Thráinsson 2007: 143)

(29) NP-Heaviness
    a. ??*She sewed the sleeve with lace around the cuff on.*   English
    b. *She sewed on the sleeve with lace around the cuff.*
       (Olsen 1996: 279)

(30) The news value of the direct object affects its position
    Michael laboriously puts DOWN the bags, pushes wide the door, picks the
    bags *UP again and enters, ...*
    (Dehé 2002: 130; example from Stephen Fry, *Making History*)

The alternation between the V-particle-object order and the V-object-particle order possible with non-pronominal objects in English, Norwegian, Icelandic and Faroese has been referred to as *particle shift* (PS; e.g., Svenonius 1994, 1996a, 1996b; Thráinsson 2007). On the basis of the similarities between PS in English and Icelandic, Johnson (1991) suggests that English has object shift (OS) similar to Icelandic, allowing for overt verb and object movement. However, as Thráinsson (2007: 141 f.) shows, there are important differences between PS and Icelandic OS, among them the fact that the presence of an auxiliary blocks the latter but not the former; see (31), from Thráinsson (2007: 141). According to Thráinsson (2007), this suggests that the object moves to a lower position in PS than in OS.

(31) a. *Ég hef   aldrei flett   UPP nöfnunum.*   (no shift)
       I   have never looked Part names-the
       'I have never looked up the names.'
    b. *Ég hef aldrei flett nöfnunum UPP.*   (PS only)
    c. **Ég hef nöfnunum aldrei flett UPP.*   (OS blocked)

In a V2 context where the subject is non-initial, verb and particle must be separate and the particle immediately follows the subject or the object. This is illustrated in (32) for Icelandic (Collins and Thráinsson 1996: 432).

(32) a. *Í gær   sendu þeir peningana* UPP.
        Yesterday sent   they the money Part
        'Yesterday they sent the money up.'
   b. *Í gær sendu þeir* UPP *peningana.*
   c. **Í gær sendu* UPP *þeir peningana.*

In more complex constructions, such as double object particle constructions (here illustrated for two nominal objects in English and Icelandic), the following particle positions are possible (see (33) and (34)).

(33) a. **John sent* OUT *the stockholders a schedule.*   English
   b. *John sent the stockholders* OUT *a schedule.*
   c. **John sent the stockholders a schedule* OUT.
     (Neeleman 2002: 141)

(34) a. **Í gær   hafa þeir sent* UPP *strákunum peningana.*   Icelandic
        Yesterday have they sent Part the boys   the money
        'Yesterday they sent the money up to the boys.'
   b. *(?)Í gær hafa þeir sent strákunum* UPP *peningana.*
   g. *Í gær hafa þeir sent strákunum peningana* UPP.

As shown in (35) for Icelandic and Norwegian, modification of the particle is possible only in the V-object-particle order.

(35) Modification of the particle
   a. *Í gær   hafa þeir sent peningana beint   *UPP.   Icelandic
        Yesterday have they sent the.money straight Part.
        'Yesterday they sent the money straight up.'
    *Í gær hafa þeir sent beint UPP *peningana.*
    (Collins and Thráinsson 1996: 430)
   b. *John sparka hunden langt* UT.   Norwegian
        John kicked the.dog far   Part
        'John kicked the dog far out.'
    *John sparka langt ut hunden
    (Åfarli 1985: 76)

2.3 Danish and Swedish

In Danish and Swedish, like in the other Scandinavian languages, particles follow the verbal stem in the infinitive (e.g., Danish *vokse OP* 'grow up'; Swedish *ringa UPP* 'call up'). An important difference between Danish and Swedish on the one hand and the four languages outlined in the previous section on the other, is that in Danish and Swedish, the position of the particle with respect to a nominal object is fixed: in Danish, the particle follows the object, in Swedish the particle is verb-adjacent and precedes the object, both if the object is pronominal and if it is a full phrase. While "all particles appear to be modifiable in Danish (so long as modification is semantically plausible)" (Toivonen 2003: 161), the Swedish particle cannot be modified in its verb-adjacent position (see (36)–(37); all examples from Toivonen 2002, 2003; see references given there).

(36) a. *Han knugede sine hænder SAMMEN.*   Danish
     he   clasped his hands Part
     'He clasped his hands.'
   b. **Han knugede SAMMEN sine hænder.*

(37) a. *Simon kastade UT   soporna.*   Swedish
     Simon threw   Part garbarge.the
     'Simon threw out the garbage.'
   b. **Simon kastade soporna UT.*
   c. *... och släpar UT   honum.*
     and drag   Part him
     '... and drag him out.'
   d. **Olle sparkade [längre BORT] bollen.*
     Olle kicked   further Part ball.the
     'Olle kicked the ball further away.'

In Thráinsson's (2007: 142) terms, particle shift obligatorily applies in Danish, but it never applies in Swedish.

3 Approaches to the morpho-syntax of particle verbs in the Germanic languages

The morpho-syntactic behaviour of particle verbs, and specifically the fact that across languages they share properties with both heads and phrases, has given rise to a number of different analyses, which have been summarized, discussed and grouped by various authors (e.g., Dehé 2002; Dehé et al. 2002; Haiden 2006; Blom 2005 and Elenbaas 2007). Given these existing overviews, only a very rough overview will be provided here and the reader is referred to the references given throughout.

Approaches to particle verbs can roughly be grouped into complex predicate approaches on the one hand and non-complex-predicate approaches on the other.

Complex predicate analyses assume that verb and particle form a constituent, either a complex verbal head of the form V^0 (e.g., Johnson 1991; Koizumi 1993; Neeleman and Weerman 1993; Stiebels and Wunderlich 1994; Olsen 1997, 2000; Ackerman and Webelhuth 1998; Dehé 2002 and Blom 2005: 41–45), or a non-minimal/non-maximal verbal projection (e.g., Booij 1990; Lüdeling 2001; Zeller 2001, 2002). Non-complex-predicate approaches assume that the particle projects its own phrase, often forming a constituent with the phrase referred to as nominal object in the discussion above.

Complex head analyses have been based on their word-like properties, such as their status as a close semantic unit, the fact that particle verbs enter into word-formation processes such as derivation and compounding, their selectional requirements, and their behaviour in syntactic environments such as gapping constructions, co-ordination, quotative inversion and VP-fronting (see Blom 2005 for recent discussions). Immediate problems with this analysis include the separability of verb and particle in the syntax, and the fact that the particle may be topicalised and modified separately. These properties suggest a phrasal approach to particles. Note at this stage that Swedish has arguably a special status, since verb and particle cannot be separated in the syntax and the particle cannot be modified in its verb-adjacent position. Accordingly, Toivonen (2003) suggests that Swedish particles are non-projecting words, which are head-adjoined to the verbal head.

Particle verbs have often been compared and found to be similar to resultative as well as causative, depictive, and adverb-verb constructions (Hoekstra 1988; Neeleman and Weerman 1993; Svenonius 1996b; Haider 1997; Lüdeling 2001, among others). Similarities in particular between particles and resultatives, along with other clausal properties, have been taken as evidence by some authors for a "small clause" analysis, which assumes a subject-predicate relationship between the particle and the post-verbal nominal constituent (e.g., Kayne 1985, 1998; Hoekstra 1988; den Dikken 1995; Collins and Thráinsson 1996; Svenonius 1996a, b; Ramchand and Svenonius 2002). The problematic aspects of the small clause analysis have received much attention in the literature (see Booij 1990: 54–58; Dehé 2002: 17–36, and Farrell 2005: 109–121 for critical discussions). Based on the differences in behaviour between semantically transparent (or, specifically, resultative) particle verbs and idiomatic ones, it has been suggested that only the former are best analysed as small clauses (Aarts 1989; Wurmbrand 2000). Along with the similarities between resultatives and particles, Neeleman and Weerman (1993) outline some differences, which, they argue, a small clause analysis cannot account for. Instead, they suggest that both resultatives and particles are adjoined to the verb, accounting for the similarities between them. However, while particle adjunction is a morphological process, adjunction of resultatives takes place in the syntax, accounting for the differences between the two constructions.

Although often based on data from specific languages, very few approaches to particle verbs are explicitly language-specific and some analyses aim at a comparison between languages. Examples of the latter are given immediately below.

Zeller (2002) presents a comparative account of particle verbs in two VO languages (English, Norwegian) and two OV languages (Dutch, German). He concludes that the relevant differences with respect to particle-verb behaviour are a consequence of independent properties, such as VO/OV-parameter setting and the V2 property. Neeleman (2002) comes to a similar conclusion. In his comparative discussion of Dutch and English, he addresses the surprising observation that word order is freer in English particle constructions than in Dutch ones, despite the fact that Dutch, which allows scrambling, has less strict constituent ordering otherwise. He concludes that the two languages have identical grammars in all relevant respects, except for the setting of the OV/VO parameter. The different structures surfacing in Dutch and English are a result of the flexibility of both case and theta theory. Comparing English and German transitive particle-verb constructions, Dehé (2005) sets off from an observation similar to that made by Neeleman (2002). While English allows for PS, the only grammatical option in German V2 sentences such as (5b) is particle stranding. Dehé (2005) concludes that the syntactic differences between German and English (specifically that German but not English is a V2 language) alone do not suffice to explain obligatory particle stranding in main clause contexts such as (5b), since particle pied-piping would not violate V2. Rather, couched in the optimality-theory framework, she suggests that the differences between the two languages with respect to particle placement can best be explained in terms of the interaction of syntactic and prosodic constraints and their respective ranking. Specifically, a syntactic constraint closely related to STAY (i.e. "avoid movement", Grimshaw 1997) is outranked by prosodic constraints in English but not in German. The question of whether or not the syntactic VO/OV parameter and V2 property are enough to explain the cross-linguistic differences in syntactic behaviour will have to be seen in a larger context, also taking into account other types of complex predicates (see Haider 1997) and non-syntactic factors.

Acknowledgements

I would like to thank the following native speaker informants: Janet Grijzenhout (Dutch), Jóhannes Gísli Jónsson (Icelandic), Guðrið Poulsen (Faroese), as well as Kristina Kotcheva and Allison Wetterlin for discussion.

4 References

Aa, Leiv Inge (2020): *Norwegian Verb Particles*. Amsterdam/Philadelphia: Benjamins.
Aarts, Bas (1989): Verb-preposition constructions and small clauses in English. *Journal of Linguistics* 25: 277–290.
Ackerman, Farrell and Gert Webelhuth (1998): *A Theory of Predicates*. Stanford, CA: CSLI.
Åfarli, Tor A. (1985): Norwegian verb-particle constructions as causative constructions. *Nordic Journal of Linguistics* 8: 75–98.
Berg, Thomas (2018): Towards an explanation of the syntax of West Germanic particle verbs: A cognitive-pragmatic view. *Cognitive Linguistics* 29(4): 703–728.
Besten, Hans den and Corretje Moed-van Walraven (1986): The syntax of verbs in Yiddish. In: Hubert Haider and Martin Prinzhorn (eds.), *Verb Second Phenomena in Germanic Languages*, 111–135. Dordrecht: Foris.
Blom, Corrien (2005): *Complex predicates in Dutch. Synchrony and diachrony*. Utrecht: LOT.
Bolinger, Dwight L. (1971): *The Phrasal Verb in English*. Cambridge, MA: Harvard University Press.
Booij, Geert (1990): The boundary between morphology and syntax: Separable complex verbs in Dutch. In: Geert Booij and Jap van Marle (eds.), *Yearbook of Morphology 1990*, 45–63. Dordrecht: Foris.
Booij, Geert (2002): Separable complex verbs in Dutch: A case of periphrastic word formation. In: Nicole Dehé, Ray Jackendoff, Andrew McIntyre and Silke Urban (eds.), *Verb-Particle Explorations*, 21–41. Berlin/New York: Mouton de Gruyter.
Collins, Chris and Höskuldur Thráinsson (1996): VP-internal structure and object shift in Icelandic. *Linguistic Inquiry* 27(3): 391–344.
Czypionka, Anna and Carsten Eulitz (2018): Lexical case marking affects the processing of animacy in simple verbs, but not particle verbs: evidence from event-related potentials. *Glossa: A Journal of General Linguistics* 3(1). [Online available at: https://doi.org/10.5334/gjgl.313]
Czypionka, Anna and Carsten Eulitz (2021): Case marking affects the processing of animacy with simple verbs, but not particle verbs: An event-related potential study. In: Artemis Alexiadou and Elisabeth Sophia Maria Verhoeven (eds.), *The Syntax of Argument Structure: Empirical Advancements and Theoretical Relevance*, 69–103. Berlin/Boston: De Gruyter.
Czypionka, Anna, Felix Golcher, Joanna Błaszczak and Carsten Eulitz (2019): When verbs have bugs: lexical and syntactic processing costs of split particle verbs in sentence comprehension. *Language, Cognition and Neuroscience* 34(3): 326–350.
Dehé, Nicole (2002): *Particle Verbs in English. Syntax, Information Structure, and Intonation*. Amsterdam/Philadelphia: Benjamins.
Dehé, Nicole (2005): The optimal placement of *up* and *ab* – A comparison. *Journal of Comparative Germanic Linguistics* 8(3): 185–224.

Dehé, Nicole, Ray Jackendoff, Andrew McIntyre and Silke Urban (2002): Introduction. In: Nicole Dehé, Ray Jackendoff, Andrew McIntyre and Silke Urban (eds.), *Verb-Particle Explorations*, 1–20. Berlin/New York: Mouton de Gruyter.

Dikken, Marcel den (1995): *Particles. On the Syntax of Verb-Particle, Triadic, and Causative Constructions*. Oxford: Oxford University Press.

Diesing, Molly (1997): Yiddish VP order and the typology of object movement in Germanic. *Natural Language and Linguistic Theory* 15(2): 369–427.

Donaldson, Bruce C. (1993): *A Grammar of Afrikaans*. Berlin/New York: Mouton de Gruyter.

Elenbaas, Marion (2007): *The Synchronic and Diachronic Syntax of the English Verb-Particle Combination*. Utrecht: LOT.

Emonds, Joseph (1985): *A Unified Theory of Syntactic Categories*. Dordrecht: Foris.

Farrell, Patrick (2005): English verb-preposition constructions: Constituency and order. *Language* 81(1): 96–137.

Gries, Stefan Thomas (2003): *Multifactorial Analysis in Corpus Linguistics. A Study of Particle Placement*. New York/London: Continuum International Publishing Group.

Grimshaw, Jane (1997): Projection, heads, and optimality. *Linguistic Inquiry* 28(3): 373–422.

Haiden, Martin (2006): Verb particle constructions. In: Martin Everaert and Henk van Riemsdijk (eds.), *The Blackwell Companion to Syntax*. Vol. 5, 344–375. Oxford: Blackwell.

Haider, Hubert (1997): Precedence among predicates. *Journal of Comparative Germanic Linguistics* 1: 3–41.

Haider, Hubert (2020): VO-/OV-Base Ordering. In: Michael T. Putnam and B. Richard Page (eds.), *The Cambridge Handbook of Germanic Linguistics*, 339–364. Cambridge: Cambridge University Press.

Harbert, Wayne (2007): *The Germanic Languages*. Cambridge: Cambridge University Press.

Hoekstra, Teun (1988): Small clause results. *Lingua* 74: 101–139.

Holmberg, Anders and Jan Rijkhoff (1998): Word order in the Germanic languages. In: Anna Siewierska (ed.), *Constituent Order in the Languages of Europe*, 75–104. Berlin/New York: Mouton de Gruyter.

Jackendoff, Ray (2002): English particle constructions, the lexicon, and the autonomy of syntax. In: Nicole Dehé, Ray Jackendoff, Andrew McIntyre and Silke Urban (eds.), *Verb-Particle Explorations*, 67–94. Berlin/New York: Mouton de Gruyter.

Jacobs, Neil G. (2005): *Yiddish. A Linguistic Introduction*. Cambridge: Cambridge University Press.

Jacobs, Neil G., Ellen F. Prince and Johan van der Auwera (1994): Yiddish. In: Ekkehard König and Johan van der Auwera (eds.), *The Germanic Languages*, 388–419. London/New York: Routledge.

Johnson, Kyle (1991): Object positions. *Natural Language and Linguistic Theory* 9: 577–636.

Kayne, Richard S. (1985): Principles of particle constructions. In: Jacqueline Guéron, Hans Georg Oberauer and Jean-Yves Pollock (eds.), *Grammatical Representations*, 101–140. Dordrecht: Foris.

Kayne, Richard S. (1998): Overt vs. covert movement. *Syntax* 1: 128–191.

Koizumi, Masatoshi (1993): Object agreement phrases and the split VP hypothesis. In: Colin Phillips and Jonathan D. Bobaljik (eds.), *Papers on Case and Agreement I: MIT Working Papers in Linguistics* 18, 99–148, Cambridge, MA: MIT Working Papers in Linguistics.

Lüdeling, Anke (2001): *Particle Verbs and Similar Constructions in German*. Stanford: CSLI.

Marle, Jaap van (2002): Dutch separable compound verbs: Words rather than phrases? In: Nicole Dehé, Ray Jackendoff, Andrew McIntyre and Silke Urban (eds.), *Verb-Particle Explorations*, 211–232. Berlin/New York: Mouton de Gruyter.

McIntyre, Andrew (2007): Particle verbs and argument structure. *Language and Linguistics Compass* 1(4): 350–367.

McIntyre, Andrew (2015): Particle-verb formation. In: Peter O. Müller, Ingeborg Ohnheiser, Susan Olsen and Franz Rainer (eds.), *Word-Formation. An International Handbook of the Languages of Europe*. Vol. 1, 434–449. Berlin/Boston: De Gruyter Mouton.

Müller, Stefan (2002): *Complex Predicates. Verbal Complexes, Resultative Constructions, and Particle Verbs in German*. Stanford: CSLI.

Neeleman, Ad (2002): Particle placement. In: Nicole Dehé, Ray Jackendoff, Andrew McIntyre and Silke Urban (eds.), *Verb-Particle Explorations*, 141–164. Berlin/New York: Mouton de Gruyter.

Neeleman, Ad and Fred Weerman (1993): The balance between syntax and morphology: Dutch particles and resultatives. *Natural Language and Linguistic Theory* 11: 433–475.

Olsen, Susan (1996): Partikelverben im deutsch-englischen Vergleich. In: Ewald Lang and Gisela Zifonun (eds.), *Deutsch – typologisch*, 165–190. Berlin/New York: Mouton de Gruyter.

Olsen, Susan (1997): Über den lexikalischen Status englischer Partikelverben. In: Elisabeth Löbel and Gisa Rauh (eds.), *Lexikalische Kategorien und Merkmale*, 45–71. Tübingen: Niemeyer.

Olsen, Susan (2000): Against incorporation. In: Johannes Dölling and Thomas Pechmann (eds.), *Linguistische Arbeitsberichte* 74, 149–172. University of Leipzig: Department of Linguistics.

Ramchand, Gillian and Peter Svenonius (2002): The lexical syntax and lexical semantics of the verb-particle construction. In: Line Mikkelsen and Christopher Potts (eds.), *WCCFL 21 Proceedings*, 387–400. Somerville, MA: Cascadilla Press.

Santorini, Beatrice (1992): Variation and change in Yiddish subordinate clause word order. *Natural Language and Linguistic Theory* 10(4): 595–640.

Stiebels, Barbara and Dieter Wunderlich (1994): Morphology feeds syntax: The case of particle verbs. *Linguistics* 32: 913–968.

Svenonius, Peter (1994): Dependent nexus: Subordinate predication structures in English and the Scandinavian languages. Ph.D. dissertation, University of California, Santa Cruz.

Svenonius, Peter (1996a): The optionality of particle shift. *Working Papers in Scandinavian Syntax* 57: 47–75.

Svenonius, Peter (1996b): The verb-particle-alternation in the Scandinavian languages. Ms. University of Tromsø.

Thráinsson, Höskuldur (2007): *The Syntax of Icelandic*. Cambridge: Cambridge University Press.

Thráinsson, Höskuldur, Hjalmar P. Peterson, Jógvan í Lon Jacobsen and Zakaris Svabo Hansen (2004): *Faroese. An Overview and Reference Grammar*. Tórshavn: Føroya Fróðskaparfelag.

Toivonen, Ida (2002): Swedish particles and syntactic projection. In: Nicole Dehé, Ray Jackendoff, Andrew McIntyre and Silke Urban (eds.), *Verb-Particle Explorations*, 191–209. Berlin/New York: Mouton de Gruyter.

Toivonen, Ida (2003): *Non-Projecting Words. A Case Study of Swedish Particles*. Dordrecht: Kluwer.

Trotzke, Andreas and Stefano Quaglia (2016): Particle topicalization and German clause structure. *The Journal of Comparative Germanic Linguistics* 19: 109–141.

Trotzke, Andreas, Stefano Quaglia and Eva Wittenberg (2015): Topicalization in German particle verb constructions: The role of semantic transparency. *Linguistische Berichte* 244: 407–424.

Trotzke, Andreas and Eva Wittenberg (2017): Expressive particle verbs and conditions on particle fronting. *Journal of Linguistics* 53: 407–435.

Vikner, Sten (2001): Verb movement variation in Germanic and optimality theory. Habilitationsschrift, University of Tübingen.

Wurmbrand, Susi (1998): Heads or phrases? Particles in particular. In: Wolfgang Kehrein and Richard Wiese (eds.), *Phonology and Morphology of the Germanic Languages*, 267–295. Tübingen: Niemeyer.

Wurmbrand, Susi (2000): The structure(s) of particle verbs. Manuscript, McGill University.

Zeller, Jochen (2001): *Particle Verbs and Local Domains*. Amsterdam/Philadelphia: Benjamins.

Zeller, Jochen (2002): Particle verbs are heads and phrases. In: Nicole Dehé, Ray Jackendoff, Andrew McIntyre and Silke Urban (eds.), *Verb-Particle Explorations*, 233–267. Berlin/New York: Mouton de Gruyter.

Pierre J. L. Arnaud

7 Noun-noun compounds in French

Abstract: Although the [NN]$_N$ pattern is not predominant for the naming of combinatory concepts, the corresponding class of compounds is expanding in contemporary French. The article presents a semantically-based taxonomy of [NN]$_N$ units, followed by a survey of their grammatical characteristics. The last section examines theoretical positions with respect to their grammatical status.

1 Introduction

Languages differ in the position they accord to compounding among their lexical extension processes. In a comparison of 13 languages with respect to lexical items corresponding to 30 culture-independent concepts like 'eyelash' and 'rainbow', German had a "score" of 18 out of 30, English 12 and French, with 4, was close to the lowest score of the language sample (Arnaud 2004). A random sample of 100 English [NN]$_N$ compounds corresponds to only 8 similar (but left-headed) units in French. These differences are due to the fact that [NN]$_N$ is in competition with other patterns for the naming of combinatory concepts in French. The most important of these alternative patterns are listed below (compound glosses are literal, so in most cases the order of components is the opposite of the English one; English equivalents or explanations are given in brackets when useful):

(1)   [N prep N]$_N$ units, mainly with the vague prepositions *de* 'of, from' and *à* 'to, at'
frein à main
'brake to hand (handbrake)'

Pierre J. L. Arnaud, Lyon, France

https://doi.org/10.1515/9783111420554-007

(2) N + relational adjective
forêt pluviale
'forest pluvial (rainforest)'

(3) lexicalized N + prepositional phrase sequence
marché aux puces
'market to-the fleas (flea market)'

Obviously, French does not produce [NN]$_N$ lexical units as freely as the Germanic languages, but the pattern is available in its grammar. After a section on preliminary notions and precautions, the article presents a classification of [NN]$_N$ units based on semantic criteria, followed by a survey of the characteristics and behaviour of the different categories. The last section will be devoted to a review of theoretical positions on their grammatical status. Until then the term *compound* will be used in a theory-neutral way.

2 Definitions and restrictions

An important consideration in the analysis of NN sequences is that nominal lexical units are the names of categories of entities. Also important is the fact that the word-formation resources of a language produce items that can be lexicalized and become units of the lexicon or of a particular terminology. Word-formation processes also produce items that refer to categories that are nameworthy (Downing 1977) only in a particular communicative situation. For this reason, hapaxes or types with few occurrences will be used as examples of productive categories along with established compounds.

French [NN]$_N$ units are formally similar to syntactic NN sequences. Some of these constructions, with non-heads such as

(4) *charnière, choc, clé, modèle, phare,   record, surprise*
'hinge,   shock, key, model, lighthouse, record, surprise'

are semantically close to subordinative compounds (see section 3), but they can be distinguished from them. French nouns may undergo different degrees of conversion to adjectives and conversion entails a semantic reduction (*marron* 'chestnut' as an adjective only denotes a colour). As a result, modification by a converted N2 does not create a subclass of N1 but only qualifies it: *année clé* 'year key' does not denote a type of year as *année bissextile* 'year bisectile (leap year)' does. Conversion also goes together with the acquisition of adjectival syntax and another reason to reject an NN sequence like *année-clé* as a compound is that *clé* is found in typically adjectival positions as in the following example:

(5) *Nous sommes dans une période assez clé de l'année.*
     'We are in a rather key period of the year.'

Another precaution is necessary when collecting French NN sequences. "Telegraphic style" can result in NN sequences that are not necessarily lexical items. This is the case when N+prep+(art)+N sequences are reduced, as in the following text seen on a roadside sign:

(6) *parking cars 200m*

This is a telegraphic version of

(7) *parking des cars à 200 m*
     'park of-the coaches in 200 m (coach park in 200m)'

For this reason, NN sequences from signs, catalogues, etc. are not safe to use in a discussion of lexical units and, therefore, only examples found in normal syntactic environments or in dictionaries will be quoted here.

3 Classification

3.1 Headedness

In a discussion of $[NN]_N$ units it is necessary to distinguish different types of heads. Therefore, I will differentiate between semantic headedness and syntactic headedness, as there are a few cases where the corresponding heads do not coincide, as will be seen in section 3.4. An endocentric compound has (only) one semantic head, which is the name of the generic class of its denotatum:

(8) *Un oiseau-mouche est un oiseau.*
     'A bird fly (hummingbird) is a bird.'

Other compounds may have two or more semantically equal constituents, in which case *pluricentric* is a more adequate term than the usual *exocentric*. In other cases yet, due to a metaphoric or metonymic construal of an endocentric compound, the denotation shifts and the name of the denotatum's category is no longer present in the compound, as exemplified by (9):

(9) *poids plume*
     'weight feather (a person with a light weight)'

As *plume* initially modifies *poids* the term *exocentric* is somewhat misleading (see Bauer 2008) and *secondary exocentric* is preferable for units of this type which, due to their secondary nature, need not figure in the classification given here (Benczes 2006). Syntax-inspired terms with wide currency are *subordinative compounds* for endocentrics, and *coordinatives* for pluricentrics. These will be used below.

The top level of the classification is binary. The reason for this is that semantic headedness is an essential parameter and if we go beyond the case of French, there are significant phonological and grammatical differences between subordinative and coordinative compounds in a number of languages, like stress position and sandhi phenomena (see, for instance, Kim 2001).

3.2 Subordinative units

The classification below is supported by a number of semantic tests inspired by Cruse (1986) and Riegel (1988), and it is justified by the difference in pluralization patterns which will be examined in section 4. The first tests T1 and T2 are tests of semantic headedness: units that test positive on T1 and negative on T2 are endocentric (subordinative):

(10) (T1) *Un nœud-papillon est un nœud.*
            'A knot butterfly (bow tie) is a knot.'
      (T2) **Un nœud-papillon est un papillon.*
            'A knot butterfly is a butterfly.'

Units that satisfy neither test are secondary exocentric compounds, and units that satisfy both tests are coordinative – but see below for apparently ambiguous cases.

3.2.1 Attributive units

Test T3 tests the attribution of features from the nonhead's semantic representation to the head:

(11) (T3) *Une tente-igloo est une tente qui est (comme) un igloo.*
'A tent igloo is a tent that is (like) an igloo.'

The analogy manifested in *comme* rests on a subset of the semantic features in the representation of the denotatum of N2, namely the function and the hemispherical shape in the above example, while other features are suppressed. Analogy, however, is less perceptible in cases like *voiture-bélier* 'car-ram (a car used by thieves to shatter a shop window)' where N2 is independently metaphorized in the lexicon, and it is absent from a unit like *date-limite* 'date limit (deadline)':

(12) (T3) *Une date-limite est une date qui est (Ø) une limite.*
'A date limit is a date which is (Ø) a limit.'

In such a case, both T1 and T2 give positive results, so we are apparently close to the category of coordinative compounds. It is possible, however, using various tests which cannot be detailed here, to ascertain that a unit like *date-limite* is semantically left-headed in the same way as *tente-igloo* is.

The attributive category is productive, and hapax occurrences can be found in the media, like:

(13) *des moutons-tondeuses embauchés au fort de Dardilly.*
'sheep lawnmowers (lawnmower sheep) hired at the fort of Dardilly' (with analogical attribution)

A particular subcategory of attribution is to be found in a limited set of units like *thon-albacore* 'tuna albacore', *mésange nonette* 'tit little-nun (marsh tit)'. N2 is the name of a species while N1 is that of a genus, and N1N2 has the same denotation as N2:

(14) (T4) *Le thon albacore et l'albacore, c'est la même chose.*
'Tuna albacore and albacore, it is the same thing.'

3.2.2 Relational units

Other endocentric compounds test negative on T3:

(15) (T3) **Une assurance vie est (comme) une vie.*
'An insurance life is (like) a life.'

Semantically, the modification relation belongs to diverse types. Some cases correspond to different implicit predications which link the constituents of the compound. The following is a very limited sample:

(16) N1 consists of N2   *code barres* 'code bars (barcode)'
     N1 includes N2   *toile émeri* 'cloth emery'
     N1 originates in N2 *point jury* 'point jury (an extra point awarded by an examination jury)'
     N1 belongs to N2   *flotte client* 'fleet customer (customer's vehicle fleet)'

The relation may also be of the verb-complement type if N1 is deverbal. Examples in (17) are followed by a logical notation and a translation:

(17) *descente dames*   descend (ladies)   (women's downhill race)
     placement produit place (x, product) (product placement)

In some cases, the modification is semantically ambiguous and different relations coexist, as in *local barre* 'room helm (steering gear compartment)', N1 place of N2 and N1 for N2. As in this example, the telic relation present in compounds naming artefacts often coexists with some other relation. In other cases yet, the compound is underpinned by a complex scenario:

(18) *banane dollar*   (a banana produced in a non-euro zone)
     amphi garnison   'lecture-theatre garrison (a meeting during which officer school graduates choose their first post)'

Listing and classifying these relations with sufficient granularity is a daunting task, which has rarely been undertaken (Arnaud 2003: 61–87). A comparison with English compounds shows that some relations may be absent from French. This is apparently the case of the "habitat" relation present in *sea bream* or *marshmallow*, but it may be an effect of the smaller number of French units.

Analogy of construction results in the emergence of series of compounds with identical heads or non-heads:

(19) *compte client, fiche client, relation client, suivi client, flotte client*, etc.
     'account customer, card customer (customer knowledge sheet), relation customer, follow-up customer, fleet customer'

3.3 Coordinative compounds

In coordinative compounds N1 and N2 are co-hyponyms. As noted above, these units test positive on both T1 and T2. Tests of anaphora show that they do not include a single semantic head, and this is confirmed by the fact that, contrary to subordinatives, sentences with the constituents in reverse order are acceptable:

(20) *Un enseignant-chercheur pourrait être appelé chercheur-enseignant.*
    'A teacher researcher (an academic) could be called researcher-teacher.'

The two versions may be actually attested, like *propriétaire-dirigeant* 'owner-manager' and *dirigeant-propriétaire*, but the order is generally lexicalized and results from a combination of factors of length and pragmatic salience (Renner 2008).

Three semantic subclasses can be distinguished, as was suggested by Hatcher (1951: 32) for English:

(21) Multifunctional coordinatives denote entities that hold several functions or purposes
    boucher-charcutier
    'butcher pork-butcher'
    chasseur-bombardier
    'fighter bomber'

(22) Hybrid coordinatives denote entities that are perceived to be a mix of other entities
    baryton-basse
    'barytone bass'
    tram-train
    (a tramcar that can be used on a railway line)

(23) Additive coordinatives (dvandvas), which are rare, denote entities that are the sum of separate entities
    bains-douches
    'baths showers (public baths)'
    batterie-fanfare
    'drum-corps fanfare (a band)'

Individual examples may be categorially ambiguous like *pli-faille* 'fold fault', which could be a hybrid or a dvandva.

3.4 Intermediate units

Units like *femme médecin* 'woman doctor', *expert-comptable* 'expert accountant', *candidat médicament* 'candidate medicine (a new medicine undergoing tests)', which generally include one constituent denoting a status relative to the other constituent's denotatum, are not easy to fit into a taxonomy. Tests of semantic headedness and anaphora do not return identical results on different units and show a notable amount of disagreement among informants. It seems wiser to conclude that these units occupy various positions along a scale between attributives and coordinatives. In some cases, however, like that of *bébé* (as in *bébé-phoque* 'baby seal'), the N1 has acquired some of the characteristics of a prefix (Amiot and van Goethem 2010).

3.5 Exceptions

"In many languages there are exceptions or fuzzy transitions to non-compounding" (Dressler 2006: 24). The most numerous exceptions are semantically and syntactically right-headed units like *auto-école* 'auto school (driving school)' or *radio-balise* 'radio beacon', where N1 results from the reanalysis of a neo-classical component and may be considered an "affixoid" (Booij 2009). In *bidonville*$_{masc}$ 'can town (shanty town)', the syntactic head is *bidon*$_{masc}$ and the semantic head *ville*$_{fem}$. Other exceptions, like the graphically fused secondary exocentrics *chien-dent* 'dog tooth (couch grass)' and *chèvrefeuille* 'goat leaf (honeysuckle)', are opacified remnants of earlier patterns. The next section is devoted to non-exceptional units only.

4 Grammatical characteristics

This section presents a survey of the grammatical characteristics of French [NN]$_N$ units.

Two characteristics of French complicate the analysis of compounding: French does not have lexical stress, and noun plurals are phonetically identical to the singulars, except for a few "irregular" nouns rarely present in compounds anyway, so it is often necessary to rely on spellings and then caution is necessary with Web occurrences. When possible, examples with audible plurals have been selected (these are in bold type).

a) Syntactic headedness
French [NN]$_N$ units are syntactically left-headed with N1 communicating its gender to the compound, as in the following examples from different categories described in section 3:

(24) [chapeau$_{masc}$-*cloche*$_{fem}$]$_{masc}$
'hat bell (cloche hat)'
[*stylo*$_{masc}$ *bille*$_{fem}$]$_{masc}$
'pen ball (ballpoint pen)'
[*femme*$_{fem}$-*commissaire*$_{masc}$]$_{fem}$
'woman police-commissioner'
[*point*$_{masc}$-*virgule*$_{fem}$]$_{masc}$
'point comma (semicolon)'

b) Plural forms
Two pluralization patterns exist, but the head (N1) is always in the plural, so French units have internal plurals. Note however that, due to the non-audible nature of most plurals, there is considerable variation in the spelling of occurrences.

(25) subordinatives: relationals: plural on N1
chevaux vapeur
'horses steam (horsepower)'
œufs cocotte
'eggs pot (a recipe)'

Occurrences of some of these units are occasionally found with double plurals, which may be a sign of regularization toward a unique rule of double plurals.

(26) attributives: plural on both N1 and N2
animaux machines
'animals machines (a term of Descartes's mechanist philosophy)'
tuiles canaux
'tiles canals (Roman tiles)'

(27) coordinatives: plural on all the constituents
couvents-hôpitaux
'convents hospitals'
auteurs-compositeurs(-interprètes)
'songwriters composers (singers)'

c) Nonhead pluralization
The nonhead (N2) of a relational unit is generally in the plural if it denotes multiple entities.

(28) *train travaux*
'train works'
marché actions
'market shares'

d) Internal modification
Modification of the head is impossible.

(29) **des pneus chers neige*
'tyres expensive snow'
**un poisson noir chat*
'a fish black cat'

This, however, is not in itself a criterion for compounding but results from lexicalization and the categorizing effect of the modification by N2, as lexicalized phrases have the same characteristic.

e) Phrasal inclusions
Syntactic sequences may be included as modifiers, as in the following examples:

(30) *laitue feuille de chêne*
'lettuce leaf of oak (oakleaf lettuce)'
kit mains libres
'kit hands free (hands-free phone kit)'
responsable news, tendances et tablettes
'person-in-charge news, trends and e-pads'

f) Derivation
Derivation from compounds is a phenomenon with limited productivity, consequently very few examples based on [NN]$_N$ units are currently available. Examples where the suffix attaches to N1 like *chéquier services* 'cheque-book services (a book of vouchers for paying service workers)', *épargnant retraite* 'saver retirement (a person saving up toward his/her pension)', *assureur vie* 'insurer life (life insurance company)' are equivocal as compounding may have occurred after the derivation of N1 and so there is no firm evidence of compound-internal deriva-

tion. That external derivation is possible appears in recent isolated units with implicit noun-to-verb conversion of N2 like *capital-risqueur* 'capital risk-er (venture capital lender)', *mot-valisage* 'word portmanteau-age (lexical blending)'.

g) Recursivity
That coordinative units do not have a unique semantic head is also apparent from the fact that longer coordinatives are formed by stringing more than two nouns together in a semantically non-hierarchical fashion:

(31) *moissonneuse-batteuse*   →   *moissonneuse-batteuse-lieuse*
      'harvester thresher (combine harvester)'   'harvester thresher binder'

The following example is a hapax:

(32) *il y a aussi la technique de Laurent le prêtre-chanteur-écrivain*
      'there is also the technique of Laurent the priest singer writer'

Triple subordinatives, which are rare in the first place, may have structures that are ambiguous between [[NN]N] and [N[NN]], like *officier sécurité incendie* 'officer safety fire (fire safety officer)', *plan épargne logement* 'plan savings housing (housing savings scheme)', as *officier sécurité* and *sécurité incendie, plan épargne* and *épargne logement* are separately lexicalized and metalinguistic reflection does not produce a preferred interpretation. An example like *contrat initiative emploi* 'contract initiative employment (employment initiative contract)' appears to be structurally opaque and is not very different from a telegraphic style sequence. In contrast, very few English triple subordinatives cause hesitation about their structure. However, although the pattern's productivity is low, there exist a few examples of clearly left-branching [[NN]$_N$N]$_N$ units, such as *poisson-feuille cacatoès* 'fish leaf cockatoo (cockatoo leaf-fish)', *oiseau-mouche abeille* 'bird fly bee (bee hummingbird)', which are attributive, and *crédit impôt recherche* 'credit tax research (R&D tax credit)', a relational compound. As for *chèque emploi service* 'cheque employment service (a voucher for paying service workers)', it is right-branching.

h) Origin and expansion
Relational [NN]$_N$ units were rare before 1850, and the first author known to have mentioned them, Darmesteter (1875), provided a very limited list of examples. Although underrepresented in dictionaries, the category is undergoing expansion in Contemporary French. Jenkins (1972) noted the "sharp increase" and Noailly

(1990: 6) the "proliferation" of NN constructions, and Picone (1996: 175) considers this growth to be one of the most important recent trends of the language.

Some units are apparently calques of English compounds:

(33) *station service*
'service station'
analyste marché
'analyst market'
empreinte carbone
'footprint carbon'

Even if [NN]$_N$ compounds were rare before 1850, the existence of units like *papier formule* 'paper formula (sheets with formulas)', *laurier cerise* 'laurel cherry' (Furetière 1690) at a time when English had no influence on French proves that the pattern did not originate in another language. As Clas (1987) has remarked, recent relational units that are obvious calques are as acceptable as attributive units, which shows that the corresponding rule must be indigenous to the grammar of French.

i) Prepositional variants
From an onomasiological perspective, naming a combinatory concept attributively can only be done with the [NN]$_N$ pattern. In contrast, when the relation is of another type, the [NN]$_N$ pattern is, as noted in section 1, in stiff competition with others and [NN]$_N$ units are outnumbered. Another interesting fact is that some [NN]$_N$ units also exist in a prepositional version:

(34) *stylo-bille / stylo à bille*
'pen ball / pen to ball (ballpoint pen)'
groupe contrôle / groupe de contrôle
'group control / group of control (control group)'

In some cases, however, the prepositional variant is attested in negligible numbers in comparison with the [NN]$_N$ form, and, more conclusively, many units are without prepositional equivalents, like:

(35) *portrait robot*
(identikit portrait)
dose carrière
'dose career (the dose of radioactivity received during one's career)'

5 The status of French [NN]$_N$ compounds

Not all definitions of compounding used in French linguistics are restricted to combinations of open-class units. For example, Guilbert (1971: LXIX), Mathieu-Colas (1996), Gross (1996: 33, 49, 53), Apothéloz (2002: 18–19), Di Sciullo (2005), Riegel, Pellat and Rioul (2009: 912) consider N+prep+N units as compounds, a position criticized by Fradin (2009) on the grounds that it confuses compounding with idiomaticity. Another problem is that definitions that include binary structure as a criterion, like Benveniste's (1966), should lead to the exclusion of coordinative units if we take them to refer to semantic interpretation, since, as we saw in section 4, these can be expanded to longer sequences while keeping a "flat" interpretation.

The pioneer of French compounding studies, Darmesteter, suggested that [NN]$_N$ units represented a "clause in short form" (Darmesteter 1875: 4). The idea that compounds are syntactic was taken up by, for instance, Benveniste (1967), without formalization and outside the framework of generative grammar where the formation of compounds by transformations of underlying sentences had been introduced earlier by Lees (1960). The generative approach had an influence on French linguistics and various authors presented transformational accounts of compounding (Barbaud 1971; Guilbert 1971; Wandruszka 1972; Giurescu 1975; Rohrer 1977; Lamy 1978), some of which only mentioned presumed underlying sentences in non-formalized accounts. This approach was criticized on account of the implausibility of some of the proposed underlying sentences (Lifetree-Majumdar 1974; Noailly 1990: 34 n. 24), or on the grounds that compounds do not include clausal relations that can be asserted or modalized like those in a sentence (Riegel 1988). Because transformations were later abandoned by generative grammar and theoretical works suggesting a radical separation of morphology and syntax appeared in the 1980s (Selkirk 1982; Di Sciullo and Williams 1987), the place of compounding in the grammar became the object of attention. The characteristics of Romance compounds set them apart from Germanic ones. In particular, the left-headedness of French units led Di Sciullo and Williams (1987: 81, 83), applying William's (1981) right-hand head rule, to classify them as listed "phrasal idioms", not as compounds. Explicitly following Di Sciullo and Williams, Zwanenburg (1992) wrote that "in French, real, right-hand headed compounding is very restricted". Such approaches, which were fundamentally inspired by the structure of English, were later criticized: Ten Hacken (1999), for instance, concludes that the right-hand head rule should not be part of a cross-linguistic definition of compounds, and Guevara and Scalise (2009) criticize the restriction of the class of compounds to right-headed units as a "theory-internal construct".

Outside the generative community, Noailly (1990) distinguished four functions of syntactic NN constructions with attributive nouns, three of which, if lexicalized, correspond to compounds: qualification corresponds to attributive compounds, complementation to relationals and coordination, obviously, to coordinatives. A recent example of the syntactic view is the model presented by Barbaud (2009). While derivation belongs to morphology, compounding is a process that expands the lexicon by combining lexemes, in which speakers interpret syntactically generated sequences on the basis of their identity with a polylexemic "dicteme" memorized in the dictionary of the language (p. 31). The definition of the dicteme associates a phonetic *signifiant*, a symbolic *signifiant* (with an ontologic domain and formal features), and a prototypical *signifié* comprising a set of semes (p. 15).

The morphologist viewpoint is represented by Corbin (1992), who notes that *timbre-poste* 'stamp post (postage stamp)' exhibits a "syntactic rupture", i.e. the lack of a determinant of its N2, which differentiates it from a lexicalized phrase. In Corbin (1997), she also criticizes Zwanenburg (1992), who compared *timbre-poste* and *homme-grenouille* 'man frog (frogman)' with the phrases *le projet Delors* 'the project Delors' and *un avocat ami* 'a lawyer friend' and concluded that the former also had syntactic structure but, in having been used for the naming of entities, they have become lexicalized. Corbin notes that *poste* and *grenouille* have a categorizing effect resulting in N1 being the hyperonym of N1N2, while modifiers like *Delors* and *ami* respectively have an identifying and a qualifying effect on N1. The fact that the categorizing effect is not found in the syntactic constructions leads Corbin to the conclusion that [NN]$_N$ units like *timbre-poste* and *homme-grenouille* result from different rules, i.e. word-formation rules. Fradin in turn applies the principle that "compounds may not be built by syntax" (Fradin 2009). Like Corbin, he considers attributives like *poisson-lune* 'fish moon', *requin-marteau* 'shark hammer (hammerhead shark)' as morphologically formed, but unlike her he claims that examples like *langage auteur* 'language author', *impôt sécheresse* 'tax drought (a farm relief tax)' are formed syntactically (Fradin 2003: 195). He later (Fradin 2009) reiterates this distinction with more explicit arguments: according to him, the perceptible properties of the compound's denotatum do not cogently produce a subcategory of the head, "N2 never introduces a semantic predicate that N1 would be an argument of", and these units exist with prepositional variants. The characteristics described above in section 4 weaken these arguments: for instance, as we have seen, many relationals are without a safely attested prepositional variant.

It has become progressively apparent that compounds are problematic in models of grammar with segregated morphology and syntax. In particular, English "phrasal" compounds show that morphology may take in syntactic constructions (Lieber 1992: 14). Montermini (2008), examining Italian units like *raccolta rifiuti ingombranti* 'collection refuse$_{plur}$ cumbersome$_{plur}$ (cumbersome refuse collection)', sees in them objects that include syntactic sequences, but are in other respects morphological. This kind of consideration has led to the construction of models where the separation is less strict, for instance in the framework proposed by Di Sciullo (2005) where morphology and syntax can exchange word sequences: English compounds are derived in the morphological space, but French compounds are derived in the syntactic space before being transferred to the morphology. All categories of compounds are derived by the application of identical rules. As the derivation of French compounds is syntactic, it involves a functional projection realized as an operator that provides the semantic relation between the two nouns. In the case of coordinatives, this operator is AND/OR and in the case of relationals, it is the semantically vague SORT, which may surface in prepositional units (*épargne de précaution* 'savings of precaution') or not be realized phonologically (*épargne logement* 'savings housing') [my examples].

In construction grammar, morphology and syntax are on a continuum, which solves the disputes over their delineation. Research on compounds in cognitive linguistics has been focused mainly on semantics (Heyvaert 2009), however, and to the best of my knowledge, no construction grammar study of French [NN]$_N$ units has been published at the time of writing, but we can refer to an article by Masini (2009), who examines Italian N+prep+N and V+and+V constructions. In this study [NN]$_N$ units like *effetto serra* 'effect greenhouse' figure among phrasal nouns, an intermediate category, together with the above constructions and [NAdj]$_N$, and this would presumably apply to French [NN]$_N$ units.

From the characteristics presented in section 4, it is obvious that French [NN]$_N$ units are less prototypical compounds than the corresponding Germanic units, and they have been the object of debate. Although descriptive knowledge about them has accumulated since 1875, no definitive answer as to their status has been provided so far because opinions have been as varied as the theoretical frameworks they were formed in.

6 References

Amiot, Dany and Kristel van Goethem (2010): Le statut de *-clé* et de *sleutel-* dans *mot-clé / sleutelwoord*: Une analyse unifiée? In: Franck Neveu, Valelia Muni Toke, Jacques Durand, Thomas Klingler, Lorenza Mondada and Sophie Prévost (eds.), *Congrès mondial de linguistique française CMLF 2010*, 847–859. Paris: Institut de Linguistique Française. http://www.linguistiquefrancaise.org [last access 18 Apr 2011].

Apothéloz, Denis (2002): *La Construction du lexique français. Principes de morphologie dérivationnelle.* Gap: Ophrys.

Arnaud, Pierre J. L. (2003): *Les Composés* timbre-poste. Lyon: Presses Universitaires de Lyon.

Arnaud, Pierre J. L. (2004): Problématique du nom composé. In: Pierre J. L. Arnaud (ed.), *Le Nom composé. Données sur seize langues*, 329–353. Lyon: Presses Universitaires de Lyon.

Arnaud, Pierre J. L. (2016): Categorizing the modification relations in French relational subordinative [NN]$_N$ compounds. In: Pius ten Hacken (ed.), *The Semantics of Compounding*, 71–93. Cambridge: Cambridge University Press.

Arnaud, Pierre J. L. (2018): *Bateau phare, magasin phare*: composés [N1N2]$_N$ et séquences syntaxiques N1+N2 à N2 adjectivé. *Travaux de Linguistique* 76(1): 7–26.

Barbaud, Philippe (1971): L'ambiguïté structurale du composé binominal. *Cahiers de Linguistique* [Montréal] 1: 71–116.

Barbaud, Philippe (2009): *Syntaxe référentielle de la composition lexicale. Un profil de l'homme grammatical*. Paris: L'Harmattan.

Bauer, Laurie (2008): Exocentric compounds. *Morphology* 18: 51–74.

Benczes, Réka (2006): *Creative Compounding in English. The Semantics of Metaphorical and Metonymical Noun-Noun Combinations*. Amsterdam/Philadelphia: Benjamins.

Benveniste, Émile (1966): Formes nouvelles de la composition nominale. *Bulletin de la Société de Linguistique de Paris* 61: 82–95.

Benveniste, Émile (1967): Fondements syntaxiques de la composition nominale. *Bulletin de la Société de Linguistique de Paris* 62: 15–31.

Booij, Geert (2009): Compounding and construction morphology. In: Rochelle Lieber and Pavol Štekauer (eds.), *The Oxford Handbook of Compounding*, 201–216. Oxford: Oxford University Press.

Bourque, Yves Stephen (2014): *Toward a typology of semantic transparency: The case of French compounds*. Ph.D. dissertation, University of Toronto.

Clas, André (1987): Sur les binominaux juxtaposés. *Lebende Sprachen* 87(3): 120–121.

Corbin, Danielle (1992): Hypothèses sur les frontières de la composition nominale. *Cahiers de Grammaire* 17: 25–55.

Corbin, Danielle (1997): Locutions, composés, unités polylexématiques: Lexicalisation et mode de construction. In: Michel Martins-Baltard (ed.), *La Locution entre langue et usages*, 53–101. Fontenay-St Cloud: ENS Editions.

Cruse, D. Alan (1986): *Lexical Semantics*. Cambridge: Cambridge University Press.

Darmesteter, Arsène (1875): *Traité de la formation des noms composés dans la langue française comparée aux autres langues romanes et au latin*. Paris: Franck.

Di Sciullo, Anna Maria (2005): Decomposing compounds. *SKASE Journal of Theoretical Linguistics* 2: 14–33.

Di Sciullo, Anna Maria and Edwin Williams (1987): *On the Definition of Word*. Cambridge, MA: MIT Press.

Downing, Pamela (1977): On the creation and use of English compound nouns. *Language* 53: 810–842.

Dressler, Wolfgang U. (2006): Compound types. In: Gary Libben and Gonia Jarema (eds.), *The Representation and Processing of Compound Words*, 23–44. Oxford: Oxford University Press.

Fradin, Bernard (2003): *Nouvelles approches en morphologie*. Paris: Presses Universitaires de France.

Fradin, Bernard (2009): IE, Romance: French. In: Rochelle Lieber and Pavol Štekauer (eds.), *The Oxford Handbook of Compounding*, 417–435. Oxford: Oxford University Press.

Furetière, Antoine (1690): *Dictionnaire universel contenant généralement tous les mots françois tant vieux que modernes*. The Hague: Leers.

Giurescu, Anca (1975): *Les Mots composés dans les langues romanes*. The Hague: Mouton.

Gross, Gaston (1996): *Les Expressions figées en français. Noms composés et autres locutions*. Gap: Ophrys.

Guevara, Emiliano and Sergio Scalise (2009): Searching for universals in compounding. In: Sergio Scalise, Elisabetta Magni and Antonietta Bisetto (eds.), *Universals of Language Today*, 101–128. Dordrecht: Springer.

Guilbert, Louis (1971): De la formation des unités lexicales. In: Louis Guilbert, René Lagane and Georges Niobey (eds.), *Grand Larousse de la Langue Française*. Vol. 1, ix–lxxi. Paris: Larousse.

Gushchina Magno, Olga (2009): *Du bébé surprise aux années bonheur: les constructions (Article) + Substantif + Substantif en français moderne*. Doctoral dissertation, Université Paris IV-Sorbonne.

Hatcher, Anna Granville (1951): *Modern English Word-Formation and Neo-Latin. A Study of the Origins of English (French, Italian, German) Copulative Compounds*. Baltimore, MD: The Johns Hopkins Press.

Heyvaert, Liesbet (2009): Compounding in Cognitive Linguistics. In: Rochelle Lieber and Pavol Štekauer (eds.), *The Oxford Handbook of Compounding*, 233–254. Oxford: Oxford University Press.

Jenkins, Fred M. (1972): Double-noun compounds in contemporary French. *French Review* 46: 67–73.

Kim, Gyung-Ran (2001): Obstruent alternations in sub-compounds. *Studies in Phonetics, Phonology and Morphology* 7: 315–331.

Koga, Kentaro (2024): [N1 + N2], [N + A], and [N1 + de + N2]: Is there a tripartite competition in French endocentric naming constructions? In: Alexandra Bagasheva, Akiko Nagano and Vincent Renner (eds.), *Competition in Word-Formation*, 297–325. Amsterdam/Philadelphia: Benjamins.

Lamy, Marie-Noëlle (1978): Neological noun-noun compounds in contemporary French. *Semasia* 5: 125–147.

Lees, Robert B. (1960): *The Grammar of English Nominalizations*. Bloomington, IN: Indiana University.

Lieber, Rochelle (1992): *Deconstructing Morphology. Word Formation in Syntactic Theory*. Chicago: Chicago University Press.

Lifetree-Majumdar, Margaret J. (1974): Contribution à l'analyse des modes de composition nominale en français écrit contemporain. *Cahiers de Lexicologie* 24: 63–84.

Masini, Francesca (2009): Phrasal lexemes, compounds and phrases: A constructionist perspective. *Word Structure* 2: 254–271.

Mathieu-Colas, Michel (1996): Essai de typologie des noms composés français. *Cahiers de Lexicologie* 69: 71–125.

Montermini, Fabio (2008): La composition en italien dans un cadre de morphologie lexématique. In: Dany Amiot (ed.), *La Composition dans une perspective typologique*, 161–187. Arras: Artois Presses Université.

Noailly, Michèle. (1990): *Le Substantif épithète*. Paris: Presses Universitaires de France.

Picone, Michael D. (1996): *Anglicisms, Neologisms, and Dynamic French*. Amsterdam/Philadelphia: Benjamins.

Radimský, Jan (2019): Les composés *N-N* de subordination: un paradigme émergent. *Studia Romanica Posnaniensia* 46(1): 167–180.

Radimský, Jan (2020a): Are French NNs variants of N-PREP-N constructions? A corpus-based study of two competing patterns. *Linguistica Pragensia* 30(2): 156–185.

Radimský, Jan (2020b): A paradigmatic account of lexical innovation: The role of repeated components in French N+N compounds. In: Jenny Audring, Nikos Koutsoukos and Christina Manouilidou (eds), *Mediterranean Morphology Meetings 12*. [Online available at: https://pasithee.library.upatras.gr/mmm/article/view/3251/3511]

Renner, Vincent (2008): On the semantics of English coordinate compounds. *English Studies* 89: 606–613.

Riegel, Martin (1988): Vrais et faux noms composés: Les séquences binomiales en français moderne. In: *Actes du Troisième Colloque Régional de Linguistique, Strasbourg, 28–29 avril 1988*, 371–394. Strasbourg: Université des Sciences Humaines.

Riegel, Martin, Jean-Christophe Pellat and René Rioul (2009): *Grammaire méthodique du français*. 4th ed. Paris: Presses Universitaires de France.

Rohrer, Christian (1977): *Die Wortzusammensetzung im modernen Französisch*. Tübingen: Narr.

Scalise, Sergio and Antonietta Bisetto (2009): The classification of compounds. In: Rochelle Lieber and Pavol Štekauer (eds.), *The Oxford Handbook of Compounding*, 34–53. Oxford: Oxford University Press.

Selkirk, Elizabeth O. (1982): *The Syntax of Words*. Cambridge, MA: MIT Press.

ten Hacken, Pius (1999): Motivated tests for compounding. *Acta Linguistica Hafnensia* 31: 27–58.

Wandruszka, Ulrich (1972): *Französische Nominalsyntagmen*. München: Fink.

Williams, Edwin (1981): On the notions 'lexically related' and 'head of a word'. *Linguistic Inquiry* 12: 245–274.

Zwanenburg, Wiecher (1992): Compounding in French. *Rivista di Linguistica* 4: 221–240.

Davide Ricca
8 Verb-noun compounds in Romance

Abstract: Verb-noun compounds are a very characteristic device in Romance word-formation. The present article tries to deal briefly with most of the facets which have made verb-noun compounds the object of intense debate from the 19th century onward. Emphasis is placed on: (i) the semantic and categorial poly-functionality of the output; (ii) its borderline position on the syntax-morphology interface, although it is argued that verb-noun compounds are definitely the output of a morphological procedure; (iii) some interlinguistic discrepancies in the build-up of forms, including the long-term issue of the formal status of the verb-component.

1 Introduction: a productive exocentric strategy

The verb-noun compounds – hereafter also VNCs – in Romance (e.g., Cat. *lleva-taps*, Fr. *tire-bouchon*, It. *cavatappi*, Port. *saca-rolhas*, Sp. *sacacorchos*, all meaning 'corkscrew', to quote a beautiful example from Gather 2001: 1, with wide lexical diversity in both V and N) occupy a very peculiar place within Romance word-formation, and unsurprisingly they have been the object of a great amount of interest and scholarly work from the 19th century up to present times: it goes without saying that such an amount of work can be referred to only minimally in this article. At least the following characteristic issues have been widely discussed:

– they are a Romance innovation with respect to Latin (cf. Lloyd 1966, followed by most authors; for a contrary view see the few lines on Bork 1990 below),

Davide Ricca, Turin, Italy

https://doi.org/10.1515/9783111420554-008

but also sufficiently old to display a basically unitary character at least across all Western Romania (they are not absent in Romanian either, but apparently much less productive, see Schapira 1985, Grossmann 2012: 155);
– they offer one of the most convincing instances of a productive exocentric compounding strategy, at least in European languages;
– they display a very wide semantic spectrum in their output, both as nouns and adjectives, and at the same time interesting restrictions on the features of both V and N;
– they raise long-debated questions regarding the formal description of the V component, both synchronically and diachronically;
– they may challenge the received idea that a morphologically defined procedure is necessarily a lexeme-forming procedure as well.

Outside Romance, VNCs are attested in other Indo-European languages, but much less pervasively. Apart from the few English instances like *killjoy*, *scarecrow*, which may be dependent on French models, the type is also present at least in Ancient Greek (e.g., *pheréoikos* carry-home 'snail', proper names like *Arkhélaos*, lit. 'lead-people') and in Slavic languages (e.g., Progovac 2006 gives many examples for Serbian, like *ispičutura* drink up-flask 'drunkard', *vadičep* take out-cork 'corkscrew'; as for Czech, Štichauer 2009: 198 states that the process is not particularly productive and typically displays a jocular connotation, e.g., *kazisvět* ruin-world 'vandal').

From a diachronic point of view, Bork (1990) has challenged a long established tradition by arguing that VNCs were not unknown to Latin either (ultimately from Greek models), and therefore Romance languages should have inherited the type from Vulgar Latin. However, as remarked by Gather (2001: 202–203), Bork's investigation has yielded only a handful (precisely 16) of sure cases, mostly rare words: moreover, most of them are not formed according to the Romance pattern, but rather by a parasynthetic template which adds a derivational suffix -*i(us)* to the V and N stems, e.g., *Verticordia* turn-heart 'who changes the hearts', epithet of Venus, *poscinummius* request-coin 'eager for money'.

At any rate, it seems unlikely that the relevance of the VNCs in Romance languages could be matched by their putative Latin antecedents: as said in the heading above, VN compounding is a productive strategy in all Western Romance languages, and has been so since medieval times. Much more disputable, and most probably untrue, is the *lieu commun* repeatedly found in the literature without empirical support, that it should be the most productive compounding strategy in Romance overall. Leaving aside the well-known difficulties in assessing a quantitative notion of productivity, especially when different domains are compared, Gather (2001: 8) correctly remarks that in the rare instances in which frequency counts on comparable corpora have been made, N-N compounds have turned out to be by far more numerous. Clearly, type frequency does not coincide with productivity (cf. article 13 on productivity). However, Ricca (2010: 240) adds some evidence from a very large Italian newspaper corpus (around 330 million tokens), concerning both types and *hapax legomena*: the latter – i.e. the words occurring only once in a corpus – give an idea of a word-formation process "in real time". Comparing the figures for VNCs with those found for A-A compounds in the same corpus by Grossmann and Rainer (2009), the ratio is only about 1:6 for both types and hapaxes, which looks quite indicative, especially because N-N compounds are expected to be even more widespread than A-A compounds in Italian.

Coming to the second qualification in the heading, exocentricity is normally viewed as the exception rather than the rule in compounding (for an attempt at typologization see Bauer 2010), so it is remarkable that the VN compounding rule is productive and has been so for a long time. Exocentricity in a compound like It. *portalettere* carry-letters 'postman' seems scarcely questionable, since the head cannot be the first element, a verb, nor the second one, which is indeed a noun, but does not transfer any of its semantic and morphosyntactic features to the whole compound: *lettere* is [–animate], feminine plural, while *portalettere* is [+animate] and may be masculine or feminine, singular or plural; moreover, obviously a postman is not a kind of letter. However, perhaps just because exocentric compounding is felt as somehow anomalous, there has been much theoretical effort in trying to analyze Romance VNCs as endocentric (not just a recent suggestion anyway, as it goes back to Osthoff 1878). The reader is referred to Gather (2001: 109–136) for a survey. A possibility which has often been put forward consists in interpreting the first element not as a V, but as a deverbal (chiefly agentive) noun derived from the base verb by a conversion or zero-suffix procedure (Coseriu 1977; Grossmann 1986 for Catalan; Varela 1990 for Spanish; Zuffi 1981 and Bisetto 1999 for Italian, among others). In this way, *porta-* in *portalettere* would be on a par with *portatore* 'bearer' (some have even suggested it is a truncation of the latter), and could be treated as the head of the compound.

These kinds of proposals are probably too *ad hoc* to be convincing. However, opting for the exocentric analysis, one must at the same time recognize the hierarchical dependency between the two elements of the compound: in a sense, V behaves as an "internal" head in its relationship with N, but has no impact on the "external" syntax of the whole compound. In the recent classification proposal by Scalise and Bisetto (2009), this double level is satisfactorily captured by assigning VNCs like *portalettere* to the "subordinate exocentric" type. The label "subordinate" takes into account the governor-argument relationship which the VNCs share with the so-called "synthetic compounds" like *truck driver*, while the exo-/ endocentric distinction keeps them apart.

2 The semantic spectrum of nominal verb-noun compounds

VNCs display a very wide semantic spectrum, basically the same in the different Romance languages (except Romanian), summarized in (1):

(1) a. Agent N: Fr. *porte-drapeau*, It. *portabandiera*, Port./Sp. *porta(-)estandarte* carry-flag 'standard-bearer'
b. Instrument N: Fr. *brise-glace*, It. *rompighiaccio*, Port. *quebra-gelo(s)*, Sp. *rompehielos*, Cat. *trencaglaç* break-ice(s) 'icebreaker'
c. Location N: Fr. *coupe-gorge* cut-throat 'ill-famed place', It. *spartiacque* separate-waters 'watershed', Port. *corrimão* run-hand 'handrail'
d. Event N: Cat. *besamà*, Fr. *baise-main*, It. *baciamano*, Port. *beija-mão*, Sp. *besamanos* kiss-hand(s) 'hand-kissing'
e. Relational A: Fr. *(porte) coupe-feu*, It. *(porta) tagliafuoco*, Port. *(porta) corta-fogo*, Sp. *(puerta) cortafuego* cut-fire 'fire (door)'
f. Qualifying A: Fr. *casse-gueule* break-face 'dangerous, risky', It. *mozzafiato* cut-breath 'breathtaking', Sp. *rompepiernas* break-legs 'very tiring (esp. in cycling)'

Among the four main nominal subclasses (1a–d), the most productive (at least in present-day Romance languages) are undoubtedly the first two, namely agent and instrument nouns, and particularly the latter. A common morphological meaning for the two subclasses may be formulated as 'entity that (usually/typically) performs the action V on N'. This general meaning incorporates the agentive (or at least [+dynamic]) character of V and the patient argument role of N (see section 5 for some exceptions), leaving unspecified the [±animate] feature. This section of the semantic spectrum is just another instance of systematic agent-instrument polysemy, not rarely found in derivation. Such a polysemy has intermediate steps, as is shown by the [–human, +animate] VNCs (denoting animals identified by a stereotypical property, like Cat. *pica-soques* peck-logs 'nuthatch', It. *beccafico* peck-fig 'figpecker, warbler', Port. *papa-formigas* eat-ants 'ant-eater', Sp. *chupaflor* suck-flower 'hummingbird'), and by those denoting plants/flowers, which are living things but [–animate], e.g., Fr. *attrape-mouches* catch-flies 'dionaea', It. *bucaneve* pierce-snow 'snowdrop', Rom. *suge-pin* suck-pine 'pinesap (a parasitic plant)', Sp. *detienebuey* stop-ox 'restharrow'. Further examples in Gather (2001: 64–66).

Agentive, [+human] nouns seem to group around two main lexical fields, namely those denoting regular, job-like activities, often of lowly prestige (Cat. *guardabosc* watch-wood 'forester', Fr. *porte-parole* carry-word 'spokesperson', It. *cantastorie* sing-stories 'street singer', Port. *limpa-chaminés* clean-chimneys 'chimney sweep', Sp. *limpiabotas* clean-boots 'shoeshine boy') and those identifying a kind of human character, often by a derogatory and/or jocular expression (e.g., Cat. *somiatruites* dream-omelettes 'daydreamer', Fr. *rabat-joie* reduce-joy 'spoilsport', It. *rompiballe* break-balls 'bore', *ficcanaso* put-nose 'meddler', Sp. *papanatas* eat-cream:PL 'dupe', Rom. *zgârie-brânză* scratch-cheese 'stingy person', It. *mangiapreti* = Sp. *comecuras* eat-priests 'radical anti-clerical'). In the latter category the creative component is very prominent. This is apparently the only meaning which has been (weakly) productive in Romanian as well (Schapira 1985: 26), where it may still give rise to some independent new formations: an instance from Grossmann (2012: 156) is *fură-becuri* steal-lightbulbs 'tall person'.

On the other hand, [–animate] nouns do not always denote instruments proper. For instance, a possible meaning only vaguely relatable to the prototypical instrument is '(chemical) product performing the action V on N', as in It. *levamacchie* = Port. *tira-nódoas* remove-stains 'stain remover'. The same could be said for Fr. *pousse-café* push-coffee = It. *ammazzacaffè* kill-coffee, both 'liqueur taken after the coffee'. Another unprototypical instrument subclass is given by items in which the V is [–dynamic], like Cat. *cobrellit* = Fr. *couvre-lit* = It. *copriletto* = Sp. *cubrecama* cover-bed 'bedcover'.

The agent/instrument readings are by no means mutually exclusive for a given compound. Cf. It. *portabagagli* carry-luggage:PL, both [+animate], 'porter', and [–animate], 'luggage container'; Fr. *garde-côte* protect-coast 'coastguard/coastguard vessel' (Villoing 2009: 191); Cat. *rentaplats* wash-dishes 'dish-washer/dishwashing machine' (Gràcia 2002: 797), etc.

As for gender assignment, [+human] VNCs quite naturally select the gender according to the sex of the referent: It. *il/la portabandiera* = Fr. *le/la porte-drapeau*, etc. For all other kinds of VNCs, the default gender is masculine, although counterexamples are found in all languages, usually when the most common hyperonym(s) is/are feminine. However, this is surely not a sufficient condition: cf. It. *la lavastoviglie* f. vs. Fr. *le lave-vaisselle* m., Port. *o lava-louça* m. (but often f. in Brazil), all three meaning 'dishwasher' and relatable to the feminine hyperonym *macchina/machine/máquina*.

The two further kinds of nominal outputs (1c) and (1d) deserve some more comment. Location nouns appear to be very rare in new formations (see, e.g., Villoing 2009 for French; Ricca 2010 has found pratically none in the whole 16-

year corpus of the newspaper *La Repubblica*). Moreover, locative semantics may be disputable even in many apparently clear-cut cases. For instance, It. *sparti-acque* 'watershed' has been taken as a good illustration of a location noun in (1c), as it denotes a portion of space (admittedly a linear one), but a residual instrumental flavour cannot be denied. Conversely, I would view It. *appendiabiti* hang-clothes 'coat-hanger' rather as a limiting case of instrument noun, but its Catalan synonym *penja-robes* is considered a location noun by Gràcia (2002: 797).

By the same token, a very productive subclass in all Romance languages denotes containers: in Italian the usual verbal base is *porta-* 'carry', often with no motion implied (e.g., *portacenere* carry-ash 'ashtray', *portapenne* carry-pen 'pen-case', etc.). These items, like It. *appendiabiti* above, can be viewed as borderline between instrumental and locative semantics (cf. Rainer 1993: 274), although they properly denote an object and not a place. Perhaps the same can be said of the often cited Fr. *gratte-ciel* = It. *grattacielo* = Port. *arranha-céus* = Sp. *rascacielos*, calqued on Eng. *skyscraper* (also Rom. *zgârie-nori* lit. 'scratch-clouds' like Ger. *Wolkenkratzer*), which is, probably, a bit more place-like than the instances above.

As already noted by Varela (1990: 67), a VNC like Sp. *lavacoches* lit. 'wash-cars' may be freely used with all three main meanings mentioned above: 'person who washes cars', 'instrument to wash cars' and 'place where cars are washed'. This is unsurprising, since the instrument-location polysemy is apparently quite common among derivational morphemes cross-linguistically. However, it is difficult to decide if in these cases the location interpretation has to be considered as a property of the VN-formation rule, or rather results from a common metonymic shift generally applicable to both agent and action nouns coming to denote the place where the activity is performed.

Of course, this potentially available polysemy may vary in diachrony and across languages. Fr. *coupe-gorge* lit. 'cut-throat' had developed all the three meanings 'murderer', 'large knife (as a weapon)' and 'ill-famed place' in the history of French, but apparently it is now available only with locative meaning. The Italian parallel *tagliagole* 'murderer', however, is agentive only.

Contrary to their rarity among new formations, exclusively locative VNCs are relatively common as toponyms, which are among the best attested VNCs in medieval times, and have been traditionally viewed as one of the original sources for the whole word-formation procedure. Note that in several cases the N is not a patient, but the performer of the action denoted by V: Fr. *Chanteloup* = It. *Cantalu-po/a* lit. 'sing-he/she wolf', Fr. *Hurlevent* lit. 'cry-wind' (Villoing 2009: 189), It. *Can-tarana* = Sp. *Cantarranas* lit. 'sing-frog(s)', all (originally) interpretable as 'place where N performs the action V' (although toponyms with a patient N are also attested, e.g., It. *Bagnacavallo* lit. 'wet-horse', *Serravalle* lit. 'close-valley'). The above pattern is very rare in "normal" VNCs – some cases are mentioned in section 5. Therefore, VNC toponyms do not seem to provide the main model for the contemporary formation rule.

Event VNCs belonging to type (1d) stand perhaps even more apart, because they cannot be accomodated along an equally well attested polysemic path in word-formation (although occasionally some may cross the border: Villoing 2009: 192 cites Marc Plénat's instance of Fr. *vide-bouteille* lit. 'void-bottle' as potentially having all four main meanings: 'drinker', 'instrument to void bottles', 'drinking place' and 'good drinking'). Some well established examples of event VNCs are Cat. *correbou* run-ox 'bull run', Fr. *remue-ménage* move-household 'mess', It. *volta-faccia* turn-face 'U-turn (esp. in figurative sense)', Sp. *cumpleaños* accomplish-years 'birthday'. They are undoubtedly much rarer than agent or instrument ones, and this has led several authors to consider them as plainly unproductive (cf. Corbin 2004: 1296 for French; Bisetto 1999: 509 for Italian; for Catalan, Gràcia 2002 just mentions event VNCs in a footnote). However, their productivity cannot be ruled out if one looks to sufficiently extended databases (see Villoing 2009 for French; Ricca 2010 for Italian). Ricca (2010: 251) remarks that, apart from strict analogical models, new formations among Italian event VNCs tend to concentrate in limited semantic niches (especially names of games, or activities involving body parts), but there are exceptions.

It may also be the case that several instances of event VNCs, e.g., *faire du ramasse-miettes* 'to do garbage collecting (in computer jargon)' cited in Villoing (2009: 192), are only licensed – or strongly favoured – by particular syntactic contexts (here, the *faire du …* construction). However, this cannot surely be extended to all occurrences.

A clear case of syntactic conditioning which operates across different Romance languages is the construction "*a/à* + VN" in instances like It. *correre a perdifiato* (lose-breath) 'to run at breakneck speed', Sp. *a regañadientes* grind-teeth 'unwillingly', Fr. *crier/chanter à tue-tête* lit. 'kill-head' = It. *gridare/cantare a squarciagola* rip up-throat 'to shout/sing as loud as possible', It. *sparare a brucia-pelo* lit. 'burn-hair', Sp. *disparar a quemarropa* = Port. *disparar à queima-roupa* burn-dress 'to shoot at a very short distance'. The VNCs involved normally do not exist as independent lexemes, but they are best interpretable as event nouns, even if licensed by the specific construction only. At any rate, the productivity of the pattern is minimal, and in most cases these "*a/à* + VN" sequences collocate quite rigidly with just one or very few verbs, giving rise to highly idiomatic, nearly lexicalized VPs (same ideas in Gather 2001: 155–156).

3 Adjectival verb-noun compounds and the unitary output hypothesis

The instances of adjectival VNCs as given in (1e–f) raise a different issue. A single morphological rule appears to form productively items belonging to two different syntactic categories, and thus provides a clear challenge to the unitary output hypothesis (henceforth UOH) found, e.g., in Scalise (1984: 137).

Even outside the lexicalist framework, this constraint has been considered empirically very solid, or even "inherent in an output-oriented approach" like the one of Plag (1999: 243). Probably for this reason, there is no general consensus about Romance VNCs really constituting a counterexample to the UOH.

To be sure, there can be little doubt that they can be used extensively as noun modifiers: for some further data, see, e.g., Gather (2001: 155–159). However, for many authors this does not automatically imply a substantial violation of the UOH. Several ways out are found in theoretically-oriented descriptions (especially in the Italian tradition; less unanimously, but prevalently in Spain as well, as discussed for instance in Gather 2001: 155–165). It can be argued that a modifier VNC is first formed as a noun by the compounding rule, and then transformed into an adjective by virtue of a further N → A conversion rule. Alternatively, the VNC may be considered as a noun in an appositional relationship with its head; or even as the modifier N in a N-N (loose) compound. The latter solution, proposed by Zuffi (1981), seems, however, hardly applicable to the instances in which the VNC occurs separated from its head (like It. *scatola d'argento portafiammiferi* box of-silver hold-matches 'silver matchbox').

It is not by chance that the advocates of the all-nominal approach normally refer to instances like It. *nave portacontainer* = Fr. *navire porte-conteneurs* ship carry-containers 'container carrier'. In such cases, the VNC is also widely employed autonomously as a noun, often much more widely than as a modifier. Therefore, it is easy to consider the modifier use as derived from the nominal one.

However, in many other instances the modifier function is the only one attested, or at least is largely prevailing in use. For these cases, a reductionist approach complying with the UOH becomes much less convincing (similarly Rainer 1993: 273). Perhaps it may still be feasible for the relational VNC adjectives, as the one in (1e) (many more examples in Gather 2001: 155), because – even when a corresponding nominal use is scarcely attested – they keep some nominal features: they have often an instrumental reading and they are not gradable. Moreover, the tight syntagmatic links with their head, with which they often constitute a single referential unit, may suggest a N-N compound-like interpretation of the whole sequence.

But cases like It. *mozzafiato* 'breathtaking' in (1f) cannot be treated this way. This item has all the features of a full-fledged qualifying adjective, including:

– occurring in predicate position: *quel panorama è veramente mozzafiato* 'that panorama is really breathtaking';
– occurring in coordination with other clearly qualifying adjectives: *panorama stupendo e mozzafiato* 'marvellous and breathtaking panorama';
– being gradable: *un panorama ancora più mozzafiato* 'a still more breathtaking panorama'.

Full-fledged qualifying VNC adjectives are present in all Romance languages and should suffice to rule out a rigid version of the all-nominal approach. On the other hand, they are undoubtedly a small minority among well established VNCs, as is reflected also in dictionary-based counts (cf. Gather 2001: 155). Therefore, from lexicographical data it could be argued that the UOH for VNCs still holds as a strong tendency.

However, Ricca (2010: 249–254) has shown that corpus data draw quite a different picture, at least for Italian. While they confirm the prevalence of nouns for high frequency items, the low frequency ones, and especially the *hapax legomena*, turn out to be quite balanced between nominal and modifier uses. Since, as said above, the *hapax legomena* in a very large corpus are the best approximation to the behaviour of a productive word-formation rule "in action", it seems fair to argue that the VN-compounding process in itself is better left unspecified regarding its output category. The clear preference for nouns among the firmly entrenched items can then hardly be ascribed to the formation pattern itself, and has probably to do with the different lexicalization potential between nouns (referential entities) and adjectives (property concepts) in general.

4 Non-lexical verb-noun compounds and the border with syntax

The investigations of large newspaper corpora by Ricca (2005, 2010) have put in evidence a further interesting feature of many hapax or nearly hapax VNCs, namely their markedly non-lexical features, especially when employed as modifiers.

Typical instances are constructions like the following (Ricca 2010: 252), which are quite often met in Italian newspapers (it would be interesting to verify if similar structures are common in other Romance languages as well):

(2)   a. *con il colpo di testa fissa-risultato di Fonseca*
       'with Fonseca's *result-securing* header'
      b. *alludendo alla ventilata astensione salva-Prodi*
       'alluding to the proposed *Prodi-saving* abstention'

From a communicative point of view, such items "work" more or less like a reduced relative clause. However, they undoubtedly belong to the same compounding pattern seen till now, and therefore in our view they are still the output of a morphological procedure, not a syntactic one.

But taking the view that the items in (2a–b) are compounds does not straightforwardly imply that they are lexemes: not just because they are nonce formations, but because they are also extremely poor candidates for lexical storage. A good argument for the inherently non-lexical nature of the VNCs in (2) is that they often keep the referential autonomy of the noun intact, which is patent when a proper noun is involved, as in (2b), but holds for (2a) as well. It is also significant that in this use the V element does not convey at all the habituality feature which is nearly always present in "lexical" VNCs, nonce formations included (and is usually taken as a general property of VNCs, see, e.g., Varela 1990: 65).

From these – and several other – instances of compounds, Gaeta and Ricca (2009) argue for the necessity of keeping well separated the issues of lexicalizability (i.e storage/storability as a unit in the mental lexicon) and "morphologicalness" (i.e. being the result of a non-syntactic procedure), an issue neatly raised already by Corbin (1992: 50). By the suggested two-feature analysis, instances like the VNCs in (2) would be [+morphological], [−lexical] entities, contrary to the often tacit assumption that non-inflectional morphology is always a lexeme-forming device, at least potentially.

More generally, the assignment of the whole VN compounding procedure – not just the non-lexical cases in (2) – to syntax rather than morphology has been often proposed. We cannot deal with the theoretical debate here (apart from the few hints below, the reader is referred to the survey in Gather 2001: 28–63 and 115–126). Apparently, an argument in favour of the syntactic option could be given by the well-known instances of V[NP] formations, like It. *porta-carta igienica* = Fr. *porte-papier hygiénique* = Port. *porta papel higiênico* 'toilet paper holder'. Gather (2001: 153) already reports a fairly long list for French, but innumerable instances with bases like *porta-/porte-* can now be found most easily on the Internet for all Western Romance languages, for any conceivable kind of container/holder on sale on the Web. The NP involved may well have a complex structure itself, and in particular govern a PP, as in It. *copriborsa dell'acqua calda* cover-hot water bag 'hot water bag cover' (Ricca 2005: 479), Fr. *nettoie-chaînes de vélo* 'bike chain cleaner' (quoted in Gather 2001: 153), despite the contrary statement for Spanish in NGLE (2009: 771). In many cases, as the ones above, the NP (and consequently the whole compound) can be considered a unit in the mental lexicon, but not necessarily so: instances of V[NP] formations with features like those in (2) occur as well.

Nevertheless, the morphological option for VN formations still seems us to fit better the data. Perhaps the strongest argument against the syntactic option, put forward by Corbin (1992: 48), Rainer (1993: 275) and many others, is the virtual absence of V[DP] compounds (i.e. compounds including the determiner). If VNCs were to be synchronically derived from VPs structures, they should freely allow for, or indeed prefer, a V[DP] pattern (*porta-la-carta-igienica* and the like), which is definitely not the case. Instances of lexicalized V-Det-N formations are in fact attested (e.g., Fr. *trompe-l'oeil* id.; lit. 'deceive-the-eye', It. *battiloro* beat-the-gold 'gold-beater', apart from family names like Fr. *Boileau* = It. *Bevilacqua* lit. 'drink-the-water', It. *Cantalamessa* lit. 'sing-the-mass', etc.), but they are exceedingly rare and are best treated, as Gather (2001: 22–23) argues, as a separate process, i.e. as idiosyncratic instances of univerbation from frozen clausal chunks, not qualitatively different from the types It. *nontiscordardimé* 'forget-me-not', Sp. *hazmerreír* make-me-laugh 'laughing stock'.

A further strong argument in favour of the essentially morphological nature of VN formations (the same point is raised, e.g., by Rainer 1993: 75) is given by the interesting syntactic and semantic restrictions involving both V and N, which will be discussed below in section 5. They should not be expected if the VN formations were the output of the same syntactic rule which forms VPs.

5 Constraints on V and N and "peripheral" formations

Concerning phonology, no categorical restriction appears to hold for VN compounding, although in all Romance languages a tendency may be detected which favours "short" V bases. Being "short" translates as bisyllabic in Italian and Spanish, and monosyllabic in French, due to the different phonotactics of the languages in question. So Rainer (1993: 269) reports an overwhelming majority (around 80 %) of compounds with bisyllabic V bases in his corpus, and a similar percentage (around 75 %) is found by Ricca (2010: 244) among over 2,200 Italian VNCs occurring in a large newspaper corpus. As for French, Villoing (2009: 194) obtains very similar percentages (80 %) for monosyllabic bases. Percentages become still higher if one considers that many trisyllabic bases (bisyllabic for French) begin with a vowel, which often undergoes resyllabification with the preceding word – e.g., an article – and therefore may be considered "extra-metrical".

Methodologically, this can be a tricky issue, since a prevailing number of short bases might be just a side effect of a more general tendency to avoid words that are too long. Ricca (2010: 244–245) checked out this possibility, showing that no similar preference is displayed among deverbal *derivatives* of equal length in the same corpus. Thus the preference for two-syllable verbal bases appears to be specific to VN compounding, at least for Italian. It is obviously just a tendency, which does not rule out perfectly legitimate (and attested) V bases with up to five syllables at least, like It. *macchina distribuisci-biglietti* 'ticket-dispensing machine'.

A similar tendency concerning the length of N seems harder to prove, despite some proposals along these lines (convincingly dismissed by Gather 2001: 16–17).

As another general limiting factor on VNC formation, it has been often observed that only a very small set of potential verb bases really gives rise to a significant number of VNCs. Gather (2001: 11–12) quotes some lists of the most frequent bases for French, Spanish, and Portuguese, mostly taken from lexicographic sources, which seriously limits their ability to reflect the formation process proper. For Italian, however, Ricca (2005, 2010) made counts both on lexicographical sources and on large corpora, confirming that the base distribution is very skewed. These facts are not astonishing at all, because a high skewedness is commonplace in every kind of word frequency distribution when productive processes are involved (cf. Baayen 2001). Nevertheless, it may be significant that some semantic types recur almost universally across languages and sources: the top ranked concepts include 'carry', 'protect/save', 'cover', 'cut', 'kill', 'break', 'pull', 'count', and the first two are probably the leading items. For some of the most frequent bases, there may be some potential for grammaticalization toward prefixal status (cf. Gather 2001: 11–12). This is clearly the case for the French series with *pare-*, because the corresponding verb with the meaning 'stop/protect' is no longer synchronically available, but Gather suggests a similar analysis for Sp. *porta-* as well, given the limited role played by the free verb *portar* when compared to the very high productivity and semantic autonomy of the compound base *porta-* in the sense of 'container/holder'. Even It. *porta-* could be considered from the same perspective (Ricca 2010: 247), despite the high frequency of the corresponding free verb *portare* 'to carry', because, as in Spanish, in most of its occurrences in compounds there is no motion capability implied.

The real restrictions on VNC formation, however, concern the syntactic/semantic features of both its lexical components. The overwhelming majority of VNCs, including the new formations, is formed from transitive verbs which allow for an agentive subject, and the N nearly always takes the role of the internal argument of such verb, and specifically the object (as remarked already, e.g., by

Varela 1990: 69–71 for Spanish). This is true also for plant words and the huge class of instrument compounds: although the implied subject is [–animate] in these cases, the verbal base in itself is compatible with [+animate] subjects as well.

There are obviously exceptions to the two very general constraints above, but on the whole they are really limited in number, drawing a sort of basically unproductive "periphery" around the core of the VN compounding procedure. This periphery will be briefly illustrated below (a longer discussion may be found in Gather 2001: 76–86, and, for French, in Villoing 2009).

The restriction on the agentivity of V rules out in particular those verbs which take an experiencer as their first argument. So formations like It. *odiaparenti* (hate-relatives), Sp. *quiereanimales* (love-animals, Varela 1990: 70) or Fr. *craint-étrangers* (fear-foreigners) are normally excluded, despite their semantic plausibility. Gather (2001: 86) cites as a historically relevant exception a series of French formations with *aimer* 'to love', common among literary coinings in the 16th century only.

As already said above, [–dynamic] verbs occur as long as they may allow – in a different context – for a controlling first argument, i.e. they are not stative proper. This is the case for many verbal bases like It. *porta-* 'carry', *reggi-* 'hold', *copri-* 'cover', which are in fact among the most productive of all and give rise to a host of names for containers, holders, covers. But the impossibility of formations like Sp. *tienefiebre* lit. 'have-fever' (Varela 1990: 70) or It. *pesachili* lit. 'weigh-kilos' seems to hold across all Romance languages.

Concerning the argument role of N, the exceptions are somehow more relevant, and may be divided in two classes: the instances where N is the external argument (subject) of V, which normally implies that V is intransitive, and those in which it is a non-object internal argument of V.

Well-known and often cited items in the first category include: It. *marciapiedi* walk-feet 'pavement', *batticuore* beat-heart 'heartthrob', Fr. *trotte-bébé* trot-baby 'baby walker', *pense-bête* think-idiot 'reminder', Sp. *saltacaballo* jump-horse 'arch springer', *reposacabezas* rest-head 'headrest' (together with several others with *reposa-*, cf. Rainer 1993: 270). Even from this shortlist, the peripheral nature of these items may be appreciated also looking at their unpredictable semantic output: the otherwise uncommon location and event nouns are well attested, as well as quite idiosyncratic instances of patient VN (Villoing 2009: 190), like *croque-monsieur* crunch-Mister 'toasted sandwich' (i.e. 'food to be crunched by men'). As said above, a coherent group of VNCs with subject N is found among toponyms.

As for the second type, N as an oblique argument appears in very few scattered items where N may fulfil different semantic roles, e.g., source (It. *scendiletto* go down-bed 'bedside rug'), path (the uncommon Sp. *andarríos* go-brooks 'wagtail'), direction (the name for 'sunflower' shared among most Romance languages: It. *girasole*, Sp./Cat. *girasol*, together with the now opaque Fr. *tournesol*).

However, within this periphery an interesting semantic niche appears to be cross-linguistically productive. From verbal bases meaning 'protect', two open lists of compounds may be formed, one where N is the object of V (i.e. meaning 'object protecting N', often but not exclusively a body part) and another where N is the oblique argument: 'object protecting *from* N'. This fact has been often observed for Spanish: Rainer (1993: 270) gives examples from the two bases *guarda-* (e.g., *guardabarros* 'mudguard') and *protege-* (the new formation *protege-esquinas* 'protector from edges'). Gather (2001: 83), although adding similar French examples with *garde-*, underestimates the relevance of the pattern, doubting its productivity outside strict analogy. However, there are plenty of similar formations also from Fr. *protège-* (like *protège-vent*, *protège-soleil* 'wind, sun shelter' very common on the Internet) and Italian offers a host of further examples with four different bases, not only *para-* and *proteggi-* 'protect', but also *ripara-* 'shelter' and above all the very productive *salva-* 'save'. A list of Italian items of the type 'protect from' taken from Internet data (e.g., *proteggi-/para-/salva-/ripara-vento* 'wind protecting (device)'), with more than 20 different Ns, has been presented in Ricca (2008) and is found also – with some expansion – in Magni (2010: 19), who discusses extensively the pattern for the three languages.

The same behaviour in different languages, without full overlap in the choice of the lexical bases, clearly suggests something more than strict analogy: in this case the saliency of the "oblique" argument – which often may occur alone, without overt specification of the object, as noted, e.g., by Val Álvaro (1999: 4797) – overcomes the syntactic constraint requiring the object role for N.

A different kind of peripheral formations involves recursivity. It is well known that Romance languages allow for recursive compounding in general only to a limited extent, at least in comparison with Germanic languages. The VN formations are no exception: recursive V[VN] compounds are neither ungrammatical nor unattested, but they are surely rather uncommon. Not unexpectedly, a high level of lexical entrenchment of the internal VN seems to be required, which does not mean necessarily a high level of opacity. Formations of frequent use include several compounds with the very productive base *porta-/porte-* denoting containers/holders, like It. *portastuzzicadenti* = Cat. *portaescuradents* carry-[pick-teeth] 'toothpick holder', It. *portasciugamani* = Fr. *porte-essuie-mains* carry-[dry-hands] 'towel holder', It. *portacontachilometri* = Sp. *portacuentakilómetros* carry-[count-kilometres] 'odometer holder'. Other instances often display a higher degree of opacity of the inner VNC, as It. *svuotaportafogli* empty-[carry-sheets] 'wallet-emptying (said of taxes, holidays, etc.)', Sp. *limpiaparabrisas* wipe-[protect-breezes] 'windscreen wiper'.

Notice that there are VVN sequences which cannot be analysed as recursive V[VN] compounds. These are items like It. *tergilavafari* = Fr. *lave-essuie-phares* = Sp. *limpialavafaros* 'headlight washer/wiper', It. *lavasciugabiancheria* = Sp. *lavase-carropas* 'clothes washer/dryer', in which the two verbs are in a coordinative relationship and both govern the noun. Therefore, the compound must be described according to a [[VV]N] structure. Interestingly, this template is licensed only by the whole constructional pattern, since coordinative VV compounds are exceedingly rare in Romance languages, and there are no compound verbs like It. *lavasciugare*, Sp. *lavasecar* 'to wash and dry' or It. *tergilavare*, Sp. *limpia-lavar* 'to wipe and wash'. Obviously only semantics, or perhaps just world knowledge, may distinguish the two types. For instance, It. *lavasciugamani* might be interpreted both ways, although it is currently attested with the [[VV]N] meaning, namely 'hand washer/dryer' and not 'towel washing machine'.

Both templates combined together, to give a [[VV][VN]] structure, occur at least in one Spanish well established compound, *limpia-lavaparabrisas* 'windscreen washer/wiper'.

Finally, brief mention may be made here of exocentric VAdv and VAdj compounds, because, although quite limited in number and scarcely productive at all, they show a great semantic affinity with the VNCs. A short list for Italian, Spanish and French is found in Gather (2001: 18). The adverb is not always a modifier, but often plays an argumental role in these compounds. Both main [+animate] types are represented, the job/role terms (It. *buttafuori* throw-out 'bouncer', Sp. *mandamás* command-more 'big boss') and the qualifying/derogatory terms (It. *cacasotto* shit-under 'coward', Fr. *lève-tard* wake up-late 'late riser'), as well as the instrument nouns (Fr. *passe-partout* pass-everywhere 'master key', Sp. *tirafuera* pull-out 'sort of fishing net with a long pole') and also the event nouns: It. *tagliafuori* cut-out 'boxing out in basketball', Port. *bota-abaixo* throwdown 'destructive criticism' (Río Torto and Ribeiro 2012: 136).

Among the perhaps even less numerous VAdj compounds, one could distinguish those where the adjective has in fact a nominal function (e.g., It. *menagramo* bring-bad 'jinx', Fr. *gagne-petit* earn-little 'low wage earner'), and those where the Adj has an adverbial use (It. *aprifacile* open-easy 'easy to open', Port. *falabarato* speak-cheap 'chatterbox', Sp. *cantaclaro* sing-clear 'very frank person'). Neither subtype seems to add anything to the general pattern of VNCs.

6 Formal details: interlinguistic differences within Romance

VNCs have been treated so far without making any distinction within Romance, and illustrated by examples taken more or less at random from the different Romance languages.

The very feasibility of this procedure shows the extent of the uniformity shared by VNCs within the whole (Western) Romance area. However, cross-linguistic discrepancies do exist, which are difficult to deal with in a short survey. They seem to concern essentially specific points in the build-up of forms, rather than semantic features and general restrictions. In the following, such points of detail will be briefly illustrated in a contrastive perspective between Italian and Spanish, which happen to differ extensively in these respects. French would be harder to evaluate at any rate, due to the great difference in relevance of inflectional markers between the graphematic and the spoken code (the former should not be fully disregarded in this particular domain, given that several new formations plausibly appear first in the written medium; for some discussion see Villoing 2009).

6.1 The V stem

The first and most hotly debated issue concerns the precise character of the V element. In this domain care should be taken in keeping the synchronic and diachronic perspectives well separated.

The three positions on the nature of V, as surveyed for instance in Rainer (1993: 265–268) and Gather (2001: 87–92), are: (i) V is an imperative 2nd person form; (ii) V is an indicative 3rd person form; (iii) V is a bound verbal stem. However, if formulated as above the three alternatives make sense chiefly as a diachronic issue. Clearly, this was also the main focus of the debate until the first half of 20th century. The imperative proposal was most energetically defended by Darmesteter (1894) with respect to French and, according, e.g., to Rainer (1993: 265), essentially won the contest until the revival of the indicative alternative, prompted especially by Tollemache's (1945) study of Italian. Not only historical, but also semantic arguments were put forward in defending the different options. For instance Tollemache's plea for the indicative, despite its formal implausibilty for Italian (see below), rested on the paraphrasability of most VNCs as 'entity who does the action V on N'.

From a contemporary and synchronic perspective however, the option that the V occurring in VNCs is a kind of verbal stem seems hardly questionable, as stressed, e.g., by Villoing (2009: 176–179) for French. Whatever form V takes in these compounds, it carries just its lexical content, not the meaning associated with any specific verbal inflectional marker: neither the imperative nor the indicative, and much less so a specific person value. Consequently, whatever the ultimate origin of the model(s) which triggered the morphological template (quite plausibly the imperative: for a partial re-evaluation of its role even in synchronic word-formation, see Floričić 2008), the present-day productive formation rule should inevitably be formulated in terms of a verbal stem (a morpheme in the sense of Aronoff 1994), and not of verbal inflectional forms. The question remains, however, how such a morpheme is formed, and some cross-linguistic divergence is found in this respect.

In Italian, the V stem in VNCs formally coincides with the 2nd person imperative for all verbs. There is no possibility of relating it to 3rd person indicative, because the two forms differ for all verbs in 2nd and 3rd conjugations (indicative *regge* 'holds', *apre* 'opens' vs. imperative *reggi*, *apri*). In Spanish, the opposite pattern holds: while there is a nearly complete overlap between the forms of 2nd imperative and 3rd indicative for all three conjugations, in the rare cases where they contrast (e.g., with *tenir* 'keep' and derivatives) the few instances of lexicalized compounds show the 3rd singular form, and speakers agree that possible new formations would do the same (Val Álvaro 1999: 4789).

In both languages, the stem occurring in VNCs cannot be identified with the derivational stem. In Spanish, for 3rd conjugation verbs the VNC stem ends in -*e*, but the derivational stem ends in -*i*: *abrelatas* open-cans 'can opener' vs. *abridor* 'opener'. Moreover, many verbs show stem alternations correlated with stress, and the VNC stem keeps the stressed variant, with very few exceptions: e.g., *cuentagotas* count-drop 'dropper' vs. *contador* 'counter' (Rainer 2001: 391). In Italian, the parallel vowel-diphthong alternation involves few verbs (e.g., *trattenere* 'to keep': *dispositivo trattieni-odore* '(bad) smell-keeping device' vs. *trattenimento* 'keeping'), but the same contrast occurs for the open class of verbs with the so-called -*isc*- augment, as *pulire* 'to clean': they usually keep it in VNCs, as in imperative (*pulisciorecchie* 'ear cleaner'), but never in derivatives (*pulitore* 'cleaner').

Catalan displays an even more complex picture, since for some bases two different stems coexist, e.g., *cobrellit* 'bed cover' vs. *cobriespatlla* cover-shoulder 'shawl' from *cobrir* 'cover', and both differ from the 3rd indicative/2nd imperative form, which is *cobreix* in today's Catalan (Gather 2001: 101).

To reduce the impact of the issue, it must be said that the problematic cases of V-stem formation concern essentially the basically unproductive verb classes outside the first conjugation. It is probably not irrelevant that in the productive first conjugation there is full coincidence between 3rd indicative and 2nd imperative in all Romance languages except Sardinian, which may have lead to reanalyses in the different directions.

6.2 The internal N plural

Many VNCs in all Romance languages display the N in plural form also when used in the singular, as seen in the examples above. Contrary to the V pseudo-inflectional marker, such a plural marker is generally not semantically void. The clearest proof is the – admittedly rare – occurrence of two different VNCs with singular and plural N, e.g., It. *portauovo* carry-egg 'egg cup' vs. *portauova* carry-eggs 'egg container'; Sp. *matarrata* kill-rat (a game) vs. *matarratas* kill-rats (a poison). The N plural marking occurring in Romance VNCs has been pointed out, at least since Booij (1994: 37), as a good instance of "inflection feeding word formation", and therefore as an argument for nominal Number belonging to inherent inflection. However, the details vary across the languages.

In Italian, its meaningful, non-morphomic character seems quite stable also beyond the cases of contrast like *portauovo/a*. Ns are always plural in *pluralia tantum* (e.g., *portaocchiali* bear-glasses 'glasses case'), and, more relevantly, when each single state of affairs associated with the compound (typically) involves a plurality of Ns (as in *contapassi* count-steps 'step counter'). The contrast between *schiaccianoci* crush-nut:PL 'nutcracker' and *cacciavite* thrust-screw:SG 'screwdriver' shows the area of unpredictable variation, which regards, quite naturally, VNCs whose referent acts on a single N in a given state of affairs, but on a plurality of Ns on different occasions: they could be labelled "variable-N compounds". In this subclass, both alternatives may often occur in the same item: *fermacravatta/e* hold-tie(s) 'tiepin'. Conversely, the singular N occurs quite regularly for "stable-N compounds", where the VNC typically acts on a single referent throughout (e.g., *copriletto* cover-bed:SG 'bedcover'), and categorically when N is a unique referent (*giramondo* 'globetrotter') or a mass noun (*spazzaneve* 'snow plough', *rompighiaccio* 'ice-breaker').

The pattern in Spanish is different. Singular VNCs display the -*s* plural marker on N in the great majority of cases. The -*s* has extended even to unique referents (cf. *trotamundos* 'globetrotter' vs. It. *giramondo* above) and to mass nouns (cf. Sp. *quitanieves* 'snow plough', *rompehielos* 'ice-breaker' vs. It. *spazzaneve*, *rompighiaccio*), although exceptions remain (a list in Val Álvaro 1999: 4798), not only within the "stable-N" type, but sometimes even among "variable-N" compounds (Am. Sp. *chupaflor* suck-flower 'hummingbird'). Such an extension implies a substantial change in the role of the -*s* marker. As already noted by Rainer and Varela

(1992: 130), the *-s* in Spanish VNCs has mainly taken the role of marking the composition process itself, with no consistent semantic motivation. That is, it has come a long way to becoming a morphome, similar to the linking elements familiar from the compositional processes in German and other languages (cf. article 4 on linking elements in Germanic) with the interesting difference that the *-s* marker occurs at the word's end and not at the border between the lexical morphemes. However, the generalization of *-s* in VNCs is surely not a concluded process, and probably has different relevance across the Spanish-speaking world: for a variety of Argentinian Spanish, Rainer (1993: 272) even reports the opposite tendency of omitting the *-s* in the singular only.

Catalan seems to take an intermediate position between Italian and Spanish: according to Gràcia (2002: 798–99), the plural N is the normal choice for countable Ns, but does not extend to unique referents (*rodamón* vs. Sp. *trotamundos*) or mass nouns (*llevaneu* vs. Sp. *quitanieves*).

6.3 The plural of the whole compound

The above variation in the marking of the internal N plural has obvious consequences for the possibility of marking external plurals, i.e. the plural of the whole compound. Nowhere in Romance languages is there an independent slot available for this function. Consequently, all VNCs with internal plural Ns are necessarily invariable. Very marginal exceptions may at most occur if the compound is so deeply entrenched in the mental lexicon that it may be perceived as non-analyzed unit. For instance, the Italian plural *i paracaduti* 'the:M:PL parachutes' is not found in dictionaries, but on the Internet it is about as frequent as the expected *i paracadute*. This deviant form necessarily implies a reanalysis of the (F):PL *-e* ending, occurring in the singular *il paracadute* stop-fall:PL 'parachute', as the (M):SG ending of the *-e*/*-i* inflectional class (as in *can-e* 'dog'), which in turn cannot happen without a substantial opacization of the compound.

A different state of affairs occurs with VNCs displaying a singular N in the singular. Since these are a minority in Spanish, Italian is more interesting in this respect. As a general rule, it appears that the possibility of marking the whole VNC as plural by pluralizing the internal N obeys plausible semantic distinctions. Both "variable-N" and "stable-N" compounds may display a plural N when they have plural reference, but there is great oscillation and in most cases both forms are possible and largely attested: *i cacciavite/i* thrust-screw(s) 'screwdrivers', *i copriletto/i* cover-bed(s) 'bed covers'. This makes sense semantically, since for both subclasses a plurality of VNC referents normally implies a plurality of Ns as well. Therefore, there is no need to analyse the plural *-i* in *spazzacamini* sweep-chimney:PL 'chimney sweeps' and the like – as done by Scalise (1994: 139) – as an instance of external plural implying that the compound is treated as an unanalysable whole, like *paracaduti* above. The *-i* is still an internal plural compatible with the inflectional class of N, and quite naturally licenses the plural interpretation of the whole compound.

The latter analysis is supported by the fact that when there is a gender clash between the N and the VNC, the compound is mostly invariable: *i portabandiera* carry-flag (f.) 'standard-bearers (m.)'. The clash may be overcome (a plural *i portabandiere* 'the:M.PL carry-flags' is possible, as witnessed by the many occurrences on the Internet), but always in favour of the internal plural (here the (F):PL ending *-e* of *bandiera*): a form like **i [portabandier]-i*, with the *-i* modelled on the inflectional class of masculines in *-a* (like *poeta/poeti*) is unacceptable.

6.4 Interaction with other morphological domains

Traditional lexicalist models usually order derivation before composition (cf. Scalise 1984: 115–122), which would imply that VNCs may freely take derived Ns as input, but would rule out the inverse case, apart from idiosyncratic instances of very opaque, essentially unanalyzed compounds. The first hypothesis is easily confirmed by the data, as stated also by Gather (2001: 142). To give just a single example, cf. It. *copri[te-iera]* = Fr. *couvre[thé-ière]* = Sp. *cubre[te-teras]* cover-teapot 'tea cosy'. Maybe the high frequency items are not very numerous, but in corpora many more can be found, although for Spanish the possibility of internal derivations is rejected in NGLE (2009: 747).

The further derivability of VNCs is indeed less straightforward. At least for Italian, data suggest a neat distinction between prefixal and suffixal derivation, which is probably to be expected, given the recognized higher autonomy of prefixes with respect to their bases. Obvious examples of prefixes freely combining with VNCs are *anti-* 'anti-, against', which attaches without problems to the wide subclass of [+animate] derogatory VNCs (e.g., *anti-ficcanaso* 'anti-meddler'), and *ex-* 'former', which similarly freely applies to the equally wide domain of job nouns (e.g., *ex-cantastorie* 'former storyteller'). Both types have very solid attestations on the Web.

As for suffixation, the picture seems different. Surely in every language some well established examples can be found, but often they involve partially opaque VNCs (this is the case for It. *paracadut-ista* = Sp. *paracaid-ista* 'paratrooper', It. *guardaroba* guard-thing 'wardrobe' → *guardarob-iera* 'wardrobe maid', Sp. *paraguas* protect-water 'umbrella' → *paragü-ero* 'umbrella maker', as also Gather 2001: 143–144 suggests). Similar considerations hold for N → V conversions: among the few Italian instances one could list *paracadutare* 'to parachute', *ficcanasare* 'to nose around', *rendicontare* 'to report' from the highly lexicalized *paracadute, ficcanaso* 'meddler' and *rendiconto* give-(ac)count 'report (N)'.

Such a restriction may be weakened, however, for some specific suffixes which more generally display practically no structural limitation on their input: the best example in Italian is *-ismo* '-ism'. So the model of quality nouns from [+animate] derogatory VNCs (like *rompiball-ismo*, from *rompiballe* break-balls 'bore') is presumably productive, since it is widely attested, at least on the Web, with many VNC bases. The situation is probably similar in Spanish: the only example of a derived VNC cited in the NGLE (2009: 771) is *chupamedismo*, from *chupamedias* suck-socks 'flatterer', and several quality nouns parallel to the Italian ones are abundantly present on the Web, with some even attested in dictionaries, e.g., *papanatismo* 'dumbness'.

Finally, as for the interaction of VNCs with evaluative morphology, we do not expect to find significant restrictions against diminutive/augmentative Ns serving as input for VN compounding, neither semantically nor theoretically, as long as the Ns in question have some referential autonomy, and this is certainly the case in Italian (cf. *porta[telefon-ino]* carry-telephone:DIM 'mobile holder', *guarda[port-one]* guard-door:AUGM 'doorkeeper'; examples could be multiplied). Such internal diminutivization is however ruled out in NGLE (2009: 747) for Spanish, similarly to derivation in general.

The possibility of applying evaluative morphology to the whole compound is more interesting and again displays some degree of contrast between Italian and Spanish. While the option seems rather restricted in both languages, its formal realizations differ. Spanish prefers the diminutive – when acceptable – to attach at the N, although the semantics involves the whole compound, e.g., *cortauñas* → *cortauñitas* cut-nails:DIM '[little [nail clipper]]' (NGLE 2009: 770). However, the picture is made complex by the possibility of interpreting the above formations as infixed diminutives according to the pattern *Carlos* → *Carl-it-os* (Gather 2001: 150). In Italian, on the contrary, diminutives referring to the whole compound are not as marginal as Gather (2001:150) would suggest, but they overwhelmingly apply externally: so *paracadute* → *[paracadut]-ino* 'little parachute (e.g., on hang gliders)' vs. **paracadutine, portafogli* carry-sheets 'wallet' → *portafoglino/portafoglietto* 'little wallet' (not **portafoglini), guardaroba* → *guardarobino* 'child wardrobe'. This holds surely for the denotative uses of evaluatives, while for the pragmatic use, the "landing site" may vary: so for the meaning 'little bore m./f', *rompiball-ino/a* '[break-ball(s)]-DIM:M/F:SG' alternates on the Web with *rompiballine* 'break-[ball:DIM:(F):PL]'.

7 References

Aronoff, Mark (1994): *Morphology by Itself. Stems and Inflectional Classes.* Cambridge, MA: MIT Press.

Baayen, Harald (2001): *Word-Frequency Distributions.* Dordrecht: Kluwer.

Bauer, Laurie (2010): The typology of exocentric compounding. In: Sergio Scalise and Irene Vogel (eds.), *Cross-Disciplinary Issues in Compounding,* 167–175. Amsterdam/Philadelphia: Benjamins.

Booij, Geert (1994): Against split morphology. In: Geert Booij and Jaap van Marle (eds.), *Yearbook of Morphology 1993,* 27–49. Dordrecht: Kluwer.

Bisetto, Antonietta (1999): Note sui composti VN dell'italiano. In: Paola Benincà, Alberto Mioni and Laura Vanelli (eds.), *Fonologia e morfologia dell'italiano e dei dialetti d'Italia. Atti del XXXI Congresso internazionale di studi della Società di Linguistica Italiana,* 505–538. Roma: Bulzoni.

Bork, Hans Dieter (1990): *Die lateinisch-romanischen Zusammensetzungen Nomen + Verb und der Ursprung der romanischen Verb-Ergänzung-Komposita.* Bonn: Romanistischer Verlag.

Corbin, Danielle (1992): Hypothèses sur les frontières de la composition nominale. *Cahiers de Grammaire* 17: 25–55.

Corbin, Danielle (2004): Français (Indoeuropéen: Roman). In: Geert Booij, Christian Lehmann, Joachim Mugdan and Stavros Skopeteas (eds.), *Morphology. An International Handbook on Inflection and Word-formation.* Vol. 2, 1285–1299. Berlin/New York: de Gruyter.

Coseriu, Ernesto (1977): Inhaltliche Wortbildungslehre (am Beispiel des Typs "coupe-papier"). In: Herbert E. Brekle and Dieter Kastovsky (eds.), *Perspektiven der Wortbildungsforschung,* 48–61. Bonn: Bouvier.

Darmesteter, Arsène (1894): *Traité de la formation des mots composés dans la langue française comparée aux autres langues romanes et au latin.* 2nd ed. Paris: Champion.

Floričić, Franck (2008): The Italian verb-noun anthroponymic compounds at the syntax/morphology interface. *Morphology* 18(2): 167–193.

Gaeta, Livio and Davide Ricca (2009): *Composita solvantur*: Compounds as lexical units or morphological objects? *Italian Journal of Linguistics* 21(1): 35–70.

Gather, Andreas (2001): *Romanische Verb-Nomen-Komposita. Wortbildung zwischen Lexikon, Morphologie und Syntax.* Tübingen: Narr.

Gràcia, Lluïsa (2002): Formació de mots: composició. In: Joán Solà, Maria Rosa Lloret, Joan Mascaró and Manuel Pérez Saldanya (eds.), *Gramàtica del català contemporani.* Vol. 1, 777–829. Barcelona: Empúries.

Grossmann, Maria (1986): Anàlisi dels compostos catalans del tipus *somiatruites. Estudis de Llengua i de Literatura catalanes* 12: 155–169.

Grossmann, Maria (2012): Romanian compounds. *Probus* 24: 147–173.

Grossmann, Maria and Franz Rainer (2009): Italian adjective-adjective compounds: Between morphology and syntax. *Italian Journal of Linguistics* 21(1): 71–96.

Lloyd, Paul (1966): A possible structural factor in the development of Verb-Noun Compounds in the Romance languages. *Studia Neophilologica* 38: 257–262.

Magni, Elisabetta (2010): From the periphery to the core of Romance [VN] compounds. *Lingue e linguaggio* 9: 3–39.

NGLE (2009): *Nueva gramática de la lengua española.* Madrid: Asociación de Academias de la Lengua Española.

Osthoff, Hermann (1878): *Das Verbum in der Nominalcomposition im Deutschen, Griechischen, Slawischen und Romanischen.* Jena: Costenoble.

Pellegrini, Matteo and Davide Ricca (2019): An instance of productive overabundance: The plural of some Italian VN compounds. *Word Structure* 12(1): 94–126.

Plag, Ingo (1999): *Morphological Productivity. Structural Constraints in English Derivation*. Berlin: Mouton de Gruyter.

Progovac, Ljiljana (2006): Fossilized imperative in compounds and other expressions: Possible implications for historical and evolutionary studies. In: *Online Proceedings of the First Meeting of Slavic Linguistics Society*. Bloomington, IN. http://www.docin.com/p-442356629.html and http://www.researchgate.net/publication/228732520_Fossilized_Imperative_in_Compounds_ and_Other_Expressions_Possible_Implications_for_Historical_and_Evolutionary_Studies [last access 30 Oct 2014].

Rainer, Franz (1993): *Spanische Wortbildungslehre*. Tübingen: Niemeyer.

Rainer, Franz (2001): Compositionality and paradigmatically determined allomorphy in Italian word-formation. In: Chris Schaner-Wolles, John Rennison and Friedrich Neubarth (eds.), *Naturally! Linguistic studies in honour of Wolfgang Ulrich Dressler presented on the occasion of his 60th birthday*, 383–392. Torino: Rosenberg & Sellier.

Rainer, Franz and Soledad Varela (1992): Compounding in Spanish. *Rivista di Linguistica* 4(1): 117–142.

Ricca, Davide (2005): Al limite tra sintassi e morfologia: I composti aggettivali V-N nell'italiano contemporaneo. In: Maria Grossmann and Anna M. Thornton (eds.), *La formazione delle parole. Atti del XXXVII congresso della Società di Linguistica Italiana*, 465–486. Roma: Bulzoni.

Ricca, Davide (2008): VN compounds in Italian: Data from corpora and theoretical issues. Paper presented at the CompoNet Congress on Compounding, Bologna, 6–7/6/2008.

Ricca, Davide (2010): Corpus data and theoretical implications: With special reference to Italian V-N compounds. In: Sergio Scalise and Irene Vogel (eds.), *Cross-Disciplinary Issues in Compounding*, 167–175. Amsterdam/Philadelphia: Benjamins.

Río Torto, Graça and Sílvia Ribeiro (2012): Portuguese compounds. *Probus* 24: 119–145.

Scalise, Sergio (1984): *Generative Morphology*. Dordrecht: Foris.

Scalise, Sergio (1994): *Morfologia*. Bologna: Il Mulino.

Scalise, Sergio and Antonietta Bisetto (2009): The classification of compounds. In: Rochelle Lieber and Pavol Štekauer (eds.), *The Oxford Handbook of Compounding*, 34–53. Oxford: Oxford University Press.

Schapira, Charlotte (1985): Les composés roumains à thème verbal et leur place dans l'ensemble des langues romanes. *Revue de Linguistique Romane* 49: 15–26.

Štichauer, Pavel (2009): Compounds in Czech. *Lingue e linguaggio* 8(2): 188–209.

Štichauer, Pavel (2016): Verb-noun compounds in Italian from the 16th century onwards: An increasing exploitation of an available word-formation pattern. *Morphology* 26(2): 109–131.

Tollemache, Federico (1945): *Le parole composte nella lingua italiana*. Roma: Rores.

Val Álvaro, José Francisco (1999): La composición. In: Ignacio Bosque and Violeta Demonte (eds.), *Gramática descriptiva de la lengua española*. Vol. 3, 4757–4841. Madrid: Espasa.

Varela, Soledad (1990): Composición nominal y estructura temática. *Revista española de lingüística* 20: 55–81.

Villoing, Florence (2009): Les mots composés VN. In: Bernard Fradin, Françoise Kerleroux and Marc Plénat (eds.), *Aperçus de morphologie du français*, 175–198. Saint-Denis: Presses Universitaires de Vincennes.

Zuffi, Stefano (1981): The nominal composition in Italian: Topics in generative morphology. *Journal of Italian Linguistics* 2: 1–54.

Bernhard Wälchli

9 Co-compounds

Abstract: Co-compounds are word-like tight units mostly consisting of two parts which express natural coordination and superordinate-level concepts in contrast to sub-compounds which mostly express subordinate-level concepts. In this article it is argued that co-compounds should be considered in their natural environment in texts, since they do not only have characteristic formal and semantic properties, but most importantly characteristic patterns of use. In Europe co-compounds occur particularly in Eastern languages, but also in Basque. However, cross-linguistically co-compounding forms a discrete cline rather than a parametric feature that languages have or lack.

1 Introduction

Co-compounds (also known as dvandva, copulative compounds, or pair words [Russian *parnye slova*], cf. Olsen 2015) are word-like tight units consisting of two parts (or more rarely, more than two parts) which express natural coordination, viz. coordination of things or events that often occur together with characteristic lexical domains including pairs of relatives (Rural Tok Pisin [Mühlhäusler 1979: 377] *papa-mama* 'father-mother' > 'parents', *brata-susa* 'brother-sister' > 'siblings'), body parts (*han-lek* 'hand-foot' > 'limbs'), clothes (*su-soken* 'shoe-sock' > 'footwear'), and collectives and abstract notions (*rit-rait* 'reading-writing' > 'skills learned at school'). They are not characteristic of European English or other Standard Average European languages, but can be exemplified, for instance, with Indian English:

Bernhard Wälchli, Stockholm, Sweden

https://doi.org/10.1515/9783111420554-009

(1) Indian English: reported speech in an English novel
   a. 'Are you maybe married already, captain? Got <u>wife-children</u> waiting somewhere?'
   b. 'However we can help our <u>father-mother</u> that is what it is for us to do.' (Rushdie 1981: 403, 228)

Co-compounds tend to cluster areally. They typically occur with moderate or high frequency in languages of Asia and Eastern Europe, New Guinea, and Mesoamerica. There is nothing in the structure of Standard Average European languages that prevents them from having co-compounds, as their presence in non-European varieties of English demonstrates.

Following the Sanskrit grammarians, traditional morphology considers any compound whose syntactic paraphrase is a coordination (*ca-arthé* 'and-denoting') to be a dvandva-compound, thus disregarding that coordination can be manifested in very different ways in compounds. Here it is argued that it is indispensable to consider the meaning of the whole compound in order to define compound types. While subordinate compounds (sub-compounds) typically denote subordinate-level concepts (Mari [Uralic] *kid-tup* 'hand-back, back of the hand'), co-compounds typically express superordinate-level concepts (Mari *kid=jol* 'hand=foot > hand and feet, limbs'). This was first noted in the description of coordinate compounds in American Sign Language (Klima and Bellugi 1979). Wälchli (2005) restricts the term "co-compound" to coordinative compounds denoting superordinate-level concepts. However, the superordinate-level meaning component of co-compounds is not equally strong in all examples, which is associated with the fact that the meanings of co-compounds exhibit family resemblance. There is no semantic feature that applies equally well to all examples. "Superordinate-level concept" is the closest one can come with a single criterion. However, compounds with a coordinate and appositional relationship between the parts which denote subordinate-level compounds, such as intermediate-denoting compounds (*southwest*), appositional compounds (French *wagon-restaurant*, see article 7 on noun-noun compounds in French and section 3.3) and complex numerals (*twenty-three*) are excluded.

Formally, co-compounds are tight or "word-like" units (they typically, but not universally, lack overt markers of conjunction); only in few languages are co-compounds phonological words as, for example, in Modern Greek and Classical Sanskrit. Usually co-compounds are intermediate between words and phrases, which is represented graphically in many orthographies by hyphenation. In this article hyphens are rendered as equal signs to avoid confusion with the hyphens used in the glosses for the delimitation of morphemes. Co-compounds are dealt with from a typological point of view in Wälchli (2005, 2007a), Bauer (2009), and

Arcodia, Grandi and Wälchli (2010). This article focuses on co-compounds in Europe and on the fundamental context-dependent nature of co-compounds – which is notoriously underestimated in most approaches to word-formation.

Co-compounds are properties of particular texts belonging to particular registers and cannot easily be detached from the context in which they occur. Consider, for instance, the Russian example *travka=muravka* in (2). Many texts in Russian, especially in Literary Standard Russian, do not contain any co-compounds at all. (2) is from a Bylina, an epic poem, for which the abundant use of several word-formation devices, such as diminutives and co-compounds is characteristic.

(2) *Pod nim   trav-ka=murav-ka ne topč-et-sja*   Russian (Bylina)
     Under he:INST grass-DIM=ant-DIM not crush-PRS3SG-RFL
     'Under his feet the grass and ants are not crushed'
     (Propp and Putilov 1958: 258)

The Byliny constitute part of spoken rural Russian. However, it would be wrong to say in general that *travka=muravka* 'grass=ant' is a co-compound of rural Russian, it can only be understood in the particular context from which (2) is taken. The example is about the hero Čurila Plenkovič who is so noble that he does not even crush what is below his feet when he walks. *Travka=muravka* is an excellent example for illustrating the function of co-compounds to denote concepts above the basic level of conceptualization. The general notion of 'animals and plants you can crush when you walk' is instantiated by the two prototypes 'grass' and 'ant'. In this context, *grass and ants* exemplify natural coordination. However, it is difficult to imagine any other context where 'grass-ant' would be a suitable instance of a natural pair. A further important factor in (2) favoring the use of a co-compound is the generalizing and non-referential context. We are not talking about concrete animals and plants but rather about eventualities for which collective terms are highly suitable.

Given the importance of the meaning of the whole, it is not particularly useful to classify co-compounds according to the semantic relationship between the parts. Rather, the semantic relationship between parts and whole must be considered. Wälchli (2005: 138) proposes a convenient sub-classification into ten types: *additive* (the whole C is A and B, as in (1, 5, 15)), *generalizing* (C is everything/everybody/everywhere/always with A and B as extreme components as in (6, 8)), *collective* (the whole C is represented by the prototypical members A and B, as in (2)), *synonymic* (C is in the context the same as A and as B as in (3, 4, 6, 9)), *ornamental* (B or A is misleading and does not contribute to C, as in (22)), *imitative* (B or A is phonologically similar to the other part and does not mean anything), *figurative* (C belongs to a domain that differs from the domain to which

A and B belong as in (24)), *alternative* (C is A or B), *approximative* (C is A or B or something close to A or B), *scalar* (C is a scale defined by the poles A and B as in (23)). Examples for all types are given below in passing.

The contextual character of co-compounds is particularly notable in synonymic co-compounds where the parts A and B are not general synonyms, but only happen to mean the same thing in a concrete context of usage. This is illustrated in (3) from Hungarian:

(3) *mi   ügy-e=baj-a*   *van*   Hungarian
     what thing/matter-POSS3SG=trouble-POSS3SG be:PRS3SG
     nek-i   valahol.
     DAT-POSS3SG somewhere
     '[Because why shouldn't I ask you,] what's wrong with him. [But I said nothing.]'
     (Füst 2000: 25)

The two words *ügy* 'thing/matter' and *baj* 'trouble' are far from meaning the same thing in general. However in the given context *Mi ügye van?* 'What's the matter?' and *Mi baja van?* 'What's wrong?' are nearly synonymous. This example shows that co-compounds are not formed by a combination of lexemes in abstraction of their contextual meanings. Rather co-compounds are formed by a combination of word-form tokens in a concrete speech situation. However, co-compounds are not simply a coordination reduction of two sentences. This can be seen in (3) if case marking is considered. The dative (*nek*) is idiomatic with *baj-a* 'wrong-its'. However, with *ügy-e* 'matter-its' in isolation the comitative (*vel*) would be used. Example (3) may further serve to illustrate the ways in which co-compounds denote concepts above the basic level of conceptualization. The meaning of the whole co-compound is particularly relevant. The level of the whole compound need not be more general than the meaning of the parts. If the parts denote general concepts already (and there are few nouns with more general meaning than *ügy* 'thing') there is no need for the co-compound to be more general than the simplex would be on its own.

Co-compounds can be formed from words from a large variety of non-grammaticalized word classes: nouns, verbs, adjectives, adverbs, demonstratives, and numerals. Numerals are typically used to form alternative co-compounds such as Mari *ik=kok* 'one=two > one or two' or approximative co-compounds such as Chuvash *pĕr=ikĕ* 'one=two > some' (Paasonen 1941: 197). Some languages including Mari and many Turkic languages seem to disprefer co-compounds consisting of finite verbs which may be associated with their dispreference for balanced coordination. However, occasionally verbal co-compounds with a converb in the first part may be encountered (cf. the discussion of (12) below).

It is not self-evident how co-compounds should be delimited from other phenomena. This follows quite naturally from the family resemblance character of the category and the absence of explicit formal marking in many languages (see section 2 below). The alternative type, for instance, is quite common even in Standard Average European (in English less so than in German and Italian) which otherwise avoid co-compounds. I include alternative co-compounds in particular because they are used in similar ways as other co-compounds in distributive contexts (see example (16) below). There is an old tradition of viewing co-compounds as a kind of reduplication, recently rearticulated in Inkelas and Zoll (2005). Wälchli (2007b) argues that co-compounds are clearly different from reduplication. Unlike co-compounds, reduplication has only one free lexical slot. In co-compounds the form of one part is not predictable from the form of the other part. For further delimitation problems, such as parallelism and serial verbs, see Wälchli (2005).

2 The meaning, use and form of co-compounds

Above I have argued that it is a major characteristic of co-compounds that they express natural coordination (as opposed to accidental coordination). However, natural coordination is not restricted to co-compounds. Most languages have a general tendency to express natural coordination in tighter formal units than accidental coordination, for instance, in English *to be able to read and write* (natural) vs. *to be able to read and to swim* (accidental). Put differently, tight coordination is iconic for natural coordination and loose coordination is iconic for accidental coordination. The iconic relationship between meaning and form is summarized in Table 9.1 (see also Wälchli 2005, ch. 2–3 for further discussion).

Tab. 9.1: The iconic relationship between different kinds of coordination.

	Semantic dimension	Formal dimension
Close relationship between the coordinands	Natural coordination	Tight coordination
Distant relationship between the coordinands	Accidental coordination	Loose coordination

A typical phrase-like tight coordination pattern are the so-called *bare binomials* in Germanic languages (Lambrecht 1984), such as *brother and sister, law and order*, German *Pfeil und Bogen* 'bow and arrow; lit. arrow and bow' whose essential formal property is the lack of articles (thus 'bare'). Whether bare or not, binomials tend to abound in legalese texts, e.g., *we decree and grant that all other cities, boroughs, towns, and ports shall have all their liberties and free customs; safe and secure by land and water* (Magna Charta 13; 42). Binomials differ from co-compounds in that the coordinands can consist of more than one word (e.g., *free custom*) which is not characteristic of co-compounds (except for Northwest Caucasian, see (7) below). Binomials often tend to be formulaic, e.g., French *au fur et à mesure* 'gradually as', German *an Ort und Stelle* 'in place', and this is paralleled by co-compounds. The Kazan Tatar synonymic co-compound *köç=xäl* 'power=power', for instance, tends to occur especially in the collocation *köç=xäl belän* 'power=power with > just barely, with pain and misery' (cf. German *mit Mühe und Not*):

(4) *Ğabbar köç=xäl   belän burıç-tan kot-ıl-a.*   Kazan Tatar
     Ğabbar power=power with debt-ABL save-PASS/MIDD-PRS3SG
     'Ğabbar gets away from debt only with pain and misery.'
     (Fäjsi 1993: 108)

Binomials also share the property with co-compounds that they can contain a component without any meaning of its own. English *kith* in *with kith and kin* or *fro* in *to and fro* only occur in these combinations very much like Turkish *çoluk* is restricted to the imitative co-compound *çoluk çocuk* 'IMI child > wife and family'.

While some co-compounds occur in contexts where other languages can have phrasal coordination or a phrase-like tight coordination pattern such as bare binomials as translational equivalents, there are many other co-compounds which correspond to single words in languages with few or no co-compounds. This is shown in Wälchli (2007: 163) who considers the distribution of co-compounds and coordination in 18 passages in translations of the Gospel according to Mark in a genealogically diverse sample of 41 languages from all continents. The use of co-compounds extends from typical coordinative contexts ('night and day', 'parents, father and mother', 'to come and go') to typical one-word contexts, such as 'children', 'clothes', 'fields', and 'people'. That co-compounds often correspond to words rather than to coordinate phrases can be illustrated also with their use in proverbs. In (5) from Komi, 'to sow' is expressed with the co-compound 'to plow=sow'. Of course, sowing usually presupposes that the field has been plowed first and 'plow' and 'sow' thus are a natural pair. However, for the proverb 'plowing' is completely irrelevant and it would be rather strange in English to say 'You reap what you plow and sow'.

(5) *Myj ger-an=kedź-an,*   *sija=j*   *pet-al-as.*   Komi
     what plow-PRS2SG=sow-PRS2SG, that=also result-FUT-3SG
     'You reap what you sow.'
     (Timušev 1971: 75)

As far as form is concerned, co-compounds are often not distinctively marked in
any particular way. They simply consist of a juxtaposition of unmarked parts as
in (1) and (5). However, if they are marked, it is very common for them to have
a double marking strategy where both parts of the compound bear the same
marker. Double marking is formally symmetric and hence iconic for the symmetric construction type of coordination (Haiman 1985). Double marking often derives from the same syntactic function of the two parts of the compound as in (3)
with the repeated Hungarian possessive suffix; this might be called "inflectional
harmony". However, double marking can also involve derivational morphology
as with the repeated diminutive suffix in the Russian example (2). The tendency
toward "inflectional harmony" can be so strong as to require a repeated affix
even if the affix would not occur if a simplex word was used instead of a co-
compound. In Mordvin, for instance, most co-compounds in the nominative singular indefinite, which is unmarked, will usually take the plural suffix *-t/-ť* in both
parts of the co-compound, even if only the whole co-compound is to be interpreted as a plural, not the individual parts: Erzya Mordvin *ťeťa-t=ava-t* 'father-PL=
mother-PL > parents' (lit. 'fathers-mothers'). Such co-compound-specific double
marking is particularly common for generalizing co-compounds. In Mari (6), it is
usually the possessive suffix of the third person singular or an additive focus
clitic, in Mordvin it is the otherwise non-productive comitative marker *-n'ek*
(*pokš-n'ek=viški-n'ek* 'big-COM=small-COM'):

(6) *Tid-lan verčin   Orina-n šüm=čon-žo*   Meadow Mari
     this-DAT because Orina-GEN heart=soul-POSS3
     jüd-žö=kečy-že   *tulšol* *gaj*
     night-POSS3=day-POSS3 embers like
     'Because of that Orina's heart hurt night and day like glowing embers.'
     (Šketan 1991: 16)

Example (6) from Mari further illustrates that co-compounds also can be single
marked. The synonymic co-compound *šüm=čon* 'heart=soul' in (6) bears a single
possessive suffix. Single marking is iconic for minimal distance which is typical
for tight coordination, but languages differ in their preference for double and
single marking strategies. While in Mordvin the majority of co-compounds are

Tab. 9.2: Iconicity in marking strategies for natural coordination.

	Symmetry	Minimal distance
Zero marking strategy	(+)	+
Single marking strategy	–	+
Double marking strategy	+	–

double marked, Mari and Tatar have a large proportion of single marked co-compounds.

Whether there is a co-compound-specific double marker does not depend only on the semantic subtype of the co-compound. Not all generalizing co-compounds in Mordvin are marked with -n'ek/nek (Wälchli 2005: 140). What is important to note here is that for many languages there is no single general rule that can produce the form of all co-compounds and not even of one semantic subtype of co-compounds.

The morphologically most complex co-compounds in Europe are probably found in Northwest Caucasian languages which are known for their high degree of polysynthesis. In Abkhaz it is no problem to have co-compounds with parts consisting of more than two words. However, there is usually one part repeated and one part varied as in (7). The co-compound 'ɥ-aχa='ɥə-mṣ 'two-day=two-night' is even interesting from a semantic point of view; while 'night and day' is natural coordination, be it generalizing as in (6) or additive as in Latvian *vien-u dien-nakt-i* 'one-ACC:SG day-night-ACC:SG > one day (period of 24 hours)', (7) from Abkhaz is a rather unusual kind of additive co-compound. It would be expected that 'two' should have scope over the whole co-compound, but it is part of each member.

(7) 'ɥ-aχa='ɥə-mṣ   'a-ţs'aqʷa-'ra   j-a-'ţs'ə-n   Abkhaz
     two-night=two-day its-nick-MASDAR it-it-be.in-FIN
     '[Since it (the woodpecker) knew that, if he (the hero Abrskj'yl) went to
     sleep, he would actually not so quickly wake up, it perched calmly beside
     his staff and spent] 2 days and nights chipping away at it.'
     (Hewitt 2005: 242)

In (8) the prefixes *na-* 'thither' and *a:-* 'hither' yield a typical generalizing co-compound ('> in all directions'). Similar generalizing co-compounds with alternating prefixes can also be found in Kartvelian languages (see Wälchli 2005: 201).

(8) *a-'χʷ(.)ada-'kʷa* <u>*na-p'ṣə=a:-p'ṣə-rta-n*</u>   Abkhaz
     the-hillock-PL <u>thither-look=hither-look-place-FIN</u>
     '[And it is known why Abrskj'yl would choose hillocks as hiding-place:]
     hillocks were places with an all-round view; [as soon as his enemies
     emerged, they at once fell under his sights.]'
     (Hewitt 2005: 222)

The morphologically complex co-compounds in Northwestern Caucasian are a
morphological variant of discontinuous co-compounds which are not characteristic of European languages, but occur in many languages of Asia (e.g., Hmong,
Khasi, Karen), Mesoamerica (e.g., Mixe, Chinantec) and New Guinea (e.g., Toaripi).
In discontinuous co-compounds, the parts of the compound A and B are interrupted by a repeated element C, often a word, according to the formula CACB or
ACBC. An example from Hmong Daw where discontinuous co-compounds are
very frequent is the synonymic co-compound *teb chaws* 'land land > land' as in
kuw lub teb lub chaw 'I CL land CL land, my land' or *Yawm Pus teb Yawm Pus
chaw* 'Yau Pu's land'; Bisang 1988: 36, 56, 37; Wälchli 2005: 102).

   A further peculiar feature of co-compounds in some Caucasian languages is
that they can contain affixes for 'and', which can be observed in the two synonymic co-compounds in Abkhaz in (8). Suffixes for 'and' in co-compounds can
also be found in some Nakh-Dagestanian languages.

(9) <u>*pṣa-ra-j='saχʲa-j*</u>   *χʲdzə-j='pṣa-j*   Abkhaz
     <u>look-ABST-and=face-and</u> <u>name-and=reputation-and</u>
     Ø-z-'gə-mə-z   *'pħʷəz-ba*   *ssəjr-k'*
     <u>they-whom-be.lacking-not-NFIN</u> woman-young   lovely-a
     '[Very long ago there was in Abkhazia] a wonderful maiden who lacked
     neither looks nor reputation.'
     (Hewitt 2005: 209–210)

The examples from Abkhaz show again that the form of co-compounds cannot
be generated by a single rule. Some co-compounds have overt markers of coordination, some not. While prefixes are usually repeated in co-compounds, there
is a more varied picture as far as suffixes are concerned. In some verbal co-
compounds suffixes occur on both parts, in others only on the second part as in
(8).

3 Co-compounds in Europe and elsewhere

Co-compounds are characteristic of languages of three macro-areas: Eurasia, New Guinea and Mesoamerica. In Eurasia the highest density of co-compounds is found in the easternmost continental languages (e.g., Mandarin, Vietnamese, Hmong) and the frequency of co-compounding decreases towards the west. Europe is the westernmost part of this continuum, there is no special European kind of co-compounding. Co-compounds in the Caucasus, for instance, have about the same frequency level in European and Asian Caucasian languages at least as far as non-Indo-European languages are concerned. European co-compounds are simply Eurasian co-compounds in languages with moderate, low or very low levels of co-compounding. A first question to address then is whether there are any characteristic ways in which Eurasian co-compounds differ from co-compounds in New Guinea and Mesoamerica.

For at least some languages of Mesoamerica, metaphorical co-compounds are highly characteristic. In Classical Nahuatl there are almost only metaphorical co-compounds, e.g., *yn j-petla-tzin in i-cpla-tzin* 'DEF his-mat-HON DEF his-seat-HON > throne, government' and they are characteristic devices of elaborate style (Lehmann and Kutscher 1949). Metaphorical co-compounds do occur in European languages (see, e.g., example (24)), but they are never as dominant as they can be in a Mesoamerican language.

Languages in New Guinea with co-compounds including Tok Pisin typically have a co-compound for 'people' consisting of the parts 'man-woman' and this form tends to be highly frequent in texts, e.g., Tok Pisin *man-meri* 'man-woman > people', Abau *uwr-sa* 'man-woman > people', East Kewa *oná-aa* 'woman-man > people', Kobon *nibi bi* 'woman man > people'. The same also occurs in some Australian languages with co-compounds: Wik Mungkan *pam wanch* 'man woman > people'. In all the languages mentioned here this co-compound occurs on average in about every seventh verse or more of the translation of the New Testament. Therefore, a useful simple strategy for finding co-compounds in New Guinea is to consider the expression for 'people'. This test does not work at all in Eurasia.

It is not easy to decide which European languages have and which ones lack co-compounds. Co-compounding is a continuous, not a discrete feature. Co-compounds are not evenly distributed across different registers and styles in a language. There are, for instance, huge differences between newspaper, fiction and traditional folklore in Erzya Mordvin (Wälchli 2005: 220). In Russian, most texts in the literary language lack co-compounds almost completely, while they are quite frequent in the epic Byliny (see example (2) above) and are common even in colloquial style in Modern Russian. Tkačenko (1979) observes an areal continuum across East Slavic varieties in the frequency of the co-compound *žili=byli* 'lived=were > (once upon a time there) were' in the beginning of fairy tales (even though *žili=byli* 'lived=were' originally might derive from a pluperfect, see Kiparsky 1967: 230 for discussion). For cross-linguistic comparison it is most convenient to consider parallel texts which largely represent the same register and style (Wälchli 2005, ch. 6).

The most reliable single word indicator for co-compounds in Eurasia is 'parents'. Nominal additive co-compounds are a central group of co-compounds and within them kinship terms tend to be salient and the domain 'parents' is particularly important for natural coordination of kinship terms. However, not even the 'parent'-test divides Eurasian languages into two neat groups. There are some languages such as Georgian and Turkish where 'parents' can, but need not, be expressed by a co-compound and in Latvian there is usually a co-compound for 'parents' only in folk songs (in the *dainas*) but not elsewhere. This is opposed to languages such as Avar, Mordvin and Chuvash where the co-compound is the only lexicalized option for 'parents' (see Map 6.2 in Wälchli 2005: 217).

The areal east-west distribution of co-compounds is salient for instance in Finno-Ugric and Turkic languages. Pitkanen-Heikkilä (2016) claims that dvandva compounds are the oldest type of compounds in Finnish, but the Finnic languages and Hungarian have a considerably lower frequency of co-compounds than Mordvin and Komi. Uotila (1980) observes parallels in the extent of co-compounding in Finnic and Baltic languages.

In Turkic languages across Eurasia co-compounds form an areal cline. As a tendency they are more frequent in Eastern than in Western Turkic languages irrespective of the genealogic affiliation within Turkic. It is no coincidence that co-compounds are not mentioned for Karaim in Lithuania which is strongly influenced by Slavic languages. Example (10) shows that Karaim prefers a Slavic loanword for 'parents'.

(10) *bu=mo dz'ed-łar jox juv'-d'a.*　　　　　　　　　　　　Karaim
　　　DEM=Q parent-PL NEG.EX house-LOC
　　　'Are the parents not at home?'
　　　(Kowalski 1929: 112)

An extremely simplistic and therefore inaccurate approximation to describing the occurrence of co-compounds in Europe would be to say that co-compounds are lacking in Indo-European and Semitic and are present in all other languages of Europe. In fact, if you browse through the articles in the final two volumes of Müller, Ohnheiser, Olsen and Rainer (2015–2016) you will find co-compounds described for most non-Indo European languages but not for most Indo-European languages of Europe. Notable exceptions for Indo-European include Tat and Modern Greek (and rural Russian for which there is no article).

Co-compounds in Greek are an innovation. According to Browning (1983: 99–100) dvandva compounds which first appear in late Hellenistic Greek become particularly frequent in the Turkish period. However, this does not mean that Greek co-compounds are generally due to language contacts with Turkish. Especially their form is very different. Greek co-compounds are exceptional in representing phonological words. This may be because at least some co-compounds have developed from exocentric compounds. In Classical Greek *andrógunos* 'hermaphroditic' is an adjective with a nominalized masculine form *andrógunos* 'coward, hermaphrodite'. According to Debrunner (1917) there is only one attested case in Classical Greek where, in an epigram, the adjective can be interpreted as a co-compound: *andróguna* (PL:N) *loutrá* 'baths for men and women' and there it is an adjective. It may therefore be assumed that Modern Greek *andró-guno* 'manwoman > couple' originates from an exocentric compound and not from coordination diachronically. Turkish co-compounds, however, often look very much like sequences of two words, especially in verbal co-compounds where the first part is a converb. Yet, there are some close lexical parallels between Modern Greek and Turkish, consider, e.g., (11) and (12) from the New Testament.

(11) *óso*   *pérn-i*   *na*   <u>*anigo-klisi*</u>   Modern Greek
as.much take-PRS3SG in.order.to <u>open-close:SUBJ3SG</u>
to   *máti*
DEF:SG:N eye
'in the twinkling of an eye'
(1st Corinthians 15:52)

(12) ... *göz* <u>*aç-ıp*</u>   <u>*kapa-yan-a*</u>   *dek* ...   Turkish
eye <u>open-CNV</u> <u>close-PTCP-DAT</u> as.far.as
'in the twinkling of an eye'
(1st Corinthians 15:52)

In translations into Turkic languages it is common to express the passage with two verbs 'to open' and 'to close' where the first is a converb (e.g., Kazan Tatar, Uzbek). In Kirgiz and Turkmen the collocation is hyphenated, marking in orthography that it is a co-compound. While most other translations use different strategies, "opening and closing of an eye" is not completely restricted to Turkic and Greek. In the Balkans we can add Albanian *hap e mbyll sytë* 'open and close eye:PL' and outside areal reach Portuguese *num abrir e fechar de olhos*, Spanish *en un abrir y cerrar de ojos* (only in the modern translation *en Lenguage Sencillo*) and in Africa Wolof *ci xef=ak=xippi* 'PREP blink=with=close.eyes'. The example shows that it is difficult to delimit co-compounds from other looser coordination strategies expressing natural coordination and that it is difficult to track down language contact effects beyond any doubt.

The most notable exception to the areal east-west co-compound cline in Europe is Basque which has far too many co-compounds for its western location. But if we now turn to Indo-European western languages, not even these lack co-compounds altogether as can be seen in examples (13) and (14) from French and Spanish. Additive co-compounds of adjacent periods of times such as days of the week are not unusual in Western Europe as, for instance, in (13) from French.

(13)   French
Le week-end est généralement le vendredi et le samedi dans les pays arabes, parfois jeudi et vendredi, exceptionnellement <u>samedi dimanche</u> (avec un temps laissé pour accomplir la prière le vendredi midi).
'The week-end is generally Friday and Saturday in the Arab countries, sometimes Thursday and Friday, in exceptional cases Saturday Sunday (with time left to perform the Friday noon prayer).'
(Wikipedia)

The Spanish example in (14) is more intricate:

(14) ... *el   bilingüismo   es   un   <u>vaivén</u>   y   no*   Spanish
       the   bilingualism   is   a   go:PRS3SG:and:come:IMP2SG   and   not
       sólo   un   ven ...
       only   a   come:IMP2SG
       'Bilingualism is a give and take and not only a take'
       (http://elpais.com/diario/1997/06/18/cultura/866584802_850215.html)

The masculine noun *vaivén* 'swaying, swinging, up and down, hither and thither' looks synchronically as if it was the present third singular form of 'go' (*va*) plus 'and' (*y*) plus the second person imperative of 'come' (*vén*). Since it does not make much sense if the category of the two parts is so different, the form might be a loan from Catalan *vaivé*. What is particularly interesting about (14) is that the second part of this entirely lexicalized noun becomes independent, but not in its original meaning of 'come!' A general description of the meaning of *vaivén* would be 'repeated alternative movement in more than one direction'. By "decomposing" it, the innovated part *vén* acquires the meaning of unidirectional movement. Example (14) is taken from a speech of the director of the Real Academia Española about the current situation of Spanish. It is a rhetorical device and it is convenient for the speaker in the context that the exact meaning of *vaivén* is difficult to pin down exactly. The example is, of course, a pun and hence of limited significance to the plain use of language. However, it demonstrates that co-compounds interfere with style and idiomatic language use.

4 Co-compounds as context-dependent and context-renewing units

Handbooks tend to have a bias on subject matters that can easily be generalized and abstracted from their concrete context of use. I have to break against this handbook convention here to emphasize the contextual embedding of co-compounds. The most fundamental misunderstanding many morphological approaches to compounding suffer from is the belief that categories of word-formation can be considered in abstraction of their contexts of use. An exception is Seiffert (2015) who argues that word-formation does not occur isolated as a rule. This is certainly true of co-compounds.

Even though there are few co-compounds which can only be interpreted if more than one sentence is taken into consideration, co-compounds are discourse units in the sense that they are context-dependent and context-renewing, to use a common slogan from conversation analysis (Atkinson and Heritage 1984). In order to illustrate this point, I will discuss selected co-compounds from one particular text in one European language Erzya Mordvin, the story *Vit'a Kil'd'az'even' er'amo* 'The life of Vitya Kil'djazev' (first part) by Vasilij Kudaškin published in the Erzya literary journal *S'atko* (Kudaškin 1996). It is a story of fourteen short chapters which is representative of Literary Erzya Mordvin. Vitya is a naughty schoolboy in a Mordvin village during the time of Stalinism before World War II.

The most obvious discourse structuring aspect of co-compounds is their use with proper nouns. A co-compound consisting of two names expresses that there is a close relationship between two persons; most often this is used for siblings, spouses or other pairs of relatives. In Kudaškin (1996) there are co-compounds of Vitya together with as many as four different other schoolboys and these work to structure the text into episodes of different adventures with different companions. Typically the other boy is first introduced as a simple name before the additive co-compound of proper names occurs. In (15) Mikita is Vitya's desk neighbor with whom he quarrels which is why the teacher makes the two of them stand in the corner. The co-compound illustrates the double plural marking mentioned in section 2 above.

(15) *Vit'a-t=Mikita-t*   *pr'a-n'*   *komavto-z'*   Erzya Mordvin
Vit'a-NOM:PL=Mikita-NOM:PL head-GEN bow-PTC
sirga-s-t'   *ugol-s*
set.off-PST-3PL corner-ILL
'Vitya and Mikita went to the corner bowing their heads.'
(Kudaškin 1996: 7)

The co-compounds of proper names depend on the previous context and create groups which are locally valid in episodes, not in the language as a whole, not even in one text as a whole.

Another context-dependent use of co-compounds is distributivity. Example (16) describes how Vitya as an older boy walks a long way to the school in town under difficult circumstances "through snow and dirt, through rain and storm" which is expressed by two co-compounds. While rain and storm often co-occur, snow and dirt can occasionally be combined, but more often they occur on different occasions. There is snow in winter and dirt in autumn and spring. The co-compound thus summarizes different difficult road conditions which apply on different occasions. The expression "wade through snow and dirt" does not make much sense if considered in isolation of this distributive context, marked here with the adverb *s'ejet'ste* 'often'.

(16) ... *s'ejet'ste kel'e-ms* *lov-ga=rudaz-ga,*   Erzya Mordvin
       often   wade-INF snow-PROL=dirt-PROL
piz'eme-n'=davol-on' pačk ...
rain-GEN=storm-GEN through
'[He studied in the second shift. He had to walk home in the dark and] often to wade through snow and dirt, through rain and storm.'
(Kudaškin 1996: 46)

The distributive use is particularly common with alternative and approximative co-compounds in examples such as "Each family had five-six horses".

Co-compounds often become good superordinate level concepts only in particular contexts. This can be illustrated with (17):

(17) *Paro azor-tnen'*   Erzya Mordvi
       good lord-PL:DEF:GEN
rozor-iz'=pan-s'-iz'
destroy/disown-PST3PL>3PL=chase-FREQ-PST3PL>3PL
'The good peasants were disowned and expelled'
(Kudaškin 1996: 23)

Example (17) occurs in an episode where Vitya sings a song on collectivization he has learned in school. His mother tells him to stop this, he asks why since they themselves are not kulaks (affluent farmers) and his mother replies that the others aren't either, that Stalin just made this up and that all the good peasants were disowned and expelled. It is difficult to imagine another context of use for the additive co-compound 'disown-expel' than collectivization and the formation of kolkhozes. The co-compound moreover comes with a specific evaluative attitude.

Very often co-compounds, and especially synonymic co-compounds, are emphatic. They mark important passages in the narrative structure of the text, where unexpected information is given (unexpected at least from the point of view of one or several actors in the story). In the context before (18) a rumor has circulated that the archangel Michael has sent thunder and lightning over the school because the teacher has put an atheistic play on stage, but Vitya reports that this is all nonsense. In order to emphasize that there is nothing wrong with the teacher, counter to the expectation created by the rumor, he uses the co-compound *šumbra=paro* 'healthy=well' with two contextually synonymous parts.

(18) *Men'-gak pur'gin'e aras'-el',*   *učitel'-es'*   Erzya Mordvin
      we-also   thunder NEG.EX-2ndPST, teacher-DEF
      šumbra=paro
      healthy=good
      'We hadn't any thunder, the teacher is well'
      (Kudaškin 1996: 19)

In another episode where Vitya confesses to his mother that he made a certain observation, the mother thinks, takes a deep breath and then quietly says: "Don't tell this to anybody, my son. Keep it to yourself." Emphasis is given to "think" by framing it as a co-compound: *ava-zo ars'e-s'=c'ota-s'* 'mother-POSS3SG think-PST3SG=calculate-PST3SG > his mother thought (for a while)'. The emphatic function is context-dependent and context-renewing.

Even if lexicalized uses of co-compounds make up the majority of tokens in the text, many occasional co-compounds can be found. Lexicalization is a cline rather than a discrete distinction, *ars'ems=c'otams* 'think-calculate > think', for instance, has an intermediate status on this cline. It is not listed in the dictionary, but can be regularly encountered in Literary Erzya Mordvin texts. Sometimes it is not really the co-compound in itself that is the lexicalized unit, but rather the co-compound functions as part of an idiom. This holds in particular, but not exclusively, for figurative co-compounds. The figurative co-compound *tarka= ez'em* 'place=bench' which must have originated as a contextually synonymic co-

compound in the context of a sitting accommodation, is hardly ever used other than in combination with *mujems* 'to find' in negation. In other texts in Literary Erzya Mordvin it sometimes has the metaphorical use of "not having found yet the right place in life". This co-compound is not listed in the dictionary however. Kudaškin (1996) contains two rather specific uses of it which demonstrate that the meaning of the idiom is much less fixed than the formal collocation of the co-compound with a lexical verb and negation. In the first passage it is the first day in school for Vitya, but he is so excited about the apples on the apple trees outside that he cannot concentrate on anything in the first lesson. He does not find "place-bench" (*tarka=ez'em e-z' muje* 'place-bench NEG-PST3SG find') which is meant entirely figuratively. It does not mean that he cannot find a seat. In the second passage the teacher is putting on stage an atheistic play at the end of which an actor puts a horse collar on the neck of an orthodox priest. The mother of the boy who is supposed to act the communist's role takes her son home saying that it is not good to mock people of God. This is now where the teacher does not find "place-bench": *tarka=ez'em e-z' mu-kšno* 'place-bench NEG-PST3SG find-FREQ'. He is put off his stride for a moment and does not know what to do; until he sees Vitya and so Vitya unexpectedly becomes an artist. What is interesting about this co-compound from a formal point of view is that it is never used with a suffix, there are no plural markers as is characteristic for most otherwise unmarked co-compounds and there is never a possessive suffix. This testifies to the idiomatic character of the co-compound. However, the semantics of the idiom is much less fixed than its form. The only thing that is clearly fixed is that the meaning must be metaphorical; it can mean anything ranging from 'not being concentrated' to 'being put off stride' to 'not having found one's vocation in life yet'. All these uses have a family resemblance, but the actual meaning of the co-compound can only be determined in a given context.

Preferred collocations are not restricted to figurative co-compounds, however. The common verbal co-compound *lovnoms=s'ormadoms* 'read=write' hardly ever occurs in any other context than that of learning or being able to read and write. In Kudaškin (1996: 39) it is used to state that Vitya's father learned to read and write himself without going to school.

On the opposite pole of least context-dependent lexical units we have the fully lexicalized example *t'et'a-t=ava-t* 'father-PL=mother-PL > parents' which is not only used for pairs of parents, but even in *t'et'a-n'=ava-n' promks-so* 'father-GEN=mother-GEN meeting-INE > in parents' meeting' (Kudaškin 1996: 36). However, some co-compounds of kinship terms are quite contextual. The girl Masha who replaces Mikita as Vitya's bench neighbor after the event in (15) is very quiet; she goes to school to relax from housework and her eight brothers and sisters: *kavkso sazor-tne-d'e=jalaks-tne-d'e* 'eight younger.sister-PL:DEF-ABL=younger.brother-PL:DEF-ABL'.

The co-compound tells us not only that Masha is older than all her brothers and sisters, but also that the younger sisters are somehow more prominent than the younger brothers (perhaps there are more sisters than brothers or Masha has to take care more of her sisters than of her brothers). In conventionalized co-compounds of kinship terms in Erzya the order is male-female. Masha's quiet character has the effect that her name never enters a co-compound together with Vitya, she is not a companion in any of his adventures.

5 Co-compounds and construction morphology

Here we will consider to what extent construction morphology might be useful to deal with co-compounds. At least at first glance, construction grammar seems very useful for co-compounds, given the relevance of both semantic properties (natural coordination, superordinate-level concepts) and formal properties (juxtaposition of two words) for co-compounds. Construction morphology allows for holistic properties of word structure which is appealing for co-compounds. We might therefore try to formulate a general schema for co-compounds such as (19):

(19) $<[X_iX_j]_{Xk} \leftrightarrow$ [Natural coordination of X_i and $X_j \rightarrow$
       superordinate level concept $X_k]_k>$

One difficulty is to determine whether the category labels for the parts should all be of the same category or of three different categories <X, Y, Z>. In a majority of cases the word class is the same, thus (19) is at least appropriate for prototypical co-compounds. However, it seems nearly impossible to reduce co-compounds and sub-compounds to one constructional schema which is well-in-line with Wälchli's (2005, ch. 4) claim that co-compounds are a construction type of their own and not a sub-type of compounds.

A highly problematic aspect of construction morphology, however, is that word-formation processes are viewed as parts of a hierarchical lexicon. This presupposes that word-formation is always a relation between parts and wholes which are types rather than tokens. Above I have argued that many co-compounds are not listed in the lexicon and that the parts of productive co-compounds are rather tokens than types, which means that many co-compounds are not formed in the lexicon. In order to become a useful framework for the description of co-compounds therefore, construction morphology must countenance the composition of tokens in particular given contexts.

Booij (2015, section 2) points out that in sub-compounds parts "may have lexicalized, yet productive meanings". This phenomenon is much more restricted with co-compounds. There are some schemas with productive parts. However, it is not clear whether they should be considered true co-compounds. In Erzya Mordvin there are nominal compounds of the type N-*t=mezt'* 'N-PL=what:PL > N and the like' and verbal compounds of the type V-*ms=t'eje-ms* 'V-INF=do-INF > V for a short while'. The former have a function similar to echo words in South Asia and *m*-doublets in Turkic and contact languages (see Wälchli 2005: 167–169 for a survey and further literature). Mordvin compounds with *mez'e* 'what' share a number of features with co-compounds. Generalizing examples and examples in comitative function have the suffix -*n'ek* on both parts which is characteristic for generalizing co-compounds in Mordvin: *pokš kudo-st sad-nek=mez-n'ek* 'big house-POSS3PL garden-COM=what-COM > their big house with garden and everything' (Kudaškin 1996: 22). Like co-compounds, N-*t=mezt'* 'N-PL=what:PL > N and the like' typically has a nominative indefinite plural marker on both parts if the form would be in the unmarked nominative indefinite singular otherwise. However, what seems to be peculiar to this type is that there can be wide scope semantically over a noun phrase with an adjective as in (20):

(20) *Raj-ev   ki-s'   avol'* <u>*paro*</u> *jarsamka-so=mez'e-se*   Erzya Mordvin
     paradise-LAT way-DEF NEG <u>good</u> food-INE=what-INE
     panžo-v-i
     open-MIDD-PRS3SG
     'The way to paradise does not open itself with good food and the like'
     (Doronin 1995: 52)

However, =*mez'e* '=what' is even used in a different pattern with single marking (unmarked first part) where the first part is a name and the whole has the function of an associative plural: *Vit'a=mez'e-n' šabra-st* 'Vitja=what-GEN neigbor-POSS3PL > the neighbors of Vitja and his people/his family' (Kudaškin 1996: 7). Whether or not the construction with =*mez'e* '=what' is a subtype of co-compounds, it consists in fact not of a single schema, but rather of a group of highly similar constructions with family resemblance. This is difficult to account for with a hierarchical schema-centered version of construction morphology.

The verbal compounds with =*t'ejems* '=do' has a function similar to the Russian delimitative prefix *po*-: *jarsa-s'=t'ej-s'* 'eat-PST3SG=do-PST3SG > he ate for a little while' (=Russian *po-el*). What is important for this pattern is that it cannot be abstracted from its context. It is hardly ever used at the end of a sentence; the activity is always interrupted because of a subsequent action that will take place: 'he ate (a bit) and hurried to school' (Kudaškin 1996: 39). While the construction might have originated from co-compounds and has the same double marking as verbal co-compounds, it has a quite different function from co-compounds semantically which is why it is probably best considered a construction of its own. However, it seems that this construction is not completely unrelated to co-compounds.

The two examples with lexicalized parts discussed above show that the best chance for co-compounds to undergo a development towards affixoids is with a kind of pronominal, semantically empty part that can stand in a natural coordinative relationship to any noun or any verb. A similar, more restricted pattern are alternative co-compounds of the type *N=kavto* 'N=two > one or two N': *ije-s=kavto-s* 'year-ILL=two-ILL > for a year or two' (Kudaškin 1996: 38). The noun denotes most typically a period of time. The construction is actually a variant of the alternative co-compound *vejke=kavto* 'one=two' where the numeral for 'one' remains unexpressed.

While in sub-compounds the meaning of recurrent compound parts tends to lexicalize in the same way, recurrent parts of co-compounds actually tend to have different meanings in different co-compounds depending on the different kinds of natural coordination they enter in with their other part. However, in texts with a high frequency of co-compounds, in particular in the epic register, there may be some playful variation with parallelism of two co-compounds sharing one part (see also Wälchli 2007b for co-compounds and parallelism). Example (21) contains two synonymic co-compounds in a parallel setting which share one compound member (*jalga* 'comrade, friend'), while the second part is varied (*oj* 'friend', *duga* 'friend, brother, sister'). Here the syntagmatic aspect of repetition in a text is more important than the paradigmatic aspect of a common schema in the lexicon.

(21) *Vaj, jalg-in'e-m=oj-in'e-m/*   Erzya Mordvin, epic poem
      oh   friend-DIM-POSS1SG=friend-DIM-POSS1SG/
      Vaj, jalg-in'e-m=dug-in'e-m
      oh   friend-DIM-POSS1SG=sibling-DIM-POSS1SG
      'Oh my friend, oh my friend'
      (Šaronov 1994: 232)

The same poem contains another instance of *jalg-in'e-m=oj-in'e-m* and a co-compound with inverted order *ojam=jalgin'em*, this time with the diminutive only on the second part. The example shows that the study of recurrent patterns in texts is as important for construction morphology as the study of recurrent patterns in the lexicon. Co-compounds tend to exhibit sub-patterns in texts at least as much as sub-patterns in the lexicon.

A construction morphology approach which is suitable for co-compounds should take into account that certain patterns are characteristic of certain texts rather than of a language as a whole. In Russian there is a distinction in some motion events between '(to go/lead) on foot' and '(to go/lead) by vehicle or horse'.

In the Bylina *Knjaz' Roman i Mar'ja Jur'jevna* (Propp and Putilov 1958: 106–111) Mar'ja Jur'jevna is led away by the Lithuanian Voz'jak Kotobrul'evič. This is expressed with the co-compound *u-vez=u-vel* 'away-lead.by.vehicle/horse:PV:PST:SG:M= away-lead.on.foot:PV:PST:SG:M > (he) led (her) away'. It is not specified whether Mar'ja really walks and rides while being kidnapped or whether it is a synonymic co-compound where the subtle semantic difference is a pure ornament in the epic text. However, there is another co-compound following the same pattern in the same text 28 lines later: *s-xod-i=s"-jezd-i* 'PREV-go/walk:IPV-IMP2SG=PREV-ride/ go.by.vehicle:IPV-IMP2SG > go (you to the Lithuanian land)!' The two co-compounds obviously form a pattern with holistic properties of word structure; they are both co-compounds of motion verbs with a manner alternation (on foot vs. by horse/ vehicle). However, it is difficult to generalize them into a construction grammar schema since none of the formal elements is repeated (there is no part of a compound turned into an affixoid). Furthermore, the order of manner elements is not constant, in the first case it is 'by.horse=on.foot', in the second case 'on.foot= by.horse'. The pattern cannot be said to be a construction of Russian in general, it is a construction in one particular text with two tokens in that text, and it has a clear syntagmatic, and not merely a paradigmatic component. The second co-compound of the pattern is obviously primed by the first one.

A very good kind of evidence for constructions is priming where one token increases the probability of another token to occur nearby. Co-compounds co-occurring in the same text close to each other are thus good evidence for syntagmatic construction effects. Ornamental co-compounds, such as Erzya Mordvin *vel'e=s'ado* 'village=hundred > village' where one part is misleading and does not contribute to the meaning of the whole are characteristic only of some registers of Mordvin. They occur mainly in folk poetry and in folktales. Example (22) from a fairy tale contains two ornamental co-compounds: 'forest=maple > forest' and 'to belly=to back > have a belly, be pregnant'. The co-occurrence suggests that they prime each other.

(22) *Pek-ija-s'=lang-ija-s'*   Erzya Mordvin: fairytale
belly-DENOM-PST3SG=back-DENOM-PST3SG
s'ej-ine-s',   *tu-s'*   *vir'-ev=ukštor-ov*
goat-DIM-DEF depart-PST3SG forest-LAT=maple-LAT
l'evksija-mo.
have.young-INF
'A goat was pregnant, (it) went into the forest to have young.'
(Kemajkina 1993: 24)

Due to the interconnection of groups and the family resemblance of co-compounds it is sometimes rather unclear how a subschema of co-compounds should best be delimited. In Wälchli (2005: 153) I discussed scalar co-compounds (C is a scale defined by the poles A and B) only for East and South East Asian languages (e.g., Khalkha Mongolian *urt bogino* 'long short > length') and obviously overlooked the fact that Basque has them as well:

(23) ... *eta* <u>*luze=labur-rean*</u>   *eta* <u>*lodi=mehe-an*</u>   *alde*   Basque
  and <u>long=short-INE:DEF</u> and <u>thick=thin-INE:DEF</u> side/difference
  handi-a   dute.
  great-DEF be:PRS3PL
  '([Orb-weaver spiders/Araneidae] They have eight legs) and there are great differences in length and thickness (from one species to another).'
  (http://eu.wikipedia.org/wiki/Araneido, 17.12. 2012)

The scalar co-compound *luze=labur* 'long=short > length, distance, size' is lexicalized and frequently mentioned in dictionaries and grammars. In (23) it primes another co-compound of the same kind – *lodi-mehe* 'thick=thin > thickness' which is absent in most dictionaries and has only very few hits on Google. It is, however, not obvious that the only relevant sub-schema is that of scalar co-compounds. Artiagoitia, Ortiz de Urbina and Hualde (2016 on Basque and section 3.1.2) group *luze=labur* 'long=short > length' together with *on=gaitz-ak* 'good=bad-PL > pros and cons' in a group of [Adj=Adj]$_N$ copulative compounds, despite the different form (plural) and the figurative meaning. Actually it is difficult to predict the meaning of the co-compound consisting of *on* 'good' and *gaitz* 'bad', interestingly it does not mean 'quality'. However, even *on=gaitz-ak* 'good=bad-PL > pros and cons' has some closer relatives among Adj=Adj co-compounds, such as the co-compound in (24):

(24) *Hor   ere   <u>argi=ilun</u>   handi-ak daude*   Basque
  there even <u>light=dark</u> big-PL   are
  'Although there are large uncertainties'
  (http://goiena.net/albisteak/joxe-rojas-ezin-dugu-itxoin-euskarazko-hedabideak-desagertzera-haien-garrantzia-aitortzeko/)

Hualde and Ortiz de Urbina (2003: 352–353), however, identify an even larger group of co-compounds with an antonymy relationship where even *luze=zabal* 'long-wide > extension' is included. The dominant use of this co-compound is to denote the extension of two-dimensional surfaces in examples such as *Mexiko 1.964.375 km² da* 'Mexico covers an area of 1.964.375 km²' (Wikipedia). Thus, *luze= zabal* 'long-wide' denotes two scales rather than one. Knowing that there is a [Adj=Adj]$_N$ pattern in Basque is only of limited use to predict the meanings of their exponents and this is not only due to several more specific sub-patterns in the lexicon, but also to idiosyncrasies in concrete use.

We may conclude that construction morphology might be highly useful for co-compounds if it can be modified in such a way that it can take concrete patterns of use into account.

Acknowledgements

I would like to thank Fernando Zúñiga for many useful comments.

Abbreviations

1	1st person		INF	infinitive
2	2nd person		INST	instrumental
2ndPST	2nd past		IPV	imperfective
3	3rd person		LAT	lative
ABL	ablative		LOC	locative
ABSTR	abstract		M	masculine
CL	classifier		MIDD	middle
CNV	converb		N	neuter
COM	comitative		NEG	negation
DAT	dative		NFIN	non-finite
DEF	definite, definite article		NOM	nominative
DEM	demonstrative		PASS	passive
DENOM	denominal verb		PL	plural
DIM	diminutive		POSS	possessive affix
EX	existental		PREP	omni-purpose preposition
FIN	finite verb form		PREV	verbal prefix
FREQ	frequentative		PROL	prolative
FUT	future		PRS	present
GEN	genitive		PST	past
HON	honorific		PV	perfective
ILL	illative		Q	polar interogative
IMI	imitative part of imitative		RFL	reflexive
	co-compound		SUBJ	subjunctive
IMP	imperative		X > X	subject form > object form
INE	inessive			

6 References

Arcodia, Giorgio F., Nicola Grandi and Bernhard Wälchli (2010): Coordination in compounding. In: Sergio Scalise and Irene Vogel (eds.), *Cross-Disciplinary Issues in Compounding*, 177–197. Amsterdam/Philadelphia: Benjamins.

Artiagoitia, Xabier, José Ignacio Hualde and Jon Ortiz de Urbina (2016): Basque. In: Peter O. Müller, Ingeborg Ohnheiser, Susan Olsen and Franz Rainer (eds.), *Word-Formation. An International Handbook of the Languages of Europe*. Vol. 5, 3327–3348. Berlin/Boston: De Gruyter Mouton.

Atkinson, J. Maxwell and John Heritage (eds.) (1984): *Structures of Social Action. Studies in Conversation Analysis*. Cambridge: Cambridge University Press.

Bauer, Laurie (2008): Dvandvas. *Word Structure* 1(1): 1–20.

Bauer, Laurie (2009): Dvandva. *Word Structure* 1: 1–20.

Bisang, Walter (1988): Hmong Texte. Eine Auswahl mit Interlinearübersetzung aus Jean Mottin, Contes et légendes hmong blanc (Bangkok: Don Bosco 1980). Zürich: Seminar für Allgemeine Sprachwissenschaft der Universität Zürich.

Booij, Geert (2015): Word-formation in construction grammar. In: Peter O. Müller, Ingeborg Ohnheiser, Susan Olsen and Franz Rainer (eds.), *Word-Formation. An International Handbook of the Languages of Europe*. Vol. 1, 188–202. Berlin/Boston: De Gruyter Mouton.

Breindl, Eva and Maria Thurmair (1992): Der Fürstbischof im Hosenrock. Eine Studie zu den nominalen Kopulativkomposita des Deutschen. *Deutsche Sprache* 1: 32–62.

Browning, Robert (1983): *Medieval and Modern Greek*. London: Hutchinson University Library.

Çinkılıç Detmold, Gaye and Helmut Weiß (2012): Kopulativkomposita. *Linguistische Berichte* Heft 232: 417–435.

Debrunner, Albert (1917): *Griechische Wortbildungslehre*. Heidelberg: Winter.

Doronin, Aleksandr (1995): Bajagan' suľejť. Omboc'e kn'igas. *S'atko* 1995(7): 3–63.

Fəjsi, Əxmət (1993): *Keçkenə apuş*. Kazan: Kazan tatarstan kitap nəşprijaty.

Füst, Milan (2000): *A feleségem története. Störr kapitány feljegyzései*. Budapest: Fekete Sas Kiadó.

Haiman, John (1985): *Natural Syntax*. Cambridge: Cambridge University Press.

Hewitt, George (2005): *Abkhazian Folktales (with grammatical introduction, translation, notes, and vocabulary)*. München: LINCOM Europa.

Hualde, José I. and Jon Ortiz de Urbina (eds.) (2003): *A Grammar of Basque*. Berlin: Mouton de Gruyter.

Inkelas, Sharon and Cheryl Zoll (2005): *Reduplication. Doubling in Morphology*. Cambridge: Cambridge University Press.

Kemajkina, Raisa S. (ed.) (1993): *Jovkson' kužo. Erz'an' jovkst*. Saransk: Mordovskoj kn'ižnoj izdaťeľstvas'.

Kiparsky, Valentin (1967): *Russische historische Grammatik*. Vol. 2. Heidelberg: Winter.

Klima, Edward S. and Ursula Bellugi (1979.): *The Signs of Language*. Cambridge, MA: Harvard University Press.

Kowalski, Tadeusz (1929): *Karaimische Texte im Dialekt von Troki*. Kraków: Nakładem Polskiej Akademji Umiejętności.

Kudaškin, Vasilij (1996): Viťa Kiľďaz'even' er'amozo: Vas'enc'e peľks. *S'atko* 1996(3): 3–51.

Lambrecht, Knud (1984): Formulaicity, frame semantics and pragmatics in German binomial expressions. *Language* 60(4): 753–796.

Lehmann, Walter and Gerdt Kutscher (1949): *Sterbende Götter und christliche Heilsbotschaft. Wechselreden indianischer Vornehmer und spanischer Glaubensapostel in Mexiko 1524*. Stuttgart: Kohlhammer.

Mühlhäusler, Peter (1979): *Growth and Structure of the Lexicon of New Guinea.* Pidgin Camberra: Australian National University.

Müller, Peter O., Ingeborg Ohnheiser, Susan Olsen and Franz Rainer (eds.) (2015–2016): *Word-Formation. An International Handbook of the Languages of Europe.* 5 Vol. Berlin/Boston: De Gruyter Mouton.

Olsen, Susan (2014): Coordinative structures in morphology. In: Antonio Machicao y Priemer, Andreas Nolda and Athina Sioupi (eds.), *Zwischen Kern und Peripherie. Untersuchungen zu Randbereichen in Sprache und Grammatik*, 269–286. Berlin: De Gruyter.

Olsen, Susan (2015): Composition. In: Peter O. Müller, Ingeborg Ohnheiser, Susan Olsen and Franz Rainer (eds.), *Word-Formation. An International Handbook of the Languages of Europe.* Vol. 1, 364–386. Berlin/Boston: De Gruyter Mouton.

Paasonen, Heikki (1949): *Gebräuche und Volksdichtung der Tschuwassen.* Ed. by Eino Karahka and Martti Räsänen. Helsinki: Suomalais-ugrilaisen seura.

Pitkänen-Heikkilä, Kaarina (2016): Finnish. In: Peter O. Müller, Ingeborg Ohnheiser, Susan Olsen and Franz Rainer (eds.), *Word-Formation. An International Handbook of the Languages of Europe.* Vol. 5, 3209–3228. Berlin/Boston: De Gruyter Mouton.

Propp, Vladimir Jakovlevič and Boris Nikolaevič Putilov (1958): *Byliny.* Vol. 2. Moskva: Gosudarstvennoe izdatel'stvo xudožestvennoj literatury.

Ralli, Angela (2020): Coordination in Compounds. In: Rochelle Lieber (ed.), *The Oxford Encyclopedia of Morphology*, 726–742. Oxford: Oxford University Press.

Rushdie, Salman (1981): *Midnight's Children.* London: Vintage.

Šaronov, Aleksandr Markovič (1994): *Mastorava.* Saransk: Mordovijan' kn'igan' izdat'el'stvas'.

Seiffert, Anja (2015): Word-formation and text. In: Peter O. Müller, Ingeborg Ohnheiser, Susan Olsen and Franz Rainer (eds.), *Word-Formation. An International Handbook of the Languages of Europe.* Vol. 3, 2178–2191. Berlin/Boston: De Gruyter Mouton.

Šketan, M. (1991): *Čumyren lukmo ojporo. Kokymšo tom. Ojlymaš, myskara, novella, očerk, statja, korrespondencij, fel'eton-vlak.* Joškar-Ola: Marij kn'iga izdatel'stvo.

Timušev, Dmitrij A. (ed.) (1971): *Obrazcy komi-zyrjanskoj reči.* Syktyvkar: Akademija Nauk SSSR.

Tkačenko, Orest B. (1979): *Sopostavitel'no-istoričeskaja frazeologija slavjanskich i finno-ugrorskich jazykov.* Kiev: Naukova dumka.

Uotila, Eeva (1980): Asyndeton in the baltic and finnic languages: An archaic construction in its typological periphery. *Journal of Baltic Studies* 11(1): 86–91.

Wälchli, Bernhard (2005): *Co-Compounds and Natural Coordination.* Oxford: Oxford University Press.

Wälchli, Bernhard (2007a): Lexical classes: A functional approach to "word-formation". In: Matti Miestamo and Bernhard Wälchli (eds.), *New Challenges in Typology. Broadening the Horizons and Redefining the Foundations*, 153–175. Berlin: Mouton de Gruyter.

Wälchli, Bernhard (2007b): Ko-Komposita (im Vergleich mit Parallelismus und Reduplikation). In: Andreas Ammann and Aina Urdze (eds.), *Wiederholung, Parallelismus, Reduplikation. Strategien der multiplen Strukturanwendung*, 81–107. Bochum: Brockmeyer.

Ingeborg Ohnheiser

10 Compounds and multi-word expressions in Slavic

Abstract: Slavic languages, as compared to English or German, show significant limitations with respect to the formation of nominal compounds. These limitations are often compensated for by complex designations consisting of a relational adjective and noun or by other types of multi-word expressions. To a significant extent the increase of new vocabulary in modern Slavic languages feeds on borrowings and loan translations or hybrid words, a large part of which consists of different types of compounds and compound elements of foreign origin. Most of the new compounds continue to exhibit parallel designations in terms of multi-word expressions consisting of a relational adjective+noun or noun+noun$_{gen/prep.case}$. Their occurrence is often more frequent than that of compounds and thus represents the continuation of typical preferences in designation.

1 Introduction

In a study on the structural typology of the vocabulary of various Slavic languages, Isačenko (1958) addressed the interaction of different methods of designation in modern Slavic languages. In his study he referred primarily to different structures of multi-word expressions (also in relation to different loan influences experienced by Slavic languages) as well as to possible transformations of complex designations into one-word designations (compounds or derivatives). So, while there are multi-word expressions including formations of the genitive type in Russian,

Ingeborg Ohnheiser, Innsbruck, Austria

https://doi.org/10.1515/9783111420554-010

Czech frequently exhibits word combinations consisting of a relational adjective (RA) and noun (N) or suffixations, e.g., Cz. *srdeční vada* lit. 'heart-RA defect' vs. R. *porok serdca* 'heart defect; lit. defect heart$_{gen}$', Cz. *železnice* 'rail way; lit. iron(N/RA-stem)-SUFF' vs. R. *železnaja doroga* 'id.; lit. iron-RA way'. Polish designations (genitival and prepositional types, according to Isačenko) like *trzęsienie ziemi* 'earthquake; lit. quake earth$_{gen}$' and *dziurka do klucza* 'keyhole; lit. hole-DIM for key', might be paralleled with compounds in Russian (*zemletrjasenie* 'earth-quake') or RA+N (*zamočnaja skvažina* lit. 'lock-RA hole'). Other examples presented by Isačenko have meanwhile experienced changes: so alongside the original RA+N-combination *tisková konference* 'press conference', Czech also uses borrowings without relational adjectives (*press konference*), as was formerly the case in Russian (*press-konferencija*) next to the new direct borrowing *brifing* 'briefing', to denote a press meeting. Even in the 1950s Isačenko (1958: 352) considered complex designations as an exceptionally productive method of lexical expansion, in particular in the field of terminology, found in all standard Slavic languages. The adoption of such formations for everyday use often goes hand in hand with structural simplifications as well as consequent stylistic revaluations, i.e. that colloquial formations and professionalisms may enter the standard language.

Similar issues were later reviewed by Dokulil (1962) in terms of the intralinguistic stylistic comparison of different structures (multi-word expression, compound, derivative, cf. also Štekauer 2005, 2009), e.g., Cz. *růže čajová* (N+RA) 'tea rose' in botanical nomenclature compared to the colloquial derivative *čajovka* (N ← RA) 'id.' (Dokulil 1962: 116).

In more recent Slavic grammars, the description of word-formation is usually undertaken according to word classes which are in turn classified according to methods of word-formation (compounding, derivation, etc.). The description of the derivation of the noun, adjective or verb mostly involves a subclassification according to the base word (N ← V, N ← N, etc.) and, furthermore, on the basis of the word-formation category (e.g., in the case of deverbal nouns: abstract nouns, agent nouns, etc.). Relations between the individual word-formation methods or – in a wider sense – designation methods are, for the most part, only considered in reference to word combinations as forming a basis for synthetic compounds and derivatives (from relational adjectives), partly also in reference to compounds as a basis for derivatives, but not in view of the relationship between compounds and multi-word expressions consisting of a relational adjective and noun, cf. the Russian examples in Table 10.1.

For Slavic languages there is no investigation in which compounds and designations consisting of a relational adjective and noun have been jointly considered as "complex nominals" on the basis of a corresponding inventory of relations between modifier and head, as was undertaken for English by Levi (1978). This

Tab. 10.1: Semantically identical compounds and multi-word expressions in Russian.

Compound	RA+N	
sud-o-mechanik (20,000 occurences in Yandex)	sudovoj mechanik (21,000)	'ship mechanic'
sud-o-remont (784,000)	sudovoj remont (1,000)	'ship repair'
sud-o-dvigatel' (41)	sudovoj dvigatel' (1 m.)	'marine engine'
sud-o-stroenie (2 m.)	sudovoe stroenie (238)	'ship building'

may be due to the fact that the formation types of nominal determinative compounds are limited in terms of possible relations between head and modifier.

The focus of the relationship between composition and multi-word designation – (i) N+N including a nominal modifier in the genitive case or (ii) a prepositional case or else (iii) RA+N – is therefore rather reserved for individual contrastive studies (cf. Gladrow 1998 on Russian and German, Szymanek 2009 on the comparison of Polish and English, Rainer 2013 also including evidence from Slavic languages). When considering the examples provided by Szymanek (2009: 466) alongside Russian and Czech equivalents we can see that indeed they do not have compounds – just as their Polish equivalents. There is, however, also no consistent structural correspondence between the equivalents in the closely related Polish and Czech languages, and the frequency of use of the examples can vary strongly when it comes to formal correspondences (for Polish and Czech determined via Google, for Russian via Yandex; the same holds for the following Tables), cf. Table 10.2:

Tab. 10.2: English compounds and their equivalents in Polish, Czech and Russian (adapted after Szymanek 2009: 466).

a)	E. telephone number		
N+N_gen	P. i. numer telefon-u	Čz. [číslo telefon-u]	R. nomer telefon-a (33 m.)
N+N_prep.case	P. ii. *numer do telefon-u	Čz. –	–
N+RA/RA+N	P. iii. *numer telefon-icz-n-y	Čz. telefon-n-í číslo	R. telefon-n-yj nomer (3 m.)
b)	E. computer paper		
N+N_gen	P. i. *papier komputer-a	–	R. bumaga dlja kompjutera
N+N_prep.case	P. ii. papier do komputer-a (5 m.)	Čz. [papír pro počítač]	(less frequent)
N+RA/RA+N	P. iii. papier komputer-ow-y (124,000)	Čz. počítač-ov-ý papír (11,000)	R. komp'juter-n-aja bumaga
c)	E. tooth paste		
N+N_gen	P. i. *pasta zęb-ów	–	–
N+N_prep.case	P. ii. pasta do zębów	[Čz. pasta na zuby]	R. pasta dlja zubov (20,000)
N+RA/RA+N	P. iii. *pasta zęb-ow-a	Čz. zub-n-í pasta	R. zub-n-aja pasta (3 m.)

Szymanek (2009: 467) simply states: "[...] certain functions that are served by compounding in other languages tend to be realized by syntactic, inflectional and/ or derivational means in Polish". At the same time he points out that the designations which he classified as "fixed nominal phrases" like, for instance, *drukarka laserowa* (N+RA) 'laser printer', are, according to other Polish authors (e.g., Jadacka 2006), considered as juxtapositions (P. *zestawienia*), which is "a special type of a generally conceived category of compounding".

Are there certain regularities regarding the choice of the designation method depending on the relationships that may exist between head and modifier?

On the basis of the examples presented in Table 10.2, we can first understand Isačenko's differentiation between Polish as "genitival type" and "prepositional type" and Czech as "adjectival type" (Isačenko 1958: 340). Russian, however, does not clearly appear as "genitival type" in the above examples.

As will be demonstrated later on, also in Russian or Czech, general (nonspecific) relations or purposive relations, as in b. and c., are likewise not expressed by compounds. But what then about the Polish and Czech equivalents corresponding to the Russian examples, provided in Table 10.1, which additionally exhibit "object relations" between the constituents? Equally, the Polish equivalent here is never a compound: designations of the type N+N$_{gen}$ probably represent the only equivalents (e.g., *budowa statków* 'ship building'), and in those cases where a purposive relation is expressed and the formation of N+RA is possible, this is less frequently attested, e.g., *mechanik statków* (11,000) vs. *mechanik statkowy* (3,150) 'ship mechanic'. Similarly there are no compounds in Czech, but RA+N-equivalents (*lodní mechanik* 'ship mechanic', *lodní motor* 'ship engine') and besides N+N$_{gen.pl}$ (*stavba lodí* 'ship building') a synonymous abstract noun: *loďař-ství* (← *loďař* 'shipbuilder' ← *loď* 'ship').

This does not, however, imply that there are no compounds at all: the documented types nevertheless need to be analysed with respect to the relationships realized between the constituents. And in light of Szymanek's statement: "However, there is a wealth of evidence to demonstrate that nominal compounding is, relatively speaking, a living process in Polish, too", it remains to be examined which tendencies emerge in the formation of neologisms compared to the established compounds. This question should also be considered in regard to Czech. As a basis for the following discussion we will focus our attention on Russian which, in adapting more recent borrowings, appears to be especially open to compounds.

2 Relations between modifier and head in the traditional Slavic compounds

In the following we will confine ourselves to a brief outline of the formation of determinative noun-noun compounds (with and without the linking vowel *o/e*, particularly in recent calques), because only here can we establish parallels to word combinations consisting of RA+N (possibly also $N+N_{gen}$ or $N+N_{prep.case}$).

Referring to English nominal compounds, Plag (2009: 148) presents different possibilities of classifying semantic relations between constituents, as, e.g., 'location', 'cause', 'possessor', 'material', 'instrument', whilst considering such attempts as "somewhat futile". One should rather ask the question as to which interpretations are possible, since N+N-compounds are basically ambiguous and can take on different meanings depending on the context (cf. contributions to the topic in Lieber and Štekauer 2009). This evaluation of English might also be true of German, yet cannot be applied to compounding in Slavic languages. Plag's observation concerning the description of isolated compounds in English (i.e. without context) – which are usually interpreted in terms of a typical relationship between the constituents – is, however, more likely to apply to Slavic compounds. Slavic grammars exclusively proceed from isolated compounds, provided this question is at all subject to discussion. This relates to the restrictions on the formation of compounds as well as to the limited, if not impossible, textually dependent semantic interpretations. Consequently, none of the German compounds with a nominal modifier presented in Ortner and Ortner (2015), Table 59.1 "Types of noun-noun and verb-noun compounds in German", can have a compound equivalent in Russian, Polish or Czech.

In Slavic languages the formation of compounds including a verbal modifier is impossible.

2.1 N+N-compounds

In its description of determinative N+N-compounds (e.g., R. *zvuk-o-režisser* 'sound operator', most formations including a deverbal head noun, e.g., R. *dač-e-vladelec* 'dacha owner', *tepl-o-otdača* 'heat emission'), the "Russian Grammar" (*Russkaja grammatika* 1980: 242 ff.) completely ignores the semantic relations between the constituents.

Tab. 10.3: Russian compounds and synonymous RA+N combinations and their equivalents in Polish and Czech.

Russian		Polish, Czech
Compound	**RA+N**	**Compound, derivative, RA+N/N+RA, N+N$_{gen}$**
N+N$_{non\text{-}derived}$	R. *zvuk-o-režisser* (2 m.) 'sound editor'	R. *zvukovoj režisser* (600)	P. N+RA *operator dźwiękowy* (← *dźwięk* 'sound') (321) P. N+N$_{gen}$ *operator dźwięku* (23,000) Cz. derivative *zvukař* (← *zvuk* 'sound')
N+N$_{<v}$ N1 = agent (non-pers.)	R. *korabl-e-krušenie* (392,000) 'ship wreck'	R. *korabel'noe krušenie* (66)	P. derivative *zatonięcie* (← *zatonąć* 'to sink') Cz. N+N$_{gen}$ *stroskotání lodi*
N1 = object	R. *dom-o-vladelec* 'house owner'	–	P. N+N$_{gen}$ *właściciel domu* Cz. N+N$_{gen}$ *majitel domu*
	ryb-o-lovlja (48,000) 'fishing'	R. *rybnaja lovlja* (553,000)	P. N+N$_{gen}$ *połów ryb* Cz. compound *rybolov*
	žir-o-zamenitel' (305) 'fat substitute'	R. *žirnyj zamenitel'* (10)* R. *žirovoj zamenitel'* (957)	N+N$_{gen}$ P. *substytut tłuszczu* Cz. *náhrážka tuku*
	ovošč-e-chranilišče (224,000) 'vegetable store'	*ovoščnoe chranilišče* (1,000)	N+ N$_{gen}$ P. *magazyn warziw* Cz. *sklad zeleniny* RA+N Cz. *zeleninový sklad*
N1=instrument (means)	*vod-o-lečenie* (304,000) 'hydrotherapy'	R. *vodnoe lečenie* (765)	Compound P. *wodoleczenie* Cz. *vodolečba* N+RA P. *leczenie wodne* RA+N Cz. *vodní lečba*

* The reduced occurrence frequency is obviously due to the development of the qualitative meaning of *žirnyj* as 'fat, greasy'.

In "pure compounds" of the N+N-type, the "Czech Grammar" (*Mluvnice češti-ny* 1986: 456 ff.) distinguishes between:

a) compounds whose heads do not denote actions, e.g., Cz. *vod-o-znak* 'water-mark', *dřev-o-průmysl* 'wood(working) industry', including numerous technical terms as well as older loan translations (*-o-* is the linking vowel). What is very revealing in this context is that some compounds marked as archaic have been replaced by RA+N (*par-o-stroj* 'steam engine' > *parní stroj* 'id.; lit. steam-RA machine'), by a prepositional phrase (*kav-o-mlýnek* 'coffee mill' > *mlýnek na kávu* 'id.; lit. mill-DIM for coffee') or by a derivative (*par-o-loď* 'steamboat' [> *parní loď* lit. 'steam-RA boat'] > *parník* 'steamer'), see also section 5;

b) compounds whose heads denote an action (mostly action nouns), including calques, e.g., Cz. *jazyk-o-věda* 'linguistics; lit. language-o-science', *těl-o-výchova* 'physical education; lit. body-*o*-education', *vod-o-lečba* 'water cure', beside *vodní lečba* lit. 'water-RA cure'.

Complex words comparable to Czech formations belonging to the group described under b) are, according to the "Grammar of Modern Polish" (*Gramatyka* 1998: 457 ff.), among the most frequently attested patterns of determinative compounds in Polish. The syntactic relations between the constituents are taken as a basis for the description of compounds representing the structure "N(N1+N2)" (with the linking vowel *-o-*), e.g.: "N1 denotes the object of the action performed by N2" (P. *mit-o-twórca* 'myth-*o*-creator', *projekt-o-dawca* 'project developer; lit. project-*o*-giver')"; "N1 = medium, instrument of the action performed by N2" (*par-o-statek* 'steam ship'), "N1 = location of N2" (*ląd-o-lod* '(continental) ice sheet; lit. (main)land ice'), etc. At the same time the dominant role of such formations in terminology is pointed out.

The previous explanations indicate fundamental systemic parallels, which, however, do not necessarily result in a structural correspondence between the equivalents. In anticipation of section 3, we have already included designations consisting of relational adjectives, which parallel the examples provided in the "Russian Grammar", as well as the Polish and Czech equivalents, cf. Table 10.3 (above).

2.2 Synthetic compounds

"Synthetic compounds are complex words that contain at least three morphemes, with neither the combination of the first two nor of the last two existing as free words" (see article 5 on synthetic compounds in German). In Slavic languages formations belonging to the group of synthetic compounds are traditionally more productive and can partly compensate for the lower productivity of "pure" word-/root-compounds, but rarely express relations between the constituents that go beyond "pure" compounds.

The "Grammar of Modern Polish" (*Gramatyka* 1995: 463 f.) points out the following relations between the constituents expressed by the structure "N(N1+V)": N1 denotes the object, the instrument or the place of the action (V), by means of the suffix (including the zero-suffix) categorial roles like 'agent' (also non-personal nouns), 'instrument', 'place', etc., are expressed, e.g., P. *list-o-nosz-Ø* 'postman; lit. mail-*o*-carrier', *wod-o-oczyszcz-acz* 'water purifier', *kwas-o-ryt-Ø* 'copperplate print; lit. acid-*o*-etch-Ø', *dom-o-krąż-c-a* 'peddler, door-to-door salesman; lit. house-*o*-back and forth go-er'.

Similar relationships can be found in Czech and Russian formations:

Cz. *vin-o-bra-ní* 'vintage; lit. grape-*o*-taking', *dřev-o-rub-ec* 'woodcutter', the calque *tepl-o-měr-* 'thermometer; lit. warmth-*o*-measur-er' (however, cf. Kavka 2009: 19, who proposes to view recurrent constituents such as Cz. *-měr* '-meter', etc. "as suffixes [...] rather than genuine compound elements"); R. *ryb-o-lov-stv-o* 'fishing; lit. fish-*o*-catch-ABSTR', *kanat-o-chod-ec* 'ropewalker; lit. rope-*o*-go-AGENT', *sud-o-pod''em-nik* 'ship elevator; lit. ship-*o*-elevate-INSTR', *piv-o-var-n-ja* 'brewery; lit. beer-*o*-brew-LOC'.

3 Relations between modifier and head in combinations of relational adjectives and nouns

3.1 General overview

As was demonstrated in section 2.1, the relations between constituents which in Russian, Polish and Czech can be expressed by means of "pure" N+N-compounds are limited in number.

a) If the heads are non-derived nouns, final relations between head and modifier dominate.

b) If the heads are deverbal nouns, the modifiers correspond to arguments of the base verb, such as subject, object, less frequently instrument or place. A decisive restriction is to be found in the fact that deverbal personal nouns rarely appear as heads (but cf. section 2.2 on the formation of personal nouns in the group of synthetic compounds with a second verbal component).

On the one hand, Slavic relational adjectives can express relations that have also been proven to exist in compounds, though restricted in terms of the expression of the object (see section 3.2). The "Grammar of Modern Polish" (*Gramatyka* 1998: 485 ff.), however, separately mentions the expression of the relationship rooted in formations based on the respective action-object relation, e.g., P. *widowisko filmowe* 'screening; lit. see-ABSTR film-RA', *szkolenie harcierskie* 'scout training; lit. training scout-RA'.

On the other hand, relational adjectives in Slavic languages represent compensatory possibilities for expressing relations specified in section 2.1 with reference to English compounds, e.g., 'location', 'possessor', 'material', 'source', etc. The grammars of Slavic languages considered here (*Russkaja grammatika* 1980: 272 ff.; *Mluvnice češtiny* 1986: 316 ff.; *Gramatyka* 1998: 482 ff.) present the same observations concerning the semantic description of relational adjectives, as have been made for English compounds. Besides the expression of unspecified relationships (e.g., in R. *vodnyj krizis* 'water-RA crisis') relational adjectives can also be interpreted differently in context and depending on the determined noun as well as on the root word of the adjective, cf.: R. *vodn-yj nalog* 'water tax' (final), -*ye resursy* 'water resources' (content), -*yj sport* 'water sports' (local); lacking compounds as **vodokrizis*, but recently: *Vodosport* as business name, occasionally *vodonalog* 'water tax'.

In compounds with the modifier *vod-* and an exclusively deverbal head, however, object/purposive relations and instrumental relations are expressed, e.g., R. *vod-o-chranilišče* 'reservoir; lit. water-*o*-reservoir', *vod-o-snabženie* 'water supply', *vod-o-lečenie* 'hydrotherapy'; synonymous word combinations consisting of RA+N represent a minority here (cf. also section 3.2 on the historical development of the usage of Russian relational adjectives).

Temporal and local relations between modifier and head, relations of origin, possession and affiliation, are not expressed by compounds in Slavic languages (final and instrumental relations between modifier and head less frequently), but rather by combinations of RA+N or by N+N$_{gen/prep.case}$ (particularly in Polish when expressing final relations) as well as by derivatives (see section 5).

Using the example of Czech, Townsend (1996) describes in detail the development of the distribution and specialization of suffixes for the formation of relational adjectives as depending on the semantic group of underlying nouns. The subject matter of the present discussion does not seem to require such differentiation. Yet, a brief outline of the semantic groups of nouns, from which relational adjectives may derive, can still prove insightful (cf. Townsend 1996: 397 ff.):
– Persons, professions, animals, parts of the body, organs of the body,
– time, place, dress, foods, agricultural products,
– diseases, plants, natural phenomena,

- technical apparatus, buildings, parts of the house, objects of construction
- institutions,
- actions (abstract nouns).

This implies that there is not just the previously mentioned comparable breadth of fixed or contextual meanings of relational adjectives, as they are, for instance, described for English and German compounds, but also an abundance of motivational possibilities for Slavic relational adjectives (e.g., derivations of names for plants, fruits, foods, body parts, natural phenomena), as known from English and German compounds not, however, from relational adjectives.

With a high degree of regularity relational adjectives in Slavic languages are also derived from recent borrowings and thus constitute an important factor in their integration into further multi-word expressions (cf. R. *ofšornyj* 'offshore-RA', *press-reliznyj* 'press-release-RA'; P. *barterowy* 'barter-RA', *dealerski* 'dealer-RA'; Cz. *dabingový* 'dubbing-RA', *píárový* 'PR [public relations]-RA'). The interaction of compounds and designations consisting of a relational adjective and noun will be treated in section 4.1.

3.2 Relational adjectives: possibilities and restrictions

None of the descriptions of relational adjectives mentioned in section 3.1 refers to restrictions on expressing possible relations between head and modifier. Such restrictions include the "direct-object-lacuna" of Slavic relational adjectives as commented on by Rainer (2013: 19 f.) and explained by Mezhevich (2002) referring to Russian.

In the case of Slk. *výroba sriebra* (N+N_{gen}) 'silver production', not however *strieborna výroba* (RA+N) (cf. Rainer 2013: 19), confirmation of the direct object-lacuna may be additionally reinforced by the fact that the adjective is mainly associated with the meaning 'made of, consisting of'. Also Slk. *ocelová výroba* 'steel-RA production' is not attested. Instead the structure N+N_{gen} *výroba oceli* 'steel production' once again is. Confer, however, Cz. *ocelová výroba* (RA+N) 'id.', with 308 occurrences less frequent than the genitive construction *výroba ocele* and the abstract noun *ocelářství* 'id.'. Also cf. N+RA in P. *produkcja stalowa, metalowa* 'steel, metal production' besides a higher frequency of N+N_{gen} (*produkcja stali, metalu* 'id.').

As mentioned in section 1, with reference to a typology of designation patterns Isačenko (1958) divided the Slavic languages into a genitival type (e.g., Russian) and an adjectival type (e.g., Czech). Compare R. *analiz krovi* lit. 'analysis blood$_{gen}$' (the genitival type here also dominates in Slovak) vs. Cz. *krevní zkouška* lit. 'blood-RA analysis'. The conception of the adjectival type, however, clashes with the more frequent Cz. *odběr krve*_{gen} 'blood draw'. The avoidance of interference with the qualitative meaning of 'bloody' can be excluded in both cases since *krvní* has an exclusively relational meaning, whilst *krvavý* is the qualitative adjective.

According to Mezhevich (2002: 96 f.) the Russian equivalents to English compounds such as *van driver* and *bookseller* can only have the structure N+N_{gen} (*voditel' furgona, prodavec knig*), but not RA+N; **furgonnyj voditel'* and **knižnyj prodavec* are ungrammatical on the following grounds: "Deverbal nouns may inherit the argument structure of their base verbs, but the internal argument cannot be expressed by an adjective" (p. 109).

For formations such as R. *avtoprodavec* (at least 664 occurrences) 'car salesman' this statement could provide proof that they are compounds with a clipped nominal (← *avtomobil'*) rather than an adjectival modifier (← *avtomobil'nyj*) and that, as a consequence of that, *avto-* should not be treated as "analytical adjective" (see section 4.3). But a RA+N-combination *avtomobil'nyj prodavec* (152) is also documented. Both occurrences are still less frequent than *prodavec avtomobilej* lit. 'seller cars_{gen}' (27,000). Even today, the existence of R. **furgonnyj voditel'* cannot be attested. There is, however, a neologism R. *avtomobil'nyj voditel'* meaning 'driving simulator; lit. car-RA driver'. Also cf. R. *knižnaja prodaža* (RA+N) 'book selling' (16,000) as opposed to *prodaža knig* (N+N_{gen}) 'id.' (195,000), and *knižnyj prodavec* (750) marked with an asterisk by Mezhevich; the compound *knigoprodavec* is obsolete, while the genitive construction *prodavec knig* (14,000) again dominates. Yet occurrences of the type RA+N in place of a compound or N+N_{gen} can be found more often in Russian online forums. This could quite possibly be indicative of a certain tendency within the Russian vernacular, such as was already noted by Zemskaja (1992), to re-activate the use of possessive adjectives (e.g., *Tanina jubka* 'Tanja's skirt') instead of genitive constructions (*jubka Tani* 'id.; lit. skirt Tanja_{gen}').

While – apart from studies of the parallels between word combinations consisting of RA+N and compounds with clipped initial components mainly of foreign origin (see section 4.2) – there are hardly any articles in the respective Slavic literature dealing with the relation between compounds and RA+N-structures, the number of investigations dedicated to the relation between RA+N and N+N_{gen/prep.case} is much higher.

On the one hand there are the contributions to historical grammar and language history. Buslaev (2009 [1862–63]: 173), for example, points out that already in the earliest translations from Greek into Old Church Slavonic relational adjectives (in particular: possessive adjectives) were frequently used in place of the genitive or prepositional case, e.g., *strach božij* 'fear of God; lit. fear God-POSS.ADJ'.

The frequent use of adjective instead of case constructions is also characteristic of Old Russian texts, e.g., *vodnaja žažda* 'thirst for water; lit. water-RA thirst' instead of *žažda vody* lit. 'thirst water$_{gen}$', *smertnaja pamjat'* 'memory of death; lit. death-RA memory' vs. contemporary Russian: *pamjat' o smerti* lit. 'memory about death', *strel'naja rana* 'arrow wound; lit. arrow-RA wound' vs. *rana ot strely* 'id.; lit. wound from arrow$_{gen}$', *strach tatarskъ* 'fear of the Tatars; lit. fear Tatar-RA' vs. *strach ot tatar* 'fear of the Tatars'.

According to Buslaev's investigations, combinations including possessive adjectives still occurred in Russian literature of the 18th century, e.g., *Kartiny Del'-Sartovy, Venera Ticianova i pročich masterov* (Fonvizin) 'paintings of del Sarto, the Venus of Tizian and of other masters; lit. paintings del Sarto-POSS.ADJ, the Venus Tizian-POSS.ADJ and other masters$_{gen}$' (particularly interesting in this context is the parallel use of possessive adjectives in naming individual painters and the genitive (plural) when generally referring to further masters).

In his history of the Russian language in the 18th and 19th century, Vinogradov (1982: 70) points out a detail of the Petrine period which proves relevant for the topic of our discussion: tables of direct borrowings from German were found to include – solely for the purpose of clarification – additional translations, e.g., *buchgalter* 'bookkeeper' (o r *knigoderžatel'* lit. 'book-o-holder'), *kamer-junker* 'groom of the bedchamber' (o r *komnatnyj dvorjanin* lit. 'room-RA noble man'). In the first case we also find a compound in Russian, which corresponds to the typical expression of the argument (object) by means of the modifier of a deverbal head, in the second case the equivalent of the German nominal modifier is a relational adjective.

In examining the changes of the usage of relational adjectives and the increasing distribution of functions between Russian RA+N and N+N$_{obl.case}$ in the 18th and 19th century, Belošapkova and Zemskaja (1962) reached the following conclusions:

a) In cases, where a relational adjective continues to be used, no individual reference can be established (as opposed to the genitive), e.g., *okonnoe steklo* 'window glass'.

b) Specific semantic relations such as object relations are less and less frequently expressed by relational adjectives but instead by use of the genitive case; also cf. ORuss. *plat'janoe myt'e* lit. 'dress-RA washing' vs. contemporary *myt'e plat'ja* lit. 'washing dress$_{gen}$', *krestnoe celovanie* vs. *celovanie kresta* 'kissing of the cross' (p. 8 f.).

c) At the end of the 18th and beginning of the 19th century, we can still encounter R. *vinnaja prodaža* 'wine-sale; lit. wine-RA sale', *notnyj perepisčik* 'copyist of notes; lit. note-RA copyist', but in the second half of the 19th century the number of occurrences decreases, especially in combination with person nouns used as head, e.g., *baletnyj ljubitel'* 'ballett lover' (p. 12).

Combinations of relational adjectives and (also non-deverbal) nouns are active to the present day, e.g., designations of firms in which object and purposive relations interact, R. *obuvnaja fabrika* 'shoe factory', R. *kirpičnyj zavod* 'brickyard'. Similarly also instrumental relations are exploited, e.g., R. *televizionnaja peredača* (besides *telepredača*) 'telecast' (p. 14).

For synonymous and competitive occurrences between RA+N and N+N$_{obl.case}$ in contemporary Russian see Zibrova (1984), where we can also prove the lack of expression of object relations by means of relational adjectives in normative language use.

4 Types of compounds without a linking vowel and their adjectival competitors

4.1 Compounds without a linking vowel

As shown in Table 10.3, apart from several Russian compounds which follow the traditional formation types (with a linking vowel and a deverbal head), there are (possibly) also word combinations of RA+N. The same applies to (borrowed) compounds without a linking vowel.

With regard to these formations the "Russian grammar" (*Russkaja grammatika* 1980: 253) still confines itself to a list of examples. In most cases they are direct borrowings or calques, whose use is frequently abandoned in favor of the RA+N combination. Cf. Table 10.4.

Neologisms show an activation of this formation type. While, for example, the Russian borrowing *komp'juter* 'computer' was made available for further designations or rather calques in the 1980s and 90s by means of the relational adjective (cf. *komp'juternaja technika* 'computer technology'), in more recent designations with *internet* as modifier the compound without a linking vowel dominates: R. *internet-opros* (also cf. P. *internet-ankieta*) 'Internet survey', *internet-reklama* 'Internet advertising'. In Russian, parallel formations with the relational adjective *internetovskij/internetnyj* occur, unlike in Polish (e.g., *reklama internetowa*), only marginally.

As part of the internationalization of vocabulary that has taken place during the last two decades, such formations (in the form of direct borrowings or hybrid calques) have also significantly increased in other Slavic languages. Consider ne-

Tab. 10.4: N+N compounds without linking vowel.

Russian		Polish, Czech	
Compound	RA+N	Compound	N+RA/RA+N
N+N	R. *dizel'-motor* (16,000) 'diesel engine'	R. *dizel'nyj motor* (88,000)		[P. *diesel* (metonym)] Cz. *Dieselův* (poss. adj.) *motor*
	R. *vakuum-kamera* (3,000) 'vacuum chamber'	R. *vakuumnaja kamera* (24,000)		P. *komora próżniowa* (← *próżnia* 'vacuum') Cz. *vakuová* komora*
	R. *džaz-orkestr* (90,000) 'jazz orchestra'	R. *džazovyj orkestr* (34,000)	P. *jazz-orkiestra* [Cz. *jazz-orchestr*]	P. *orkiestra jazzowa* Cz. *jazzový orchestr*

* In Czech derivatives from foreign words in *-um* this element is deleted.

ologisms including frequent constituents like R. *bisnes*, P. *biznes*, Cz. *byznys* 'business', documented in all three languages, e.g., in connection with R. *proekt*, P./ Cz. *projekt* and R./P. *plan*/Cz. *plán* 'business project/plan', but R. *biznes-otnošenija* 'business relations' vs. P. *stosunki biznesowe* (N+RA) 'id.', R. *biznes-pravo* 'business law' vs. P. *prawo biznesowe* 'id.'. New compounds of this type, which consist exclusively of native components and are not loan translations, however, have not been documented. Since both constituents are known as single words, examples of the above kind can also be perceived as independent Russian formations. Unlike parallel designations such as R. *dizajner-narkotiki* and *dizajnerskie narkotiki* 'designer drugs' (cf. also the examples below) there are also fewer synonymous combinations with a relational adjective competing with compounds with *biznes* as modifier: R. *biznesnye/biznesovye otnošenija* have been documented with approximately 800 occurrences, including combinations with adverbs (*čisto biznesovye otnošenija* 'mere business relations', but **čisto biznes-otnošenija*). The compound is furthermore more frequent in combinations with an additional, adjectival modifier: *političeskie i biznes-interesy* 'political and business interests'.

The occurrences that have been cited so far and many further examples show that the modern Slavic languages (and in this context particularly Russian) are not so much enriched by new types of compounds as they are influenced by a strong activation of those (already existent) compounding methods that are most suited to the integration of new borrowings/internationalisms. Several choices of designation may thereby be available (also beyond word-formation), see below.

As was established on the basis of an analysis of the "Russian Newspaper Corpus" of the 1990s, the number of new noun compounds exceeded the number

Tab. 10.5: Loan compound, prepositional word combination, RA+N.

	Compound	Prepositional word combination	RA+N/N+RA
a)			
R.	džip-safari 'jeep safari' (474,000)	safari na džipach 'id.; lit. safari on jeeps' (43,000)	džipovoe safari 'id.; lit. jeep-RA safari' (1)
P.	džip safari (233)	safari na džipach (7)	–
Cz.	džíp safari (30,000)	safari na džípech (1,360)	džípové safari (9)
b)			
R.	serfing-kostjum (272) 'surfing clothes'	kostjum(y) dlja serfinga (600) lit. 'clothes for surfing'	serfingovyj kostjum (11) 'id.'
P.	–	strój do serfingu	strój serfingowy
Cz.	–	oblečení na surfing	surfingové oblečení
c)			
R.	demping-ceny (3,000) 'dumping prices'	–	dempingovye ceny (20,000) 'id.'
P.	dumping-ceny	–	ceny dumpingowe
Cz.	dumping-ceny	–	dumpingové ceny

of the remaining nominal neologisms by more than 10 % (Kukuškina, Polikarpov and Toktonov 2007).

Yet, with respect to such evaluations, we have to consider that the activation of specific patterns – as reflected in the entries of neologism dictionaries (cf. Uluchanow and Belentschikow 2007; Worbs, Markowski and Meger 2007; Martincová 1998, 2004) – does not necessarily have to go hand in hand with an increased occurrence frequency of formations based on these patterns.

Besides new borrowed compounds, we can often find variants in the form of prepositional constructions and/or in the form of (fixed) word combinations on the basis of RA+N, cf. Table 10.5.

In a), the loan compound is also more frequently documented in Polish and Czech. In many other cases we can, however, encounter a higher frequency of synonymous multi-word expressions, cf. b). In Czech and Polish an analogous compound could not be documented. As is representative of the expression of final relations, combinations consisting of $N+N_{prep.case}$ dominate (in this case also in Russian), besides individual occurrences of RA+N: P. *strój serfingowy*, Cz. *surfin-*

gové oblečení. The reasons for a preference of RA+N/N+RA in c) are to be found in the enhanced syntactic availability. In oblique singular and plural cases the ratio of the borrowed compound is considerably lower, e.g.: R. dative plural *demping cenam* (59) vs. *dempingovym cenam* (59,000), and the genitive plural R. *demping cen*, P./Cz. *dumping cen* is obviously entirely avoided due to its homonymy with N+N$_{gen.pl}$ 'price dumping'.

Finally we can recognize tendencies towards the use of the compound as a constituent of proper names (e.g., R. *inžiniring kompanija* 'engineering company' in business names as *Inžiniring kompanija "Merkurij"* 'Mercury Engineering'. (The RA+N combination *inžiniringovaja kompanija* is more frequently attested as common noun.) The preference for such formations in the nominative case is also visible in new compounds of other formation types. Consequently, we may encounter compounds, for instance in names of Internet domains, which have not (yet) been established as part of the general vocabulary (R. *Vodosport* 'water sports' as opposed to the common appellative construction *vodnyj sport* (RA+N), P. *Autosprzedawca* 'car salesman', but normally: *sprzedawaca samochodów* lit. 'seller cars$_{gen}$'). The choice may also vary depending on the text type (cf. Ohnheiser 2012).

Apart from such cases of (partial) competition, combinations of RA+N are often the only way to translate English compounds with nominal modifiers. In Russian the common occurrence of new borrowed compounds and synonymous multi-word expressions of the form RA+N is more frequently documented than in Polish or Czech.

4.2 Compounds with clipped modifiers

International word-formation elements (confixes) like *astro-*, *avto-/auto-* 'self', *mini-*, *mono-*, etc. – which the "Russian Grammar" (*Russkaja grammatika* 1980: 242 ff.) describes as "international bound components" – are, in the field of compounding, contrasted with formations with "clipped roots" functioning as modifiers, "clipped" because there exist parallel designations in the form of relational adjectives. Formations with clipped modifiers are presently very productive in the Slavic languages. This further reinforces compounding and at the same time extends the traditionally possible semantic relations between head and modifier, cf. Table 10.6.

Moreover, combinations of clippings (mostly syllables) of the adjectival (also non-borrowed) modifier and the head of a multi-word expression to form a "clipped-compound word" are specifically characteristic of Russian, cf. *detsad* 'kindergarten' (← *detskij* RA from *deti* 'children' + *sad* 'garden'; a calque of the

Tab. 10.6: Compounds with clipped modifiers and RA+N/N+RA combinations.

	Russian		Polish, Czech	
	Compound	RA+N	Compound	N+RA, RA+N; N+N$_{gen}$
avto- (avtomobil'nyj RA/ avtomobil' N) 'car'	*avtodviženie* (34,000) 'car traffic'	*avtomobil'noe* *dviženie* (13 m.)	Cz. *autoprovoz*	P. *ruch samochodowy*
	avtorynok (878,000) 'car market'	*avtomobil'nyj* *rynok* (530,000)	P. *autorynek** Cz. *autotrh*	P. *rynek samochodowy*
	avtoškola (2 m.) 'driving school'	*avtomobil'naja* *škola* (78,000)	P. *autoszkoła,* *auto-szkoła** Cz. *autoškola*	P. *ośrodek szkolenia* *kierowców* lit. 'centre for the training of drivers'
tele- (televizionnyj RA/ televidenie N) 'TV'	*telereportaž* (47,000) 'TV report'	*televizionnyj* *reportaž* (14,000)	P. *telereportaż* Cz. *telereportáž*	P. *reportaż telewizyjny* Cz. *televizní reportáž*
	telezritel' (142,000) 'TV viewer'	*televizionnyj zritel'* (521)	P. *telewidz* Cz. *teledivák* (occasionally; coll.)	P. *widz telewizyjny* Cz. *televizní divák*

* Frequently as part of proper names.

German compound), *gosuniversitet* 'state university' (← *gosudarstvennyj* 'state-RA' + *universitet* 'university'). Formations with this structure are still frequently found today in political and administrative domains in the transition from common to proper nouns, cf. *mosgortransport* (← *moskovskij gorodskoj transport* 'Moscow municipal transport'). Some occurrences in other Slavic languages, e.g., with the components *soc-* 'socialist' such as P. *socrealizm*, Cz. *socrealismus* 'socialist realism' or *spec-* 'special', e.g., P. *speckomando* 'special forces unit', are considered to be borrowings/loan translations stemming from Russian. One of the motives for the active formation of words such as those above in Russian may also be found in the fact that they frequently enable the derivation of relational adjectives, which are syntactically more economical than, for instance, other multi-word expressions, e.g., *detsadovskij vozrast* 'preschool age' instead of *vozrast detej, poseščajuščich detsad* 'id.; lit. age of children attending a kindergarten'; occ. *mosgortransportskie bilety* instead of *bilety na Moskovskij gorodskoj transport* 'tickets for (lines of) the Moscow municipal transport'. (Additionally there are a variety of occurrences of exclusively clipped components to be found in the administrative domain like R. *Rosminzdrav* ← *Ministerstvo zdravoochranenija Rossijskoj Federacii* lit. 'Ministry health protection$_{gen}$ Russian$_{gen}$ Federation$_{gen}$'.)

4.3 Multi-word expression or compound?

4.3.1 On the notion of "analytical adjectives" in Russian studies

Particularly in Russian studies, some authors consider elements like *avto-*, *tele-*, etc. mentioned in section 4.2 (which are described by the "Russian grammar" as clipped compound elements going back to an N or a RA) as "analytical adjectives". They hence agree with Panov (2004 [1971] amongst others) who treated components which mainly stem from borrowings as "indeclinable adjectives" or "indeclinable modifiers", respectively, e.g., R. *radio- i televizionnye centry* (Panov 2004 [1971]: 137) lit. 'radio- and television-RA centres'. In elements of this kind Panov saw an increase in analytic traits in Russian morphology, i.e. grammatical categories such as gender, number and case (when establishing the congruity between an adjective and a noun) are not expressed in endings but exclusively contextually, the formation of compounds lacks linking vowels, etc.

Panov (2004 [1971]: 138 ff.) did not only classify the initial constituents in formations such as *partbilet* 'party membership book' (← *partijnyj bilet* RA+N), *kinoscenarij* 'script; lit. film-script', *telepostanovka* 'TV production' as analytical adjectives. Although we have the noun *pressa*, *press-officer* 'military press officer' would not be considered a compound because the initial constituent ends in a consonant (that is to say there is no linking vowel, I. O.). In the "adjective" *super* as in *superkrizis* 'supercrisis' one could only diachronically recognize a prefix, today such elements have already obtained all features of a word and as such have fallen into the category of analytical adjectives, which may freely merge with nouns. Compounds, however, would always exhibit (a certain) idiomaticity. But also *chlebouborka* 'corn harvest', *lesozagotovki* 'timber cutting; lit. timber preparation' are, according to Panov, combinations consisting of an "analytical adjective" and a noun (p. 143). Judging by their origin *leso-* and *chlebo-* would be constituents of a compound, but since they do not possess a restricted (idiomatic) connectivity, they have to be treated as "pseudo words" and *chlebouborka*, *lesozagotovki* synchronically as (analytical) word combinations.

As we could see from the observations presented in section 4.2, the authors of the "Russian grammar" (*Russkaja grammatika* 1980) did not agree with Panov's views, but despite this fact they prevail in Russian studies to this day. Golanova

(1998) referred to R. *VIP-zal* 'VIP hall' and others as "alleged compounds" and Zemskaja (1997: 190) also included the initial components of borrowings/loan formations like *šou-programma* 'show program', *top-fil'm* 'top film', for which there are no equivalent adjectives in Russian, into the entities now identified as "analytics" (a seemingly innocuous term that is not limited to a specific word class). With regard to R. *kompaktdisk* 'compact disc', *videoklip* 'videoclip', Kostomarov (1999: 272) spoke of a new type of word combinations conceived of as univerbation. (Cf. also Vačkova 1999 on Bulgarian.) In more recent studies on Russian (e.g., Rochtchina 2012: 74) occurrences such as R. *mul'timedia technika* 'multimedia technology' and *onlajn-novosti* 'online news', *SMS-soobščenija* 'SMS messages' are considered as "analytic formations". (Cf. also Cz. *SMS-zprávy* 'id.', but P. *wiadomości SMS-owe* lit. 'news SMS-ra'.)

Benin'i [Benigni] (2007: 74 ff.), on the other hand, advocates the idea that "analytical adjectives" do not correspond to the syntactic criteria of the word class and that the respective formations are more closely related to compounds rather than syntagms. She thus focuses on examination of the possible isolation of the modifier (e.g., R. *fitnes oborudovanie* 'fitness equipment' – *Kakoe oborudovanie?* 'What kind of equipment?' – **Fitnes.* *'Fitness.') and – with reference to Giegerich (2009: 193) – on coordination tests (R. *pop- i rok-muzyka* 'pop and rock music').

4.3.2 Observations on further Slavic languages

Without using the term "analytical adjective", also in other Slavic studies separate spelling and syntactic functions (i.e. "attribute", although the initial component is formally not recognizable as adjective) are considered to be criteria according to which designations on the basis of borrowings can be determined as word combinations (cf. Nábělková 1999). These conceptions are contrasted with the classification as compounding.

a) Classification as indeclinable adjectives as part of multi-word expressions
The attempt to differentiate the syntactical and word-formation functions of such invariant components has, e.g., been undertaken by the authors of the dictionary of Czech neologisms (Martincová 1998; 2004). Accordingly, *bio* is, on the one hand, listed as (indeclinable) adjective (Cz. *bio celozrnná mouka* 'organic wholemeal flour; lit. bio wholemeal-ra flour'), and, on the other hand, (under *bio-*) as initial part of compounds. Consequently the obvious variants Cz. *bio brambory* und *biobrambory* 'organic potatoes', which are distinct only in spelling, receive a different structural explanation. Cf. also Gester (2001); Bozděchová (1997) on *on line* as

an adjective in designations like Cz. *on line systém*, besides *onlinový* (RA); on Polish: Worbs, Markowski and Meger (2007).

A broad conception of indeclinable adjectives is represented by Doleschal (2000), where she gives special weight to the criterion of separate spelling (e.g., *nonstop* in Cz. *nonstop automobilová pout'* 'non-stop automobile pilgrimage'). Among other things, she points out that "a peculiar type of pseudo-compound structure", whose initial component had to be considered as "uncommon conversion of a noun into an indeclinable adjective", developed on the basis of loan translations (p. 288). So-called indeclinable adjectives were for the most part business or brand names, their occurrence was strictly confined to advertising texts, e.g., Slk. *Crisan protilupinové vlasové tonikum* 'Crisan Anti-Dandruff Hair Tonic; lit. Crisan antidandruff-RA hair-RA tonic' (p. 289 ff.). Doleschal (p. 295) regards the expansion of uninflectable adjectives as the "at the moment probably most interesting question of grammatical change in the Slavic languages", which is "advanced by intensive borrowing processes". Cf. also Hinrichs (2000) on analytic tendencies in the languages of Eastern and Southeastern Europe; Ohnheiser (2004).

b) Identification as compound (reinforcement of compound patterns)

According to Selimski (2003) a demarcation between word combinations and compounds in neologisms is difficult to achieve, since the relation between the constituents is not expressed formally as is usually the case in Slavic languages (i.e. absence of the linking vowel in compounds or of an adjectival suffix in an agreeing or, respectively, of the case marker in a non-agreeing adjunct). The older formation with a linking vowel Bulg. *gazostancija* lit. 'petrol/gas-*o*-station' is contrasted with, e.g., the more recent compound *gazstancija* (as English *gas station*) (p. 120). Nevertheless, Zelimski holds that a new type of c o m p o u n d is thus emerging in the Slavic languages, in which the relations between the constituents are only expressed by their position, independently of whether the formations are spelled separately, with a hyphen or as one word (cf. Sln. *Slovenijales, Slovenija-les, Slovenija les* lit. 'Slovenia-wood/timber'; name of a Slovene timber company (p. 121)). This kind of composition would be particularly suitable for formations whose modifier is an abbreviation (e.g., Sln. *TV-studio, -chronika* 'TV studio, chronicle'), but also in other cases of more recent designations, compounds are the preferred structure, e.g., Bulg. *baskettitla* 'basket title' (instead of RA+N *basketbolna titla*), *basketfinal* 'basket final'. Such phenomena are, according to Selimski, especially representative of the "analytic languages" Bulgarian and Macedonian, which are also close to Serbian, but less frequently found in other South Slavic languages or in Czech. (Cf. however also Cz. *diskohudba* 'disco music', *diskooděv* 'disco clothes', etc.)

Jadacka (2001: 93 ff.) describes Polish formations with constituents such as *euro-*, *eko-*, *narko-*, *porno-*, *seks-*, *tele-*, *wideo-* as "zrosty", i.e. a special type of compound, and makes reference to proper names like P. *Sopotfestiwal* 'Sopot festival' and *Inwestbank* (= *Bank Inwestycyjny* N+RA) 'investment bank' (p. 143) as an additional formation type among neologisms, lacking formal markers of composition (linking vowel). (See also Waszakowa 2005.)

For typological tendencies in modern Slavic languages cf. also Gutschmidt (2003).

5 Derivatives from multi-word expressions (RA+N) and denominal derivatives

In section 3.1, we have looked at the relations between head and modifier which, in Slavic languages, are not expressed by compounds, but by RA+N (or Polish N+RA). Restrictions in nominal composition (N+N) are thus often compensated for. The multi-word expressions can themselves form the basis for synonymous suffixal derivations from relational adjectives. In many cases mediated motivation might be assumed on the basis of the noun, e.g., R. *doždevik* 'raincoat' (← *doždevoj* 'rain-RA' *plašč* 'id.'); cf. several examples given in Table 10.7 which at the same time illustrate certain preferences for individual semantic relations. In addition to that there are several cases of ellipsis of the head noun and nominalization of the relational adjective.

Factors pertaining to the economy of language such as brevity and easier syntactic availability as opposed to multi-word expressions enhance the productivity of synonymous derivatives, primarily in technical jargon but also in colloquial language; the frequency of use might lead to their being stylistically neutralized. The following recent formations however might still exhibit a colloquial tinge, e.g., R. *okonnik* 'window air conditioner' (← *oknonnyj*-RA *kondicioner* 'id.'), *vidik* 'video player' (← *videokassetnyj plejer*/*videoplejer* 'id.'; with clipping of the modifier), Cz. *digitálky* 'digital watch' (← *digitální hodinky* 'id.'), P. *mikrofalówka* 'microwave' (← *kuchenka mikrofalowa* 'id.').

Derivatives (← RA) formed on the basis of multi-word expressions (RA+N) are not, however, always synonymous with their source, cf., for example, personal nouns such as R. *neftjanik* 'oil worker' (← *neftjanoj* 'oil-RA', semantically referring to *neftjanaja promyšlennost'* 'oil industry'), or P. *naftowiec* 'id.' (← *naftowy*/*przemysł naftowy*).

As could be learned from the above descriptions and tables, in Slavic languages not only combinations of RA+N or N+N$_{obl.case}$, but also derivatives can be

Tab. 10.7: Multi-word expressions and derivatives.

	Multi-word expression (RA+N/N+RA)	Derivative (or ellipsis of the head + nominalization of the RA)
'made of/ consisting of'	R. *solomennaja* (← *soloma* 'straw') *šljapa* 'strawhat'	
	Cz. *slaměný* (← *sláma* 'straw') *klobouk* 'id.'	Cz. *slamák* 'id.'
'temporal'	Cz. *noční* (← *noc* 'night') *směna* 'night shift'	Cz. *noční* 'id.' (ellipsis of the head + nominalization of the RA)
	R. *večernjaja* (← *večer* 'evening') *gazeta* 'evening newspaper'	R. *večerka* 'id.'
	P. *gazeta popołudniowa* (← *popołudnie* 'afternoon') 'id.'	P. *popołudniówka* 'id.'
	Cz. *večerní* (← *večer* 'evening') *noviny* 'id.'	Cz. *večerník* 'id.'
	R. *utrennij* (← *utro* 'morning') *spektakl'* 'morning matinee'	R. *utrennik* 'id.' (also in the meaning 'morning frost' referring to *utrennij moroz*)
'temporal-final'	Cz. *jarní* (← *jaro* 'spring') *kabát* 'spring coat'	Cz. *jarník* 'id.'
'final'	R. *učitel'skaja* (← *učitel'* 'teacher') *komnata* 'teachers' room'	R. *učitel'skaja* (ellipsis of the head + nominalization of the RA)
'instrumental'	R. *motornaja* (← *motor*) *lodka* 'motorboat'	R. *motorka* 'id.'
	Cz. *motorní* (← *motor*) *vlak* 'motor train'	Cz. *motorák* 'id.'
	R. *parusnoe* (← *parus* 'sail') *sudno* 'sailing boat; lit. sail-RA boat'	R. *parusnik* 'id.'
	P. *łódź żaglowa* (← *żagiel* 'sail') 'id.; lit. boat sail-RA'	P. *żaglówka* 'id.'

found as equivalents of English (or German) compounds. In some cases there are certain regularities, e.g., in the word-formation category of p l a c e   n o u n s (implying final relations), which is also why there are fewer parallel RA+N-combinations, e.g., E. *cowshed* – R. *korovnik*/Cz. *kravín* (← *korova/kráva* 'cow'), E. *vineyard* – R. *vinogradnik* (← *vinograd* 'vine, grape'), P. *winnica*/Cz. *vinice* (← *wino/vino* 'vine, grapevine'); E. *teapot, teakettle* – R. *čajnik*/Cz. *čajník* (← *čaj* 'tea'), etc.

Denominal p e r s o n a l   n o u n s also have to be mentioned in this context, whose implicit actional meaning is explicated in their English compound-equivalents, e.g., R. *parketčik*, P. *parkieciarz*, Cz. *parketář* 'parquet floor layer' (← *parket/ parkiet* 'parquet'), R. *spletnik* and P. *plotkarz* 'scandalmonger' (← *spletnja/plotka* 'gossip'). While in English we can find both designation types (*footballer* and *football player*) in certain names (e.g., those of athletes), Slavic languages here too usually have derivatives, be it on the basis of borrowings (Cz. *fotbalista, volejbalista*), loan translations or calques (P. *piłkarz* 'footballer' ← *piłka nożna* 'football; lit. ball foot-RA', *siatkarz* 'volleyball player' ← *siatka* 'net' respectively *piłka siatkowa* 'volleyball; lit. ball net-RA').

6 Conclusion

To a significant extent the increase of new vocabulary in the modern Slavic languages feeds on borrowings and loan translations or hybrid formations, a large part of which consist of compound patterns and compound elements of foreign origin. Direct borrowings or loan translations are not only to be found in the domains of technology, economy, finances, etc., but also increasingly in colloquial vocabulary.

New compounds, which consist exclusively of native components and do not represent loan translations, are, however, rarely documented or never. Yet the foreignness of neologisms is mitigated in so far as one or both components are usually already known as borrowings; the compound can consequently also be perceived as an autonomous formation.

Comparing new c o m p o u n d s with the traditional models of composition, the following conclusions can be drawn:
a) The productivity of the formations with a clipped international component (← RA or N) continues.
b) Influenced by the borrowing of more recent English compounds (including partial and complete calques), the frequency of compounds in Slavic languages is increasing, which creates the impression of heightened productivity of one model in particular – the formation of compounds without a linking vowel.
c) Related to borrowing processes, the number of compounds with a non-derived head is increasing (as opposed to the dominant number of deverbal derivations as heads in older compounds).
d) Most of the recent compounds formed or borrowed according to the models a) and b) possess parallel designations in the form of RA+N/N+RA, whose

occurrence is often more frequent than that of the compounds. In this context we can observe cases of functional-stylistic differentiation between compounds (of direct borrowing) and RA+N/N+RA (or also $N+N_{\text{obl.case/prep.case}}$) structures.

e) The scope of formation and use of new compounds are restricted by the given theme and communicative domain (specifically in the case of model b). They predominantly fulfil a designatory function, while text functions such as that of syntactic condensation (with few occasional exceptions) are as alien to them as to the traditional Slavic compounds.

The productivity of the derivation of relational adjectives from new borrowings is not affected by borrowed compounds. With a high degree of regularity, relational adjectives are first derived from recent single-word borrowings, in order to integrate them into further designation processes and, in many cases, combinations of RA+N/N+RA are the only way to reproduce English compounds.

As can be deduced from the examples provided, besides the many correspondences in the structures of the equivalents of newer English borrowings in the languages considered there are also differences which represent a distinct conservation of traditional designation patterns (RA+N/N+RA or $N+N_{\text{gen/prep.case}}$ instead of N+N) and/or also a different functional-stylistic integration.

While Isačenko (1958) could trace certain discrepancies or preferences in the methods of designation in the individual Slavic languages back to different loan influences (German vs. French), more commonalities seem to develop under the present dominant influence of one language, that is English. Isačenko's suggestion to establish a structural typology for the vocabularies of all Slavic languages, however, still has to be put into practice.

7 References

Belošapkova, Vera A. and Elena A. Zemskaja (1962): Iz istorii funkcionirovanija otsubstantivnych prilagateľnych. In: Viktor V. Vinogradov, Elena A. Ivančikova, Jurij S. Sorokin and Nataľja Ju. Švedova (eds.), *Materialy i issledovanija po russkomu literaturnomu jazyku*. Vol. 5, 4–25. Moskva: Izdateľstvo AN SSSR.

Benin'i [Benigni], Valentina (2007): Analitičeskie prilagateľnye: Rasprostranenie inojazyčnoj modeli "opredeljajuščee suščestviteľnoe + opredeljaemoe suščestviteľnoe". In: Elena A. Zemskaja, Marija L. Kalenčuk, Marija Ja. Glovinskaja, Svetlana M. Kuz'mina and Anna V. Zanadvorova (eds.), *Jazyk v dviženii. K 70-letiju L. P. Krysina*, 68–82. Moskva: Jazyki slavjanskoj kuľtury.

Bozděchová, Ivana (1997): Vliv angličtiny na češtinu. In: František Daneš (ed.), *Český jazyk na přelomu tisíciletí*, 271–279. Praha: Academia.

Bozděchová, Ivana (2010): Kompozita v proměnach moderní české slovní zásoby odborné a neologické. In: Nina F. Klymenko and Jevgenija A. Karpilovs'ka (eds.), *Vidodbražennja istoriї ta kul'tury narodu v slovotvorenni*, 35–46. Kyïv: Vydavnyčyj dim Dmytra Burago.

Buslaev, Fedor I. (2009 [1862–63]): *Istoričeskaja grammatika russkogo jazyka. Sintaksis.* Moskva: Direkt-Media. http://x86watch.com/istoricheskaya-grammatika-russkogo-yazyika-sintaksis/110/

Dokulil, Miloš (1962): *Tvoření slov v češtině.* Vol. 1: *Teorie odvozování slov.* Praha: Nakladatelství ČSAV.

Doleschal, Ursula (2000): Das Phänomen der Unflektierbarkeit in den slawischen Sprachen. Habilitationsschrift, Wirtschaftsuniversität Wien, Wien.

Gester, Silke (2001): *Anglizismen im Tschechischen und im Deutschen. Bestandsaufnahme und empirische Analyse der Rezeption im Jahre 2000.* Frankfurt/M.: Lang.

Giegerich, Heinz (2009): Compounding and Lexicalism. In: Rochelle Lieber and Pavol Štekauer (eds.), *The Oxford Handbook of Compounding*, 178–200. Oxford: Oxford University Press.

Gladrow, Wolfgang (ed.) (1998): *Russisch im Spiegel des Deutschen. Eine Einführung in den russisch-deutschen und deutsch–russischen Sprachvergleich.* Frankfurt/M.: Lang.

Golanova, Elena I. (1998): O "mnimych složnych slovach" (razvitie klassa analitičeskich prilagatel'nych v sovremennom russkom jazyke). In: Marija Ja. Glovinskja (ed.), *Liki jazyka*, 31–39. Moskva: Nasledie.

Gramatyka 1998 = Grzegorczykowa, Renata, Roman Laskowki and Henryk Wróbel (eds.) (1998): *Gramatyka współczesnego języka polskiego. Morfologia. 2.* Warszawa: Wydawnictwo PWN.

Gutschmidt, Karl (2003): Tipologični tendencii. In: Ingeborg Ohnheiser (ed.), *Komparacja systemów i funkcjonowania współczesnych języków słowiańskich. 1. Słowotwórstwo/Nominacja*, 339–355. Opole: Uniwersytet Opolski.

Hinrichs, Uwe (2000): Prolegomena zu einer Theorie des Analytismus I + II (anhand der Sprachen in Ost- und Südosteuropa). In: Uwe Hinrichs and Uwe Büttner (eds.), *Die Südosteuropa-Wissenschaften im neuen Jahrhundert. Akten der Tagung vom 16.–19.10. 1999 an der Universität Leipzig*, 107–128. Wiesbaden: Harrassowitz.

Isačenko, Aleksandr V. (1958): K voprosu o strukturnoj tipologii slovarnogo sostava slavjanskich literaturnych jazykov. *Slavia* 27: 334–352.

Jadacka, Hanna (2001): *System słowotwórczy polszczyzny (1945–2000).* Warszawa: Wydawnicto naukowe PWN.

Jadacka, Hanna (2006): *Kultura języka polskiego. Fleksja, słowotwórstwo, składnia.* Warszawa: Wydawnictwo Naukowe PWN.

Kavka, Stanislav (2009): Compounding and idiomatology. In: Rochelle Lieber and Pavol Štekauer (eds.), *The Oxford Handbook of Compounding*, 19–33. Oxford: Oxford University Press.

Kostomarov, Vitalij G. (1999): *Jazykovoj vkus épochi.* 2nd ed. Sankt-Peterburg: Zlatoust.

Kukuškina, Ol'ga V., Anatolij A. Polikarpov and Anton G. Toktonov (2007): Analiz sistemnych charakteristik slovoobrazovatel'nogo processa. (Na osnove analiza novych leksičeskich edinic gazetnogo materiala "Polistilevogo korpusa sovremennogo russkogo jazyka"). http://www.philol.msu.ru/~humlang/articles/novgazlex.html

Levi, Judith N. (1978): *The Syntax and Semantics of Complex Nominals.* New York: Academic Press.

Lieber, Rochelle and Pavol Štekauer (eds.) (2009): *The Oxford Handbook of Compounding.* Oxford: Oxford University Press.

Martincová, Olga (ed.) (1998): *Nová slova v češtině. Slovník neologizmů.* Vol. 1. Praha: Academia.

Martincová, Olga (ed.) (2004): *Nová slova v češtině. Slovník neologizmů.* Vol. 2. Praha: Academia.

Mezhevich, Ilana (2002): English compounds and Russian relational adjectives. In: Geoffrey S. Morrison and Les Zsoldos (eds.), Proceedings of the North West Linguistics Conference 2002. http://edocs.lib.sfu.ca/projects/NWLC2002/NWLC2002_Proceedings_Mezehvich.pdf

Mluvnice češtiny 1986 = Dokulil, Miloš, Karel Horálek, Jiřina Hůrkova and Miloslava Knappová (1986): *Mluvnice češtiny*. Vol. 1. Praha: Academia.

Nábělková, Mira (1999): Internacionálne v novej adjektívnej lexike v slovenčine. In: Ján Bosák (ed.), *Internacionalizácia v súčasných slovanských jazykoch. Za a proti*, 100–115. Veda: Bratislava.

Ohnheiser, Ingeborg (2004): Analytische Tendenzen in der Wortbildung slawischer Gegenwartssprachen? In: Uwe Hinrichs (ed.), *Die europäischen Sprachen auf dem Wege zum analytischen Sprachtyp*, 97–111. Wiesbaden: Harrassowitz.

Ohnheiser, Ingeborg (2012): Slovosloženie v sisteme slovoobrazovanija i v tekste. In: Jerzy Sierociuk (ed.), *Słowotwórstwo słowiańskie. System i tekst*, 101–111. Poznań: Wydawnictwo PTPN.

Ortner, Hanspeter and Lorelies Ortner (2015): Schemata and semantic roles in word-formation. In: Peter O. Müller, Ingeborg Ohnheiser, Susan Olsen and Franz Rainer (eds.), *Word-Formation. An International Handbook of the Languages of Europe*. Vol. 2, 1035–1056. Berlin/Boston: De Gruyter Mouton.

Panov, Michail V. (2004 [1971]): Ob analitičeskich prilagatel'nych. In: Michail V. Panov, *Trudy po obščemu jazykoznaniju i russkomu jazyku*. Vol. 1, 137–150. Moskva: Jazyki slavjanskoj kul'tury. http://danefae.org/lib/panov/trudy/selecta-i.pdf

Plag, Ingo (2009): *Word-Formation in English*. 5th ed. Cambridge: Cambridge University Press.

Rainer, Franz (2013): Can relational adjectives really express any relation? An onomasiological perspective. *SKASE Journal of Theoretical Linguistics* 10(1): 12–40. http://www.skase.sk/

Rochtchina, Julia (2012): Morphology and lexicology interface. Latest Russian neologisms: The next step towards analytism? In: Veronika Makarova (ed.), *Russian Language Studies in North America. New Perspectives from Theoretical and Applied Linguistics*, 71–84. Cambridge: Cambridge University Press.

Russkaja grammatika 1980 = Švedova, Natal'ja Ju. (ed.) (1980): *Russkaja grammatika*. Vol. 1. Moskva: Nauka.

Selimski, Ludvig (2003): Projava na tendencijata kăm internacionalizacija v južnoslavjanskite ezici. In: Ingeborg Ohnheiser (ed.), *Komparacja systemów i funkcjonowania współczesnych języków słowiańskich. 1. Słowotwórstwo/Nominacja*, 103–126. Opole: Uniwersytet Opolski.

Szymanek, Bogdan (2009): IE, Slavonic: Polish. In: Rochelle Lieber and Pavol Štekauer (eds.), *The Oxford Handbook of Compounding*, 464–477. Oxford: Oxford University Press.

Šlosar, Dušan (1999): *Česká kompozita diachronně*. Brno: Masarykova univerzita.

Štekauer, Pavol (2005): Onomasiological Approach to Word-Formation. In: Pavol Štekauer and Rochelle Lieber (eds.), *Handbook of Word-Formation*, 207–232. Dordrecht: Springer.

Štekauer, Pavol (2009): Meaning predictability of novel context-free compounds. In: Rochelle Lieber and Pavol Štekauer (eds.), *The Oxford Handbook of Compounding*, 272–297. Oxford: Oxford University Press.

Townsend, Charles E. (1996): Some pecularities of Czech relational adjectives. In: Barbara H. Partee and Petr Sgall (eds.), *Discourse and Meaning. Papers in honor of Eva Hajičová*, 393–403. Amsterdam/Philadelphia: Benjamins.

Uluchanow, Igor and Renate Belentschikow (eds.) (2007): *Russisch–deutsches Wörterbuch der neuen Wörter*. Moskva: Azbukovnik.

Vačkova, Kira (1999): Internacionalizacionni procesi v bălgarskija ezik ot kraja na XX vek. In: Ján Bosák (ed.), *Internacionalizácia v súčasných slovanských jazykoch. Za a proti*, 59–66. Veda: Bratislava.

Vinogradov, Viktor V. (1982): *Očerki po istorii russkogo literaturnogo jazyka XVII–XIX vv.* Moskva: Vysšaja škola.

Waszakowa, Krystyna (2005): *Przejawy internacjonalizacji w słowotwórstwie współczesnej polszczyzny*. Warszawa: WUW.

Worbs, Erika, Andrzej Markowski and Andreas Meger (eds.) (2007): *Polnisch-deutsches Wörterbuch der Neologismen*. Wiesbaden: Harrassowitz.

Zemskaja, Elena A. (1992): *Slovoobrazovanie kak dejatel'nost'*. Moskva: Nauka.

Zemskaja, Elena A. (1997): Aktivnye tendencii slovoproizvodstva. In: Evgenij Širjaev (red.), *Najnowsze dzieje języków słowiańskich. Russkij jazyk*, 167–201. Opole: Uniwersytet Opolski.

Zibrova, Raisa V. (1984): Semantika ad"ektivnych i genetivnych odnokornevych opredelenij v sovremennom russkom jazyke. Ph.D. dissertation, State University Voronež. http://cheloveknauka.com/semantika-adektivnyh-i-genetivnyh-odnokornevyh-opredeleniy-v-sovremennom-russkom-yazyke

Heike Baeskow

11 Rules, patterns and schemata in word-formation

Abstract: The observation that word-formation is systematic to a relatively high degree has inspired generations of linguists to identify patterns, rules and schemata and to describe regularities as well as idiosyncrasies from different perspectives. This article presents selected approaches, which have successfully contributed to the scientific attractiveness of word-formation, and takes account of morpho-syntactic, semantic, phonological and cognitive considerations.

1 Introduction

Since the early seventies of the last century, word-formation has opened up a highly complex and continually expanding field of research, which owes its attractiveness to the fact that the combination of morphemes is not restricted to morpho-syntactic considerations, but also involves aspects of other linguistic components, especially of phonology and semantics. Since the interaction of these components is most striking in derivation, this article will concentrate on the rules, patterns and schemata involved in word-formation processes of this type. For instance, from a morpho-syntactic point of view, the derivative *writer* consists of the verbal base *write* and the nominalizing suffix *-er*, which constitutes the head of the complex word because it determines its categorial properties. Semantically, the deverbal derivative *writer* is an agent noun because it refers to the class of individuals actively or habitually involved in a writing event. Of course, the properties depicted here rather pre-theoretically are not individual properties of *writer*, but apply to a whole range of derivatives, as examples like *driver, reader,*

Heike Baeskow, Frankfurt/M., Germany

https://doi.org/10.1515/9783111420554-011

singer, runner, producer and many more suggest. Moreover, sets of data like these, which are easily retrievable from reverse dictionaries (e.g., Lehnert 1971, Muthmann 2002 or the *OneLook Reverse Dictionary* provided by the internet), reveal the selectional preferences of a suffix. Thus, although the highly productive suffix *-er* is relatively flexible with respect to its input (cf. *potter, stranger, upper* 'antidepressant pill', *fiver* 'five pound note', *penny-a-liner* 'journalist'), it prototypically combines with verbal bases.

The interaction between derivation and phonology becomes evident in pairs like *divine* [dɪˈvaɪn] : *divinity* [dɪˈvɪnəti], *serene* [səˈriːn] : *serenity* [səˈrenəti] or *profound* [prəˈfaʊnd] : *profundity* [prəˈfʌndəti]. Unlike the functionally similar native suffix *-ness*, which preserves the sound pattern of its base, (e.g., *serene* : *sereneness*), the Latinate suffix *-ity* often reduces a long vowel or diphthong contained in the final syllable of a polysyllabic adjectival base. Since it is the antepenultimate syllable of an *-ity* derivative which is affected by vowel reduction, this rule is referred to as trisyllabic shortening.

Of course, prefixation is an "interactive process" as well. In English, prefixes do not normally change the categorial properties of their bases because they occur in the non-head position, but they add semantic information content. For example, the prefix *un-*, which typically combines with adjectives, has a negativizing function. As observed by Jespersen 1974 [1942]: 466) and confirmed by Zimmer (1964: 36–37), *un-* shows a relatively strong preference for adjectival bases denoting positive qualities. There are derivatives like *unwise, unhealthy, unclean* or *unhandsome*, but forms like **undumb, *unill, *undirty* or **unugly* are unacceptable. According to the redundancy restriction formulated by Lieber (2004: 161), "[a]ffixes do not add semantic content that is already available within a base word (simplex or derived)". As far as *un-* is concerned, there are only a few exceptions to the redundancy restriction, including forms like *uncorrupt, unguilty, unselfish* or *unvulgar* (Zimmer 1964: 36; Lieber 2004: 159). The redundancy restriction also predicts the compatibility of *un-* with semantically neutral bases, which according to Zimmer is attested in a number of cases (*unbindable, uncountable, unseen,* etc.).

Although derivation – unlike syntax – involves a rather high degree of idiosyncrasy, which has to be listed in the lexicon or a comparable storage place, the preliminary examples provided so far illustrate that morpho-syntactic, semantic and phonological regularities, which account for well-formedness, rarely affect individual words, but operate over sets of derivatives. The observation that there are regularities in word-formation by derivation has inspired generations of linguists to identify patterns and schemata and to formulate rules which serve to generate new complex words on the one hand and to analyse existing ones on the other. However, since word-formation – like language in general – is a dynamic system, these rules do not have absolute character, but express strong tendencies which may be overridden by exceptions.

2 The pre-generative era

Before representative rules, patterns and schemata and the way they are treated in modern linguistics are dealt with in more detail, some pre-generative approaches which have had a considerable influence on subsequent morphological research will be considered briefly.

Most valuable insights, which are ascribed to modern word-formation theories nowadays, were already formulated by Hermann Paul (1846–1921). In his lecture "Ueber die Aufgaben der Wortbildungslehre" [On the tasks of word-formation theory], whose content is provided by Henne and Kilian (1998: 171–192), he convincingly argues that inflection and word-formation should be treated as different domains of morphology. This view arose from the observation that inflection is relatively systematic and functionally determined by the syntax, whereas word-formation is only partially regular. Paul does not deny an analogy between both domains: there are inflectional categories such as the genitive or the subjunctive on the one hand and word-formation categories like *nomina agentis* or *nomina actionis* on the other. However, word-formation involves aspects of meaning, which are neither predicted by the syntax nor reducible to dictionary entries. Moreover, in word-formation, the relation between form and function is often obscured by lexicalization, as in the case of German *Schöpfer* 'Creator', whose relation to *schöpfen* 'to create' is only etymologically traceable. By emphasizing the necessity to identify the morphological and functional aspects which favour or restrict the productivity of a suffix, Hermann Paul anticipates the mechanisms of generative word-formation.

Paul's differentiation between form and function or meaning is mirrored by Ferdinand de Saussure's (2005 [1916]: 98–102) view of the linguistic sign. According to Saussure (1857–1913), whose name is inextricably linked with European structuralism, a linguistic sign is associated with a concept (*signifié*) and a sound sequence (*signifiant*), which are related to each other in an arbitrary way. For instance, the fact that the concept HORSE is referred to as *horse* /hɔːs/ in English, *cheval* /ʃəval/ in French, *Pferd* /pfeːrt/ in German or *caballo* /kaßaʎo/ in Spanish is entirely arbitrary or unmotivated. As far as word-formation is concerned, Saussure explicitly distinguishes between semantic and grammatical functions of derivational suffixes. For example, the suffix *-tēr* of the Greek noun *zeuk-tēr* 'one who yokes' denotes an agent or initiator (*l'agent, l'auteur de l'action*). On the other hand, the suffix -*nū* as displayed by *zéug-nū(mi)* is a marker of the present tense and hence fulfils a grammatical function. Importantly, however, complex signs are never entirely motivated a) because their parts are inherently arbitrary and b) because their semantics is not strictly compositional (e.g., pain + ful), but results from the interaction of the meanings of their parts (e.g., pain × ful). This part-whole relation plays a key role in Saussure's approach.

The view that the linguistic sign or signal consists of sound and meaning is preserved by the American structuralist Leonard Bloomfield (1887–1949). In particular, sound and meaning are involved in the definition of the morpheme: "A linguistic form which bears no partial phonetic-semantic resemblance to any other form, is a *simple* form or *morpheme*" (Bloomfield 1933: 161). The meaning of a morpheme is referred to as a *sememe*, i.e. a feature of the practical world, and sememes are arbitrarily linked to phonemes. However, the description of meaning is considered to be beyond the scope of linguistics, which according to Bloomfield is an independent science. In this respect, American structuralism differs from European structuralism, where meaning was part of the linguistic description. As far as word-formation is concerned, a remarkable consequence of the purely structural Bloomfieldian approach is that *primary words* like *hammer, rudder, spider, bitter, linger* or *under*, which bear a partial resemblance to secondary words like *danc-er, lead-er* or *rid-er*, are supposed to consist of two immediate constituents, namely of a root (/hɛm-/, /rod-/, /spajd-/, etc.) and an affix-like constituent -*er* (1933: 240–241). The constituent which resembles the derivational suffix -*er* is referred to as a *primary affix* because it occurs in *primary words*, i.e. in words which contain no free forms among their immediate constituents. Further examples of primary affixes are -*ow* (e.g., *furrow, yellow, borrow*), -*ock* (e.g., *hummock, mattock, hassock*) or *de-* (e.g., *deceive, deduce, detain*). Primary affixes which convey semantic information are typically found in American Indian languages, whose analysis was the main concern of American structuralism.

The descriptive approach to language initiated in structuralism is maintained in the comprehensive works on English word-formation presented by Koziol (1971 [1937]), Jespersen (1974 [1942]) and Marchand (1969). These works include large sets of data, which are annotated with diachronic and synchronic information. Koziol lists his examples in chronological order, beginning with Old English. Jespersen's work on morphology, which is part of his *Modern English Grammar* in seven volumes, is based on historical principles, but focuses on present-day English and thus on "living, i.e. productive formations" (1974: 4), including their phonological behaviour. A milestone in the literature on English word-formation is Marchand's synchronic-diachronic approach first published in 1960. Since this book provides a wealth of data, it offers a solid, corpus-like basis for morphological analyses. As far as the theoretical framework is concerned, Marchand's (1969) work ranges between traditional and generative approaches. On the one hand, it is in the tradition of Koziol and Jespersen in that it includes etymological aspects. On the other hand, it is already partly influenced by Lees (1960), who derived nominalizations from underlying sentences via transformations. Thus, Marchand refers to complex words as "grammatical syntagmas" (1969: 2) and assumes that a denominal agent noun like *potter* derives from an underlying sentence *He makes pots* (1969: 276). However, since the complex machinery of early transformational grammar (i.e. Chomsky 1957) is not applied by Marchand, his work is closer to the traditional than to the generative school of thought. Although concrete mechanisms of word-formation are not developed by Koziol, Jespersen and Marchand, their works constitute reference books of great value, which are consulted in international research up to the present, as for instance in Bauer, Lieber and Plag (2013).

3 Generative approaches

The idea that nominalizations are derived from underlying sentences via transformations as suggested by Lees (1960) and accepted, e.g., by Marchand (1969) and Lakoff (1970) was criticized by Chomsky in his influential article "Remarks on nominalization" (1970). Although it was Chomsky himself who developed generative transformational grammar, he claims that the idiosyncrasies involved in word-formation should be dealt with in the lexicon.

In the seventies of the last century, this position gave rise to the lexicalist hypothesis, according to which the lexicon functions not only to store the idiosyncratic properties of lexical items, but also to accommodate word-formation processes. Unlike the authors of traditional works, who confined themselves to descriptive, etymologically oriented analyses of complex words, the representatives of generative approaches have always attempted to reveal morpho-syntactic, semantic and phonological generalizations over patterns of word-formation, some of which will be presented in the following sections.

3.1 Derivational mechanisms

3.1.1 Word-formation rules, adjustment rules and word-formation patterns

A major achievement of generative word-formation theories is the explicit formalization of the observation anchored already in traditional approaches that the combination of derivational affixes with bases is not arbitrary, but somehow systematic. Morris Halle was the first to introduce word-formation rules (WFRs) as a formal device which tells us "how the morphemes are to be arranged in sequence to form actual words" (1973: 4) and which – together with a list of morphemes – provides the potential words of a language. The actual words are separated from potential words by means of a filter and find their way into the dictionary. Potential words (e.g., *derival, *confusal, *arrivation) are marked as [–lexical insertion] by the filter and thus prevented from entering the dictionary. The filter also accounts for idiosyncratic semantic and phonological information associated with lexical items. It ensures that only well-formed actual words are listed in the dictionary. Halle's pioneering model of word-formation, which de-scribes regular patterns as well as idiosyncrasies without making use of syntactic transformations, was elaborated by Jackendoff (1975), Aronoff (1976) and later on by Bochner (1993). However, contrary to the morpheme-based approach presented by Halle, these authors prefer a full-entry theory, i.e. a theory of derivation in which WFRs take actual words from the dictionary as their input instead of mor-phemes. Thus, they avoid the problem of assigning lexical properties to *hapax legomena* such as *butch* (in *butcher*) or non-native roots like *mit* (in *permit*, *sub-mit*, *transmit*, etc.). According to Aronoff (1976: 49), both the input and the output of a WFR are members of major lexical categories. The following WFR combines the suffix *-er* with actual words of the category "verb". More precisely, the verb serving as an input may be either transitive (e.g., *teacher*) or intransitive (e.g., *sleeper*). The output of the WFR belongs to the category "noun" and receives an agentive interpretation, which is "a function of the meaning of the base" (Aronoff 1976: 50).

(1) $[X]_V$ → $[[X]_V \quad \#er]_N$
     [±transitive]   [±transitive]

'one who Vs habitually, professionally, …'

As indicated already by Halle (1973: 16), a high proportion of complex words from the dictionary are stored already in the speaker's permanent memory, so that strictly speaking, a WFR is activated only when he/she encounters or forms new words. Aronoff (1976: 31) explicitly accounts for this observation by claiming that WFRs function not only to generate new words, but also constitute redundancy rules, i.e. rules which help to analyze existing words. For example, the rule in (1) reveals that *baker* consists of the verb *bake* and the nominalizing suffix *-er* and thus has the structure $bake_V\#er_N$. The structurally similar form *butcher* is analysa-ble only as $butch\#er_N$. Since *butch* does not exist in English, this string – unlike $bake_V$ – cannot be assigned a categorial label by the relevant WFR.

A problem with the word-based approach is that the output of a WFR is not always well-formed and may require adjustment before the rules of phonology apply. For instance, the rule which combines verbs like *nominate, evacuate, vaccinate*, etc. with the suffix *-ee* generates the sequences **nominatee, *evacuatee* or **vaccinatee*, which do not exist in this shape. Aronoff (1976: 88–98) solves this problem by introducing a truncation rule, i.e. an adjustment rule which deletes the verb-forming suffix *-ate* to yield the well-formed sequences *nominee, evacuee* or *vaccinee*. Another type of adjustment rule is the allomorphy rule, which serves to adjust the form of a morpheme to its phonological environment. For example, this type of rule determines the distribution of the phonologically conditioned variants *+Ation, +ion*, and *+tion* associated with the suffix *-ion*.

Aronoff's comprehensive work has set a standard for generative word-formation. By separating the lexical component from the syntax, Aronoff – like Halle (1973) and Jackendoff (1975) – explicitly accounts for the fact that words are more than syntactic building blocks and that the speakers of a language are well aware of their internal structure and their interaction with other linguistic components.

The full-entry theory proposed by Jackendoff (1975), in which idiosyncratic information is measured by relating derivatives to their bases via redundancy rules (e.g., *decide* ↔ *decision*), inspired Motsch (2004) to describe word-formation processes on the basis of word-formation patterns. A complex word consists of a semantic pattern ("semantisches Muster") and a phonological form. In the lexicon, these components are paired with syntactic and morphological information respectively. The potential to form neologisms is inherent to the semanticosyntactic patterns. As shown in (2), such a pattern is conceived of as a predicate-argument structure containing a categorial label, e.g., (N), and an argument position (x). In the course of a word-formation process, the categorial label is replaced by a concrete lexical item, e.g., HUND ('DOG'). The semantic representation of the newly generated word *hündisch* 'dog-like', which is predicated of the referent of (x), is specified in the form of the paraphrase 'a referent x has prominent properties of N (e.g., of dogs)'.

(2)   SEMANTISCHES MUSTER:
      [WIE (N)] (x)
      'ein Bezugswort x hat prominente Eigenschaften von N'
      SEMANTISCHE REPRÄSENTATION VON WORTBILDUNGEN:
      hündisch
      [WIE (HUND)] (x)
      'ein Bezugswort x hat prominente Eigenschaften von Hunden'

Word-formation patterns allow for a direct mapping of meaning structures onto sound structures and thus render mediating syntactic rules redundant.

3.1.2 Subcategorization frames

The introduction of a lexicon as an autonomous component of the grammar removed from the syntax the burden of handling word-formation processes with all their idiosyncrasies. However, the generative theories presented so far indicate that the shift of word-formation from the syntax to the lexicon coincided with the introduction of quite a few morphological devices. Halle's model requires a filter, and the output of Aronoff's WFRs may be forced to undergo truncation or allomorphy rules.

A less costly and more elegant description of derivational processes is achieved by Lieber's (1981) morpheme-based approach, which provides lexical entries for the idiosyncratic properties of free and bound morphemes. The lexical entry of a morpheme is composed of its phonological and semantic representation, categorial information and diacritical features (e.g., [+Latinate]). Significantly, the entries of affixes display subcategorization frames which specify the category of their input and output, e.g.,

(3) -ee: $]_V$ ___ $]_N$

Subcategorization frames have their origin in generative transformational grammar (e.g., Chomsky 1965), where they revealed the number and category of the complements required by verbs. A considerable advantage of Lieber's model is that it dispenses not only with WFRs, but also with adjustment rules. Since affixes have access to bound morphemes, truncation is no longer required. Thus, -ee directly selects the bound root *nomin-* of the verb *nominate* and inserts it into its subcategorization frame. The abolishment of truncation is advantageous especially for languages whose verbs have infinitival endings (e.g., German *fahren* → *Fahr-er*, French *danser* → *dans-eur*, Spanish *pensar* → *pensa-miento*). Allomorphy rules are no longer required either because according to Lieber (1981: 141), all allomorphy in English is confined to stems. Analogously to inflectional morphology, she postulates lexical classes for ordered pairs of Latinate stem allomorphs, which are defined over morpho-lexical rules (e.g., *Xduce* ~ *Xduct*, *Xscribe* ~ *Xscript*, *Xmit* ~ *Xmis* etc). In the lexical entry of -ion (and -ive), it is stated that these suffixes combine with the marked member of each pair, i.e. with the one which does not occur independently (e.g., *reduct-ion*, *inscript-ion*, *permiss-ive*). Given this mechanism, the shapes of the suffixes remain invariable. Although Lieber's approach is morpheme-based, it does not imply that morphemes must be meaningful.

A morpheme-based, lexicalist approach in the sense of Lieber (1981) is also favoured by Selkirk (1982), Olsen (1986), Dalton-Puffer (1996) and Baeskow (2002).

In Selkirk's model, the notion of subcategorization is extended to include the selectional behaviour of bound roots like *-ceive* (as in *deceive, receive, conceive,* etc.) or *moll-* (as in *mollify*), whose combination with other morphemes is as obligatory as the addition of an affix to an appropriate base.

3.2 Semantic restrictions in generative word-formation

The constraints imposed upon derivational processes by lexicalists affect not only the subcategorial behaviour of affixes, but also the interpretation of their output. In generative word-formation, semantic aspects of derivation are usually expressed in terms of argument structure, thematic relations and mechanisms which co-ordinate the word-internal assignment of thematic information. Although it is widely accepted today that argument structure is associated not only with verbs, but also with nouns, adjectives and prepositions (cf., e.g., Williams 1981; Higginbotham 1985; Rauh 1988; Zwarts 1992; Lieber 2004), the focus of attention has for a long time been on deverbal derivatives in research on word-formation.

3.2.1 Absorption and inheritance

In lexicalist approaches (e.g., Olsen 1986: 78; Randall 1988: 143–145) it is assumed that the much discussed suffix *-er* absorbs the theta-role of the external argument of its verbal base. As a result, this role is no longer assignable outside the derivative. Thus, a phrase like **the builder of the ship by John* is ill-formed because the agent role of *build* is absorbed by *-er* and simultaneously assigned to the prepositional phrase *by John*, which leads to a violation of the theta-criterion postulated by Chomsky (1993: 36). According to this restriction on theta-role assignment, "[e]ach argument bears one and only one theta-role, and each theta-role is assigned to one and only one argument". Formally, the process of absorption may be represented as follows:

(4)   a. [[build <E<AGENT, THEME>>] -er <R>]
       b. [[build <E<$\emptyset_i$, THEME>>] -er <R<AGENT$_i$>>]
          |⎯⎯⎯⎯⎯⎯⎯↑

Apart from the referential argument <E>, which indicates that *build* denotes an event, (4a) specifies the theta-roles AGENT and THEME, which the verb assigns to its external and internal argument respectively. This representation is referred to as the verb's theta-grid.

Since *-er* derivatives denote sets of entities in the world (i.e. human beings or objects), this suffix is associated with the referential argument <R> introduced by Williams (1981: 86). In the course of the derivation, the AGENT role of *to build* is absorbed by *-er* and hence added to the suffix's theta-grid, as shown in (4b). The process of absorption (first introduced by Jaeggli 1986 for passive constructions) may be considered a kind of morphological licensing because it ensures the interpretation of derivatives like *builder, writer, singer*, etc. as agent nouns. Since *-er* specifically (though of course not exclusively) refers to the base verb's external argument, Burzio (1986) claims that unaccusative verbs like *fall, die* or *arrive*, which only have an internal argument in their argument structure, are excluded from being selected by this suffix.

The THEME role of *to build* is passed on to the derivative *builder* by inheritance (e.g., Selkirk 1982: 33; Olsen 1986: 78–88; Rappaport Hovav and Levin 1992: 130–131). In contrast to an absorbed role, an inherited role is available for the assignment to a modifier (e.g., *shipbuilder*) or a syntactic phrase (e.g., *a builder of ships*). This process, however, is semantically restricted. As noted by Rappaport Hovav and Levin, English instrument nouns do not inherit the internal argument of their base verb, with the result that there are no corresponding phrases introduced by *of* which convey an instrumental reading. For example, *a wiper of windshields* does not refer to an instrument. Only an agentive reading would be possible here, but this is blocked by extralinguistic considerations. If *wiper* is extended to *windshield wiper* or *a wiper for windshields*, the noun *windshield* does not realize the internal argument of *to wipe* <E <AGENT, THEME>> because *wiper* did not inherit this argument from its base verb and hence cannot assign the THEME role. Thus, the instrumental role for *windshield* has to be reconstructed via inference. The word-internal assignment of the THEME role is also blocked in the case of instrument nouns like *tin opener, hairdryer, vegetable steamer*, etc. (but assigned via the inference process just mentioned). Moreover, there is a correlation between inheritance and the event interpretation of *-er* nominals. For example, the agentive reading of a phrase like *a grinder of imported coffees* presupposes that an event of grinding has actually occurred. On the other hand, instrument nouns like *grinder* or *coffee grinder* emphasize the purpose of a machine rather than an event in which it is used. Thus, instrument nouns (or non-event nominals) are incompatible with adverbs of frequency such as *frequent* or *constant* (e.g., *I know that Dan is a frequent waxer of parquet floors* vs. **I know that this mop is a frequent floor waxer*).

As observed by Olsen (1986: 82–83) for German, inheritance is not generally optional. If the derivative generated by *-er* constitutes a relational noun, which requires complementation, its THEME role has to be saturated word-internally. Examples are **Hemmer, *Vertilger* or **Treter,* which are well-formed only in synthetic compounds like *Appetithemmer* 'appetite suppressant', *Unkrautvertilger* 'herbicide' or *Balltreter* 'football player, kicker'.

Although absorption and inheritance successfully restrict the semantic output of regular derivational processes, a problem with these mechanisms is that there is not always a one-to-one relation between a suffix and a particular argument position of the base. For instance, established derivatives like *roaster, fryer, broiler* or formations like *wilter, dyer* or *fader* collected by Ryder (1999) from everyday contexts violate Burzio's generalization because the suffix *-er* makes reference to the internal argument of its unaccusative verbal bases. The same problem is observable for the suffix *-ee,* which typically, but not necessarily absorbs the role of the base verb's first internal argument, i.e. of the argument which syntactically occupies the position of the direct object. This behaviour is responsible for the passive character of many *-ee* derivatives (e.g., *employee, trainee, visitee*). Nevertheless, there are nouns like *addressee, experimentee, amputee, escapee* or *attendee,* which cannot be linked to this particular argument position. Moreover, as far as denominal derivatives like *potter, Marxist* or *festschriftee* are concerned, there is no thematic argument position for the suffix to correspond with because the nominal bases only have a referential argument <R> in their argument structure.

Authors of more recent generative approaches have attempted to solve this matching problem. Barker (1998) postulates an individual theta-role for the suffix *-ee,* which episodically links the sentient, non-volitional referent of an *-ee* derivative to the event denoted by or associated with the base. This approach will be dealt with in more detail in article 18 on semantic restrictions on word-formation: the English suffix *-ee.* In Lieber's (2004, 2006) lexical semantic approach, the input and output of word-formation processes is defined over sets of well-motivated semantic features. An outline of this approach will be presented in the following section. Like Barker's proposal, Lieber's treatment of *-ee* derivatives is also part of article 18.

3.2.2 The anatomy of lexical items: semantic skeleton and semantic body

In lexicalist approaches, lexical entries specify the ensemble of orthographic, phonological, morpho-syntactic and semantic information associated with individual morphological building blocks (words or morphemes). The most delicate matter is the representation of meaning. On the one hand, the referents of many lexical items have highly specific extra-linguistic properties which require complex definitions. Scientific or technical terms are a case in point. Even the definition of the apparently simple item *dog* goes beyond the listing of properties like 'has four legs', 'has fur' and 'barks' if biological and evolutionary facts are taken into consideration. On the other hand, the profundity of world knowledge differs considerably among the speakers of a language. As pointed out by Moravcsik (1981), a child's understanding of objects and concepts is definitely incomplete, and so is the knowledge of the layperson in comparison to the knowledge of the expert. However, despite the discrepancy between the infinite complexity of facts, causal relations and events in the world and the relative narrowness of human knowledge, people are able to communicate more or less successfully. Thus, the mental lexicon in the generative sense should not be expected to deal scientifically with the referents of lexical items. Instead, it makes more sense to distinguish between semantic knowledge and world knowledge, the latter of which is also referred to as conceptual or encyclopedic knowledge. This distinction is at the heart of Lieber's (2004, 2006) lexical semantics model of word-formation. In this model, lexical items are assumed to consist of two components: the semantic skeleton and the semantic body. The skeleton provides elementary lexical information such as an item's category membership and argument structure. The body consists of substantial encyclopedic information which differs from one speaker to another – as pointed out above. The focus of attention is on the semantic skeleton. Significantly, skeletal properties are defined over cross-categorial semantic features like [+material] (*man, chair, book*), [−material] (*peace, time, love*), [+dynamic] (*sing, write, teach*), [−dynamic] (*know, own; tall, intelligent*) or [dynamic], the latter of which is a privative nominal feature, i.e. it is present only in nouns which imply activity, like *author, mother* or *effort*. These features instantiate the ontological categories SUBSTANCES/THINGS/ESSENCES and SITUATIONS that structure the extralinguistic reality in a very abstract but universal way. Another feature, namely [+IEPS] "Inferable Eventual Position or State", adds a PATH component of meaning to the skeleton of verbs denoting a change of position (e.g., *descend, fall, go*) or change of state (e.g., *evaporate, forget, grow*). A sample of semantic skeletons, which include placeholders for argument positions, is given in (5).

(5) a. *chair*   [+material, ([ ])]
     b. *mother*   [+material, dynamic ([ ])]
     c. *employ*   [+dynamic ([ ], [ ])]
     d. *grow*   [+dynamic, +IEPS ([ ])
     e. *happy*   [−dynamic, +scalar ([ ])]

Affixes, like simplex lexical items, are defined by means of semantic features as well. In the following lexical entry postulated by Lieber (2004: 62), the suffix *-er* is specified for the features [+material] and [dynamic]. The brackets are place-holders for the referential argument <R>:

(6)   *-er*
       Syntactic subcategorization: attaches to V, N
       Skeleton: [+material, dynamic, ([ ], <base>)]

An essential ingredient of Lieber's lexical semantics is the principle of co-indexa-tion (2004: 61), which accounts for the interpretation of derivatives independently of the category of their input.

(7)   **Principle of co-indexation**
       In a configuration in which semantic skeletons are composed, co-index the highest nonhead argument with the highest (preferably unindexed) head argument. Indexing must be consistent with semantic conditions on the head argument, if any.

Applied to suffixation, this principle states that the highest argument of the base is co-indexed with the highest argument of the head-forming suffix provided that these arguments are semantically compatible. The resulting derivative absorbs whatever thematic interpretation the base argument has. In the case of a deverb-al *-er* derivative like *driver*, the external argument of *drive* is co-indexed with the referential argument <R> of the suffix, and the derivative assumes an agentive interpretation.

(8)   *driver*
       [+material, dynamic ([$_i$], [+dynamic]([$_i$], [ ]))]
       -er   *drive*

If the base of an *-er* derivative is an unaccusative verb (e.g., *sink*), the principle of co-indexation links the verb's internal argument to the referential argument of the suffix. Since unaccusative verbs lack an external argument, the internal argument is the highest one.

(9)   *sinker*
       [+material, dynamic ([$_i$], [+dynamic, +IEPS ([$_i$]))]
       -er   *sink*

As suggested by (8) and (9), *-er* does not impose a semantic restriction on the non-head argument it is co-indexed with. In the case of *-ee*, the situation is different (cf. article 18 on the English suffix *-ee*).

Subcategorization frames of a morpho-syntactic design gradually lose their significance in Lieber's works on lexical semantics. The reason is that selection on the basis of syntactic category (c-selection) is replaced by semantic selection (s-selection), according to which affixes are sensitive to the semantic categories of their potential bases (cf. Lieber 2006: 266–267).

3.3 From affix ordering to lexical phonology

The compatibility of affixes with bases is determined not only by the individual selectional behaviour of affixes and semantic mechanisms, but also by more general constraints, which have an impact on the structure of the lexicon.

3.3.1 Affix classes

As first observed by Siegel (1974), there are several aspects which suggest that the English affix inventory falls into two classes – class I affixes (10) and class II affixes (11):

(10) in+, con+, de+, sub+, dis+; +ity, +ion, +ate, +al, +or, etc.

(11) un#, be#, non#, fore#; #ness, #hood, #less, #ful, #en, etc.

The distinction between these affix classes was basically a phonological one. The morpheme-boundary "+" and the word-boundary "#" were introduced by Chomsky and Halle (1968) in order to restrict the application of phonological rules. Since these rules operate across morpheme-boundaries, but not across word-boundaries, only class I affixes are able to change the phonological properties of their bases. Moreover, class I affixes themselves may be subject to phonological processes. The negative prefix *in-* is a case in point (e.g., *inactive, impossible, irrelevant, illegal*). On the other hand, class II affixes are phonologically neutral. From a morphological point of view, class I affixes combine with words (e.g., *parent-al, modern-ity, de-limit*) and with bound roots (e.g., *astr-al, vivac-ity, de-duce*), whereas class II affixes predominantly occur in the context of words (e.g., *happi-ness, child-hood, un-kind*). As a result, the former are nearer to the root than the latter in words which contain affixes of both classes (e.g., *credul-ous-*

ness, romant-ic-ism). Moreover, while derivatives formed by class II affixes are semantically transparent, the semantics of derivatives displaying class I affixes is not always predictable. For example, as observed by Riddle (1985), derivatives ending in *-ness* (*ethnicness, Africanness, pinkness*, etc.) ascribe an embodied trait to the individuals they are predicted of, whereas *-ity* derivatives mainly denote abstract entities, i.e. names of concepts, situations, and of characteristics in the generic sense (*ethnicity, hyperactivity, sectility*). Sporadically, however, *-ity* derivatives also refer to concrete entities, e.g., *curiosity* in the sense of 'an object of interest; any object valued as curious, rare, or strange', *cavity* 'a hollow place; a void or empty space within a solid body' or *oddity* 'an odd or peculiar person', 'an odd, peculiar, or grotesque thing' (*Oxford English Dictionary*). The "concrete entity" reading is idiosyncratic and has to be specified in the lexicon.

The most influential observation formulated by Siegel (1974) is that class I affixation precedes class II affixation in English. This ordering hypothesis, which was extended by Allen (1978) to include compounding, served as a basis for Kiparsky's (1982) lexical phonology, in which a close interaction of morphological and phonological processes is assumed. The lexicon consists of three levels (or "strata"): Level 1 accommodates class I affixation (*divine → divin+ity*) as well as irregular inflection (*keep ~ kept, index ~ indices*). At level 2, class II affixation and compounding take place (*sahib → sahib#hood; house#boat*). Level 3 is reserved for regular inflection (*dance ~ danced; book ~ books*). Significantly, the output of the morphological processes taking place at a particular level is subject to a set of phonological rules of the same level. Since the rules of lexical phonology (e.g., trisyllabic shortening, velar softening) interact with morphological processes at each level of the lexicon, they are intrinsically cyclic and thus differ from rules of postlexical phonology (e.g., coalescence, insertion of intrusive *-r*). According to the bracket erasure convention (BEC), the internal structure of words generated at a particular level is invisible to subsequent levels. A hallmark of lexical phonology is the blocking effect. For instance, both the agent noun *assist+ant* and the irregular plural form *oxen* are generated at level 1, where they are lexically specified as [assistant]$_{N \text{ [Agent]}}$ and [oxen]$_{N \text{ [Plural]}}$ respectively. The BEC and the lexical information that *assistant* is an agent noun prevent the verb *assist* from being combined with the productive agent-noun forming suffix *-er* at level 2 (**assister*). Likewise, the formation of **oxes* is blocked at level 3 because the plural form *oxen* was idiosyncratically formed at level 1. The non-application of a general rule, which is due to the application of a specific rule on an earlier level, is referred to as the "elsewhere condition".

3.3.2 Problems with lexical phonology and alternative models

Although lexical phonology was quite influential especially in the eighties of the last century and beyond (cf. Rubach 1984; Mohanan 1986; Booij 1997; McMahon 2000), it has been subject to severe criticism. As shown convincingly by Giegerich (1999), one major problem is that there are quite a few English suffixes which display dual class membership because their morphological or phonological behaviour enables them to select bases at level 1 and level 2. Idiosyncrasy resulting in dual class membership is particularly striking in the following contexts identified by Giegerich:

- an affix which predominantly selects free morphemes sporadically occurs in the context of bound morphemes (e.g., *gorm-less, wist-ful, scrib-er, astrolog-er, un-couth*)
- the phonological neutrality of a suffix is overridden (e.g., *compárable* vs. *cómparable, wild* [waɪld] → *wilderness* [wɪldənəs])
- an affix assigned to class I gains productivity and semantic transparency in certain jargons (e.g., *-ant* in chemo-technical/medical terms like *depressant, digestant, propellant, coolant* or in legal agent nouns such as *defendant, consultant, complainant, claimant*)
- an affix which qualifies for class II membership precedes a class I affix (e.g., *govern#ment+al, un#grammatical+ity*).

Obviously, it is problematic to generalize over the morphological, phonological and semantic properties of affixes and to aim at a neat division of the affix inventory, which eventually determines the structure of the lexicon. Since there is too much idiosyncrasy involved, the lexical properties of affixes do not constitute a reliable criterion for level ordering. Nevertheless, it cannot be denied that lexical phonology provided valuable insights into the complexity of morphological structure and the proceedings at the morphology-phonology interface. Moreover, numerous alternatives have been proposed which preserve the basic insights of this theory.

Apart from revealing the shortcomings of affix-driven stratification, Giegerich (1999) develops an alternative which is intended to overcome the difficulties described above. On the basis of the observation formulated by Selkirk (1982: 98–99) that English morphology distinguishes between the categories "root" and "word", Giegerich proposes a theory of base-driven stratification, according to which the levels (or strata) of the lexicon are no longer determined by affixes, but by their potential input. Significantly, the problem of dual membership, which blurred the distinction between class I and class II affixes in the earlier models of lexical phonology, does not arise in this approach. While the number and nature of lexical levels is fixed in a language (the German lexicon, for instance, consists of three strata which are determined by the categories "root", "stem" and "word", cf. Wiese 1996: 129), affixes may combine with their bases on more than one stratum.

Influential works which entirely dispense with level ordering have been presented by Plag, who discovered a significant correlation between selectional restrictions and stacking. For example, Plag (1999: 67–69) shows that the incompatibility of nominalizing suffixes like *-age, -al, -ance, -ment* or *-y* with verbs ending in *-ize, -ify* or *-ate* (e.g., **magnify-ation, *verbalize-al, *concentrate-ment*) is not due to a selectional restriction which these suffixes impose on their bases, but follows from a base-driven selectional restriction: Complex bases ending in *-ize, -ify* or *-ate* typically select the suffix allomorphs *-ation* (*verbalization*), *-cation* (*identification*) and *-ion* (*concentration*) of the morpheme *-ation* and thus block the attachment of other nominalizers.

An attractive phonological alternative to level ordering is offered by Raffelsiefen (1999), who claims that suffixes differ with respect to whether or not they form a phonological word (*pword*) with their base, where the pword is defined as the domain for syllabification. The idea behind this assumption is that only suffixes which trigger phonological rules, i.e. the former class I suffixes, are integrated into the pword of the base they operate on, e.g., (*medícinal*)$_\omega$. On the other hand, phonologically neutral suffixes, i.e. the former class II suffixes, appear outside the pword of their base, e.g., ((*áccurate*)$_\omega$ *ness*)$_\omega$. This approach accounts for the observation that so-called stem-affixes are generally closer to their bases than word-affixes.

Referring to an observation formulated already by Booij (1985), Raffelsiefen assumes that in English the suffixes which fuse with their bases usually begin with vowels, whereas consonant-initial suffixes are phonologically neutral. This is what she refers to as the "law of initials". However, since there are some vowel-initial suffixes which are not integrated into the pword of their bases – examples are provided by ((*vínegar*)$_\omega$ *ish*)$_\omega$ or ((*ínjur*)$_\omega$ *able*)$_\omega$ – Raffelsiefen concludes that "[n]ot all, but only vowel-initial suffixes can induce stress shift" (1999: 229).

The numerous attempts which have been made to preserve and reformulate the achievements of lexical phonology reveal the impact which this model has on contemporary morphology. The fruitful discussions triggered by this theory, which was doomed to extinction, will most probably serve as an input to further research.

4 Schemata in word-formation (an outline)

In cognitive approaches to word-formation (e.g., Ungerer 2002; Ryder 1999; Panther and Thornburg 2002), grammatical information associated with the input and output of derivational processes is of secondary relevance. In these models, the compatibility of affixes with bases is primarily described by means of schemata, i.e. mental representations of the knowledge which human beings share about objects and events in the world. Schemata, which were first introduced by Sir Frederic Bartlett (1997 [1932]), can be activated any time and help to process new information, impressions and situations on the basis of former experience. In cognitive grammar, each linguistic building block is conceived of as a bipolar symbolic unit, consisting of a phonological and a semantic structure. Since cognitive grammar does not differentiate between linguistic and extra-linguistic information, the knowledge associated with an entity is a continuum ranging from salient to marginal properties. Importantly, abstract units function as schemata for specific units. Complex words such as the *-er* nominalization *pencil sharpener* discussed by Langacker (1988: 19–20) form constructional schemata in which highly abstract symbolic units like [THING/X], [PROCESS/Y] and [ER/-er] are instantiated by specific symbolic units.

The shift of emphasis from grammatical information to world-knowledge enables adherents of cognitive approaches to describe a wide range of regular and idiosyncratic word-formation processes. As indicated already in section 1, the input of the productive suffix *-er* is not restricted to verbs. Evidence comes from derivatives like *potter, stranger, upper, fiver, empty nester*, etc., which weaken the classical generative assumption that a suffix is subcategorized for bases belonging to a particular category. Moreover, although a high proportion of *-er* derivatives constitute agent nouns, a variety of non-agentive readings are available. Apart from denoting human beings (e.g., *singer, potter, left-hander*), nouns ending in *-er* may refer to animals (e.g., *retriever, pointer, sitter*), plants (*creeper, (late) bloomer, bedder*), physical objects, especially instruments (e.g., *toaster, receiver, tin-opener*), articles of clothing (e.g., *slipper, jumper, rompers*), locations (e.g., *sleeper, diner, kneeler*) and events (e.g., *no-brainer, thriller, laugher*). Even a single *-er* derivative like *birthdayer* may be highly polysemous. According to Ryder (1999: 284), this form is associated with the meaning components 'person having the birthday, person giving the party, person attending the party, present given' or 'birthday cake'.

As far as their ambiguity is concerned, *-er* derivatives are comparable to noun-noun compounds, which Ryder (1994) describes on the basis of semantic information schemas. A noun-noun compound like *garage man* evokes multiple event schemas in which the referents of the nominal constituents participate.

Thus, a *garage man* may be 'a man who works in a professional garage, builds garages, hangs around in garages, is shaped like a garage', etc. The most plausible interpretation is retrievable either from the context or from world knowledge. As far as derivatives are concerned, the interpretation is complicated by the fact that the referent of the head constituent, i.e. of the suffix *-er*, is indeterminate.

Referent ambiguity is observable even for deverbal *-er* derivatives if they are presented context-independently. For example, the form *smasher* may me associated with a variety of meanings. The verbal base *smash* evokes an event schema which involves a number of participants. Prototypically, there is an agent who performs the activity of smashing (e.g., *George*) and a patient, i.e. an entity which is affected by the destructive activity (e.g., *the rock*). Optionally, the agent may use an instrument to smash the object (e.g., *a sledge-hammer*), and there may even be a benefactive for whom he does the smashing (e.g., *George's wife*). Moreover, since events are located in space and time, the smashing event may have occurred in the backyard yesterday evening. In principle, the noun *smasher* could refer to the agent, the patient, the instrument, the benefactive or the place or time of the smashing event. However, according to Ryder (1999: 285), there are two conceptual factors which restrict the reference of such a derivative, namely *salience* and *identifiability*.

Salience refers to the degree to which something is noticeable in comparison with its surroundings. As far as the smashing event is concerned, the agent, the patient and the instrument are more salient than the benefactive and the spatial or temporal location. Identifiability refers to the extent to which a participant is readily identifiable by mention of the event alone. Although the patient is one of the salient entities in the smashing event, it is unlikely to be identified as the referent of *smasher* because patients are identifiable only in very specific contexts (e.g., *roaster* and *broiler* are identifiable as patients of different cooking events). Likewise, *smasher* is unlikely to receive an instrument reading because the smashing event (unlike, for instance, the event of putting nails into a wall or the event of cutting a piece of wood) is not associated with a particular tool. Thus, the agent is the participant most readily identifiable as the referent of *smasher*.

Panther and Thornburg, two further representatives of cognitive word-formation, consider the suffix *-er* to be a polysemous symbolic unit with the central sense "a human Agent who performs an action or engages in an activity to the degree that doing so defines a primary occupation" (2002: 285), to which all other *-er* nominals are related. Given the central sense of the suffix, *-er* derivatives evoke a prototypical transitive scenario, which, like Ryder's event schema, constitutes a knowledge representation. The prototypical transitive scenario has a setting (i.e. a place and a time in which an event takes place) and two distinct participants that are in an asymmetrical interaction. One participant is an intentionally acting human, whereas the other is directly affected/effected by the action. Significantly, the parameters of this multidimensional model are scalar, so that the scenario can be extended or reduced in various ways. Representative derivatives like *teacher*, *baker*, *brewer*, *steel-worker*, etc. range high on the transitivity scale because they fully correspond to the idealised cognitive model of human activities. The verbal bases serve as a reference point in that they allow mental access to other components of the respective scenario. This idea is the starting-point for Panther and Thornburg's argumentation that the denotatum of a non-verbal base serves as a reference point from which the activity performed by the agent is accessed either metonymically (e.g., *Wall Streeter* 'person professionally employed on Wall Street') or via a combination of metonymy and metaphor (e.g., *hoofer* 'professional (vaudeville/chorus) dancer', *upper* 'anti-depressant pill').

There are, however, a number of idiosyncrasies in derivation which are not accounted for by schemata alone. For instance, although Panther and Thornburg attempt to dispense with morpho-syntactic information, they correctly state (in a non-cognitive way) that the suffix *-ist* shows a preference for non-native bases (e.g., *nihilist*, *analyst*). Moreover, they observe that agent nouns ending in *-ant* or *-ent* are mainly derived from intransitive verbs (e.g., *emigrant*, *convalescent*), whereas instrument and patient nouns in *-ant/-ent* are restricted to transitive verbs (e.g., *defoliant*, *ingestant*). Observations like these suggest that word-formation is not entirely reducible to conceptual information – although this kind of information certainly plays an important role. The rules, patterns and schemata presented in this article, which are achievements from decades of morphological research, rather suggest that word-formation processes are determined by the interaction of morpho-syntactic, phonological and conceptual-semantic information.

Acknowledgement

I would like to thank the Deutsche Forschungsgemeinschaft (DFG), whose support of my project on word-formation enabled me to write this article.

5 References

Alexiadou, Artemis and Hagit Borer (eds.) (2020): *Nominalization. 50 years on from Chomsky's Remarks*. Oxford: Oxford University Press.

Allen, Margaret R. (1978): Morphological investigations. Ph.D. dissertation, University of Connecticut.

Aronoff, Mark (1976): *Word Formation in Generative Grammar*. Cambridge, MA: MIT Press.

Aronoff, Mark and Andrea D. Sims (2023): The relational nature of morphology. In: Davide Crepaldi (ed.), *Linguistic Morphology in the Mind and Brain*, 7–25. London/New York: Routledge.

Baeskow, Heike (2002): *Abgeleitete Personenbezeichnungen im Deutschen und Englischen. Kontrastive Wortbildungsanalysen im Rahmen des Minimalistischen Programms und unter Berücksichtigung sprachhistorischer Aspekte*. Berlin/New York: de Gruyter.

Baeskow, Heike (2024): The competition between noun-verb conversion and *-ize* derivation: Contrastive analyses of two productive English verb-formation processes. *Review of Cognitive Linguistics* 22(1): 258–288.

Barker, Chris (1998): Episodic *-ee* in English: A thematic role constraint on new word formation. *Language* 74(4): 695–727.

Bartlett, Frederic Charles (1997 [1932]): *Remembering. A Study in Experimental and Social Psychology*. Cambridge: Cambridge University Press.

Bauer, Laurie (2019): Notions of paradigm and their value in word-formation. *Word Structure* 12(2): 153–175.

Bauer, Laurie, Rochelle Lieber and Ingo Plag (2013): *The Oxford Reference Guide to English Morphology*. Oxford: Oxford University Press.

Bloomfield, Leonard (1933): *Language*. New York: Hold, Rinehart and Winston.

Bochner, Harry (1993): *Simplicity in Generative Morphology*. Berlin/New York: Mouton de Gruyter.

Booij, Geert (1985): Coordination reduction in complex words: A case for prosodic phonology. In: Harry van der Hulst and Norval Smith (eds.), *Advances in Nonlinear Phonology*, 143–159. Dordrecht: Foris.

Booij, Geert (1997): Allomorphy and the autonomy of morphology. *Folia Linguistica* 31(1–2): 25–56.

Booij, Geert (2019): The role of schemas in Construction Morphology. *Word Structure* 12(2): 385–395.

Brdar, Mario (2017): *Metonymy and Word-Formation. Their interactions and complementation*. Newcastle upon Tyne: Cambridge Scholars Publishing.

Burzio, Luigi (1986): *Italian Syntax. A Government-Binding Approach*. Dordrecht: Reidel.

Chomsky, Noam (1957): *Syntactic Structures*. The Hague: Mouton.

Chomsky, Noam (1965): *Aspects of the Theory of Syntax*. Cambridge, MA: MIT Press.

Chomsky, Noam (1970): Remarks on nominalization. In: Roderick A. Jacobs and Peter S. Rosenbaum (eds.), *Readings in English Transformational Grammar*, 184–221. Waltham, MA: Blaisdell.

Chomsky, Noam (1993): *Lectures on Government and Binding. The Pisa Lectures*. Reprint 7th ed. 1st ed. 1981. Berlin/New York: Mouton de Gruyter.

Chomsky, Noam and Morris Halle (1968): *The Sound Pattern of English*. New York: Harper and Row.

Dalton-Puffer, Christiane (1996): *The French Influence on Middle English Morphology. A Corpus-based Study of Derivation*. Berlin/New York: Mouton de Gruyter.

Giegerich, Heinz (1999): *Lexical Strata in English. Morphological Causes, Phonological Effects*. Cambridge: Cambridge University Press.

Halle, Morris (1973): Prolegomena to a theory of word-formation. *Linguistic Inquiry* 4: 3–36.

Henne, Helmut and Jörg Kilian (eds.) (1998): *Hermann Paul. Sprachtheorie, Sprachgeschichte, Philologie. Reden, Abhandlungen und Biographie*. Tübingen: Niemeyer.

Higginbotham, James (1985): On semantics. *Linguistic Inquiry* 16: 547–593.

Huyghe, Richard and Marine Wauquier (2021): Distributional semantics insights on agentive suffix rivalry in French. *Word Structure* 14(3): 354–391.

Jackendoff, Ray (1975): Morphological and semantic regularities in the lexicon. *Language* 51: 639–671.

Jaeggli, Oswaldo (1986): Passive. *Linguistic Inquiry* 17: 587–622.

Jespersen, Otto (1974 [1942]): *A Modern English Grammar on Historical Principles. Part VI: Morphology.* London: Allen & Unwin.

Kiparsky, Paul (1982): From cyclic phonology to lexical phonology. In: Harry van der Hulst and Norval Smith (eds.), *The Structure of Phonological Representations (Part I)*, 131–175. Dordrecht: Foris.

Körtvélyessy, Lívia, Alexandra Bagasheva and Pavol Štekauer (eds.) (2020): *Derivational Networks across Languages.* Berlin/Boston: De Gruyter.

Koziol, Herbert (1971 [1937]): *Handbuch der englischen Wortbildungslehre.* Heidelberg: Winter.

Lakoff, George (1970): *Irregularity in Syntax.* New York: Holt, Rinehart and Winston.

Langacker, Ronald W. (1988): An overview of cognitive grammar. In: Brygida Rudzka-Ostyn (ed.), *Topics in Cognitive Linguistics*, 3–47. Amsterdam/Philadelphia: Benjamins.

Lees, Robert B. (1960): *The Grammar of English Nominalizations.* The Hague: Mouton.

Lehnert, Martin (1971): *Rückläufiges Wörterbuch der englischen Gegenwartssprache.* Leipzig: VEB Verlag Enzyklopädie.

Lieber, Rochelle (1981): On the organization of the lexicon. Bloomington, IN: Indiana University Linguistics Club.

Lieber, Rochelle (2004): *Morphology and Lexical Semantics.* Cambridge: Cambridge University Press.

Lieber, Rochelle (2006): The category of roots and the roots of categories: What we learn from selection in derivation. *Morphology* 16: 247–272.

Lieber, Rochelle (2016): *English Nouns. The ecology of nominalization.* Cambridge: Cambridge University Press.

Marchand, Hans (1969): *The Categories and Types of Present-Day English Word-Formation. A Synchronic-Diachronic Approach.* 2nd ed. München: Beck.

McMahon, April (2000): *Lexical Phonology and the History of English.* Cambridge: Cambridge University Press.

Mohanan, Karuvannur P. (1986): *The Theory of Lexical Phonology.* Dordrecht: Reidel.

Moravcsik, Julius M. (1981): How do words get their meanings? *Journal of Philosophy* 78: 5–24.

Motsch, Wolfgang (2004): *Deutsche Wortbildung in Grundzügen.* 2nd ed. 1st ed. 1999. Berlin/New York: de Gruyter.

Muthmann, Gustav (2002): *Reverse English Dictionary. Based on Phonological and Morphological Principles.* Berlin/New York: Mouton de Gruyter.

Olsen, Susan (1986): *Wortbildung im Deutschen.* Stuttgart: Kröner.

Olsen, Susan (2020): The relatedness of meaning in derivational patterns. In: Jenny Audring, Nikos Koutsoukos and Christina Manouilidou (eds.), *Proceedings of Mediterranean Morphology Meetings*, 2019, Vol. 12: 64–76.

OneLook Reverse Dictionary (online): http://www.onelook.com/reverse-dictionary.shtml [last access 24 Aug 2010].

Oxford English Dictionary (online): http://dictionary.oed.com [last access 24 Aug 2010].

Panther, Klaus-Uwe and Linda Thornburg (2002): The roles of metaphor and metonymy in English -er nominals. In: René Dirven and Ralf Pörings (eds.), *Metaphor and Metonymy in Comparison and Contrast*, 279–319. Berlin/New York: Mouton de Gruyter.

Plag, Ingo (1999): *Morphological Productivity. Structural Constraints in English Derivation.* Berlin/New York: Mouton de Gruyter.

Raffelsiefen, Renate (1999): Phonological constraints on English word formation. In: Geert Booij and Jaap van Marle (eds.), *Yearbook of Morphology 1998*, 225–287. Dordrecht: Kluwer.

Randall, Janet (1988): Inheritance. In: Wendy Wilkins (ed.), *Syntax and Semantics 21. Thematic Relations*, 129–146. San Diego: Academic Press.

Rappaport Hovav, Malka and Beth Levin (1992): *-Er* nominals: Implications for the theory of argument structure. In: Tim Stowell and Eric Wehrli (eds.), *Syntax and Semantics 26. Syntax and the Lexicon*, 127–153. San Diego: Academic Press.

Rauh, Gisa (1988): *Tiefenkasus, thematische Relationen, Thetarollen. Die Entwicklung einer Theorie von semantischen Relationen*. Tübingen: Narr.

Riddle, Elizabeth M. (1985): A historical perspective on the productivity of the suffixes *-ness* and *-ity*. In: Jacek Fisiak (ed.), *Historical Semantics Historical Word-Formation*, 435–461. Berlin: Mouton.

Rubach, Jerzy (1984): *Cyclic and Lexical Phonology*. Dordrecht: Foris.

Ryder, Mary Ellen (1994): *Ordered Chaos. The Interpretation of English Noun-Noun Compounds*. Berkeley: University of California Press.

Ryder, Mary Ellen (1999): Bankers and blue-chippers: An account of *-er* formation in present-day English. *English Language and Linguistics* 3(2): 269–297.

Saussure, Ferdinand de (2005 [1916]): *Cours de linguistique générale*. Paris: Payot.

Selkirk, Elizabeth (1982): *The Syntax of Words*. Cambridge, MA: MIT Press.

Siegel, Dorothy (1974): Topics in English morphology. Ph.D. dissertation, MIT.

Ungerer, Friedrich (2002): The conceptual function of derivational word-formation in English. *Anglia* 120(4): 534–567.

Wiese, Richard (1996): *Phonology of German*. Oxford: Clarendon Press.

Williams, Edwin (1981): Argument structure and morphology. *Linguistic Review* 1: 81–114.

Zimmer, Karl (1964): *Affixal Negation in English and Other Languages. An Investigation of Restricted Productivity*. Supplement to *Word* 20, Monograph 5. New York: Clowes.

Zwarts, Jost (1992): *X'-Syntax – X'-Semantics. On the Interpretation of Functional and Lexical Heads*. Utrecht: OTS Dissertation Series.

Sabine Arndt-Lappe

12 Word-formation and analogy

Abstract: The article discusses the much-debated status of analogy in contemporary theories of synchronic word-formation. It provides an overview of the key assumptions made in pertinent theoretical camps as well as of the major phenomena that have featured prominently as evidence in the debate. Theories can broadly be classified into those which assume that analogy is active only as a complementary mechanism, and those which assume that analogy is the central mechanism of productive word-formation. Among the latter, we can distinguish between general theoretical and computational analogical models. Based on a detailed definition and discussion of the analogical equation, different usages of analogy in the literature are shown to be closely tied to theory-dependent conceptualisations of productivity, predictability, and (ir-)regularity.

1 Introduction

The term *analogy* is used in many different senses and in many different contexts within morphological theory. One subdiscipline with which analogy is frequently associated is diachronic morphology, where, ever since the Neogrammarian revolution, analogical change has been seen as a central mechanism of morphological change (cf., e.g., Hock 2003 for a summary). Developments which have come to be associated with analogy are, especially, analogical extension and levelling.

In synchronic morphological theory, the type of analogy that is the subject of discussion is proportional analogy, i.e. a heuristic mechanism in which a new complex word is formed on the basis of a perceived similarity with existing base-

Sabine Arndt-Lappe, Trier, Germany

https://doi.org/10.1515/9783111420554-012

derivative pairs (cf. section 2 below for a more detailed definition). The central question that has been debated in the contemporary literature is whether analogy is an active mechanism in synchronic morphology, and, if it is, what its relation is to other mechanisms in synchronic morphology, such as rules or constraints or schemas. Much of this debate, which has its origins far back in the history of morphological research (cf., e.g., Becker 1990; Anttila 2003 for a summary), has taken place in inflectional morphology. In this debate, the term *analogy* has come to be used in different senses, which are often heavily dependent on the underlying theory. In particular, senses of analogy are often tied to particular assumptions about central theoretical notions such as regularity, productivity, variability, and the nature of lexical representations.

Thus, we find approaches that claim that analogy is the basis of any rule-based, productive behaviour in morphology (cf., e.g., Blevins and Blevins 2009b for an overview), whereas at the same time we find, especially generative, approaches that appeal to analogy exactly in those cases in which linguistic behaviour is not rule-governed, but exceptional, unproductive, unpredictable, or irregular (cf., e.g., Prasada and Pinker 1993; Pinker and Prince 1994). Also within word-formation theory, analogy has come to be used as a term opposite to the concept of the linguistic rule (cf. Bauer 1983, 2001). In usage-based and constructionist approaches, by contrast, it is argued that analogy forms the underlying principle of exemplar-based reasoning or the beginnings of low-level schematisation (Booij 2010: 88–93). Crucially, the implication in this latter group of approaches is that analogies in word-formation are regularly based on subsymbolic aspects of lexical representations. However, this assumption is not inherent in the definition of analogy per se, as we will see.

This article is concerned with concepts of analogy in synchronic word-formation. The focus is on providing an overview of the different notions of analogy as they are used in different theories of word-formation, and of the different phenomena that have featured prominently in references to analogy in the word-formation literature. Reference to parallel developments in theories of inflection will be made occasionally, where necessary.

The structure of the article is as follows: We will begin with a general definition of proportional analogy as a heuristic device (section 2). Section 3 will then provide an overview of the status of analogy in different theories of word-formation. We will see how different theories operationalise different aspects of the structure of proportional analogy in different ways, resulting in radically different views about the regularity, productivity, and predictability of analogical formations. Based on this overview, theories will be grouped broadly into a) theories that consider analogy to be an irregular or exceptional process and b) those that consider analogy to be the basic process underlying word-formation. Sections 4 and 5 will then be devoted to these two classes of theories, respectively, discussing pertinent word-formation phenomena for which analogy has been invoked. The discussion in section 5 will specifically focus on computational analogical models, which will be shown to provide interesting solutions to some of the criticism that has traditionally been mounted against analogy-based models, but will also be shown to be limited in terms of the range of processes covered in such approaches to date. The article ends with a conclusion (section 6).

2 Definition and terminology

Analogy as used in the word-formation literature is usually described in terms of a proportion (proportional analogy), as in (1).

(1) $a : b = c : x$

In this equation, 'x' is the new form, i.e. a morphologically complex word that is about to be coined. 'a', 'b', and 'c' are forms that already exist in the lexicon. 'a' and 'c' are (potential) base forms, whereas 'b' is an existing complex form. What happens in an analogical formation, then, is that the relationship between 'a' and 'b' is used as a model example for the formation of 'x'.

As an example, consider the English compound *chairperson*, which we may plausibly assume to have been formed on the basis of analogy with the existing compound *chairman*. In this case, we can fill the variables in the equation above as in (2).

(2)   *chair* : *chairman* = *chair* : *chairperson*

Interestingly, there is no established terminology in the morphological literature to refer to most parts of the analogical equation. The only established term seems to be *analogue*, which is usually used to refer to the complex form on which a newly coined word is modelled ('b' in (1), *chairman* in (2)). In order to facilitate further discussion, however, it is useful to have labels to refer to the other parts of the equation as well. These labels are presented in Figure 12.1, again using *chairperson* as an example.

In accordance with most of the literature, we will use the term *analogue* to refer to the complex word that serves as a model for the coining of a new complex word. The new word that is about to be coined will be referred to as the *new word*. Finally, there are two bases involved in an analogy, for which we will use the terms *base of the analogue* and *base of the new word*, respectively.

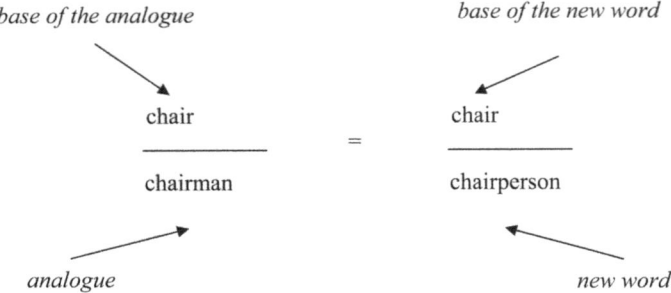

Fig. 12.1: Elements of the analogical equation.

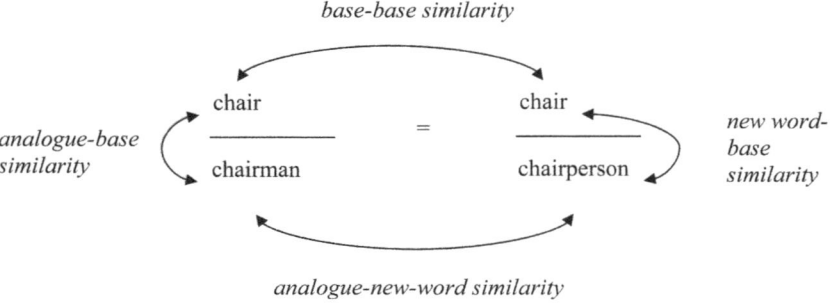

Fig. 12.2: Similarity relations in the analogical equation.

As is clear from the example, a key role in the process of analogy is played by the (perceived) similarity between the elements of the equation. Figure 12.2 provides an overview of (and labels for) the similarity relations we find within the analogical equation.

In the example *chairperson* the base of the analogue and the base of the new word are identical (both *chair*). Hence, it is easy to see that they may be perceived as being similar to each other by the hypothetical speaker(s) who coined *chairperson*. The second aspect where similarity plays a role is the relation between the base of the analogue (*chair*) and the analogue (*chairman*), which must be perceived as being similar to the relation between the base of the new word (*chair*) and the new word (*chairperson*). In *chairperson*, the relation between the analogue and its base is a morphological relation, pertaining to both the form and the meaning of the two lexemes. The form of the base, *chair*, appears as the first constituent of the compound *chairman*. Semantically, we could broadly say that the relation between the analogue and its base is that between a role (*chair*) and

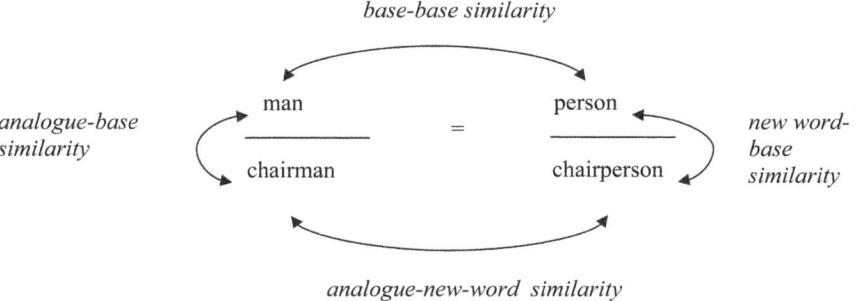

Fig. 12.3: *chairman – chairperson –* an alternative.

the occupant of that role, who is human and male (*chairman*). Like the relation between *chair* and *chairman*, the relation between *chair* and *chairperson* (i.e. that between the new form and its base) also pertains to both the form and the meaning of the elements involved. Again, *chair* appears as the first constituent of a compound. Semantically, the relation between the new word and its base is that between the role (*chair*) and the occupant of that role, who is human but, crucially, not necessarily male.

Our example already indicates that similarity is not only a key determinant of a morphological analogy, but that it is also one of the key problems in defining and explaining analogies, and, on a theoretical level, a key challenge for any morphological theory that is based on analogies. The reason is that the basis for the computation of similarity is not part of the equation.

Whereas the word-formation literature generally agrees that in cases of analogy similarity must be given both in terms of form and in terms of meaning, there is almost no restriction on precisely which formal and semantic properties can make an analogue and a potentially corresponding new word similar. In addition, there is no agreement about how analogical similarity relations (those schematised in Fig. 12.2) map onto morphological complexity relations. For example, when discussing *chairperson* as a product of analogical reasoning on the basis of *chairman*, we assumed that the relation between *chair* and *chairman* was the base for the analogy. At the same time, however, it is also clear that *chairman* is related to *man* as much as it is related to *chair*, and that the relation between *man* and *chairman* is similar to the relation between *person* and *chairperson*. Thus, Fig. 12.3 above is another plausible representation of an analogical relation between *chairman* and *chairperson*.

What this tells us is that it is not always clear what exactly the base of an analogy is. There is, from a theoretical point of view, no restriction on which of the multiple similarity relations that exist between words in the mental lexicon may form the basis of an analogical formation.

In sum, we see that *analogy* as a heuristic formalism does not say much about many of the issues that morphological theory needs to be explicit about. Specifically, it does not say anything about a) which features (formal, semantic, syntactic, etc.) establish similarity relations on which analogies may be based, and b) which of the existing similarity relations may or will form the basis of a new analogical formation. Furthermore, as we will see later in this article, it does not say anything about c) how many lexemes are involved in an analogy. This explains, in part, the great diversity of usages of the term *analogy* in the literature, to which we will now turn.

3 Senses of *analogy* in word-formation theory

The focus in this section will be on showing the scope of senses in which analogy has been used in the literature on synchronic word-formation. Rather than attempting to be exhaustive, the discussion will be restricted to a sample of representative theories.

Analogy is often discussed in the context of the theoretical divide between word-based, paradigmatic, and syntagmatic approaches to morphology (cf., e.g., Becker 1990, 1993a and references therein for discussion). It is clear that approaches to word-formation which attribute a systematic role to analogy are all word-based approaches. However, not every word-based approach assumes that analogy is an active mechanism in productive word-formation. This is true in spite of claims often made in the literature that the mechanisms underlying word-based formalisms can be described in terms of a proportional analogy. Word-based approaches are divided in terms of whether they consider rules or analogy to be the central mechanism in productive word-formation. In rule-based approaches of this type, analogy is often invoked to explain irregular, or unproductive behaviour. In analogy-based approaches, analogy is invoked to explain regular, productive behaviour. The term *paradigmatic* approaches to morphology is difficult to apply here, because it is used in different senses in the literature. Whereas it is assumed to be synonymous with 'word-based' approaches by some authors, others use it rather in the sense that has been labelled 'analogy-based' above. In what follows we will discuss senses of *analogy* in word-based theories.

One type of approach that takes an extreme position with respect to the rule-analogy divide is comprised of, mostly generative, paradigmatic frameworks which make a radical distinction between analogical formations and regular processes of word-formation. Regular processes are the product of an abstract formalism that operates independently from individual lexemes, on symbolic features that are shared by pertinent lexemes (cf., e.g., Aronoff 1976). Analogy, in this view, is always local in the sense that it affects only few and very specific lexical items. Productivity is rule-application, with the consequence that a low degree of variation is predicted for morphological rules. Unlike regular and productive word-formation, then, processes of analogy are unpredictable and unproductive. A clear expression of this view, which is found frequently in the generative literature, is found, for example, in Bauer's (1983) textbook on English word-formation (but cf. also Bauer 2001: 75–97, where this view has been relativised considerably):

> If instances of word-formation arise by analogy then there is in principle no regularity involved, and each new word is produced without reference to generalizations provided by sets of other words with similar bases or the same affixes: a single existing word can provide a pattern, but there is no generalization. [...] If it is true that there are in principle no generalizations, then a generative account of word-formation is at best a convenient fiction and at worst an irrelevancy. (Bauer 1983: 294)

At the other end of the divide we find approaches that assume that analogy with existing lexemes is used regularly and productively in the formation of new words. In what follows I will refer to such approaches as "analogical" approaches. Conceptually, they are rooted mainly in two traditions: One is the Neogrammarian and the American descriptivist tradition (cf. esp. Becker 1990 for details and discussion), the other comprises functionalist, exemplar-based, and usage-based theories of grammar, i.e. theories that are grounded in the assumption that analogy constitutes a central cognitive mechanism that is active in human cognition in general, and in language in particular (cf. esp. Bybee 2001, 2010; Gahl and Yu 2006; Blevins and Blevins 2009a). Work in both types of theories has traditionally focussed on inflection and on diachronic language development. Recent times, however, have seen a growing number of publications devoted to word-formation phenomena.

For example, Becker (1990, 1993a, 1993b) proposes for both inflection and derivation that all morphological operations are analogical, in the sense that they describe relations between existing words, on the basis of which speakers productively coin new words by means of proportional analogy (e.g., Becker 1990: 187). His proposal builds on and extends those of especially van Marle (1985, 1990), who also claims a synchronic relevance for analogical formation in word-formation, but distinguishes between (rule-based) productivity and (analogy-based) creativity, the former producing regularity, and the latter allowing for some degree of unpredictability.

One obvious characteristic of approaches that do not embrace the distinction between analogical and rule-based word-formation is that they consider variability and gradience to be a key property of morphological operations. This variability has often been identified with unpredictability, and the failure of many analogical approaches to be predictive constitutes one of the key points of criticism against these approaches (cf. above and Bauer 2001: 75–97 for a summary of pertinent arguments – and counterarguments). However, there is also a growing body of literature springing from mainly quantitative work in morphology that challenges the view that analogical models must necessarily be non-predictive (cf., e.g., Baayen 2003; Hay and Baayen 2005). The main argument is that variability in general and different degrees of variability in particular can be predicted in a probabilistic approach to linguistic categorisation. One major class of such probabilistic approaches explicitly draws on analogy as the fundamental underlying principle of morphology and has produced a growing number of studies that model word-formation phenomena with the help of computational implementations of analogical models of grammar (specifically: AM(L); Skousen 1989, 1992; Skousen, Lonsdale and Parkinson 2002; TiMBL; Daelemans et al. 1999 ff.). What these models have in common is that they apply similarity-based, analogical reasoning, creating new forms on the basis of the similarity of the base of the new form with existing forms in the lexicon. Analogies are therefore very rarely local; the idea advanced in many rule-based approaches that analogies must be based on a single lexical item is conceived to be only one of many possibilities. Much more frequently analogues in such approaches are sets of words in the lexicon. Behaviour that is described as rule-based in other approaches emerges exactly in situations in which analogues for a given new form comprise a large set. Details of such models will be discussed in section 5.2.

Whereas the said analogical models fundamentally differ from rule-based models in the way in which they view variability, however, not all of them differ from rule-based models in terms of the way in which they conceptualise lexical representations. Thus, in some analogical approaches it is assumed that similarity relations between words are established on the basis of symbolic features (e.g., Becker 1990: 63–71). In some exemplar-based models, by contrast, it is assumed that the exemplars that serve as potential analogues also comprise information that is more detailed and specific than the abstract features traditionally associated with rule-based grammatical models (cf., e.g., work on compounding, esp. Krott, Baayen and Schreuder 2001, 2002; Plag, Kunter and Lappe 2007; Arndt-Lappe 2011).

An intermediate position between views that consider analogy to be exceptional and those that consider it to be the basis of regular word-formation is found in constructionist theories. The interesting question here is how analogy is related to schemas or schematisation, which are considered to be the central mechanism in word-formation. A clear view on this is found in Booij's recent proposal (Booij 2010). Here it is claimed that schemas and subschemas may operate on symbolic features, and that the crucial difference between analogical formations and schema-based formations lies in their making reference to different degrees of abstraction. Analogy in this model is defined as strictly local analogy, which is complementary to schemas and may constitute an initial stage of the development of a schema (cf. esp. Booij 2010: 88–93 and section 4.1 for examples). Thus, Booij's constructionist approach is different from both analogical and non-analogical approaches outlined above. There are differences between what happens in productive word-formation and what happens in an analogical formation in his sense, but this difference is a gradual difference, and not, as in the generative tradition, a difference that concerns the fundamental nature of the system.

In the remaining two sections of this article I will provide an overview of the type of word-formation phenomena for which analogy has been invoked in the literature. Section 4 will deal with analogical formation in approaches which attribute a complementary role to analogy, i.e. rule- or constraint- or schema-based approaches in the sense outlined above. Section 5 will be devoted to phenomena discussed in analogical approaches, both non-computational and computational.

4 Complementary analogy

We find pertinent appeals to analogy mainly in three domains. The first comprises relatively local analogies, explaining the emergence of small-scale patterns (section 4.1). Such small-scale patterns are often seen as the precursors to morphological processes proper. The second domain comprises apparent cases of re-analysis (section 4.2). The third domain is affix selection (section 4.3).

4.1 Local analogies

An analogy is usually considered to be local if a) the analogue is restricted to one particular lexeme, b) a very high degree of similarity is involved, and c) the productivity of the process is very limited, in the extreme case producing only one new word. Needless to say, 'locality' of an analogy is a gradual notion.

Traditionally, many such cases are of the type *chairman* : *chairperson* discussed in section 2 above, where both formally and semantically there is complete identity of one of the bases involved. A representative recent analysis is Booij's (2010) constructionist approach, where a distinction is made between "analogical word-formation in the strict sense" on the one hand and constructional schemas on the other hand. Booij's examples of analogical word-formation are given in (3). They are all from Dutch.

(3) Examples of analogical word-formation (glosses are taken from the original)

new word	analogue
paniek-haas lit. 'panic-hare, panicky person'	angst-haas lit. 'fear-hare, terrified person'
vader-taal lit. 'father-language, native language of father'	moeder-taal lit. 'mother language, native language'
muis-vaardig lit. 'mouse-able, with mouse-handling skills'	hand-vaardig lit. 'hand-able, with manual skills'
oud-komer lit. 'old-comer, immigrant who arrived a long time ago'	nieuw-komer lit. 'new-comer, recent immigrant'

(Booij 2010: 89)

For the distinction between analogical word-formation and constructional schemas, Booij considers it to be crucial that

> [f]or these words [i.e. those in (3), S. A.-L.] we can indeed point to one particular existing compound as the model for the formation of the new compound, and the meaning of this new compound is not retrievable without knowing the (idiomatic) meaning of the model compound. (Booij 2010: 90)

Even in approaches using the term *analogy* in such a restrictive sense, it is often noted that analogies of the type exemplified in (3) can give rise to new word-formation patterns (cf. Booij 2010: 90–91, Szymanek 2005 for examples and pertinent references). The claim in many theories is, however, that once a new pattern has been created, its description in terms of analogy is no longer appropriate.

There are two conceptual problems involved for an analogical description of the new pattern. One is that, once a pattern has arisen, it is impossible to trace the analogy back to one single analogue lexeme. Another problem is that many of the examples that are usually quoted in the literature involve reanalysis of either the analogue or the base of the analogue as morphologically complex. The problem of reanalysis will be discussed in section 4.2 below. For the problem of analogue selection, reconsider our example *chairperson* from section 1, where we have assumed that its analogue is *chairman*. However, there also exists *chairwoman*, which, like *chairman*, predates *chairperson* (the *Oxford English Dictionary*, henceforth: OED, records 1699 as the date of the earliest attestation of *chairwoman* and 1971 as the corresponding date for *chairperson*). It is, therefore, unclear whether *chairperson* was modelled on *chairman* or on *chairwoman*. Indeed, the definition of the OED as 'a chairman or chairwoman' (OED, s. v.) suggests that it may have been modelled on both.

On a theoretical level, the example shows that the assumption that the distinction between "analogy in the strict sense" and a pattern is not without problems. Thus, if we take Booij's approach, we would assume the existence of a schema to account for the triplet *chairman – chairwoman – chairperson*. Apart from the apparent stipulation that bases of analogy must be single lexemes, it is, however, unclear why *chairperson* should be attributed a different status in the word-formation system than cases like *paniek-haas* (cf. (3) above). An alternative approach would assume that analogues may be sets of lexemes, which is, for example, inherent in many traditional, analogy-based accounts of cases of reanalysis, to which we now turn.

4.2 Reanalysis based on analogy

The reason why analogy is often invoked in reanalysis cases lies in the fact that reanalysis obviously happens on the basis of similar lexemes that are stored in the lexicon. There are two pertinent classes of processes: certain cases of backformation and affix secretion (Marchand 1969: 210–214). Note that for both classes also rule-based accounts have been proposed. Examples of backformation are given in (4).

(4)   Cases of backformation

new word	*base of new word*	*analogue/base*
burgle	burglar	write/writer, sing/singer, etc.
(Marchand 1969: 391)		
televise	television	act/action, revise/revision, etc.
(Marchand 1969: 395)		
self-destruct	self-destruction	cases of noun-verb pairs where *-ion* is added to the verbal base
(Bauer 2001: 83)		

Cases like *to burgle* (derived from: *burglar*) are commonly analysed as involving reanalysis of the base word as morphologically complex, on the basis of analogy with existing pairs of lexemes. In this case, the bases of the analogue and the new word share a form, *-er*, but this form does not have the same meaning in the two bases. Note, however, that still there is a semantic similarity between the two bases: In the case of *burglar* and its analogues, for example, they all denote agents.

One major theoretical issue in approaches to backformation cases is whether back-formation is a diachronic process (cf. Becker 1993a for discussion and a review). Examples like those in (4) have been used convincingly to demonstrate the synchronic relevance of the process. The basis of this argument is semantic complexity. Whereas, for example, *to burgle* means 'to act the burglar', the noun *burglar* does not mean 'one who burgles' (Marchand 1963, as discussed in Becker 1993a: 4–8).

Another case of apparent backformation which has been analysed by appealing to analogy is the case of bracketing paradoxes. A well-known representative is Spencer's analysis of certain English person-denoting adjective-noun phrases (Spencer 1988). Pertinent data are given in (5).

(5) Bracketing paradoxes
     new phrase   *analogue*
     transformational grammarian   transformational grammar
     atomic scientist   atomic science
     moral philosopher   moral philosophy

The phrases in (5) are part of a group of phrases that, for some morphological theories, form bracketing paradoxes because it is unclear to which base the person-noun forming suffix (in the examples in (5): *-ian*, *-ist*, *-er*) is attached. Thus, the morphological base for *-ian* suffixation is the noun *grammar*, while the semantic base is the phrase *transformational grammar*.

According to Spencer, formations such as those in (5), which are clearly productive in English, pose a challenge to rule-based morphological theories because the derived person noun cannot be convincingly related to their bases via a syntagmatic morphological rule (which would, for example, involve suffixation in *grammarian* and suffix substitution in *philosopher*). He therefore argues that the relation between bases and derivatives is an analogical relation, pertaining between lexicalised phrases in the mental lexicon. Unlike in the "traditional" back-formation cases discussed further above, then, Spencer's claim is that analogical processes may be productive.

Another group of reanalysis cases where analogy is often assumed to play a role involves cases where new morphological patterns emerge (affix secretion, in Marchand's terminology, cf. Szymanek 2005: 431, 435–436 for English). Similarly to the backformation cases, in these cases the semantics of the base for the analogical formation arises through reanalysis of the analogue-base relation as morphologically complex. Unlike the cases in (4) and (5), however, analogue forms are not morphologically complex, at least not before the advent of secretion. Some of the pertinent cases have also been described as blends. Examples are given in (6).

(6) cases of affix secretion
    new word   *analogue*   *meaning*
    candy<u>teria</u>   caf<u>eteria</u>   'shop, store, or establishment selling food x'
    (Marchand 1969: 211)
    Monica<u>gate</u>   Water<u>gate</u>   'political scandal involving x'
    (Szymanek 2005: 436)

There is a formal overlap between the new word and the analogue (*-teria*, *-gate*). This form, however, is not a unit of meaning in the analogue base, but becomes a unit of meaning in the new word, i.e. the moment it is extended to other words. This is precisely the situation for which Booij (2010: 88–93) argues that schematisation takes place, which in his view replaces analogy as the underlying mechanism.

4.3 Affix selection on the basis of analogy

A third group of processes where analogy has been invoked in the literature is affix selection. Pertinent examples are given in (7).

(7) Irregular affix selection
    new word   *analogue*
    a. orienteer   volunteer
    (Bauer 1983: 290)
    b. womanity   humanity
    (Baeskow 2012: 9–10)

For examples like those in (7), analogy is often invoked to explain affix selection. The underlying assumption is that this selection is irregular or unproductive. Thus, in both cases in (7), the affix selected to derive an agent noun (*-eer*) and an abstract nominalisation (*-ity*) is allegedly unproductive for the bases *orient* and *woman*, respectively. Bauer (1983: 285–291) assumes that *-eer* is generally unproductive in Modern English, and appeals to analogy to provide an explanation for the form *orienteer*, which is an apparent counterexample. The basis for the analogy here is phonological similarity between *volunt-* and *orient*, i.e. the base of the analogue and the base of the new word.

The form *womanity* (7b) is an apparent counterexample to the generalisation that English *-ity* attaches to Latinate bases (cf., e.g., Baeskow 2012 and Arndt-Lappe 2014) for discussion and further counterexamples). Like in the case of (7a), phonological and perhaps also semantic similarity between the bases of analogue and new word, *woman* and *human*, plays a large part in motivating the analogy. Unlike in (7a), the two bases are also semantically similar.

Apart from affix selection, also other types of selection between grammatical alternatives have traditionally been explained with the help of analogy. A case in point is stress in English nominal compounds, where two types of stress are available: left stress and right stress. Whereas left stress has traditionally been assumed to be the default pattern, cases of right stress have often been explained to be the product of analogy. Oft-cited textbook examples are compounds denoting street names. The examples in (8) are taken from Plag (2003). Stress is marked by an acute accent on the pertinent vowel.

(8) Stress in English noun-noun compounds
     Óxford Street Madison Ávenue
     Fóurth Street Fifth Ávenue
     (Plag 2003: 139)

The analogical effects exemplified in (8) differ in two important ways from the affix selection cases in (7). Thus, in (8) analogue bases are sets of words, not isolated words (i.e. all compounds whose second constituent is *street* or *avenue*, respectively). Also, within their domain, analogies in (8) are productive.

In sum, we have seen in this section that appeals to analogy in rule-, constraint-, or schema-based theories by no means form a homogeneous group. What they have in common, is that analogy is conceived to be relatively local, usually affecting lexical items which are highly similar both phonologically and semantically. However, approaches differ in terms of whether they define elements involved in the analogy as single lexemes or sets, and in terms of which similarity relation exactly they view as being crucial to trigger an analogical formation. Also, they vastly differ in terms of whether they view analogy as a (potentially) productive process.

In the next section we turn to a group of theoretical approaches which not only assumes that analogy may be productive in morphological grammar, but that it in fact forms its underlying principle.

5 Analogy in analogy-based approaches to word-formation

Two groups of phenomena feature prominently in analogical approaches to word-formation: productive replacive formations, and cases of variability that affect the formal properties of outputs of word-formation. The former has been the object of discussion in much of the general theoretical literature, whereas the latter has been in the focus of the literature working with computational analogical models.

5.1 Productive replacive formations

The term *replacive formation* refers to a pattern where new words are coined from existing complex words via affix replacement (Becker 1993a: 9–12). The phenomena discussed in the literature are in part the same as the phenomena discussed in sections 4.1 and 4.2. The issue under debate between analogical and non-analogical approaches here is, however, the productivity of these phenomena. Whereas in much of the generative literature it is claimed that analogical patterns of the type discussed in section 4 are not productive, it is claimed in the analogical literature that they are productive. In addition, it is claimed that the distinction between analogy and rule-based behaviour cannot be upheld on formal grounds.

An explicit discussion of the theoretical implications that the existence of productive replacive formation has in terms of an analogical approach to word-formation is found in Thomas Becker's work (Becker 1990, 1993a, 1993b). The key argument has two parts: a) There are productive replacive word-formation patterns (Becker 1993a, 1993b), b) they are not different from patterns which have traditionally been described as rule-governed.

An example of a productive replacive formation pattern is the pattern producing *in-* and *ex-* prefixed words in German (discussed in Becker 1993b: 194). Examples are given in (9).

(9) German pairs of *in-* and *ex-*prefixed words
Immatrikulation 'immatriculation' Exmatrikulation 'exmatriculation'
Inkardination 'incardination' Exkardination 'excardination'
Internat 'boarding school' Externat 'a school that accepts day students'
(Becker 1993b: 194)

In- and *ex*-prefixation is replacive in the sense that one prefixed word is derived from the other prefixed word. In all examples in (9), the *ex-* derivative has been coined on the basis of the *in-* derivative, but there are also examples in which the reverse is the case. The pattern constitutes evidence in favour of a paradigmatic approach to word-formation because, as Becker convincingly shows, many pertinent cases cannot be described in terms of a concatenation of *in-* or *ex-* and a base. For example, *ternat* is attested only in the pair *Internat* and *Externat* in German, which makes it difficult to analyse it as a base for prefixation.

The second part of Becker's argument, i.e. that replacive formations are not different from other, allegedly rule-governed patterns, is more difficult. In Becker's analogical approach, both types of pattern are described in terms of a rule format that Becker shows to be formally equivalent to a proportional analogy, especially since the format crucially employs traditional symbolic representations of lexemes. For Becker, the only difference between word-formation patterns that have been described as rule-governed and those that have been described as analogical in the generative literature lies in their different degrees of productivity. However, like many strands of traditional generative theory, which claim exactly the opposite, also Becker's theory is lacking a testable means to predict which patterns will be more productive and which ones will be less productive.

5.2 Cases of formal variability

Testability of degrees of variability is one of the key issues that has been addressed in simulation studies employing computational analogical models. The discussion here will focus on work based on the two analogical algorithms which are most widely used to model word-formation phenomena: the Tilburg Memory Based Learner (TiMBL, Daelemans et al. 1999 ff.; cf. Daelemans and van den Bosch 2005) and Skousen's analogical model of language (AM; Skousen and Stanford 2007; cf. Skousen 1989, 1992; Skousen, Lonsdale and Parkinson 2002). Another algorithm that has been used in much work on inflection is the generalized context model (Nosofsky 1986, 1990). Furthermore, there is also work investigating the role of analogical factors using statistical modelling, without the implementation of a formal analogical model (cf., e.g., Plag 2006, 2010 on English compound stress).

An obvious question is what the exact nature of the analogical theory is that is implemented by algorithms like TiMBL and AM. We will address this issue after we have discussed relevant studies.

Like many analogical models, the key focus in the initial stages of pertinent morphological research was on problems of inflection (cf. esp. Daelemans and van den Bosch 2005; Skousen, Lonsdale and Parkinson 2002 for a summary of central issues). Issues of word-formation addressed in the literature always concern cases in which outputs of word-formation exhibit some sort of semi-regular variability. They are "semi-regular" in the sense that deterministic rule-based models fail to predict the attested variability. In contrast to work on inflection where there is a wealth of literature exploring the predictive power of computational analogical models (cf. relevant references in Skousen, Lonsdale and Parkinson 2002, the AM bibliography at http://humanities.byu.edu/am/am-biblio.html, Daelemans and van den Bosch 2005, and, in particular, work on the English past tense, e.g., in Skousen 1989; Eddington 2000; Keuleers 2008), pertinent research on word-formation phenomena is still in its infancy. Existing research has focussed mainly on two word-formation phenomena: compounding and allomorphy in derivation. Pertinent studies are most often based on corpus data and, in some cases, on data in which novel complex words have been generated by experimental subjects.

Simulation studies devoted to variability in compounding have investigated linking morphemes in Dutch and German (esp. Krott, Baayen and Schreuder 2001, 2002; Krott et al. 2007; cf. Krott 2009 for a summary) and stress assignment in English noun-noun compounds (esp. Plag, Kunter and Lappe 2007; Arndt-Lappe 2011; cf. also Plag 2006, 2010). Both TiMBL and AM were used as algorithms.

The three options that are available as linking morphemes in Dutch are: -s-, -en-, and -Ø- ('zero, no linking morpheme'). Examples are given in (10). For easier reading but contrary to orthographic conventions, the relevant morphological components in the Dutch words are separated by spaces.

(10) Variability in Dutch linking morphemes (from Krott, Schreuder and Baayen 2002: 55 f.)

thee-bus	'teabox'
papier-handel	'paper trade'
plaatje s boek	'picture book'
tabak s rook	'tobacco smoke'
krent en brood	'currant bread'
boek en kast	'book case'

In English noun-noun compounds, two options are available: stress on the first constituent ("left stress") or stress on the second constituent ("right stress", sometimes also referred to as "level stress"). Examples are given in (11). Stress is marked by an acute accent.

(11) Variability in stress assignment in English noun-noun compounds

ópera glasses	steel brídge
wátch-maker	morning páper
clássroom	silk tíe
Óxford Street	Madison Ávenue

In spite of the fact that they are concerned with different phenomena, the two groups of simulation studies show surprising agreement in terms of their findings. Thus, predictive power of the computational analogical models employed was greater than that of traditional rule-based models. Furthermore, the most important determinant of the variation was the constituent family. This means that linking morphemes or stress assignment of a given novel compound can be predicted best on the basis of the pertinent behaviour of existing compounds that share either the first or the second constituent with the novel compound. In addition, it was found in most studies that, apart from constituent family, also semantic factors, if included in the simulation, served to enhance predictive power.

Another group of phenomena that has been studied is affix selection and allomorphy in derivation. Pertinent studies include, for example, work on diminutives (Daelemans, Berck and Gillis 1997 on Dutch; Eddington 2002, 2004 on Spanish), negative prefixation (Chapman and Skousen 2005, with a diachronic perspective), nominalisation (Eddington 2006 on Spanish; Arndt-Lappe 2014 on English) and comparative formation (Elzinga 2006) in English. A representative study is Eddington's study of diminutives (Eddington 2002, 2004). Examples are given in (12).

(12) Variable allomorph selection in Spanish diminutives

minut-ito	←	minuto	'minute'
gallet-ita	←	galleta	'cookie'
vidri-ecito	←	vidrio	'glass'
yerb-ecita	←	yerba	'grass'
pastor-cito	←	pastor	'shepherd'
joven-cita	←	joven	'young girl'
normal-ito	←	normal	'normal'
naric-ita	←	nariz	'nose'
pec-ecito	←	pez	'fish'
flor-ecita	←	flor	'flower'
lej-itos	←	lejos	'far away'
Luqu-itas	←	Lucas	'Luke'
patron-cita	←	patrona	'patron saint'

(Eddington 2002: 402)

Variability affects at least two dimensions: the form of the diminutive suffix (mainly *-ito/a*, *-cito/a*, *-ecito/a*), and the form of the stem allomorph (truncated, not truncated).

In Eddington's simulation experiment AM is able to predict correctly some 92 % of the data. In addition, it is shown that the variability predicted by AM is plausibly similar to the variability that exists in real life. Thus, uncertainty in the model's predictions occurs exactly where uncertainty in allomorph selection in real life manifests itself, for example, by the existence of doublets.

Eddington's study of Spanish diminutive allomorphy is also representative of this type of analogical approach in terms of the features that were given to the algorithm as its information source. These typically involve mainly the phonological (i.e. segmental and prosodic) shape, but also the relevant grammatical categories of the base words in the dataset. In Eddington's study, the latter comprised gender information.

In general, the studies that have been introduced here are representative of work employing computational analogical algorithms to model variability in word-formation. An obvious difference to much previous work in analogy is that analogical algorithms are predictive mechanisms. In what follows we will briefly address the question of how this is achieved. Major differences between AM and TiMBL will be mentioned, but will not be in the focus of the discussion.

Like in all approaches discussed in this article, analogical word-formation is assumed to be the product of a perceived formal and semantic similarity between a form that is about to be coined and its analogue (cf. section 2 above). Unlike in other approaches, however, the scenario that the analogue is only a single form or a small set of forms that is maximally similar to the new form is only one of several potential scenarios. Instead, analogies are based on those exemplars in the lexicon that are informative with respect to the given task. This group of exemplars is often called the "analogical set" of a new form (esp. in the AM-based literature) or the "nearest neighbour set" (in the TiMBL-based literature). Often, exemplars in the analogical set will differ in terms of their similarity with the given item. Classification of a new form will therefore always incorporate an effect of (type-) frequency because all members of the analogical set will influence classification. Thus, one element that makes algorithms like AM and TiMBL predictive is the fact that, unlike other analogical approaches, they have a principled way of determining which exemplars in the lexicon will serve as analogues, i.e. will be part of the analogical set.

The second element that makes the models predictive is that they have a principled method at their disposal to determine which types of similarity are relevant for a given classification. The basis of all computation of similarity is formed by those elements of lexical representations which are provided by the researcher as a set of coded features for each exemplar in the database. The nature of these features is, in principle, a matter of choice, and it is still an unresolved question, which types of features lead to the best predictive power of a model. Existing studies of compounding have successfully used features encoding aspects of the compositional semantics of the compound, as well as features encoding the particular identity of the compound constituents. Existing studies of derivational allomorphy have typically used syllable-based phonological representations of base words (e.g., phonemes of onset, nucleus, coda of the ultima, penult, etc.) as well as, in some cases, grammatical information such as gender, word class, etc. Crucially, the question of how abstract or symbolic representational features are is still a matter of debate.

The problem of determining which exemplars end up in the analogical set for a given new form is resolved in different ways by TiMBL and AM. What they have in common, though, is that the analogical set / nearest-neighbour set comprises those items which are similar to the new form in terms of exactly those features that are most useful for the given task. To do this, most varieties of TiMBL weigh the coded features of all exemplars in their lexicon in terms of how informative they are with respect to the given task, and treat items that share more informative features as more similar to a given new form than items that share less informative features. This means, then, that the importance of a given feature for the computation of similarity is the same for the whole lexicon. This is different in AM, where the decision of which coded features are relevant for a given exemplar to end up in the analogical set is made for each new form on an individual basis. For each new form the algorithm determines which combinations of features shared or not shared with that new form behave in a homogeneous way with respect to the given task (cf., e.g., Skousen 2002a, 2002b for a discussion of "homogeneity").

A crucial property of computational analogical models that is particularly relevant for grammatical theory in general and morphological theory in particular is that they have been claimed to be able to account for both types of effect: one that has traditionally been described as local analogy and one that has traditionally been described as rule-governed behaviour. This point has explicitly been made mainly for inflection (cf. esp. Derwing and Skousen 1994; Eddington 2000; Keuleers 2008), but is also often alluded to in work on derivation and compounding. Recall from section 4 above that in non-analogical, rule-based approaches it has often been claimed that the distinguishing feature between regular and analogical processes is productivity. In an analogical model, however, there exists only a gradual distinction between local analogies and less local analogies. A local analogy arises if only exemplars which share many features with the new form are incorporated in the analogical set. Typically, then, analogical sets will be very small, and members of these sets will be highly similar in terms of both their phonological structure and their meaning. By contrast, behaviour that looks like rule-governed behaviour in the traditional sense will arise if the analogical set is large, with exemplars in that set sharing fewer features. Thus, members of the analogical set will be less similar to each other both phonologically and semantically.

6 Summary and conclusion

This article has presented an overview of approaches to analogy in word-formation theory. It has become clear that we have to distinguish *analogy* as a heuristic device from *analogy* as a construct in word-formation theory. The former is a mechanism that is very open and, in principle, underspecified in terms of many issues that need to be addressed in morphological theory. This openness of analogy is reduced in the specific usages of analogy as a construct in word-formation theory. These usages are closely tied to the theories' basic assumptions about productivity, regularity, and variability. Strikingly, analogy has often been used in a narrow sense to denote local analogies, where both formally and semantically a very high degree of similarity is involved. The implication of this usage is that it is assumed that less local generalisations are non-analogical, because they involve higher degrees of abstraction (in terms of representations, rules, constraints, or schemas).

This view is not shared by analogical approaches, where local analogies are considered to be only a special case of analogy. Here emphasis is put on the generality of analogy as a mechanism, with the implication that predictability and regularity of morphological operations is gradient. Constraints on analogy are often seen as a consequence of the nature of lexical representations and usage-based factors. In computational analogical theories, we furthermore observe that analogy is conceptualised as a predictive mechanism, where predictability emerges from the fact that analogues are not selected by chance, but by algorithms that have a principled, information-theoretic method at their disposal to distinguish informative and non-informative features and select sets of analogues accordingly.

7 References

AM research group (ed.) (AM bibliography): http://humanities.byu.edu/am/am-biblio.html [last access 20 Oct 2014].

Anttila, Raimo (2003): Analogy: The warp and woof of cognition. In: Brian D. Joseph and Richard D. Janda (eds.), *The Handbook of Historical Linguistics*, 425–440. Malden, MA: Blackwell.

Arndt-Lappe, Sabine (2011): Towards an exemplar-based model of stress in English noun–noun compounds. *Jounal of Linguistics* 47(11): 549–585.

Arndt-Lappe, Sabine (2014): Analogy in suffix rivalry – the case of -ity and -ness. *English Language and Linguistics* 18(3): 497–547.

Arndt-Lappe, Sabine (2023): Different lexicons make different rivals. *Word Structure* 16(1): 24–48.

Aronoff, Mark (1976): *Word Formation in Generative Grammar.* Cambridge, MA: MIT Press.

Baayen, Harald R. (2003): Probabilistic approaches to morphology. In: Rens Bod, Jennifer Hay and Stefanie Jannedy (eds.), *Probabilistic Linguistics*, 229–287. Cambridge, MA: MIT Press.

Baeskow, Heike (2012): -Ness and -ity: Phonological exponents of n or meaningful nominalizers of different adjectival domains? *Journal of English Linguistics* 40(1): 6–40.

Bauer, Laurie (1983): *English Word-Formation.* Cambridge: Cambridge University Press.

Bauer, Laurie (2001): *Morphological Productivity.* Cambridge: Cambridge University Press.

Becker, Thomas (1990): *Analogie und morphologische Theorie.* München: Fink.

Becker, Thomas (1993a): Back-formation, cross-formation and 'bracketing paradoxes' in paradigmatic morphology. In: Geert Booij and Jaap van Marle (eds.), *Yearbook of Morphology 1993*, 1–25. Dordrecht: Kluwer.

Becker, Thomas (1993b): Morphologische Ersetzungsbildungen im Deutschen. *Zeitschrift für Sprachwissenschaft* 12(2): 185–217.

Blevins, James P. and Juliette Blevins (eds.) (2009a): *Analogy in Grammar.* Oxford: Oxford University Press.

Blevins, James P. and Juliette Blevins (2009b): Introduction: Analogy in grammar. In: James P. Blevins and Juliette Blevins (eds.), *Analogy in Grammar*, 1–12. Oxford: Oxford University Press.

Bonami, Olivier and Jana Strnadová (2019): Paradigm structure and predictability in derivational morphology. *Morphology* 29(2): 167–197.

Booij, Geert (2010): *Construction Morphology.* Oxford: Oxford University Press.

Booij, Geert (ed.) (2018): *The Construction of Words.* Cham: Springer.

Bybee, Joan (2001): *Phonology and Language Use.* Cambridge: Cambridge University Press.

Bybee, Joan (2010): *Language, Usage and Cognition.* Cambridge: Cambridge University Press.

Chapman, Don and Royal Skousen (2005): Analogical modeling and morphological change: The case of the adjectival negative prefix in English. *English Language and Linguistics* 9(2): 333–357.

Daelemans, Walter, Peter Berck and Steven Gillis (1997): Data mining as a method for linguistic analysis: Dutch diminutives. *Folia Linguistica* 31: 57–75.

Daelemans, Walter and Antal van den Bosch (2005): *Memory-Based Language Processing.* Cambridge: Cambridge University Press.

Daelemans, Walter, Jakub Zavrel, Ko van der Sloot and Antal van den Bosch (1999 ff.): *TiMBL: Tilburg Memory Based Learner.* Available from http://ilk.uvt.nl/timbl/.

Derwing, Bruce I. and Royal Skousen (1994): Productivity and the English past tense: Testing Skousen's analogical model. In: Susan D. Lima, Roberta Corrigan and Gregory K. Iverson (eds.), *The Reality of Linguistic Rules*, 193–218. Amsterdam/Philadelphia: Benjamins.

Eddington, David (2000): Analogy and the dual-route model of morphology. *Lingua* 110: 281–298.

Eddington, David (2002): Spanish diminutive formation without rules or constraints. *Linguistics* 40(2): 395–419.

Eddington, David (2004): *Spanish Phonology and Morphology. Experimental and Quantitative Perspectives.* Amsterdam/Philadelphia: Benjamins.

Eddington, David (2006): Look Ma, no rules: Applying Skousen's analogical approach to Spanish nominals in -ión. In: Grace Wiebe, Gary Libben, Tom Priestly, Ron Smyth and H. S. Wang (eds.), *Phonology, Morphology, and the Empirical Imperative. Papers in Honour of Bruce L. Derwing*, 371–407. Taipei: Crane.

Elzinga, Dirk (2006): English adjective comparison and analogy. *Lingua* 116(6): 757–770.

Gahl, Susanne and Alan C. L. Yu (eds.) (2006): *Special Issue on Exemplar-based Models in Linguistics. The Linguistic Review* (23). Berlin: Mouton de Gruyter.

Hathout, Nabil and Fiammetta Namer (2022): ParaDis: a family and paradigm model. *Morphology* 32(2): 153–195.

Hay, Jennifer and Harald R. Baayen (2005): Shifting paradigms: Gradient structure in morphology. *Trends in Cognitive Science* 9: 342–348.

Hock, Hans H. (2003): Analogical change. In: Brian D. Joseph and Richard D. Janda (eds.), *The Handbook of Historical Linguistics*, 441–460. Malden, MA: Blackwell.

Jackendoff, Ray and Jenny Audring (2020): *The Texture of the Lexicon – Relational Morphology and the Parallel Architecture*. Oxford: Oxford University Press.

Keuleers, Emmanuel (2008): Memory-Based Learning of Inflectional Morphology. Ph.D. dissertation, University of Antwerp.

Krott, Andrea (2009): The role of analogy for compound words. In: James P. Blevins and Juliette Blevins (eds.), *Analogy in Grammar*, 118–136. Oxford: Oxford University Press.

Krott, Andrea, Harald R. Baayen and Rob Schreuder (2001): Analogy in morphology: Modeling the choice of linking morphemes in Dutch. *Linguistics* 39: 51–93.

Krott, Andrea, Rob Schreuder and Harald R. Baayen (2002): Analogical hierarchy: Exemplar-based modeling of linkers in Dutch noun-noun compounds. In: Royal Skousen, Deryle Lonsdale and Dilworth B. Parkinson (eds.), *Analogical Modeling*, 181–206. Amsterdam/Philadelphia: Benjamins.

Krott, Andrea, Rob Schreuder, Harald R. Baayen and Wolfgang U. Dressler (2007): Analogical effects on linking elements in German compounds. *Language and Cognitive Processes* 22: 25–57.

Marchand, Hans (1963): On content as a criterion of derivational relationship with backderived words. *Indogermanische Forschungen* 68: 170–175.

Marchand, Hans (1969): *Categories and Types of Present-Day English Word-Formation. A Synchronic-Diachronic Approach*. 2nd ed. München: Beck.

Mattiello, Elisa (2017): *Analogy in Word-formation. A Study of English Neologisms and Occasionalisms*. Berlin/Boston: De Gruyter Mouton.

Nosofsky, Robert M. (1986): Attention, similarity, and the identification-categorization relationship. *Journal of Experimental Psychology: General* 115: 39–57.

Nosofsky, Robert M. (1990): Relations between exemplar similarity and likelihood models of classification. *Journal of Mathematical Psychology* 34: 393–418.

OED = *Oxford English Dictionary*. http://www.oed.com [last access 30 Sept 2011].

Pinker, Steven and Alan Prince (1994): Regular and irregular morphology and the status of psychological rules in grammar. In: Susan D. Lima, Roberta Corrigan and Gregory K. Iverson (eds.), *The Reality of Linguistic Rules*, 321–351. Amsterdam/Philadelphia: Benjamins.

Plag, Ingo (2003): *Word-Formation in English*. Cambridge: Cambridge University Press.

Plag, Ingo (2006): The variability of compound stress in English: Structural, semantic, and analogical factors. *English Language and Linguistics* 10(1): 143–172.

Plag, Ingo (2010): Compound stress assignment by analogy: The constituent family bias. *Zeitschrift für Sprachwissenschaft* 29(2): 243–282.

Plag, Ingo, Lea Kawaletz, Sabine Arndt-Lappe and Rochelle Lieber (2022): Analogical modeling of derivational semantics. Two case studies. In: Sven Kotowski and Ingo Plag (eds.), *The Semantics of Derivational Morphology. Theory, Methods, Evidence*, 103–141. Berlin/Boston: De Gruyter.

Plag, Ingo, Gero Kunter and Sabine Lappe (2007): Testing hypotheses about compound stress assignment in English: A corpus-based investigation. *Corpus Linguistics and Linguistic Theory* 3(2): 199–233.

Prasada, Sandeep and Stephen Pinker (1993): Generalization of regular and irregular morphological patterns. *Language and Cognitive Processes* 8: 1–56.

Rainer, Franz (2018): Patterns and niches in diachronic word-formation: the fate of the suffix -MEN from Latin to Romance. *Morphology* 18(3): 397–465.

Skousen, Royal (1989): *Analogical Modeling of Language*. Dordrecht: Kluwer.

Skousen, Royal (1992): *Analogy and Structure*. Dordrecht: Kluwer.

Skousen, Royal (2002a): An overview of analogical modeling. In: Royal Skousen, Deryle Lonsdale and Dilworth B. Parkinson (eds.), *Analogical Modeling*, 11–26. Amsterdam/Philadelphia: Benjamins.

Skousen, Royal (2002b): Issues in analogical modeling. In: Royal Skousen, Deryle Lonsdale and Dilworth B. Parkinson (eds.), *Analogical Modeling*, 27–48. Amsterdam/Philadelphia: Benjamins.

Skousen, Royal, Deryle Lonsdale and Dilworth B. Parkinson (eds.) (2002): *Analogical Modeling*. Amsterdam/Philadelphia: Benjamins.

Skousen, Royal and Thereon Stanford (2007): *AM: Parallel.* Available from http://humanities.byu.edu/am/.

Spencer, Andrew (1988): Bracketing paradoxes in the English lexicon. *Language* 64(4): 663–682.

Szymanek, Bogdan (2005): The latest trends in English word-formation. In: Pavol Štekauer and Rochelle Lieber (eds.), *Handbook of Word-Formation*, 429–448. Dordrecht: Springer.

van Marle, Jaap (1985): *On the Paradigmatic Dimension of Morphological Creativity*. Dordrecht: Foris.

van Marle, Jaap (1990): Rule-creating creativity – analogy as a synchronic morphological process. In: Wolfgang U. Dressler, Hans C. Luschützky, Oskar E. Pfeiffer and John R. Rennison (eds.), *Contemporary Morphology*, 267–273. Dordrecht: Foris.

Livio Gaeta and Davide Ricca

13 Productivity

Abstract: The article deals with the many facets of the concept of productivity in word-formation, focusing on the one hand on the recent elaboration of various statistical quantitative measures made possible by the availability of large textual corpora. On the other hand, the article will provide a brief account of the qualitative impact on productivity given by the different kinds of system-related and cognitively rooted restrictions on word-formation. The distinct, but related, notion of productivity of inflectional classes is also discussed.

1 Introduction

Productivity is a central issue in linguistics which has been traditionally of relevance for morphology but has recently gained attention in other domains of language as well (for instance, in syntax, cf. Barðdal 2008). In a nutshell, productivity in word-formation can be conceived of as the capacity of natural languages to form an in principle uncountable number of new words with the help of morphological means in an unintentional way, as in Schultink's (1961) classical definition. Several objections have been raised against this definition. First, it is not clear what "an in principle uncountable number" really means, because the potential of creating new words is normally restricted by the size of the input domain selected. Thus, if a certain word-formation rule (henceforth, WFR) takes as an input only, let's say, kinship terms, then its productivity can be quite high because it can freely form derivatives in this domain, but the number of words formed is perfectly countable and in fact corresponds to the whole set of kinship terms of the language. The latter is usually limited to at most a couple dozens of words.

Livio Gaeta, Turin, Italy
Davide Ricca, Turin, Italy

https://doi.org/10.1515/9783111420554-013

As we will see below, this problem leads us to the distinction between qualitative aspects of productivity focusing on the selectional properties of the WFRs and quantitative aspects focusing on the concrete number of lexical units involved. It is not entirely clear what the relation should be between these two faces of the coin.

Second, it is not clear at all what a new word definitely is. This depends very much on a number of idiosyncratic factors relating among others to the personal education of the speakers, to his/her familiarity with specific speech registers or experiential (ontological) domains, etc. Thus, what is new for one speaker can sound perfectly familiar to another. As we will see, there are several proposals for approximating the intuitive idea of 'new formation'.

Third, "unintentional" refers to the fact that the productivity of a WFR cannot be attested by nonce formations expressly created by the speakers to reach particular stylistic effects, as in the well-known Heideggerian expression: *Wahrnis des Wesens der Wahrheit* 'true-ness of the essence of truth' (cf. Fleischer 1975: 71), in which *Wahrnis* is Heidegger's genuine creation but cannot seriously be taken to testify to the productivity of the suffix *-nis* because the philosopher is well known for his attitude towards coining affected (and we may add: abstruse) expressions. As commented upon by Bauer (2001: 56), "it would not be expected that such words would be adopted by the speech community, since they would run counter to the rules accepted by the speech community". On the other hand, it is not at all clear whether a creation, even Heidegger's *Wahrnis*, has to be considered as the result of an intentional, conscious process. At any rate, even if Heidegger had created *Wahrnis* unconsciously, the term could not signal the productivity of the suffix *-nis* in German. Conversely, it is not necessarily true that intentional, conscious creations could not be instantiations of productive WFRs (cf. Bauer 2001: 66–68). The latter is normally the case with terminologies, which are the result of the intentional agreement of a special speech community on a certain way of denominating referents familiar to the community.

Finally, Schultink's definition does not reflect the scalar character of productivity, whereby WFRs are often available to different degrees to form new words, because it characterizes productivity as an absolute property (cf. Bauer 2005: 330).

To cope with the multifaceted nature of productivity, Rainer (1987) identifies at least six different meanings associated with this term in the domain of word-formation:

(1)   a. the number of words formed with a certain WFR;
      b. the number of new words coined with a certain WFR in a given time span;
      c. the possibility of coining new words with a certain WFR;

d. the probability of coining new words with a certain WFR;
e. the number of possible (or generatable by rule) words formed with a certain WFR;
f. the relation between occurring and possible words formed with a certain WFR.

The six meanings highlight different properties of productivity, and in particular: (1a) simply equates productivity with the vocabulary size of the words formed with a certain WFR; (1b) introduces the variable of time thus rendering productivity basically a diachronic notion; (1c) and (1d) focus on the speakers' competence by referring respectively to their capacity to use a certain WFR and to the probability that a certain WFR is used; (1e) attempts to quantify the concept of possible word and finally (1f) relates it to the mere quantitative count provided by (1a).

These meanings cross-cut the main distinction between a qualitative and a quantitative understanding of productivity. In fact, the qualitative approach basically sees productivity as inversely relating to the number of selectional restrictions of a WFR (cf. Booij 1977): with their increase we generally observe the decrease of the productivity, namely the possibility of using the WFR, which relates qualitative productivity essentially with the meaning (1c) above. Clearly, the idea of a possible word is strictly related to such an approach. Given the indirect relation between qualitative properties and quantitative factors, this relation is at least difficult to spell out on a precise basis.

The other meanings besides (1c) focus on a quantitative understanding of productivity, and in fact the discussion has centered on how to elaborate precise methods to measure the quantitative impact of the WFRs. In what follows, we will first discuss in section 2 the quantitative side of the issue, and we will especially focus on recent attempts to find reliable methods to measure productivity in large text corpora. Subsequently, in section 3 we will devote our attention to the qualitative perspective, trying to assess those qualitative factors which also influence the quantitative instantiation of WFRs. Finally, in section 4, we will briefly discuss the inflectional side of productivity, to the extent that it is relevant for word-formation as well.

2 Quantitative approaches

The earlier attempts to deal quantitatively with the notion of productivity have mainly relied upon the use of large dictionaries (including frequency dictionaries) and, less commonly, on text samples to substantiate intuitions about the degree of productivity of individual WFRs, especially in English (cf. Neuhaus 1973; Plag 1999: 115; Anshen and Aronoff 1999; Bauer 2001: 157), but also in Italian (e.g., Iacobini and Thornton 1992; Thornton 1998), Dutch (Al and Booij 1981), German (Wellmann 1975).

However, reflection and research on a quantitative, measurable correlate to the notion of productivity in word-formation has undergone a dramatic development starting from the early nineties of last century under the decisive impulse of Baayen's work (e.g., Baayen 1992, 1993; Baayen and Renouf 1996; more recent references are found in the following discussion of the article). The key strategy introduced by these works, made possible by the availability of very large, computer-analyzable corpora, mainly relies on the role of *hapax legomena*, i.e. words occurring only once in such corpora (typically sized in tens or hundreds of millions of tokens), as will be seen below.

The basic concept underlying corpus-based approaches to productivity is the notion of *vocabulary growth curve* of a given affix or morphological procedure, namely the plotting of the number $V(N)$ of different *types* of derivatives formed with that affix as a function of the total number N of the *tokens* of the same affix occurring in the corpus. This assumes of course that the figures for the function $V(N)$, as those for N itself, are computed progressively as long as the corpus is being processed. To give an idea of the shape of the vocabulary growth curves, four instances of $V(N)$ are reported in Fig. 13.1, taken from Gaeta and Ricca (2006: 58): they refer to the Italian suffixes *-mente*, forming adverbs, and *-mento*, *-(t)ura* and *-nza*, forming action nouns, progressively sampled from three years of the Italian newspaper *La Stampa*.

If an affix is even minimally productive, new types will be encountered as long as the sampling proceeds: mathematically $V(N)$ is a non-decreasing monotonic function. However, for every affix the slope of the curve $V(N)$ will progressively decrease, since it will become more and more probable that new tokens of the affix will be occurrences of already attested types.

The curves in Fig. 13.1 have been taken from a procedure of real progressive sampling of a newspaper corpus. Fortunately, at present several statistic models and packagings are available (although the mathematics behind them is far from obvious, cf. Baayen 2001; Evert 2004; Evert and Baroni 2007) which provide reliable fittings for the growth curves, at least for interpolations: extrapolating the curves beyond the real sample size raises much more difficult and debated reliability issues, which cannot be mentioned here. These fitting algorithms need as input just data obtainable from the full corpus sampling, which makes things operationally much easier.

From Fig. 13.1, it is evident that the curves $V(N)$ for the four suffixes increase at different rates. Whereas the curve of the suffix *-nza* immediately reaches al-

V(N)

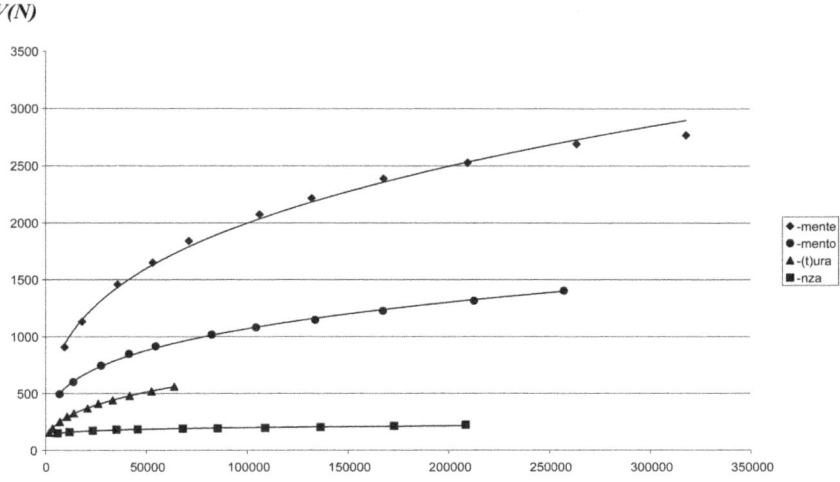

N: Token number of the suffix

Fig. 13.1: Vocabulary growth curve V(N) for four Italian derivational suffixes (from Gaeta and Ricca 2006: 58).

most the whole number of possible types and then approximates a horizontal line, for the other suffixes the curve is clearly still increasing, although with different slopes, at the end of the sampling procedure.

The behaviour of the curve for *-nza* illustrates the case of a qualitatively unproductive suffix: once all (or nearly all) the well-established items derived with the suffix occur in a (sufficiently large) corpus, there is no expectation of finding instances of new types. All three other curves display the behaviour expected for qualitatively productive word-forming procedures, although they differ according to several measurable parameters.

The simplest parameter to measure and understand is the type frequency V in the full corpus, which can be seen as the size of the morphological category (Baayen 2009: 901). A high value of V means that many items have been derived with that affix and are currently in use in the language community. A corpus-based value of V may be compared with the type frequency resulting from lexicographical counts, and usually is much more indicative of the real "currency" of the given affix than the latter, assuming we are dealing with a sufficiently large and balanced corpus which can reasonably approximate real language behaviour. This is because a corpus will not include many obsolete words that dictionaries record plenty of, will not overstate the impact of special language terminologies, and, for productive procedures, will contain many new formations too "regular" and unnoticeable to become quickly registered in dictionaries. A large-scale comparison between type frequency data taken from corpora and dictionaries is provided for Italian in Gaeta and Ricca (2003).

However, *V* is an indication of how much success a morphological procedure has enjoyed in a given language, and in this regard it roughly corresponds to Corbin's (1987: 177) notion of *rentabilité* 'profitability' ("la possibilité de s'appliquer à un grand nombre de bases" [the possibility of applying to a large number of bases]), but does not tell the whole truth about how easily the given procedure is currently available to form new items, which is intuitively the very core of the notion of productivity. An affix which has been very fashionable in the past may keep a trace of its past relevance by still displaying a relatively high *V*, even if speakers do not use it anymore to form new words. That's why Baayen (2009: 901) suggests the label "realized productivity" for the notion measured by *V*. As a matter of fact, considering the bulk of Italian derivation taken into account in Gaeta and Ricca (2003: 83–84), this effect is much less significant than expected. The (nearly) unproductive suffixes with highest *V* in the Italian corpus examined are the denominal agentive -*aio* (*giornale* → *giornalaio* 'newspaper seller') and the deverbal potential adjectival -*evole* (*piegare* → *pieghevole* 'folding'), and they are ranked rather low in the list. Clearly, the distortion effect would be much more important if dictionary-based type frequency were considered, for the reasons mentioned above. Indeed, most productive formation rules tend to produce such a high amount of *hapax legomena* and very low-frequency items registered in a corpus (but not in a dictionary!), that the well-established items which survive the marginalization of their word-formation procedure cannot really reverse the picture.

This leads to the consideration of the central role of the *hapax legomena* in measuring productivity. Mathematically, the hapax number *h* after *N* occurrences of an affix have been processed is directly connected to the slope of the curve *V(N)*, which can be demonstrated (Baayen 1992: 115) to be equal to the ratio *h/N*. Measuring the slope of the growth curve at a given point *N* means evaluating the speed at which new types of a certain affix emerge in the sample: the steeper the slope, the higher the production rate of new types. For this reason, comparing the slopes of the growth curves of two affixes for a given value of *N* is a way of comparing the contribution of the two affixes to the growth rate of the vocabulary in a corpus, i.e. it is a way to rank their productivities. As stressed by Gaeta and Ricca (2006), who applied the procedure to a significant portion of productive Italian derivational morphology, the slope comparison at equal values of *N* allows one to plausibly rank the productivity of affixes with different *token* frequencies, whose overall growth curves in a fixed corpus differ substantially in length (for instance, the nearly synonymous -*tura* and -*mento* in Fig. 13.1). Gaeta and Ricca define their procedure as "variable corpus approach", because, in order to compare at equal token number two affixes of different token frequency, one has to process subcorpora of different size.

Baayen terms this facet of productivity "expanding productivity", contrasting it with the "realized productivity" measured by the sheer V value, and confirms that the former measure produces rankings which are "reasonable reflections of linguists' overall intuitions about degrees of productivity" (Baayen 2009: 905). However, he states that the same results can be obtained by a still simpler measure, namely by comparing directly the absolute values of h in the whole corpus for any two (or more) affixes. On the basis of his suggestion, Gaeta and Ricca (2006: 73–74) verified that there is indeed a high correlation between the two measures; however, they also showed that this is not always the case. In particular, comparing the two Italian deverbal suffixes -*tore* for male/generic agent and -*trice* for female agent, the simple number of hapaxes h strongly favours the more frequent suffix -*tore*, which has twice as many hapaxes as -*trice*, while the two display about the same value for Gaeta and Ricca's "variable corpus" measure. Being essentially linked with *hapax legomena*, the expanding productivity may be related to Corbin's (1987: 177) notion of *disponibilité* 'availability', although the latter ("la possibilité de construire des dérivés non attestés" [the possibility of forming unattested derivatives]) can also be interpreted as a purely yes/no notion, as done for instance by Bauer (2001: 205).

A third, quite different measure originally suggested by Baayen is the h/N value calculated for each affix at the full corpus value, which means the slope of the growth curves in Fig. 13.1 at their endpoints. Given that for any growth curve, the slope steadily decreases for increasing N, this measure would get lower results for the very frequent affixes (e.g., for -*mente* and -*mento* compared with -*tura* in Fig. 13.1). The resulting rankings are quite perplexing from the point of view of linguists' intuitions, as shown by Gaeta and Ricca (2006: 72). For instance, the adverbial suffix -*mente* '-ly' is unanimously considered extremely productive. Its generality locates it at the border between derivation and inflection, and for some even beyond it, analogously to its English counterpart (see, e.g., Haspelmath 1996: 49–50). But according to this measure, -*mente* would be ranked below some clearly derivational suffixes, and particularly below the relatively infrequent female agent suffix -*trice*, which in turn would result as over five times more productive than its male agent counterpart -*tore*. Similar considerations are entertained by Plag (1999: 113) about the data for English -*ly* in Baayen and Renouf (1996).

However, Baayen (2009) gives an interpretation of the measure above: the ratio h/N at full corpus should essentially measure how far a given procedure is from saturating its domain of application. This is reflected by his proposed label of "potential productivity".

From this point of view, there is a further way to evaluate the grade of saturation. An estimation of the maximal size S (in types) of the domain of a given morphological procedure, for an ideally infinite corpus, can be provided by statistical models, such as those proposed in Evert (2004). Then the ratio $I = S/V(N)$ would measure the inverse of the saturation ratio, which Baayen (2009: 907) claims to show a high positive correlation with his potential productivity.

The narrow connection between the number of *hapax legomena* in a corpus and the productivity measures has often been criticized with the objection that hapaxes in a corpus are not necessarily new formations. On the one hand, this is undoubtedly true, but becomes progressively less relevant as corpus size increases: for corpora of many tens of millions of tokens, most hapaxes indeed turn out to be un-established words (cf. Baayen and Renouf 1996 on a 80 million-word *Times* corpus). On the other hand, as Baayen (2009: 906) puts it, "*hapax legomena* are not a goal in itself, they only function as a tool for a statistical estimation method aimed at gauging the rate of expansion of morphological categories". For hapaxes to be a reliable tool, however, it is necessary that corpus data are carefully and time-consumingly checked by manual inspection: a fully automatic listing of items associated with a given ending in a corpus would indeed produce huge distortions (cf. Evert and Lüdeling 2001). Suffice it to think that most misprints would turn out as hapaxes, thus heavily polluting any quantitative measure based on them.

A more serious operational problem met with any quantitative approach is establishing what exactly counts as a type of a given affix. For instance, to what extent should opaque derivations be included? More intriguingly, as pointed out by Bauer (2001: 151), should *underdevelopment* be counted as a different type of *-ment* (considering it as derivation from the verb *underdevelop*), or should its occurrences be merged with those of *development* into a single type? The latter instance raises another problem. Should *underdevelopment* count as a type of *under-*, of *-ment*, or of both?

These issues have been tackled at length in Gaeta and Ricca (2006), to which we refer. The most interesting is perhaps the third one, namely how to deal coherently with multiply affixed words, like *conventionalize* or *reprintable*. The standard choice in these cases (defended explicitly in Plag 1999: 29) has always been to select as affix tokens only those words in which the affix is attached last (i.e. *-ize* and *-able* in the examples given above, called "outer cycles" in Gaeta and Ricca 2006). The main reason for this choice – which is also often operationally easier – is that it keeps the tokens of the different affixes as independent subsets within the corpus, thus allowing for statistical testing (Baayen 2009: 903–904).

Linguistically, however, it would be preferable to count both *re-* and *-able* in *reprintable* as occurences of the respective affixes. Fortunately, Gaeta and Ricca (2006: 79–83) have shown that in most cases their "variable corpus" productivity measure is practically insensitive to the inclusion of the inner derivational cycles, even when these amount to a great number of tokens. In the latter case, however, the same does not hold for Baayen's potential productivity.

The brief discussion above should have made clear that there is not a unique quantitative concept of productivity in word-formation. Different facets of this complex phenomenon may be reflected quantitatively by different statistical measures. However, there can be little doubt that statistical work on large corpora has contributed decisively to a deeper understanding of the notion of productivity and to the disentanglement of its diverse components. Moreover, quantitative methods make it possible to rank and compare effectively with each other different morphological procedures competing in the same domain (and perhaps also in different domains) by means of reproducible and falsifiable data. Finally, statistical corpus-based methods, dealing with large amounts of real language production, have the great merit of stressing that the coinage of new words is deeply rooted in the external communicative needs of the speech community, and therefore can hardly be treated as a prevailingly system-based phenomenon, contrary to what is suggested in approaches like the one in Dressler and Ladányi (2000). This opens the wide issue of comparing the morphological productivity of the same procedures across genres and registers, not to speak of the spoken-written distinction. In principle, a careful construction and comparative investigation of corpora contrasting along genre/register dimensions may be the ideal empirical tool to reach sound and reliable conclusions in this domain, although much is still to be done (cf. Plag, Dalton-Puffer and Baayen 1999).

Another aspect in which much research work remains to be done is the systematic cross-linguistic collection and comparison of quantitative data on productivity, especially in the light of the increasing availability of large electronic corpora in many languages other than English. First results in this direction are available at least for Dutch (Baayen 1994; Baayen and Neijt 1997), German (Lüdeling and Evert 2005; from a diachronic perspective, see Scherer 2005), Italian (Gaeta and Ricca 2003; diachronically, see Štichauer 2009), and French (cf. Dal 2003 and the papers contained there).

3 Qualitative approaches

Following Aronoff (1976), a number of investigations have focused on the idea that productivity should be strictly related to the concept of possible word. From this perspective, productivity depends on the possibility offered by the grammar of a WFR to apply to a certain set of bases. Accordingly, Booij (1977) suggests to inversely relate the productivity of WFRs to the number of restrictions pertaining to a certain WFR when applied to a set of bases. These restrictions constrain the theoretically unlimited application of a WFR, and therefore have an impact on its productivity. However, the number of restrictions pertaining to a WFR cannot be directly reflected in quantitative terms, as argued by Booij, because their quantitative impact does not relate in linear terms with the selectional properties displayed by the WFRs. Thus, it is not safe to claim that a WFR displaying more restrictions is also quantitatively less productive than a WFR displaying a smaller number of restrictions.

The restrictions can come from every level of linguistic analysis, from phonology to syntax, including semantic and pragmatic aspects (cf. article 14 on restrictions in word-formation). To mention only a couple of cases with an immediate impact on the quantitative dimension, it has been observed that the interaction of prefixation and suffixation creates interesting telescoping effects, which limit or enhance the productivity of WFRs when they are considered in connection with each other. Thus, in Italian deverbal potential adjectives formed with a negative prefix like *invendibile* 'unsalable' display an apparent distortion of the quantitative measure of their expanding productivity as discussed in section 2. Notice that these adjectives display a clear derivational sequence, because the prefix cannot take verbs as an input:

(2) a. *vendere* 'to sell' → *vendibile* → *invendibile*
     b. *vendere* → **invendere* → *invendibile*

If the inner derivational cycles are taken into account, the calculation of the expanding productivity of the suffix *-bile* varies considerably (cf. Gaeta and Ricca 2003, 2006 for details). In fact, the inclusion of the inner cycles (thus for instance the prefixed [*in*-[*vendi*-*bile*]]) strongly lowers the expanding productivity of *-bile* with regard to the value obtained including the outer cycles only. Far from undermining the reliability of the whole procedure, Gaeta and Ricca argue that this is due to the fact that many derivatives formed with *-bile* are current only if co-occurring with a further prefixal derivation. This is shown by cases like *introvabile* 'untraceable', *instancabile* 'tireless', *imperturbabile* 'imperturbable', etc., whose unprefixed bases (??*trovabile*, ??*stancabile*, ??*perturbabile*) are at most marginal due to pragmatic reasons. Therefore, the exclusion of the inner cycles has the effect of introducing many "spurious" hapaxes not flanked by their much commoner prefixed counterparts, which considerably overestimates the productivity value of *-bile*. Thus, although the question of the inclusion of the inner/outer derivational cycles can be generally kept under control by the procedure described in the previous section, in some cases the interaction of the qualitative properties of prefixation and suffixation can lead to apparently distorted results.

A second example has to do with the stratification of the vocabulary which is often neglected or marginalized in the theoretical debate. For instance, Japanese has borrowed a significant part of its lexicon from Chinese. This includes especially VN compounds (3a), which are at odds with the native NV compounds (3b) (cf. Kageyama 1982):

(3)   a. *satu-zin* 'killing a man'   b. *yama-nobori* 'mountain climbing'
         kill-man   mountain-climb
         hoo-bei 'visiting the USA'   *booru-nage* 'ball throwing'
         visit-US   ball-throw

The pattern in (3a) has become productive in Japanese, but it is still restricted only to items of Chinese origin. Thus, a VN compound containing a lexical unit not belonging to the Chinese stratum is unacceptable: **hoo-Amerika* 'visiting America'. Therefore, to judge the quantitative relevance of these compounds, one should preliminarily know the size of the Chinese stratum in the Japanese lexicon. Furthermore, the comparison with the productivity of the native compounds is not obvious because it crucially depends on the mechanism of borrowing, which is in a way extra-grammatical. Similar problems are found in many other languages as well, most notoriously in the case of the English suffixes *-ive*, *-ity*, *-ous* and *-al* (as in *dialectal*, *parental*, etc.) which are mostly restricted to Latinate bases; unfortunately, they are scarcely considered in quantitative works on productivity.

From a more general perspective, a number of universal restrictions have been suggested which allegedly limit the productivity of WFRs besides the aforementioned ones concerning individual, language-specific cases. Accordingly, one can distinguish (i) general claims relating to the general format of the WFRs, (ii) specific claims relating to particular properties of the grammar, (iii) predictions resulting from the particular format of the grammar, and (iv) general properties of the lexical items depending on their accessibility at the cognitive level. These restrictions are of a very different nature, going from those reflecting a certain view of WFRs or of grammar, i.e. the way in which our language competence is structured, to those relating to more general properties of our cognitive endowment when it performs linguistic operations. In the following a quick survey of the different theoretical options will be offered, which also reflects the historical trend from more competence-oriented approaches typical of the early discussions on the productivity of WFRs to the more performance-oriented views which characterize recent research carried out with the help of large electronic corpora (cf. Bauer 2005 and Rainer 2005 for more detailed recent surveys).

With regard to general claims relating to the format of the WFRs, they clearly have an impact on their potential application. For instance, Aronoff's (1976) unitary base hypothesis (UBH) severely constrains the input base to a single word category. Given the very different size of, for instance, the nominal with regard to the verbal lexical class normally present in a language, it is straightforward to expect that, at least in purely absolute numbers, denominal WFRs will be more productive than deverbal WFRs. In spite of its coarseness, this estimation should not be forgotten when WFRs based on nouns and verbs are compared to each other. On the other hand, it has been suggested that the UBH might be a reflex of the semantics of the WFRs (cf. Plag 1998: 237): if it is true, this casts some doubts on the relevance of the UBH as an independent universal constraint.

As for specific claims relating to the particular properties of the grammar, several universal restrictions have been suggested like the adjacency condition (Siegel 1977), the atom condition (Williams 1981), etc. As commented upon by Rainer (2005: 336): "Most of these constraints were flawed from the beginning by an insufficient empirical underpinning, and when the conditions-on-rules approach went out of fashion in generative grammar, they met the quiet death they deserved."

Other predictions result from the particular format of the grammar assumed by a certain framework. In this perspective, it may for instance be relevant which stance the researcher takes on the question of whether restrictions are generally affix- or base-driven. The former approach has been by far the most common in lexicalist frameworks, but Plag (1999: 67–76, 2002) suggests on the contrary a generalized base-driven approach, giving by way of illustration the treatment of the complex domain of English deverbal abstracts. Accordingly, the selective correlation between the verbs formed with the suffix -*ize* and the nominalizing suffix -*ation* is taken to be driven by -*ize*, which at the same time accounts for the restriction on deverbal abstracts displaying the sequence *-*ize-ment*. This approach is more economic than the former because it does not require one to explicitly state the restriction on *-*ize-ment* among the selectional properties of -*ment*. On the other hand, it crucially excludes doublets of derivatives from the same base, which appears to be contradicted by the Italian verbalizing suffix -*eggia*- selecting -*mento* (*corteggiare* 'to court' → *corteggiamento*), -*tura* (*tinteggiare* 'to paint' → *tinteggiatura*) and -*io* (*lampeggiare* 'to blink' → *lampeggìo*, see Gaeta 2005 for a detailed discussion of the question based on Italian).

Finally, a number of restrictions have been claimed to be due to general properties of the lexical items insofar as they are more or less easily parsable or accessible at the cognitive level. In this regard, Hay (2000, 2002) has suggested that the whole question of selectional restrictions be conceived from a perspective dubbed by Plag (2002) "complexity-based ordering". Accordingly, the prediction is made that the more easily parsable affixes should be normally less restricted than (and accordingly should occur after) the less easily parsable ones. In other words, words containing less easily parsable affixes are more likely to be stored in our mental lexicon and therefore directly accessed as units. Factors influencing the ease of parsability are frequency, and especially relative frequency, namely the frequency of a derivative with respect to its base, and phonotactics. The latter is more difficult to operationalize, but generally has to do with the occurrence of less frequent sound clusters resulting from the combination of two morphemes. They are a better cue for detecting and parsing a morphological boundary than more frequent sound clusters which often occur inside morphemes. Taking into consideration these parameters allows Hay to construct a hierarchy which expresses the combinability potential of the individual affixes with regard to the base: affixes scoring higher in terms of relative frequency and phonotactics are normally placed closer to the base. This shows that the selectional properties of the affixes can in principle be explained only with the help of these performance-oriented factors. However, Hay and Plag (2004: 590) observe that this approach is in fact unable to exclude all impossible combinations and conclude that "both selectional restrictions and processing constraints are instrumental in determining suffix ordering".

A further example of the impact of cognitive aspects relating to our storage memory is given by blocking, which for instance causes the relatively marginal status of °*stealer* with respect to *thief*. As shown by Rainer (1988), the main factor influencing synonymy blocking due to a well-established lexical item is the frequency of the latter. As it decreases, doublets of synonymous words become acceptable. For instance, the German suffix -*heit* forms quality nouns from monosyllabic adjectives, but it is blocked when an adjective forms a quality noun with another unproductive suffix: *reich* 'rich' → *Reichtum/*Reichheit*. However, the strength of the blocking effect decreases in correlation with the frequency of the established quality noun: *herb* 'acerb' → *Herbe/Herbheit*, because *Herbe* is comparatively uncommon.

It is precisely the relevance of frequency to blocking that shows that blocking is a qualitatively different phenomenon from the grammar-related restrictions discussed above, since it is not a constraint on *formation* proper, but rather on the lexicalization/entrenchment chances of a given word. While a word like **dier* (from *die*) may be considered ill-formed due to a semantic restriction on the base, a word like °*stealer* is not ill-formed, it is simply unlikely to get established in the mental lexicon due to the existence of the well-entrenched synonym *thief.*

4 Productivity of inflectional classes

A different notion of productivity which is perhaps only tangentially relevant to word-formation concerns the productivity of inflectional classes. However, the topic is worth mentioning in the context of this handbook, because the inflectional classes are obviously a partition of a major word class, and consequently their (in)accessibility to new entries has long-range consequences on the general shape of the lexicon in a given language. Thus, for instance, if it can be shown that a certain WFR is sensitive to a constraint on the inflectional class to which its input base belongs, the productivity of the inflectional class has a great impact on the productivity of the WFR. In Classical Latin, the two adverbializing suffixes *-ē* and *-iter* took as an input adjectives belonging to the first and to the second inflectional class (cf. respectively *lentus/-a/-um* 'slow' → *lentē* vs. *fortis/-e* 'strong' → *fortiter*). Given the different distribution of the two classes, this has a consequence on the productivity of the two adverbializing suffixes.

Probably the qualitative approach has been dominant in dealing with this facet of productivity (especially due to the massive work by Wolfgang U. Dressler and his school in this domain); however, there are also quantitative considerations which can corroborate some relevant points of the issue (see Gaeta 2007 discussed below).

Dressler's approach to productivity in inflectional classes, although qualitative, is not really two-valued, but rather based on a gradual scale of criteria, which test the accessibility of a new item to the given inflectional class (or single microclass, according to Dressler's terminology, cf. Dressler 2003). Hierarchically, the strictest criteria concern the integration of loanwords. Following Wurzel (1984), Dressler further distinguishes the integration of those loanwords that do not originally fit in the class they enter (according to phonological and/or structural properties) from those which already have fitting properties. For instance, the integration of English verbs into Italian (*to dribble* → *dribblare, to set* → *settare*; similarly for Spanish) requires also the insertion of the thematic vowel *-a-* to comply with the system adequacy requirement for Italian verbs (Dressler 2003: 37). The integration of unfitting loanwords is seen by Dressler as marking the highest level of productivity, which can obviously get lost in diachrony. As an illustration, in older Italian the masculine nominal class identified by sg. *-o*/pl. *-i* usually received loanwords also ending in a consonant (e.g., *stoccafisso/-i* 'stockfish' < Old Dutch *stocvisch*, 15th century, *tallero/-i* < Ger. *Thaler* (an old currency), 16th century) but nowadays these items are put in the invariable class (*killer* → It. *killer/*killero*, Ger. *Blitz* 'flash' → It. *blitz/*blitzo* 'swoop, police raid'). According to Dressler's approach, this means that the *-o/-i* class is now only intermediately productive and no longer fully productive.

Notice that even a fitting loanword is not necessarily integrated into an existing inflectional class. A clear case is given by the contrast between feminine and masculine loanwords ending in -*a* in Italian: feminines like *dacia* 'dacha', *sauna*, *geisha* vs. masculine *lama* (both the Tibetan monk and the animal), *koala*, *tanga* 'thong underwear'. Italian has two inflectional classes whose singular ends in -*a*, namely the nouns with pl. -*e* (all feminines, e.g., *casa/e* 'house(s)'), and those with plural -*i* (all masculines, e.g., *poeta/i* 'poet', barring two exceptions). Feminine loanwords in -*a* enter the -*a/-e* class without exceptions, while masculine loanwords never enter the -*a/-i* class, but remain invariable. Like the case of the -*o/-i* class seen above, the impossibility of integrating into the -*a/-e* class the unfitting feminine loanwords like *la jeep*, pl. *le jeep* (never *la jeeppa/*le jeeppe*) makes this class only strongly productive, not fully so. On the other hand, the masculine -*a/-i* class is labelled as plainly unproductive, because it answers negatively also to a weaker test posited by Dressler: the integration of indigenous non-derivational lexemes (i.e. those arising from "extramorphological" procedures like clippings or acronyms, or from conversions). The partially positive response to the latter criterion (the conversions from verb infinitives like *sapere* 'to know' → *il sapere* 'the knowledge', pl. *i saperi* 'the knowledge fields') together with a negative response to the stronger first two, locates a further Italian noun class, the -*e/-i* of f. *fronte* 'forehead' and m. *ponte* 'bridge', in an intermediate position between the -*a-/e* and the -*a/-i* classes and thus defines it as "slightly productive".

The Italian -*a/-i* noun class only responds positively to a last criterion: new items steadily enrich it via the very productive suffix -*ista* '-ist'. However, in Dressler's model this just testifies to the stability, not the productivity of the class, because in this case the productivity is seen as a property of the derivational suffix only (Dressler 2003: 43). Similarly, in Polish the neuter microclass in -*e* is considered as unproductive, despite the existence of a productive word-formation process, abstract nouns in -*anie.* The same is said of German neuter nouns forming the plural by umlaut + -*er* (e.g., *Land* 'country' → *Länder*), although the derivational suffix -*tum* (pl. -*tümer*) is productive.

By the same token, instances of class shift (like Ger. *der Mops* 'the pug', older plural *die Mops-e* > today's Umlaut plural *die Möps-e*) may at most distinguish between stable and recessive classes (Dressler 2003: 43) – and not necessarily so, as shown by the example above, where the two classes involved are said to display the same level of productivity.

Dressler's approach provides the field with a comprehensive framework which has been thoroughly applied to a number of languages, e.g., Italian (Dressler and Thornton 1996; Gardani 2013), Polish (Dressler, Dziubalska-Kołaczyk and Fabiszak 1997), Russian (Dressler and Gagarina 1999), French (Kilani-Schoch and

Dressler 2005) and recently also in a wider diachronic perspective from Latin to Old Italian (Gardani 2013). However, many open points remain, for instance:

(i) There is still limited support for the claim that the above criteria can be ordered hierarchically according to an implicational scale, which is crucial for the cross-linguistic reliability of pseudo-quantitative evaluations like 'strongly > weakly > slightly productive'.

(ii) The qualitative approach, although being discrete in principle, cannot conceal the existence of grey areas between the grades. For example, in Italian, a minority of -*o* masculines are apparently integrated in rare cases (*i/dei torna-do* has ten times the occurrences of *i/dei tornadi* on the web), and conversely a minority of -*e* nouns usually do (*i/dei droni* from *il drone* 'military crewless airplane' is largely dominant, despite the fact that the borrowing is quite recent); in general what impact the variable time may have on the integration of lexical material is not discussed, especially when a language also has inflectional classes exploiting zero marking (see below).

(iii) It is unclear whether in a given language the invariable class has to be considered as a mere default reservoir of non-integrated items, or rather as a full inflectional class on its own. For instance, Russian has basically no native indeclinable nouns, so an indeclinable *pal'to* 'coat' (< Fr. *paletot*) has to be considered a non-integrated loanword, which does not initiate a productive class; but the same item *paltò* in Italian goes into an open class of the native vocabulary (enrichable via the productive suffix -*ità* '-ity'), and in doing so it fully reflects system adequacy given its phonetic shape (all Italian words ending in a final stressed vowel are invariable). Invariable nouns are rightly considered a productive class in Italian (Dressler and Thornton 1996: 7); however, it is a bit paradoxical that by the criteria discussed above they turn out to be the *only* fully productive class in the language.

A different approach to the productivity of inflectional classes is taken by Gaeta (2007), who for the first time applies the quantitative, corpus-based methodology sketched in section 2 systematically to the domain of inflection. Some of his results concern inflection proper, and appear to strongly support the validity of the "variable corpus" method developed in Gaeta and Ricca (2006). In particular, Gaeta shows that the "variable corpus" productivity values for different endings varying along a dimension of contextual inflection (in the sense of Booij 1996) are exactly the same, as should be expected linguistically: the growth curves for the types of 3rd sg. imperfect -*ava* and 3rd pl. imperfect -*avano* can be superposed, although the tokens of the former are three times more numerous, and consequently its growth curve is much longer. No similar result is obtained by applying the other measures of productivity described in section 2. Variation in the inherent inflection component (e.g., 3rd sg. imperfect *-ava* vs. 3rd conditional sg. *-erebbe*) has an impact on the productivity values (see Gaeta 2007 for its evaluation) but interestingly the different values are all ranked above those of the most productive derivational affixes, another linguistically meaningful result not matched by the other measures.

The main relevance of Gaeta (2007) for the topic under discussion here, however, concerns the sharp contrast which emerges in quantitative productivity data among the productive verb class of *-are* verbs, and the other two conjugations (*-ere* and *-ire* verbs). Dressler and Thornton (1991) merge the latter into a single essentially unproductive macroclass, a theoretical and descriptive proposal shared also outside the framework of natural morphology (cf., e.g., Vincent 1988: 294; Maiden 1992: 309). Contrary to *-are* verbs, in Gaeta's work the productivity values for the inflections of *-ere* and *-ire* verbs are very low, in the range of those of the scarcely productive derivational suffixes. This result validates quantitatively the qualitative distinction between productive and unproductive inflectional classes, and also the "polarization" effect in productivity when inflection is concerned, suggested, e.g., by Aronoff and Anshen (1998: 246–247).

5 References

Al, Bernard and Geert Booij (1981): De produktiviteit van woordvormings-regels: Enige kwantitatieve verkenningen op het gebied van de nomina actionis. *Forum der Letteren* 22: 26–38.

Anshen, Frank and Mark Aronoff (1999): Using dictionaries to study the mental lexicon. *Brain and Language* 68: 16–26.

Arndt-Lappe, Sabine, Angelika Braun, Claudine Moulin and Esme Winter-Froemel (eds.) (2018): *Expanding the Lexicon. Linguistic Innovation, Morphological Productivity, and Ludicity.* Berlin/Boston: De Gruyter.

Aronoff, Mark (1976): *Word-Formation in Generative Grammar.* Cambridge, MA: MIT Press.

Aronoff, Mark and Frank Anshen (1998): Morphology and the lexicon: Lexicalization and productivity. In: Andrew Spencer and Arnold M. Zwicky (eds.), *The Handbook of Morphology*, 237–247. Oxford: Blackwell.

Baayen, R. Harald (1992): Quantitative aspects of morphological productivity. In: Geert Booij and Jaap van Marle (eds.), *Yearbook of Morphology 1991*, 109–149. Dordrecht: Kluwer.

Baayen, R. Harald (1993): On frequency, transparency and productivity. In: Geert Booij and Jaap van Marle (eds.), *Yearbook of Morphology 1992*, 181–208. Dordrecht: Kluwer.

Baayen, R. Harald (1994): Productivity in language production. *Language and Cognitive Processes* 9: 447–469.

Baayen, R. Harald (2001): *Word-Frequency Distributions.* Dordrecht: Kluwer.

Baayen, R. Harald (2009): Corpus linguistics in morphology: Morphological productivity. In: Anke Lüdeling and Merja Kytö (eds.), *Corpus Linguistics. An International Handbook.* Vol. 2, 899–919. Berlin/New York: Mouton de Gruyter.

Baayen, R. Harald and Anneke Neijt (1997): Productivity in context: A case study of a Dutch suffix. *Linguistics* 35: 565–587.

Baayen, R. Harald and Antoinette Renouf (1996): Chronicling the Times: Productive lexical innovations in an English newspaper. *Language* 72: 69–96.

Barðdal, Jóhanna (2008): *Productivity. Evidence from Case and Argument Structure in Icelandic*. Amsterdam/Philadelphia: Benjamins.

Bauer, Laurie (2001): *Morphological Productivity*. Cambridge: Cambridge University Press.

Bauer, Laurie (2005): Productivity: Theories. In: Pavol Štekauer and Rochelle Lieber (eds.), *Handbook of Word-Formation*, 315–334. Dordrecht: Springer.

Berg, Kristian (2020): Changes in the productivity of German word-formation patterns. Some methodological remarks. *Linguistics* 58(4): 1117–1150.

Booij, Geert (1977): *Dutch Morphology*. Lisse: De Ridder.

Booij, Geert (1996): Inherent versus contextual inflection and the split morphology hypothesis. In: Geert Booij and Jaap van Marle (eds.), *Yearbook of Morphology 1996*, 1–16. Dordrecht: Kluwer.

Corbin, Danielle (1987): *Morphologie dérivationelle et structuration du lexique*. Tübingen: Niemeyer.

Dal, Georgette (2003): Productivité morphologique: Définitions et notions connexes. In: Georgette Dal (ed.), *La productivité morphologique en questions et en expérimentations*. Special issue of *Langue Française* 140: 3–23.

Dressler, Wolfgang U. (2003): Degrees of grammatical productivity in inflectional morphology. In: Mark Aronoff and Livio Gaeta (eds.), *Morphological Productivity*. Special issue of *Italian Journal of Linguistics* 15(1): 31–62.

Dressler, Wolfgang U., Katarzyna Dziubalska-Kołaczyk and Małgorzata Fabiszak (1997): Polish inflection classes within Natural Morphology. *Bulletin de la Société Polonaise de Linguistique* 53: 95–119.

Dressler, Wolfgang U. and Natalia Gagarina (1999): Basic questions in establishing the verb classes of Contemporary Russian. In: Lazar Fleishman, Mikhail Gasparov, Tatiana Nikolaeva, Alexander Ospovat, Vladimir Toporov, Alekseï Vigasin, Ronald Vroon and Andrej Zaliznjak (eds.), *Essays in Poetics, Literary History and Linguistics. Presented to Viacheslav V. Ivanov on the Occasion of his Seventieth Birthday*, 754–760. Moscow: OGI.

Dressler, Wolfgang U. and Mária Ladányi (2000): Productivity in word-formation (WF): A morphological approach. *Acta Linguistica Hungarica* 47: 103–144.

Dressler, Wolfgang U. and Anna M. Thornton (1991): Doppie basi e binarismo nella morfologia italiana. *Rivista di Linguistica* 3(1): 3–22.

Dressler, Wolfgang U. and Anna M. Thornton (1996): Italian nominal inflection. *Wiener Linguistische Gazette* 55–57: 1–24.

Evert, Stefan (2004): A simple LNRE model for random character sequences. In: Gérald Purnelle, Cédrick Fairon and Anne Dister (eds.), *Le Poids des Mots. Proceedings of the 7th International Conference on Textual Data Statistical Analysis*, 411–422. Louvain-la-Neuve: UCL.

Evert, Stefan and Marco Baroni (2007): ZipfR: Word frequency distributions in R. In: Annie Zaenen and Antal van den Bosch (eds.), *Proceedings of the 45th Annual Meeting of the Association for Computational Linguistics. Posters and Demonstrations Session*, 904–911. East Stroudsburg, PA: ACL.

Evert, Stefan and Anke Lüdeling (2001): Measuring morphological productivity: Is automatic preprocessing sufficient? In: Paul Rayson, Andrew Wilson, Tony McEnery, Andrew Hardie and Shereen Khoja (eds.), *Proceedings of the Corpus Linguistics 2001 Conference*. Special issue of *UCREL Technical Paper* 13: 167–175. Lancaster: Lancaster University.

Fleischer, Wolfgang (1975): *Wortbildung der deutschen Gegenwartssprache*. 4th ed. Tübingen: Niemeyer.

Gaeta, Livio (2005): Combinazioni di suffissi in italiano. In: Maria Grossmann and Anna M. Thornton (eds.), *La formazione delle parole. Atti del XXXVII Congresso Internazionale di Studi della Società di Linguistica Italiana*, 229–247. Roma: Bulzoni.

Gaeta, Livio (2007): On the double nature of productivity in inflectional morphology. *Morphology* 17: 181–205.

Gaeta, Livio and Davide Ricca (2003): Frequency and productivity in Italian derivation: A comparison between corpus-based and lexicographical data. In: Mark Aronoff and Livio Gaeta (eds.), *Morphological Productivity*. Special issue of *Italian Journal of Linguistics* 15(1): 63–98.

Gaeta, Livio and Davide Ricca (2006): Productivity in Italian word-formation: A variable-corpus approach. *Linguistics* 44(1): 57–89.

Gardani, Francesco (2013): *Dynamics of Morphological Productivity. The Evolution of Noun Classes from Latin to Italian*. Leiden: Brill.

Hartmann, Stefan (2016): *Wortbildungswandel. Eine diachrone Studie zu deutschen Nominalisierungsmustern*. Berlin/Boston: De Gruyter.

Hartmann, Stefan (2018): Derivational morphology in flux: A case study of word-formation change in German. *Cognitive Linguistics* 29(1): 77–119.

Haspelmath, Martin (1996): Word-class-changing inflection and morphological theory. In: Geert Booij and Jaap van Marle (eds.), *Yearbook of Morphology 1995*, 43–66. Dordrecht: Kluwer.

Hay, Jennifer (2000): Causes and consequences of word structure. Ph.D. dissertation, Northwestern University.

Hay, Jennifer (2002): From speech perception to morphology: Affix-ordering revisited. *Language* 78: 527–555.

Hay, Jennifer and Ingo Plag (2004): What constrains possible suffix combinations? On the interaction of grammatical and processing restrictions in derivational morphology. *Natural Language and Linguistic Theory* 22: 565–596.

Iacobini, Claudio and Anna M. Thornton (1992): Tendenze nella formazione delle parole nell'italiano del ventesimo secolo. In: Bruno Moretti, Dario Petrini and Sandro Bianconi (eds.), *Linee di tendenza dell'italiano contemporaneo. Atti del XXV Congresso della Società di Linguistica Italiana*, 25–55. Roma: Bulzoni.

Kageyama, Taro (1982): Word-formation in Japanese. *Lingua* 57(2–4): 215–258.

Kempf, Luise (2016): *Adjektivsuffixe in Konkurrenz. Wortbildungswandel vom Frühneuhochdeutschen zum Neuhochdeutschen*. Berlin/Boston: De Gruyter.

Kempf, Luise (2021): Methoden der Produktivitätsmessung in diachronen Korpusstudien. In: Christine Ganslmayer and Christian Schwarz (eds.), *Historische Wortbildung. Theorien – Methoden – Perspektiven*, 23–52. Hildesheim: Olms.

Kilani-Schoch, Marianne and Wolfgang U. Dressler (2005): *Morphologie naturelle et flexion du verbe français*. Tübingen: Narr.

Lombard, Alizée, Richard Huyghe and Pascal Gygax (2024): Morphological productivity and neological intuition. *Glossa Psycholinguistics* 3(1): 18, 1–41.

Lüdeling, Anke and Stefan Evert (2005): The emergence of productive non-medical *-itis*. Corpus evidence and qualitative analysis. In: Stephan Kepser and Marga Reis (eds.), *Linguistic Evidence. Empirical, Theoretical, and Computational Perspectives*, 351–370. Berlin/New York: Mouton de Gruyter.

Maiden, Martin (1992): Irregularity as a determinant of morphological change. *Journal of Linguistics* 28: 285–312.

Neuhaus, Heinz Joachim (1973): Zur Theorie der Produktivität von Wortbildungssystemen. In: Abraham P. ten Cate and Peter Jordens (eds.), *Linguistische Perspektiven. Referate des VII. Linguistischen Kolloquiums*, 305–317. Tübingen: Niemeyer.

Plag, Ingo (1998): The polysemy of *-ize* derivatives: On the role of semantics in word-formation. In: Geert Booij and Jaap van Marle (eds.), *Yearbook of Morphology 1997*, 219–242. Dordrecht: Kluwer.

Plag, Ingo (1999): *Morphological Productivity. Structural Constraints in English Derivation.* Berlin/New York: Mouton de Gruyter.

Plag, Ingo (2002): The role of selectional restrictions, phonotactics and parsing in constraining suffix ordering in English. In: Geert Booij and Jaap van Marle (eds.), *Yearbook of Morphology 2001*, 285–394. Dordrecht: Kluwer.

Plag, Ingo, Christiane Dalton-Puffer and R. Harald Baayen (1999): Morphological productivity across speech and writing. *English Language and Linguistics* 3: 209–228.

Rainer, Franz (1987): Produktivitätsbegriffe in der Wortbildungslehre. In: Wolf Dietrich, Hans-Martin Gauger and Horst Geckeler (eds.), *Grammatik und Wortbildung romanischer Sprachen*, 187–202. Tübingen: Narr.

Rainer, Franz (1988): Towards a theory of blocking: The case of Italian and German quality nouns. In: Geert Booij and Jaap van Marle (eds.), *Yearbook of Morphology 1988*, 155–185. Dordrecht: Foris.

Rainer, Franz (2005): Constraints on productivity. In: Pavol Štekauer and Rochelle Lieber (eds.), *Handbook of Word-Formation*, 335–352. Dordrecht: Springer.

Salvadori, Justine, Rossella Varvara and Richard Huyghe (2024): Measuring affix rivalry as a gradient relationship. In: Alexandra Bagasheva, Akiko Nagano and Vincent Renner (eds.), *Competition in Word-Formation*, 104–138. Amsterdam/Philadelphia: Benjamins.

Scherer, Carmen (2005): *Wortbildungswandel und Produktivität. Eine empirische Studie zur nominalen -er-Derivation im Deutschen.* Tübingen: Niemeyer.

Schultink, Henk (1961): Produktiviteit als morfologisch fenomeen. *Forum der Letteren* 2: 110–125.

Siegel, Dorothy (1977): The adjacency condition and the theory of morphology. In: Mark J. Stein (ed.), *Proceedings of the Eighth Annual Meeting of the North East Linguistic Society*, 189–197. Amherst, MA: North East Linguistic Society.

Štichauer, Pavel (2009): *La produttività morfologica in diacronia. I suffissi* -mento, -zione *e* -gione *in italiano antico dal Duecento al Cinquecento.* Praha: Karolinum.

Thornton, Anna M. (1998): Quali suffissi nel "Vocabolario di Base"? In: Federico Albano Leoni, Daniele Gambarara, Stefano Gensini, Franco Lo Piparo and Raffaele Simone (eds.), *Ai limiti del linguaggio*, 385–397. Roma/Bari: Laterza.

Varvara, Rossella (2019): Misurare la produttività morfologica: i nomi d'azione nell'italiano del ventunesimo secolo. In: Bruno Moretti, Aline Kunz, Silvia Natale and Etna Krakenberger (eds.), *Le tendenze dell'italiano contemporaneo rivisitate. Atti del LII Congresso Internazionale di Studi della Società di Linguistica Italiana (Berna, 6–8 settembre 2018)*, 187–201. Milano: Officinaventuno.

Varvara, Rossella (2020): Constraints on nominalizations: investigating the productivity domain of Italian -mento *and* -zione. *Zeitschrift für Wortbildung / Journal of Word Formation* 4(2): 78–99.

Vincent, Nigel (1988): Italian. In: Martin Harris and Nigel Vincent (eds.), *The Romance Languages*, 279–313. London: Routledge.

Wellmann, Hans (1975): *Deutsche Wortbildung. Typen und Tendenzen in der Gegenwartssprache. 2. Hauptteil: Das Substantiv.* Düsseldorf: Schwann.

Williams, Edwin (1981): On the notions 'lexically related' and 'head of a word'. *Linguistic Inquiry* 12: 245–274.

Wurzel, Wolfgang U. (1984): *Flexionsmorphologie und Natürlichkeit.* Berlin: Akademie Verlag.

Livio Gaeta

14 Restrictions in word-formation

Abstract: The main factors taken to be responsible for constraining or restricting the application of word-formation rules are surveyed. On the one hand, constraints of a general nature will be discussed which may be due to several distinct reasons ranging from our concrete cognitive abilities to different views of approaching word-formation from a theoretical point of view. On the other, a typology of more specific restrictions will be provided which result from the interaction of the different levels of linguistic analysis.

1 Introduction

Word-formation rules (WFRs) are typically subject to a number of general constraints or more specific restrictions conditioning or limiting their productivity, the latter intended in a broad sense as the possibility of applying to lexical bases serving as an input (see article 13 on productivity for a survey). Rainer (2005a: 335) observes that the question of restrictions only arises for productive WFRs, for which the application domain has to be defined intensionally, i.e. by indicating one or more features that any potential base must or should possess as well as additional factors from outside the pattern itself that may be relevant. For unproductive rules the domain is generally described extensionally by enumerating the set of bases to which the rule applies. However, this does not exclude that intensionally defined features may also synthetically summarize the properties shared by the enumerated bases, especially when the latter are quite numerous. What is more, productivity is likely to be a gradient notion to the effect that in some cases a very low degree of productivity approximates unproductivity.

The question of the restrictions on WFRs has been the object of wide investigations ever since; surveys can be found in Bauer (2005) and Rainer (2000, 2005a).

Livio Gaeta, Turin, Italy

https://doi.org/10.1515/9783111420554-014

As a matter of fact, a big part of the research carried out in word-formation focuses on the restrictions displayed by WFRs. They can be approached by adopting two different, although interwoven, perspectives: theory-driven restrictions or constraints of a general nature, and specific restrictions empirically resulting from the analysis of individual language-specific patterns. The latter also come from the interaction of morphology with the other components of the language.

In what follows, a survey of the different aspects of the question will be offered starting (i) with different views of looking at constraints and restrictions and subsequently (ii) developing a typology of restrictions resulting from the interaction of the different levels of the linguistic analysis. In this regard, it must be observed that constraints are usually considered to be those absolute limitations on WFRs which are of a rather general nature while restrictions have a more narrow scope (cf. Rainer 2005a). On the other hand, in the wake of optimality theory constraints can also be taken to be violable, much more limited in scope and hierarchically ordered (cf. Bauer 2001: 126). However, the literature is not always consistent with these distinctions; in this article I will follow Rainer's distinction and generally speak of constraints with regard to general limits on WFRs which are independent of the particular linguistic level considered while restrictions are held to be of a more reduced scope.

2 Constraints on word-formation rules

Generally, there are two possible ways of looking at the question of constraints on WFRs: the first view adopts a top-down perspective, according to which there are constraints due to the format of the grammar and more generally of the language faculty; this view is accordingly competence-oriented. The opposite view is performance-oriented and treats the constraints as resulting in a bottom-up fashion from the way in which our language faculty concretely treats lexical items when they are processed by our cognitive equipment. From the interplay of these two opposite views four possible families of constraints can be identified, which also reflect the historical trend from more competence-oriented approaches typical of the early models of word-formation to the more performance-oriented views characterizing more recent research supported by the use of large electronic corpora.

2.1 Constraints relating to the format of the word-formation rules

A first type of constraints directly depends on how WFRs are generally conceived. In this regard, a question which has been discussed at length concerns the input of WFRs, whether they select as a base a possible or an actual word or rather an abstract morpheme. In a nutshell, while nothing seems to hinge *a priori* on whether a word is possible or actual, i.e. stabilized or entrenched in our mental lexicon, the question of word- or morpheme-based WFRs is much thornier. As to the first point, it can be easily shown that possible but unattested words can constitute the input of WFRs, as in *decaffeinate* which presupposes the unattested °*caffeinate*. On the other hand, WFRs may be sensitive to the actual status of the base, as in the cases of paradigmatic word-formation pointed out by Rainer (1993: 29) in which a complex word is formed on the basis of another complex word as in the German compound *Volkszählung* 'population census, lit. population count' → *Volkszähler* 'person carrying out the census', which can only be interpreted with regard to the idiosyncratic meaning of the base. Thus, a conceivable form ??*Volksberechner* is odd because no base ??*Volksberechnung* 'population count' occurs. Furthermore, bases that are stabilized in the lexicon and give rise to instances of paradigmatic word-formation may also be larger than one word, as in *baroque flute* → *baroque flutist*, while ??*wooden flutist* is odd because *wooden flute* is not stabilized in the lexicon (cf. Spencer 1988). This latter example calls into play another family of constraints which aim at limiting the access of syntactic patterns and rules below the word level and go under various names such as "lexical integrity principle", "no phrase constraint", etc. (see Gaeta 2006 for a recent survey).

As to the second point, Aronoff (1976) launched the slogan of a word-based word-formation intending that the input of WFRs cannot consist of (bound) morphemes but rather must consist of full lexemes (possibly deprived of their inflectional endings). This is motivated by word pairs like *aggression/aggressive* which are not to be derived from a bound stem **aggress-* but rather form a series of derivatives *Xion/Xive*, in which the adjective is formed on the basis of the action noun. Substantive evidence in support of this analysis is provided among other things by those cases in which an available verb stem cannot be the base of the adjective which is rather formed from the action noun: *induction* → *inductive* in spite of *induce* (cf. Aronoff 1976: 28–30). However, although words intended as lexemes are undoubtedly the prototypical input of WFRs, the restriction against bound stems cannot be universal as is shown on the one hand by bound stems like *log-* occurring in *logic*, *logistics*, etc. On the other, for languages of the polysynthetic or strongly fusional (including the introflecting) type, the concept of lexeme may be much more difficult to define. For instance, in Montagnais, an Algic language spoken in Canada, a strictly morpheme-based approach has been defended (cf. Drapeau 1980). However, morphological templates characterizing non-concatenative processes might be more easily treated in a word-based fashion rather than in a morpheme-based framework which can only accommodate a linear concatenation of morphemes intended as atomic units. For instance, in Hindi/Urdu the anticausative verb form is claimed to be straightforwardly obtained by shortening the root vowel: $[XV_1V_1]_V$ 'A causes B to happen' $\leftrightarrow$ $[XV_1]_V$ 'B happens', as in *maar-/mar-* 'to kill/die' (cf. Haspelmath 2002: 49).

This question has gained more relevance in recent times after Aronoff's (1994) "morphomic" turn especially from the perspective of a realizational approach to inflectional morphology as suggested by Stump (2001: 2). This view has repercussions for WFRs that manifest themselves in a general tendency towards the maximization of base allomorphy with respect to affix allomorphy (cf. Loporcaro 2012 for a discussion with regard to inflectional morphology). The base allomorphy is accordingly dealt with in terms of different "morphomes", i.e. concrete formats of a certain lexeme, selected by the affix. In this way, a bias arises towards favoring as input to WFRs existing morphomes, while abstract, underspecified morphemes like stems which increase affix allomorphy are taken to be costly. In brief, the problem is how to deal with cases which allow different interpretations going back to different input bases. This also implies a different format for the affix. For instance, there are at least two different allomorphs for the Italian suffix forming agent or instrument nouns found in *stampare* 'to print' → *stampatore* 'printer' or *udire* 'to hear' → *uditore* 'hearer' in contrast with *aggredire* 'to attack' → *aggressore* 'mugger', *distribuire* 'to distribute' → *distributore* 'distributor', etc. The latter derivatives select as base the Latinate perfect participle which does not match the actual past participle (cf. **aggresso* vs. *aggredito*, **distributo* vs. *distribuito*). On the other hand, the former may be either analyzed as formed by *-tore* plus the so-called verbal stem (formed in turn by the root plus the thematic vowel: *stampa-tore*), or by *-ore* plus the stem of the past participle (cf. *stampat-ore*). The latter analysis presents the advantage of minimizing the suffix allomorphy at the expense of the base allomorphy for which two distinct morphomes have to be assumed. In addition, it also accounts for derivatives like *diffondere* 'to diffuse' → *diffusore* 'diffuser' based on the Italian past participle *diffuso*. However, this choice leaves unexplained on the one hand those cases which require as a base the verbal stem instead of the past participle as *scoprire* 'to discover' → *scopritore* 'discoverer' (cf. the past participle *scoperto*), and on the other new formations which are based neither on the Latin nor on the Italian participle but are rather formed from the parallel action nouns suffixed with *-ione* like *estorcere* 'to extort' → *estorsore* 'blackmailer' / *estorsione* 'extortion' (cf.

the Latin and Italian past participles *extortus/estorto*, see Rainer 2001), possibly under the influence of Neo-Latin patterns.

A second type of constraints on the format of WFRs focuses on their possible input or output, and maintains that any WFR should be limited to one single word category in input (unitary base hypothesis, UBH, cf. Aronoff 1976: 47) or in output (unitary output hypothesis, UOH, cf. Scalise 1984: 137). As for the UBH, it has been pointed out that practically any combination of features such as [±N], [±V] and the like has been suggested, which means that "by choosing the appropriate feature system the UBH can be immunized against refutation" (Plag 1999: 48). Furthermore, the process of base selection is most likely guided by rule-specific semantic principles (cf. Plag 1998: 237) rather than by purely abstract features. Finally, WFRs are often sensitive to well-defined lexical sub-domains on the basis of a unitary meaning of the process (cf. Plank 1981: 43–65, Rainer 2005b). At any rate, in many cases the decision of considering two derivatives from different bases (like for instance the denominal *fashion-able* and the deverbal *accept-able*) as related to the same or to a different WFR depends on whether we look with favor at the occurrence of affixal homonymy or whether we rather prefer the assumption of rules of semantic extension such as those discussed in Rainer (2015) on agent and instrument nouns.

While the UBH has been discussed at length, the UOH has received much less discussion and has been, to a large extent, taken for granted. In principle, the UOH opens two different perspectives depending on whether the formal or the semantic aspect of the WFR is in focus. From the formal perspective, the UOH is strictly connected to the degree of allomorphy one is willing to tolerate before considering two affixes as distinct. For instance, in the Italian case discussed above one might be tempted to postulate two different WFRs, a first one selecting a suffix *-tore* and a second one selecting *-ore*. In virtue of their identical meaning, however, this choice is likely to be inadequate. On the other hand, nobody would postulate a unitary WFR for two utterly different affixes sharing the same meaning such as *-ant* in *inhabit* → *inhabitant* and *-er* in *sleep* → *sleeper*. In other words, suppletion is generally admitted for lexical bases (e.g., the French pair *eau* 'water' / *hydr-ique* 'hydric', cf. Schwarze 1970) but much less so for derivational affixes. Notice that this does not hold for inflectional rules (e.g., the Hungarian second person singular suffix of the indefinite present takes the form *-ol* after sibilants or affricates and *-(a)sz* elsewhere, cf. Carstairs 1988: 70), probably because of the stronger paradigmatic force displayed by inflection vs. that of word-formation.

Scalise (1984) suggests that the UOH might be valid only for the formal aspect of WFRs, not for their semantic aspect. However, that the question is much more complex is shown by the Italian suffix *-ino* which gives rise to several different sorts of derivatives: *mare* 'sea' → *mar-ino* 'marine', *tavolo* 'table' → *tavol-ino* 'table-DIM', *bocca* 'mouth' → *bocch-ino* 'mouthpiece' and *stagno* 'tin' → *stagn-ino* 'tinker'. The first case can be explained away as an instance of affixal homonymy because the output word category is clearly different (an adjective vs. a noun), although this criterion is not uncontroversial as the objections raised against the UBH above also apply here. The other three examples are more complicated, because the purely diminutive value found in *tavolino* can also be traced back in instrument nouns like *bocchino* that denote little objects, and even the agent nouns like *stagnino* generally refer to humble, in a way "little" professions. Even worse, these cases are paralleled by deverbal instrument and agent nouns like, respectively, *cancellare* 'to erase' → *cancellino* 'eraser' and *spazzare* 'to sweep' → *spazz-ino* 'street sweeper', which display exactly the same properties. It is not easy to decide whether all of this should be assigned to the same or to different WFRs. Similar to what we observed above for the UBH, the decision depends on the plausibility of assuming rules of semantic extension; as an alternative, one might also think of a relationship in terms of family resemblance of a Wittgensteinian kind among the several nominal types that can in any case be kept apart from the adjectival homonym.

Finally, a further constraint generally assumed is the open-class base hypothesis which requires that only major lexical classes can be input of WFRs, namely nouns, verbs, adjectives and adverbs. This excludes, for instance, adpositions and pronouns from being involved in WFRs, which forces an analysis of certain patterns like German *hinauf* 'thereon', *darunter* 'there:below', etc. as resulting from a process different from word-formation proper. Moreover, it does not lead us to expect to find cases like Spanish *le* 'her' → *leísmo* 'use of the form *le* for direct objects', in which a pronoun serves as the input of a WFR. However, one can conclude that the major word classes represent the most common or prototypical input of WFRs, although this restriction probably has to be related to the main function of vocabulary enrichment typical of word-formation. In this light, words belonging to the minor word classes usually display grammatical meaning which is only in restricted cases salient enough to be used in word-formation as shown by the Spanish example mentioned above or by numerals.

2.2 Constraints relating to general properties of the grammar

In the light of its general value, the last constraint might also be treated in this section, which discusses constraints depending on general properties usually held to shape our language faculty. One such property is expressed by the compositionality or Frege's principle, because the German logician Gottlob Frege is generally credited for its first modern formulation (but see Klos 2011): it requires that the meaning of a complex word resulting from a WFR be a function of the meaning of the rule and the base. Against Frege's principle, clear cases of analogical formations have been mentioned which require a holistic reference to another complex word like the German compound *Doktormutter* 'female thesis supervisor' with regard to its male counterpart *Doktorvater*. In general, a holistic approach has to be assumed when affix substitution occurs like the Italian verb *svitare* 'to unscrew' which can only be interpreted by making reference to a previous *avvitare* 'to screw' (cf. **vitare*), or with instances of bracketing paradoxes like *multiconfessional* which is formally derived by prefixation [[*multi*]*confessional*] but semantically requires the analysis [[*multiconfession*]*al*]. At any rate, this anisomorphism between form and meaning can be treated in terms of the paradigmatic relations mentioned above and is not substantially different from a strictly compositional approach on condition that the lexical status of the pattern is duly taken into account. In other terms, the compositionality and the holistic approach simply reflect the two different routes followed by the speakers when they access complex words, namely decomposition or full lexical access (cf. Baayen and Schreuder 2003 for a recent survey).

Further constraints focus on the limits imposed on WFRs which result from the interaction with other components of the language. In particular, general trends favoring haplology have been observed for many languages, which block the application of a WFR if a phonological string is replicated by the addition of an affix. For instance, the Italian deanthroponymic suffix *-iano* is normally blocked when the base ends with the same string: *Gadda* → *gaddiano*, but *Flaiano* → *??flaianiano*. In spite of the apparently universal character of this tendency towards the avoidance of cacophonic repetitions, formulating a general rule is not an easy task (see section 3.6).

A second more debated case concerns recursion which is normally widely present in syntax, but much less so in word-formation. Recursion seems to be generally possible in compounding (although languages may differ as to its extent) but much more restricted in affixation. In contrast to syntactic recursion, recursion in word-formation is strongly limited by two aspects: on the one hand, WFRs often are property-changing, which prevents their immediate reapplication to the output. On the other, the systematic reapplication of WFRs leads to long chains of morphemes which may present problems from the viewpoint of their processing, especially when property-changing affixes occur as, for instance, in *organizationalization*. When the last two factors do not intervene, recursion can be generally observed as in the case of the Italian evaluatives *casa* 'house' → *casetta* 'small house' → *cas-ett-ina* 'small small house'. Finally, while the reapplication of two identical suffixes seems quite rare (again with the remarkable exception of evaluative suffixes as in the colloquial Spanish examples *ahora* 'now' → *ahor-it-ita* 'right now', *amigo* 'friend' → *amig-az-azo* 'close friend', cf. Rainer 1993: 108), prefixes are in general more liberal, probably because they are mostly not property-changing, as in *re-rewrite* and the like.

Finally, general constraints can also come from the interaction with factors external to the language faculty but of high relevance with regard to the function of lexical enrichment generally assigned to word-formation. A first constraint has to do with the demand of new words which is of greatest importance for those WFRs which are more connected with the naming function rather than with other functions carried out by WFRs like the mere transcategorization. This is clearly the case with WFRs forming agent or instrument nouns which presuppose the existence of a certain profession or device. This fact contributes to a large extent to shape our lexicon as the result of our cultural historical development and to motivate the varied degree of acceptability of certain formations which synchronically lack a referent like Spanish *arzobispa* lit. 'archbishop (fem.)', *calienta-ojos* lit. 'eyes-warmer', etc. (cf. Rainer 1993: 113). The possible unacceptability of these formations is likely to be guided not by grammatical – i.e. competence-oriented – principles, but rather by performance-oriented conditions, also connected with our world knowledge (see section 3.6 and article 19 on dissimilatory phenomena in French word-formation).

Similar observations also hold for a constraint such as neophobia which has been invoked to account for the low acceptability of new formations simply because they are unusual words (cf. Gyurko 1971 on Spanish). This is especially the case with neologisms which are launched in creative writing (intending on the one hand literary works and on the other products which involve the conscious manipulation of language like advertisements). What appears more acceptable in certain contexts allowing for more creativity may be rejected in contexts requiring a stricter subscription to a shared norm.

2.3 Constraints relating to the particular format of the grammar

While the former constraints can be considered to be theory-independent and therefore universal, the constraints discussed in this section are strictly related to a certain format attributed to the grammar. For instance, in the late seventies a number of locality conditions were formulated which aimed to restrict the number of features visible to a certain WFR in a given domain like Siegel's (1977) adjacency principle, Williams' (1981) atom condition, or Kiparsky's (1982) bracket erasure convention (cf. Plag 1999: 45–46 for a brief survey). As repeatedly emphasized in the literature, these constraints were flawed by serious problems, due among others to an insufficient empirical basis underlying their formulation. At any rate, when the interest in generative grammar sailed towards theoretical shores different from conditions on rules, these constraints were simply abandoned. A similar problem concerns the binary branching hypothesis (cf. Scalise 1984: 146–151), which – far from being universal – is systematically falsified by coordinative compounds like *German-French-English* (*corporation*) and therefore best to be viewed as consequence of the semantics of determinative compounds rather than as the result of a formal constraint on the grammar format (cf. Barri 1977).

Stratal conditions on WFRs deserve a partially different discussion. The latter were originally formulated to account for the well-known fact that WFRs may be sensitive to certain sets of lexical items (lexical strata, cf. Saciuk 1969) characterized for instance in etymological terms (e.g., "of Latin origin"). This idea was further expanded by assuming at least two different and serially ordered derivational strata or levels to which the affixes belong (cf. Siegel 1979). Accordingly, the properties shared by different groups of affixes result from the specific level assigned to them and need not be specified for the individual WFRs. Against the stratal view it has been generally objected that it is largely impossible to account for the severe restrictions on the combinability of the affixes especially when they belong to the same level (cf. Fabb 1988). Furthermore, in several cases affixes have to be assigned to more than one stratum in order to account for their selective and allomorphic properties. This weakens the stratal approach considerably. On the other hand, there are surely languages in which the lexicon is sharply compartmentalized into separate strata displaying robustly different properties. For instance, in German the native WFRs do not generally produce prosodic changes on the bases, while the non-native WFRs are largely characterized by stress shifts: *Wissenschaft* 'science' → *Wissenschaftler* 'scientist' vs. *Térror* 'terror' → *Terroríst* 'terrorist'.

An orthogonal question relates to the source of the selective properties, whether they must be sought in the WFRs, i.e. in the affixes, as generally assumed by those who support a stratal approach, or in the bases, as maintained by Plag (1999: 67–76) who defends a generalized base-driven approach. Accordingly, the selective correlation between the German non-native noun-forming suffix *-ität* and the non-native adjectival bases as in *banal* 'banal' → *Banalität* 'banality' is taken to be driven by the latter. This approach is more economic than the former because it does not require us to assume a complex mechanism of rule-by-rule blocking to account for the oddness of the conceivable form **Banalheit*. Furthermore, it also accounts for cases in which the non-native suffix is selected by native bases like *schwul* 'gay, queer' → *Schwulität* 'embarrassing situation', which violate a rigid stratal view (see section 2.4). However, doublets of derivatives from the same base should in principle be excluded, but exceptions of this kind are not uncommon, as shown by cases like *absurd* 'absurd' → *Absurdität/Absurdheit* 'absurdity', *naiv* 'ingenuous' → *Naivität/Naivheit* 'ingenuity', etc.

2.4 Constraints depending on lexical accessibility

The problems relating to the lexical strata and their ordering have been approached recently from a completely different perspective, which has been termed by Plag complexity-based ordering. This refers to the general properties displayed by the lexical items when they are processed by our cognitive capacities. In particular, Hay (2000, 2002) suggests that more easily parsable affixes should be normally less restricted than less easily parsable ones and accordingly should occur more externally. On the other hand, words containing less easily parsable affixes are more likely to be directly accessed as units entrenched in our mental lexicon. The ease of parsability, or its counterpart lexical entrenchment, are influenced by factors like frequency, especially relative frequency, i.e. the frequency of a derivative with respect to its base, and phonotactics. The latter refers to the occurrence of less frequent sound clusters resulting from the combination of two morphemes which are a better cue for detecting and parsing a morphological boundary than sound clusters occurring frequently inside morphemes. Relying on these parameters, Hay provides a hierarchy expressing the combinability force of the individual affixes with regard to the base: affixes scoring higher in terms of relative frequency and phonotactics are likely to be placed closer to the base. In spite of the attractiveness of this entirely performance-oriented approach, it is empirically insufficient because of the fact that specific selectional restrictions are also required to account for the number of impossible combinations normally observed (cf. Hay and Plag 2004).

A second family of constraints relating to lexical accessibility goes under the broad label of blocking, although substantially different concepts are to be understood here. First of all, one must distinguish between homonymy and synonymy blocking: the first type has been suggested to account for the non-occurrence of denominal verbs like *spring* → *to spring, fall* → *to fall* parallel to *summer* → *to summer, winter* → *to winter* because of the mere presence in our mental lexicon of the corresponding homophonous verbs. However, the non-occurrence – at least in British English, see Bauer (1983: 97) – of *to autumn* in the absence of any homonymous verb casts doubt on the reliability of this explanation. More in general, "this approach fails to expound why language tolerates innumerable ambiguities, but should avoid this particular one" (Plag 1999: 50).

Much more relevance has been attributed to the second type of synonymy blocking. Two cases have to be distinguished: word or (perhaps slightly emphatically) Paul's blocking, in which the occurrence of one synonymic lexeme in our mental lexicon is made responsible for the non-occurrence of a possible derivative as in the classic example of *thief* blocking the formation of ??*stealer*. In this case, which is a true instance of lexical blocking as already envisaged by Hermann Paul (1896: 704), the accessibility of the established word is of crucial relevance: as argued by Rainer (1988: 163), the blocking force of the established word is a direct function of its frequency and of the productivity of the intervening WFR. On the other hand, the blocked word is not really ill-formed, but a potentially usable word – and indeed often attested – provided that for some reason a speaker fails to retrieve the established word responsible for the blocking and/or is in search of a particular meaning effect as in *scene-stealer* (cf. Rainer 2012). Notice that potential words like ??*stealer* are different from possible words like °*caffeinate* seen in section 2.1 also because they are usually inert to further derivation as shown by the impossibility of ??*stealerless* with regard to pairs like *leader* → *leaderless*, *teacher* → *teacherless*, etc., while °*caffeination* is a possible word exactly like its base. In this regard, Rainer (2005a: 337) formulates a possible-base constraint according to which bases of WFRs must be possible words, while merely potential words are excluded.

The second case is more complicated and can be referred to as rule or Pāṇini's blocking, because the non-occurrence of a derivative is accounted for by the fact that a synonymous pattern takes precedence provided that both patterns are productive. This reminds us very closely of the so-called Pāṇini's, or elsewhere principle whereby the application of a more specific rule blocks that of a more general one, as already envisaged by the Indian grammarian Pāṇini (cf. Kiparsky 1973; for a different view see Giegerich 2001). Rainer (1988) suggests to account in these terms for the lexical domain of the German quality nouns formed on the basis of end-stressed adjectives. The latter select different suffixes depending on a set of features restricting in a cumulative way their scope of application. Thus, the suffix *-heit* normally combines with end-stressed adjectives: *gewiss* 'sure' → *Gewissheit* 'sureness', *ordinär* 'vulgar, common' → *Ordinärheit* 'vulgarity', etc., unless they display a learned flavor; in this case they select *-ität*: *binär* 'binary' → *Binarität* 'binarity'/??*Binärheit*, cf. also ??*Ordinarität*, only possible with a mathematical meaning: 'the property of being a common event'. Finally, if a learned, end-stressed adjective ends with the bound stem *-phil*, it selects the suffix *-ie*: *xenophil* 'xenophile' → *Xenophilie* 'xenophilia'/??*Xenophilität*/??*Xenophilheit*. Notice that the simple occurrence of an ending /-fil/ does not trigger the application of *-ie* and the superordinate preference for *-ität* applies in the light of the learned flavor: *monofil* 'unifilar' → *Monofilität* 'unifilarity'/??*Monofilie*/??*Monofilheit*.

Although they rely on a similar synonymic mechanism, Paul's and Pāṇini's blocking are two completely different phenomena because the former refers to the degree of entrenchment of a word in our mental lexicon which is measurable in frequency terms, while the latter is due to the selective specificity of two rules applying to (portions of) the same set of lexical bases. In fact, Rainer (2005a: 337) observes that Pāṇini's blocking may also "apply even when no actual blocking word formed according to the rival pattern exists". Furthermore, while a word like ??*Xenophilheit* can be said to be ill-formed because of the conditions on the selected base, ??*stealer* is not ill-formed *stricto sensu*, as discussed above. At any rate, frequency may also play a role in the case of Pāṇini's blocking as shown by the occurrence of doublets of derivatives from the same end-stressed adjectives if the latter "have become part of a more colloquial register" (Rainer 2005: 338): *debil* 'stupid' → *Debilheit* 'stupidity', beside established *Debilität*, *skurril* 'droll' → *Skurrilheit* 'drollery', beside established *Skurrilität*, etc. (see the pairs *Absurdität*/ *Absurdheit*, etc. mentioned in section 2.3). Clearly, the property of becoming part of a more colloquial register is also connected with an increase of frequency, which has the effect of relaxing the strict condition on learnedness.

On the other hand, Rainer (1988: 172) has suggested that frequency may interfere in cases of affix rivalry systematically blocking a derivative when a clearly more frequent competitor occurs. This is allegedly the case of the Italian deadjectival nouns formed with the two highly productive suffixes *-ismo* and *-ità*, whereby frequent quality nouns selecting *-ismo* (by dropping the ending *-ico* of the base) are said to block the possible formation of *-ità* derivatives: *cinico* 'cynic' → *cinismo* 'cynism'/??*cinicità*, *patriottico* 'patriotic' → *patriottismo* 'patriotism'/??*patriotticità*, etc. Although Rainer maintains that this should be interpreted as a case of Paul's blocking, the high productivity of the two WFRs might be regarded as a clue that indeed an intertwining of the two types of blocking is going on here, because the frequency of the individual derivatives cannot be kept totally distinct from the availability of the two synonymic WFRs expressed by productivity. The latter is in fact related to frequency (see article 13 on productivity). In other words, a productive WFR can be blocked by the intervention of another productive WFR forming more frequent derivatives.

3 Domain-specific restrictions

Let us now turn to specific restrictions relating to the different levels of linguistic analysis which have been pointed out in the literature. The discussion will be in some cases brief because several issues have been already touched upon in the foregoing sections.

3.1 Phonological restrictions

Besides the constraint on haplology mentioned above in section 2.2, there are generally three types of restrictions of a phonological nature. First, there may be selectional restrictions of a positive or a negative value relating to the segmental make-up of the base. For instance, a certain stem ending or the occurrence of certain segments within a stem may favor or hinder the combination with a certain suffix: respectively, the suffix -eer preferably selects bases ending with a dental voiceless obstruent: *musketeer, profiteer*, etc. (cf. Rainer 2005a: 344), while the Dutch noun-forming suffix -te as in *koelte* 'coolness' cannot be added to adjectives ending in a vowel (cf. Bauer 2001: 129). More complex and much discussed especially from the viewpoint of an autosegmental approach to phonology is the case of the Latin suffix -*ālis* in *capitālis* 'capital', *nāvālis* 'naval', etc., which takes the form -*āris* if the base contains a lateral: *lūnāris*/**lūnālis* 'lunar' (cf. Cser 2010). Notice that prefixes are generally held to be far less sensitive to base-driven phonological restrictions (cf. Rainer 2000: 881).

Second, the selectional restrictions may relate to the prosodic shape of the base; in particular word stress may play a role guiding, for instance, the positive selection of the suffix -al with regard to verbs stressed on the final syllable: *arrival, rebuttal*, etc. On the other hand, this restriction might also be seen as due to the preference for Latinate prefix-root verbs, which all happen to have final stress (cf. Malicka-Kleparska 1992: 437). Word stress is relevant for the derivation of circumfixal abstract nouns in German, insofar as only bases displaying initial stress are possible: *klatschen* 'to clap' → *Geklatsche* 'clapping' but *applaudieren* 'to clap' → **Geapplaudiere*, etc. Third, the length of the base computed in syllables may be relevant, as in the suffix -$C_1 oj$ '-ish' found in the Mayan language Tz'utujil spoken in Guatemala, which only selects monosyllabic adjectives *rax-roj* 'greenish', *q'eq-q'oj* 'blackish' (cf. Bauer 2001: 129). The stress position and the syllable number may also form a joint restriction as in the case of the suffix -eer mentioned above which preferably selects bisyllabic trochaic bases: *cameleer* vs. **giraffeer, profiteer* vs. **gaineer, racketeer* vs. **fraudeer*, etc. (cf. Rainer 2005a: 344).

3.2 Morphological restrictions

We have already seen some examples of morphological restrictions above when stratal constraints were discussed. In general, three types of morphology-driven restrictions can be determined. First, the base can belong to a class which is morphologically well-defined by means of stratal constraints or some other morphological feature like gender as in the case of the Hebrew sarcastic diminutive of the form CCaCCaC which can only be formed from masculine nouns: *zakan* 'beard' → *zkankan* 'little beard' (cf. Bauer 2001: 130). In this regard, the reference to "etymological" information such as "of foreign origin" and the like mentioned in section 2.3 above might also be labeled as morphological (or lexical, possibly) because "most speakers do not have in their mental lexicons information about the sources of the words they use" (Bauer 2001: 130). Rather, the latter "are perceived as belonging to various synchronic classes" which "mimic etymological provenance (because that is their origin), but the mental listing involves assigning them to classes which are as random as (perhaps more random than) gender classes" (Bauer 2001: 131). In fact, we have also seen above that the etymological categorization often "leaks", insofar as words of a wrong etymological type are included. Notice incidentally that reference to some information about the base, including when the latter already contains an affix, comes into conflict with those approaches which are typically represented by Anderson's (1992) "a-morphous morphology", because they assume that a process of bracketing erasure cancels any morphological information contained in the base, which is therefore inaccessible to further WFRs. This view is too radical, as shown by the highly productive selectional solidarity of *-ize* and *-ation* which does not hold when the ending has no morphological status: *to realize* → *realization*, but *to surmise* → **surmisation*, etc. (cf. Rainer 2005a: 345).

Second, the base may have to show a particular morphological structure. In this regard, examples are found in which an affix only applies to complex bases, as the Punjabi prefix *gair-* 'un-', which only selects derived bases, e.g., deriving *gairsarkaarii* 'non-governmental' from *sarkaarii* 'governmental', itself derived from *sarkaar* 'government' (cf. Bauer 2001: 131).

The third possible case of morphological restrictions relates to the presence or the absence of a particular affix in the base, as in the case of the Dutch female suffix *-ster* which requires the presence of the suffix *-aard* '-er' in the base: *wandelaarster* 'female hiker' (cf. Bauer 2001: 131), or, conversely, the German suffix *-heit* which can be combined with compounds (e.g., *Schreib-faul-heit* 'the quality of being a bad correspondent; lit. write-lazy-ness'), prefixed adjectives (*un-gleich* 'un-equal' → *Ungleichheit* 'inequality') or circumfixed past participles (*ge-schloss-en* 'closed' → *Geschlossenheit* 'closure'), but does not generally apply to already suffixed bases as shown by *freund-lich* 'friend-ly' → **Freundlichheit* vs. *Freundlichkeit* 'friendliness', *ein-sam* 'lonely' → **Einsamheit* vs. *Einsamkeit* 'loneliness', in which the allomorph *-keit* has to be selected (cf. Aronoff and Fuhrhop 2002: 459), although sparse exceptions like *blei-ern* 'lead-en' → *Bleiernheit* 'leadenness' are attested. A positive correlation can give rise to the phenomenon of potentiation when the productivity of an affix is reinforced by the productivity of the affix in the base (cf. Williams 1981: 250). On the other hand, a negative correlation has been referred to in terms of closing morphemes, namely morphemes that "'close' the construction to other morphemes" (Nida 1949: 85, cf. Marle 1985: 234–238 for Dutch, and Aronoff and Fuhrhop 2002 for German). The closing property is considered an idiosyncratic feature of the individual affixes which has the effect of pre-empting the application domain of another affix as, for instance, in the case of the Bulgarian suffix -*ski* forming denominal adjectives like *pisatel* 'writer' → *pisatelski* 'writer's' which cannot be further derived although there are recent Russian borrowings like *rus-sk-ost* 'Russian-like style', *svet-sk-ost* 'worldly-minded style', etc. (see article 20 on closing suffixes for a detailed discussion).

3.3 Syntactic restrictions

Although at first sight one might expect to observe a number of clear-cut restrictions resulting from the interaction of morphology and syntax, in practice this turns out to "be more illusory than real" (Bauer 2001: 133). The often mentioned importance of the syntactic category of the base as a milestone for the WFRs has been overestimated, as pointed by several authors (see for instance Plank 1981: 43–45), while Plag (1998: 237) even dismisses it as "a by-product of the semantics of the process". More generally, allegedly syntactic restrictions can always be reinterpreted as morphological (or possibly lexical) in nature because of the way in which "a word is used depends to some extent upon the class it belongs to" and therefore "it might seem preferable to merge these two" (Bauer 2001: 133). However, in a more loose parlance one may treat under the label of syntactic restrictions those instances which refer to abstract properties of the bases which have an immediate effect on their syntactic behavior. One such case is represented by examples in which the argument structure of the verbal base is involved as suggested by the so-called "constructional" approaches to argument structure according to which "meaning resides in the syntactic context" (cf. Levin and Rappaport Hovav 2005: 18). For instance, it has been repeatedly claimed that the suffix -*able* normally combines only with transitive verbs: *visitable* vs. **goable*, *observable* vs. **lookable*, etc. On the other hand, depending on the theory, transitivity has also be seen as a semantic, not a syntactic feature (cf. Rainer 2005a: 348). Similarly, in Apalai, a Cariban language spoken in Brazil, two different suffixes are used to form agent nouns, -*ne* with transitive and -*kety* with intransitive verbs (cf. Bauer 2001: 133): *parata wo-ne* 'rubber cutt-er' and *wa-kety* 'danc-er'.

Finally, a particularly tricky example is provided by the Australian language Diyari in which the attributive suffix *-kaɲɟi* is used on "the set of common nouns which take the inchoative verbalizer and appear in the ergative case when used predicatively" (Austin 1981: 39) as in *ɲudu* 'power' → *ɲudukaɲɟi* 'powerful one'.

3.4 Lexical restrictions

Since the role of the lexicon is ubiquitous in word-formation, it is difficult to identify genuinely lexical restrictions. One might conceive of two different sources for lexical restrictions. First, considering that unproductive WFRs normally give rise to shorter or longer lists of words in our mental lexicon, these lists have been generally assumed to form the lexical restrictions of the WFRs. Particular blatant are those cases in which the domain of a WFR is restricted to one or two single entries, as in *bishopric*, the only English word testifying of a suffix *-ric*, or *laughter* and *slaughter* which testify of the suffix *-ter*. Similarly, in Punjabi the nominalizing suffix *-aapaa* is found only in the noun *kuʈaapaa* 'beating' from the verb *kuʈʈ* 'to beat', and in Abkhaz the intensifier *-samsal* appears only in the adjective *àyk°ac°'a-samsal* 'very black' (Bauer 2001: 135).

Second, lexical restrictions may relate to class properties of the bases which have to do with their status within our mental lexicon. One example is given by the stratal conditions repeatedly discussed above, which can also be treated as lexical in nature if one thinks that they refer to the architecture of our mental lexicon rather than to form-specific properties of the words. A similar conclusion can also be reached if a "projectionist" approach to argument structure is adopted, which maintains that the latter results from the projection onto syntax of lexically specified information contained in the verb (cf. Levin and Rappaport Hovav 2005: 18).

3.5 Semantic restrictions

Similarly to the lexicon, also the role of semantics is ubiquitous because any WFR displays a meaning side which selects portions of the lexicon on the basis of their content. In this light, since a projectionist approach to argument structure may also be interpreted as involving a semantic restriction on the possible input, this would subsume under semantics all the examples discussed above.

In general, semantic restrictions are invoked when highly specific meaning aspects of the base domain are required in order to delimit the input of a WFR. For instance, the Italian suffix *-eto* combines only with plant or fruit names and forms nouns referring to the corresponding grove: *canna* 'reed' → *canneto* 'grove of reeds', *arancia* 'orange' → *aranceto* 'orange grove', etc. Similarly, in the Australian language Mangarayi the ethnic suffix *-ɲuɲuŋ* combines only with bases referring to a place name or a language: *Guwiɲilen-ɲuɲuŋ* 'Queenslander' (cf. Bauer 2001: 134).

A certain debate has been kindled by the question of the boundary between word meaning and world knowledge insofar as this is relevant for WFRs. For instance, the reversative prefix *un-* can only be applied to verbal bases displaying a reversible meaning: *unfold, unscrew* vs. **unswim, *unkill*. While for the unacceptability of *unswim* a true semantic restriction may be invoked because the atelic process of swimming cannot give rise to any reversative interpretation, the unacceptability of *unkill* might be due to our encyclopedic knowledge which tells us that death is an irreversible state. The latter condition, however, might not hold in other possible worlds: for instance in the jargon of video-game aficionados *unkill* is a possible verb consisting in bringing back to life a character.

3.6 Pragmatic restrictions

As briefly hinted at in the previous section, a lively debate has focused on the possible distinction of the word meaning from our encyclopedic knowledge which is necessary in order to correctly understand "the nature of the real-world referent of the word" (Bauer 2001: 135) when it is used in a certain context. The latter perspective can also open the door for investigating the role of pragmatically-oriented restrictions on WFRs. For instance, the Dyirbal suffix *-ginay* meaning 'covered with, full of' is normally restricted to bases denoting something dirty or unpleasant as in *gunaginay* 'covered with faeces'. Similarly, in Kusaie, an Austronesian language spoken in Micronesia, the inchoative suffix *-yak* combines typically with names of insects (with the meaning 'to become infested with') or diseases (with the meaning 'to be badly affected by'). In Kannada, the adverbializing suffix *-vaːra* is generally restricted to a bureaucratic language, as in *koːmu-vaːra* 'community-wise' (Bauer 2001: 135 and further references there). This reminds us of the German suffix *-ität* seen in section 2.4 above, which is sensitive to the stylistic register in which the base is employed. A full-fledged system of restrictions relating to stylistic-sociolinguistic features is provided by the Javanese "cromification" rules (cf. Becker 1990: 20–23).

Finally, restrictions of an "aesthetic" nature have been invoked for the speakers' rejection of certain words which are theoretically well-formed: for instance, Guilbert (1975: 191) discusses an aesthetic reaction against very long words in French as the reason preventing the formation of the adverb **oppositionellement* 'oppositionally' from its base *oppositionel* 'oppositional'. In this vein, an aesthetic reason might be made responsible for the haplological blocking of *sillily in English. However, in the absence of solid investigations these observations have an impressionistic flavor.

4 References

Anderson, Stephen R. (1992): *A-Morphous Morphology*. Cambridge: Cambridge University Press.

Aronoff, Mark (1976): *Word-Formation in Generative Grammar*. Cambridge, MA: MIT Press.

Aronoff, Mark (1994): *Morphology by Itself*. Cambridge, MA: MIT Press.

Aronoff, Mark and Nanna Fuhrhop (2002): Restricting suffix combinations in German and English: Closing suffixes and the monosuffix constraint. *Natural Language and Linguistic Theory* 20: 451–490.

Austin, Peter (1981): *A Grammar of Diyari, South Australia*. Cambridge: Cambridge University Press.

Baayen, Harald and Robert Schreuder (2003): *Morphological Structure in Language Processing*. Berlin/New York: Mouton de Gruyter.

Bagasheva, Alexandra, Akiko Nagano and Vincent Renner (eds.) (2024): *Competition in Word Formation*. Amsterdam/Philadelphia: Benjamins.

Barri, Nimrod (1977): Giving up word formation in structural linguistics. *Folia Linguistica* 11: 13–37.

Bauer, Laurie (1983): *English Word-formation*. Cambridge: Cambridge University Press.

Bauer, Laurie (2001): *Morphological Productivity*. Cambridge: Cambridge University Press.

Bauer, Laurie (2005): Productivity: Theories. In: Pavol Štekauer and Rochelle Lieber (eds.), *Handbook of Word-Formation*, 315–334. Dordrecht: Springer.

Becker, Thomas (1990): *Analogie und morphologische Theorie*. München: Fink.

Carstairs, Andrew (1988): Some implications of phonologically conditioned suppletion. In: Geert Booij and Jaap van Marle (eds.), *Yearbook of Morphology 1988*, 67–94. Dordrecht: Kluwer.

Cser, András (2010): The *-alis/-aris* allomorphy revisited. In: Franz Rainer, Wolfgang U. Dressler, Dieter Kastovsky and Hans Christian Luschützky (eds.), *Variation and Change in Morphology. Selected Papers from the 13th International Morphology Meeting, Vienna, February 2008*, 33–51. Amsterdam/Philadelphia: Benjamins.

Drapeau, Lynn (1980): Le rôle des racines en morphologie dérivationnelle. *Recherches Linguistiques à Montréal* 14: 299–326.

Fabb, Nigel (1988): English suffixation is constrained only by selectional restrictions. *Natural Language and Linguistic Theory* 6: 527–539.

Fernández-Domínguez, Jesús, Alexandra Bagasheva and Cristina Lara-Clares (eds.) (2020): *Paradigmatic Relations in Word Formation*. Leiden: Brill.

Gaeta, Livio (2006): The lexical integrity principle as a constructional strategy. *Lingue e Linguaggio* 5(1): 1–16.

Giegerich, Heinz J. (2001): Synonymy blocking and the elsewhere condition: Lexical morphology and the speaker. *Transactions of the Philological Society* 99: 65–98.

Guilbert, Louis (1975): *La créativité linguistique*. Paris: Larousse.

Gyurko, Lanin A. (1971): Affixal negation in Spanish. *Romance Philology* 25(2): 225–239.

Haspelmath, Martin (2002): *Understanding Morphology*. London: Arnold.

Hay, Jennifer (2000): Causes and consequences of word structure. Ph.D. dissertation, Northwestern University.

Hay, Jennifer (2002): From speech perception to morphology: Affix-ordering revisited. *Language* 78: 527–555.

Hay, Jennifer and Ingo Plag (2004): What constrains possible suffix combinations? On the interaction of grammatical and processing restrictions in derivational morphology. *Natural Language and Linguistic Theory* 22: 565–596.

Huyghe, Richard, Alizée Lombard, Justine Salvadori and Sandra Schwab (2023): Semantic rivalry between French deverbal neologisms in -*age*, -*ion* and -*ment*. In: Sven Kotowski and Ingo Plag (eds.), *The Semantics of Derivational Morphology. Theory, Methods, Evidence*, 125–158. Berlin/Boston: De Gruyter.

Huyghe, Richard and Rossella Varvara (2023): Affix rivalry: theoretical and methodological challenges. *Word Structure* 16(1): 1–23.

Kempf, Luise (2016): *Adjektivsuffixe in Konkurrenz. Wortbildungswandel vom Frühneuhochdeutschen zum Neuhochdeutschen*. Berlin/Boston: De Gruyter.

Kiparsky, Paul (1973): "Elsewhere" in phonology. In: Stephen R. Anderson and Paul Kiparsky (eds.), *A Festschrift for Morris Halle*, 93–106. New York: Holt, Rinehart and Winston.

Kiparsky, Paul (1982): Lexical morphology and phonology. In: In-Seok Yang (ed.), *Linguistics in the Morning Calm*, 3–91. Seoul: Hanshin.

Klos, Verena (2011): *Komposition und Kompositionalität. Möglichkeiten und Grenzen der semantischen Dekodierung von Substantivkomposita*. Berlin/New York: de Gruyter.

Levin, Beth and Malka Rappaport Hovav (2005): *Argument Realization*. Cambridge: Cambridge University Press.

Loporcaro, Michele (2012): Stems, endings and inflectional classes in Logudorese verb morphology. *Lingue e Linguaggio* 11(1): 5–34.

Malicka-Kleparska, Anna (1992): Against phonological conditioning of WFRs. In: Jacek Fisiak and Stanislaw Puppel (eds.), *Phonological Investigations*, 423–442. Amsterdam/Philadelphia: Benjamins.

Marle, Jaap van (1985): *On the Paradigmatic Dimension of Morphological Productivity*. Dordrecht: Foris.

Nida, Eugene A. (1949): *Morphology. The descriptive analysis of words*. Ann Arbor: University of Michigan Press.

Paul, Hermann (1896): Über die Aufgaben der Wortbildungslehre. *Sitzungsberichte der philosophisch-philologischen und der historischen Classe der königlichen bayerischen Akademie der Wissenschaften zu München, Jahrgang 1896*, 696–713 [Reprinted in: Leonhard Lipka and Hartmut Günther (eds.), *Wortbildung*, 17–35. Darmstadt: Wissenschaftliche Buchgesellschaft, 1981].

Plag, Ingo (1998): The polysemy of -*ize* derivatives: On the role of semantics in word-formation. In: Geert Booij and Jaap van Marle (eds.), *Yearbook of Morphology 1997*, 219–242. Dordrecht: Kluwer.

Plag, Ingo (1999): *Morphological Productivity. Structural Constraints in English Derivation*. Berlin/New York: Mouton de Gruyter.

Plank, Frans (1981): *Morphologische (Ir-)Regularitäten*. Tübingen: Narr.

Rainer, Franz (1988): Towards a theory of blocking: The case of Italian and German quality nouns. In: Geert Booij and Jaap van Marle (eds.), *Yearbook of Morphology 1988*, 155–185. Dordrecht: Foris.

Rainer, Franz (1993): *Spanische Wortbildungslehre*. Tübingen: Niemeyer.

Rainer, Franz (2000): Produktivitätsbeschränkungen. In: Geert Booij, Christian Lehmann and Joachim Mugdan (eds.), *Morphology. An International Handbook on Inflection and Word-Formation*. Vol. 1, 877–885. Berlin/New York: Mouton de Gruyter.

Rainer, Franz (2001): Compositionality and paradigmatically determined allomorphy in Italian word-formation. In: Chris Schaner-Wolles, John Rennison and Friedrich Neubarth (eds.), *Naturally! Linguistic studies in honour of Wolfgang Ulrich Dressler presented on the occasion of his 60th birthday*, 383–392. Torino: Rosenberg & Sellier.

Rainer, Franz (2005a): Constraints on productivity. In: Pavol Štekauer and Rochelle Lieber (eds.), *Handbook of Word-Formation*, 335–352. Dordrecht: Springer.

Rainer, Franz (2005b): Semantic change in word formation. *Linguistics* 43(2): 414–441.

Rainer, Franz (2012): Morphological metaphysics: Virtual, potential, and actual words. *Word Structure* 5: 165–182.

Rainer, Franz (2015): Agent and instrument nouns. In: Peter O. Müller, Ingeborg Ohnheiser, Susan Olsen and Franz Rainer (eds.), *Word-Formation. An International Handbook of the Languages of Europe*. Vol. 2, 1304–1316. Berlin/Boston: De Gruyter Mouton.

Rainer, Franz, Francesco Gardani, Wolfgang U. Dressler and Hans Christian Luschützky (eds.) (2019): *Competition in Inflection and Word-Formation*. Cham: Springer.

Ruz, Alba E., Cristina Fernández-Alcaina and Cristina Lara-Clares (eds.) (2022): *Paradigms in Word Formation: Theory and Applications*. Amsterdam/Philadelphia: Benjamins.

Saciuk, Bohdan (1969): The stratal division of the lexicon. *Papers in Linguistics* 1: 464–532.

Salvadori, Justine and Richard Huyghe (2023a): Affix polyfunctionality in French deverbal nominalisations. *Morphology* 33(1): 1–39.

Salvadori, Justine and Richard Huyghe (2023b): D'une frontière à une autre: la délimitation aspectuelle dans le domaine nominal. *Verbum* 45(2): 167–194.

Scalise, Sergio (1984): *Generative Morphology*. Dordrecht: Foris.

Schwarze, Christian (1970): Suppletion und Alternanz im Französischen. *Linguistische Berichte* 6: 21–34.

Siegel, Dorothy (1977): The adjacency condition and the theory of morphology. In: Mark J. Stein (ed.), *Proceedings of the Eighth Annual Meeting of the North East Linguistic Society*, 189–197. Amherst, MA: North East Linguistic Society.

Siegel, Dorothy (1979): *Topics in English Morphology*. New York: Garland.

Spencer, Andrew (1988): Bracketing paradoxes and the English lexicon. *Language* 64: 663–682.

Stump, Gregory T. (2001): *Inflectional Morphology. A Theory of Paradigm Structure*. Cambridge: Cambridge University Press.

Williams, Edwin (1981): Argument structure and morphology. *The Linguistic Review* 1: 81–114.

Holden Härtl
15 Argument-structural restrictions on word-formation patterns

Abstract: The implementation of argument-structural effects on word-formation is a vital aspect in modeling the lexical system and the interface between morphology and syntax. The current article provides an overview of theoretical perspectives in the field and presents analyses of structural principles holding in the domain. A number of test cases relating to fundamental operations, e.g., in compounding and nominalization are discussed, as well as specific conditions restricting the formation of morphologically complex words.

1 Introduction

The relation between argument structure (AS) and word-formation patterns is a central topic in the theoretical description of the structural operations available in language. In particular, a correspondence between full sentences and certain types of nominalizations (cf. *John described the city* and *John's description of the city*), where each of the predicates' arguments link systematically to specific structural positions, has long been assumed in the literature (e.g., Lees 1960; Levi 1978; Marchand 1969). For example, Marchand's (1969) classification of compound nouns is based upon the syntactic function of the compound's head constituent, so that *beer drinker* classifies as subject-type nominalization and *eating apple* as object-type. The parallels between nominalizations and sentences are also evident when aspectual properties of a verbal predicate are inherited by a nominal (cf. *giving* vs. *gift*), which, at the same time, have been argued to determine the argument realization qualities of the head noun, cf. *The frequent expression *(of one's*

Holden Härtl, Kassel, Germany

https://doi.org/10.1515/9783111420554-015

feelings) *is desirable*, in which the event reading of *expression* forces the object argument to be realized overtly, cf. Grimshaw (1990: 50).

The examples illustrate that a deeper understanding of AS regularities in processes of word-formation can also give us a broader insight into the characteristics of the interfaces between the different structure-building components of grammar. Specifically, an investigation can help us find an answer to the intensely debated assumption of an autonomous morphological, word-formation component, which is attached to the lexical system and as such isolated from syntax. The various perspectives on this matter, as will be shown in the next section, can differ radically in their assumptions about the general architecture of grammar and the locus of word-formation, as well as in their theoretical presuppositions (for outlines see, among others, Carstairs-McCarthy 2010; Meyer 1993; Olsen 1989). This is also reflected in the terminological conventions used in the literature, e.g., when the labels of "external argument" from a syntactic angle and "agentive role" from a lexical-semantic perspective are used to denote the same thing, i.e. a "subject" nominal of some kind. Hence, discussing word-formation regularities in a theory-neutral fashion is rather difficult.

2 Word-formation and the syntax-morphology interface

According to the classical lexicalist-morphological stance, word-formation is part of an autonomous component of grammar, i.e. the lexical system, which organizes the formation of novel lexemes and can, as such, be seen as the basis of lexical productivity. The history of the debate about the appropriateness of this perspective leads us back to Chomsky's seminal "Remarks on Nominalization" (Chomsky 1970), in which he localizes nominalizations and word-formation in general as part of the lexicon and thus deprives the lexicon of regular syntactic structure building mechanisms, see article 11 on rules, patterns and schemata in word-formation; Bauer (1983: 75 ff.); Roeper (2005). Initially, word-formation was considered for the most part idiosyncratic, and it was only later that such a lexicalist approach to word-formation was bolstered with systemic lexical and AS rules in their own right as have been developed, for example, by Di Sciullo and Williams (1987), Jackendoff (1975), Lieber (2004), Williams (1981a). Marchand (1969) can be considered a precursor of lexicalism, cf. Kastovsky (2005).

To consolidate the assumption that morphological rules are different from syntactic transformations (cf. Scalise and Guevara 2005: 150), often the principle of lexical integrity is employed (cf. Anderson 1992). The principle states that syntactic operations cannot access word-internal structures and thus explains, for instance, the ungrammaticality of "stranded" noun-noun compounds as in **Morphology, she would never give a ___ lecture* (see Spencer 2005: 78). However, apparent counter-examples as they are related, e.g., to the bracketing paradox (evident in phrases like *transformational grammarian*, where the adjective forms a constituent with a subpart of the head noun, i.e. *grammar*, cf. Booij 2009a for discussion) can be utilized to promote the exact opposite, non-lexicalist position, in which the internal structure of complex words is indeed open to syntactic operations. According to such an integrative view, products of word-formation are generated by the same recursive mechanisms as syntactic phrases, with the implication that syntactic operations like movement or binding apply at word level as well. In this manner, for example, Lieber investigates cases of sublexical binding as in *Max's argument was point$_i$less, but Pete's did have one$_i$*, which displays pronominal binding below the level of X^0 through reference between *one* and the sublexical noun *point* in *pointless* (cf. Lieber 1992: 130).

The origins of the syntactic approach can be traced back to transformationalist accounts of nominalization as we find them in Lakoff (1970). Several theoretical variants of the integrative view of word-formation have been implemented in quite different grammar models since then, among them distributed morphology (cf. Harley 2008; Lieber 2006) and also construction grammar (cf. Booij 2009a, 2009b; Schlücker and Plag 2011; Borer 2003). A position mediating between the syntactic and the lexicalist stance is taken by Borer (1991), who promotes a parallel architecture. Here, internal word-structure is subject to a separate morphological rule system whose output, however, is visible to syntax in the derivation of the structural environment as well as the subcategorization features of complex words.

3 Structural principles

In order to capture the argument-structural characteristics of complex expressions in a principled manner, proponents of the different theories sketched above have formulated a number of rules relating to issues like the following: How is the AS of a verbal stem transferred to a derived form? What linking regularities underlie the linear and thematic organization of an output form? And what types of modifiers can a complex noun host? Certain answers to these questions might entail, for instance, that a phrasal modifier cannot occur within a synthetic compound: **apple on a stick taster*, cf. Roeper (1988). Lieber (1992: 59 f.) explains this behavior on syntactic grounds when she argues that a phrase, i.e. a maximal projection like *apple on a stick*, is case-licensed in the complement position to the right of the head only and, therefore, cannot be moved leftward.

3.1 Principles of argument projection

A central research question in the word-formation domain under discussion concerns the process by which AS features are projected up from lexical entries to produce complex word structures and, thus, grasp the intuition that the AS of a compound verb like *pan-fry* is a function of the AS of its head. Lieber (1983) conceives of this in terms of a feature percolation mechanism, which transfers the morpho-syntactic features (including the AS features) to the first non-branching node dominating that morpheme, see (ibid.: 252) and, for critical discussion, Lieber (1992: 86 ff.). Specific AS realizations are then derived from her argument linking principle see Lieber (1983: 258). It dictates that if a verbal head appears as sister to a (potential) internal argument that is the logical object, this argument slot will be linked (i.e. satisfied), thus bringing about the configuration of synthetic compounds like *beer drinker* as [[beer$_N$ drink$_V$] -er$_N$]. In the case of a semantic argument of the head, e.g, the instrument *hand* in *hand-weave*, the verb's AS features percolate to the compound verb, which then satisfies its internal role outside the compound, as in *hand-weave the cloth* (cf. Spencer 1991: 331 f. for critical discussion). One problem with this analysis is that in the derivation of deverbal synthetic compounds like *beer drinker* a verbal element would be involved, which, however, is not a possible expression: **John likes to beer-drink*, cf. Carstairs-McCarthy (2010: 26 ff.) for discussion. Hence, in Lieber (2004), the theoretical focus shifts to lexical-conceptual aspects of synthetic compounding when the author formulates her principle of co-indexation. This maintains that the head's highest argument, in our case the referential argument of *-er*, and the non-head's (*drink-*) highest argument, are co-indexed, which renders an agentive interpretation of *drinker* with the internal argument role still active (for the details see article 11 on rules, patterns and schemata in word-formation; Lieber 2004: 83, 2005: 382 f.).

3.2 Thematic regularities

A significant number of scholars take into account thematic criteria in their description of the AS regularities in word-formation. For example, Baker (1998: 190) refers to Chomsky's (1981) theta criterion to rule out cases like **a truck-driver of 14-wheelers*, where the PATIENT role of *drive* is realized twice, which violates the criterion and, at the same time, illustrates that it governs not only phrasal syntax but the construction of compound structures as well. Also, again from a syntactic perspective, Lieber (1992: 61) exploits Baker's (1988) uniformity of theta assignment hypothesis to motivate the deep-structural identity of phrases and compounds of the type *quencher of thirst* and *thirst quencher*, respectively.

Grimshaw (1990: 14) refers to the specific semantic content of thematic roles when she formulates her prominence theory. According to this approach, for example, a GOAL argument is more prominent than a THEME argument and a non-head of a compound must realize the least prominent argument. This is illustrated by the ungrammaticality of **child-giving of gifts* in which *child* denotes a GOAL. Consequently, *gift-giving to children*, which has the THEME argument inside the compound, is grammatical. Note, however, that Selkirk (1982: 37) considers an equivalent example like **toy-giving to children* unacceptable (see Härtl 2001: 82 f. for further discussion). Another aspect Grimshaw examines in this context is the syntactic type of a noun's argument: Sentential complements of a deverbal nominal are always optional, cf. *The announcement (that an investigation has been initiated) was inaccurate*, even if the underlying verb takes an obligatory complement, i.e. an object NP, cf. **They announced* (see Grimshaw 1990: 74). The author concludes that nouns do not directly theta-mark sentential complements; an assumption which is also supported by the unavailability of sentential complements to -*er* nominals, cf. **the observer that water boils at a certain pressure* (see Grimshaw 1990: 101 ff.).

As a final matter, the theta-assigning behavior of affixes shall be mentioned here. Lieber (1992: 57) assumes that affixes like *de-* and *en-* as in *defuzz* and *encase* assign a theme and a location role, respectively, to their base nouns. In contrast, a suffix like -*ize* does not assign a role to its base but rather assigns a theme role to a word-external NP, cf. *modernize the monarchy*, and Lieber concludes that only verbalizing prefixes can assign theta-roles word-internally. Later, Lieber (1998) revises this position in reference to examples like *apologize* or *texturize*, in which the nominal base seems indeed to be assigned a theme role, which leads the author to favor a lexical-semantic analysis over a purely syntactic approach.

3.3 Linearization regularities

The question of whether and how affixes assign thematic roles hinges on whether an affix figures as head or not. Williams (1981b: 248) formulated a righthand head rule for English, which defines the right-hand member of a complex word as the head of that word. Hence, for example, the suffix -*ion* in *construction* functions as the head. The rigidity of this (parameterized) rule is called into question by apparently left-headed complex verbs containing prefixes like *en-*, which seem to determine the syntactic category of an output form, cf. *entomb*, [[en-$_V$ tomb$_N$]$_V$]; see Lieber (1992: 31), Selkirk (1982), and Williams (1981a: 249 f.). Addressing this problem, Olsen (1992: 12), following Wunderlich (1987), argues for German prefixed forms like [[Ge-$_N$ spött$_V$]$_N$] ('mockery') or [[ver-$_V$ arm$_A$]-en$_V$] ('to impoverish') that they do not contradict the righthand head rule. On diachronic grounds, Olsen characterizes cases like these as instances of a conversion, which triggers a categorical change of the head, with the assumption that it is the right-hand element, i.e. *spott-* and *arm*, respectively, which functions as the head of the complex word. To guarantee a match between morpho-syntactic and morpho-phonological configurations applying to affixes and heads, Ackema and Neeleman (2004: 140) assume a linear correspondence principle, which controls the linear organization of complex words, cf. also Spencer (2005: 91).

From a transformational standpoint, Roeper and Siegel (1978) assume a first sister principle, which states that verbal compounds always incorporate the first sister of the underlying verb, thus excluding ungrammatical forms like **quickly-smoker*, in which *quickly* does not figure as first sister, cf. *John smokes cigarettes quickly*. Bauer (1983: 180 f.) argues that the first sister principle is empirically incorrect because it does not predict examples of verbal compounds like *evening smoker*, in which an adverbial occurs as non-head. Bauer's more general proposal implies that any noun can be used in the formation of synthetic compounds containing a transitive verb (for discussion see also Lieber 1983: 282 f.; Spencer 1991: 326 f.). A refined ordering principle, which is related to the first sister principle, was formulated by Selkirk (1982: 37). Her first order projection condition states that all internal arguments need to be realized "within the first order projection of X$_i$", thus excluding cases like **pizza restaurant eating*, where the internal argument *pizza* of the verb *eat* is realized outside the first projection of the compound's head, cf. Olsen (2000: 907 f.); Spencer (1991: 328 f.).

4 Conditions and operations

Word-formation operations that are associated with the AS of lexical elements are restricted by mechanisms of quite different provenance. AS can be affected in many ways when a complex word is produced and, thus, we find operations in which AS features are simply passed on to some output form (*describe sth.* → *the description of sth.*), but also operations of AS reduction (*tell sb. sth.* → *retell sth.*) and AS extension (*grow* → *outgrow sth.*), cf. Bauer (1983: 177 ff.). Williams (1981a) was the first to formalize AS operations in terms of an externalization and internalization of arguments. He assumes, for example, the rule in (1) for suffixation with *-able*, which implies two stages: (i) the promotion of a new external argument (cf. Williams 1981a; Spencer 1991: 192 f.):

(1) *read* (AGENT, THEME) → *readable* (AGENT, THEME)

Rules like this enable us to capture meaning relations between sentences like *John read the book* and *The book is readable* in structural terms. Structural configurations are central as well for the interpretation of complex expressions. For example, the compound noun *soldier brother* is interpreted as denoting a brother of a soldier due to the fact that the relational noun *brother* contains an argument slot to be obligatorily filled, cf. *The brother* ??*(of Max) smokes*. In contrast, the interpretation of *computer brother*, because of the inanimate non-head noun, can only be deduced by referring to conceptual knowledge and, thus, be possibly understood as the brother who is a computer expert (cf. Meyer 1993: 104 ff.; Štekauer 2005: 28 ff.). Along with the mere presence of an argument slot, it is also the thematic content of the slot, which governs the interpretation of complex words. From a processing perspective, Gagné and Shoben (1997) have developed a thematic relation model based on the assumption that thematic information associated with a noun is a key factor in the interpretation of noun-noun compounds. For instance, the noun *mountain* in *mountain cabin*, has a locative role as its primary thematic function (as part of its qualia structure, see Pustejovsky 1995) and, thus, tends to be interpreted as a cabin on a mountain.

Word-formation operations are also sensitive to the number of arguments. This is evident in compounding where a restriction holds that no compound can be formed from a verb that has two obligatory arguments, cf. the example **the book-putting on the table*, which can be explained under reference to Selkirk's (1982) first order projection condition, see section 3.3 and Baker (1998: 191 ff.) for details. Further, Di Sciullo (2005) formulates a restriction which holds that as soon as an argument position is satisfied within a compound it is no longer accessible to any compound-external NP as **bike-ride a scooter* illustrates (cf. Di Sciullo 2005: 27). In this context, cases of apparent double argument saturations are challenging as in *Personenbeschreibung der Täter* 'person description of the culprits', where the predicate's THEME role is associated with two nominals expressions, i.e. *Person* and *Täter*, and where the distinction between a synthetic and root compound is blurred, cf. Solstad (2010).

Moreover, Randall (2010) observes that the grammatical difference between argument and adjunct affects compound formation. In passive compounds, for example, the left-hand element must be an adjunct, cf. *hand-sewn clothes* vs. **away-given clothes*, and the externalized argument must be internal to the verb, *machine-washed fabrics* vs. **hoarse-shouted throat* (cf. Randall 2010: 210). Further, only (resultative) arguments but not adjuncts can occur as right-hand member in a passive compound: *watered-flat tulips* vs. **picked-late grapes* (ibid.: 148 f.). Note, however, that Randall's restriction is possibly subject to parameterization, as the availability of corresponding German examples indicates: *der heisergeschrieene Hals* 'the hoarse-shouted throat', *die weggegebene Kleidung* 'the away-given clothes'.

4.1 Prefixation and suffixation

The connection between AS and the various operations of prefixation and particle verb formation are well described in the literature, cf., among others, Booij (1992), Dehé et al. (2002), Günther (1987), McIntyre (2003), Olsen (1997a, 1998), Stiebels (1996), Wunderlich (1987) as well as article 6 on particle verbs in Germanic. For example, in Germanic languages like German and Dutch, the prefix *be-* attached to an intransitive verb like *gehen* 'to walk' introduces an internal argument, cf. *Sie begehen die Insel* 'they walk the island', which Booij (1992) considers the outcome of a rule applying at the level of lexical-conceptual structure. A similar modification is the locative alternation, which is morphologically marked in German and Dutch but not in English, cf. Rappaport and Levin (1988), Olsen (1994) for an analysis:

(2) a. Er pflanzte Blumen auf das Beet.
     b. Er bepflanzte das Beet mit Blumen.

(3) a. He planted flowers in the bed.
     b. He planted the bed with flowers.

Likewise, the prefixes *ver-* and *über-* in German affect AS in that the output form is always a transitive verb while the input's AS can be intransitive, cf. *schreiten* 'step' → *etwas überschreiten* 'to step over sth.; lit. to over-step sth.'. In contrast, particles like *ab-* or *aus-* do not introduce a new argument slot, cf. *fahren* 'to drive' → *abfahren* 'to depart', *schlafen* 'to sleep' → *ausschlafen* 'to sleep in'. Particles like *zu-* add a dative argument, which is inserted to the lexical representation of the base via its goal argument *P*, (cf. the simplified representation in 4, see Olsen 1997b: 317 and Wegener 1991):

(4) a. *werfen* 'throw'
         $\lambda P \, \lambda y \, \lambda x \, [\text{THROW}(x,y) \text{ and } P(y)]$
     b. *zu* 'to'
         $\lambda z_{\text{DATIVE}} \, \lambda y \, [\text{BECOME}(\text{LOC}(y,\text{AT}(z)))]$

c. *zuwerfen* 'throw to; lit. to$_{PART}$-throw'

λz_{DATIVE} λy λx [THROW(x,y) and BECOME(LOC(y,AT(z)))]

The dative argument must be satisfied by an expression denoting an animate goal in German, see (5a). Inanimate entities can link with a corresponding (directional) prepositional phrase only, see (5b), cf. Olsen (1997b: 325), Witt (1998: 85 f.):

(5) a. *den Ball dem Kind | *dem Korb zuwerfen*
     the ball the child$_{DATIVE}$ / the basket$_{DATIVE}$ to$_{PART}$-throw
   b. *den Ball zu dem Korb werfen*
     the ball to the basket throw

Similarly, particle verbs with the particle *ein-* 'in' do not accept animate goals linked with a PP, cf. ibid.:

(6) *das Gebiss *in den Patienten | in den Mund | dem Patienten einlegen*
    the denture into the patient$_{ACCUSATIVE}$ / in the mouth / the patient$_{DATIVE}$ insert

In addition to such systematic derivational constraints, any theory of linking in prefixation must also allow for specific lexical differences between the derived forms. For example, the internal argument slot of the verb *believe* can be realized by an ACI, cf. *I believe him to be smart*, whereas the prefixed form *disbelieve* cannot, **I disbelieve him to be smart*, cf. Bauer (1983: 60), Carlson and Roeper (1981).

Like prefixation, suffixation affects the AS of the input form. For instance, the suffix *-ize* attaches to nominal and adjectival bases and produces a verb with an internal argument, i.e. causative/transitive verbs like *symbolize*, *modernize* or inchoative/unaccusative verbs like *oxidize*, *aerosolize*. Despite their wide-ranging polysemy (cf. Lieber 2004: 77), Plag (1999: 137) assumes a unified lexico-conceptual representation for *-ize* verbs, which can realize both a transitive and an unaccusative verb form achieved through the optionality of the constant CAUSE. Note, though, that the implication of this assumption, i.e. the non-causativity of inchoative verbs, is subject to constant debate, cf. Bierwisch (2006), Chierchia (2004), Härtl (2013), Koontz-Garboden (2009), Levin and Rappaport-Hovav (1995). Lieber (2004) proposes a unitary lexical template for *-ize* and *-ify* verbs as well but derives their individual differences from the semantic category of the base and specific co-indexation configurations holding between the arguments of the affix and the base, cf. Lieber (2004: 81 ff.). A more abstract perspective is taken by Williams (1981a), where an *-ize* derivation is achieved through the mechanisms of externalization and internalization of argument slots, cf. also Spencer (1991: 193) and section 4 above:

(7)   *modern* (THEME) → *modernize* (AGENT, THEME)

As we have seen, any theorizing about the link between word-formation and AS has to consider a wide range of linguistic phenomena, such as thematic role content, animacy, case, morpho-syntactic marking, etc., as well as structural configurations like transitivity or externalization. Another word-formation domain where the interplay of a broad variety of linguistic factors is particularly evident is that of nominalization, which we shall have a more detailed look at in the following section.

4.2 Nominalization

The term *nominalization* covers a broad range of morpho-syntactic operations, which all produce a nominal of some kind. Thus, e.g., gerunds like *criticizing*, agent and instrument nouns (*opener*), deverbal nouns (*description*) in general as well as synthetic compounds (*car driver*) fall under this category, with the question being relevant here if and how they inherit the AS of the underlying verb. The perspectives on this issue vary radically: from the assumption that deverbal nouns do not contain any AS features or that they have their own AS to the classical view that the AS of the underlying verb is fully inherited by the derived form; for overviews see Alexiadou (2010), Spencer (1991: 324 ff.) and article 5 on synthetic compounds in German.

   According to the standard view, i.e. that the AS of the verb is copied over to the deverbal nominal, linking conditions control the verb's internal argument, which is assigned structural accusative case in languages like German, to be realized as a structural genitive, cf. *die Stadt beschreiben* 'to describe the city' → *die Beschreibung der Stadt* 'the description of the city', cf. Olsen (1986). Such canonical linking postulations, however, are challenged by deviations where the internal argument links with a PP in a derived nominal, cf. *die Feinde hassen* 'to hate the enemies' → *der Hass *der Feinde / auf die Feinde* 'the hatred of the enemies / towards the enemies', cf. Lindauer (1995), Ehrich and Rapp (2000). This has led some researchers to conclude that derived nominals are equipped with their own AS, which is determined by semantic aspects like the event-structural properties of the nominal, cf. Grimshaw (1990), or the affectedness of the lowest argument, cf. Ehrich and Rapp (2000) and section 4.2.3 for further details.

   On the other end of the theoretical spectrum we find approaches in which no verbal AS features are present in the grammatical representation of derived nominals. To substantiate this conception, in many cases the ontological differences between nouns and verbs are brought forward and, in particular, the optionality of the arguments of nouns, cf. Dowty (1998), Kayne (2008). Kaufmann (2002) argues that nouns do not exhibit a fixed array of linkers and considers the "arguments" of nouns to be semantic attributes instead, for which certain interpretative defaults apply. Likewise, Fanselow (1988) employs what he calls prominent meaning relations holding between the constituents of complex nouns, thus, making lexical-semantic argument positions redundant. According to Fanselow, this applies to derived nominals like *Verfasser des Buches* 'composer of the book' as well, for which a stereotypical relation like WRITE needs to be deduced thus explaining its parallels in meaning to non-derived nouns like *Autor des Buches* 'author of the book' (cf. Olsen 1992 for critical discussion). Problematic for such concept-based approaches are linking differences between deverbal nominals like *Jill's shock* vs. *Jill's attempt*. Here, parallel prominence relations link crosswise such that the genitive NP of a nominalized psych-predicate like *shock* links with an internal experiencer argument, whereas with *attempt* the genitive is linked with the external agent argument (cf. Bauer 1983: 77). This behavior can only be explained by dint of the predicates' lexical-semantic properties, which have to be somehow active in the derivation.

4.2.1 Linking conditions on nominalization

According to several theories, inter alia Grimshaw's (1990) prominence theory, external arguments cannot be realized within synthetic compounds, cf. **gourmet-eating*, **tourist-arriving*, **child-sleeper*. A similar restriction is implemented by Selkirk (1982), where the author employs her subject condition to allow only internal arguments to appear within a synthetic compound (cf. also Chomsky 1970). Borer (2003) doubts the validity of a general constraint against external arguments occurring within derived nominals, providing examples of *-ion* nouns, where a genitive NP is linked with an agent role, i.e. an apparent external argument, cf. *the enemy's destruction of the city*. Also, Di Sciullo (1992) questions the rigidity of the constraint in reference to examples like *expert-tested*, in which the noun contained in the compound is associated with the external argument role of the base verb as well (ibid.: 66). Baker (1998) makes the same observation although with a different interpretation: According to Baker, the linking behavior of such adjectival constructions (i.e. *expert-tested* as in *expert-tested guide*) is expected under the subject condition because the agent role of a past participle form does not figure as an external argument but as an internal one. Rather, it is the theme (i.e. *guide*), which functions as the external argument of the adjectival predicate (ibid.: 191). Note, however, that AS based approaches, in general, are weakened by the noticeable degree of non-productivity of the construction. While, for example, constructions like *expert-tested guide* or *chef-cooked dish* may well be acceptable, a less stereotypical relation between the roles involved renders the expression odd, cf. ??*grandmother-knitted sweater*, ??*professor-taught subject*. Alternatively, what seems to play a role here is the conceptual salience of the property expressed with the adjective, which determines its interpretability and which makes its analysis as synthetic compound in the narrow sense redundant. Such a view is compatible with approaches which favor an analysis based on free interpretation, like Marantz's (1997). These assume, along the lines of Grimshaw (1990) and the above restriction against external arguments, that agent-like genitives in phrases like *the King's separation of the family* should rather be characterized as POSSESSORS, which happen to correspond to an agent interpretation based on conceptual knowledge, cf. Borer (2003) for critical discussion. The accessibility of such agent readings independent of AS is also evident in NPs like *the German invasion*, where the modifier *German* can receive both an agent interpretation as well as a theme interpretation, cf. Roeper and van Hout (1999). It is clear, however, that the adjective does not function as an argument, at least on the theme interpretation: as soon as an explicit agent is provided, the theme reading of *German* is no longer available, cf. **the German invasion by France* (ibid.: 8).

4.2.2 Nominalization with *-er* and *-ee*

The structural status of the arguments as external or internal is also relevant in *-er* nominalizations. A standard assumption comes from Levin and Rappaport (1988: 1068), who formulate a requirement for the bases of *-er* nominals that they contain an external argument, cf. *appealer* vs. **appearer*, which is bound by the affix (cf. Di Sciullo 1992: 73). The specific thematic content of the role is not decisive, see Fleischer and Barz (1995: 151 ff.), Lieber (2004: 17) for lists of possible meanings of *-er* nominals. Furthermore, instrument interpretations are grammatical if this role can also be realized as subject of a corresponding proposition, cf. Levin and Rappaport (1988: 1071 f.), Rainer (2005: 348 f.):

(8) a. A metal gadget opened the can.
         → can opener_INSTRUMENT
     b. *A silver fork ate the meat.
         → *meat eater_INSTRUMENT

It is commonly assumed that deverbal *-er* nominals (or a subset of them, see below), in some way, inherit the object arguments of the base, cf. *baker of bread*, *giver of presents to children*, which Lieber (2004: 61 f.) captures using her principle of co-indexation, see also section 3.1 above. Object arguments are not inherited in compound expressions containing a gerund, cf. **baking man of bread*, **frying pan of meat*, cf. Di Sciullo and Williams (1987). Besides, there are also several instances of *-er* nominals like *villager* and *Londoner*, which are not related to a verbal base, cf. Booij and Lieber (2004), Fleischer and Barz (1995: 154 f.) and, for diachronic aspects relevant in this context, Meibauer, Guttropf and Scherer (2004).

Di Sciullo (1992) examines Italian verb-noun compounds like *taglia-carte* 'paper cutter; lit. cut-paper' and claims that the external argument of the verbal part is realized as *pro* (existent in Italian but not in English or German) inside the compound. According to Di Sciullo, this explains the unavailability of synthetic *-ore* '-er' compounds in Italian, as this affix, too, binds an external argument role. As a result, the external argument would be satisfied twice in a synthetic *-ore* compound thus producing a theta criterion violation, cf. *tagliatore-carte (ibid.: 72). Note that Di Sciullo uses this argumentation to strengthen her reservations against the subject condition, which bans external arguments from being realized within compounds, see the previous section.

A concept-based restriction on deverbal *-er* nominals (and synthetic compounds in general) is that they cannot contain cognate objects as non-head, cf. *tear crier, *dream dreamer, as they render the compound's meaning tautological. Instead, a cognate object requires a taxonomic specification of the argument expression: *false tears crier, nightmare dreamer*. Similar observations have been made for unacceptable noun-noun compounds like *furniture chair or *animal horse, with the explanation that a modifier of a compound must always bring about an ontological specification of the head noun's extension, cf. Meyer (1993: 102), Štekauer (2005: 11).

Along with event structural factors, which we shall examine in the next section, it is also the optionality of the predicate's internal argument, which determines the interpretation of deverbal *-er* nominals. Olsen (2000: 907) observes that, for example, *tree devourer*, due to the obligatory internal argument of *devour*, receives an interpretation of an entity that devours trees, whereas *tree* in *tree eater*, which contains a predicate with an omissible internal argument, is open for an interpretation as a locative modifier, i.e. an eater in trees.

Nouns with the *-ee* suffix (present in English but not in Dutch and as a less productive equivalent *-ling* in German, as in *Prüfling* 'test-ee', *Ankömmling* 'arrivee') can be derivatives of transitive verbs, cf. *employee, trainee*. In these cases, the derived noun is related to the object argument of the predicate. But we also find subject-oriented *-ee* nouns, like *escapee, attendee*, and nouns that derive from genuinely intransitive verbs, like *standee*, again questioning conventional accounts based on AS inheritance (cf. Barker 1998, Spencer 2005 and article 18 on semantic restrictions on word-formation). The selectional characteristics of *-ee* have also led to several semantic treatments of the derivation, where semantic-conceptual features associated with volitionality and sentience are put in focus of the theoretical description, cf., e.g., Booij and Lieber (2004).

Note that *-er* nominals with an *of*-complement cannot receive an instrument reading as only an agentive-eventive interpretation is possible with them: **open-er*$_{\text{INSTRUMENT}}$ *of cans*, **sharpener*$_{\text{INSTRUMENT}}$ *of knives*. This has led to the well-known assumption that only eventive *-er* nominals inherit the verbal AS and can hence realize an *of*-complement, whereas non-eventive ones cannot, cf. van Hout and Roeper (1998), Levin and Rappaport (1988). Thus, for instance, *destroyer of the city* denotes somebody who has actually destroyed something at some time, whereas a *destroyer*, i.e. a warship, may never destroy anything (ibid.: 1069). Olsen (1992: 23 f.), however, points to the influence of the determiner semantics in this context and discusses examples like *closer of gates*, which, although an *-er*$_{\text{AS}}$ nominal in Levin and Rappaport's conception, receive a non-eventive, generic interpretation, cf. also Alexiadou and Schäfer (2010) for a related aspectual analysis as well as McIntyre (2010) for discussion. Generic qualities are also reflected in compounds and in the well-described non-referentiality of the modifier of a compound (cf. Lawrenz 1996; Meibauer 2007), which, in turn, promotes the instrument reading of a synthetic *-er* compound like *knife sharpener*.

4.2.3 Event structural conditions on nominalization

Event structural properties have long been argued to determine the availability of AS in nominalizations. One of the standard assumptions can be traced back to Grimshaw (1990). She assumes that the presence of AS in a deverbal nominal depends on whether the nominal denotes a process, i.e. a complex event, or rather a non-eventive result of some event (ibid.: 49):

(9) a. The examination$_{\text{PROCESS}}$ of the student was in the office at 12:00.
     b. The exam$_{\text{RESULT}}$ (??of the student) was in the drawer.

Process nominals can be identified in time and space and can hence combine with temporal and spatial modifiers, cf. (9a), whereas result nominals can only be spatially identified, as (9b) illustrates. The underlying idea is that complements in NPs are not altogether optional; instead, only nominals lacking aspectual structure do not exhibit AS. A number of grammatical criteria have been isolated to substantiate the grammatical distinction displayed in (9), one of them being that a genitive NP in process nominals is linked with an agent role, whereas it is linked with a possessor role in result nominals, cf. *the teacher's examination of the student* vs. *the teacher's exam*, cf. (ibid.: 51) and Alexiadou (2001: 10 ff.), Alexiadou and Grimshaw (2008) for overviews of the differences between the two types. Criticism raised against Grimshaw's original concept holds that, among other things, process nominals, too, do not necessarily require all their roles to be realized, as is illustrated in *An unskilled instructor's examination will take a long time*, where the internal argument of *examine* is not realized, cf. Pustejovsky (1995: 257 f.).

Problematic for the above distinction is also the significant number of deverbal nouns which realize their internal argument overtly but can still receive a result interpretation as in *The written description of the painting is in the drawer*, cf. Bierwisch (1989), (2009). As McIntyre (p.c.) notes, however, the problem dissolves under the assumption that the PP *of the painting* in this example does not link with the object argument of the verbal base but rather figures as an *of*-complementation to a relational noun on a par with non-deverbal nouns like *replica*, as in *replica of the painting*. A related assumption is implied in Grimshaw's (1990) distinction between *of*-phrases functioning as arguments ("a-adjuncts" in her terminology) and those functioning as "modifiers". For example, *of the girl* in *picture of the girl* containing the relational noun *picture* is described as a modifier by Grimshaw (1990: 144). Following this logic, the PP *of the painting* in *description*$_{\text{RESULT}}$ *of the painting* figures as a modifier just as it figures as a modifier of the noun *replica* or *picture*. The distinction between *of*-modifier and *of*-argument is reflected in the separability of *of*-modifiers from their head, cf. *The picture was of the girl* vs. **The destruction was of the city*, which Grimshaw attributes to the locality restriction of theta-assignment holding for arguments but not for modifiers. This, in turn, predicts that the above *-ion* noun with a result reading can be separated from a (non-argument) *of*-phrase, whereas the corresponding process nominal is predicted not to be detachable from the *of*-phrase. This is indeed supported by the following contrast:

(10) a. The written description$_{\text{RESULT}}$ was [of the painting]$_{\text{MODIFIER}}$.
   b. *The frequent description$_{\text{PROCESS}}$ was [of the painting]$_{\text{ARGUMENT}}$.

Alternative perspectives on the correlation between nominalization and AS realization put a stronger focus on the lexical-semantic qualities of the nouns involved. For example, Ehrich and Rapp (2000) consider verbal and nominal ASs to be completely independent of each other, each equipped with its own individual linking rules. Here, the linking properties of a deverbal noun, process nominal or not, are not derived from the underlying verb and, as the authors assume, it is the feature of affectedness, which determines the linking properties of arguments.

The basic idea is that the interpretation of a postnominal genitive NP, in German, depends on whether the noun's semantic representation contains a BECOME-operator: a postnominal genitive will always be interpreted, when present, as the lowest argument under BECOME, i.e. as an affected theme. This explains why postnominal genitives in NPs like *Hinrichtung des Henkers* 'execution of the hangman', which involve an affected object, can only be interpreted as theme, while non-affecting predicates can realize any role in this position, cf. *Entdeckung des Seefahrers*AGENT/THEME 'discovery of the sailor', *Verehrung der Mädchen*EXPERIENCER/THEME 'adoration of the girls', cf. (ibid.: 279 f.). The factor of affectedness has also been observed to have an impact on the preposing of object NPs, which are banned from a prenominal position in a deverbal nominal if they denote an unaffected object: **the fact's knowledge* vs. *the city's destruction*, cf. Anderson (1977, 2007: 121 ff.). It has been argued that the affectedness constraint on preposed NPs is subject to parameterization as no restriction in terms of NP-internal fronting is active, for example, in Greek, cf. Alexiadou (2001: 94 ff.) for discussion.

Event-structural conditions on AS linking can be found to be active elsewhere in word-formation. For instance, aspectual properties have also been described as a key factor determining the locative alternation (see section 4.1) and producing the meaning differences anchored in the alternating pairs, cf. Olsen (1994). This illustrates, all in all, that only a wide-ranging and interrelated view on the different components of the linguistic system and its interfaces will contribute to a full understanding of the lexical productivity in human language.

5 References

Ackema, Peter and Ad Neeleman (2004): *Beyond Morphology. Interface Conditions on Word Formation.* Oxford: Oxford University Press.

Alexiadou, Artemis (2001): *Functional Structure in Nominals. Nominalization and Ergativity.* Amsterdam/Philadelphia: Benjamins.

Alexiadou, Artemis (2010): Nominalizations: A probe into the architecture of grammar. *Language and Linguistics Compass* 4: 496–511.

Alexiadou, Artemis and Jane Grimshaw (2008): Verbs, nouns and affixation. In: Florian Schäfer (ed.), *SinSpeC* 1. *Working Papers of the SFB 732*, 1–16. Stuttgart: OPUS.

Alexiadou, Artemis and Florian Schäfer (2010): On the syntax of episodical vs. dispositional -er nominals. In: Artemis Alexiadou and Monika Rathert (eds.), *Nominalizations Across Languages and Frameworks*, 9–38. Berlin: Mouton de Gruyter.

Anderson, Mona (1977): NP preposing in noun phrases. *North-Eastern Linguistic Society* 8: 12–21.

Anderson, Mona (2007): Affectedness. In: Martin Everaert and Henk van Riemsdijk (eds.), *The Blackwell Companion to Syntax*, 121–141. Malden, MA: Blackwell.

Anderson, Stephen R. (1992): *A-morphous Morphology.* Cambridge, MA: Cambridge University Press.

Baker, Mark (1988): *Incorporation. A Theory of Grammatical Function Changing*. Chicago, IL: University of Chicago Press.

Baker, Mark (1998): Comments on the paper by Sadock. In: Steven G. Lapointe, Diane K. Brentari and Patrick M. Farrell (eds.), *Morphology and its Relation to Phonology and Syntax*, 188–212. Stanford, CA: CSLI.

Barker, Chris (1998): Episodic *-ee* in English: A thematic role constraint on new word formation. *Language* 74: 695–727.

Bauer, Laurie (1983): *English Word-Formation*. Cambridge, MA: Cambridge University Press.

Bierwisch, Manfred (1989): Event nominalizations: Proposals and problems. In: Wolfgang Motsch (ed.), *Wortstruktur und Satzstruktur*, 1–73. Berlin: Akademie Verlag.

Bierwisch, Manfred (2006): German reflexives as proper and improper arguments. In: Patrick Brandt and Eric Fuß (eds.), *Form, Structure, and Grammar. A Festschrift Presented to Günther Grewendorf on Occasion of his 60th Birthday*, 15–36. Berlin: Akademie Verlag.

Bierwisch, Manfred (2009): Nominalization – lexical and syntactic aspects. In: Anastasia Giannakidou and Monika Rathert (eds.), *Quantification, Definiteness, and Nominalization*. Oxford: Oxford University Press.

Booij, Geert (1992): Morphology, semantics, and argument structure. In: Iggy Roca (ed.), *Thematic Structure. Its Role in Grammar*, 27–50. Dordrecht: Foris.

Booij, Geert (2009a): Lexical integrity as a formal universal: A constructionist view. In: Sergio Scalise, Elisabetta Magni and Antonietta Bisetto (eds.), *Universals of Language Today*, 83–100. Berlin: Springer.

Booij, Geert (2009b): Phrasal names: A constructionist analysis. *Word Structure* 2: 219–240.

Booij, Geert and Rochelle Lieber (2004): On the paradigmatic nature of affixal semantics in English and Dutch. *Linguistics* 42: 327–357.

Borer, Hagit (1991): The causative-inchoative alternation: A case study in parallel morphology. *The Linguistic Review* 8(2–4): 119–158.

Borer, Hagit (2003): Exo-skeletal vs. endo-skeletal explanations: Syntactic projections and the lexicon. In: John Moore and Maria Polinsky (eds.), *The Nature of Explanation in Linguistic Theory*, 31–67. Stanford, CA: CSLI.

Borer, Hagit (2023): Argument structure and derived nominals. In: Peter Ackema, Sabrina Bendjaballah, Eulàlia Bonet and Antonio Fábregas (eds.), *The Wiley Blackwell Companion to Morphology*, 137–202. Wiley-Blackwell.

Carlson, Greg and Thomas Roeper (1981): Morphology and subcategorization: Case and the unmarked complex verb. In: Teun Hoekstra, Harry van der Hulst and Michael Moortgat (eds.), *Lexical Grammar*, 123–164. Dordrecht: Foris.

Carstairs-McCarthy, Andrew (2010): *The Evolution of Morphology*. Oxford: Oxford University Press.

Carston, Robyn (2022): Words: Syntactic structures and pragmatic meanings. *Synthese* 200(430): 1–28. [Online available at: https://doi.org/10.1007/s11229-022-03861-1]

Chierchia, Gennaro (2004): A semantics for unaccusatives and its syntactic consequences. In: Artemis Alexiadou, Elena Anagnostopoulou and Martin Everaert (eds.), *The Unaccusativity Puzzle*, 22–59. Oxford: Oxford University Press.

Chomsky, Noam (1970): Remarks on nominalization. In: Roderick A. Jacobs and Peter S. Rosenbaum (eds.), *Readings in English Transformational Grammar*, 184–221. Waltham, MA: Blaisdell.

Chomsky, Noam (1981): *Lectures on Government and Binding*. Dordrecht: Foris.

Dehé, Nicole, Ray Jackendoff, Andrew McIntyre and Silke Urban (eds.) (2002): *Verb Particle Explorations*. Berlin: Mouton de Gruyter.

Di Sciullo, Anna Maria (1992): Deverbal compounds and the external argument. In: Iggy M. Roca (ed.), *Thematic Structure. Its Role in Grammar*, 65–78. Dordrecht: Foris.

Di Sciullo, Anna Maria (2005): Decomposing compounds. *SKASE Journal of Theoretical Linguistics* 2(3): 14–33.

Di Sciullo, Anna Maria and Edwin Williams (1987): *On the Definition of Word.* Cambridge, MA: MIT Press.

Dowty, David (1989): On the semantic content of the notion thematic role. In: Gennaro Chierchia, Barbara Partee and Raymond Turner (eds.), *Properties, Types and Meanings. Semantic Issues,* 69–129. Dordrecht: Kluwer.

Ehrich, Veronika and Irene Rapp (2000): Sortale Bedeutung und Argumentstruktur: *ung*-Nominalisierungen im Deutschen. *Zeitschrift für Sprachwissenschaft* 19(2): 245–303.

Fanselow, Gisbert (1988): Word syntax and semantic principles. In: Geert Booij and Jaap van Marle (eds.), *Yearbook of Morphology 1988,* 95–122. Dordrecht: Foris.

Fleischer, Wolfgang and Irmhild Barz (1995): *Wortbildung der deutschen Gegenwartssprache.* 2nd ed. Tübingen: Niemeyer.

Gagné, Christina L. and Edward J. Shoben (1997): The influence of thematic relations on the comprehension of non-predicating conceptual combinations. *Journal of Experimental Psychology: Learning, Memory, and Cognition* 23: 71–87.

Grimshaw, Jane (1990): *Argument Structure.* Cambridge, MA: MIT Press.

Günther, Hartmut (1987): Wortbildung, Syntax, *be*-Verben und das Lexikon. *Beiträge zur Geschichte der deutschen Sprache und Literatur* 109: 179–201.

Harley, Heidi (2008): Compounding in distributed morphology. In: Rochelle Lieber and Pavol Štekauer (eds.), *The Oxford Handbook of Compounding,* 129–144. Oxford: Oxford University Press.

Härtl, Holden (2001): *CAUSE und CHANGE. Thematische Relationen und Ereignisstrukturen in Konzeptualisierung und Grammatikalisierung.* Berlin: Akademie Verlag.

Härtl, Holden (2013): Generic rescue: Argument alternations and the monotonicity condition. In: Patrick Brandt and Eric Fuß (eds.), *Repairs. The Added Value of Being Wrong,* 95–130. Berlin/ New York: Mouton de Gruyter.

Hout, Angeliek van and Thomas Roeper (1998): Events and aspectual structure in derivational morphology. *MIT Working Papers in Linguistics* 32: 175–220.

Jackendoff, Ray (1975): Morphological and semantic regularities in the lexicon. *Language* 51(3): 639–671.

Kastovsky, Dieter (2005): Hans Marchand and the Marchandeans. In: Pavol Štekauer and Rochelle Lieber (eds.), *Handbook of Word-Formation,* 99–124. Dordrecht: Springer.

Kaufmann, Ingrid (2002): Infinitivnominalisierungen von reflexiven Verben: Evidenz gegen Argumentstrukturvererbung? In: Claudia Maienborn (ed.), *(A)Symmetrien – (A)Symmetries. Beiträge zu Ehren von Ewald Lang / Papers in Honor of Ewald Lang,* 203–232. Tübingen: Stauffenburg.

Kayne, Richard (2008): Antisymmetry and the lexicon. *Linguistic Variation Yearbook* 8: 1–32.

Koontz-Garboden, Andrew (2009): Anticausativization. *Natural Language and Linguistic Theory* 27: 77–138.

Lakoff, George (1970): *Irregularity in Syntax.* New York: Holt, Rinehart and Winston.

Lawrenz, Birgit (1996): *Der Zwischen-den-Mahlzeiten-Imbiß* und *der Herren-der-Welt-Größenwahn*: Aspekte der Struktur und Bildungsweisen von Phrasenkomposita im Deutschen. *Zeitschrift für Germanistische Linguistik* 24: 1–15.

Lees, Robert B. (1960): *The Grammar of English Nominalizations.* Bloomington, IN: Indiana University Press.

Levi, Judith N. (1978): *The Syntax and Semantics of Complex Nominals.* New York: Academic Press.

Levin, Beth and Malka Rappaport (1988): Non-event *-er* nominals: A probe into argument structure. *Linguistics* 26: 1067–1083.

Levin, Beth and Malka Rappaport Hovav (1995): *Unaccusativity. At the Syntax-Lexical Semantics Interface.* Cambridge, MA: MIT Press.

Lieber, Rochelle (1983): Argument linking and compounds in English. *Linguistic Inquiry* 14(2): 251–285.

Lieber, Rochelle (1992): *Deconstructing Morphology. Word Formation in Syntactic Theory.* Chicago: University of Chicago Press.

Lieber, Rochelle (1998): The suffix -*ize* in English: Implications for morphology. In: Steven G. Lapointe, Diane K. Brentari and Patrick M. Farrell (eds.), *Morphology and its Relation to Phonology and Syntax*, 12–33. Stanford, CA: CSLI.

Lieber, Rochelle (2004): *Morphology and Lexical Semantics.* Cambridge: Cambridge University Press.

Lieber, Rochelle (2005): Word formation processes in English. In: Pavol Štekauer and Rochelle Lieber (eds.), *Handbook of Word-Formation*, 375–427. Dordrecht: Springer.

Lieber, Rochelle (2006): The category of roots and the roots of categories. What we learn from selection in derivation. *Morphology* 16: 247–272.

Lindauer, Thomas (1995): *Genitivattribute. Eine morphosyntaktische Untersuchung zum DP/NP-System.* Tübingen: Niemeyer.

Marantz, Alec (1997): No escape from syntax. *University of Pennsylvania Working Papers in Linguistics* 4(2): 201–225.

Marchand, Hans (1969): *The Categories and Types of Present-Day English Word-Formation. A Synchronic-Diachronic Approach.* 2nd ed. München: Beck.

McIntyre, Andrew (2003): Preverbs, argument linking and verb semantics. In: Geert Booij and Jaap van Marle (eds.), *Yearbook of Morphology 2003*, 119–144. Dordrecht: Kluwer.

McIntyre, Andrew (2010): Agentive Nominals and Argument Structure. Ms. Université de Neuchâtel.

Meibauer, Jörg (2007): How marginal are phrasal compounds? Generalized insertion, expressivity, and I/Q-interaction. *Morphology* 17: 233–259.

Meibauer, Jörg, Anja Guttropf and Carmen Scherer (2004): Dynamic aspects of German -*er*-nominals: A probe into the interrelation of language change and language acquisition. *Linguistics* 42(1): 155–193.

Meyer, Ralf (1993): *Compound Comprehension in Isolation and in Context. The Contribution of Conceptual and Discourse Knowledge to the Comprehension of German Novel Noun-Noun Compounds.* Tübingen: Niemeyer.

Olsen, Susan (1986): *Wortbildung im Deutschen.* Stuttgart: Kröner.

Olsen, Susan (1989): *Zur Stellung der Wortbildung in der Grammatik.* Drei Theorien der Affigierung. *Papiere zur Linguistik* 40(1): 3–22.

Olsen, Susan (1992): Zur Grammatik des Wortes: Argumente zur Argumentvererbung. *Linguistische Berichte* 137: 3–32.

Olsen, Susan (1994): Lokativalternation im Deutschen und Englischen. *Zeitschrift für Sprachwissenschaft* 13: 201–235.

Olsen, Susan (1997a): Zur Kategorie ‚Verbpartikel'. *Beiträge zur Geschichte der deutschen Sprache und Literatur* 119(1): 1–32.

Olsen, Susan (1997b): Der Dativ bei Partikelverben. In: Christa Dürscheid, Monika Schwarz and Karl-Heinz Ramers (eds.), *Festschrift für Heinz Vater*, 307–328. Tübingen: Niemeyer.

Olsen, Susan (1998): *Semantische und konzeptuelle Aspekte der Partikelverbbildung mit* ein-. Tübingen: Stauffenburg.

Olsen, Susan (2000): Composition. In: Geert Booij, Christian Lehmann and Joachim Mugdan (eds.), *Morphology. An International Handbook on Inflection and Word-Formation.* Vol. 1, 897–916. Berlin/New York: de Gruyter.

Plag, Ingo (1999): *Morphological Productivity. Structural Constraints in English Derivation.* Berlin/New York: Mouton de Gruyter.

Pustejovsky, James (1995): *The Generative Lexicon*. Cambridge, MA: MIT Press.
Rainer, Franz (2005): Constraints on productivity. In: Pavol Štekauer and Rochelle Lieber (eds.), *Handbook of Word-Formation*, 335–352. Dordrecht: Springer.
Randall, Janet (2010): *The Geometry of Argument Structure*. Dortrecht: Springer.
Rappaport, Malka and Beth Levin (1988): What to do with theta-roles. In: Wendy Wilkins (ed.), *Thematic Relations*, 7–36. New York: Academic Press.
Roeper, Thomas (1988): Compound syntax and head movement. In: Geert Booij and Jaap van Marle (eds.), *Yearbook of Morphology 1988*, 187–228. Dordrecht: Foris.
Roeper, Thomas (2005): Chomsky's remarks and the transformationalist hypothesis. In: Rochelle Lieber and Pavol Štekauer (eds.), *Handbook of English Word-Formation*, 187–228. Dordrecht: Springer.
Roeper, Thomas and Muffy Siegel (1978): Lexical transformation for verbal compounds. *Linguistic Inquiry* 9: 199–260.
Roeper, Thomas and Angeliek van Hout (1999): The impact of nominalization on passive, *-able* and middle. Burzio's generalization and feature-movement in the lexicon. In: Liina Pylkkänen, Angeliek van Hout and Heidi Harley (eds.), *Papers from the UPenn/MIT Roundtable on the Lexicon*, 185–211. Cambridge, MA: MIT Press. Online: http://people.umass.edu/roeper/online_papers/NOM-PASSIVE%20MITWPL%20VAN%20HOUT00.pdf [last access 7 Jan 2015].
Schlücker, Barbara and Ingo Plag (2011): Compound or phrase? Analogy in naming. *Lingua* 121: 1539–1551.
Scalise, Sergio and Emiliano Guevara (2005): The lexicalist approach to word-formation and the notion of the lexicon. In: Pavol Štekauer and Rochelle Lieber (eds.), *Handbook of Word-Formation*, 147–187. Dordrecht: Springer.
Selkirk, Elisabeth O. (1982): *The Syntax of Words*. Cambridge, MA: MIT Press.
Solstad, Torgrim (2010): Postnominal genitives and prepositional phrases in German: A uniform analysis. In: Artemis Alexiadou and Monika Rathert (eds.), *The Syntax of Nominalizations across Languages and Frameworks*, 219–252. Berlin: Mouton de Gruyter.
Spencer, Andrew (1991): *Morphological Theory*. Oxford: Blackwell.
Spencer, Andrew (2005): Word-formation and syntax. In: Pavol Štekauer and Rochelle Lieber (eds.), *Handbook of Word-Formation*, 73–97. Dordrecht: Springer.
Štekauer, Pavol (2005): *Meaning Predictability in Word Formation. Novel, Context-Free Naming Units*. Amsterdam/Philadelphia: Benjamins.
Stiebels, Barbara (1996): *Lexikalische Argumente und Adjunkte. Zum semantischen Beitrag von verbalen Präfixen und Partikeln*. Berlin: Akademie Verlag.
Wegener, Heide (1991): Der Dativ – ein *struktureller* Kasus? In: Gisbert Fanselow and Sascha W. Felix (eds.), *Strukturen und Merkmale syntaktischer Kategorien*, 70–103. Tübingen: Narr.
Williams, Edwin S. (1981a): Argument structure and morphology. *The Linguistic Review* 1: 81–114.
Williams, Edwin S. (1981b): On the notions 'lexically related' and 'head of a word'. *Linguistic Inquiry* 12: 245–274.
Witt, James (1998): Kompositionalität und Regularität im System der Partikelverben mit *ein-*. In: Susan Olsen (ed.), *Semantische und konzeptuelle Aspekte der Partikelverbbildung mit ein-*, 27–104. Tübingen: Stauffenburg.
Wunderlich, Dieter (1987): An investigation of lexical composition: The case of German *be*-Verbs. *Linguistics* 25: 283–331.

Renate Raffelsiefen

16 Phonological restrictions on English word-formation

Abstract: Word-formation rules differ from syntactic rules in that they, apart from obeying morphological and semantic constraints, can also be – and often are – restricted phonologically. The present article includes an overview of the relevant phenomena in English and discusses the consequences for the representation of words in the mental lexicon and for grammar.

1 Introduction

Phonological restrictions on word-formation, as commonly understood, concern cases where affixation rules are sensitive to sound structure. The existence of such restrictions in English is not well established. The relevant sections in current English grammars with fairly comprehensive sections on word-formation, in particular Quirk, Greenbaum and Leech (1972) and Huddleston and Pullum (2002), contain little, and often inaccurate relevant information. There is indeed not a single phonological restriction on affixation which is noted in both grammars; even the rather sparse information on phonological restrictions found in traditional handbooks (Jespersen 1942; Marchand 1969) goes unmentioned.

This neglect is remarkable in view of the abundant evidence for phonological restrictions on English affixation. Before delving into this subject it is worth inspecting more marginal types of word-formation where phonological restrictions can hardly be overlooked. The formation of acronyms (e.g., *DOS, NAFTA*), as op-

Renate Raffelsiefen, Mannheim, Germany

https://doi.org/10.1515/9783111420554-016

posed to initialisms (e.g., *GRE*, *BMX*), appears to be conditioned by the organizability of the relevant segments into wellformed prosodic constituents. That is, if the phonemes associated with the sequence of letters can be grouped into unmarked syllables, in which a vocalic nucleus is flanked by single consonants, acronyms can be formed as in (1a, b). (Syllables are grouped into feet in English. Every phonological word includes minimally one foot. "ω" = phonological word, "Σ" = foot, "σ" = syllable, "S" = strong, "W" = weak, "O" = onset, "N" = nucleus, "C" = coda.)

(1) a.   b.

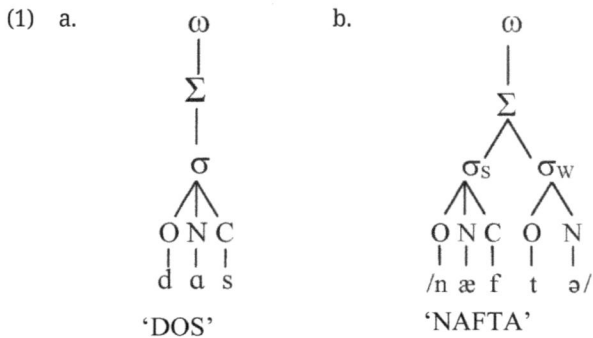

'DOS'   'NAFTA'

If the relevant sequences – due to the distribution of vowels and consonants – cannot be parsed into such syllables, a copulative compound of the names of the letters is formed instead. In such compounds the last member receives primary stress:

(2) (dʒi)ω (aɹ)ω (í)ω 'GRE'
     (bi)ω (ɛm)ω (éks)ω 'BMX'

A second example for conspicuous phonological restrictions concerns certain blends, in which the initial onset of one word is combined with the complete structure, except for the initial onset, of another word. In such cases the choice and order of the parts is restricted phonologically: the word whose initial onset is complex supplies that onset, the other word supplies the remaining structure, cf. (3).

(3) smoke + fog   smog   *foke
     breakfast + lunch   brunch   *leakfast
     stalker + fan   stan   *falker
     sneeze + fart   snart   *feeze
     brother + romance   bromance   *rother

If neither word has a complex onset, blending appears to be inhibited, unless the onsets are followed by identical VC-sequences (e.g., *Bi̱ll* + *Hi̱llary* → *Billary*, *gue̱ss* + *e̱stimate* → *guesstimate*). In such cases, the order is still determined phonologically, such that both the properties of the onsets (e.g., minimal sonority) and foot structure play a role.

The best-known cases of non-affixational word coinage are perhaps clippings (cf. Marchand 1969; Lappe 2007). The examples in (4) suggest a preference for reducing the word to the first syllable, unless the second syllable carries main stress. In the latter case, that syllable is included in the clipped form.

(4) a. fábulous   →   fab   b. obítuary   →   obít
        rádical   →   rad   exécutive   →   exéc
        pícture   →   pic   celébrity   →   celéb
        Jàpanése   →   Jap   delícious   →   delísh
        síster   →   sis   legítimate →   legít
        géntleman   →   gent   ridículous →   ridíc

The patterns in (4) indicate a particular solution to the conflicting goals of shortening the word as much as possible while preserving as much of the salient sound structure of the base as possible. The conflict is solved by retaining the word-initial segmental material including the first stressed syllable. (The few counter-examples generally reflect a preference for the first syllable, regardless of stress, or a preference for the stressed syllable, regardless of its position, e.g., *spagétti* → *spag*, *detéctive* → *tec*.) There appears to be a preference for the clipped form to end in a consonant with relatively low sonority, with the result that certain postvocalic clusters are typically preserved (e.g., *chìmpanzée* → *chimp*, *Yánkee* → *Yank*, but *cústomer* → *cus*) while words with single postvocalic /r/, /l/, or /n/ tend to resist clipping altogether (*rélevant* → ??*rel*, *itínerary* → ??*itín*, *facílity* → ??*facíl*).

Regardless of whether or not the above formations are recognized as word-formation proper, they do exhibit systematic properties that need to be described in a comprehensive grammar of English. Moreover the types of phonological constraints observed in these word coinages shed light on the sort of constraints to be expected in more ordinary affixation. Here, too, it is the prosodic organization of segments, which can be shown to play a central role. The sort of structure referred to is precisely the one seen in the above investigation of more marginal morphology: phonological word, foot, and syllable structure, as well as the sonority of phonemes.

2 Background

Descriptions of word-formation in traditional handbooks are typically organized in form of a list of affixes, each individually detailed with the affix's historical development and combinatory potential. For some affixes, the relevant entry also includes phonological stem properties as is illustrated in (5):

(5) Suffix   restricted to:
   -ive   stems ending in -t, -s
   (Jespersen 1954: 454; Marchand 1969: 316)
   -al (nominal)   stems with final stress
   (Jespersen 1954: 386)
   -en (verbal)   stems ending in stop or fricative
   (Marchand 1969: 272)

The already fragmentary information given in the handbooks is largely ignored in modern grammars. One reason for neglecting the relevant rules may concern the distinction between the actual and the potential. For example, the restriction on -al-suffixation stated in (5) could be overlooked because of apparent counter-examples among English nouns ending in -al. Here it is significant, that none of the relevant exceptions originate from native -al-suffixation; the noun *burial*, for instance, goes back to the Old English noun *buriels* meaning 'burying-place, tomb'. While the change in the spelling (<buriels> → <burial>) along with the meaning change ('bury-ing-place' → 'act of burying') indicate the likely historical reanalysis of the ending /əl/ as the suffix -al, the fact remains that no word has been coined in English by attaching -al to a verbal stem with non-final stress. To capture this generalization it is necessary to treat separately the conditions for "analysis", including the condi-tions for affix recognition and the conditions for recognizing paradigmatic related-ness between words, and "synthesis", which concerns the rules for forming new words based on known words as well as the ability to judge the grammaticality of non-existing words (cf. Aronoff 1976). Significantly, phonological restrictions on word-formation concern synthesis, that is, the potential for forming new words, not the analysis of given, that is inherited or borrowed, words.

    A second obstacle to the detection of phonological restrictions on word-forma-tion can be traced to the indiscriminate use of the notions "stem" and "base". The remarkable restriction on -ive-suffixation stated in (5) contrasts hence with the more fuzzy one offered in Huddleston and Pullum (2002), where the relevant do-main is identified as "mostly Latinate verbs in /d/, /t/ or /s/" (2002: 1711). The relative weakness of the latter restriction results from the lack of distinction between "bas-es", which concern paradigmatic relations between whole words such as the adjective *evasive* and the verb *evade*, as opposed to "stems", which concern syntagmatic part-whole relations such as *evas-* and *evasive*. A stem is accordingly the part of a word which remains after an affix has been stripped off. Significantly, the sort of requirements illustrated in (5) concern stems, not bases, a point easily overlooked in English due to the frequent occurrence of so-called "free stems", which are homophonous to bases (e.g., *disrúpt-*), as opposed to "bound stems", which are not (e.g., *suscépt-* from *suscépt-ible*). The restriction relevant to *-ive*-suffixation in English concerns the availability of a stem, free or bound, which ends in *-t* or *-s*. If such a stem exists, *-ive*-suffixation may occur as is shown by the native coinages *obséssive*, *sécretive*, *caréssive*, *púrposive*, *excúsive* (not because of the verb *excú/z/* 'excuse', but because of the noun *excú/s/* 'excuse'), even *sticktóitive* ('stick to it + -ive'), where a quotation of a phrase is treated as a stem. If there is no such stem, native *-ive*-suffixation is ruled out, even for Latinate verbs in /d/ such as *encode* (e.g., **encódive*, because the stem *encód-* ends in a phoneme other than /t/ or /s/, **encósive*, **encótive* because there are no stems **encós-*, **encót-*).

The third and perhaps most important obstacle to the detection of phonological restrictions on word-formation lies in the common assumption that word-formation rules are properly described by specifying *inputs*, that is, the items that potentially undergo the rule, along with the relevant operations. From that perspective, the exclusion of certain items from the domain of a rule for strictly phonological reasons appears to have no function and seems whimsical at best. The crucial generalization, missed also in traditional work, concerns the observation that phonological constraints on affixation typically refer to only those aspects of stem structure which are part of the prosodic constituents encompassing the affixes in *output* forms. For instance, the targeting of the stem-final consonant in *-ive*-suffixation relates to that consonant's role in the output, where it forms the onset of the syllable encompassing the suffix, cf. (6a). The observation that nominalizing *-al* attaches only to verbs with final stress relates to the fact that the relevant syllables together build a trochaic foot in the output, cf. (6b):

(6) a.

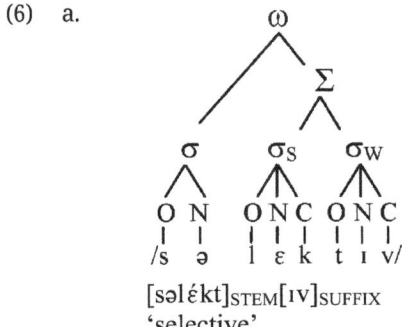

[səlékt]STEM[ɪv]SUFFIX
'selective'

b.

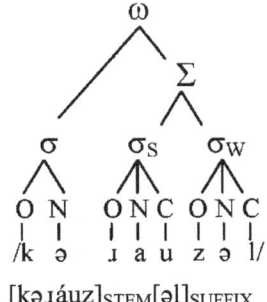

[kəɹáuz]STEM[əl]SUFFIX
'carousal'

From the perspective of output-oriented grammar models, in particular optimality theory, the restrictions observed in (5) indicate the interaction of independently motivated phonological markedness constraints such as foot binarity (a foot must consist of two syllables) and paradigm uniformity constraints (Prince and Smolensky 1993). The latter constraints are crucial for explaining the unacceptability of coinages such as *caróu/s/ive or *promísal. These derivations are ruled out because of the non-identity between the segments (caróu/s/ive – caróu/z/) or the stress patterns (promísal – prómise) in the derived forms compared to the respective base words. Such deviations violate a constraint, referred to as "uniform exponence" (Flemming 1995), which requires derivational paradigms to be associated with a single stem form.

Once phonological restrictions are conceived of as expressions of markedness constraints on output forms, it becomes evident that besides positive requirements (trochee in (6)) there can also be negative ones, that is, the avoidance of word-formation for phonological reasons. For instance, there are numerous systematic gaps in English word-formation which indicate constraints against identical or near-identical segments within adjacent syllable constituents. Also many stressed suffixes will not attach to stems with final stress, apparently to avoid a stress clash. Some examples are listed in (7) (the symbol "#" marks the end of the stem):

(7) a. -ish   sheepish,   b. *[cor fric]#   *horse-ish,
                  oldish   *fresh-ish
        -ése   Sudanese,   *[cor fric]#   *Bangladesh-ese,
                  Nepalese   *Greece-ese
        -ity   oddity,   */t/#   *acute-ity,
                  torpidity   *concrete-ity
        -al   withdrawal,   */l/#   *appeal-al,
                  referral   *result-al
        -ifý   gasify,   */f/#   *shelf-ify,
                  nullify   *stiff-ify
        -ée   trainee,   */i/#   *free-ee,
                  divorcee   *pity-ee
        -éer   pistoleer,   *ó#, */ɹ/#   *gún-eer,
                  rocketeer   *revolver-eer
        -étte   kitchenette,   *ó#, */t/#   *garáge-ette,
                  wagonette   *closet-ette
        -ésque   Pinteresque,   *ó#, */s/#   *Camús-esque,
                  Kafkaesque   *Wallace-esque

None of the restrictions in (7) are noted in Jespersen (1942) or Marchand (1969), apparently due to the fact that they are not easily expressed as selection (rather than avoidance). It is also significant that Aronoff, who did note the absence of stem-final coronal fricatives in -*ish*-suffixation and offered an explanation in terms of output constraints, went on to assert the existence of general constraints against coronal fricatives in adjacent syllables in English phonology, insisting that these constraints do not pertain to word-formation proper (Aronoff 1976: 82). There are many counter-examples to this assertion, including the words listed in (8a). Additionally, there are several affixation rules which appear to be insensitive to the constraint in question. The formations in (8b) show that -*ship* freely attaches despite the presence of a coronal fricative in the stem-final syllable.

(8)   a. hashish, shashlik, thesis, seize, zest, scissors, missis, sizzle, season, assassin
      b. musicianship, professorship, censorship, citizenship, lectureship, apprenticeship

Unlike Aronoff, Dressler (1977) relegates dissimilation to morphology. His constraint stated in (9), where # represents the boundary between a stem and a derivational suffix, accounts for ungrammatical derivations like **fishish*, without affecting the well-formed words in (8):

(9) $*XV_iC_j\#V_iC_jY$

However, as a result of requiring identity of both vowel and consonant, the constraint in (8) is too specific to account for any of the ungrammatical examples in (7b). Generalizing the constraint to the effect that suffix-initial vowels may not be flanked by identical consonants would solve that problem, but falsely rule out the suffixations illustrated in (10):

(10) -ic   hierarchic, anarchic, monarchic, psychic
      -able   bribable, (in)describable, (im)perturbable, clubbable
      -er   bearer, explorer, admirer, caterer, murderer, sufferer

It appears then that phonological restrictions in English word-formation concern output-oriented markedness constraints associated with individual affixes. Dressler's (1977: 42) observation that, unlike sequences of the type in (9), those of the type $XC_iV_j\#C_iV_jY$ occur frequently indicates the insensitivity of consonant-initial suffixes to dissimilatory constraints.

The wider generalization is that consonant-initial syllabic suffixes are generally rather insensitive to phonological structure in English. The causal connection between the sound shape of affixes and their potential sensitivity to phonological structure is the topic of the next section.

3 Prosodic structure

In English derivational morphology, the occurrence of phonological restrictions appears to be linked to certain properties of affixes. Phonological sensitivity is typical for vowel-initial or vowelless suffixes, less so for consonant-initial suffixes which form a separate syllable (cf. Raffelsiefen 1999; Plag 2003). This generalization indicates the relevance of the prosodic organization of affixes to their potential sensitivity to sound structure. Significantly, vowel-initial or vowelless suffixes form a prosodic domain together with the stem, a property referred to as "coherence". Other suffixes are non-cohering, in that they are prosodified separately (cf. Booij 1985 for a similar generalization in Dutch). The trees in (11) illustrate the basic connection between morphological and prosodic structure: prosodic word boundaries regularly coincide with stem boundaries as in (11b, c), unless a cohering suffix follows as in (11a) ("C" = clitic group).

(11)

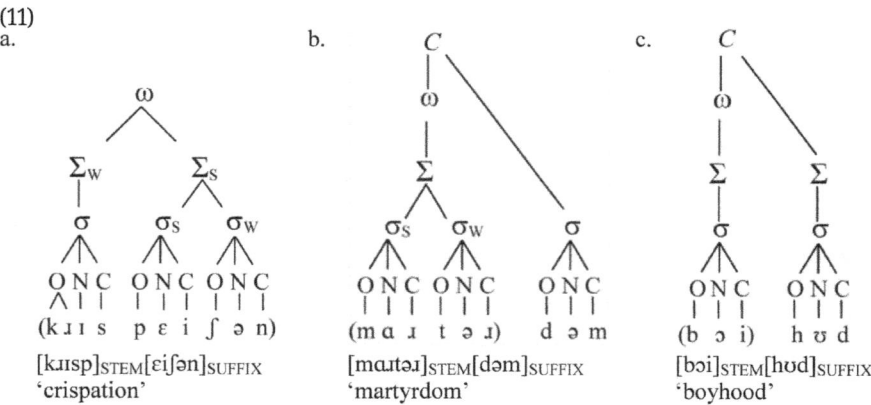

The terms "cohering" vs. "non-cohering" suffixes were introduced by Dixon (1977) to capture the morphophonological behavior of monosyllabic vs. disyllabic suffixes in Yidiny. The insight is that suffixes which are in some sense deficient cohere, in that they form a single domain for prosodic organization together with the stem, whereas non-deficient suffixes form a separate prosodic domain. In English, vowel-initial suffixes are deficient in that syllables formed from them lack an onset, whereas vowelless suffixes are deficient in that they lack a potential nucleus. Consequently both of these suffixes cohere, cf. (11a). Other suffixes are prosodically organized separately and are attached outside of the phonological word of the stem, cf. (11b, c).

The importance of the division between cohering and non-cohering suffixes for the purpose of the present article lies in the causal connection between prosodic representation and potential phonological restrictions. It is plausible that affixes which form a prosodic domain together with the stem interact with that stem more extensively than do suffixes which are not part of that domain. Before further reviewing the relevant evidence from English, it is in order to discuss the strictly phonological motivation for the different prosodic groupings illustrated in (11). The fundamental division between cohering and non-cohering suffixes is motivated both on phonological and on phonetic grounds.

A rather striking generalization following from the notion of suffix coherence is that only vowel-initial suffixes can bear main stress in English. This is because vowel-initial suffixes, as a consequence of being integrated into the phonological word of the stem, are part of the domain for foot formation: in *crispation* the last two syllables form a binary foot, which regularly attracts main stress, cf. (11a). Some monosyllabic suffixes, including those in (12a), are lexically marked for carrying main stress in their respective domain. Suffixes with more than one syllable can also be lexically associated with secondary or no stress, cf. (12b):

(12) a. /ésk/ '-esque', /ét/ '-ette', /í/ '-ee', /íz/ '-ese', /íɹ/ '-eer'

 b. /ìzəm/ '-ism', /ətɔ̀ɹi/ '-atory', /ɪfài/ '-ify', /ɪti/ '-ity', /əbəl/ '-able', /ənsi/ '-ancy'

 c. /ɪv/ '-ive', /íz/ '-ese', /àiz/ '-ize', /ɪʃ/ '-ish', /ɪdʒ/ '-age' /θ/ '-th'

By contrast, non-cohering suffixes are never lexically marked for stress. Unlike the bi- or trisyllabic cohering suffixes in (12b), non-cohering suffixes always form a single syllable, which is organized outside of the phonological word and consequently outside of the domain of foot formation. Single syllables are not grouped into feet and are therefore stressless, cf. (11b). The only exception is the suffix *-hood* shown in (11c), which forms a separate foot due to the necessary alignment of the phoneme /h/ with a left foot boundary in English. The presence of the foot is accordingly conditioned by segmental structure, not by lexical marking. A complete list of English non-cohering suffixes illustrated with native coinages is given in (13). English non-cohering suffixes are nominal or adjectival; none are verbal.

(13) a. /fəl/ '-ful'   purposeful, harmful

       /dəm/ '-dom'   kingdom, sheriffdom

       /səm/ '-some'   frolicsome, fearsome

       /mənt/ '-ment'   ailment (= bereavement)

       /mən/ '-man'   craftsman, infantryman

       /uəɹd/ '-ward'   northward, downward

       /iəɹ/ '-ior', '-ure'   failure, behavior

   b. /lɪŋ/ '-ling'   youngling, nursling

       /nɪk/ '-nik'   peacenik, fashionnik

       /ʃɪp/ '-ship'   courtship, governorship

       /lɪs/ ~ /ləs/ '-less'   goalless, effortless

       /nɪs/ ~ /nəs/ '-ness' stubbornness, foulness

       /lɪt/ ~ /lət/ '-let'   leaflet, streamlet

   c. /li/ '-ly'   orderly, scholarly

   d. /hʊd/ '-hood'   parenthood, priesthood

A closer examination of the phonological structure of the non-cohering suffixes reveals a remarkable degree of neutralization of phonemic contrast. Certain marked consonants such as voiced fricatives or dental fricatives are entirely absent, in contrast to the full range of fricatives found in cohering suffixes, cf. (12c). Apart from the presence of alveolar obstruents in marginal positions in *-ment* and *-ward*, the non-cohering suffixes generally have a simple onset-nucleus-coda structure as is illustrated in (14a). The phonemic representations of the suffixes *-ward* and *-ior*/*-ure* in (14b) is based on the assumption that high tense vowels can occur in syllable margin positions in English, where they are phonetically realized as glides [j] and [w]. The suffix -/iəɹ/ constitutes a borderline case in that its prosodic coherence is contextually conditioned: it systematically fuses with stems ending in an alveolar obstruent (e.g., (ɹɹéis)ω 'erase' – (ɹɹéiʃəɹ)ω 'erasure', (kəmpóuz)ω 'compose' – (kəmpóuʒəɹ)ω 'composure' – (feil)ω 'fail' – (féil)ωiəɹ 'failure'). Such dual behavior is perhaps generally restricted to suffixes with an initial high front vowel.

(14) a.   b.   c.   d.

The most striking constraints on the distribution of phonemes in non-cohering suffixes, compared to cohering suffixes, concern the syllable nucleus. Here the default vowel conditioned by the stresslessness is schwa (cf. 13a), which in specific segmental contexts alternates with high vowels. The front high lax vowel [ɪ] is the regular allophone of schwa before the velar nasal, cf. (13b), (14c); in non-cohering suffixes that vowel appears before all coda obstruents, where it varies with schwa before alveolars, cf. (13b). Schwa is also banned from foot-initial syllables in English: here the back high lax vowel appears (/hʊd/ '-hood', cf. (11c)), in accordance with the general affinity of back high vowels with stress in English (cf. the acronym *SNAFU*, with final stress, vs. *MORI*, with non-final stress). The occurrence of tense /i/ in /li/ -*ly* appears to be conditioned by the absence of a following consonant. Assuming that high tense vowels alone associate with both nucleus and coda as in (14d), the /i/ ensures syllable closure. The occurrence of vowels in non-cohering suffixes is then determined entirely by the consonantal structure, with no potential contrast.

The constraints on the phonemic make-up of suffixes illustrated in (14) hold only for true suffixes. So-called semi-suffixes (Marchand 1969: 356–358), which correspond to free-standing words, form separate phonological words and exhibit the full range of phonemic contrasts (e.g., /laik/ -*like*, /uaiz/ -*wise*, /fʊl/ -*ful*).

Apart from the phonemic structure of the suffixes themselves, there are additional phonological differences between cohering and non-cohering suffixation. The latter exhibit various juncture effects, that is, phoneme combinations and stress patterns resulting from the combination of stem and suffix, which occur neither within simplexes nor within cohering suffixations. These include "deviant" consonant clusters (e.g., non-homorganic nasal-stop clusters (/ŋd/, /nf/), obstruent clusters which differ in voicing (/ds/, /gf/), fricative clusters (/sʃ/, /fs/), and irregular stress patterns (e.g., *góvernorship*, which ends in three unstressed syllables). A particular characteristic of non-cohering suffixation is the frequent occurrence of overly complex rhymes preceding the suffix, including rhymes with two consonants (e.g., [ɑrm] in *harmless*), tense vowel plus consonant (e.g., [iːm] in *teamster*), or diphthong plus consonant (e.g., [eim] in *aimless*). Significantly, such juncture effects are generally stable for as long as a non-cohering suffix is recognized, regardless of whether or not there is a free stem, as is illustrated in (15) (cf. Raffelsiefen 2005: 241–242).

(15) (gɔɹm)_ωləs   'gormless'   (cf. †*gome* 'attention', 'care')
  (uɪst)_ωfəl   'wistful'   (cf. †*twistly* 'with close attention')
  (ɔint)_ωmənt   'ointment'   (cf. †*oint* 'to smear with oil')
  (gæst)_ωli   'ghastly'   (cf. †*gast* 'to frighten')

Consonant-initial suffixes fuse regularly with the stem only when they are non-recurring and therefore cannot be learned and recognized, cf. (16a). Apart from such cases of systematic fusion, there are isolated cases of prosodic fusion in non-cohering suffixation, illustrated in (16b). These cases, like occasional fusion of compounds (e.g., *cupboard, shepherd, necklace, nothing*), are rather rare historical changes affecting individual words. They thereby differ sharply from the prosodic fusion of cohering suffixes, which is entirely systematic, conditioned by the phonological shape of the suffix (i.e. vowel-initial or vowelless).

(16) a. (nɑ.lɪdʒ)$_\omega$ 'knowledge'   (cf. *know, -lɪdʒ*)
        (hɛi.tɹəd)$_\omega$ 'hatred'   (cf. *hate, -rəd*)
     b. (hæn.səm)$_\omega$ 'handsome'   (cf. *hand*)
        (wuɹ.ʃɪp)$_\omega$ 'worship'   (cf. *worth*)
        (bɪz.nəs)$_\omega$ 'business'   (cf. *busy*)

Additional evidence for the fundamental distinction between cohering and non-cohering suffixation pertains to phonetic realization. The narrow phonetic transcription of the word *ransom* in (17a), compared to the lexical phonemic representation, illustrates the processes of schwa reduction and stop epenthesis, which applies between a nasal and a homorganic fricative in foot-internal position. The fact that neither of these processes applies in *winsome* indicates accordingly the non-integration of the suffix *-some* into the foot of the stem (the phonetic transcriptions are adopted from the *Cambridge English Pronouncing Dictionary* (Jones 2011) and Muthmann 1999). Similarly, the duration of the stressed vowels in *lawful* or *freeness*, compared to that of the corresponding vowels in *offal* or *Venus*, respectively, indicate the non-integration of the suffix *-ful* into the foot of the stem, cf. (17b, c). This is because stressed vowels at the end of a phonological word are longer than word-internal stressed vowels.

(17)   Non-cohering suffixation   Simplex
     a. Phonemic: (uɪn)$_\omega$səm 'winsome'   (ɹænsəm)$_\omega$ 'ransom'
        Phonetic: [wínsəm]   [ɹæn^{t}s^{ə}m]
     b. Phonemic: (lɑ)$_\omega$fəl 'lawful'   (ɑfəl)$_\omega$ 'offal'
        Phonetic: [lɑ:fəl]   [ɑf^{ə}l]
     c. Phonemic: (fri)$_\omega$nəs 'freeness'   (vinəs)$_\omega$ 'Venus'
        Phonetic: [fri:nəs]   [vi:nəs]

In general it holds that words which include non-cohering suffixes *never* rhyme perfectly with other words in careful speech, even when the relevant phoneme sequences are identical (cf. *lawful* and *offal, freeness* and *Venus*). This is because the separate prosodic organization of stem vs. suffix phonemes necessarily yields subtle differences in the phonetic realization compared to the joint organization of the entire phoneme sequence. By contrast, words with cohering suffixes can rhyme perfectly with simplexes. This is illustrated with the vowel-initial suffixes in (18a) and the vowelless suffixes in (18b):

(18) a. [[fiud]$_{STEM}$[əl]$_{SUFFIX}$]$_{WORD}$ → (fiudəl)$_{\omega}$ [nudəl]$_{WORD}$ → (nudəl)$_{\omega}$
                                        'feudal'   'noodle'

      [[hɛl]$_{STEM}$[ɪʃ]$_{SUFFIX}$]$_{WORD}$ → (hɛlɪʃ)$_{\omega}$ [ɹɛlɪʃ]$_{WORD}$ → (ɹɛlɪʃ)$_{\omega}$
                                          'hellish'   'relish'

      [[sɹpənt]$_{STEM}$[ain]$_{SUFFIX}$]$_{WORD}$ → (sɹpəntain)$_{\omega}$ [tɹpəntain]$_{WORD}$ → (tɹpəntain)$_{\omega}$
                                        'serpentine'   'turpentine'

  b. [[tɹu]$_{STEM}$[θ]$_{SUFFIX}$]$_{WORD}$ → (tɹuθ)$_{\omega}$ [buθ]$_{WORD}$ → (buθ)$_{\omega}$
                                      'truth'   'booth'

      [[gɹəu]$_{STEM}$[θ]$_{SUFFIX}$]$_{WORD}$ → (gɹəuθ)$_{\omega}$ [bəuθ]$_{WORD}$ → (bəuθ)$_{\omega}$
                                      'growth'   'both'

      [[hai]$_{STEM}$[t]$_{SUFFIX}$]$_{WORD}$ → (hait)$_{\omega}$ [fait]$_{WORD}$ → (fait)$_{\omega}$
                                      'height'   'fight'

The assumption of a fundamental division between English affixes into prosodically cohering vs. non-cohering ones is then independently motivated by phonetic structure. Phonetic evidence for prosodic organization is particularly valuable because, unlike phonotactic rules, phonetic processes are free of lexical exceptions.

4 Cohering suffixation

The importance of the division between cohering and non-cohering suffixes for English word-formation is reflected in the correlations listed in (19), which indicate the relatedness of phonological restrictions to other morphophonological phenomena in the language (cf. Raffelsiefen 1999, 2004, 2007; Plag 2003).

(19) (i)   only cohering suffixes can be sensitive to the phonological shape of the stem, resulting in gaps
   (ii)   only cohering suffixes can trigger stem allomorphy
  (iii)   only cohering suffixes may exhibit allomorphy
  (iv)   only cohering suffixes can attach to bound stems (of other suffixations)
   (v)   cohering suffixes cannot follow non-cohering suffixes
  (vi)   only cohering suffixes may "fuse" with other suffixes

The relatedness of the phenomena in (19) concerns the prominent role of phonological markedness constraints. These apply only within specific prosodic domains, which include cohering, but not non-cohering suffixes. The close relation between gaps and allomorphy can be illustrated by comparing the suffixes *-eer* and *-ese*. The suffix *-eer*, which has been somewhat productive in English in certain semantic fields, including military jargon, attaches only to trochaic stems as in (20a).

(20) a. pístol+éer → (pìstoléer)$_\omega$ b. Vietnám+ése → (Viètnamése)$_\omega$
     rócket+éer → (ròcketéer)$_\omega$ Sudán+ése → (Sùdanése)$_\omega$
     wéapon+éer → (wèaponéer)$_\omega$ Nepál+ése → (Nèpalése)$_\omega$
     platóon+éer → Ø   Saigón+ése → (Sàigonése)$_\omega$

The avoidance of stems with final stress such as *platóon* is indicative of an inherent conflict: attaching the suffix would either violate a phonological markedness constraint against adjacent stressed syllables (cf. **platòonéer*), or would lead to non-uniform paradigms, where the stressed syllables in the stem of the derived form and in the base fail to correspond (cf. *plàtoonéer* – *platóon*), yielding multiple stem forms (cf. {*platóon-*, *plátoon-*}). To avoid violation of either of these constraints, the suffix is not attached. Instead there is a gap.

The suffix *-ese* also does not tolerate a stress clash. The suffixes differ, in that the constraint on paradigm uniformity is violated in *-ese*-suffixation to ensure a phonologically well-formed alternating stress pattern, cf. (20b). Consequently, there are no gaps in *-ese*-suffixation. Instead there is stem allomorphy (e.g., {*Vietnám-*, *Viétnam-*}).

The third possibility concerning the interaction of the markedness constraint against adjacent stressed syllables and the relevant paradigm uniformity constraint can be illustrated by *-ee*-suffixation:

(21) a. ábsent+ée → (àbsentée)$_\omega$ b. seléct+ée → (selèctée)$_\omega$
     lícense+ée → (lìcensée)$_\omega$ divórce+ée → (divòrcée)$_\omega$
     pátent+ée → (pàtentée)$_\omega$ advíse+ée → (advìsée)$_\omega$

The suffix *-ee* attaches to any stems, including stems with final stress, without adjustments of the foot structure. As a result, *-ee* is like the suffix *-eer* in that there is no stem-allomorphy, and like the suffix *-ese*, in that there are no stress-related gaps. The suffixes *-eer*, *-ese*, and *-ee*, all of which are lexically marked for carrying main stress, hence illustrate the basic possibility space observed in the interaction of phonological markedness constraints and paradigm uniformity constraints as well as the claim that such interactions are suffix-specific.

Phonologically conditioned gaps and stem allomorphy are rarely found in non-cohering suffixation. One of the few examples is the adverbial suffix -*ly*, which does not attach to stems ending in /li/ (e.g., **sillily*, **holily*). The suffix -*ful* avoids stems ending in /f/ or /v/ (e.g., **loveful*, **griefful*, cf. Chapin 1970: 54). Avoidance of (near-)identical phonemes in junctures is not generally characteristic of non-cohering suffixation (cf. *goalless, embalmment, stubbornness, fashionnik*). There are no systematic cases of stem-allomorphy in non-cohering suffixation other than "degemination", often with schwa loss, in stems ending in /əl/ before adverbial -*ly*-suffixation (e.g., /bɹutəl/ 'brutal' – /bɹutəli/ 'brutally', /sʌtəl/ 'subtle' – /sʌt(ə)li/ 'subtly', but /kul/ – /kulli/ 'coolly'). All other relevant examples concern historical prosodic fusion in individual words (e.g., the "stress shift" in (evidéntly)$_\omega$ or (insíghtful)$_\omega$, compared to regular nonfused (élegant)$_\omega$ *ly*, (cónfident)$_\omega$ *ly*, (púrpose)$_\omega$ *ful*, (wórship)$_\omega$ *ful*).

Allomorphy in cohering suffixes mentioned in (19iii) is illustrated with the homophonous suffixes in (22). While deverbal /əl/ does not attach to stems with final /l/ to avoid violation of the constraint against nuclei flanked by identical segments, the denominal suffix satisfies that constraint by violating suffix uniformity in a minimal manner: the phoneme /l/ is substituted by the other liquid, /ɹ/. Consequently, there are no gaps in the latter suffixation.

(22) a. withdráw+al → (withdráwal)$_\omega$ b. séason+al → (séasonal)$_\omega$
           revérse+al → (revérsal)$_\omega$ bride+al → (brídal)$_\omega$
           renéw+al → (renéwal)$_\omega$ coast+al → (cóastal)$_\omega$
           revéal+al → Ø   prótocòl+ar → (prótocòlar)$_\omega$
           fulfíll+al → Ø   enámel+ar → (enámelar)$_\omega$
           inhále+al → Ø   corólla+ar → (coróllar)$_\omega$

Additional examples of allomorphy in cohering suffixation are given in (23). The suffix /əɹi/ appears without the initial schwa in (23a) to avoid words ending in three unstressed syllables (cf. Marchand 1969: 285). To satisfy the same constraint, the suffix /ənsi/, which replaces the suffix /ənt/, appears without the final /i/ in (23b). (When attaching to verbs, the suffix is always /əns/, regardless of stress, e.g., *gúidance, occúrrence, útterance, inhéritance*.)

(23) a. bribe+ery → (bríbery)$_\omega$ b. prégn-ant+ancy → (prégnancy)$_\omega$
           forge+ery → (fórgery)$_\omega$ stríd-ent+ency → (strídency)$_\omega$
           can+ery → (cánnery)$_\omega$ delínqu-ent+ency → (delínquency)$_\omega$
           rével+ery → (révelry)$_\omega$ ímman-ent+ence → (ímmanence)$_\omega$
           húsband+ery → (húsbandry)$_\omega$ sáli-ent+ence → (sálience)$_\omega$
           mímic+ery → (mímicry)$_\omega$ hésit-ant+ance → (hésitance)$_\omega$

The selection and "replacement" of certain suffixes illustrated in (23b) is another property distinguishing cohering from non-cohering suffixes. Some of these relations, referred to as "correlative derivation" (Marchand 1969: 216), are asymmetrical and less regular (*nutrit-ion* licenses *nutrit-ious*, cf. (24a)), others are symmetrical and fully regular in that either suffixation licenses the word with the other suffix (e.g., *femin-ism* licenses *femin-ist* as *femin-ist* licenses *femin-ism*, cf. (24b)). Phonemic alternation in the relevant suffix pairs appears to be confined to coronals and vowels differing in stress.

(24) a. /ən/ → /əs/   nutrition – nutritious, caution – cautious, oblivion – oblivious

  /ənt/ → /ənsi/   blatant – blatancy, redundant – redundancy, lenient – leniency

  /ət/ → /əsi/   prophet – prophesy, pirate – piracy, secret – secrecy

   b. /ɪst/ ↔ /ɪzəm/   feminist – feminism, tourist – tourism, nudist – nudism

  /ɛit/ ↔ /ɛiʃən/   frustrate – frustration, exacerbate – exacerbation

  /ɪfai/ ↔   purify – purification, falsify – falsification

  /ɪfɪkɛiʃən/

The examples in (24) illustrate the ability of cohering suffixes to combine with bound stems. That ability is further illustrated by the native coinages in (25a), where the respective suffixed words which qualify as plausible sources of the relevant bound stems are listed in (25b). While it is true that there are also a few cases of bound stems in non-cohering suffixation, listed in (25c), there is a crucial difference between the relevant coinages: according to the *Oxford English Dictionary* (2012) all of the coinages with non-cohering suffixes were based on a free stem, when the words were first coined. The relevant words, listed in (25d), became obsolete only after the suffixed words had come into existence. By contrast, native word-formation with cohering suffixes can in many cases be shown to involve bound stems (that is, stems found in words with other suffixes), from the start:

(25) a. Nat. coinage: b. Hist. base: c. Nat. coinage: d. Hist. base:

  (àmput-ée)$_\omega$ (ámput-àte)$_\omega$ (ruth)$_\omega$less   † *ruthe* 'pity'

  (aggréss-ive)$_\omega$ (aggréss-or)$_\omega$ (gorm)$_\omega$less   † *gome* 'attention'

  (biógraph-er)$_\omega$ (biógraph-y)$_\omega$ (feck)$_\omega$less   † *feck* 'efficacy'

  (cóal-ìze)$_\omega$ (còal-ítion)$_\omega$ (grate)$_\omega$ful   † *grate* 'agreeable'

  (compétit-ive)$_\omega$ (compétit-or)$_\omega$ (wist)$_\omega$ful   † *wistly* 'intently'

  (skélet-al)$_\omega$ (skélet-on)$_\omega$ (dole)$_\omega$ful   † *dol* 'pain, grief'

  (sýphil-òid)$_\omega$ (sýphil-is)$_\omega$ (bale)$_\omega$ful   † *bale* 'evil influence'

Suffixation to bound stems, although frequently attested in English, is generally tied to specific conditions. In the formations in (26a), bound stems are selected to avoid identical onsets; in (26b) the purpose is to yield output forms with alternating stress. The respective examples to the right show that the relevant suffixes attach to morphologically complex free stems otherwise.

(26) a. ámput-àte+ée   (àmput-ée)$_\omega$ éduc-àte+ée   (èduc-àt-ée)$_\omega$
          áppet-ìte+ìze   (áppet-ìze)$_\omega$ páras-ìte+ìze   (páras-ìt-ìze)$_\omega$
      b. sénsit-ive+ìze   (sénsit-ìze)$_\omega$ colléct-ive+ìze   (colléct-iv-ìze)$_\omega$
          áccur-ate+ìze   (áccur-ìze)$_\omega$ prív-ate+ìze   (prív-at-ìze)$_\omega$

Bound stems are accessible only if a word contains a recognizable suffix that can be stripped off. Since suffixes are inherently tied to certain syntactic categories, the same phoneme sequences may function as suffixes in some words but not in others. Final /ənt/ or /i/ function as suffixes in abstract nouns and adjectives (*delinquent, agent, modesty, scrutiny*), but not in verbs. Consequently, the relevant bound stems are accessible in (27a), to satisfy constraints on word length in the relevant suffixations, but not in (27b).

(27) a. néglig-ent]$_A$ (néglig-able)$_\omega$ b. órient]$_V$ (órient-able)$_\omega$
          astrónom-y]$_N$ (astrónom-er)$_\omega$ accómpany]$_V$ (accómpani-er)$_\omega$

A closer examination of the conditions for selecting bound stems shows that in English all verbal suffixation, be it verb-based or verb-deriving, satisfies paradigm uniformity. This generalization is obscured when comparing native suffixation as in (28a) with the corresponding free stems in (28b), as paradigm uniformity violations appear to be rampant. The claim that the suffixes satisfy phonological constraints (e.g., no adjacent stressed syllables for -*ize*-suffixation and no adjacent unstressed syllables for -*ify*-suffixation) by selecting the underlined bound stems in (28c), rather than by inducing stress shifts, is supported by the fact that words containing the relevant bound stems can always be shown to be attested in English prior to the coinage of verbs, often as foreign loanwords (cf. the earlier attested French loans *Japonnais, sublimation, rigidité, angelique, bovarysme*). The claim that the word-formation in (28a) involves the bound stems in (28c), not adjustments of the free stems in (28b), is further demonstrated by the observation that word-formation fails when there are no suitable stems, cf. (28d).

(28) a. (Jápan-ìze)$_\omega$ b. Japán   c. (Jàpan-ése)$_\omega$ d. Tibét – *Tíbet-ìze
          (súblim-ìze)$_\omega$ sublíme   (súblim-àte)$_\omega$ extréme – *éxtrem-ìze
          (rigíd-ify)$_\omega$ rígid   (rigíd-ity)$_\omega$ rándom – *randóm-ifỳ
          (angél-ify)$_\omega$ ángel   (angél-ic)$_\omega$ túnnel – *tunnél-ify
          (Bóvar-ìze)$_\omega$ Bóvary   (Bóvar-ìsm)$_\omega$ Kénnedy – *Kénned-ìze

Paradigm violations in English native word-formation are accordingly found only when no verbs participate, as in (29); truly productive cases of word-formation involving paradigm uniformity violations are mostly limited to formations based on proper nouns. Suffixation which induces paradigm violations supplies novel bound stems, underlined in (29b), which can then be used in other suffixation when needed to satisfy phonological markedness constraints (e.g., Viétnam-ìze, Darwín-ifỳ).

(29) a. Vietnám+ése   →   (Vìetnamése)$_ω$ b. {Vietnám-, Viétnam-}
      Dárwin+ian   →   (Darwínian)$_ω$ {Dárwin-, Darwín-}
      Íceland+ic   →   (Icelándic)$_ω$ {Íceland-, Icelánd-}
      cónsonant+al   (cònsonántal)$_ω$ {cónsonant-, cònsonánt-}
      téchnical+ity   →   (tèchnicálity)$_ω$ {téchnical-, tèchnicál-}
      hórmòne+al   →   (hormónal)$_ω$ {hórmòne-, hormón-}
      phónème+ic   →   (phonémic)$_ω$ {phónème-, phoném-}

The last two correlations in (19) concern the combinability of suffixes, which is also sensitive to coherence. The observation that cohering suffixes cannot follow non-cohering suffixes, illustrated in (30a), indicates that cohering suffixes attach only when they can be integrated into a phonological word. This restriction does not concern non-cohering suffxes, which can follow one another. Apparent counter-examples are rare individual words, where the location of main stress indicates complete prosodic fusion (e.g., (devèlopméntal)$_ω$, (gòvernméntal)$_ω$, as opposed to ungrammatical *(púnish)$_ω$ment-al, *(encóurage)$_ω$ment-al, *(embá-rass)$_ω$ment-al).

(30) a. *(kind)$_ω$ness+y   b.   (grate)$_ω$ful+ness
        *(free)$_ω$dom+al   (reck)$_ω$less+ness
        *(grate)$_ω$ful+ize   (world)$_ω$ly+ness
        *(establish)$_ω$ment+al   (pen)$_ω$man+ship
        *(suck)$_ω$ling+ish   (govern)$_ω$ment+less
        *(court)$_ω$ship+ous   (gentle)$_ω$man+ly
        *(child)$_ω$hood+ish   (book)$_ω$let+less
        *(gorm)$_ω$less+ity   (lone)$_ω$some+ness
        *(man)$_ω$ly+ize   (free)$_ω$dom+less

The final characteristic of cohering suffixes to be illustrated here concerns the potential development of strong productivity with respect to specific other suffixes (cf. 19vi). The suffix *-ation*, for instance, occurs only in a few native suffixations based on simplexes, all of which end in an unstressed syllable or are monosyllabic (e.g., *hỳphenátion, defòrestátion, flỳrtátion, stàrvátion*). The suffix is however very productive with stressed verbal suffixes, including *-ize* (*victimization, computerization, vulgarization*). Similarly, *-ity*-suffixation occurs only sporadically in native formations based on simplexes with final stress (*oddity, queerity*), but prevails over the generally much more productive *-ness*-suffixation with respect to bases ending in *-able* (*corruptibility, readability, drinkability*). In English, such cases of hyperproductivity, where words automatically license the attachment of a specific, somewhat fossilized affix, involve cohering suffixes only.

The force behind the development of such affinities among suffixes appears to be phonological: when a suffix causes allomorphy in a preceding suffix, without causing a stress clash or stress allomorphy in the preceding stem, the two suffixes are likely to "fuse" (cf. (31a), where the relevant allomorphy is boldfaced). This fusion is then apparently grounded in the preference for uniform stems, which favors the segmentation *mèmor-izátion* (cf. *mémor-y, mémor-ìze*) over *mèmoriz-átion*, as the latter would involve stem allomorphy ({*mémorize-, mèmoriz-*}). Fused suffixes in relation to their first member may develop into fully productive correlative patterns, as is shown in (31b).

(31) a. (stándard-<u>ìze</u>)ω → (stàndard-<u>iz</u>-átion)ω   b. /aiz/ ↔ /ɪzéiʃən/
     (respóns-<u>ible</u>)ω → (respòns-<u>ibíl</u>-ity)ω   /əbəl/ ↔ /əbíləti/

The suffix sequences *-izátion* and *-abílity* will never cause a stress clash or stress allomorphy in the preceding stem, as they start with a stressless syllable. These suffix sequences thereby differ from those illustrated in (32a), where, due to the initial stress, constraint violations would be unavoidable whenever there is a stem with final stress, cf. (32b). The existence of such a conflict appears to inhibit the development of hyperproductivity even when there is no stem-final stress as in (32c). There is no automatic licensing of the second cohering suffix in such cases; instead non-cohering suffixes are often preferred (*bóisterousness, nátural-ness, intúitiveness*).

(32) a. sócial-ist   → (sòcial-íst-ic)ω   b. deféat-ist / *-íst-ic
     vírtu-ous   → (vìrtu-ós-ity)ω   enórm-ous / *-ós-ity
     whímsic-al → (whìmsic-ál-ity)ω   parént-al / *-ál-ity
     sénsit-ive → (sènsit-ív-ity)ω   aggréss-ive / *-ív-ity
   c. théor-ist / *-íst-ic
     bóister-ous / *-ós-ity
     nátur-al / *-ál-ity
     intúit-ive / *-ív-ity

The development of hyperproductivity in English suffixation, while basically determined by stress, can have specific segmental restrictions. The data in (33a) demonstrate the automatic licensing of *-ation*-nominalization for *-ize*-suffixation in English, except when the stem ends in a coronal fricative, as in (33b). The avoidance of such stems appears to be due to the presence of a single unstressed vowel between the coronal fricatives in cases like **fànta/sɪz/átion*, as opposed to the stressed diphthong in *fánta/sàiz/*. All *-ize*-formations in (33) are native and involve bound stems, inferred by affix stripping (e.g., *fántas-y, crític-ism, mémor-y, émphas-is*).

(33) a. mémor-ìze   →   (mèmor-iz-átion)_ω   b. fánta/s/-ìze / *-iz-átion
       hármon-ìze   →   (hàrmon-iz-átion)_ω   críti/s/-ìze / *-iz-átion
       metábol-ìze   (metàbol-iz-átion)_ω   éxor/s/-ìze / *-iz-átion
       plágiar-ìze   (plàgiar-iz-átion)_ω   óstra/s/-ìze / *-iz-átion
       epítom-ìze   →   (epìtom-iz-átion)_ω   émpha/s/-ìze / *-iz-átion
       mésmer-ìze   (mèsmer-iz-átion)_ω   públi/s/-ìze / *-iz-átion
       súbsid-ìze   (sùbsid-iz-átion)_ω   sýmpa/θ/-ìze / *-iz-átion
       monópol-ìze →   (monòpol-iz-átion)_ω   éner/dʒ/-ìze / *-iz-átion
       metrópol-ìze →   (metròpol-iz-átion)_ω   apólo/dʒ/-ìze / *-iz-átion

The gap in nominalization illustrated in (33b) indicates the satisfaction of a markedness constraint against nuclei flanked by coronal fricatives. A rough classification of the phonological markedness constraints playing a role in English suffixation is given in (34):

(34) a. Syllable wellformedness (onset, sonority thresholds, hiatus avoidance, identity avoidance)
     b. Foot well-formedness (*clash, *lapse, size constraints)
     c. Phonological word (size constraints)
     d. Alignment constraints

Identity avoidance typically refers to phonemes in specific syllable positions, including the segments flanking the nucleus, the onsets in adjacent syllables, or the codas in adjacent syllables. English suffixes associated with dissimilatory constraints were listed in (7).

     The stem restrictions on the suffixes *-en* and *-ive* stated in (5) are examples for onset constraints. The restriction to obstruent-final stems associated with verbal *-en* satisfies a phonological constraint concerning sonority thresholds: due to their low sonority, obstruents constitute optimal onsets. (The constraint in question concerns only verbal *-en*, not the homophonous adjectival suffix *-en*, cf. *wool-*

en.) The restriction to stems ending in *-s* or *-t* associated with *-ive* satisfies an additional constraint on place of articulation: alveolar consonants are least marked. Apart from suffixes which are associated with constraints favoring particular unmarked onsets there are others, such as *-eer* and *-ese*, which accept any onset, requiring only that the stem end in a consonant.

While the suffixes *-en* and *-ive* attach only to stems ending in a phoneme with low sonority, the suffix *-th* attaches only to stems ending in a segment with relatively high sonority, such as liquids or vowels, cf. (35). This difference is prosodically conditioned: in vowel-initial suffixation, the stem-final consonant forms an onset, where minimal sonority is preferred, whereas before a consonantal suffix, maximally sonorous stem-final consonants are preferred to ensure a maximal sonority decrease among the two consonants.

(35) (illth)$_\omega$ (< ill)   (tilth)$_\omega$ (< till)
      (spilth)$_\omega$ (< spill)   (coolth)$_\omega$ (< cool)
      (blowth)$_\omega$ (< blow)   (sloth)$_\omega$ (< slow)

Apparent counter-examples have cognates in other Germanic languages (cf. Engl. *depth*, Gothic *diupiþa*, Dutch *diepte*; Engl. *length*, Swedish *längd*, Dutch *lengte*; Engl. *breadth*, Icelandic *breidd*, Dutch *breedte*), presumably originating at a time when the suffix was still vowel-initial. (Its reconstructed form in Germanic is *-iþō*.) As was noted above, inherited words are not expected to satisfy the constraints associated with synchronic rules for novel word-formation.

Regarding sensitivity to foot structure, the stressed suffixes *-ize* and *-ify* differ in that *-ize* tolerates so-called stress lapses, that is sequences of unstressed syllables as in (36a), while *-ify* does not, cf. (36b). The other examples show that *-ize*-suffixation must not exhibit a stress clash: as a result the suffix attaches neither to monosyllabic nor to iambic stems, cf. (36c, d).

(36) a. (rádical-ìze)$_\omega$ b. *féudal-ifỳ   c. *stríct-ìze   d. *obscúr-ìze
         (prímitiv-ìze)$_\omega$ *áctiv-ifỳ   *crísp-ìze   *concrét-ìze
         (skéleton-ìze)$_\omega$ *cárbon-ifỳ   *púr-ìze   *cafféin-ìze
         (cánnibal-ìze)$_\omega$ *tríbal-ifỳ   *bóld-ìze   *robúst-ìze

Size constraints can be illustrated by comparing the unstressed suffixes *-en* and nominal *-al* in (37). Both suffixes select stems with final stress, to yield a word which ends in a branching foot; they differ in that *-en*-suffixation has two syllables while *-al*-suffixation has three syllables:

(37) a. (tóugh-en)$_\omega$ b. (caróus-al)$_\omega$

     (swíft-en)$_\omega$ (survív-al)$_\omega$

     (héight-en)$_\omega$ (perús-al)$_\omega$

     (thréat-en)$_\omega$ (appráis-al)$_\omega$

The restriction on -*en*-suffixation indicates a constraint requiring the alignment of foot and word boundaries in the output. The restriction to three syllables could be expressed by associating nominal -*al*-suffixation with a requirement for binary branching structure both within and above the foot level, cf. (6b). Alternatively, the number of syllables within the phonological word could also play a role. Evidence for relevant maximality constraints can be gleaned from the formations in (38), where bound stems are preferred to free stems if this serves to avoid words with more than four syllables:

(38) a. déleg-<u>àte</u>+able (déleg-able)$_\omega$ b. dón-<u>àte</u>+able (dón-àte-able)$_\omega$

     ségreg-<u>àte</u>+able (ségreg-able)$_\omega$ díl-<u>àte</u>+able (díl-àte-able)$_\omega$

     váccin-<u>àte</u>+able (váccin-able)$_\omega$ nárr-<u>àte</u>+able (nárr-àte-able)$_\omega$

     precípit-<u>àte</u>+able (precípit-able)$_\omega$ vác-<u>àte</u>+able (vác-àte-able)$_\omega$

5 Prefixes vs. modifiers

The distinction between modifying and head prefixation in English is characterized by a number of correlating properties, concerning morphosyntactic, semantic and phonological structure. *Modifying prefixes* combine with words without affecting the category of the derived word and can therefore be freely omitted without affecting grammaticality (*she was ✓unable/✓able to leave*). In accordance with their optionality modifying prefixes have inherent meaning (e.g., *un-* 'not'). By contrast, *head prefixes* determine the resulting category – mostly verbs, but also adverbs and prepositions (e.g., *anew, ago, behind*) – and cannot be omitted (*they ✓enabled/*abled her*). Head prefixes often lack inherent meaning. For instance, the causative meaning in the verb *enable* is not necessarily associated with the prefix *en-*, as this meaning component appears to be present whenever a transitive verb has a recognizable adjectival base (cf. *becalm, deepen, slenderize, intensify, corrupt*).

Modifying prefixes, but not head prefixes, form separate phonological words. The prosodic organization of *unable* in (39a) is manifest both in the word-initial secondary stress and in the potential juncture before the stem-initial vowel. By contrast, the lack of initial stress together with the pronunciation of the prefix-final consonant as the onset of the stem-initial syllable indicates the integration of the head prefix *en-* into the phonological word of the stem, cf. (39b). In native word-formation, both modifying and head prefixes combine with free stems only.

(39) a.   b.   c.

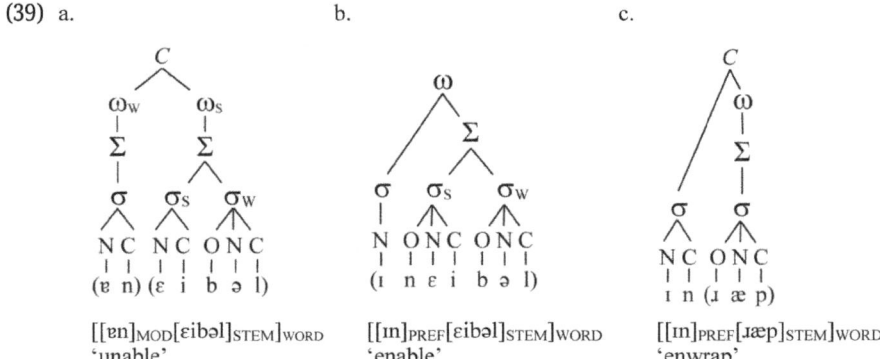

[[ɐn]ᴍᴏᴅ[ɛibəl]ꜱᴛᴇᴍ]ᴡᴏʀᴅ   [[ɪn]ᴘʀᴇꜰ[ɛibəl]ꜱᴛᴇᴍ]ᴡᴏʀᴅ   [[ɪn]ᴘʀᴇꜰ[ɹæp]ꜱᴛᴇᴍ]ᴡᴏʀᴅ
'unable'   'enable'   'enwrap'

Whether head prefixes are always prosodically cohering, or whether they are integrated only when necessary for supplying an onset, is not clear. In either case, the representation, also that with an unintegrated head prefix as in (39c), differs from the prosodic organization of modifying prefixes, which form separate phonological words. These prosodic differences are reflected in how much the prefixes are sensitive to the phonological structure of the stem: there are no phonological restrictions on modifying prefixation (cf. (40a)), while head prefixation has phonologically conditioned gaps. In English, head prefixes attach only to stems consisting of a single foot consisting of one or two syllables as is illustrated in (40b):

(40) a. (ùn)_ω(fít)_ω   b. em(pówer)_ω   c. (il)_ω(lógical)_ω
         (ùn)_ω(belíef)_ω   em(bódy)_ω   (ir)_ω(repláceable)_ω
         (ùn)_ω(pópular)_ω   en(mésh)_ω   (ìm)_ω(bálance)_ω
         (ùn)_ω(méntionable)_ω   en(nóble)_ω   (ìm)_ω(méasurable)_ω
         (ùn)_ω(nécessary)_ω   en(líst)_ω   (ìm)_ω(precíse)_ω

Modifying prefixation never exhibits gaps nor stem allomorphy. There is one such prefix, the negative prefix *in-* illustrated in (40c), whose final sonorant assimilates fully to a following liquid and partially to a following stop or nasal; curiously this prefix assimilates even more strongly than the head prefix, cf. (40b, c). Assimilation does not indicate prosodic fusion here as is shown by the evidence from stress: secondary stress before following main stress as in *imbálance* and final main stress in *imprecíse* indicate the organization of the prefix as a separate stress domain, with weaker stress than the stem (Wells 1990). The absence of phonologically conditioned gaps follows from this organization.

There are various word-formation rules which are sensitive to the distinct prosodic organization between modifying and head prefixations. Verb-to-noun conversion is rather productive in modifing prefixation with a monosyllabic stem, cf. (41a, b), much less so in head prefixation, cf. (41c). The latter formations would involve a dilemma: the derived noun either has final main stress and thereby deviates from regular stress patterns in nouns or there is violation of paradigm uniformity in that the main stress in the noun corresponds to a syllable which is unstressed in the base. No such conflict is present in the conversions in (41a, b), which involve a mere reversal of relative prominence among phonological words.

(41) a. V
$(mìs)_\omega(prínt)_\omega$
$(prè)_\omega(bóil)_\omega$
$(rè)_\omega(chárge)_\omega$
$(sùb)_\omega(léase)_\omega$

b. N
$(mís)_\omega(prìnt)_\omega$
$(pré)_\omega(bòil)_\omega$
$(ré)_\omega(chàrge)_\omega$
$(súb)_\omega(lèase)_\omega$

c. V
$be(stów)_\omega$
$en(rích)_\omega$
$re(néw)_\omega$
$de(fróst)_\omega$

While generally organized as unstressed syllables, head prefixes can form separate phonological words when participating in antonymic relations as in (42b) (Eckert and Barry 2002: 115).

(42) a. $de(dúce)_\omega - in(dúce)_\omega$
$ex(plóre)_\omega - im(plóre)_\omega$

b. $(dè)_\omega(créase)_\omega$ ↔ $(ìn)_\omega(créase)_\omega$
$(èx)_\omega(pórt)_\omega$ ↔ $(ìm)_\omega(pórt)_\omega$

Antonymic verbs are also more prone to be converted to nouns (with concomitant relative prominence reversal). The observation that, here, too, conversion correlates with the prosodic organization of the base verb suggests that word-formation is sensitive to prosodic organization itself, rather than the underlying morphosyntactic or semantic differences.

6 Implications for the mental lexicon

The phonological restrictions observed in English word-formation lend themselves to an analysis based on interacting phonological markedness constraints and paradigm uniformity constraints referring exclusively to output forms. These restrictions moreover provide insight into the sort of structure and level of phonological abstractness to be associated with those output forms. The presence of prosodic organization in the relevant representations is reflected in various restrictions on word-formation, including sensitivity to the location of feet and to the number of syllables in a phonological word. Regarding the level of abstractness of segmental structure, phonological constraints requiring segmental nonidentity need to refer to phonemic representations, from which all contextually determined allophony has been abstracted. For instance, the ungrammaticality of formations in which a nucleus is flanked by identical segments such as *appéalal* indicates reference to the phonemic level, where the two liquids are indeed identical (i.e. /ləl/), not the phonetic level, where the liquids may differ quite strongly in many varieties of English as a result of their appearance in onset vs. coda position (i.e. "clear [l]" vs. "dark [ɫ]" in [ləɫ]).

The evidence for reference to phonemic representation in word formation, along with the desirability of limiting such reference to a single level, calls for a close inspection of alleged counter-evidence. Dressler (1977) argues that the regular truncation of the sequence *-er* in German *-in*-suffixation as in *Zauberin* 'sorceress' (*Zaubererin*), but not in *-er*-suffixation as in *Zauberer* 'sorcerer', can only be explained with reference to phonetic representations. Specifically, he claims that the constraint against sequences of identical CV-strings would be violated only in *Zaubererin*, where both instances of /ʀ/ occur in onset position and therefore are pronounced alike. Consequently truncation applies. By contrast, in *Zauberer* the final /ʀ/ occurs in coda position, being subject to /ʀ/-vocalization. Consequently the relevant strings are phonetically distinct, obliterating the need for truncation.

(43) Phonemic: /tˢáubəʀəʀ/ /tˢáubəʀɪn/ */tˢáubəʀəʀɪn/
     Phonetic: [tˢáubəʀɐ] [tˢáubəʀɪn] *[tˢáubəʀəʀɪn]

Dressler's analysis, if correct, would indeed refute the generalization that word-formation is sensitive to phonemic representation only, as /ʀ/-vocalization is clearly allophonic. However, his conclusion is not cogent because the relevant words also exhibit a difference at the phonemic level: unlike *Záuberer*, *Záubererin* includes a sequence of three syllables following the main stress. Similar restrictions are observed in English *-ess*-suffixation (e.g., *sórcerer* – *sórceress* (*sórcereress*), *múrderer* – *múrderess* (*múrdereress*)). All of these instances of "truncation" lend themselves to an analysis where bound stems are selected if necessary to satisfy phonological constraints in word-formation. Significantly, bound stems are inferred by stripping affixes from the phonemic representations of complex words (cf. the examples in (6) or (11)), with no reference to phonetic form.

The question of which level of abstractness is referred to in word-formation is of considerable theoretical significance. If there is no evidence for any reference to allophonic structure in word-formation, this would support a model of the lexicon, which recognizes a separate level of "post-lexical" phonetic implementation. This conclusion is consistent with standard assumptions in lexical phonology (cf. Kiparsky 1982; Mohanan 1982).

The exclusive reference to (prosodically organized) phonemic representations in word-formation has also been challenged by those who posit more abstract morphophonemic representations. The alleged claims are based on putative correlations between affixes which are "stress-shifting" and combine with bound stems (so-called "level 1" affixes) vs. those which combine with free stems and are "stress-neutral" (so-called "level 2" affixes) (cf. Newman 1948; Chomsky and Halle 1968; Siegel 1974; Kiparsky 1982; Mohanan 1982). The relevant distinction is captured by representing bound stems abstractly, such that phonemic form and prosodic structure are created only in the course of stress-shifting affixation. Empirically, this approach is flawed in that stress neutrality and stem selection (free vs. bound) do not in fact correlate. Indeed there are many suffixes which never shift stress, yet select bound stems when necessary to satisfy phonological constraints, e.g., *-able, -ee, -er, -ize, -ify*, cf. (26), (36), (38). Moreover, the two-level models predict that stress-neutral suffixes can be sensitive to prosodic stem structure; yet consonant-initial suffixes, all of which are stress-neutral, are in fact never sensitive to such structure. Those models further predict that stress-shifting suffixes cannot follow stress-neutral suffixes; yet the cases of hyperproductivity identified in (31) are precisely of that kind. The evidence from phonological restrictions on English word-formation hence supports a "one-level" model where affixes and stems, free or bound, are represented phonemically, including prosodic organization.

Phonological restrictions on word-formation also shed light on the acquisition of morphological rules. Here, the idea that novel word-formation is best described as a proportional analogy (Becker 1990), where pairs of related words serve as a concrete model for new coinages (e.g., *explain : explanation = compláin :* X) is not supported. There is no reason to doubt that learners recognize the relatedness between the inherited loans in *-ation* and the relevant iambic verbs in (44a) and yet analogous stems are strictly avoided in native *-ation*-suffixation.

(44) a. èxplanátion – expláin
pèrturbátion – pertúrb
ìnspirátion – inspíre
àdorátion – adóre
cònsultátion – consúlt
còndensátion – condénse
èxhalátion – exhále

b. compláin / *complanation
distúrb / *disturbation
desíre / *desiration
ignóre / *ignoration
insúlt / *insultation
incénse / *incensation
assáil / *assalation

The rejection of the starred forms in (44) indicates the association of *-ation*-suffixation with necessary paradigm uniformity in the minds of English learners, despite the dozens of apparent exceptions to this constraint in existing noun-verb pairs as in (44a). As was noted above, the recognition of the paradigmatic relations in (44a) and the rejection of analogous formations are easily reconciled: one concerns analysis of the given while the other concerns synthesis of the new. Regarding the latter, it appears that paradigm uniformity functions as some kind of default constraint on English word-formation, which is "demoted" only for certain affixes, in fact never for word-formation involving verbs.

It appears then that the potential for analogy is restricted by specific structural constraints, including those on prosodic organization. For instance, citing the examples *beatnik, beachnik, peacenik*, Bauer (1983: 260) notes the original prevalence of the phonetic pattern /i/ + obstruent in the base, which however soon dissolved (e.g., *jazznik, folknik, so-whatnik, draftnik, fashionnik, computernik*). Bauer's remark that the pattern /i/ + obstruent "can never have provided more than a preference" makes sense in view of the prosodic structure: being consonant-initial and therefore non-cohering, the suffix *-nik* is prosodified outside of the phonological word of the stem and therefore is unlikely to be sensitive to stem phonology. Hence the pattern can only function as a fleeting model for sporadic coinages, but cannot become encoded in grammar.

7 Summary

Phonological restrictions on English word-formation manifest both as allomorphy and as gaps, that is, abstention from word-formation for phonological reasons. The occurrence of such restrictions can be linked to certain phonological properties of suffixes and to morphosyntactic properties of prefixes. The observation that in English phonological restrictions are characteristic for vowel-initial or vowelless suffixes, which are integrated into the phonological word of the stem, but are not characteristic for consonant-initial syllabic suffixes, which are not integrated, indicates the relevance of prosodic organization. Modifying prefixes, which form separate phonological words, and consonant-initial suffixes, which are also prosodically organized separately from the phonological word of the stem, are attached in virtual absence of any phonological restrictions; presumably this is a consequence of their being comparatively separate prosodically.

The range of phonological restrictions indicates the satisfaction of certain constraints, including phonological markedness constraints, in output forms. The reference to outputs also explains the reason behind the relevant restrictions: the goal is to yield phonologically wellformed words. Phonological wellformedness is thereby assessed neither at the phonetic level, nor is there any reference to putative abstract morphophonemic representations. The evidence from phonological restrictions on English word-formation supports a model of the lexicon, where all morphological units – words, stems, and affixes – are represented phonemically and word-formation is completed prior to phonetic implementation.

8 References

Aronoff, Mark (1976): *Word Formation in Generative Grammar.* Cambridge, MA: MIT Press.
Bauer, Laurie (1983): *English Word-formation.* Cambridge: Cambridge University Press.
Becker, Thomas (1990): *Analogie und morphologische Theorie.* München: Fink.
Booij, Geert (1985): *The Phonology of Dutch.* Oxford: Clarendon Press.
Chapin, Paul (1970): On affixation in English. In: Manfred Bierwisch and Karl-Erich Heidolph (eds.), *Progress in Linguistics*, 51–63. The Hague: Mouton.
Chomsky, Noam and Morris Halle (1968): *The Sound Pattern of English.* New York: Harper & Row.
Dixon, Robert M. W. (1977): Some phonological rules in Yidiny. *Linguistic Inquiry* 8(1): 1–34.
Dressler, Wolfgang U. (1977): Phono-morphological dissimilation. In: Wolfgang U. Dressler and Oskar E. Pfeiffer (eds.), *Phonologica* 1976, 41–48. Innsbruck: Institut für Sprachwissenschaft.
Eckert, Hartwig and William Barry (2002): *The Phonetics and Phonology of English Pronunciation.* Trier: Wissenschaftlicher Verlag.
Flemming, Edward (1995): The analysis of contrast and comparative constraints in phonology. Talk presented at MIT Phonology Circle lecture.
Huddleston, Rodney and Geoffrey K. Pullum (2002): *The Cambridge Grammar of the English Language.* Cambridge: Cambridge University Press.
Jespersen, Otto (1942): *A Modern English Grammar on Historical Principles. Part VI: Morphology.* London: Allen & Unwin.
Jones, Daniel (2011): *Cambridge English Pronouncing Dictionary.* Ed. by Peter Roach, James Hartman and Jane Setter. 8th ed. Cambridge: Cambridge University Press.
Kiparsky, Paul (1982): From cyclic phonology to lexical phonology. In: Harry van der Hulst and Norval Smith (eds.), *The Structure of Phonological Representations.* Part 1, 131–175. Dordrecht: Foris.
Lappe, Sabine (2007): *English Prosodic Morphology.* Dordrecht: Springer.
Marchand, Hans (1969): *The Categories and Types of Present-Day English Word-Formation. A Synchronic-Diachronic Approach.* 2nd ed. München: Beck.
Mohanan, Karuvannur Puthanveettil (1982): Lexical phonology. Ph.D. dissertation, MIT.
Muthmann, Gustav (1999): *Reverse English Dictionary. Based upon Phonological and Morphological Principles.* Berlin/New York: Mouton de Gruyter.
Newman, Stanley S. (1948): English suffixation: A descriptive approach. *Word* 4, 24–36.
Oxford English Dictionary online: http://www.oed.com [last access 9 Mar 2012]
Plag, Ingo (2003): *Word-Formation in English.* Cambridge: Cambridge University Press.
Prince, Allen and Paul Smolensky (1993): *Optimality Theory. Constraint Interaction in Generative Grammar.* Technical Report CU-CS-696-96. RuCCS-TR-2. [2002, as ROA-537].

Quirk, Randolph, Sydney Greenbaum, Geoffrey Leech and Jan Svartvik (1972): *A Grammar of Contemporary English*. London: Longman.

Raffelsiefen, Renate (1999): Phonological constraints on English word formation. In: Geert Booij and Jaap van Marle (eds.), *Yearbook of Morphology 1998*, 225–288. Dordrecht: Kluwer.

Raffelsiefen, Renate (2004): Absolute ill-formedness and other morphophonological effects. *Phonology* 21: 91–142.

Raffelsiefen, Renate (2005): Paradigm uniformity effects versus boundary effects. In: Laura Downing, Tracy Allan Hall and Renate Raffelsiefen (eds.), *Paradigms in Phonological Theory*, 211–262. Oxford: Oxford University Press.

Raffelsiefen, Renate (2007): Morphological word structure in English and Swedish: The evidence from prosody. In: Geert Booij, Luca Ducceschi, Bernard Fradin, Emiliano Guevara, Angela Ralli and Sergio Scalise (eds.), *On-line Proceedings of the Fifth Mediterranean Morphology Meeting, Fréjus, 15–18 September 2005*, 209–268. University of Bologna. (http://mmm.lingue.unibo.it/mmm-proc/MMM5/MMM5-Proceedings_full.pdf)

Raffelsiefen, Renate (2023): Morphophonological Asymmetries in Affixation. In: Peter Ackema, Sabrina Bendjaballah, Eulàlia Bonet and Antonio Fábregas (eds.), *The Wiley Blackwell Companion to Morphology*, Vol. III, 1483–1538. Hoboken, NJ: Wiley & Sons.

Siegel, Dorothy C. (1974): Topics in English morphology. Ph.D. dissertation, MIT.

Wells, John C. (1990): *Longman Pronunciation Dictionary*. Harlow: Addison Wesly Longman.

Lothar Peter
17 Morphological restrictions on English word-formation

Abstract: Morphological restrictions have been dealt with in traditional accounts of English word-formation as well as in more recent and theoretically-oriented studies. The present article gives an overview of the history of the treatment of morphological restrictions and the major theoretical questions and concepts involved. Its focus is on studies pertaining to the complex issue of restrictions on English multiple affixation, or, more precisely, multiple suffixation. The linguists' debate suggests that reliable findings are more likely when a combination of morphological, phonological and speech perception parameters as well as the parameter of frequency of occurrence are applied in the investigation process.

1 Introduction

The study of morphological restrictions (or constraints) in the system of English word-formation has been the subject of scholarly research, with varying approaches, for more than sixty years.

Among the early studies mentioning problems of restriction, we find Jespersen (1961 [1942]) and Marchand (1969). However, neither of these works deals with restrictions in a systematic way. Koziol (1937, 1972), a diachronic and more formally oriented description of English word-formation, includes no theoretical discussion of the issue of productivity and restrictions at all. Nonetheless, the early scholars were all inspired by Paul's (e.g., 1896, 1920) pioneering works. In Paul (1896: 694–697), for example, we find an elaboration of the idea that competing word-formation patterns interfere with each other's productivity. He also es-

Lothar Peter, Berlin, Germany

https://doi.org/10.1515/9783111420554-017

tablishes the fact that agent nouns of a specific type (e.g., *Weiner* 'crier') cannot be derived from certain verbs of Modern German (Paul 1896: 698). Paul's treatment of word-formation thus already points towards correlations between different levels of language – an idea he exemplifies by making reference to Germanic languages. As for English, Jespersen (1961 [1942]: 418–420), in his discussion of the suffix *-ful*, also mentions the aspect of competition between English *-ful* and the foreign suffix *-able*. Such findings, obviously, lead Hansen et al. (1982: 33–34), when outlining the principles that underlie the production of new complex words, to assume that morphological restrictions are intertwined with etymological and semantic restrictions. They also say that (systematic) morphological restrictions are predominantly related to the morphological structure of derivational bases and thus explain the combinability of, e.g., *-ful* with, almost exclusively, simple stems and that of *-ness* with both simple and complex stems, the use of which, however, blocks any subsequent formation (Hansen et al. 1982: 34). Pertaining to the same patterns, we find an analogous passage in Kastovsky (1982: 161). The aspect of blocking in *-ness* derivations also raises the question of whether this is caused by the morphological structure or, e.g., by the prosodic structure of the complex word. More recently, this phenomenon was explained by the concepts of "closure" in Stump (1998) and "closing morphemes" in Szymanek (2000) (cf. also article 20 on closing suffixes and Stein 2009: 238).

Hansen et al. (1982: 34) conclude their short general introduction to morphological restrictions by saying that (a) the potential of derivational options are the fewer, the more derivational stages are already contained in a stem, and (b) the upper limit of derivation is formed by the result of four successive derivational processes, such as in the word *decentralization*.

Apart from these structure-related aspects, the issue of etymology is discussed fairly early on with a view towards affixation. Marchand (1969: 318–321) and Jespersen (1961 [1942]: 318–320), for example, examine whether the suffix *-ize/-ise* can only be combined with bases of Latinate and Greek (or other foreign) origin and, after examination, find a number of counter-examples. Jespersen (1961 [1942]: 319), however, fails to give evidence for his statement that "[a] great many derivatives formed from Engl[ish] roots are in common use".

The study of origin and diachronic development seems to be one of the keys to a number of questions involved in the study of word-formation constraints. However, with massive, deep-reaching foreign inputs entering the lexicon of English in the Middle English and Early Modern English periods, the potential for productive word-formation patterns was enormously widened and equipped with a wealth of new options. Early and Late Modern English, at least until ca. 1750, had no strict rules as to the use of certain affixes. This often resulted in the existence of two, three or even four formations expressing the same concept with the same degree of complexity. Many of the rules and restrictions of interest in our realm are, then, the result of later standardisation/rationalisation (e.g., the principle of blocking) and the course of "pure" morphological development. With regard to the process commonly referred to as "standardisation", I agree with Kastovsky (2006: 170) when he says, "[...] the rivalry of these competing patterns and their sorting out in the eighteenth and nineteenth centuries are in need of further investigation, especially with regard to their distribution among text types and the influence of prescriptive grammar".

However, this article will be concerned with the aspect of synchrony only, i.e. it will focus on the problem of morphological restrictions in Present-Day English.

2 Morphological restrictions on compounding and derivation

2.1 Defining and delimiting morphological restrictions

Traditionally, morphological restrictions are conceived of as structural restrictions that are due to morphological properties of the constituents of a word-formation, e.g., those of a (potential) derivational base or those of an affix (potentially) attaching to some base. In the history of the study of English word-formation, the notion of what morphological properties comprise has varied to some extent. This is especially true of the relationship between morphology and etymology. Thus, in certain publications on (English) word-formation, the etymological aspect is discussed as a separate phenomenon as in Marchand (1969, sections 3.1.2, 3.1.3 and 4.1.4–8). Sometimes restrictions that are caused by the etymology of, for instance, specific affixes are considered to be outside morphological restrictions (cf., e.g., Schmid 2011: 119 and Hansen et al. 1982: 34–35).

In this article, however, morphological restrictions are understood to include issues of the origin (source language/s) of affixes as well as formal development of affixes. We find this to be in accordance with most linguistic accounts of the issue of morphological restrictions.

Another general issue concerns the questions of where exactly these restrictions are "located". In some publications, we find that morphological restrictions are similarly addressed as pattern-related (e.g., in Schröder and Mühleisen 2010) or "model-specific" (Schmid 2011: 118). In other words, they only consider the morphological combination of, e.g., a base and an affix in the sense of the affix attaching or not attaching, for one reason or the other, to some base. Schmid (2011), in this context, discusses Aronoff's (1976) example of the adjectival suffix

-al, which can only be attached to complex nouns ending in -ment if -ment itself is not a suffix but part of a morpheme.

However, one of the most researched problems in this respect is multiple affixation and the order in which affixes occur therein, particularly when the same affixes vary their order in different complex words (cf. Hay and Plag 2004, also Schmid 2011: 119).

In some earlier studies, we find that a distinction is made between restrictions relating to individual words and others concerning a pattern. Thus Neuhaus (1971, ch. 3) develops a model of level I to level III restrictions, in which, e.g., on level II various systematic conditions are shown (Neuhaus 1971: 35). A similar approach is developed in Hansen et al. (1982: 33), in which a division was introduced between non-systematic (item-specific) and systematic (pattern-related) restrictions. Consequently, they explain the impossibility of the formation *friendlinessful on the basis of two systematic restrictions: (1) -ness blocks any further formation, and (2) -ful can only (almost exclusively) be attached to simple stems.

2.2 Compounding and derivation

The study of the relevant literature shows that the two major fields of English word-formation, compounding and derivation, have attracted interest in restrictions in an unbalanced way.

As regards compounding, no paper has been written which systematically deals with morphological restriction. It is, therefore, not surprising that all recent handbook-type publications address affixation only, or, more precisely, suffixation. This is why such comments cannot be found in Schmid (2011: 115–120), Lieber and Štekauer (2009) or Štekauer and Lieber (2005). In Lieber and Štekauer (2009), a handbook of compounding, any reference in its index to restrictions or constraints is even missing altogether.

However, since the publication of Gold's (1969) article on the competing patterns with a (de)verbal first constituent as represented by the compounds frypan and frying pan, there has been some awareness of the implications. Apart from different preferences in the various national varieties of English, there seem to be certain restrictions on the use of verbal or nominal constituents. We notice, for example, that only the pattern V + N is used to form a compound with verbal blow as determinant; cf., e.g., blow-pipe, blowhole and blowlamp. Conversely, compounds with a (de)verbal determinant and the noun method as the determinatum only follow the $(V + -ing_N) + N$ pattern: cf., e.g., learning method, sampling method and teaching method.

As mentioned before, most of the research work concerned with morphological restrictions on English word-formation has been done in the field of affixation in general and multiple affixation in particular. Here only a small number of publications are concerned with special issues of prefixation; cf. from among the established works, e.g., Marchand (1969: 134–137) and Hansen et al. (1982: 67–71). One of the few topics addressed is the morphological and semantic interpretation of denominal verbs, e.g., *unbutton* (with a reversative meaning), *encage* (directional/locative) and *disarm* (privative), in connection with which, according to Marchand (1969: 134), "the formula AB is B does not apply". A similar pattern is discussed by Hansen et al. (1982: 68–70) with regard to complex words such as *postcentral* in the meaning 'related to something behind the centre' or *transcontinental* 'related to something across (the) continents'. For these formations, they assume a structure with a "prepositional" prefix, a nominal stem and an adjectival suffix, determining the word-class. Because a regular morphological analysis of the formations and their semantic analysis contradict each other, they consider most of the formations in question pseudo-prefixations and categorise them as zero-derivations.

Among the more recent publications, there are very few on problems of prefixation. Lehrer (1995) is one of greater general interest in that she raises several questions pertaining to the general status of prefixes, their combinability with one another and the role of semantic and pragmatic restrictions relevant to their use. Schröder (2011) is a study combining the issue of productivity of selected verbal prefixation patterns and their occurrences in several corpora as well as the statistical measurement thereof. When reflecting on the theoretical basis of her study, she discusses restrictions as "limitations of productivity" in general (section 2.4) and language-specific and rule-specific aspects in particular (Schröder 2011: 43–45). A result of her analysis with relevance to our problems is that prefixed verbs, in relation to (in certain respects) functionally equivalent particle verbs (e.g., *underperform* vs. *go under*), are morphologically more versatile than the latter in that they can generate structurally more diverse derivations or derivations at all (Schröder 2011: 81–82). In her conclusion (sections 7.3 and 7.4), she revisits such problems, saying, "[a]lthough [...] productivity cannot be defined on the basis of rule restrictions alone, these nevertheless have an influence on the productivity of a word-formation rule" (Schröder 2011: 246). Otherwise, she reports no morphological restrictions (also cf. section 7.3).

Returning to Lehrer (1995), she examines, in the context of prefixation, two major issues: selectional restrictions and whether affixes can be regarded as having the status of signs. However, her study is also concerned with combinations of prefixes. In addition, she raises the point of "bracketing paradoxes" (Lehrer 1995: 143), referring to the problem of whether the principle that all affixation takes place before compounding found elsewhere is applicable to prefixation as well (cf., e.g., *anti-animal rights* with the meaning 'against animal rights'), an idea she rejects concerning the pattern in question. She also discusses combinations of prefixes and suffixes as in *anti-racism* and *anti-liberialism*, revisiting the aspects dealt with by Marchand (1969) and Hansen et al. (1982). To turn to her initial issues again, Lehrer (1995: 147) argues in her summary that "many limitations on recursion and combination of word-formation processes should be explained in terms of pragmatic and processing factors, as well as in terms of the semantics of the affix and the base" and adds that, in tendency, "affixes are similar to lexemes". The latter idea is emphasised by her observation of the obvious parallelism among certain prefixes, on the one hand, and certain prepositions, adjectives and adverbs on the other.

This short discussion may serve to show why the problem of morphological restrictions on English prefixation is so difficult to deal with. It is apparent that the use of prefixes is not only determined by simple structural rules and restrictions, but also by a combination of linguistic structure and meaning properties as well as by mental processing and, possibly, extralinguistic factors.

As pointed out earlier, however, compounding and prefixation have not been in the focus of most studies which have been concerned with morphological restrictions on English word-formation. Relevant publications in the field, in different traditions and stages, have, on other hand, been written about suffixation. The following section will deal with various approaches towards restrictions on suffixation.

3 Combinability, selectional restrictions and parsing in (multiple) affixation

Apart from the concepts of the earlier publications discussed here in sections 1 and 2 (e.g., Jespersen 1961 [1942]; Marchand 1969; Hansen et al. 1982), the problem of restrictions on multiple affixation, particularly suffixation, has attracted much attention over the last four decades. As will be shown, this issue is not easy to clarify.

The first studies addressing this problem in a more or less systematic way are Stein (1971) and Neuhaus (1971). Other or new aspects of multiple affixation are discussed by, e.g., Burgschmidt (1978), Siegel (1979), Kiparsky (1982), Fabb (1988), Giegerich (1999), Plag (1996, 1999, 2002, 2003), Hay (2000, 2002), Hay and Baayen (2002), Aronoff and Fuhrhop (2002), Hay and Plag (2004), Rainer (2005), Kastovsky (1986, 2005), Bauer (2001, 2005), Plag and Baayen (2009), and Stein

(2009). Most of the more recent investigations are enriched and made more reliable concerning the results they yield by the use of large electronic corpora and/ or databases, such as the *British National Corpus* or the *Oxford English Dictionary* in one of its electronic versions.

3.1 Early studies on English multiple affixation

Stein (1971) is probably the first comprehensive and systematic study of French and English adjectival suffixation and prefixation, as well as of English word-formations with a very high degree of morphemic complexity. In this work, she introduces the distinction between primary or non-derived and derived adjectives as secondary, tertiary, quaternary and quinary word-formations. This work is largely based on theoretical notions developed by Marchand and Coseriu. The basic question posed is that of whether secondary adjectives behave in the same way as primary adjectives. Another goal was to identify typological differences between the two languages. Also (and with special regard to English), the study is designed to give more detailed information about the kinds of words (derived and non-derived) in which further word-formation is not possible. A corresponding issue is to develop a theoretical basis for a new classification of prefixes and suffixes. This classification is presented as a detailed listing of (adjectival) prefixes and affixes in word-formations with indices stating the degrees of complexity in the use of the respective affix and thus its highest possible degree (cf., e.g., *-able$_4$* in *depolarizable* vs. *-wise$_1$* in *clockwise*, i.e. fourth stage of formation vs. first stage). The lists also contain information about their combinability with stems of varying complexity (nouns, verbs and adjectives) and other affixes. Thus, through implication, the reader gains access to information concerning restrictions as well.

With regard to her basic question, Stein (1971: 267) summarises that "the morphological and conceptual structures of primary and secondary adjectives are different. The difference in their behaviour becomes most obvious at the level of word-formation: While derivational options of primary adjectives are relatively open, those of secondary adjectives become more and more restricted. The more word-formation stages an adjective has undergone, the fewer the chances of subsequent affixation" (my translation). However, much of the value of her study lies in the detailed findings pertaining to specific affixes.

Neuhaus (1971) is designed to develop a framework for a generative morphology of English affixations and for finding restrictions on English word-formation, using the example of *-ish* suffixations. In analogy to phonotactic rules, he uses the term *morphotactic rules* and seeks to describe the combination of certain affixes (Neuhaus 1971: 47–50). He thus shows that the suffixes -*al*, -*ist* and -*ic* and their combination with nouns like *nature, terror* and *period* may occur in different "cycles" of word-formation in various ways. The major part of his work is an exemplary grammar of the system of suffixations ending in -*ish*. It uses corpus-oriented and computer-based methods developed to process data that were gained from the Finkenstaedt, Leisi and Wolff (1970) chronological dictionary of English. Before the suffixations are examined, they are semantically classified, in an approximative way, as to their derivational bases. By comparing his data with those of other dictionaries on historical principles, he is able to show that the productivity rates of the sub-types vary according to historical periods and socio-cultural foci of society (Neuhaus 1971: 159–161). In addition, he stresses the mutual influence of competing word-formation models. A typical example here is the current use of the words *Indian* and *Greek* that have rendered suffixations like *Indish* and *Greekish* obsolete, although the latter clearly fulfil the criterion of morphological well-formedness (and display a greater regularity than the former). Based on this and the discussion of language change, i.e. typological change of the meanings of -*ish* suffixations, he stresses that chronological indicators are absolutely essential for an adequate description of the various types of restriction (Neuhaus 1971: 166).

However, this also raises the general question of the interplay between morphological and extralinguistic factors.

3.2 Principles of affix-ordering

The first studies examining restrictions on multiple affixation within the framework of generative linguistics appeared in the 1970s using a stratification theory with a distinct phonological orientation.

Drawing largely from principles described by Chomsky and Halle (1968), Siegel (1979) is an early attempt to combine aspects of derivational morphology and generative phonology, involving issues of stress rules and their influence on affixation. One of its aims is to describe how lexical entities, i.e. stems, affixes, etc., are represented in the lexicon (Siegel 1979: 101). Furthermore, affixes are classified and discussed with regard to differences in their properties. Siegel (1979: 111–148) identifies and elaborates two classes of affixes, which then, in turn, break down into prefixes and suffixes. The classification is based on the criterion of whether the affix is introduced with a + boundary (= morpheme boundary) or with a # boundary (= word boundary). Accordingly, she distinguishes Class I suffixes and Class II suffixes. Class I suffixes are introduced with the + boundary and Class II suffixes with the # boundary. According to Siegel, Class I suffixes are "all suffixes which satisfy the environment of the cyclic stress assignment rules and influence the placement of primary stress assignment rules" (Siegel 1979: 112). In other words, they cause and are affected by a shift of primary stress, such as nominal *-y* and *-ation*. Class II suffixes were considered to not be involved in such processes, e.g., adjectival *-y* and *-less* or nominal *-al*. In analogy, Class I prefixes and Class II prefixes were distinguished. These two classes of affixes are also called, with the notion of the corresponding strata, level 1 and level 2 affixes.

In essence, the distinction implied a grouping of non-Germanic (i.e. mostly Latin or French) affixes as level 1 and Germanic affixes as level 2 with different morphological and phonological properties. With respect to these criteria, Spencer (1991: 79) lists the most mentioned affixes, in accordance with Siegel, in the following table:

Tab. 17.1: Class I and class II affixes.

Class I suffixes:	+ion, +ity, +y, +al, +ic, +ate, +ous, +ive
Class I prefixes:	re+, con+, de+, sub+, pre+, in+, en+, be+
Class II suffixes:	#ness, #less, #hood, #ful, #ly, #y, #like
Class II prefixes:	re#, sub#, un#, non#, de#, semi#, anti#

Among the studies influenced by Siegel's theory are Aronoff (1976) and Kiparsky (1982 and later). Aronoff's book is the first published generative study of English word-formation. Siegel's stratification model was included in Kiparsky's version of lexical phonology. He assumed that the lexicon of English, in correspondence to Siegel, has primary morphology (involving word-stress and trisyllabic shortening) and secondary morphology, including compounding (with compound stress). With reference to the suffix *-ism*, for instance, Kiparsky (1983: 4) states that it "does not participate in the assignment of word stress and is not followed by primary suffixes because it is added at level 2, where word stress does not apply and primary suffixes are not available" and concludes that *-ism* "could not be sensitive to the difference between an underived base and a primary derivative".

Although Siegel's theory was relatively influential, it was soon criticised because it was considered too restrictive and prone to make the wrong predictions.

Fabb (1988) reconsiders Siegel's level-ordering hypothesis and the potential outcomes of the rules based on this theory. He examines them with regard to the behaviour of 43 frequently used suffixes, studying their combinability. Using the assumptions of level-ordering, he predicts 459 suffix pairs. He finds, however, that there are, in fact, only about 50 attested pairs of suffixes (combinations in complex words). Thus he concludes that "[s]ome other constraint must be at work ruling out the other ca 400 suffix pairs. It can be seen that level-ordering of suffixes achieves relatively little in predicting which suffix pairs exist and which do not" (Fabb 1988: 530). Also, he identifies four groups of suffixes: (a) suffixes which never attach to an already-suffixed word (e.g., deverbal -*al*), (b) suffixes which attach outside one other suffix (adjective-forming -*ary*), (c) freely attaching suffixes and (d) according to him, a problematic group of six semi-productive suffixes (e.g., noun-selecting -*al* combining with -*ion*, -*ment* and -*or*). Based on his findings, he rejects the feasibility of level-ordering with the argument: "In each case a suffix seems to have a particular affinity for another suffix; we are not dealing with affinities between sets of suffixes, as in level-ordering" (Fabb 1988: 535). He exemplifies his reasoning by postulating selectional restrictions and chooses the categorical statement "English suffixation is constrained only by selectional restrictions" as the title of his article.

Nevertheless, various more recent publications relativise Fabb's findings. One reason for this criticism is the small empirical basis of his study because he only uses Walker's (1924) rhyming dictionary and his own personal collection of word-formations.

The first response to Fabb (1988) is by Plag (1996). Plag formulates his fundamental criticism of Fabb on two levels, theoretical and empirical. For his own study, he uses a large database that draws from Lehnert's (1971) reverse dictionary of the English language and the second edition of the *Oxford English Dictionary on CD-Rom* as well as from handbooks of English word-formation. This allows him to identify a number of counter-examples to Fabb's claims. In addition, three general aspects established by Plag are of interest:

1   The regular distinction between an unrestricted domain (-*ness* suffixations with a high combinability) and specific restricted domains limiting the applicability of the suffixes to a linguistically determined set of bases;
2   The postulation of "base-driven" restrictions in contrast to "affix-driven" restrictions, the latter forming Fabb's only perspective in his analysis;
3   The notion of "lexical rules" for rules of (multiple) affixation and the "fact that lexical rules are often subject to exceptions" (Plag 1996: 794).

In sum, he dismisses many of Fabb's generalisations, particularly the ones pertaining to Fabb's four groups of suffixes, as having no theoretical significance. Plag (1996: 795) concludes that the incapability of specific suffixes to combine with certain stems is mainly due to some important property of the putative base rather than to a feature of the suffix itself and adds: "Taking this point seriously means to question any strictly affix-driven approach as put forward by standard lexical morphology or other stratum-oriented approaches."

The last aspect is emphasized again in Plag (1999: 91): "These constraints, in particular base-driven selectional restrictions and general morphological constraints like the Latinate constraint and blocking, regulate the applicability of derivational processes to given domains, ruling out a great many logically possible combinations of stems and affixes."

In spite of its weaknesses, Fabb (1988) and some of his observations have continued to attract attention from researchers, particularly his thoughts about certain affixes that do not attach to already affixed words. This was because his findings and their explanation implied a number of important issues concerning the roles of the base, the affix(es) and the new complex word as a whole in the over-all picture of restrictions.

3.3 Corpus evidence, psycholinguistics and parsing

Hay (2002), methodologically based on Hay (2000) and Hay, Pierrehumbert and Beckman (2003) and corresponding experimental work, offers a new approach to the understanding of suffixal restrictions by including aspects of speech perception and the frequency with which the given stems and affixes occur. Within the framework of her model of morphological processing she raises the question of how a morphologically complex word is accessed (perceptively analysed). Hay (2002: 528) thus identifies two perceptive "access routes", "a decomposed access route (e.g., *climber* may be accessed via the representations for *climb* and *-er*), or a nondecomposed whole-word access route (e.g., *climber*)". Which of the two really applies, according to Hay, has to do with, among more factors, "the phonotactics across the morpheme boundary, and the relative frequency of the derived form and the base". She assumes the existence of a phonological prelexical processor with sensitivity to distributional cues. Consequently, she regards certain suffixations to have different probabilities for either of the access routes, depending on whether or not the boundary between base and suffix is more likely to be perceived as a word-internal morpheme boundary and the respective suffixation to be accessed via decomposition. Such a case is given in the word *pipeful* because the phonemic sequence /pf/ has to be interpreted as a signal of transition from the base *pipe* /paɪp/ to the suffix *-ful* /f(ə)l/, whereas *bowlful* is more often interpreted as less complex.

Hay's second point is that frequent words are accessed faster (Hay 2002: 529). These assumptions together with others form a framework of hypotheses. Among the others, we find that suffixes beginning with a consonant tend to be more separable than those beginning with a vowel and that more separable affixes occur outside less separable affixes. She discusses these hypotheses in the light of her and other linguists' experiments and relevant publications and concludes

(Hay 2002: 552) that the issue of restrictions on English affix-ordering is mainly one of parsability:

> The overall result is that the less phonologically segmentable, the less transparent, the less frequent, and the less productive an affix is, the more resistant it will be to attaching to already affixed words. This prediction accounts for the pattern of the original affix-ordering generalization it was intended to explain. Importantly, the prediction also extends to the parsability of affixes as they occur in specific words. This accounts for the so-called dual-level behavior of some affixes. An affix may resist attaching to a highly decomposable complex word but be acceptable when it attaches to a comparable complex word that favors the direct route in access. Understanding affix ordering, then, requires a full understanding of factors influencing the parsing and storage of individual words. [...] it appears clear that the properties of affixes cannot be sensibly detached from the properties of the specific words in which they appear.

Hay and Baayen (2002) complement these generalisations by identifying a critical ratio of base frequency and the frequency of corresponding derived forms, which can be calculated and represented by a parsing line, above which (in a graph) derived forms are likely to be parsed.

Hay and Plag (2004), then, is meant to confirm the applicability of Hay's parsability theory. This research report is based on Hay (2002) and Plag (2002), the latter of which captures the essence of Hay's theory as "complexity based ordering" (CBO). In their article, Hay and Plag test the following contrary hypotheses: (1) the hierarchy hypothesis (based on hierarchy of juncture strength) and (2) the selectional restriction hypothesis. The hypotheses are examined with regard to the combinability behaviour of 15 English suffixes (13 of which are taken from Aronoff and Fuhrhop 2002), e.g., to check all 210 potential two suffix-combinations for attestations in several very large databases, such as the British National Corpus, and on the Internet. According to their findings, Hay and Plag (2004: 591–592) summarise that Hay's (2000, 2002) CBO predictions are largely compliant with the attestations. They find suffixes with weaker boundaries located closer to the base and those with stronger boundaries further away from the base. They also see a clear correspondence between selectional restrictions and parsing restrictions and add: "Overall, it was observed that only combinations that are well processable are possible combinations, and that this range of possible combinations is further curtailed by suffix-particular phonological, syntactic and semantic restrictions."

However, they relativise this statement by saying that the correlation between boundary strength and affix-ordering is very strong, but not absolute, as shown in the cases of -less and -ness: "-less is more separable than -ness by all measures considered. And yet -ness is very clearly positioned after -less in the ordering hierarchy" (Hay and Plag 2004: 590).

In a follow-up study, Plag and Baayen (2009) basically confirm the Hay and Plag (2004) findings and also show that there is a correlation to the productivity of the suffixes in question. In addition, they focus on the issue of perception, i.e. (time-related) processing costs in the mental analysis of complex words, to find that "constituent-driven processing is not necessarily the most time-efficient way of processing. In particular, constituent-driven processing (as gauged in terms of rank in the hierarchy) does not stand in a linear relationship with processing costs" (Plag and Baayen 2009: 146).

All of these research projects have been focused on English. However, Hay and Plag (2004) express the need to compare their findings to those in other languages. In this respect, Aronoff and Fuhrhop (2002) is the first attempt to examine, within the framework of the theories discussed in this article, restrictions on suffix combination in two languages, German and English. Their study is largely based on assumptions in Aronoff (1976) and uses the data set of the *Oxford Dictionary of English on CD-Rom*. The major finding is that German and English are typologically different with respect to suffix combination: English has the monosuffix constraint, i.e. roughly the tendency for a word to have no more than one suffix, whereas German has closing suffixes. More precisely, in English a suffix only combines with a Germanic base when the base has no suffix as a constituent. Concerning typology, they hold that "German morphology is closer to the Latinate morphology than to the Germanic morphology of English" (Aronoff and Fuhrhop 2002: 487–488). The study has been strongly criticised by several publications because of its theoretical and empirical weaknesses as well as its descriptive inadequacies (cf. Hay and Plag 2004: 592–593 and Stein 2009: 239–247).

Stein (2009), similar to, e.g., Hay (2002) and Hay and Plag (2004), also proposes a multiple-parameter approach. She favours a combination of ten factors, such as language origin, linguistic form, position of the affix, word class (as determined by the suffix), base structure, meaning, effect (whether the base remains intact or is caused to change), productivity, valency (combining properties of affixes) and closure.

In sum, these combined approaches towards a problem that is so complex and difficult to pin down at least raises the question of whether the concept of morphological restrictions in the traditional sense can still be upheld. It has become clear that the explanation routes via the morphological pattern, i.e. via base and/or affix properties, do not suffice to solve the issue adequately.

4 Conclusion

First and foremost, it can be said that the concept of morphological restrictions has become blurred as a consequence of the general finding that the factors constraining English affixation are not purely morphological, even if one extends the notion of morphology in word-formation to matters of etymology and morphonology. A number of restrictions traditionally considered to be of the morphological type can be thought of as having a combination of causes.

It has been shown that recent multiple-parameter studies involving morphological, phonological and speech-perception aspects as well as frequency of occurrence of word-formation elements (as attested in large electronic databases) have produced more detailed and more reliable results in comparison to the findings in traditional word-formation research, most of which were based on observation rather than systematic empirical investigation. These studies also yield more than the theories that are primarily or exclusively based on phonologically-based stratification models.

In addition, the degree of "granularity" has been enhanced in the recent studies by going beyond mere attestations of the given formations in the corpora in that they include psycholinguistic methods, such as native speakers' parsing of potential words. However, the exceptions remain despite the high degree of granularity and complexity of conditioning factors applied in the examination of English affixations. We thus agree with Schmid (2011: 119) that "the reasons for gaps in principally productive word-formation patterns have not been definitively clarified". However, in contrast to, e.g., Schmid (2011) and Mühleisen (2010) we do not think that this is caused by the English language being flexible or elusive. Rather, we hold the view that "natural morphology" (in the extended sense above, including competition between functionally equivalent patterns) is intertwined with historical decisions ruling out certain word-formations (cf. Kastovsky's remark discussed in section 1) and other extralinguistic factors. Nevertheless, it remains to discover whether linguistically predictable cases of restriction have increased in new complex words of Present-Day English in comparison to those that are the result of word-formation over several previous developmental stages of English.

Also, it is to be hoped that the research work discussed in this article is extended, with a similar degree of intensity, to the study of restrictions on English compounds.

5 References

Aronoff, Mark (1976): *Word Formation in Generative Grammar.* Cambridge, MA: MIT Press.

Aronoff, Mark and Nanna Furhop (2002): Restricting suffix combination in German and English: Closing suffixes and the monosuffix constraint. *Natural Language and Linguistic Theory* 20: 451–490.

Bauer, Laurie (2001): *Morphological Productivity.* Cambridge: Cambridge University Press.

Bauer, Laurie (2005): Productivity: Theories. In: Pavol Štekauer and Rochelle Lieber (eds.), *Handbook of Word-Formation*, 315–334. Dordrecht: Springer.

Burgschmidt, Ernst (1978): *Wortbildung im Englischen.* Dortmund: Lensing.

Chomsky, Noam and Morris Halle (1968): *The Sound Pattern of English.* New York: Harper and Row.

Fabb, Nigel (1988): English suffixation is constrained only by selectional restrictions. *Natural Language and Linguistic Theory* 6: 527–539.

Finkenstaedt, Thomas, Ernst Leisi and Dieter Wolff (1970): *A Chronological Dictionary of the English Language.* Heidelberg: Winter.

Giegerich, Heinz J. (1999): *Lexical Strata in English. Morphological causes, phonological effects.* Cambridge: Cambridge University Press.

Gold, David L. (1969): Frying pan versus frypan: A trend in English compounds? *American Speech* 44(4): 299–302.

Hansen, Barbara, Klaus Hansen, Albrecht Neubert and Manfred Schentke (1982): *Englische Lexikologie. Einführung in Wortbildung und lexikalische Semantik.* Leipzig: Verlag Enzyklopädie.

Hay, Jennifer (2000): Causes and consequences of word structure. Ph.D. dissertation, North Western University.

Hay, Jennifer (2002): From speech perception to morphology: Affix ordering revisited. *Language* 78(3): 527–555.

Hay, Jennifer and Harald Baayen (2002): Parsing and productivity. In: Geert Booij and Jaap van Marle (eds.), *Yearbook of Morphology 2001*, 203–235. Dordrecht: Kluwer.

Hay, Jennifer, Janet Pierrehumbert and Mary Beckman (2003): Speech perception, wellformedness, and the statistics of the lexicon. In: John Local, Richard Ogden and Rosalind Temple (eds.), *Phonetic Interpretation*, 58–74. Cambridge: Cambridge University Press.

Hay, Jennifer and Ingo Plag (2004): What constrains possible suffix combinations? On the interaction of grammatical and processing restrictions in derivational morphology. *Natural Language and Linguistic Theory* 22(3): 565–596.

Huyghe, Richard and Rossella Varvara (2023): Affixal rivalry: Theoretical and methodological challenges. *Word Structure* 16(1): 1–23.

Jespersen, Otto (1961 [1942]): *A Modern English Grammar on Historical Principles. Part VI: Morphology.* London: Allen & Unwin.

Kastovsky, Dieter (1982): *Wortbildung und Semantik.* Düsseldorf: Bagel-Francke.

Kastovsky, Dieter (1986): The problem of productivity in word formation. *Linguistics* 24: 585–600.

Kastovsky, Dieter (2005): Hans Marchand and the Marchandeans. In: Pavol Štekauer and Rochelle Lieber (eds.), *Handbook of Word-Formation*, 99–124. Dordrecht: Springer.

Kastovsky, Dieter (2006): Typological changes in derivational morphology. In: Ans van Kemenade and Bettelou Los (eds.), *The Handbook of the History of English*, 151–176. Oxford: Blackwell.

Kiparsky, Paul (1982): *Explanation in Phonology.* Dordrecht: Foris.

Kiparsky, Paul (1983): Word-formation and the lexicon. In: Frances Ingemann (ed.), *Proceedings of the Mid-America Linguistics Conference*, 3–29. Lawrence: University of Kansas.

Kjellander, Daniel (2018): Cognitive constraints in English lexical blending: A data collection methodology and an explanatory model. *Pragmatics & Cognition* 25(1): 142–173.

Koziol, Herbert (1972): *Handbuch der englischen Wortbildungslehre*. 2nd ed. Heidelberg: Winter.

Lehrer, Adrienne (1995): Prefixes in English word formation. *Folia Linguistica* 29(1–2): 133–148.

Lieber, Rochelle and Pavol Štekauer (eds.) (2009): *The Oxford Handbook of Compounding*. Oxford: Oxford University Press.

Marchand, Hans (1969): *The Categories and Types of Present-Day English Word-Formation. A Synchronic-Diachronic Approach*. 2nd ed. München: Beck.

Mühleisen, Susanne (2010): *Heterogeneity in Word Formation Patterns. A Corpus-Based Analysis of Suffixation with -ee and its Productivity in English*. Amsterdam/Philadelphia: Benjamins.

Neuhaus, H. Joachim (1971): Beschränkungen in der Grammatik der Wortableitungen im Englischen. Ph.D. dissertation, Universität des Saarlandes.

Paul, Hermann (1896): Ueber die Aufgaben der Wortbildungslehre. In: *Sitzungsberichte der philosophisch-philologischen und historischen Classe der k. b. Akademie der Wissenschaften zu München, Jahrgang 1896, Heft 4*, 692–713.

Paul, Hermann (1920): *Deutsche Grammatik. Band V. Teil V. Wortbildungslehre*. Halle/S.: Niemeyer.

Plag, Ingo (1996): Selectional restrictions in English suffixation revisited: A reply to Fabb (1988). *Linguistics* 34: 769–798.

Plag, Ingo (1999): *Morphological Productivity. Structural Constraints in English Derivation*. Berlin/New York: Mouton de Gruyter.

Plag, Ingo (2002): The role of selectional restrictions, phonotactics and parsing in constraining suffix ordering in English. In: Geert Booij and Jaap van Marle (eds.), *Yearbook of Morphology 2001*, 285–315. Dordrecht: Kluwer.

Plag, Ingo (2003): *Word-Formation in English*. Cambridge: Cambridge University Press.

Plag, Ingo and Harald Baayen (2009): Suffix ordering and morphological processing. *Language* 85(1): 109–152.

Rainer, Franz (2005): Constraints on productivity. In: Pavol Štekauer and Rochelle Lieber (eds.), *Handbook of Word-Formation*, 335–352. Dordrecht: Springer.

Schmid, Hans-Jörg (2011): *English Morphology and Word-Formation. An Introduction*. 2nd ed. Berlin: Schmidt.

Schmid, Hans-Jörg (2016): *English Morphology and Word-Formation. An Introduction*. 3rd ed. Berlin: Schmidt.

Schröder, Anne (2011): *On the Productivity of Verbal Prefixation in English. Synchronic and Diachronic Perspectives*. Tübingen: Narr.

Schröder, Anne and Susanne Mühleisen (2010): New ways of investigating morphological productivity. *Arbeiten aus Anglistik und Amerikanistik* 35(1): 43–58.

Siegel, Dorothy (1979): *Topics in English Morphology*. New York/London: Garland.

Spencer, Andrew (1991): *Morphological Theory. An Introduction to Word Structure in Generative Grammar*. Oxford: Blackwell.

Stein, Gabriele (1971): *Primäre und sekundäre Adjektive im Französischen und Englischen*. Tübingen: Narr.

Stein, Gabriele (2009): Classifying affixes and multiple affixation in Modern English. *Zeitschrift für Anglistik und Amerikanistik* 57(3): 233–253.

Štekauer, Pavol and Rochelle Lieber (eds.) (2005): *Handbook of Word-Formation*. Dordrecht: Springer.

Stump, Gregory (1998): Inflection. In: Andrew Spencer and Arnold M. Zwicky (eds.), *The Handbook of Morphology*, 13–43. Oxford: Blackwell.

Szymanek, Bogdan (2000): On morphotactics: Closing morphemes in English. In: Bożena Rozwadowska (ed.), *PASE Papers in Language Studies. Proceedings of the 8th Annual Conference of the Polish Association for the Study of English*, 311–320. Wrocław: Aksel.

Walker, John (1924): *The Rhyming Dictionary*. Revised by Lawrence H. Dawson. London: Routledge and Kegan.

Heike Baeskow
18 Semantic restrictions on word-formation: the English suffix -ee

Abstract: English derivatives ending in -ee are of particular morphological and semantic interest because their suffix has developed from a Romance inflectional ending to a productive element of English word-formation. Moreover, the referents of -ee derivatives, which are typically, though not exclusively human beings, play a variety of roles in the events denoted by or associated with the bases. As a result, the semantic description of these derivatives constitutes a challenge for representatives of different linguistic schools. In this article, substantial theories which aim at a restriction of derivational processes involving -ee will be presented after a brief historical overview.

1 Introduction

In classical generative approaches to word-formation (e.g., Williams 1981; Selkirk 1982; Lieber 1983; Olsen 1986; Burzio 1986; Randall 1988; Rappaport Hovav and Levin 1992) it is assumed that argument structure and thematic relations play a role not only in the syntax, but also in word-formation processes. In particular, it is claimed that derivational suffixes which preferably occur in the context of verbs are sensitive to the argument structure and theta-grid of their input. A frequently discussed example is the suffix -er, which prototypically realizes the external argument of its verbal base – i.e. the argument which occupies the position of the subject in the syntax – and absorbs the theta-role associated with this

Heike Baeskow, Frankfurt/M., Germany

https://doi.org/10.1515/9783111420554-018

argument position. The theta-role which is most likely to be absorbed by *-er* is the role of the AGENT (e.g., *driver, singer, producer*). The suffix *-ee*, which may be considered the passive equivalent to *-er* (and *-or*) in many contexts, frequently refers to an internal argument of the base verb and thus to an argument which surfaces as the direct or indirect object in the syntax (e.g., *employee, examinee, congratulatee; sendee, addressee, explainee*).

However, these observations reflect strong tendencies rather than absolute properties of the suffixes concerned. A number of recent approaches to word-formation (e.g., Ryder 1999; Lieber 2004, 2006; Plag 2004; Barker 1998) convincing-ly show that there is no constant one-to-one relation between a suffix and a particular argument position of the input. As far as *-er* is concerned, examples like *roaster, wilter, diner* or *laugher* (Ryder 1999) suggest that this suffix is by no means restricted to an agentive reading. The discrepancy between the semantics of a derivational suffix and the argument structure of its input is even more striking in the case of *-ee*. As stated already by Jespersen (1974 [1942]: 221–222), a number of *-ee* derivatives are not interpretable as direct or indirect objects of their verbal bases, e.g., *absentee, debauchee, devotee, fusee* or *refugee*. This view is shared by Bauer (1983: 243–250), who identifies four grammatically defined patterns involved in *-ee* derivation: Pattern 1 and 2 capture the "direct" and "indi-rect object" reading exemplified above. Pattern 3 gives rise to derivatives which realize the object of a preposition (e.g., *laughee* 'someone who is laughed at'), and pattern 4 applies to derivatives which make reference to the subject (e.g., *dilutee* 'unskilled worker used to dilute a skilled work-force'). Moreover, Bauer recogniz-es that there are forms which do not fit either of these patterns (e.g., *biographee, amputee*) or which are ambiguous between a passive and an active reading (e.g., *embarkee, retiree*). The examples presented so far clearly show that the reference of *-ee* goes beyond the semantics of the most common derivatives belonging to pattern 1 (type *employee*) or pattern 2 (type *addressee*).

2 A brief historical overview

The suffix *-ee* goes back to the inflectional ending *-é* (extended to *-ée* in feminine forms), which marks the *participe passé* in French, and entered Middle English via legal terms such as *appellee* (< French *appelé*), *feoffee* (< Anglo-French *feoffé*), *lessee* (< Old French *lessé*) or *assignee* (< Old French *a(s)signé*). Passive nouns like these, some of which have an agentive pendant in *-or* (e.g., *feoffor, lessor, assign-or*), still reflect the strong influence which French exerted on legal English after the Norman Conquest (Koziol 1972 [1937]: 227; Marchand 1969: 267–268; Baeskow 2002: 539–543).

In Early Modern English, *-ee* began to assume the status of an English derivational suffix. According to Jespersen (1905: 111), the derivative *vendee* is symbolic of this process because it imitates the French pattern regardless of the fact that the second participle of *vendre* 'to sell' is *vendu(e)* and not **vendé(e)*.

Initially, the formation of *-ee* derivatives was restricted to bases of Romance origin, and derivatives with native bases are not attested before the 17th century (e.g., *trustee, pawnee*). However, in the 19th century, *-ee* became a very popular suffix which was no longer confined to the legal vocabulary. Among the 19th century formations, there are derivatives like *sendee, addressee, employee, visitee, kickee, jokee, conferee, laughee, biographee* and many more. Likewise, the 20th century gave rise to numerous neologisms ending in *-ee* such as *recoveree, meetee, relaxee, pickpocketee, lovee, followee* or *inquisitee*. Quite a few of these neologisms have the character of creative ad hoc-formations and were introduced in the context of corresponding nouns in *-er*. The following examples are provided by Bauer (2001: 72).

(1) "Maybe", he offered, "they didn't want the follower and the followee to meet."

(2) The inquisitor becomes the inquisitee.

(3) If there was any conning to be done, Jack was supposed to be one of the conners, not one of the connees.

According to Bauer, *-ee* derivatives like these result from paradigmatic pressure, i.e. they are required as equivalents to established *-er* derivatives, and their paradigmatic relation to these derivatives allows for easy processing. The paradigmatic dimension of word-formation has always played a key role in the Netherlands School (cf. especially Marle 1985). Because of its semantic flexibility and its compatibility with non-native and native bases, *-ee* has replaced the Germanic suffix *-ling* in its passive reading. In Modern English, there is only a small set of patient nouns ending in *-ling*, including *hireling, foundling, suckling* and *starveling*.

3 The morpho-syntactic "blindness" of *-ee*

A comprehensive analysis of *-ee* derivatives performed by Barker (1998) on the basis of data from the *Wall Street Journal* confirms the observation formulated for example by Jespersen (1974 [1942]) and Bauer (1983) that this suffix realizes not only the direct or indirect object of its verbal input. It also refers to the object of a governed preposition (e.g., *conferee, consultee, gazee*), to the subject of intransitive verbs (e.g., *escapee, arrivee, resignee*) and even to the subject of transitive verbs (e.g., *attendee, forgettee, signee* 'someone who has signed a contract or register'). Moreover, *-ee* derivatives occasionally denote individuals which are in a part-whole relation to an unexpressed entity (e.g., *amputee, erasee* 'someone whose mind has been erased', *drainee* 'person involved in brain drain'). Although the majority of *-ee* derivatives have a verbal input, a few denominal forms are attested as well (e.g., *biographee, festschriftee, blind datee, asylee* 'person granted political asylum').

According to Barker's (1998: 705) statistics, 53 % of the *-ee* derivatives under consideration realize the direct and 16 % the indirect object of transitive verbs, whereas the other types mentioned above are less central or even marginal. Nevertheless, the statistics indicate that there is not generally a one-to-one relation between an *-ee* derivative and a particular argument position of the base. Deverbal *-ee* derivatives are problematic because their referents do not form a natural class from a syntactic point of view. The following sentences from Barker (1998: 705) illustrate this point:

(1)   a. The city employed the employee.
      b. She addressed the letter to the addressee.
      c. The psychologist experimented on the experimentee.
      d. The retiree retired.
      e. The attendee attended the concert.

Derivatives of the type *amputee, erasee* do not realize a syntactic argument of their verbal base at all although, (parts of) their referents are definitely involved in the events denoted by the verbs. In the case of denominal derivatives like *biographee, asylee*, there is no syntactic argument to be realized by *-ee*. These are Barker's core arguments against models of word-formation which associate suffixes with particular syntactic argument positions.

4 A suffix-specific theta-role and its components

The problems addressed in the preceding section caused Barker (1998) to describe person-denoting nouns ending in *-ee* from a purely semantic perspective and thus independently of syntactic argument positions projected by the input. Significantly, he postulates an individual theta-role for *-ee*. Influenced by Dowty's (1991) view that theta-roles are cluster concepts rather than discrete categories, Barker defines the suffix-specific role via three interacting semantic constraints: sentience, episodic linking and lack of volitional control.

The first constraint, "sentience", requires the referent of an -*ee* derivative to be human. This requirement holds for most, though not for all derivatives ending in -*ee*. Exceptions listed by Barker (1998: 710) are *actee, causee, controllee* and *governee*, all of which constitute linguistic terms. Moreover, *catapultee* 'a catapulted aeroplane' and *raisee* 'a war-ship or vessel reduced in height by the removal of her upper deck or decks' do not refer to human beings either. Another exception not mentioned by Barker is *settee* 'a long, soft seat like a sofa, with sides and back, for two or more persons'. However, since most of the -*ee* derivatives referring to non-sentient entities are domain-specific because they belong to the linguistic vocabulary, they are not an obstacle to the "sentience" requirement.

The second constraint, "episodic linking", requires that the referent of an -*ee* derivative has participated in the event denoted by or associated with the base for a certain period of time. Analogously to Carlson's (1977) description of individual-level predicates (e.g., *intelligent, tall, brown-haired*) and stage-level predicates (e.g., *drunk, sad, nervous*), the temporally determined involvement of an individual x in the event e denoted by the base is represented in the form of a stage, i.e. an ordered pair $<x,e>$, in the following definition of episodic linking (Barker 1998: 712):

> A derived noun N is EPISODICALLY LINKED to its stem S iff for every stage $<x,e>$ in the stage set of N, e is a member of the set of events that characterizes S.

For instance, John qualifies for the noun *trainee* if and only if e is a training event and if John has participated in this event – which is referred to as a qualifying event – in the appropriate manner.

A significant aspect of "episodic linking" is its reference to time because the extension of -*ee* derivatives is determined by aspectual properties of the base verb. For example, the referent of *employee* remains in the extension of this noun only for the duration of employment. On the other hand, the referents of nouns like *adoptee* or *retiree* are permanently involved in the qualifying events denoted by the base verbs from a particular point in time. It is precisely the correspondence between the duration of involvement in an event denoted by the base and the extension of -*ee* derivatives which gives rise to the episodic character of these person-denoting nouns.

Since the argument structure of the base is inaccessible to this purely semantic constraint, episodic linking ensures a uniform description of all -*ee* derivatives independently of the morpho-syntactic properties of their bases. Moreover, episodic linking applies not only to concrete events and participants, but also to implicit constituents, which are conceptually present although they are not spelled out. This property makes it a suitable device for the description of *-ee* derivatives which do not correspond to any of the arguments projected by the verbal base (e.g., *amputee, erasee*) and for the description of denominal *-ee* derivatives (e.g., *biographee, asylee*).

A further characteristic of the referents of *-ee* derivatives is that they are involved rather passively in the qualifying events. At any rate, they have no control over the activities performed. This property is expressed by the third constraint defining the theta-role for *-ee*, namely "lack of volitional control". Evidence for this constraint comes from the observation that numerous nouns ending in *-ee* fall within the domain of compulsion and obligation. Barker's corpus comprises not only legal terms such as *debtee, evictee, warrantee*, but also nouns relating to personal violence (e.g., *beatee, hittee, knockee*), crime and police work (e.g., *abductee, arrestee, blackmailee*), prisons and punishment (e.g., *escapee, offendee, releasee*) or military and war (e.g., *bombee, enlistee, invadee*).

As far as apparent agent nouns like *escapee, enlistee* or *arrivee* are concerned, Barker (1998: 718) argues that the referents act volitionally, but do not have control over the immediate consequences of the qualifying events. However, Barker does not consider this solution to be optimal because it relativizes the efficiency of one constraint, namely "lack of volitional control". This problem is solved by Lieber (2004), whose account of *-ee* derivatives will be presented in the following section.

5 Ranking of constraints and the principle of co-indexation

The semantic analysis of *-ee* derivatives proposed by Barker (1998) is compatible with Lieber's (e.g., 2004, 2006) lexical semantics approach to word-formation, which is discussed in some detail in article 11 on rules, patterns and schemata in word-formation. In Lieber's approach, lexical items are defined via sets of cross-categorial semantic features such as [+material] (*man, chair, book*), [−material] (*peace, time, love*), [+dynamic] (*sing, write, teach*), [−dynamic] (*know, own; tall, intelligent*), which instantiate the ontological categories SUBSTANCES/THINGS/ESSENCES and SITUATIONS. Another feature, namely [+IEPS] "inferable eventual position or state", is introduced for verbs denoting a change of state (e.g., *evaporate, forget, grow*) or a change of position (e.g., *descend, fall, go*).

Semantic feature constellations are also involved in the description of affixes. As illustrated in (5) and (6), both *-er* and *-ee* are lexically specified for [+material] because the derivatives they form denote concrete entities. In traditional terminology, these suffixes serve to form concrete nouns. Moreover, their entries display a non-binary feature [dynamic], which signals that the referents of nouns ending in -er and -ee are typically involved in some activity. This privative feature is absent in non-processual nouns, i.e. in nouns which do not imply activities (e.g., *happi-ness, modern-ity, child-hood*).

The crucial difference between -er and -ee is that only the latter imposes semantic restrictions on its input, namely sentience and non-volitionality. In principle, these restrictions, which are integrated into the suffix's semantic skeleton, correspond to Barker's (1998) constraints "sentience" and "lack of volitional control".

(5) *-er*
     Syntactic subcategorization: attaches to V, N
     Skeleton: [+material, dynamic ([ ], <base>)]

(6) *-ee*
     Syntactic subcategorization: attaches to V, N
     Skeleton: [+material, dynamic ([sentient, non-volitional], <base>)]

The adequate interpretation of -er and -ee derivatives naturally follows from the principle of co-indexation (Lieber 2004: 61), which is defined in article 11. Applied to suffixation, this principle states that the highest argument of the non-head (i.e. of the base) is co-indexed with the highest argument of the head-forming suffix provided that these arguments are semantically compatible. As demonstrated in article 11, this mechanism straightforwardly accounts for the well-formedness of a derivative like *driver*, whose suffix does not impose a semantic restriction on the non-head argument it is co-indexed with. The external argument of the dynamic verb *drive* is co-indexed with the referential argument <R> of the suffix, and the derivative assumes an agentive interpretation. The referential argument <R> occupies the placeholder in the semantic skeleton of -er.

(7) *driver*
     [+material, dynamic ([$_i$], [+dynamic] ([$_i$], [ ]))]
        -er   *drive*

In the case of -ee (e.g., *employee*) the situation is different because this suffix requires the referent of the non-head argument it is co-indexed with to be sentient and non-volitional. This requirement is specified in the position for the referential argument <R> of -ee. As a consequence, co-indexation with the highest argument of the base (e.g., of *employ*) is blocked because the referent of this argument is generally sentient and acts volitionally. Instead, *-ee* is co-indexed with the internal argument, which meets the requirements specified by the suffix, e.g.,

(8) *employee*
　　[+material, dynamic ([$_{\text{sentient, non-volitional}}$ i], [+dynamic ([ ], [$_i$])])]
　　-ee　　　　　　　　　　　　　　　　　　　　　　*employ*

As far as the noun *escapee* is concerned, there is a mismatch between the requirement "non-volitional" of *-ee* and the base *escape*, whose first argument refers to a volitional being and whose second argument generally denotes a non-sentient entity such as an institution. Nevertheless, according to Lieber (2004: 65–66), the acceptability of *escapee* is accounted for if we assume that the requirement of non-volitionality is weaker than the requirement of sentience and therefore violable. Since the first argument of *escape* at least meets the requirement of sentience, it is this argument which is co-indexed with the referential argument of *-ee*. Mismatches of this kind, which were considered problematic by Barker (1998), are idiosyncratic and hence dealt with in the lexicon.

(9) *escapee*
　　[+material, dynamic ([$_{\text{sentient, non-volitional}}$ i], [+dynamic ([$_i$], [+Loc ([ ])])])]
　　-ee　　　　　　　　　　　　　　　　　　　　　　*escape*

A semantic mismatch is also observable for the derivative *amputee*, which refers to an implied argument of the base verb *amputate*. The referent of the highest argument of this verb is a sentient being who acts volitionally (i.e. the surgeon). The second argument position is occupied by a noun denoting a limb (e.g., *arm*, *leg*). Thus, both positions are incompatible with the semantic requirements specified by *-ee* at first sight. However, nouns denoting body parts open semantic argument structures themselves. For example, since the referent of *leg* is in a part-whole relation with a human being, this noun has not only a referential argument <R>, but also an argument position for the possessor of the leg. It is this argument which is eventually co-indexed with the referential argument of the suffix *-ee* in order to yield the appropriate reading for *amputee*.

In Lieber's feature-based model, denominal *-ee* derivatives of the type *biographee* are described analogously to deverbal ones. Significantly, *biography* is conceived of as a processual abstract noun, which is typically associated with the activity of writing. Furthermore, *biography* opens two argument positions. The first position is occupied by the referential argument <R>. Since a biography is always written about someone, the second position is opened for the argument which would be realized as the complement of the preposition *of* in a syntactic phrase like *a biography of Dr. Samuel Johnson*. If *-ee* combines with the noun *biography*, the referential argument of the suffix, which is semantically specified for "sentience" and "non-volitionality", is co-indexed not with the first, but with the second argument of *biography*, which fulfils at least the stronger requirement of "sentience".

(10) *biographee*
　　 [+material, dynamic ([$_{\text{sentient, non-volitional}}$ **i**], [−material, dynamic ([ ], [$_i$])])]
　　 -ee　　　　　　　　　　　　　　　　　　　　　*biography*

Importantly, *-ee* derivatives involving constraint ranking (e.g., *escapee*), multi-layered semantic skeletons (e.g., *amputee*) or nominal bases (e.g., *biographee*) are not a result of productive word-formation but of paradigmatic pressure. Like Bauer's (2001) examples *followee*, *inquisitee* and *connee* in (1)–(3), they were formed in order to denote concepts for which no words have existed so far.

The semantically oriented works of Barker (1998) and Lieber (2004) provide an attractive and well-founded alternative to the morpho-syntactic view that derivational suffixes like *-er* or *-ee* are inextricably linked to specific argument positions of their bases. In both models, idiosyncrasies such as denominal *-ee* derivatives or deverbal *-ee* derivatives which do not correspond to any of the arguments of their bases are accounted for by general principles, namely episodic linking on the one hand and the principle of co-indexation on the other.

6 Prototypes – a recent trend in derivational word-formation

The semantic approaches presented in the previous sections reveal that there is a tendency to accept the lexical diversity of productive suffixes like *-er* and *-ee* and to relativize the significance of the argument structure associated with the bases. The decreasing relevance of morpho-syntactic information is particularly obvious in approaches to word-formation which incorporate aspects of prototype theory as developed by Eleanor Rosch (e.g., Rosch 1977). The meaning of complex concepts involved in compounding has been constructed on the basis of prototypes for quite a long time (e.g., Cohen and Murphy 1984; Smith et al. 1988; Štekauer 2005). In derivation, too, prototype theory is beginning to gain importance because it helps to account for the numerous deviations from regular word-formation patterns. Evidence comes from various works, which were developed independently of each other. Until recently, the application of prototypes to derivation was restricted to -er derivation (cf. Ryder 1991; Panther and Thornburg 2002; Baeskow 2010).

A highlight in the analysis of -ee derivatives is the work of Susanne Mühleisen (2010), whose formal synchronic description is based on the notion of "semantic prototype" as defined by Lyons (1995). According to Mühleisen, the prototypical -ee derivative of the type *interviewee* has the following properties: verb-derived, with existing correlative -er noun, direct-object relation to the verb, sentient and probably human, role participant, non-volitional and non-active part in the event, can be used in a legal as well as more general contexts (2010: 57). Formations such as *retiree, festschriftee* or *benefactee* are less central examples, but nevertheless belong to the class of -ee derivatives. By tracing the development of -ee suffixation from Middle English legal terms to 20th century neologisms from the world wide web, Mühleisen convincingly shows that the synchronic heterogeneity of -ee derivatives is diachronically motivated. The anglicized French past participles, which belonged to the legal vocabulary (cf. section 2), are described as a result of a language contact situation "in which English gradually took over domains like the legal sphere from the erstwhile hegemonic French" (Mühleisen 2010: 13). Once the nativized French loanwords were established in the 14th/ 15th century, -ee began to assume the status of an English derivational suffix. At this early stage, -ee derivatives were formed analogously to agent nouns in -or with verbal bases. This kind of correlative noun formation smoothed the way to deverbal -ee derivation without mediating nouns in -or, which prevailed in the 17th century. During the process of nativization, -ee was subject to significant morpho-syntactic and semantic changes, which are responsible for the synchronic diversity of -ee derivatives and which may be summarized as follows:

Most of the derivatives formed by the speakers of English in the 15th and 16th century realize the indirect object or the prepositional object of their base verbs, e.g., *lessee, grantee, donee, vendee, vowee, debtee*. In this respect, they differ from the Anglo-French participial nouns, which made reference to the direct object. Moreover, the effective use of the coinage *absentee* (< French *s'absenter* 'to withdraw') first attested in 1537 gave rise to a new but weak pattern: the agentive -ee derivative, which is further instantiated by later formations like *submitt(i)e, refugee, escapee, standee*, etc.

In the 17th century, further borrowings from French induced a shift towards direct object formations (e.g., *seducee, cheatee, challengee, transplantee, nominee*). The meanings of these derivatives began to generalize, and the bases were no longer restricted to non-native verbs. In 1691, the sense of the established noun *patentee* 'person to whom letters patent have been granted' (1442), 'the inventor, proprietor of something' (1616) was extended to include the invention itself. This is the first instance of a non-human -ee derivative.

After a century of lexical stagnation, a wealth of -ee derivatives was produced by the speakers of British and American English in the 19th century. Apart from semantically neutral derivatives (e.g., *addressee, employee, consultee, pardonee*), there are quite a few playful, humorous or ironic imitations of the established French borrowings. Examples of the creative use of -ee are *kissee, drivee, kickee, gazee* or *shavee*. From a morpho-syntactic point of view, most of the 19th century coinages refer to the direct object of their verbal input.

Semantically, many new words in -ee formed in the 20th century may be ascribed to the military jargon because they were coined during the two World Wars (e.g., *enlistee, internee, bombee, selectee, returnee*). The inventory of humorous -ee derivatives initiated in the 19th century was extended (*rushee, crackupee, squeezee, quizzee*, etc.), and a morpho-syntactic innovation is the formation of -ee nouns on the basis of compounds (e.g., *handshakee, blind datee, moneylendee, return addressee*).

The fact that representative late-twentieth-century dictionaries of new words fail to provide a sufficient number of more recent neologisms in -ee caused Mühleisen to perform an efficient internet-based search of -ee derivatives of the late 1990s and early 2000s. The aim of this empirical study was to test the productivity of contemporary patterns of -ee formation on the basis of 1,000 potential -ee words which are listed neither in the *Oxford English Dictionary* nor in other reference books. 748 words turned out to be successful new -ee formations displaying different degrees of frequency. Mühleisen's analysis, which is founded on a careful distinction between actual words, possible words, creativity and various types of productivity, reveals that the coinages provided by the world wide web largely adhere to the synchronically defined -ee prototype described above. Mühleisen (2010: 147–149) also provides reasons for the non-occurrence of certain -ee words. For example, bases ending in <-ee> or <-e> are prevented from combining with -ee for orthographic and phonological reasons (**see-ee, *free-ee, *lie-ee, *eye-ee*). Semantically, some -ee derivatives are blocked because they would refer to either non-events (e.g., **uneducatee, *untamee*) or negative events (e.g., **discouragee, *misguidee*). Apart from presenting formal, historical and innovative empirical aspects of -ee derivation, Mühleisen also examines the distribution of -ee words in certain varieties of English and thus accounts for the fact that language contact, which once brought about the English derivational suffix -ee, still plays a role in word-formation processes involving this suffix.

7 A symbolic approach to deverbal -*ee* derivation

A unified cognitive account of -*ee* derivatives is offered by Heyvaert (2006), who identifies a relationship between the different types of deverbal -*ee* derivatives discussed in the previous sections and the functions of the English past-participle morpheme -*ed*.

It is a well-known fact that the past participle may occur in adjectival, passive or perfect constructions, as shown by the sentences in (11)–(13). In its adjectival use, it attaches either to intransitive verbs (11a) or to transitive verbs (11b).

(11) a. Maturing and *matured* birds were on free range.
   b. Psychotherapy and analysis can sometimes help the more *motivated* patient who is curious to understand him- or herself.

(12) They were *captured* on the 5th day.

(13) She has *painted* all three of her children.

Following Langacker (1982, 1991), Heyvaert distinguishes four uses of the past participle. Adjectival PERF1, which attaches to intransitive verbs, profiles a stative relation in which the *agentive* participant finds himself/herself after he/she has undergone an (internal) change of stage, e.g.,

(14) Diana Tether is a newly *enlisted* Friend who makes good use of Kew gardens.

PERF2, which is adjectival in nature as well, profiles a relation in which the *non-agentive* participant finds himself/herself through the intervention of another, agentive entity, e.g.,

(15) Tens of thousands of refugees, including Rwandans, and *displaced* persons are in fear of their safety.

According to Langacker (1991: 203), PERF2 enhances the salience of a "terminal participant" or a participant "that lies downstream from another with respect to the flow of energy".

PERF3 is the passive variant of the past-participle morpheme -*ed*. Unlike PERF2, it profiles not only a final state, but all the stages of a process. This difference is reflected by the following sentences, which include Perf2 (16a) and Perf3 (16b):

(16) a. The town was (already) destroyed (when we got there).
     b. The town was destroyed (house by house).

Perf4, which is the perfect variant of the past-participle morpheme -ed, shares properties with Perf1 and Perf3. On the one hand, it behaves like Perf1 in that it does not imply that a participant is acted upon by another participant. On the other hand, it is like Perf3 in that it profiles all the stages of a process, including its termination, e.g.,

(17) Damon Hill already has been out testing the new Renault engine [...].

According to Heyvaert (2006: 352), the crucial characteristic of Perf4 is that "it invokes a temporal reference point and indicates that the process designated by the content verb is prior to that reference point".

Heyvaert's theory is based on the assumption that the participial constructions presented above constitute "agnates" of -ee nominalizations. Following Gleason (1965), she defines agnation as systematic or paradigmatic relations among large numbers of constructions. Significantly, all the functions identified for the past-participle are reflected by deverbal -ee derivatives. The most common -ee derivatives, i.e. those which realize the direct object of their verbal base in traditional terminology, correlate with clausal Perf3 – the passive use of the past participle.

(18) a. *employee*   (s)he is employed
     b. *detainee*   (s)he is detained
     c. *payee*   (s)he is payed
     d. *experimentee*   (s)he is experimented on
     e. *nominee*   (s)he is nominated

Because of their conceptual relation to Perf3, these nouns profile all the stages of the underlying processes in which the non-agentive participants are involved. In this respect, they differ from nouns like *adoptee* 'an adopted child' or *electee* 'an elected member', which behave like adjectival Perf2 in that they emphasize the final state in which the participants find themselves as the result of some change. However, some -ee derivatives are ambiguous between a Perf3 and a Perf2 reading. For example, the noun *abusee* may be interpreted as 'a woman who is (being) abused' (passive interpretation in the sense of Perf3) or 'an abused woman' (adjectival interpretation in the sense of PERF2, which focuses on the final state).

In Heyvaert's approach, agentive *-ee* derivatives do not constitute a problem because they also correlate with functions of the past-participle morpheme. Heyvaert distinguishes between two types of agentive *-ee* derivatives. The first type shifts the profile to a state in which the agentive participant finds himself/herself and thus correlates with PERF1, the adjectival variant of the past participle:

(19) a. *retiree*   a retired officer
      b. *escapee*   an escaped prisoner
      c. *enlistee*   an enlisted soldier
      d. *enrollee*   an enrolled student

The second type of agentive *-ee* derivatives correlates with PERF4, the perfect variant of the past-participle morpheme. These nouns, some of which are listed in (20), do not have an adjectival equivalent.

(20) a. *resignee*   (s)he has resigned
      b. *returnee*   (s)he has returned
      c. *forgettee*   (s)he has forgotten
      d. *deferee*   (s)he has deferred

To summarize, Heyvaert's analysis of deverbal *-ee* derivatives does not rely on a matching relation between the meaning of the suffix and a particular syntactic argument position of the base. In this respect, it differs from classical generative approaches like Bauer (1983), who was the first to develop concrete patterns for *-ee* derivation, or Rappaport Hovav and Levin (1992), who concentrated on the suffix *-er*. Unlike the theories proposed by Barker (1998) and Lieber (2004), Heyvaert's analysis does not make use of independent semantic constraints or principles either. Instead, it reveals a symbolic, i.e. a formal and semantic relation between the functions of the past-participle morpheme *-ed* and four types of deverbal *-ee* derivatives, which is diachronically motivated because *-ee* originated as an anglicized version of the French past participle *-é(e)*. In cognitive terminology, non-agentive *-ee* derivatives profile a participant that is downstream with respect to the flow of energy (e.g., *employee, experimentee*) or with respect to the flow of time (e.g., *adoptee, electee*). On the other hand, agentive *-ee* derivatives are downstream with respect to the flow of time and profile the final state in which the referent finds himself/herself after some change (e.g., *enlistee, returnee*). Of course, the approaches presented in this article are not mutually exclusive, but rather reflect the complexity of English *-ee* nominalization and the interaction of morpho-syntactic, semantic and cognitive constraints involved in the restriction of the derivational processes under consideration.

Acknowledgement

I am much indebted to the Deutsche Forschungsgemeinschaft (DFG), whose support of my project on word-formation enabled me to write this article.

8 References

Albrespit, Jean (2009): Is the trust-*ee* trust-*able*? On English suffixes with a passive meaning. *Groninger Arbeiten zur Germanistischen Linguistik* 49: 251–273.
Baeskow, Heike (2002): *Abgeleitete Personenbezeichnungen im Deutschen und Englischen. Kontrastive Wortbildungsanalysen im Rahmen des Minimalistischen Programms und unter Berücksichtigung sprachhistorischer Aspekte.* Berlin/New York: de Gruyter.
Baeskow, Heike (2010): Derivation in generative grammar and neo-construction grammar: A critical evaluation and a new proposal. In: Susan Olsen (ed.), *New Impulses in Word-Formation*, 21–59. Hamburg: Buske.
Barker, Chris (1998): Episodic -*ee* in English: A thematic role constraint on new word formation. *Language* 74(4): 695–727.
Bauer, Laurie (1983): *English Word-Formation.* Cambridge: Cambridge University Press.
Bauer, Laurie (2001): *Morphological Productivity.* Cambridge: Cambridge University Press.
Burzio, Luigi (1986): *Italian Syntax. A Government-Binding Approach.* Dordrecht: Reidel.
Carlson, Gregory Norman (1977): Reference to kinds in English. Ph.D. dissertation, University of Massachusetts, Amherst.
Cohen, Benjamin and Gregory L. Murphy (1984): Models of concepts. *Cognitive Science* 8: 27–58.
Dowty, David R. (1991): Thematic proto-roles and argument selection. *Language* 67: 547–619.
Dressman, Michael R. (1994): The suffix -*ee*. *Publication of the American Dialect Society* 78(1): 155–161.
Gleason, Henry A. (1965): *Linguistics and English Grammar.* New York: Holt, Rinehart and Winston.
Heyvaert, Lisbeth (2006): A symbolic approach to deverbal -*ee* derivation. *Cognitive Linguistics* 17(3): 337–364.
Jeong, Haeja (2017): -*ee* derivatives in English: Focusing on dual role of -*ee* suffix. *Studies in English Language & Literature* 43(3): 167–183. [Online available at: https://www.kci.go.kr/kciportal/landing/article.kci?arti_id=ART002253963]
Jespersen, Otto (1905): *Growth and Structure of the English Language.* Leipzig: B.G. Teubner.
Jespersen, Otto (1974 [1942]): *A Modern English Grammar on Historical Principles. Part VI: Morphology.* London: Allen & Unwin.
Koziol, Herbert (1972 [1937]): *Handbuch der englischen Wortbildungslehre.* Heidelberg: Winter.
Langacker, Ronald W. (1982): Space grammar, analysability, and the English passive. *Language* 58(1): 22–80.
Langacker, Ronald W. (1991): *Foundations of Cognitive Grammar. Descriptive Application.* Stanford: Stanford University Press.

Lieber, Rochelle (1983): Argument linking and compounds in English. *Linguistic Inquiry* 14(2): 251–285.

Lieber, Rochelle (2004): *Morphology and Lexical Semantics.* Cambridge: Cambridge University Press.

Lieber, Rochelle (2006): The category of roots and the roots of categories: What we learn from selection in derivation. *Morphology* 16: 247–272.

Lyons, John (1995): *Linguistic Semantics. An Introduction.* Cambridge: Cambridge University Press.

Marchand, Hans (1969): *The Categories and Types of Present-Day English Word-Formation. A Synchronic-Diachronic Approach.* 2nd ed. München: Beck.

Marle, Jaap van (1985): *On the Paradigmatic Dimension of Morphological Creativity.* Dordrecht: Foris.

Mühleisen, Susanne (2010): *Heterogeneity in Word-Formation Patterns. A Corpus-Based Analysis of Suffixation with -ee and its Productivity in English.* Amsterdam/Philadelphia: Benjamins.

Olsen, Susan (1986): *Wortbildung im Deutschen.* Stuttgart: Kröner.

Panther, Klaus-Uwe and Linda Thornburg (2002): The roles of metaphor and metonymy in English -er nominals. In: René Dirven and Ralf Porings (eds.), *Metaphor and Metonymy in Comparison and Contrast,* 279–319. Berlin/New York: Mouton de Gruyter.

Plag, Ingo (2004): Syntactic category information and the semantics of derivational morphological rules. *Folia Linguistica* 38(3–4): 193–225.

Randall, Janet (1988): Inheritance. In: Wendy Wilkins (ed.), *Syntax and Semantics 21. Thematic Relations,* 129–146. San Diego: Academic Press.

Rappaport Hovav, Malka and Beth Levin (1992): -Er nominals: Implications for the theory of argument structure. In: Tim Stowell and Eric Wehrli (eds.), *Syntax and Semantics 26. Syntax and the Lexicon,* 127–153. San Diego: Academic Press.

Rosch, Eleanor (1977): Human categorization. In: Neil Warren (ed.), *Studies in Cross-Cultural Psychology.* Vol. 1, 1–49. London/New York: Academic Press.

Ryder, Mary Ellen (1991): Mixers, mufflers, and mousers: The extending of the -er suffix as a case of prototype reanalysis. In: Laurel A. Sutton, Christopher Johnson and Ruth Shields (eds.), *Proceedings of the Seventeenth Annual Meeting of the Berkeley Linguistics Society, February 15–18, 1991: General session and parasession on the grammar of event structure,* 299–311. Berkeley: Berkeley Linguistics Society.

Ryder, Mary Ellen (1999): Bankers and blue-chippers: An account of -er formation in present-day English. *English Language and Linguistics* 3(2): 269–297.

Selkirk, Elizabeth (1982): *The Syntax of Words.* Cambridge, MA: MIT Press.

Smith, Edward E., Daniel N. Osherson, Lance J. Rips and Margaret Keane (1988): Combining prototypes: A selective modification model. *Cognitive Science* 12: 485–527.

Štekauer, Pavol (2005): *Meaning Predictability in Word Formation. Novel, Context-Free Naming Units.* Amsterdam/Philadelphia: Benjamins.

Trevian, Ives (2020): The suffix -ee: history, productivity, frequency and violation of stress rules. *Anglophonia. French Journal of Linguistics* 30 [Online available at: https://journals.openedition.org/anglophonia/3504]

Williams, Edwin (1981): Argument structure and morphology. *Linguistic Review* 1: 81–114.

Marc Plénat
19 Dissimilatory phenomena in French word-formation

Abstract: The present article provides an overview of the ways in which the universal tendency to avoid the repetition of similar consonants manifests itself in French word-formation. Phonological reactions include consonant dissimilation, truncation, haplology and epenthesis. Morphological reactions may consist in the choice of another suffix or stem, or in the insertion of an interfix. Dissimilation is also shown to play a major role in word games such as "javanais".

1 Introduction

The main finding of Grammont's doctoral thesis on consonant dissimilation in Indo-European and Romance languages (1895) was the awareness that all observed cases of dissimilation can be traced back to "a unique and very general principle: If in a word (or a closely knit word group) one and the same articulatory gesture has to be repeated twice, one of these gestures must be omitted" (Meillet 1904: 461; our translation). By conferring on this principle of dissimilation the status of a law – or a series of laws – governing exclusively phonetic changes, Grammont has restricted its scope and oriented the debate towards a discussion of the formulation of these laws (cf. Posner 1961) and their validity for historical phonetics (cf. Togeby 1964). It is obvious, however, that in its general form such a principle may have other phonological and morphological effects, both in synchrony and in diachrony, than that of changing the words of the lexicon (cf. Maiden 1997). As a modern descendant of this principle, the obligatory contour principle (Goldsmith 1976), conceived of originally as a constraint on underlying

Marc Plénat, Valence d'Albigeois, France

https://doi.org/10.1515/9783111420554-019

representations, has turned out to be useful for blocking or, on the contrary, triggering certain phonological processes (McCarthy 1986; Yip 1988). The present contribution follows this modern line of research by establishing the range of effects for which the principle of dissimilation can be held responsible in the formation of new words in Modern French. Due to space limitations, we can only illustrate each of these effects with a short analysis of some cases of consonantal dissimilation. The reader can find more detailed accounts and more numerous references in Roché et al. (2011: chapter 4).

The study of dissimilatory phenomena is impeded by the small number of relevant data in dictionaries. The main effect of the principle of dissimilation is to dissuade speakers from coining lexemes which would be rendered awkward or in need of repair by a cacophonic repetition. In the dictionaries, for example, the prefix *re-* or *ré-* expressing repetition does not precede a verb that begins with an *r*. This restraint does not work for all speakers alike, however, which is why many find themselves in a situation where they have to avoid the immediate repetition of two similar consonants. Systematic investigations on the Internet allow one to find a number of new forms which in one way or another avoid an expected repetition. These, mostly occasional, neologisms have little chance of ever entering the dictionary. However, due to their large numbers and homogeneity, they constitute a solid starting point for a synchronic study of dissimilatory phenomena.

We will classify the numerous and varied effects of the principle of dissimilation in French according to the stage at which they interfere with word-formation. Certain phonological processes correct repetitions which arise from the concatenation of elements in morphology. These phonological changes, however, are not the only possibility: An unexpected morphological combination of elements may also preempt the appearance of cacophonic repetitions. Finally, the principle of dissimilation can be seen at work even in secret languages after the phonology has given a word its canonical shape.

2 Phonological reactions

A priori, there are several ways of avoiding a sequence containing two similar consonants in neighbouring onsets or in the onset and rhyme of one and the same syllable. One can act on the presence or the identity of the neighbouring consonants by altering or deleting one of them; alternatively, one can take advantage of the distance which separates them and avoid a deletion that would bring them closer together by inserting, for example, an epenthetic consonant between them.

2.1 Progressive and regressive dissimilations

Dissimilation proper is rarely found in complex words. Grammont (1895: 16) has even claimed that "no dissimilation occurs when the etymology of the different parts of the word is transparent for the speakers". Nevertheless, we have found two good cases of dissimilation, one concerning progressive dissimilation, the other regressive dissimilation. Both manifest themselves in the suffixation of *-esque* '-esk', which derives adjectives from nouns (e.g., *Courteline* (name of a playwright) → *courtelinesque*, *funambule* 'tightrope walker' → *funambulesque*).

(1)   a.   Bakayoko /bakajoko/ (name of a football player) → bakayokeste, cirque /sirk/ 'circus' → cirqueste, blague /blag/ 'joke' → blagueste, blog /blɔg/ 'id.' → blogueste, bling-bling /bliŋbliŋ/ 'ostentatious' → blingeste, jogging /dʒɔgiŋ/ 'id.' → joggineste

b.   Bakayoko /bakajoko/ → bakayotesque, Facebook /fɛsbuk/ → facebootesque, gloubi-boulga /glubibulga/ (imaginary food) → gloubibouldesque, nov-langue /nɔvlɑ̃g/ (imaginary language) → novlandesque, bling-bling /bliŋbliŋ/ → bling-blinesque, jogging /dʒɔgiŋ/ → jogginesque

If the final consonant of the base is a velar stop (/k/, /g/ or /ŋ/), the ending *-esque* (/-ɛsk/) is sometimes replaced by *-este* (/-ɛst/), cf. (1a), or the velar stop of the base may be replaced by the corresponding dental stop (/t/, /d/, /n/), cf. (1b). In both cases the feature [+velar] of one of the velar stops disappears, and the consonant concerned takes on the unmarked place of articulation, which is the normal case in dissimilation. Maybe this is why dental suffixes, which are the most numerous, seem to shun dissimilation. Note that the large majority of cases of regressive dissimilation affect polysyllabic stems, while half of the derivatives in *-este* are formed from monosyllabic stems which an alteration would render unrecoverable.

2.2 Deletions and haplologies

The deletion of one of two similar consonants constitutes a radical remedy against repetition, but its consequences with respect to the syllabification and intelligibility of the derivative limit its application.

Let us use again for illustration suffixation by *-esque*. This suffix does not tolerate the presence of a sibilant at the end of the stem any better than that of a velar stop.

(2) a. Rolls /rɔls/ (trade mark) → rollsesque, pin's /pins/ 'id.' → pinsesque,
     lynx /lɛ̃ks/ 'id.' → lynxesque, ronce /rõs/ 'blackberry bush' → roncesque

   b. Beatles /bitœls/ → beatelesque, Dickens /dikɛns/ → dickeneste, Bill Gates /
     bilgɛts/ → bill-gatesque, Brassens /brasɛ̃s/ → brassinesque, Camoëns /
     kamɔɛ̃s/ → camoïnesque

   c. bidasse /bidas/ 'soldier' → bidassesque, saucisse /sosis/ 'sausage' → sau-
     cissesque, Pangloss /pɑ̃glɔs/ (figure in Voltaire) → panglossesque, Nim-
     bus /nɛ̃bys/ (comic figure) → nimbusesque

   d. Juliénas /ʒyljenas/ (wine from Burgundy) → juliénesque, Toutatis /tutatis/
     (god of the Gauls) → toutatesque, tétanos /tetanos/ 'tetanus' → téta-
     nesque, Cosinus /kɔsinys/ (comic figure) → cosinesque

When the final sibilant of the base is preceded by another consonant or a nasal
vowel that can give rise to a nasal consonant, its deletion does not affect syllabification. However, this deletion (sometimes) only takes place if the base contains
at least two syllables (cf. 2b); the very rare monosyllabic bases of this type always
retain their sibilant (cf. 2a). When the sibilant is preceded by an oral vowel, its
deletion would provoke the appearance of a hiatus if it were not accompanied
by the deletion of the vowel. But generally this double deletion only takes place
if the base has at least three syllables (cf. 2d); if it has only two, the last rhyme
is normally maintained intact (cf. 2c).

   This kind of behaviour is not infrequent. The deletion of the final rhyme of
a polysyllablic string for reasons of dissimilation affects consonants other than
sibilants (for example stops, cf. *Goldorak* → *goldorakeste* ~ *goldoresque*, *cosmonaute* 'cosmonaut' → *cosmonette* 'female cosmonaute'), and may be triggered by suffixes other than *-esque* (for example suffixation of *-issime* 'very', cf. *rigoureux*
'rigorous' → *rigourissime*, or suffixation of *-iste* '-ist', cf. *rhinocéros* 'id.' → *rhino-
cériste*). The two-syllable threshold below which the dissimilatory constraint does
not apply is normally rigorously respected (cf. *Chirac* → *chiraquesque*, *heureux*
'happy' → *heureusissime*).

   There is nevertheless one condition under which the two-syllable threshold
often seems to be ignored, *viz.* when the final rhyme of the base is identical with
the suffix or its initial part.

(3) (Louis de) Funès /fynɛs/ → funesque, DS /deɛs/ (game console) → déesque,
     Lewis /lewis/ → lewissime, propice /prɔpis/ 'favourable' → propissime

It is tempting to analyze these forms as cases of haplology rather than as cases
of deletion by postulating, for example, that in *propissime* (cf. section 3) the sequence /is/ represents at the same time the end of the stem /prɔpis/ and the

beginning of the suffix /isim/. In this case, the derivative would faithfully respect its base and the two-syllable threshold, only infringing the constraint of a one-to-one correspondence which requires that each phoneme of the derivative corresponds to one of the phonemes of its constituents.

2.3 Non-truncation

The strength of the principle of dissimilation is not only sensitive to the number of similar phonemes concerned, but also to the distance which separates them: The more distant the two phonemes are from one another, the better their presence is tolerated. We have conducted two experiments showing that the difficulty of deleting the first of two vowels in a hiatus is dependent on the degree of similarity between the two consonants surrounding it.

In the first study (Plénat 1996: 590 ff.), we asked 12 speakers to choose between the derivative in -*esque* with a truncated stem and the derivative in -*esque* with a non-truncated stem corresponding to di- or trisyllabic bases ending in /u/ or /o/. The subjects had to choose, for example, between *gourou-esque* and *gour-esque* (← *gourou* 'guru'), or between *kangourou-esque* and *kangour-esque* (← *kangourou* 'kangaroo'). The 18 consonants constituting possible onsets in French were represented twice each in front of the two vowels both in the disyllables and in the trisyllables.

In the second experiment (Roché et al. 2011: chapter 4), we collected from the Internet all the derivatives we could find in -*esque* derived from a base ending in a velar consonant + *a* or a sibilant + *a* with two and three syllables (907 items containing a velar consonant + *a* and 161 items with a base ending in a sibilant + *a*), and for each of the other consonants the derivatives from a di- and trisyllabic base were chosen at random (705 derivatives in all), in order to determine for each category the percentage of cases of truncation, hiatus and epenthesis.

Neither of the two experiments was entirely satisfactory. In the first one, the speakers were placed in a rather unnatural situation; in the second one, the origin of the derivatives was too diverse (there were numerous loan words). However, in spite of these shortcomings, these experiments show clearly not only that the presence of a sibilant or of a velar stop hinders the deletion of the final vowel of the base (for example, while *yakuzaesque* is attested, one only finds *loyolesque*), but also that this deletion is sensitive to the degree of resemblance between the final consonant of the base and the consonants of the suffix: Sonorants tolerate deletion better than obstruents, and among these, voiced obstruents tolerate deletion better than unvoiced ones.

2.4 The choice of epenthetic consonants

If, for whatever reason, the final vowel of a word is retained before a vowel-initial suffix, a hiatus is very often avoided by the epenthesis of a consonant. It seems likely that the choice of this consonant is determined by dissimilatory constraints, but lexical constraints sometimes work against this tendency.

Consider the distribution of the two most frequent epenthetic consonants of French, /t/ and /z/ (as shown in Table 19.1), when they are inserted between the disyllabic bases *gaga* 'senile', *bébé* 'baby', *neuneu* 'stupid', *bobo* 'bourgeois' and the suffixes *-ité* '-ity', *-isme* '-ism', *-esque* and *-itude* (Google search, December 18, 2010):

Tab. 19.1: Epenthetic consonants before *-ité*, *-isme*, *-esque* and *-itude*.

	-s-ité	-t-ité	-s-isme	-t-isme	-s-esque	-t-esque	-s-itude	-t-itude
gaga	0	0	0	2690	0	353	9	960
bébé	1	0	0	25	0	50	0	40
neuneu	46	0	1	307	0	57	4	1680
bobo	7	0	0	215	0	32	8	554

As one can see, the distribution of /t/ and /z/ is not random. /t/ almost never appears in front of *-ité*, nor does /z/ occur in front of *-isme* or *-esque*: One normally says *neuneusité*, but *neuneutisme* and *neuneutesque*. This distribution can only be attributed to the dissimilatory constraints prohibiting the repetition of two onsets or of an onset and a similar coda.

However, as one can also see, *-itude* is regularly preceded by /t/: One says *neuneutitude* rather than *neuneusitude*. This anomaly is undoubtedly due to the frequency of the ending *-titude* in the mental lexicon. The majority of lexicalized nouns in *-itude* (*aptitude, beatitude, certitude, exactitude, promptitude*, etc.), which are often borrowings from Latin, have a stem in /-t/. This explains the "gang effect" imposing the choice of /t/ as an epenthetic consonant to prevent a hiatus. Such gang effects sometimes appear locally even with suffixes normally sensitive to the dissimilatory constraints. For example, the epenthetic /s/ of *bétacisme, deltacisme* or *zétacisme* is borrowed from *iotacisme* and *la(m)dacisme*, which in turn were borrowed from Greek through Latin. The French pronunciation of these words has introduced a repetition of /s/ into the final sequence /sism/, which has been extended to the other members of the small series in spite of the dissimilatory constraints (cf. Roché 2007: 50).

3 Morphological reactions

Languages often prefer prevention to cure. In such a case, a sequence of two similar articulations may be avoided by choosing an unexpected suffix or stem. Alternatively, a meaningless segmental chain may be inserted between the base and suffix.

3.1 The choice of another suffix

The choice of a suffix other than the one required by the type of base and the meaning of the derivative is not infrequent (cf. already Roché 1997). It can be found with verbs, nouns and adjectives.

(4)   a. tunisien 'Tunisian' → tunisifier, rather than tunisianiser /tynizjanize/ vs. algérien 'Algerian' → algérianiser, marocain 'Maroccan' → marocaniser, and mauritanien 'Mauritanian' → mauritaniser
   b. champignon 'mushroom' → champignonniste, and not champignonnier /ʃɑ̃piɲɔnje/ vs. betterave 'sugar beet' → betteravier, céréales 'cereals' → céréalier, houblon 'hop' → houblonnier
   c. Molière → moliéresque, rather than moliérien /mɔljerjɛ̃/ vs. Corneille → cornélien, Pascal → pascalien, Racine → racinien

French has a series of verbs in -*iser* '-ize' derived from the Latinate variant of relational adjectives corresponding to names of countries and conveying the meaning that some institutions are given a national character which lacked it before (cf. 4a). In the case of Tunisia, the two sequences /niz/ of *tunisianiser*, though distant, are subjected to the principle of dissimilation. Choosing the noun instead of the adjective (*tunisiser*) would not make things better. Therefore, the only other verb-forming suffix, -*ifier* '-ify' is resorted to.

French also possesses a series of nouns in -*ier* derived from plant names and yielding nouns referring to people who grow them (cf. 4b). But when mushroom growers needed to be designated, *champignonniste* was preferred over *champignonnier*, which is awkward because of the sequence of a palatal nasal and an onset formed by a nasal and a palatal. Since it is used for productively deriving agent nouns from nouns, -*iste* was the most suitable suffix for replacing -*ier* in its function as an agentive suffix.

The most common way of deriving a relational adjective from a proper name in French consists in adding -*ien* to its Latinate stem (cf. 4c). However, if the base noun contains a palatal in its final onset, the risk of having to pronounce a palatal immediately following another is reason enough for speakers to prefer another suffix. That is why one says *le théâtre cornélien* 'Corneille's plays', *le théâtre racinien* 'Racine's plays', but *le théâtre moliéresque* 'Molière's plays'. Due to its frequent use in Italian loanwords such as *caravagesque, dantesque* or *pétrarquesque*, *-esque* is a good choice of replacement for *-ien*.

The replacement of one suffix by another only constitutes a remedy for the risk of repetition of similar articulations if the language has recourse to a suffix similar in function to the one that causes the difficulties. The suffix *-iste*, for example, which serves to designate human beings, cannot replace *-ier* if this suffix is used for deriving a place noun (cf. *une champignonnière* 'mushroom bed') or a noun designating a tree (if mushrooms grew on trees, these would be called *champignonniers*, cf. *brugnons* 'white nectarines' → *brugnoniers*). At the same time, French, the "language of Molière", which is sometimes jokingly called *moliérien*, could not be dubbed *moliéresque*. That is why one and the same suffix can sometimes be replaced by another suffix or can itself sometimes replace another suffix. So *-ien*, which gives way to *-esque* after a palatal in relational adjectives derived from names of persons, itself replaces *-ais* and *-ois* after a sibilant in inhabitant names (cf. *Parisien, Calaisien* vs. *Marseillais, Lillois*) and *-iste* in agent nouns derived from a stem ending in a sibilant (cf. *physicien* 'physicist' vs. *chimiste* 'chemist', see Lignon and Plénat 2009).

3.2 The choice of another stem

The choice of a stem different from the expected one can take on two forms. Sometimes a sequence of two similar articulations is avoided by violating the restrictions on the affix that selects the stem on which the derivative is based; on other occasions, a substitute stem is borrowed from the derivational paradigm of the base lexeme.

Lexemes – written here in small caps – are represented in the lexicon, not by a single form, but by a set of stem-forms each allotted to one or more slots in their inflectional or derivational paradigm. Adjectives, for example, have a Latinate stem-form which by default takes over the stem-form used for the feminine gender, but which can also be deduced from the default stem-form or can be unpredictable. Since the suffix *-ité* requires such a stem-form, the adjective RIGOUREUX 'rigorous' will yield, depending on the speaker, *rigorosité* /rigɔroz-ite/ (borrowed from Latin), *rigourosité* /riguroz-ite/ (backing of the last vowel), or *rigoureusité* /rigurøz-ite/ (default form). The superlative suffix *-issime* is one of those suffixes which require a Latinate stem (cf. RIGOUREUX → *rigorissime*, according to certain speakers).

Let us consider now the form taken on by the superlatives of adjectives in *-ique* /-ik/, whose specific Latinate stem-form is assibilated, yielding /-is/ (e.g., ÉROTIQUE 'erotic' → *érotic-ité* /erɔtis-ite/):

(5) a. DRAMATIQUE 'dramatic' → dramatissime ~ dramatiquissime, ÉROTIQUE → érotissime ~ érotiquissime, PSYCHÉDÉLIQUE 'psychedelic' → psychédélissime ~ psychédéliquissime

b. COMIQUE 'comical' → comiquissime, LUBRIQUE 'sensual' → lubriquissime, PRATIQUE 'practical' → pratiquissime

c. MAGIQUE 'magical' → magissime ~ magiquissime, MERDIQUE 'lousy' → merdissime ~ merdiquissime, MYTHIQUE 'mythical' → mythissime ~ mythiquissime

When the base contains three or more syllables (5a), the superlative, as expected, selects either the default stem-form or a stem derived by truncation or haplology from the stem-form ending in a sibilant (ÉROTIQUE cannot yield *erotic-issime* /erɔtisisim/, only *érot-issime* /erɔtisim/). When, on the contrary, the base has only two syllables – and is not transparent – (5b), the stem selects the default form in /-ik/ (COMIQUE → *comiquissime* /kɔmikisim/). Neither the stem ending in a sibilant nor its shortened variant are attested (neither *comicissime* /kɔmisisim/, nor *comissime* /kɔmisim/). Assibilation – and, as a consequence, haplology – are blocked due to the existence of the default form.

When, on the contrary, the disyllabic base is transparent, the superlative can again take either a short form or the default form (cf. MAGIE 'magic' → MAGIQUE 'magical' → *magissime* /maʒisim/ ~ *magiquissime* /maʒikisim/). Assibilation and shortening are not sufficient explanations in this case for the short form. This form is somehow licensed by the existence in the family of the base lexeme (MAGIQUE) of a lexeme with a different lexical category but the same meaning as the short form (MAGIE /maʒi/).

In the case of *magissime*, it is the noun which provides the stem of the derivative of the corresponding relational adjective. In the same way MAURITANIEN yields *mauritaniser* (← *Mauritanie* 'Mauritania') instead of *mauritanianiser* (cf. 4a). But the inverse case also exists:

(6) a. CLAUSEWITZ → clausewitzianisme, KEYNES → keynésianisme, LEIBNIZ → leibnizianisme, MALTHUS → malthusianisme

b. BERGSON → bergsonisme, CALVIN → calvinisme, ERASME → érasmisme, MONTAIGNE → montaignisme

Roché (2007) has shown that the names of philosophical and religious systems – but not political and artistic ideologies – derived from the name of a philosopher take the stem of the corresponding relational adjective if this name ends in a sibilant (6a): *malthusianisme* /maltyzjanism/ avoids the repetition of sibilants that would arise in *malthusisme* /maltyzism/. Inversely, the names of philosophers ending in a nasal phoneme directly take the suffix *-isme* (6b): *bergsonisme* /bɛrgsɔnism/ avoids the repetition of nasals that would arise in *bergsonianisme* /bɛrgsɔnjanism/. In these cases, the risk of having two sibilants is not the only determining factor (cf. *marxisme*, *debussysme*, etc.), the selection of the relational adjective also obeys a lexical constraint favouring *-ianisme* at the expense of *-isme* in the philosophical and religious sphere (cf. *luthérianisme*, *zwinglianisme*, *hégélianisme*, etc.). But this lexical logic must yield to the risk of an accumulation of nasals.

3.3 Shifted suffixation

A last remedy against the repetition of similar consonants consists in inserting a segmental string between base and suffix which takes on the form of a suffix but is devoid of meaning, a process referred to as "shifted suffixation" (*suffixation décalée*, in French). We will limit ourselves here to some short remarks about the diminutive suffix *-ette* (cf. Plénat 2005). Shifted suffixation is treated more in detail in article 3 on interfixes in Romance.

The suffix *-ette* is shifted to the right if the base is short, generally monosyllabic. But in addition to size constraints, which tend to impose a disyllabic stem, dissimilatory constraints also come into play. In fact, 1) the frequency of the phenomenon depends on the degree of similarity between the final consonant of the base and the consonant of the suffix. Shifting is rare after sonorants, but dominates after bases ending in /d/ and occurs regularly after bases in /t/ (e.g., *goutte* 'drop' → *goutt-el-ette*, etc.); 2) the consonant of the inserted segmental string is as different as possible from the consonants separated by this chain. In the case of the derivation in *-ette*, it is always a sonorant (cf. *boîte* 'box' → *boît-el-ette*, *boît-in-ette*, *boît-oun-ette*); 3) the only disyllabic bases which admit shifting are those whose final consonant is identical or almost identical to the consonant of the suffix. Hence we find derivations such as *patate* 'potato' → *patat-in-ette*, *patat-oun-ette*, *salade* 'salad' → *salad-in-ette*, *salad-oun-ette*. Shifted suffixation ensures more distance between similar articulations.

4 Dissimilatory phenomena in *javanais*

"Javanais" refers to language games which are often described as relying on infixation, but should rather be conceived of, as we will see, as associating the sounds of the source word with partly prespecified schemata. If the prespecified schema contains one or several phonemes identical to phonemes of the source word, dissimilatory phenomena can often be observed. These language games are of particular interest to us since they do not operate over lexemes, but over inflected words. This shows that the principle of dissimilation is also operative after morphology and phonology have provided inflected words with their canonical form. We will study here a javanais in *-av-* for which we have recordings, and a javanais in *-guede-* which we have found on the web.

4.1 Haplologies and reduplications in the javanais in *-av-*

French has a javanais associating the sounds of the source word with a series of disyllabic schemata of the form /C(C)avV(C(C))/.

(7) a. Frédo /fredo/ (hypocoristic) → /frave davo/, maton /matõ/ 'warder' → /mava tavõ/

  b. garde-à-vous /gardavu/ 'attention' (in the military sense of the word) → /gavar davu/, désespoir /dezɛspwar/ 'despair' → /davɛs pavwar/, relevé /rœlœve/ 'raised' → /ravœ lave/, à un /aɛ̃/ 'to one' → /avɛ̃/

  c. gradé /grade/ 'NCO' → /grave dave/, locataire /lɔkatɛr/ 'tenant' → /lavɔ kavo tavɛ ravœ/, Follenfant /fɔlãfã/ (family name) → /favɔ lavo favã/, souvenance /suvœnãs/ 'memory' → /savu navœ navã savœ/

If this javanais relied on infixation, the coded word should always have twice as many syllables as the original word and, apart from the occurrences of the coding sequence *-av-*, contain the same number of phonemes as the source word, as in *Frédo* → *Fr-av-é d-av-o* (cf. 7a). However, this is not always the case. Sometimes (cf. 7b) the coded word has fewer disyllabic schemata than the source word has syllables. This happens when the latter contains the sequence /av/ (cf. *garde-à-vous*), or when it contains two similar consecutive VC sequences (cf. *désespoir*), two identical consecutive vowels and a /v/ (cf. *relevé*), or two identical consecutive onsets and an /a/ (cf. *à un*, with two empty onsets). In other cases (cf. 7c), one of the phonemes of the source word appears twice in the javanais. In most cases, we find a vowel preceding or following an /a/ (cf. *gradé* and *locataire*), or followed by two identical vowels (cf. *Follenfant*); but some examples have also been found where a consonant is preceded by a /v/ which is repeated (cf. *souvenance*).

It is clear (cf. Plénat 1991) that all these apparent deviations allow one and the same general description: pairs of identical phonemes figuring both in the source word or one in the source word and the other in the coding sequence /av/ are represented by a single phoneme in the javanais. When a pair of vowels and a pair of consonants are merged in this way into one unit, the javanais can dispense with one disyllabic schema. In /gavar davu/, for example, the disyllable /davu/ simultaneously codes the syllable /da/ and the syllable /vu/ of *garde-à-vous*, at the same time respecting the schema /CavV/. When, on the contrary, only a pair of vowels or a pair of consonants are merged into a unit, this reduction necessarily provokes the reduplication of a consonant or of a vowel in the javanais. So in /grave dave/ the two vowels of *gradé*, /a/ and /e/, both figure in the first disyllable /grave/, but since the /d/ is not represented, coding must have recourse to a second disyllable which takes up the /e/.

These haplologies are often subject to multiple conditionings. Metrical constraints can play a role in explaining cases where haplology allows the reduction of the number of syllables. If, for example, *ô désespoir!* becomes *avô davespavoir!*, in our materials this serves to yield the second hemistich of an alexandrine. But this certainly is not the kind of constraint which explains the cases where the simplification is compensated by reduplication. It is reasonable to assume that the main *raison d'être* of these haplologies is to diminish the number of repetitions or to distribute them in a more harmonious manner. If all speakers of a javanais produce /gavar davu/ instead of /gavar dava vavu/, this is probably due to the fact that they avoid in this way having to pronounce a sequence of three /a/ and three /v/ one after the other. This certainly constitutes another manifestation of the principle of dissimilation.

4.2 Metathesis in the javanais in *-degue*

There is a second type of javanais whose coding sequence is based on a consonantal skeleton containing a /d/ and a /g/. These two consonants can appear in the order /d … g/ or in the order /g … d/ and be separated or not by a vowel. All the vowels of one and the same trisyllable or of one and the same disyllable are borrowed from the coded syllable. The syllable /la/ can therefore be coded as /ladaga/, /lagada/, /ladga/ or (probably) /lagda/, but when coding an utterance the speaker normally will stick to one of these variants.

(8) a. jeguede trouguoudou veguede quedegue tugudu èguèdè condonguon
(corresponding to: je trouve que tu es con 'I think that you are stupid')

  b. sadaga vadaga tudugu [faidaigais] kiodiogio [sic] degede bodogo (corresponding to: Ça va ? Tu fais quoi de beau ? 'How are you? What are you
doing?')

  c. tugdu peudgeu endgan chandgan geandgan lesdges autgo togolangan
(corresponding to: Tu peux en changeant les autocollants 'You can by
changing the stickers')

However, if the coded syllable starts with a velar stop, one often observes that
the order of the sequence /g ... d/ is reversed (cf. *que* → *quedegue* instead of
queguede, con → *condongon* instead of *congondon* in (8a), and, in a parallel fashion, that the order of the sequence /d ... g/ is reversed if the onset is a dental stop
(cf. *de* → *degede* instead of *dedegue* in (8b) and *tu* → *tugdu* instead of *tudgu* in
(8c). Not all speakers resort to this kind of metathesis, and those who practice it
do not do so consistently (cf. *tu* → *tudugu* in (8b). But, as far as I know, one never
observes inversions in contexts other than those described. It is furthermore note-
worthy that other anomalies appear if the normal coding would lead to a repetition of two similar onsets. So, for example, the disyllable *togo* in (8c) codes at the
same time the syllables *to* and *co* of *autocollants* (which ought to be coded as
audgo todgo codgo landgants): A sort of haplology conflates the expected syllables
with a velar onset *go* and *co*, while the *d* of the coding sequence, which would
partially repeat the initial *t*, is omitted. Both the distribution of the metatheses
and their co-occurrence with anomalies analogous to those which we find in the
javanais in -*av*- speak in favour of the idea that they are also a consequence of
the principle of dissimilation. They do not suppress the repetitions of velars and
dentals, but by widening the distance which separates the occurrences of these
phonemes they render these repetitions more tolerable.

We have not found dissimilatory metatheses outside the javanais in -*degue*-.
This is probably due to the fact that, since the infix is devoid of semantic content,
it does not matter whether the order of its elements is reversed or not.

5 Conclusion

In French it is frequently the case that, when an articulatory gesture in a derivative has to be repeated immediately, these two gestures are kept at a distance
from one another or merged into a single articulation. The facts can be described
in process terms: On the one hand, we observe progressive and regressive dissim-

ilations, cancellations and haplologies, unexpected choices of suffixes and stems; on the other, the absence of truncations, epentheses, shifting of suffixes, and metatheses. But this conspiracy speaks in favour of the existence of the general principle already vaguely alluded to by Grammont. The strength of this principle of dissimilation, which seems to affect all consonants, varies according to the degree of similarity between the phonemes involved, the distance which separates them in the word, and their number.

Frequently, one and the same derivative may take on several forms. Although we could not go into more detail here, it nevertheless turns out that the distribution of these forms is not due to chance: Short stems are more resistant than long ones and favour the widening of the distance between the similar articulations over the suppression of one of them; it is also only in case the suffix is somehow unique that the stem-building rules are infringed upon; and it is no coincidence that metathesis only affects elements devoid of meaning.

These facts taken together speak against a serial approach of morphology and phonology. The principle of dissimilation not only affects the contextual adaptation of the elements concatenated in word-formation, but also, beforehand, the very choice of these elements, as well as, further down, the deformation of words in word games. In order to be successful, the principle of dissimilation not only has to outdo other phonological principles, but also lexical regularities and the mechanics of javanais; in this task, it finds allies in other principles and rules. The complexity of these interactions speaks in favour of the idea that phonology and morphology proceed in parallel.

6 References

Goldsmith, John (1976): Autosegmental phonology. Ph.D. dissertation, MIT.

Grammont, Maurice (1895): *La Dissimilation consonantique dans les langues indoeuropéennes et dans les langues romanes*. Dijon: Darantière.

Lignon, Stéphanie and Marc Plénat (2009): Échangisme suffixal et contraintes phonologiques (Cas des dérivés en -*ien* et en -*icien*). In: Bernard Fradin, Françoise Kerleroux and Marc Plénat (eds.), *Aperçus de morphologie du français*, 65–81. Saint-Denis: Presses Universitaires de Vincennes.

Maiden, Martin (1997): La dissimilation à la lumière des pronoms clitiques en roman. *Zeitschrift für romanische Philologie* 113(4): 531–562.

McCarthy, John J. (1986): OCP effects: Gemination and antigemination. *Linguistic Inquiry* 17(2): 207–263.

Meillet, Antoine (1904): Note sur quelques recherches de linguistique. *L'année psychologique* 11: 457–467.

Plénat, Marc (1991): Le javanais: Concurrence et haplologie. *Langages* 25: 95–117.

Plénat Marc (1996): De l'interaction des contraintes: Une étude de cas. In: Jacques Durand and Bernard Laks (eds.), *Current Trends in Phonology. Models and Methods*, 585–615. Salford: ESRI, University of Salford.

Plénat, Marc (2005): *Rosinette, cousinette, starlinette, chipinette*: Décalage, infixation et épenthèse devant *-ette*. In: Injoo Choï-Jonin, Myriam Bras, Anne Dagnac and Magali Rouquier (eds.), *Questions de classification en linguistique. Méthodes et descriptions. Mélanges offerts au Professeur Christian Molinier*, 275–298. Bern: Lang.

Posner, Rebecca (1961): *Consonantal Dissimilation in the Romance Languages*. Oxford: Blackwell.

Roché, Michel (1997): *Briard, bougeoir* et *camionneur*: Dérivés aberrants, dérivés possibles. In: Danielle Corbin, Bernard Fradin, Benoît Habert, Françoise Kerleroux and Marc Plénat (eds.), *Mots possibles et mots existants. Actes du colloque de Villeneuve d'Ascq (Forum de morphologie, 1res rencontres, 28–29 avril 1997)* [= *Silexicales* 1], 241–250. Lille: SILEX, Université Lille 3.

Roché, Michel (2007): Logique lexicale et morphologie: La dérivation en *-isme*. In: Fabio Montermini, Gilles Boyé and Nabil Hathout (eds.), *Selected Proceedings of the 5th Décembrettes. Morphology in Toulouse*, 45–58. Somerville, MA: Cascadilla Press.

Roché, Michel, Gilles Boyé, Nabil Hathout, Stéphanie Lignon and Marc Plénat (2011): *Des unités morphologiques au lexique*. Paris: Hermès-Lavoisier.

Togeby, Knud (1964): Qu'est-ce que la dissimilation? *Revue de philologie* 17: 642–667. [Also in: Togeby, Knud 1968 Immanence et structure. Recueil d'articles publié à l'occasion de son cinquantième anniversaire. *Etudes Romanes* 2: 96–121].

Yip, Moira (1988): The obligatory contour principle and phonological rules: A loss of identity. *Linguistic Inquiry* 19(1): 65–100.

Stela Manova
20 Closing suffixes

Abstract: Closing suffixes are a topic related to affix ordering. A closing suffix closes the word to further suffixation. The article discusses a number of theoretical issues relevant to closing suffixation and considers examples from different languages. It is shown that there are closing suffixes in inflection and closing suffixes in derivation and that in derivation attention should also be paid to evaluative suffixes, since they are not always trivially closing.

1 Introduction

Closing suffixes or closing suffixation (I use the two terms as interchangeable) is a topic related to affix ordering. The latter is a central issue in linguistics and many theories have been suggested to account for the way affixes combine (see the overviews in Manova and Aronoff 2010 and Rice 2011). According to Manova and Aronoff (2010), there are eight types of approaches to affix order: 1) phonological; 2) morphological; 3) syntactic; 4) semantic; 5) typological (or statistical); 6) psycholinguistic; 7) cognitive; and 8) templatic. Phonological affix ordering uses phonological information, morphological ordering relies on morphological information, etc., and templatic ordering means that there is some order but it is (usually) inexplicable. Following this classification, closing suffixes are a subtype of morphological ordering, since the definition of closing suffixation relies on morphological information such as the existence of suffixes (morphemes). The idea of closing suffixation is thus an additional attempt to explain restrictions on

Stela Manova, Vienna, Austria

https://doi.org/10.1515/9783111420554-020

affix ordering. The logic behind it is the following. On the one hand, diagrammatic affixation (i.e. affixation by addition of an overt affix) is the most natural way of expressing addition of meaning (i.e. new semantics) in a natural language; on the other hand, the words are not always formed by the addition of affixes to already affixed words. This fact provides evidence, among other things, that some of the affixes a language possesses may serve to stop further affixation. Such affixes seem to "close" the word to the addition of further affixes and are therefore termed *closing*. In the literature, the issue has been discussed only with respect to suffixation, therefore the term *closing suffixes*. However, as we will see below, prefixation also appears compatible with the idea of closing morphemes.

2 History of research

The first mentioning of the term *closing* with respect to morphological material is usually referred to Eugene Nida's book *Morphology* (1946, 1949 2nd ed.). Nida (1949: 85) differentiated closing and non-closing morphemes and used the label "closing" to describe the role of the inflectional suffixes in morphology, i.e. the fact that after an inflectional suffix no derivational suffixes can be added:

> Certain morphemes close the construction to further formation. For example, in English the use of a genitive suffix closes the noun to further suffixation. No suffix may follow the genitive.
> [...]
> [T]he addition of the plural *-s* closes any form to further derivation by such suffixes as *-ment, -ity, -ence, -ion, -ian, -ize, -er*. A genitive suffix does the same thing. This break in structure in English coincides with the division between inflectional and derivational formations.

Thus, Nida's definition of a closing suffix is a version of Greenberg's "*Universal 28*: If both the derivation and the inflection follow the root, or they both precede the root, the derivation is always between the root and the inflection" (Greenberg 1963: 93).

In his 1985 Ph.D. dissertation, van Marle reported the "inability" of some Dutch derivational suffixes "to constitute the starting point for further morphological coining" (p. 236). However, van Marle did not use the term *closing suffix* but spoke of suffixes the morphological valence of which is either low or zero (cf. Schultink 1962: 132 f.).

> The characteristic trait of *low-valence [derived] words* is that their morphological valence is (i) either highly restricted, or (ii) zero. In the case that their morphological valence is *not*

equal to zero, there is a proviso that further coining is restricted to categories with a predominantly – or even exclusively – 'syntax-directed' nature. (van Marle 1985: 236)

In a similar fashion, in the more recent literature on affix ordering closing suffixes are usually defined as derivational suffixes that do not allow addition of further derivational suffixes. A number of linguists have reported the existence of closing suffixes in various languages: Szymanek (2000) is on closing morphemes (the term Szymanek uses) in English and Polish; Aronoff and Fuhrhop (2002) report a phenomenon that bans the further derivation in German and explain it in terms of closing suffixes; Manova (2008, 2010) provides evidence for closing suffixes in Bulgarian and Russian; Plungian and Sitchinava (2009) speak of closing suffixes in Russian; Melissaropoulou and Ralli (2010) acknowledge the existence of closing suffixes in Greek derivational morphology; and Manova and Winternitz (2011) discuss closing diminutive suffixes in Bulgarian and Polish. (Note, however, that these studies, though dealing with closing suffixes, are not thorough investigations of the phenomenon of closing suffixation.)

It should also be mentioned that the term *closing suffix* is difficult to find in reference sources. Even reference books devoted exclusively to morphological terminology (e.g., Laurie Bauer's *A Glossary of Morphology* from 2004) do not have an entry for "closing suffix". I could find "closing suffix" only in the glossary of Aronoff and Fudeman's book *What is Morphology?* (2005).

Finally, some approaches to affix ordering, without explicitly mentioning closing suffixes, are perfectly compatible with the phenomenon of closing suffixation. Approaches of this type are: the monosuffix constraint (Aronoff and Fuhrhop 2002); the parsability hypothesis (Hay 2001, 2002, 2003) and the elaboration of it termed "complexity-based ordering" (Plag 2002; Hay and Plag 2004; Plag and Baayen 2009). Finally, an analysis that relies on morphological selectional restrictions (Plag 1996) is also compatible with closing suffixes.

According to the monosuffix constraint, in English "suffixes that select Germanic bases select unsuffixed bases" (Aronoff and Fuhrhop 2002: 473), i.e. the Germanic part of the English derivational morphology allows only one derivational suffix and that single derivational suffix is thus a closing suffix. This issue is also discussed in Szymanek (2000) who illustrates it with copious examples and who, in contrast to Aronoff and Fuhrhop (2002), provides an analysis in terms of closing morphemes. Aronoff and Fuhrhop's (2002) argument as to why they speak of the monosuffix constraint in English and of closing suffixes in German is the following: "If English Germanic suffixes were all closing suffixes, then all the adjectival suffixes would have to be viewed as exceptionally non-closing only when they are followed by *-ness*. When not followed by *-ness*, the same suffixes would be closing suffixes. So the exceptionality of *-ness* cannot be expressed prop-

erly within the closing suffix framework" (p. 475). Note that the English suffix
-ness is closing.

The parsability hypothesis claims that a set of factors are responsible for
morphological parsing, such as phonology, productivity, regularity, semantic
transparency, and relative frequency. Since parsability depends on a number of
factors, it is a gradual notion and allows affixes to be ordered hierarchically
according to their degree of parsability. Parsability determines affix order in the
sense that a more parsable affix should occur outside a less parsable affix because this order is easier to process. As a parsable affix adds morphological structure to a base, making the latter more complex morphologically, Plag (2002)
termed affix ordering that depends on parsability *complexity-based ordering*.
Thus the parsability hierarchy (or complexity-based ordering) of the suffixes A,
B, C, D and E (see Table 20.1), where A is the least parsable suffix and E is the
most parsable one, predicts that all combinations in which A is followed by the
suffixes B, C, D and E should be possible (e.g., ACE), whereas combinations such
as *CAD and *EAB should be impossible. This way of ordering of affixes assigns
to the suffix E the status of a closing suffix. Table 20.1 illustrates this type of affix
ordering with a hypothetical example of a parsability hierarchy:

SUFF2 SUFF1	A	B	C	D	E
A		+		+	
B			+		+
C				+	+
D					
E					

Tab. 20.1: A hypothetical parsability hierarchy ("+" marks existing combinations).

Note that in the parsability hierarchy more than one suffix can be closing. For
example, in Table 20.1 both D and E are closing.

Plag (2002) and Hay and Plag (2004) also demonstrate that parsability works
in conjunction with selectional restrictions on affix order. An example of a selectional rule is the fact that the English suffix *-ization* always selects the suffix *-al*.
On the role of selectional restrictions in English word-formation, see Plag (1996).
Thus, a selectional rule may also state that a particular suffix is never followed
by another suffix, i.e. that it is a closing suffix.

3 Delimiting the phenomenon and providing a precise definition

3.1 Delimiting closing suffixation

3.1.1 Terminal suffixes

A terminal suffix is the last suffix in a word form. However, since there may be a suffix that is terminal in one word and followed by a suffix in another word, not all terminal suffixes are closing. For example, the English suffix *-ation* is terminal in *organiz-ation* but followed by *-al* in *organiz-ation-al*.

3.1.2 Blocking

Another phenomenon related to closing suffixation is blocking. We speak of blocking if the existence of one lexeme prevents the derivation of another lexeme with the same or similar semantics (Aronoff 1976, and many others). For example, the existence of *glory* in English blocks the derivation of **gloriousity* (Aronoff 1976: 44) and thus also the suffix combination *-ous + -ity* in this particular case. However, if one of the combinations of the suffix *-ous* is blocked, it does not mean that *-ous* is closing. Consider, for example, *gloriousness*, where *-ous* is followed by *-ness*. Blocking refers to a single combination of two particular suffixes, often only in a single word (on blocking, see also Rainer 1988). Closing suffixation refers to the general combinability of a suffix, that is closing suffixation accounts for the non-combinability of a suffix with all other suffixes in a language. Additionally, while there is a clear semantic explanation of blocking, a closing suffix cannot be always successfully defined with the help of semantics only. The role of semantics in closing suffixation is discussed in section 4.2.

3.2 Closing suffixes and morphological organization

In this subsection I discuss closing suffixation in relation to various issues that I label "morphological organization": base-driven vs. affix-driven morphology, morphological language types, derivation vs. inflection, evaluative morphology and suffixation vs. prefixation.

3.2.1 Base-driven vs. affix-driven morphology

In morphological theory, affixation is seen as being either (i) base-driven, i.e. it is the base that selects the affix and the direction of the derivation is thus from the base to the affix, or as (ii) affix-driven, i.e. it is the affix that selects the base and the direction of the derivation is from the affix to the base. Classical descriptive sources are affix-driven – they list suffixes and explain to what bases a suffix attaches to express a particular semantic meaning associated with that suffix. An example of a statement of this type is: the English suffix -*(at)ion* attaches to verbs derived by the suffix -*ize* to form abstract nouns, as in *nasalize* → *nasalization*. Studies on affix ordering are often base-driven, i.e. they would describe the same combination as starting with the suffix -*ize* (a verb derived with -*ize*, that is a base) to which then the suffix -*ation* is attached. Since closing suffixes stop the attachment of further suffixes but a closing suffix can follow other suffixes and bases, closing suffixation is base-driven by definition. This could be the explanation of why many sources, especially classical grammars and textbooks that provide affix-driven descriptions of morphology, do not mention closing suffixes.

3.2.2 Closing suffixes and morphological language types

In the literature so far, closing suffixes have been discussed primarily in relation to the inflecting languages (recall the history of research). Closing suffixes have not been reported in agglutinating and incorporating languages, though they should be compatible with these morphological types too. This conclusion has the following motivation. There are two ways to produce morphological structure – template morphology and layered morphology. A template is a linear set of slots and each slot accommodates particular suffixes which can be substituted in that slot but never co-occur. Thus, the last slot in the template hosts the closing suffixes. On templates, see Stump (2006). Layered morphology is usually semantically compositional and also scopal by nature. In a scopal affix order, a suffix with a broader semantic scope follows a suffix with a narrower scope. Thus, the suffix(es) with the broadest scope in a language will be the closing one(s). On semantic scope in affix ordering, see Rice (2000). An accessible explanation of template and layered morphology with a comparison of these two types of morphological organization can be found in Manova and Aronoff (2010).

3.2.3 Derivation vs. inflection

A language that distinguishes between derivational and inflectional suffix slots usually allows more than one derivational and more than one inflectional suffix. Such a situation is found in the Slavic family. (1) is a schema of the structure of the Slavic word. In (1), a slot that is associated with more than one arrow can host more than one affix. The term *evaluative* is used after Scalise (1984) and denotes diminutive and augmentative suffixes.

(1)   The structure of the Slavic word

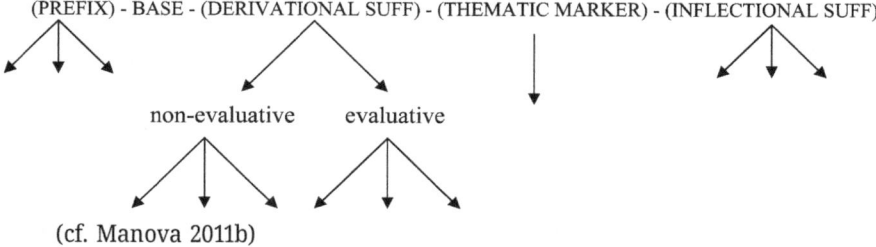

(PREFIX) - BASE - (DERIVATIONAL SUFF) - (THEMATIC MARKER) - (INFLECTIONAL SUFF)

non-evaluative   evaluative

(cf. Manova 2011b)

For German, a language that, like Slavic languages, distinguishes between derivational and inflectional suffixes, Aronoff and Fuhrhop (2002: 468) argue for two types of closing suffixes – closing suffixes in derivation and closing suffixes in inflection. We will also adopt this differentiation of closing material. A derivational suffix that is never followed by another suffix of the same type (i.e. another derivational suffix) is a closing derivational suffix, whereas an inflectional suffix that is never followed by another inflectional suffix is a closing inflectional suffix. A closing derivational suffix can be followed by inflection.

As regards inflection, in Slavic languages a word has either a single inflectional suffix or if there is more than one inflectional suffix, the order of the inflectional suffixes is fixed. (2) is an example of a fixed (also called templatic) order of inflectional morphemes. The template in (2) gives the order of the adjectival inflectional suffixes in Bulgarian; note that GEND and NUM share the same slot, i.e. are cumulatively expressed (Matthews 1972):

(2)   BASE–GEND/NUM–DEF
    a. *krasiv-ø-ø*   'beautiful' (masculine)
       krasiv-ø-ijat   'beautiful-DEF'
    b. *krasiv-a-ø*   'beautiful-FEM/SG'
       krasiv-a-ta   'beautiful-FEM/SG-DEF'

c. *krasiv-o-ø*   'beautiful-NEUT/SG'
   krasiv-o-to   'beautiful-NEUT/SG-DEF'
d. *krasiv-i-ø*   'beautiful-PL'
   krasiv-i-te   'beautiful-PL-DEF'

These examples show that the definite article (DEF) is a closing suffix in inflection. Let us now look into the order of the suffixes that occupy the evaluative derivational subslot in (1).

3.2.4 Evaluative suffixes

As indicated in (1), Slavic derivational suffixes are of two types – non-evaluative and evaluative; and as already mentioned, the latter type includes diminutive and augmentative suffixes. Aronoff and Fuhrhop (2002) exclude diminutive suffixes from their investigation of closing suffixes in German because according to these authors diminutive suffixes are closing by definition, which is due to the fact that a German noun can have only one diminutive suffix which is also always the last derivational suffix in the word form. In the Slavic languages, however, only the augmentative suffixes are like the German diminutive suffixes. The Slavic diminutive suffixes combine with each other (Szymanek and Derkach 2005; Manova 2011c; Manova and Winternitz 2011). Consider the following double diminutives: Russian *kartina* 'picture' → DIM1 *kartin-ka* 'small picture' → DIM2 *kartin-oč-ka* 'very small picture'; Polish *dom* 'house' → DIM1 *dom-ek* 'small house' → DIM2 *dom-ecz-ek* 'very small house'; and Ukrainian *dub* 'oak' → DIM1 *dub-ok* 'small oak' → DIM2 *dub-oč-ok* 'very small oak'. Thus, in Slavic languages not all diminutive suffixes are closing.

Table 20.2 gives the exact combinations of diminutive suffixes in Bulgarian, a language in which also triple diminutives are possible: *dete* 'child' → DIM1 *det-ence* 'little child' → DIM2 *det-enc-ence* 'very little child' → DIM3 *det-enc-enc-ence* 'very very little child'.

From Table 20.2, we see that there are diminutive suffixes that are clearly closing: *-ec, -čica* and *-ička*. These suffixes are never followed by another diminutive (or other derivational) suffix. It is, however, not the case with the suffix *-ence* that is never followed by another diminutive suffix but can be repeated on adjacent cycles. (Recall also the examples of double diminutives from Russian, Polish and Ukrainian cited above.) In order to account properly for the repetition of a diminutive suffix, we should allow the recursive use of a closing derivational suffix.

Tab. 20.2: Combinability of the Bulgarian diminutive suffixes (from Manova and Winternitz 2011).

Nouns in	DIM1 suffixes	DIM2 suffixes	DIM3 suffixes
in -C	-ec (unproductive)		
	-le (unproductive) -če	-ence	-ence
	-čica (unproductive)		
in -a	-ica	-ka	
	-ka	-ica	-ica
	-ička (unproductive)		
in -o	-ce	-ence	-ence
in -e	-ence -ice (unproductive)		

Clearly, the suffixes -ica and -ka that occur in both orders, -ica + -ka and -ka + -ica, are both non-closing.

3.2.5 Are there closing prefixes?

In the literature, there is no information on closing prefixes but there are studies on prefixation that seem to offer evidence for the existence of closing prefixes. A closing prefix will be the last prefix, outward from the root, in a sequence of prefixes. The account of the English prefixes in Zirkel (2010) where a complexity-based ordering hierarchy of prefixes is provided (recall Table 20.1) gives the closing prefixes in English. The assignment of the Slavic prefixes into different groups, such as lexical, super-lexical and perfectivizing (Babko-Malaya 1999; Svenonius 2004, among others) also seems to speak for the existence of closing prefixes, since the prefixes of the different groups combine in a specific way and there are prefixes that are always in the last position, outward from the root, in a sequence of prefixes. Thus, closing prefixation is an issue for future research.

3.3 Precise definition of closing suffixation

The following definition accounts for all instances of closing suffixes we discussed above:

Closing suffixation is a base-driven morphological phenomenon whereby a suffix closes the word to the addition of further suffixes of the same type: a closing derivational suffix is never followed by another derivational suffix, except by itself, i.e. a closing derivational suffix can be repeated on adjacent cycles or followed by inflection. A closing inflectional suffix is never followed by another suffix, be it derivational or inflectional.

4 Form and semantics in closing suffixation

4.1 The role of morphotactics

Homophonous suffixes can be used to check the role of morphotactics in closing suffixation. Put differently, if homophonous suffixes are always closing, morphotactics defines the feature [+/-closing]. The Polish suffixes $-k_1-a$ and $-k_2-a$ in (3) below are an instance of homophonous suffixes. The suffix $-k_1-a$ derives objects, whereas the suffix $-k_2-a$ subserves the formation of nouns for female humans from male humans. Intriguingly, the nouns derived by $-k_1-a$ can be further derived (3a), whereas nouns derived by the suffix $-k_2-a$ do not serve as bases for further derivation (3b).

(3) a. *kołys-k_1-a* 'cradle' → ADJ *kołys-k_1-ow-y* 'cradle-'
       kołys-k_1-a 'cradle' → DIM *kołys-ecz_1-k-a*
     b. *trener-k_2-a* 'female trainer' → ADJ ø
       trener-k_2-a 'female trainer' → DIM ø

Thus, (3) provides evidence that morphotactics cannot define closing suffixation.

However, Aronoff and Furhop's (2002) account of German closing suffixes relies on morphotactics. Following the tradition of generative morphology, they related the German closing suffixes to a non-semantic fact – the presence of a linking element in a compound with as first constituent a derived noun that terminates in a closing suffix. To exemplify:

(4) *Üb-ung-s-sache*
     to train-ing-linking element-matter
     'a matter of training'

In this example, *-ung* is a closing suffix and *-s-* is a linking element. Note that German is a language with very productive compounding and almost every noun can be used as a first constitutent of a compound. Therefore, Aronoff and Fuhr-hop (2002) had to provide an explanation for why a closing suffix is followed by word-formation material in compounds, and they claimed that the German link-ing elements "reopen" closing suffixes. However, linking elements are not a per-fect diagnostic criterion for the feature [+/−closing]. For example, they cannot explain the closing character of the suffix -ismus that derives abstract nouns, as in the German noun *Real-ismus* 'realism', but does not require a linking element in a compound, e.g., *Real-ismus-streit* 'polemic on realism'. Intriguingly, the suffix -ismus (English -ism, Russian -izm, Polish -i/yzm, Bulgarian -izăm, etc.) is one of the very few instances of a suffix that seems to be cross-linguistically closing.

Thus, we will conclude that morphotactics is not a sufficient diagnostic for the definition of a suffix as [+/−closing].

4.2 The role of morphosemantics

In order to check the role of semantics in closing suffixation, Manova (2009) compares the German closing suffixes from Aronoff and Fuhrhop (2002) with their semantic homologues from two Slavic languages, Bulgarian and Russian. In what follows, I will use the same strategy and some of Manova's examples of closing suffixes in Bulgarian.

According to Aronoff and Fuhrhop (2002: 461), six German suffixes are clos-ing: -e, -heit/-keit/-igkeit, -in, -isch, -ling, and -ung. With respect to the categories of the base and the output, we can define these German suffixes in the following way:

(5) V   + -e   →   N
     ADJ   + -heit/-keit/-igkeit   →   N
     N males   + -in   →   N females
     N person   + -isch   →   ADJ
     V, ADJ   + -ling   →   N
     V   + -ung   →   N

The German pattern V + -e → N, as in *pflegen* 'to care for' → *Pflege* 'care', can be compared with Bulgarian derivations of the type *griža se* '(I) care for' → *griž-a* 'care'. Such derivations are, however, conversions in Bulgarian where the Bulgari-an suffixes parallel to the German -e are purely inflectional (consider Bulgarian *griž-a* – PL *griž-i*), which explains why the suffix -a cannot be followed by deriva-tional suffixes in Bulgarian.

The German pattern ADJ + -heit/-keit/-igkeit → N, e.g., *schön* 'beautiful' → *Schön-heit* 'beauty', has a clear parallel in Bulgarian derivations such as *xubav* 'beautiful' → *xub-ost* 'beauty'. In the two languages, N is an abstract noun expressing a property. However, the Bulgarian parallels to the German closing suffix -heit (-keit/-igkeit) allow further suffixation. Consider, Bulgarian *cjal* 'whole' → *cjal-ost* 'wholeness' → *cjalost-en* 'complete' → *cjalostn-ost* 'completeness'. The Bulgarian suffix -ost can also be followed by the suffix -nik. This unproductive pattern derives human nouns with negative characteristics, e.g., Bulgarian *xubav* 'beautiful' → *xubost* 'beauty' → *xubost-nik* 'rascal'. Thus, the suffix -ost is not closing. Note that also the German suffix -heit can be followed by other suffixes, e.g., *ein-heit-lich* 'uniform'. Such instances are, however, exceptions in German (Aronoff and Fuhrhop 2002: 460).

The German closing suffix -in derives female humans from male humans. Over ninety percent of all female humans in German are derived by the attachment of -in. Additionally, formations with other suffixes often have -in doublets or allow the addition of -in, e.g., *Baron-esse* and *Baron-in*, as well as *Prinzess-in* (cf. Wellmann 1975: 107 ff.). In other words, the fact that the suffix -in is closing is sufficient to determine the semantic meaning 'a female human derived from a male human' as closing in German. Bulgarian, however, possesses a set of suffixes for deriving female humans from male humans: -ka, -inja, -kinja, -ica, -esa, -isa, and -va (cf. Stojanov 1993). Manova (2008) establishes that the Bulgarian suffixes are closing only if the suffix is native and added to a base denoting a male person (except for the unique suffix -va which only forms a single noun). Suffixes deriving female animals are not closing, e.g., *magare* 'donkey' → FEM *magar-ica* → DIM *magarič-ka*. Female humans derived from foreign bases differ from those derived from native bases and can also be diminutivized, e.g., *princ* 'prince' → FEM *princ-esa* → DIM *princes-ka*, *poet* 'poet' → FEM *poet-esa* → DIM *poetes-ka*, etc. Another exception to the closing character of the pattern of female humans constitute lexicalizations, e.g., *daskal* 'teacher (archaic)' → *daskal-ica* 'female teacher and female pupil' → DIM *daskalič-ka* 'little female teacher and little female pupil'.

The German -isch, as in *Schriftsteller* 'writer' → *schriftsteller-isch* 'literary; lit. writer-REL.ADJ', corresponds to Bg. -ski, e.g., *pisatel* 'writer' → *pisatel-ski* 'literary; lit. writer-REL.ADJ'. The Bulgarian suffix -ski is closing, but since the same suffix is not closing in Russian (R. -skij), recent borrowings from this language could be analyzed as exhibiting the suffix combination -ski + -ost = -skost. Consider: *rus-sk-ost* 'Russian-like style', *svet-sk-ost* 'worldly-minded style', *det-sk-ost* 'child-like style'. However, as such nouns are borrowings and used only in highly specialized texts, it is difficult to decide whether they should count as evidence for changing combinability of -ski in Bulgarian (see the discussion in Manova 2010).

The German -*ling* has no parallel in Bulgarian. It is also unclear whether the suffix is closing in German. On the Internet one can find: *prüfen* 'to examin' → *Prüfling* 'the examined person' → FEM *Prüflingin, lehren* 'to teach' → *Lehrling* 'the taught person' → FEM *Lehrlingin, Haft* 'prison' → *Häftling* 'prisoner' → FEM *Häftlingin*. For an alternative explanation of the peculiar behavior of the German -*ling*, see Plank (2012).

The last German closing suffix -*ung* derives action nouns as in *bewegen* 'to move' → *Bewegung* 'moving, movement'. This German suffix has two corresponding suffixes in Bulgarian, the suffix -*Vne*, e.g., *dviža (se)* '(I) move' → *dviž-ene* 'moving', and the suffix -*Vnie*, e.g., *dviža (se)* '(I) move' → *dviž-enie* 'moving, movement'. Curiously, only -*Vnie* nouns can be diminutivized, e.g., DIM *dviž-eni-jce* whereas the suffix -*Vne* cannot be followed by other suffixes, *dvižene* 'moving' → *DIM. This different behavior of the two suffixes with respect to diminutivization can be explained as due to the more lexicalized character of the -*nie* pattern, i.e. -*nie* nouns often exhibit lexicalized semantics and denote objects instead of actions (cf. Radeva 1991: 139), e.g., *piša* '(I) write' → *pis-anie* 'a piece of writing' (cf. *pis-ane* 'writing'). In other words, the Bulgarian -*Vne* is closing while -*Vnie* is not. Lexicalizations of -*ne* nouns are seldom. The reverse dictionary of Bulgarian (Andrejčin 1975) lists only *prane* 'laundry', *piene* 'drink', *jadene* 'food', and *imane* 'wealth'. Some native speakers use diminutivized forms of these nominalizations. (For lexicalizations of action nouns in English and Polish and how they relate to closing suffixation, see Szymanek 2000.)

In sum, meanings that are closing in German are not always closing in Bulgarian, which thus speaks against the existence of semantic patterns that are universally closing. However, we can define a specific closing suffix in a particular language by its semantics, e.g., the suffix -*Vne* that derives action nouns in Bulgarian is closing, as is the suffix -*ung* in German. We can even define sets of semantically related closing suffixes in one language and in different languages, e.g., native suffixes deriving female humans from male humans are closing in Bulgarian (except the suffix -*va*) and in German. However, due to the exceptions found, we cannot conclude that closing suffixes can be defined properly on the basis of their semantics only.

So far, we have seen that closing suffixes could have exceptions. However, the exceptions we had to deal with above were primarily due to borrowing and lexicalization. The role of lexicalization in closing suffixation is discussed in some detail in Szymanek (2000) who systematically differentiates between a semantics that is compositional and a semantics that is lexicalized (i.e. non-compositional). Szymanek argues that if only instances of compositional semantics are considered, closing suffixes do not have exceptions. However, I will now give examples of closing suffixes from Bulgarian that allow exceptions and which share the semantics of the closing pattern, i.e. exceptions that are also semantically compositional. The Bulgarian suffixes *-ina* and *-ota* both derive abstract nouns from adjectival bases, as in *dobrina* 'good deed' and *dobrota* 'goodness', both formed from the adjective *dobăr* 'good'. Nevertheless, while the suffix *-ina* easily diminutivizes, one even does not need a basic word in order to produce the corresponding suffix combination *-in-ka* (as in *dobrinka* 'little good deed'), the suffix *-ota* is hard to diminutivize. Perhaps the only exception is *krasotička* 'little beautiful place' (found on the Internet), which is, however, a diminutive form of the lexicalized *krasota* 'beautiful place'. In addition, despite the existence of the suffix *-oten*, e.g., *straxoten* 'terrific' (note that there is no **straxota*, i.e. *-oten* is not a combination of *-ota*$_N$ + *-en*$_{ADJ}$), abstract nouns in *-ota* do not adjectivize, i.e. there is no **dobroten* in Bulgarian. In other words, the suffix *-ota* seems to be a good example of a closing suffix. Nevertheless, two words that are clearly semantically compositional are exceptions to the closing character of *-ota*: (*sam* 'alone' →) *sam-ota* 'loneliness' → *sam-ot-en* 'lonely' and (*čest* 'frequent' →) *čest-ota* 'frequency' → *čest-ot-en* 'frequency-'. Thus, semantic compositionality is not a perfect diagnostic for the feature [+/–closing] either.

In sum, closing suffixes allow exceptions. If one of a set of suffixes with synonymous semantics is closing, the other suffixes of the set are not all closing. Lexicalizations always behave as exceptions but also semantically compositional derivations, including borrowings, that match a closing semantic pattern could allow further derivations. Nevertheless, there seems to exist some relation between closing suffixes and semantics. Suffixes that derive female humans as well as action and abstract nouns tend to be closing even in languages (such as Bulgarian and German) that do not belong to the same language family.

5 Closing suffixation and word-class specification

Of the six German closing suffixes in Aronoff and Fuhrhop (2002), five derive nouns; and this fact is neither because of the suffixes selected nor by chance. In what follows I will try to explain why nominal suffixes tend to be closing, while verbal and adjectival ones do not. For illustration of my argument, I will refer to word-formation in two Germanic languages, English and German, and three Slavic languages, Bulgarian, Russian, and Polish.

Germanic and Slavic languages have very productive patterns for derivation of deverbal nouns and suffixes that derive verbs always combine with at least one nominalizing suffix, which thus explains why Slavic and Germanic verbal suffixes are not closing. Of the above listed five languages, Bulgarian is the only language with a closing verbal suffix, the suffix -*Vsa-m* that is of a Greek origin. Then, Germanic and Slavic languages possess very productive patterns for derivation of abstract nouns from adjectives and in English, Russian and Polish every adjectival suffix combines with at least one nominalizing suffix (E. -*ness*, R. -*ost'* and P. -*ość*). Bulgarian and German, compared above, are rather exceptional in this respect; both languages have an adjectival suffix that is closing (-*isch* in German and -*ski* in Bulgarian). Thus, we come to suffixes that derive nouns in Germanic and Slavic. Nouns are the only word class with a potential for closing suffixes, which explains why closing suffixes usually have this syntactic specification.

6 Closing suffixes and diachrony

A language's morphology changes over time and one of the visible results of this process is the changed morphological status of some affixes. For example, in the diachronic development of a language, an inflectional suffix may be reanalyzed as a derivational formative. Such neo-derivational suffixes are closing. A good illustration of this type of closing suffixes is provided by the Slavic family. The example below is from Bulgarian, the situation is, however, the same in the other Slavic languages (Manova 2011a). In Bulgarian, the suffix -*in* that is found in singular forms of ethnicity terms, as in *bălgarin* 'a Bulgarian' (PL *bălgari* '(the) Bulgarians') is classified as a derivational suffix in the grammars (Stojanov 1993: 174). However, the suffix -*in* was originally a singulative (Georgiev 1969: 111–115); and since there is no other singulative suffix in Bulgarian, -*in* has been assigned to the class of derivational suffixes. This is the explanation for why -*in* is never followed by another derivational suffix in Bulgarian (and in the other Slavic languages).

7 Are conversion and subtraction closing rules?

In this section, I briefly discuss whether there is some relation between conversion (when new meaning is expressed by the same form) and subtraction (when new meaning is expressed by some deletion of form) and closing suffixation. On conversion and subtraction as morphological rules, see Manova (2011a).

We devote attention to this issue, since when morphology "re-uses" the same form (as in conversion) or shortens a form (as in subtraction), it, like in closing suffixation, avoids further suffixation; and one thus expects that conversion and subtraction could be closing operations too.

There are linguists who do claim that conversion (or zero suffixation) closes the word to further derivation in the way closing suffixation does (Sitchinava and Plungian 2009 for Russian; Szymanek 2000 based on Myers 1984 for English). This claim, however, seems unjustified. There are enough Russian conversions that allow further derivation, but since Russian is an inflecting language, Russian conversions involve deletion and addition of inflection and this makes conversion in Russian more difficult to identify than in English. Thus, in the limited space of this article, I will discuss only English conversions, as such examples are well known from the literature. In English, the level-ordering or stratal approach (Siegel 1979; Allen 1978; Kiparsky 1982) divides the lexicon in levels or strata that are ordered in a specific way: level-II affixes can follow both level-I and level-II affixes, but after a level-II affix no level-I affix can be attached. According to Kiparsky (1982), English verb-to-noun derivations are level-I, while noun-to-verb derivations are level-II. This analysis thus assigns conversions to nouns and verbs to different levels, conversions to nouns being level-I, which means that at least conversions to nouns should serve as bases for further derivation. This is indeed the case and can be illustrated with the following examples: *alarm-ist*, *escap-ism*, *segment-al*, etc. (Kiparsky 1982). In these examples, the bases *alarm*, *escape* and *segment* are derived by verb-to-noun conversion and then suffixed by an overt suffix. Examples such as these undoubtedly show that conversion is not a closing rule. For a discussion of these and similar issues within level-ordering, I refer the reader to Don (1993: 29–35).

As regards subtraction, the situation is similar to that for conversion. There are subtractions that allow further derivations and such that do not. Consider the following examples from Bulgarian (see Manova 2011a): *biologija* → *biolog* (derived by subtraction) → *biolož-ki* 'biologist's' and *mečka* 'bear' → *meči* 'bear-' (with subtraction of *-k-*) → Ø, i.e. no further derivation is possible. However, we cannot attribute the missing further derivations from *meči* 'bear-' to the subtractive origin of this adjective, as the adjective *biložki*, which is formed by affixation with an overt affix, cannot be further derived either.

8 Conclusion

Closing suffixation is a specific instance of affix ordering. There are closing suffixes in derivation and closing suffixes in inflection. A closing suffix closes the word to the addition of further suffixes of the same type but a closing derivational suffix may be repeated on adjacent cycles. There is evidence that closing suffixes exist in a number of languages, but it is hard to define semantic patterns that are cross-linguistically closing, though semantics is of importance to closing suffixation. Moreover, closing suffixation allows for exceptions. Therefore, closing suffixes seem best describable as a tendency, i.e. as suffixes that tend to prohibit further suffixation.

Acknowledgements

This article uses data collected for the project *(De)composing the Slavic word* that was carried out at the University of Vienna (2007–2011), PI Stela Manova. The project was supported by the Austrian Science Fund (FWF), Grant V64-G03. The support is hereby gratefully acknowledged.

9 References

Allen, Margaret (1978): Morphological Investigations. Ph.D. dissertation, University of Connecticut.
Andrejčin, Ljubomir (ed.) (1975): *Obraten rečnik na săvremennija bălgarski ezik.* Sofija: BAN.
Aronoff, Mark (1976): *Word Formation in Generative Grammar.* Cambridge, MA: MIT Press.
Aronoff, Mark and Kirsten Fudeman (2005): *What is Morphology?* Malden, MA: Wiley-Blackwell.
Aronoff, Mark and Nanna Fuhrhop (2002): Restricting suffix combinations in German and English: Closing suffixes and the monosuffix constraint. *Natural Language and Linguistic Theory* 20: 451–490.
Babko-Malaya, Olga (1999): *Zero Morphology. A Study of Aspect, Argument Structure and Case.* Piscataway, NJ: Rutgers University Press.
Bauer, Laurie (2004): *A Glossary of Morphology.* Washington, D.C.: Georgetown University Press.
Don, Jan (1993): *Morphological Conversion.* Utrecht: OTS.
Georgiev, Vladimir (1969): *Osnovni problemi na slavjanskata diaxronna morfologija.* Sofija: BAN.
Greenberg, Joseph (1963): Some universals of grammar with particular reference to the order of meaningful elements. In: Joseph Greenberg (ed.), *Universals of Language,* 40–70. Cambridge, MA: MIT Press.
Hay, Jennifer (2001): Lexical frequency in morphology: Is everything relative? *Linguistics* 39: 1041–1070.
Hay, Jennifer (2002): From speech perception to morphology: Affix ordering revisited. *Language* 78(3): 527–555.
Hay, Jennifer (2003): *Causes and Consequences of Word Structure.* London: Routledge.
Hay, Jennifer and Ingo Plag (2004): What constrains possible suffix combinations? On the interaction of grammatical and processing restrictions in derivational morphology. *Natural Language and Linguistic Theory* 22: 565–596.
Kiparsky, Paul (1982): Lexical morphology and phonology. In: In-Seok Yang (ed.), *Linguistics in the Morning Calm,* 3–91. Seoul: Hanshin.

Manova, Stela (2008): Closing suffixes and the structure of the Slavic word: Movierung. *Wiener Slavistisches Jahrbuch* 54: 91–104.

Manova, Stela (2009): Closing suffixes in Bulgarian, Russian and German: The role of semantics. In: Mónika Farkas Baráthi (ed.), *Bulgarian Language and Literature in Slavic and non-Slavic Contexts*, 286–292. Szeged: JATE Press.

Manova, Stela (2010): Suffix combinations in Bulgarian: Parsability and hierarchy-based ordering. *Morphology* 20(1): 267–296.

Manova, Stela (2011a): *Understanding Morphological Rules. With Special Emphasis on Conversion and Subtraction in Bulgarian, Russian and Serbo-Croatian.* Dordrecht: Springer.

Manova, Stela (2011b): A cognitive approach to SUFF1-SUFF2 combinations: A tribute to Carl Friedrich Gauss. *Word Structure* 4(2): 272–300.

Manova, Stela (2011c): Affix ordering in Bulgarian, Russian and Polish double diminutives. Paper presented at the 6th Annual Meeting of the Slavic Linguistics Society, Aix-en-Provence, France, 1–3 September 2011.

Manova, Stela and Mark Aronoff (2010): Modeling affix order. *Morphology* 20(1): 109–131.

Manova, Stela and Kimberley Winternitz (2011): Suffix order in double and multiple diminutives: With data from Polish and Bulgarian. *Studies in Polish Linguistics* 6: 117–140.

Matthews, Peter H. (1972): *Inflectional Morphology. A Theoretical Study Based on Aspects of Latin Verb Conjugation.* Cambridge: Cambridge University Press.

Melissaropoulou, Dimitra and Angela Ralli (2010): Greek derivational structures: Restrictions and constraints. *Morphology* 20(2): 343–357.

Myers, Scott (1984): Zero derivation and inflection. In: Margaret Spears and Richard Sproat (eds.), *MIT Working Papers in Linguistics. Papers from the January 1984 MIT Workshop in Morphology.* Vol. 7, 53–69. Cambridge, MA: Department of Linguistics and Philosophy, MIT.

Nida, Eugene (1949): *Morphology.* 2nd ed. Ann Arbor: The University of Michigan Press.

Plag, Ingo (1996): Selectional restrictions in English suffixation revisited: A reply to Fabb (1988). *Linguistics* 34: 769–798.

Plag, Ingo (2002): The role of selectional restrictions, phonotactics and parsing in constraining suffix ordering in English. In: Geert Booij and Jaap van Marle (eds.), *Yearbook of Morphology 2001*, 285–314. Dordrecht: Kluwer.

Plag, Ingo and Harald Baayen (2009): Suffix ordering and morphological processing. *Language* 85: 109–152.

Plank, Frans (2012): Why *-ling-in*? The pertinacity of a wrong gender. *Morphology* 22(2): 277–292.

Radeva, Vasilka (1991): *Bălgarskoto slovoobrazuvane.* Sofija: Universitetsko izdatelstvo "Sv. Kl. Oxridski".

Rainer, Franz (1988): Towards a theory of blocking: The case of Italian and German quality nouns. In: Geert Booij and Jaap van Marle (eds.), *Yearbook of Morphology 1988*, 155–186. Dordrecht: Foris.

Rice, Keren (2000): *Morpheme Order and Semantic Scope.* Cambridge: Cambridge University Press.

Rice, Keren (2011): Principles of affix ordering: An overview. *Word Structure* 4(2): 169–200.

Scalise, Sergio (1984): *Generative Morphology.* Dordrecht: Foris.

Schultink, Henk (1962): *De morfologische valentie van het ongelede adjectief in modern Nederlands.* The Hague: Van Goor.

Siegel, Dorothy (1979): *Topics in English Morphology.* New York: Garland.

Sitchinava, Dmitri and Vladimir Plungian (2009): Closing suffixation patterns in Russian, with special reference to the Russian National Corpus. Paper presented at the 2nd Vienna Workshop on Affix Order: Affix Order in Slavic and Languages with Similar Morphology, Vienna, 5–6 June 2009.

Stojanov, Stojan (1993): *Gramatika na bălgarskija knižoven ezik.* 5th ed. Sofija: Universitetsko izdatelstvo "Sv. Kl. Oxridski".
Stump, Gregory T. (2006): Template morphology. In: Keith Brown (ed.), *Encyclopedia of Language and Linguistics.* Vol. 12, 559–563. Oxford: Elsevier.
Svenonius, Peter (2004): Slavic prefixes and morphology. Introduction to *Nordlyd* 32(2). *Special issue on Slavic prefixes*, 177–204. Tromsø: University of Tromsø.
Szymanek, Bogdan (2000): On morphotactics: Closing morphemes in English. In: Bożena Rozwadowska (ed.), *PASE Papers in Language Studies*, 311–320. Wrocław: Aksel.
Szymanek, Bogdan and Tetyana Derkach (2005): Constraints on the derivation of double diminutives in Polish and Ukrainian. *Studies in Polish Linguistics* 2: 93–112.
van Marle, Jaap (1985): *On the Paradigmatic Dimension of Morphological Creativity.* Dordrecht: ICG Printing.
Wellmann, Hans (1975): *Deutsche Wortbildung. Typen und Tendenzen in der Gegenwartssprache. Eine Bestandsaufnahme des Instituts für deutsche Sprache. Forschungsstelle Innsbruck. Zweiter Hauptteil: Das Substantiv.* Düsseldorf: Schwann.
Zirkel, Linda (2010): Prefix combinations in English: Structural and processing factors. *Morphology* 20(1): 239–266.

Index

https://doi.org/10.1515/9783111420554-021

www.ingramcontent.com/pod-product-compliance
Lightning Source LLC
Jackson TN
JSHW022111190625
86369JS00004B/18